THE OTHER GREAT GAME

THE OTHER GREAT GAME

*The Opening of Korea and the Birth
of Modern East Asia*

SHEILA MIYOSHI JAGER

THE BELKNAP PRESS OF
HARVARD UNIVERSITY PRESS

Cambridge, Massachusetts
London, England

2023

First printing

Library of Congress Cataloging-in-Publication Data

Names: Jager, Sheila Miyoshi, author.
Title: The other great game : the opening of Korea and the birth of modern
East Asia / Sheila Miyoshi Jager.
Description: Cambridge, Massachusetts : The Belknap Press of
Harvard University Press, 2023. | Includes bibliographical references and index.
Identifiers: LCCN 2022038640 | ISBN 9780674983397 (hardcover)
Subjects: LCSH: Korea—Foreign relations—1864–1910. | Korea—History—1864–1910. |
Eurasia—History—19th century. | Eurasia—History—20th century. |
Eurasia—Relations. | East Asia—History. | East Asia—Relations.
Classification: LCC DS910.18 .J34 2023 | DDC 327.51905—dc23/eng/20221003
LC record available at https://lccn.loc.gov/2022038640

For my beloved children,
ISAAC HENDRIK, HANNAH MARIJKE,
EMMA KATARINA, *and* AARON ROLFE

CONTENTS

MAPS

NOTE ON ROMANIZATION, NAMES, AND DATES

Throughout the book I have employed the McCune-Reischauer romanization system for Korean and pinyin for the romanization of Chinese. Throughout I have followed the Japanese, Korean, and Chinese convention of family name or surname preceding given or personal name. Some exceptions were made for place names and personal names long familiar in the West, such as Syngman Rhee (Yi Sŭng-man), Chiang Kai-shek (Jiang Jieshi), and Mikhail Muravev (Mikhail Muravyov) Finally, all dates are in the Gregorian calendar unless otherwise noted. Some references provide two dates, Gregorian and Julian for Russian and/or Gregorian and lunar for Chinese and Korean sources. This is because many of the sources did not provide a Gregorian date. The Julian calendar is thirteen days behind its corresponding Gregorian date, whereas the lunar year of twelve months runs about eleven or twelve days shorter than the solar year.

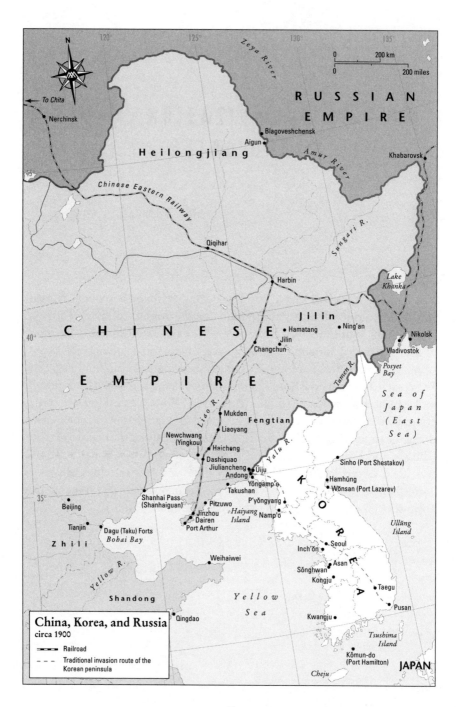

N

To Chita ←
• Nerchinsk

120°   125°   130°   135°

Zeya River

RUSSIAN
EMPIRE

0   200 km
0   200 miles

• Blagoveshchensk
Aigun •

H e i l o n g j i a n g

Amur River

• Khabarovsk

Chinese Eastern Railway

45°

Sungari R.

Lake Khanka

• Qiqihar

• Harbin

J i l i n
• Hamatang   • Ning'an
Jilin •
• Changchun

• Nikolsk
Vladivostok •

C H I N E S E

40°

Posyet Bay

*S e a   o f
J a p a n
(E a s t
S e a)*

E M P I R E

Liao R.

Tumen R.

• Mukden
• Liaoyang
F e n g t i a n

Newchwang
(Yingkou) •
• Haicheng
Dashiquao •
Jiuliancheng •
Andong • • Uiju
• Yöngamp'o
Takushan •

Yalu R.

• Sinho (Port Shestakov)

• Hamhǔng
• Wǒnsan (Port Lazarev)

K
O
R
E
A

35°

Shanhai Pass
(Shanhaiguan) •
• Pitzuwo
Jinzhou •
Dairen •
Port Arthur •

• P'yǒngyang
*Haiyang
Island*   Namp'o •

*Ullǔng
Island*

• Beijing

• Tianjin
• Dagu (Taku) Forts
Bohai Bay

Z h i l i

Yellow R.

• Weihaiwei

Inch'ǒn •
• Seoul
Sǒnghwan • • Asan
Kongju •
Kwangju •

• Taegu

• Pusan

S h a n d o n g

• Qingdao

*Y e l l o w
S e a*

*Tsushima
Island*

J A P A N

Kǒmun-do
(Port Hamilton) •

Cheju

China, Korea, and Russia
circa 1900

━━━ Railroad

╌ ╌ ╌ Traditional invasion route of the
Korean peninsula

PREFACE

One of the best-known struggles of the nineteenth century was the Great Game, when Russia's threat to British interests in India initiated a lasting rivalry and bloodshed that would continue until the beginning of the twentieth century. While the dramatic geopolitical struggle between these two Great Powers has been the subject of numerous books, the Great Game in East Asia is less well known but just as remarkable. Britain did not play a primary role in this struggle, but it became aligned with a rising Japan, which did. Moreover, whereas the ultimate prize of the Great Game was India—the crown jewel of the British Empire—in East Asia, China, Japan, and Russia fought for control over the impoverished yet strategically important Korean Peninsula. The intricate chessboard on which this "other" Great Game was played at the close of the nineteenth and early twentieth centuries caused two major wars—the First Sino-Japanese War and the Russo-Japanese War—that changed the East Asian region, and the world, forever. Since ancient times, China had held a position of supremacy as the Middle Kingdom. By 1911, one year after Korea became a colony of Japan, the Qing dynasty collapsed and Meiji Japan had risen up to take the Celestial Empire's place as the dominant power in the region.

My narrative chronicles this great transformation in East Asia. The story begins in the year 1860, because this was the period of Russia's eastward expansion when Russia first came to share a border with Korea. Some may find this choice surprising. They might point, instead, to the decades of the 1840s and 1850s as decisive, when both China and Japan witnessed threats to the old order as they confronted the foreboding intrusion of Western gunboats on their shores. But I argue that actual transformation occurred in full measure only when Korea emerged from its isolation to become the object of regional competition. Russia's eastward expansion set in motion a series of events that not only fractured the previous regional harmony within the Confucian world order but provided Western countries with both the incentive and the opportunity to intervene more vigorously in East Asian affairs.

By the end of the nineteenth century the United States and Japan stepped forward onto the world stage as two non-European Great Powers that would come to dominate the Asia-Pacific region, eclipsing the European military and economic powers that had prevailed before. This took place due to the widespread fear that a weakened China was about to be carved up by the Great Powers and that Russia would absorb all of Korea and Manchuria for itself. So pervasive was this fear that earlier promoters of Russo-American cooperation, like Theodore Roosevelt, cast their lot with Japan and defined Russia as America's chief rival in East Asia. Concern over Russia's expansion into Manchuria and the breakup of China thus unexpectedly earned Japan new allies in its war with Russia in 1904–1905. It was this unwitting alliance between these two rising non-European powers during the latter half of the nineteenth century that set the stage for Japan's continental expansionism.

The first of these conflicts occurred when Japan began to encroach on China's tributary state of Korea and succeeded in acquiring Taiwan. The second major war was waged by Japan against the Russian Empire and paved the way for Japan's takeover of Korea. In between these imperial clashes, Spain and the United States fought a war that left the latter in temporary possession of the Philippines, Guam, and a number of small islands in the Pacific. There was also the China Relief Expedition undertaken by the Eight-Nation Alliance, a multinational military coalition that invaded northern China in 1900 to relieve the foreign legations in Beijing from Boxer militia, and the Russo-Chinese War that handed over control of Manchuria to Russia in August 1900. As the insurgent power, Japan participated directly and indirectly in all but one of these conflicts, while China and Korea remained at the receiving end of the scramble for concessions and territory. These large-scale conflicts created a new sense of national identity and a more genuinely national politics, even in nations with much older pedigree. They also gave rise to a new cadre of elite economic and military reformers in Japan, China, Russia, and Korea, whose job it was to help navigate their nations' response to the rapidly changing environment. Their stories are the subject of this book.

What follows is a narrative history in which I have tried as much as possible to capture the flow of historical action in time and to impart some feeling about the lives of the historical actors as well as a sense of place in which they lived. This approach was due in part to an intellectual debt to two books—Rudyard Kipling's *Kim* and Peter Hopkirk's *The Great Game: The Struggle for Empire in Central Asia*. Kipling's 1901 novel, which made the Great Game popular, was set during the Second Afghan War and captures perfectly the paranoid mood of the Anglo-Russian contest. (The phrase Kipling used—"Now I shall go far and far into the North, playing the Great Game"—was actually coined by Arthur Conolly, one of the players of the game, who in 1842 was tortured and beheaded by the Khan of Bokhara). *Kim* was one of the first novels I read as a child, and I enjoyed it immensely. I read Hopkirk's *The Great Game* for the first time in university—and in one sitting. Hopkirk was a writer of the old school, an inveterate journalist-historian-explorer-adventurer-anthropologist, and I see my book as a kind of homage to both these authors.

I begin my story with Russia's eastward expansion, an important theme. Traditionally Russia has not figured prominently in the histories of China, Japan, and Korea. If Russia is dealt with at all, its contributions are noted almost perfunctorily, a side story to the bigger story of these nations' singular development and their relations to each other. Much of the history we will be examining in this book is a *regional* history—that is, an examination of how Russia, Japan, China, and Korea interacted with each other, with inputs from the Western powers. To the extent that I include Russia in this regional history, I wish to draw attention to its vital identity as an Eastern power.

Much like the Great Game proper, the Other Great Game was largely about war and conflict, another important theme in the book. I devote a considerable amount of space to describing military campaigns, recounting in detail some of the more intricate military operations of many key battles during the Sino-Japanese War of 1894–1895, the China Relief expedition of 1900, the Russo-Chinese War of 1900, and the Russo-Japanese War of 1904–1905. I believe it is important to flesh out this military history, partly because a detailed study of all four military campaigns and operations has not been extensively covered together in one book, and partly because I believe one cannot adequately appreciate this history without reckoning with the enormous consequences of these wars and their impact on societies. In the case of the Russo-Japanese War, that conflict changed the character of war itself. The sheer drama of this struggle—the huge numbers of soldiers and sailors involved, and the introduction of innovations such as extensive use of barbed wire, rapid-fire weapons, and even poison gas—revolutionized the very character of warfare itself to usher in modern war that presaged the utter horror of blood and destruction of the Great War of 1914–1918.

In my descriptions of these wars, I also wished to convey how they were experienced on the ground. At its deepest level, the resort to war signals the failure of political systems to settle human conflict, and to the extent that East Asia from the middle of the nineteenth century onward was an extremely violent age, the study of war must make up a significant part of that history. How soldiers and civilians alike struggled to make sense of these conflicts, and the lessons they took away from them, are a central concern of *The Other Great Game*.

I understand a "modern" East Asian order to be synonymous with the "Westphalian" system of modern nation-states with sovereign rights over their own territory and people. The transformation of the old Confucian order of international relations to a modern Westphalian one was fraught with conflict in which the Korean Peninsula played an outsized role. One simply cannot understand the rise of modern Japan and China without engaging with the role and perception of Korea among these countries' elites. At the same time, these changes to the traditional order came about due to the struggles *between* the regional powers, how they sought to define themselves as modern nations not only in relation to the West but in their relations to each other. Korea played a central role in this transformational drama because the turmoil it created for the region had worldwide implications. In particular, the two decades that began with Korea's first modern treaty, in 1876 with Japan, and that ended with the Triple Intervention of 1895 was especially critical. Due to these events, the international situation in East Asia changed drastically, ushering in unprecedented developments in the region as the final stages of the old Confucian order began to give way to a modern international system of sovereign states. By the first decade of the twentieth century, China was reduced from being the Middle Kingdom at the center of its universe to being a semi-colony, and Korea had lost its sovereignty altogether. This book tells the story of how and why this happened.

The notion of "opening" Korea was in standard use by diplomats and historians during the nineteenth century. Scholars, travelers, and observers of this period referred to Korea as the "hermit kingdom" in need of being "opened," something we see repeatedly evoked in contemporary commentary about North Korea. Such terms are rarely used in academic circles today, as they are considered both ahistorical and anachronistic. Ahistorical in the sense that Korea's political culture and economy were opened in all sorts of ways before the 1860s, and anachronistic in the sense that the portrayal of Koreans as being in the waiting room of history to be acted upon by the Great Powers is simply not accurate. A key argument of *The Other Great Game* is to underscore precisely this point—that far from being acted upon (like a "shrimp among whales"), Koreans were key players in this history and the *source* of transformational change. The "opening of Korea" that appears in the subtitle of this book is thus evoked ironically, not only as a throwback to nineteenth-century depictions of the "hermit nation" but also to underscore how they continue to influence the way Korea is often perceived and depicted in contemporary policy circles.

Finally, the presence of the past can also be seen in other ways. I hope that the focus on the geopolitical struggles over the Korean Peninsula that took place during the late nineteenth and early twentieth centuries will make clear just how much this history illuminates the present, especially in light of the fact that the Korean Peninsula continues to remain the locus of conflict in the Asia-Pacific region. We can see how in 1894, again in 1904, and yet again in 1950, Great Power rivalries gave the struggle over the Korean Peninsula its international significance, opening the way for an uncertain passage to a new era and leading to the rise and fall of Great Powers. Armed with the knowledge of these earlier struggles, we may gain a sharper understanding of the forces now confronting contemporary East Asia, by showing how these earlier conflicts and rivalries continue to influence the region's present and future.

THE OTHER GREAT GAME

PROLOGUE

THE RISE OF RUSSIA IN ASIA

They said that when Kyiv fell in 1240, the noise produced by the invading hurricane of horses, camels, and men was so great that the people of the city could not hear each other's screams. When the Mongols took a town, they slaughtered without mercy. "Some were impaled, some shot at with arrows for sport, others were flayed . . . priests were roasted alive, and nuns and maidens ravished in the churches before their relatives." They spread such panic that the people in nearby towns would flee their homes in terror, or even kill themselves, rather than be caught alive by the dreaded enemy. Once the Mongol storm had descended upon the land, wrote the chronicler of Kostroma, "no eye remained open to weep for the dead."[1]

Sweeping into Russia in the early thirteenth century, which then consisted of a dozen or so principalities, the Mongol domination of the Russian people lasted for more than two hundred years. The experience left deep and long-lasting scars on the Russian soul. Aside from the material destruction wrought by the invaders—also known as the Tatars or the Golden Horde—the Mongols introduced despotic methods of administration.[2] Cut off from the liberalizing influences of Europe, the tyrannical storm from the Asiatic steppe moved swiftly through the length and breadth of the land. It was Tatar ideas and administrative practices that paved the way for the establishment of the "semi-oriental despotism" of the Muscovite tsars. The experience goes far in explaining the Russians' stoic acceptance of tyranny at home, their historic xenophobia, aggressive

I

foreign policy, and perennial fear of invasion (which the onslaughts of Napoleon and Hitler would later reinforce). The effects of the Tatar domination in Russian history were felt long after the Golden Horde vanished from the Russian frontier into the ancient steppes from whence they came.

The man who finally delivered his country from the hateful foreign yoke was Ivan the Great, then the Great Prince of Moscow, who in 1480 won a bloodless victory against the enemy. The two armies had faced each other across the River Ugra and a ferocious battle appeared inevitable. But then an extraordinary thing happened. The weather suddenly turned cold. As the terrible Russian winter descended upon the land, the lightly clad Tatars appeared to have lost their stomach for the fight.[3] By the time his son, Ivan IV, known as Ivan the Terrible, assumed the title of tsar in 1547, the Mongol hordes, once so feared, were no longer thought invincible. The Tatar grip was at last broken when Ivan IV's troops stormed the fortress of Kazan on the upper Volga in 1552 and opened up the Caspian Sea in the south and the Urals in the east, thus leaving the way open for Russia's great march into the far reaches of East Asia.

The conquest of Siberia was carried out during the second half of the sixteenth century and was led by a band of adventurous Cossacks, whose trek into this stark wilderness secured a vast realm east of the Urals for Imperial Russia. By the middle of the following century, Russian power had extended as far as Lake Baikal and beyond to the Amur River. By the late seventeenth century the conquest of Siberia was complete. But there the Russian advance stopped. The Chinese, objecting to Russian colonization, concluded an agreement with Saint Petersburg. In 1689, at Nerchinsk, the two countries signed a treaty in which Russia agreed to give up its claims to the area north of the Amur River as far as the Stanovoy Mountains, and the entire Amur territory was officially recognized as part of China.[4]

By the early part of the eighteenth century, the Russians were on the move again. Under the leadership of Peter the Great, and his successor, Catherine II (wife of his grandson, Peter III, who ruled a little less than a year), Russia this time turned its gaze southward toward the Caucasus and Central Asia. Following the ascension of Nicholas I in 1825, the Russians had subdued the wild Muslim and Christian tribesmen in their march toward Persia.

It was during this period that Anglo-Russian antagonism began in a contest that became known as the Great Game. Leaders in Britain and

Calcutta took notice of Russia's southern advance, for it seemed only a matter of time before Russian troops would march on India, the Crown Jewel of the British Empire. Before long this political no man's land—which stretched from the snow-capped peaks of the Caucasus in the west, across the great deserts and mountains of Central Asia, to Chinese Turkestan and Tibet—became, as Peter Hopkirk put it, "a vast adventure playground for ambitious young officers and explorers of both sides as they mapped the passes and desert along which their armies would have to march if war came to the region."[5]

But the Russian march on British India never came. Instead, Russia began moving eastward again. For 150 years, Russian colonizers in Siberia were restricted to the territory lying north of the Amur along the Argun River and Stanovoy Mountains, but in 1846 Nicholas I ordered an investigation of the sources of the Amur River as well as its adjacent territory.[6] An expedition was organized in 1849, and the tsar selected the young and energetic governor-general of Siberia, Nikolai Nikolaevich Muravev, to lead it.

At the time, it was believed that the Amur was inaccessible to seagoing vessels. The island of Sakhalin was thought to be a peninsula that precluded sea access to the Amur from the south, and the river itself was thought to be unfit for navigation at its mouth, rendering the river of limited strategic value for Russia. Following China's loss to the British in the First Opium War (1839–1842) and the subsequent opening of treaty ports, Nicholas I was stimulated to reinvestigate the question of the Amur's nature and accessibility, because he feared that Russia might be forestalled by Britain, whose occupation of the mouth of the Amur could permanently impede Russia's eastern expansion to the Pacific.

Muravev directed Captain Gennady Nevelskoy to sail to the mouth of the Amur on the ship *Baikal* to lead the exploratory expedition. The two men were supposed to link up on Sakhalin in late August 1849 after Nevelskoy had sailed from Petropavlovsk on the Kamchatka Peninsula, but the *Baikal* was nowhere to be found. Muravev proceeded to Ayan Bay alone, hoping to hear some news of the captain. After waiting for nearly two weeks, Muravev began to fear that that the *Baikal* may have been lost either on the way from Petropavlovsk or in the shallow sandbanks of the Amur estuary. But then, on the morning of September 3, the *Baikal* suddenly appeared in the waters of the bay. Unable to restrain his impatience, and relief, Muravev went out to meet the vessel in a rowboat. He was hailed by Nevelskoy through a speaking-trumpet with the following words: "God has assisted us! . . . The main question is happily solved . . . Saghalien [Sakhalin] is an island, and sea-going ships can penetrate into the estuary of the Amur both from north and south. An ancient error is completely dissipated. I now report to you that the truth has been discovered."[7]

Nevelskoy also notified Muravev that on his own responsibility he had boldly hoisted the Russian flag over the Bay of Iskai [Good Fortune] at the mouth of the river, proclaiming "the whole Amur region down to the Korean frontier as well as Sakhalin Island as Russia's possession."[8]

Muravev quickly recognized that securing the use of the Amur was indispensable for the future development of the Russian Far East. Nevelskoy's discovery proved that eastern Siberia was connected with the East Sea by the Amur River and therefore to the Pacific Ocean. He was convinced that Russia must have a secure port on the Pacific, because if it should forfeit control of the entrance to the river to another power—namely Britain—Russia would forfeit control of Siberia. "In order to have total control of trade in China, the English, without question, must control the mouth of the Amur," Muravev declared. "All I can say is that whoever controls the mouth of the Amur controls Siberia, at the very least all the way to Baikal—and controls it firmly. The English need only keep the mouth under lock and key, and all Siberia, its settlements, its potential for bountiful agriculture and industry, will be a tributary and slave to that power that holds the key."[9] Although many of the tsar's advisors were outraged by Muravev's bold pronouncements, for fear that they might precipitate a war with China, Nicholas I approved, proclaiming that "where once the Russian flag has flown, it must not be lowered again."[10]

Tsar Alexander II had no reason to think differently. When he succeeded his father Nicholas in 1855, Russia possessed the largest and most powerful army in Europe, and its claim to membership in the European community of Great Powers was Russian military strength. A defeat in Crimea the following year had seriously undermined that claim, however. Many saw this defeat as a summons for renewed modernization along Western lines, but for others Russia's humiliation gave rise to a small but influential group of frontier generals who argued that Russia must turn eastward to redeem its martial glory. Lieutenant General Ivan Blaramberg, a military topographer and consummate player in the Great Game, spoke for many of these officers when he proclaimed, "Russia's future does not lie in Europe: It must look to the East."[11]

The Russian desire to expand into Asia was not new, of course. Ever since Ivan the Terrible vanquished the Tatars and extended his sovereignty to Siberia, Russia had succeeded in resuscitating its national fervor. In the eighteenth century, Peter the Great had enlarged the limits of Russia's territory almost from the Baltic to the Pacific but he had no sympathy with Muscovite ideals. Under Peter, Russia sought to redefine itself as a European empire with a presence in the West. Nevertheless, Russia still could not escape its deeply ambivalent attitudes toward Asia.[12] Educated Russians preferred to see themselves as Europeans, in every way equal to the West. And yet, although they might have defined themselves as Europeans with regard to Asia, they were considered "Asiatic" in the eyes of the Europeans.[13] "Let him conceive of the idea of half-savage people who have been enrolled and drilled, without having been civilized," wrote the Marquis de Custine, the French aristocrat who traveled to Russia in 1839, "and he will be able to understand the social and moral state of the Russian nation."[14] Russian intellectuals themselves cursed their country's Asiatic backwardness, believing that nothing good had ever come from their Mongol past.[15]

But beginning in the early nineteenth century, many Russian intellectuals and writers began to reconsider Russia's Asian identity.[16] In 1822 Alexander Pushkin published his poem "The Prisoner of the Caucasus," which the renowned Russian literary critic Vissarion Belinsky described as transforming the region from a decrepit backwater into "the cherished land not only of wide, expansive freedom but of inexhaustible poetry, the country of boiling life and bold dreams."[17] Other writers followed suit: Mikhail Lermontov's *Hero of Our Time* (1840) was likewise set in the Caucasus, and Leo Tolstoy's *The Prisoner of the Caucasus* (1872) continued Pushkin's tradition of portraying the region as one that could offer freedom to the Russians. By making Asia part of Russia again, Pushkin became, in the words of Nikolai Gogol, "a national [*natsionalen*] because true nationality [*natsional'nost*] consists not in the description of a *sarafan*, but in the very soul of the people."[18]

The discovery of the "Russian soul" in the 1830s and 1840s was predicated upon Russia having a distinctive mission in the world. Count Sergei Semenovich Uvarov, then a young nobleman working as an attaché in Vienna and later Nicholas I's long-serving minister of education, later wrote that Russia, by virtue of its contact with "all the peoples of the Orient," was destined to become the mediator between East and West. He paid considerable attention to Russia's Asian lands and introduced the study of Eastern languages and cultures to Russian universities, primarily as a means for training Russians to administer their growing empire. These

Slavophiles espoused a cult of Russian exceptionalism, believing that Russia had a special role to play in the world, while distaining the "flaccid, decadent West."[19]

Not surprisingly, Russia's expansion into Central Asia and the Far East was also seen as a tonic for the empire's wounded pride in the aftermath of the Crimean debacle. Russia's defeat by the British in the Crimean War (1853–1856) gave rise to a new and aggressive breed of frontier officers, much like the Byronic hero of Lermontov's novel.[20] These officers were consummate Anglophobes who burned to settle their country's score with the British. Thus Murarev, later to become known as Count Muravev-Amursky in honor of his conquests in the Amur, fit in perfectly with other advocates of Russian nationalism and imperial expansionism on the continent. In 1855 Muravev embarked upon another expedition to the mouth of the Amur. By the end of 1857 his troops had occupied the upper Amur, the original Manchu heartland of the Qing Empire.

At the time, the Qing emperor, Xianfeng, being fully embroiled in the Taiping Rebellion (1850–1864) and fighting off British and French demands for concessions and other privileges, was in no position to stop him. In May 1858, less than a decade after Nevelskoy's brilliant discovery, Muravev proposed to the Chinese emperor that the river Amur should be the frontier between the two empires. After several "long sittings," the emperor's ministers finally yielded and the Treaty of Aigun was signed on May 28. The Chinese negotiator, I-Shan, bitterly reflected: "We dared take the liberty to grant their [Russians] desires by signing and exchanging the treaties as a temporary way to pacify the bestial hearts of the barbarians and thereby extricate ourselves from a dire situation."[21] Although the Chinese insisted that they had merely "lent" the "uninhabited" portions of the north bank of the Amur for "temporary habitation," it served Muravev's purposes in paving the way for Russia's permanent annexation of the region.

During the negotiations, Muravev justified his demands on the basis of Russia's "protection of China" against Britain. "Rapid conquests made by England in various parts of the world have brought her nearer to us . . . The perfidious roads traveled by Britain are well known to the Government of China," he proclaimed. He then added, disingenuously, "But do not believe, gentlemen, that Russia is greedy for expansion of her frontiers. Such a plan is not within the scope of our intentions. All Russia cares for is the security of her boundaries."[22]

Two years later the Russians were again at China's door. Fearful that the British might gain possession of Alexander II's ill-guarded possessions

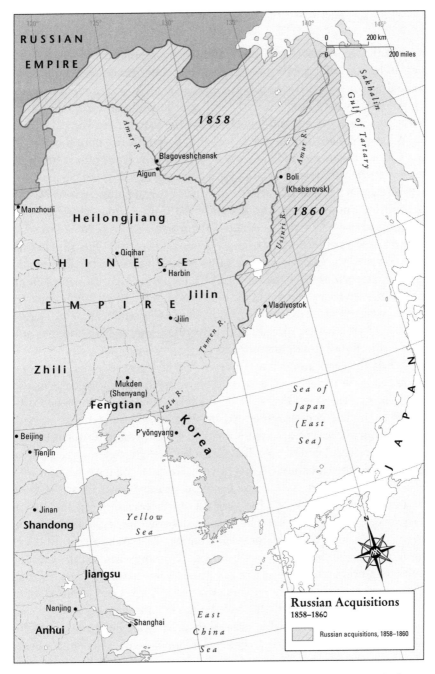

In 1860, following China's humiliating loss in the Second Opium War, Russia acquired an enormous territory north of the Amur River. The 1860 Treaty of Peking extended Russia's territory to the Pacific Ocean and the border of Korea.

in the Far East, the tsar sent Count Nikolai Ignatiev, another brilliant frontier officer, to Beijing. His mission was to coerce the Chinese emperor to formally cede to the Russian Empire the new territories temporarily acquired by Muravev in 1858. In the spring of 1859, Ignatiev, aged twenty-seven, set out by sleigh and horseback for the Chinese capital.

What he discovered upon his arrival in Beijing was a nation in chaos, for China was in the midst of a war with Britain and France. In 1856, four years before Ignatiev's fateful journey, war had erupted between the Chinese against the British and the French in the so-called Arrow War, or Second Opium War. The British had seized Canton in 1856. They then went on to take the strategic Dagu forts in 1858 and threatened to seize Tianjin, the northern coastal city port. By June 1858 the British had strong-armed the Qing government into signing a new treaty, this one imposing extraordinarily strict terms on China, including the opening of an additional ten treaty ports and the concession that Christian missionaries be allowed to proselytize anywhere in the Chinese interior. The Tianjin Treaty (1858) also stipulated lower transit taxes on foreign imports and standardized duty on opium imports.[23]

When the Qing refused to abide by the new treaty terms, hostilities reopened in the summer of 1859. This time French forces joined the British and attacked the Dagu Forts. The Qing forces rallied and beat the Europeans back. The British responded by sending a team of negotiators to Beijing, but they were arrested and some were tortured and executed.[24] This infuriated Lord Elgin, Britain's chief treaty negotiator, and he promptly formed a combined Anglo-French expeditionary force of thirty-five hundred men to march into Beijing to teach a lesson that the Qing would never forget. When the Anglo-French force entered the city in October 1860, Elgin ordered his men to destroy one of the Chinese emperor's most prized possessions, the Summer Palace, known as the Yuanmingyuan. No blood was to be spilled. Elgin only wanted the Chinese emperor's pride, and with it China's pride, to be crushed. "The burning of the palace was not a proceeding to my taste," Elgin later admitted, "but it was a necessary act and has proved quite helpful in its results."[25]

This was the spectacle that greeted Ignatiev when he reached the Chinese capital, and he immediately saw his opportunity. By then Emperor Xianfeng, along with his concubine, Cixi, had already fled Beijing, leaving his younger brother, Yixin, or Prince Gong, to deal with the enemy. Ignatiev at once offered his services as a mediator between the prince and his European foes. Fearing the wholesale destruction of the city, Prince Gong reluctantly agreed although he suspected that Ignatiev might be playing a double game.[26]

Prince Gong's suspicions proved correct. Ignatiev assisted the European invaders with maps and with intelligence from inside the city, and then, when the British and French had already decided to leave due to the onset of the Manchurian winter, kept that vital information from the Chinese in order to play on their fears that the foreign troops would stay put. The plan worked wonders. Ignatiev was able to convince Prince Gong that he alone had hastened the British and French troops' departure.[27] For his services, Ignatiev demanded not only the territory north of the Amur that had been nominally secured in the Treaty of Aigun (1858), but the region lying east and south of the river, the so-called Ussuri coastal region.

The Treaty of Peking, signed in 1860, was a dazzling Russian triumph.[28] Following the signing of the treaty, Russia founded a new city on the bay where the British had first landed in 1856 (Port May). The new Russian outpost, established in 1860, was renamed Vladivostok—"Ruler of the East." In one fell swoop Ignatiev had acquired for Russia a vast domain of about four hundred thousand square miles, roughly the size of France and Germany combined. Without the use of force and only with subtle diplomacy, he had succeeded in extending Russia's territory to the Pacific and the border of Korea.[29]

These were ominous developments. Despite Russia's assurances to the Celestial Empire that it had no hostile intentions toward the Korean Peninsula—the "lips protecting China's teeth"—and that each advance was the last, it looked to many as though Russia's relentless move eastward was part of a grand scheme to bring the whole of Northeast Asia under tsarist sway. Fear of that precise scenario was shared by Japan, making the Korean Peninsula the center of major convulsions in East Asia as regional powers embarked on their own Great Game.

PART ONE

NEW FRONTIERS

FOR THE FIRST HALF of the Chosŏn dynasty (1392–1910), Koreans maintained close relations with Ming China (1368–1644). Following the invasion of the Ming by northern Jurchen tribesmen who called themselves the Manchus, the Koreans were forced to submit to Manchu rule under the new Qing Empire (1644–1912). Beyond the periodic diplomatic tribute missions that served to regulate the relationship between the two countries, most Koreans saw little of their northern neighbor. To minimize contact between the two peoples, Korea and China agreed to a no man's land along both sides of the Yalu and Tumen Rivers that formed the border. This area was designated a neutral territory and off-limits to all settlements.

This situation changed abruptly in 1860 with the signing of the Convention of Peking (Beijing) that brought the Second Opium War to an end. Russia came into possession of a huge swath of Chinese territory in the Ussuri and Amur regions, now known as the Russian Far East, which included the lower reaches of the Tumen River that formed a border between Russia and Korea. The new border brought Russians and Koreans into direct contact for the first time in history. It also introduced a completely new dynamic to East Asia by evoking novel security concerns for Korea.

The sudden appearance of Russian soldiers across the Tumen River could not have occurred at a more inopportune time for Korea. In 1863 the Korean king died unexpectedly, and because he had no heir, a distant relative of the late king was selected to succeed him. But the heir was only twelve years old, so his father, the Taewŏn'gun, or "Grand Prince" was put in charge as regent until the young king came of age. The Taewŏn'gun immediately faced the problem of what to do about the Russian threat. He was worried not only about potential Russian incursions, but about Korean emigrants colluding with Russian authorities to act against the Korean government.

At the same time, the Taewŏn'gun was facing internal challenges to his rule posed by an ardent group of Korean Catholic converts. The teachings of Catholicism had been introduced into Korea by Jesuit priests sometime in the early eighteenth century, and over the years Korean Catholics had been intermittently purged or tolerated depending on the vagaries of the Korean court. China's loss to Anglo-British forces in the Second Opium War (1856–1860) had emboldened Korea's clandestine Catholic community, and seeking new ways to proselytize their faith, some Korean Catholic leaders saw an opportunity to take advantage of the Russo-Korean border problem. They proposed that the Taewŏn'gun initiate an alliance with France, with French missionaries acting as intermediaries, to counter the looming Russian threat. In exchange the Korean Catholics requested complete freedom of religion.

At first the Taewŏn'gun was receptive to the idea, but when the anti-Catholic faction in the Korean Court got wind of it, he reversed his position, and then initiated a purge of Catholics, including the execution of seven French missionaries in 1866.

When the French chargé d'affaires in China received news of the executions, he ordered a punitive expedition to be sent to Korea. But the paltry French force of a few hundred men was soundly defeated. To celebrate this victory, the Taewŏn'gun ordered the purge of several thousand Korean Catholics. Instead of forcing the Korean government to squarely acknowledge the realities of the changing world and Korea's increasingly dire circumstances, as the sacking of the Summer Palace had done for China, Korea's illusory "triumph" over France merely hardened its resolve to keep the world at bay.

This was the context for Korea's rude treatment of Japanese envoys when they sought to establish new relations with the Korean government following the establishment of the Meiji Restoration in 1868. The Koreans belittled the Western appearance of the Japanese envoys and disparaged Japan as a "country without laws." Angered and insulted, the Japanese threatened war. It was at this point that King Kojong, then twenty-one years old, assumed direct rule and reversed his father's, the Taewŏn'gun's, isolationist foreign policy. With China's vigorous encouragement, Kojong opted for nonconfrontation, and in 1876, under the threat of Japanese gunboats, Korea and Japan signed the Kanghwa Treaty, which ostensibly normalized relations between the two countries and opened Korea to foreign trade. It was a pivotal moment for Korea and, as it turned out, for all of East Asia.

Meanwhile, the looming danger to Korea from Russia grew unchecked. Forced out of its isolation by Japan, Korea was fast becoming an international security conundrum as competition for influence and control over the peninsula transformed the regional Great Powers' centuries-old diplomatic practices in the region.

CHAPTER ONE

KOREA'S PYRRHIC VICTORY

The new border between Korea and Russia had unexpected consequences for relations between Korea and China. Ever since 1637, Korea had more or less cut itself off from the world, and seclusion became the cardinal principle of its foreign policy. That date marked the end of the Manchu invasions, the last of a series of calamitous foreign wars on the peninsula. Because of Korea's strategic position on China's eastern frontier, nearly every change of China's dynastic fortunes had brought with it large-scale conflicts on the peninsula. In 1254, for example, the Mongols slaughtered two hundred thousand Korean men, women, and children as they embarked upon their scorched earth policy to make Korea their tributary state before establishing the Yuan dynasty in China in 1271.[1] In 1274 and again in 1281, the Korean Peninsula became the staging ground for the Mongolian invasion of Japan, which failed—twice. Thirty thousand Koreans were drafted to build nine hundred ships for the Mongols, while five thousand Koreans were forcibly conscripted for the invasion effort. A powerful typhoon—which the Japanese called *kamikaze,* "divine winds"—had miraculously saved Japan from the Mongolian hordes in 1274. The typhoon struck again in 1281, sending another fleet of Korean-built ships to the bottom of the sea for the second, and last, time.[2]

But the most significant destruction on the Korean Peninsula was wrought by the Japanese invasions of the late sixteenth century. Nearly two million Koreans, a staggering 20 percent of the population, perished during the Imjin Wars, Toyotomi Hideyoshi's campaigns of 1592–1598 to subjugate the Korean Peninsula.[3] Hideyoshi's object was the conquest of Ming China (1368–1644) but the result was to turn Korea into a ruined land. With the help of the Ming, the Koreans were finally able to beat back the Japanese, but peace did not last long. Almost as soon as Hideyoshi's army withdrew from the peninsula, the rising Manchus began gathering their forces for their own planned conquest of the Ming. In 1636, Manchu troops crossed the Yalu border into Korea, the second such invasion by the northern barbarians in less than ten years. The Korean court capitulated and agreed to recognize the Manchu Qing Empire as the rightful dynasty of China. This betrayal of the Ming was a bitter pill for the Korean court to swallow, but after so much devastation, court officials became convinced that compliance, not resistance, to Manchu demands was the only way to guarantee their country's existence. The Korean people were, by this time, utterly exhausted.

Korea's betrayal of the Ming paid off. Because of its military superiority and size, the Qing dynasty (1644–1912) established an extraordinarily stable diplomatic system that provided a way to regulate foreign relations within its own Celestial Empire.[4] Except for Koreans' own independent relationship with the Japanese, who had withdrawn into their own policy of seclusion, Korean external contacts were maintained through China. Korean emissaries performed the highest level of kowtow to the Chinese emperor, received imperial edicts, and presented tributes that consolidated the tributary relationship (*zongfan*) between the two countries but also helped to establish Qing bona fides as the newly civilized Central Kingdom (*zhongguo*).[5]

This did not mean that relations between Korea and the Qing were particularly close. Contact between Korean and Qing officials were irregular. Beyond the occasional Chinese diplomatic missions that were received in Seoul, Koreans saw very little of their northern neighbor. When periodic envoys from Beijing came to the Korean capital for ritual purposes, they were received as superiors and accorded the finest accommodations but in seclusion. In times of crisis the Chinese envoys would bring Beijing's friendly advice to Korean officials but the Koreans were under no obligation to follow their counsel. Under the terms of the tributary relationship, China had no right to interfere in Korea's domestic affairs.

To minimize contact between the two nations, China and Korea agreed to a no man's land along both sides of the Tumen and Yalu River frontiers. Following the Qing conquest of the Ming in 1644, the Manchus established a policy of isolating its northeast region from Han Chinese subjects. The Kangxi emperor (r. 1661–1722) ordered the construction of a Willow Palisade—made up of gates and outposts—to restrict the people's movement to Manchuria. The area north of the Yalu and Tumen River near Changbai Mountains (located in Jilin Province at the border of China and North Korea) was subject to especially rigorous restrictions. The area of roughly 200 kilometers wide and about 500 kilometers long was considered by Emperor Kangxi as the "sacred birthplace" of the imperial court and therefore off-limits to all settlements or cultivation.[6] A body of regulations to enforce Korea's strict seclusion policy gained the force of law. Violators of the frontier were subjected to harsh punishments to deter trespassers. Chosŏn authorities made every effort to uphold Qing regulations regarding this empty buffer zone. In one case, two Korean fugitives who were returned by Qing authorities "were decapitated, their heads hung by the river bank as a warning to others."[7]

Russia's new border with Korea changed all this. The 1860 Treaty of Peking had added an immense territory to the Russian Empire, and the task before the Russian administrators was how to make these far eastern regions their own. This required a colossal effort to populate the region. What Russia acquired in 1858–1860 was a vast territory with a population that, according to most official accounts, did not exceed fifteen thousand people. "It was a huge emptiness, with no agriculture, no trade, no roads, and of course, no industry."[8] If the Amur and Ussuri region were to be developed into an outpost of Russian power, it would need cities, towns, and ports. But under the reign of Alexander II a mass migration of peasants to the Far East was impossible, for there were simply not enough people from European Russia to populate this vast region. The Russians thus experienced a severe workforce shortage, and if they were to make something out of their new imperial acquisitions, they would need help to settle and cultivate the land. Under such conditions, local Russian authorities were more than happy to accept new immigrants from the northern provinces of Korea.

In the 1860s several natural disasters struck Hamgyŏng-do, the northeast Korean province that borders the Tumen River. Already suffering from extreme poverty, local corruption, and oppressive rule, the opportunity to cross the new border into Russia and build a new life there was tempting. To encourage these Korean emigrants, Lieutenant Rezanov was put in charge of building a small outpost on Posyet Bay. Writing in November 1863 to his superior O. V. Kazakevich, governor-general of the Primorskaya

Oblast, Rezanov observed that about twenty Korean families had settled in and around Novogorodskiy, the new Russian outpost. He was pleased by their industriousness, remarking that they had begun to diligently make bread, which "might fill the garrison stores with buckwheat." Despite the Koreans' apparent lack of agricultural tools, "they still got quite a lot done," he enthused. "The settlement had quite a livable appearance, and although impoverished, one could not see any traces of the usual indicators of poverty—that is, of dirt and idleness."[9] The Russian imperial geographer Nikolai Przhevalsky noted that in 1863 twelve Korean families had already settled in the new Russian territories. The "poverty and rude despotism" of Korea, "proximity to our territory," and "fertile ground" were sufficient incentives for the Koreans to leave their homes. These early settlements, he explained, "had a powerful effect on the Korean population at the border and now there are many who wish to join our country."[10]

By 1864 the number of families had grown to 30, and roughly 140 Koreans lived in the Tizinhe River valley. The following year, another 65 families, or 343 people, moved to the basin of the river Tizinhe. By 1866, an additional 90 families—546 people—entered the Russian territory. In 1867 Korean settlers numbered 185 families, with 999 people.[11] Russian authorities in the region were so pleased that Kazakevich ordered Rezanov "to give the Koreans who want to settle *en masse* within our borders his patronage and assistance." "These Koreans, in their first year, got settled and produced so much bread that they could get along without any help from us . . . It's clear that these are people distinguished by an unusual love of work and propensity for agriculture."[12]

The Russian intrusion constituted a real challenge to the Korean government and to traditional Sino-Korean relations. At the rate at which Koreans were emigrating, there would be few families left in the northern province. Korean authorities responded by complaining loudly to Qing officials to intervene on Korea's behalf. Russian officials declared that border issues, and particularly the escape into Russian territory of Korean emigrants, was not the Qing's concern and repeatedly invited the Koreans to discuss the border issue directly with them instead.[13] On this point, Chinese authorities agreed with the Russians. Distracted by troubles at home, the Qing stated that it was not China's policy to directly intervene in internal matters like the emigration of Korean nationals into Russian territory, and they urged the Koreans to settle their own affairs.

But the Koreans did not want to deal with the Russians directly, so they responded by tightening border security instead. "The Korean government has tried and continues to try to put a stop to these settlers and uses the strictest measures, including shooting at the Koreans who manage to cross into our territory," Przhevalsky wrote. "Despite this, however, the Koreans leave their *fangzi* [homes], swim quietly at night across the Tumen River, and once there, sometimes even find protection from our soldiers."[14]

KING KOJONG AND HIS FATHER

Border security and Korean emigration were just some of the many problems the Korean government was facing during this period. The Russian exploits had coincided with a time of tremendous upheaval in Korea. In 1863, three years years after the signing of the Treaty of Peking, the Korean king, Ch'ŏljong (r.1849–1863), died unexpectedly. Leaving no heir, the eldest living dowager queen, by custom, had the power to appoint a successor. Dowager Queen Cho, the wife of the deceased King Ikchong, had settled upon a distant relative of her husband's family, a twelve-year-old boy, Kojong, and put him on the throne. Being far too young to rule on his own, the Dowager Queen appointed herself as the boy's regent Actual day-to-day governing of state affairs, however, was left to Kojong's father, Yi Ha-ŭng, also known as the Taewŏn'gun, or Grand Prince, whom the queen appointed as co-regent.[15] Whatever grand bargain the Dowager Queen and the Taewŏn'gun had come up with to settle the succession affair—to this day no one knows for sure—it was a highly unusual arrangement.[16] Never before in the history of the dynasty had a king been so designated with his father still living. In 1866 the Dowager Queen relinquished her regency. Since Kojong was only fourteen years old, the Taewŏn'gun became the de facto ruler of Korea.

The ascendency of the Taewŏn'gun to power must have come as a shock to his family. His son's selection to the pinnacle of power had given the forty-four-year-old ne'er-do-well a new lease on life. Until then, few had believed the Taewŏn'gun would ever amount to much. As a member of an obscure branch of the royal line, the Taewŏn'gun had spent most of his adult life in idle and frivolous pursuits. "He associated with hooligans and led a dissipated life, frequented the entertainment quarter and quarreled with commoners, drank and gambled," wrote the late nineteenth-century chronicler Pak Che-gyŏng. "All people called him bad names and never thought of him as a King's relative or a gentleman."[17] Although the Taewŏn'gun had received a thorough education in Confucian studies, his relatives saw him as hopelessly inept. He had neither the inclination nor the ability to pass the civil service examination that was required for a career in government. Apart from his dabbling in calligraphy and painting, the Taewŏn'gun enjoyed few of the other scholarly pursuits that were an essential prerequisite of the governing class.

It was therefore astonishing to everyone that the Dowager Queen decided to conspire with such a person to put his son on the throne. Some have surmised that the Taewŏn'gun's libertine ways and unassuming persona must have all been a clever act to hide his true talents and ambitions, for Taewŏn'gun turned out to be a capable leader. Once in power, the Taewŏn'gun resolutely began reorganizing the traditional bureaucracy by widening the opportunity for office holding, promoting the efficient collection of taxes, and eliminating corruption. "He is undoubtedly the most powerful man of Korea," observed George Foulk, America's first attaché to Korea.[18]

Upon his ascension as regent in 1864, the Taewŏn'gun faced the immediate problem of what to do about the Russian threat to the nation's northern borders. But another although less pressing problem also loomed: the spread of Catholicism in Korea. During the first two years of the Taewŏn'gun's rule, the Russian and Catholic challenges would be dealt with together.

The Catholic problem was not new. Catholicism had surreptitiously made its way to Korea via China through the teaching of Jesuit priests as early as the eighteenth century. Over the years, Catholic converts were intermittently purged or tolerated depending upon the Korean court's vagaries. Under the reign of Ch'ŏljong's predecessor, King Hŏnjong (r. 1834–1849), Korean Catholics had suffered widespread persecution and the practice of the Catholic faith was officially banned. A terrible massacre of Korea's Catholics occurred in 1839. But Ch'ŏlchong had reversed this trend, displaying unusual toleration toward the foreign faith. This reversal may have been due to the fact that his immediate family had suffered terribly during an earlier Catholic purge. In 1801 Ch'ŏlchong's grandfather, the half-brother of King Chŏngjo (r.1776–1800), had been forced into exile to Kanghwa Island. His wife, Ch'ŏlchong's grandmother, and oldest daughter-in-law had secretly converted to the Catholic faith. The women were forced to drink poison, and shortly thereafter the distraught old man committed suicide. Ch'ŏlchong grew up on the remote island where his late grandfather and father had been banished until he was unexpectedly summoned to the capital to assume the throne following the sudden death of the childless Hŏnjong.[19] Ch'ŏlchong's toleration of Catholicism thus had deep personal roots. When his reign began in 1849, there were about eleven thousand Catholics in Korea, and when it ended in 1864 the number of converts had nearly doubled to roughly twenty thousand.[20]

The increased number of converts was also caused by the news that the French and the British had entered Beijing and sacked the Summer Palace in 1860. Fearing that there might be a similar invasion of Korea by Anglo-French forces, many high officials sought the protection of Korea's Catholics. "Medals, crosses, and books of religion were bought in quantities. Some even publicly wore them on their dresses, hoping for safety when the dreaded invasion should come." William Griffis, one of the first Westerners to visit and write about Korea, noted the transformation. "In Kyŏngsang province a funeral procession carrying two hundred lanterns, bore aloft a huge cross, and chanted responsive prayers. In the capital, the converts paraded the sign of the Romish cult. A theological training school was established in the mountains, four new missionaries entered the kingdom through Mapo, 1,979 baptisms were made during the year, and, with much literary work accomplished, the printing press was kept busy."[21]

Although Dowager Queen Cho was a staunch opponent of the Catholic Church, the Taewŏn'gun, was not initially opposed to the faith. In fact, there were persistent rumors that his own wife had converted to Catholicism and that his son, King Kojong, had even been baptized.[22] Far more worrying for him than the spread of Catholicism in Korea was the threat of Russian expansion in the north.

The new border with Russia had concerned and confused the Taewŏn'gun. What he feared the most was that the hundreds of Koreans who had crossed the Tumen River into the new Russian territory might conspire with the Russians against the Korean government. Many of those who emigrated to Russia had experienced extreme oppression at the hands of local government authorities, so it was not far-fetched to believe that they might return to stir up trouble at home. The living standards in this province were some of the lowest in the country, and poverty was aggravated by discriminatory policies that were answered by the occasion flare-up of rebellions.[23]

At the same time, the Russians began demanding that Korean ports be opened for trade. As early as 1854 Admiral E. V. Putatin's fleet with

439 sailors visited the island of Kŏmun-do off Korea's southern coast. They then proceeded up along Korea's eastern coast, stopping in Wŏnsan, the mouth of the Tumen River and Posyet Bay. Around the same time, Przhevalsky and his men were making their way to Kyonghŭng, despite a dire warning not to cross the river. Russian intentions toward Korea were opaque.[24] These, too, were ominous developments.

The Taewŏn'gun was unsure what to do. The Korean government had never had any dealings with the Russians. Several Korean Catholics shared the regent's concern, but they also saw an opportunity to turn the situation to their advantage. The Catholic converts Nam Chong-sam and Kim Myŏn-ho secretly approached the Taewŏn'gun with a plan: Korea should forge an alliance with France, with French missionaries acting as intermediaries, in order to ward off the looming Russian threat.[25] In exchange, the Korean Catholics requested complete freedom of religion in Korea and the right to proselytize.

THE PURGE

It was a bold and audacious plan, but the Taewŏn'gun appeared amenable. Since assuming the regency in 1864, he gave no indication that he would act any differently than Ch'ŏljong had done during his tolerant reign. The French missionary Bishop Simeon François Berneux, who had come to Seoul in May 1856 to lead the underground Korean diocese, observed happily that the Taewŏn'gun "was hostile neither to the Catholic faith, which he knows is good, nor missionaries with whom he got on well." Indeed, it was widely known among religious circles in Korea that his wife had for a long time been receiving instruction and advice from Msgr. Berneux.[26] In his annual report to Europe, dated November 19, 1865, Berneux wrote confidently that "our position is good and I believe by next year, it will be better still."[27] A high-ranking official acting on behalf of the Taewŏn'gun had told Berneux that if he could prevail upon the Russians to refrain from encroaching on Korean territory, the former "would grant religious freedom to proselytize [in Korea]." Optimistic due to these developments, Berneux wrote home with good news:

> Quite recently I have been in touch with the Prince Regent through a mandarin, concerning the new demand made by the Russians for a base on the Korean coast. The Prince received our communications in a good spirit. His wife, the mother of the King, has secretly sought me to write

to our minister at Peking to come and ask for religious liberty. The leaders in the capital desire the presence of French warships. On my part, I refrain from doing a thing until I have conferred with the Regent.[28]

Some of Berneux's confrères were not quite as sanguine, however. Bishop Daveluy, who became coadjutor bishop upon Berneux's arrival in Korea in 1856, was suspicious of the Taewŏn'gun.[29] "The father of the young King," Daveluy wrote, "is not now concerned with us nor with our Christians, but how long will this [tolerance] last? He is a man of violent character, cruel, despising the people and with no regard for human life."[30] Korea's Catholics, however, were optimistic. Emboldened by the freedom they had enjoyed since the 1850s under Ch'ŏlchong, and by their belief that their influence would continue to grow under the protection of the Taewŏn'gun, they even dreamed of building in Seoul a cathedral of "imposing proportions and finished in a style worthy alike of the religion and their country."[31]

It was just at this time that the Russian threat began receding. Worried that a conflict with Korea might precipitate a British response on the peninsula that could prove to be a severe menace to Russia's holdings in the Far East, Tsar Alexander believed that no actions be taken that could further antagonize the Koreans.[32] A harsh crackdown by Korean officials on the border areas thus drew no response from the Russians when additional guard posts were emplaced with orders to shoot anyone who attempted to cross the border.[33]

Meanwhile, the anti-Catholic party, which still dominated the court under the support and influence of Dowager Queen Cho, began to mobilize against the Catholics. They accused Catholic leaders of using the Russian threat to ally with the French "to sell their country" to foreigners. Then, on January 9, 1866, the Korean court issued a warrant to arrest Nam Chong-sam (John Nam) and Hong Pong-ju (Thomas Hong), the Catholic converts who had made secret overtures to the Taewŏn'gun, accusing them of treason. "They spread enticing words to incite an evil plot to betray our country and have, without a doubt, already begun to plot a treasonous uprising."[34] News of anti-Christian persecution in China added fuel to the flames. Cries of "Death to all the Christians, death to the Western barbarians" began to be loudly heard in the streets of Seoul.

The Taewŏn'gun now found himself in dangerous political territory. His close connection to Catholic converts put him in a precarious position vis-à-vis the Dowager Queen and the political party that had brought him and his son to power. Attempting to salvage the situation, he rapidly reversed his position and, betraying his earlier promise, promulgated the old laws against the Catholics. Father Berneux was seized on February 23, 1866. By the end of March, nine of twelve French missionaries, including Berneux, and forty Korean Christian converts had been hunted down, tortured, and executed.[35]

One of the surviving missionaries, however, was able to escape. With eleven Korean Catholic followers, Father Ridel made the perilous journey out of Korea with the help of sympathetic local converts. Arriving in Tianjin on China's coast in June, he reported the terrible events to Rear Admiral Pierre-Gustave Roze, the commander of the French Far Eastern Squadron. Henri de Bellonet, the chargé d'affaires and the senior French diplomat in Beijing, was informed of the massacre in early July. The young and hot-headed Bellonet had been named chargé d'affaires due to the temporary absence of the permanent French minister to Beijing, Jules Berthémy, who had returned to France for health reasons.

The Korean purge had come on the heels of similar unrest in China. The 1860s had witnessed an outburst of anti-Christian persecution in China, predominantly anti-Catholic, which had violated the terms of the 1860 treaty signed at the end of the Second Opium War. That treaty had guaranteed Western missionaries the right to preach their faith and Chinese Christians to practice it.[36] Furious over the violation of the treaty terms, which he viewed as applicable to Korea as China's tributary, Bellonet sent a strongly worded letter to Roze. "In receiving the news of the general massacre of Christians and missionaries in Korea," he seethed, "you have no doubt thought like myself that the slightest delay in the punishment of this bloody outrage could result in serious endangerment of the hundreds of missionaries preaching in China, the example it sets may be terribly contagious."[37] Bellonet concluded the letter with an order, without authorization from Paris, to send a punitive expedition to Korea. The Chinese, through their tributary Korea, would be taught a lesson. Like Lord Elgin's punitive directive to destroy the Summer Palace in 1860, Bellonet, too, would put the Chinese on notice.

Bellonet wrote to Prince Gong, who had become the head of the Zongli Yamen, China's newly created Foreign Office. The letter was as alarming as it was blunt. Because the prince had repeatedly claimed that China was not responsible for Korea's actions, Bellonet sarcastically reminded him that the French punitive mission had nothing at all to do with China and he expected no Chinese intervention in the conflict between France and Korea.[38] "The government of His Majesty," Bellonet arrogantly declared, "cannot permit so bloody an outrage to go unpunished." He then went on to say something that would have alarmed any foreign government:

> The same day on which the king of Corea laid his hands upon my unhappy countrymen was the last of his reign; he [the king] himself had proclaimed its end which I, in turn, solemnly declare today. In a few days our military forces are to march to the conquest of Corea, and the [French] Emperor, my august Sovereign, alone has now the right and the power to dispose, according to his good pleasure, of the country and vacate the throne.[39]

Appalled and alarmed by the threats to depose the Korean king, Prince Gong promptly forwarded Bellonet's letter to Seoul with a request and advice. "If the execution of French missionaries is true, please investigate these cases and avoid the use of violence." The Chinese did not want to instigate a war. The Korean government responded coolly: "Korea has never had any conflict with France, so why would we kill their citizens without any valid reason?"[40]

Angry over Bellonet's insulting letter, the Koreans responded by unleashing a full-scale purge in Korea. The letter revived the old suspicion that the Roman Catholic Church was an agent of the French government and that converts were not only heretics but traitors serving a hostile foreign power. The Korean government then issued a public decree:

> Say no more, We must fight!
> The Taewŏng'un rose up from his seat and scribbled a war manifesto.
> Western Barbarians are making war
> Not fighting is begging for peace
> Begging for peace is selling the country.[41]

As the Koreans mobilized for war, the French squadron, which departed Chefoo (Yantai) on October 11, 1866, with the mission to depose the Korean king and overthrow his government, consisted of a paltry force of six hundred soldiers, a reflection of French arrogance and hubris. As William Griffis ironically observed, "One would have thought 600 men too small a force to root up thrones, seeing that the days of Cortez and Pizarro were passed. The Coreans were not like the Mexicans, who thought a horse and his rider were one animal. They had smelt powder and fought tigers."[42]

BATTLE OF KANGHWA, 1866

At first it appeared that the French might still win an easy victory. After receiving reports from an earlier reconnaissance mission to Korea in September to plan his assault on Seoul, Roze scrapped the plan after assessing that he did not have the forces necessary to take the capital city. Instead he settled upon a campaign to seize the island of Kanghwa, located at the delta of the Han River. Historically the island was used as the first line of defense from the sea, the last bastion against territorial threats, and a refuge for the king in times of war. During the thirteenth-century Mongolian invasion, a temporary Korean government was established on the island after Seoul was occupied. Roze believed that blockading the Han River would force the Korean court to yield to French terms.

When French troops landed to seize the island on October 15, they encountered little resistance. The soldiers simply marched into Kanghwa city unimpeded and helped themselves to booty. "Most important was the discovery of a storehouse with cases containing saucer-shaped slabs of silver . . . there were roughly 300,000 francs worth of them."[43] They also pillaged large quantities of rare books and manuscripts from the Royal Library. These treasures were transported to Paris, where they remained hidden in the National Library of France until their accidental discovery by a South Korean scholar in 1975.[44]

As the French gathered along the bank of the river to cross into the mainland, thousands of Korean soldiers on the opposite side fired upon the invaders. "The valiant Korean tiger hunters rained their bullets upon the enemy's head from both sides, killing scores of the French vanguard in an encircling movement."[45] Shocked by the unexpected Korean resistance, the French beat a hasty retreat. Shortly thereafter, on November 7, Roze received word that a Korean force had landed on the southern coast of Kanghwa, occupying a strategically important Buddhist monastery, Yongjusa. He ordered a force of 150 men to take the monastery, but it soon became clear that they were far outnumbered. Fearful his ships would be unable to escape the waters around the island, Roze ordered a full withdrawal on November 11.[46]

News that the hated Frenchmen had been driven away was celebrated in Seoul with another massacre of Catholics. Scores of these unfortunate believers, including women and children, were brought to the bank of the Han River on the site where the French vessels had anchored. There they were decapitated "so that their blood might wash away the stain of foreign pollution."[47] Official accounts of the purge place the number of those executed at two thousand, but public rumor placed the number much higher, up to eight thousand.[48]

As a warning to his people, the Taewŏn'gun ordered the erection of stone anti-heretic tablets throughout the country chiseled with this menacing message: "The barbarians from beyond the seas have violated our borders and invaded our land. If we do not fight, we must appease them. To urge appeasement is to betray the nation."[49] Henceforth, there would be no conciliation with foreign powers.

Despite what appeared to be a tremendous triumph for the Taewŏn'gun, the ultimate outcome of this "victory" was in reality a disaster for Korea. Unaware that Bellonet's real objective of the punitive mission was simply to let the Chinese know of the French minister's resolve to answer any Catholic persecution with a gun, the Taewŏn'gun believed that Korea had actually won a war against France. The result was that instead of forcing the Korean government to squarely acknowledge the realities of their changing world, as the sacking of the Summer Palace in 1860 had done for China, Koreans' "triumph" over France merely hardened their resolve to keep the world at bay.[50] The war was celebrated as a vindication of the Korean government's seclusion policy and had the effect of swelling the Taewŏn'gun's pride and resolve and that of the court with the folly of conceit, for soon thereafter they began to hurl their defiance at Japan.

CHAPTER TWO

JAPAN'S KOREA PROBLEM

Such a great revolution as the present has never taken place since the creation of Japan," Ōkubo Toshimichi announced on April 10, 1868. "How can it be judged by ordinary rules?"[1] The truth of this declaration by the former samurai from Satsuma and a guiding spirit of the Meiji Restoration was made spectacularly clear in the decades to come. The forces of social, political, economic, and industrial changes that the Restoration unleashed to transform an isolated feudal society into a modern state were breathtaking. Few could have imagined that in a span of four decades Japan would emerge to become a regional power strong enough to upstage China and then, just ten years later, a Great Power able to take on Russia—and win.

None of these momentous changes had come without rancorous opposition, of course. The loss of their special privilege and status enraged many former members of the samurai class, but more than the loss of their social and economic standing, they were troubled by the abandonment of the old ways of samurai swords and Bushido spirit. Pride in Japan's modern accomplishments also brought with it a secret shame of having to turn one's back on the nation's traditions and the deeply held beliefs that had sustained the Japanese for centuries.[2]

This is why Korea's stark refusal to recognize or even acknowledge the Meiji Restoration so enraged the Japanese leaders. When Japanese envoys announcing the Meiji Restoration were sent to Korea and were mocked for wearing Western clothing and behaving like a "country

28

without laws," the Koreans had simply confirmed to the Japanese their own private misgivings and humiliation. Their wounded pride, compounded by the unequal treaties Japan signed with the Western nations and the growing fear of Russian encroachment, were the reasons the debate over whether to launch a punitive mission against Korea—or Seikanron—took on the urgency and fierceness that it did.[3]

For nearly four centuries, official contacts between the Japanese Shogunate and the Korean court were made through the Japanese daimyo, or feudal lord, of Tsushima, an island located midway between Japan and Korea in the Korean Strait. Japan was allowed to establish a small trading post in Pusan, known as the Wakan (K. Waegwan), which literally meant "Japan house," where Japanese traders and officials were housed and worked.[4] These quarters were restricted to members of the Tsushima Domain. The walled complex subjected Japanese inhabitants to tight surveillance, and their interactions with Korean subjects were closely monitored. Joseph H. Longford, a British consular official in Japan who had heard about the Japanese settlement firsthand, wrote, "The few Japanese who were at Pusan were virtual prisoners. The resident stated that he had not been outside the limits of the settlement for over six months. Trade was represented by an occasional junk from Tsushima, and all traffic with the [Korean] natives was carried on the outskirts of the settlement, the neighboring Korean town being forbidden ground."[5] Following the overthrow of the Tokugawa Shogunate and the establishment of Meiji government in 1868, Tsushima's centuries-old intermediary role ended as the island became part of Izuhara Prefecture and the management of Korean affairs was taken over by the newly established foreign ministry.

In 1869 the Japanese foreign ministry sent a mission to Korea to inform the Taewŏn'gun and the Korean court of the change. They were rudely rebuffed. Riding high from their alleged "victory" over the French in 1866, the Koreans responded that they had always dealt with the lord of Tsushima and scornfully told the Japanese envoys that this tradition ought to continue. The Koreans also objected to the Japanese use of the Chinese character "*huangdi*" [皇帝] (emperor) to refer to the Japanese emperor, a term that they condescendingly reminded the envoys had been used exclusively to refer to the Chinese sovereign.

Meiji officials reacted with outrage. Sada Hakubo, a foreign ministry official who was in Tongnae when Japanese officials were trying to negotiate a new relationship with Japan, was so angered by Korea's treatment that he became convinced that the only option was to resort to force. "The

Koreans are conservative, stubborn, backward, unreasonable, and irascible, and they are disrespectful toward our empire both in manner and words. They are despicable people, our ultimate adversary, and should be punished." Sada advised a "massive invasion" of the Korean Peninsula.[6]

SOEJIMA'S MISSION TO CHINA

Sada's opening salvo was the first of many rancorous debates regarding the Korea problem that emerged after 1868. But the actual task of redefining Japan's new relationship with Korea fell on the new foreign minister, Soejima Taneomi, one of the architects of the Meiji Restoration and a man of unsurpassed learning and ability. Unlike Sada, Soejima did not view the Korea problem in isolated terms, distinct from the larger regional challenges that Japan was facing. In 1871 Soejima was dispatched to negotiate the boundary questions regarding Sakhalin with the Russians. The following year, he began talks with the newly appointed Russian representative in Japan, chargé d'affaires Eugene Butzov, on the Sakhalin question. The Russians had occupied the island following Nevelskoy's brilliant exploration of the Amur in the 1840s and 1850s and reports of Russian attacks on Japanese settlements there led Soejima to explore ways to end the joint occupation of Sakhalin. There was deep concern in Tokyo that the constant strife between Russian and Japanese settlers might entangle the two nations in a war.[7] Although the effort came to naught—the island remained under shared sovereignty until 1875, when Japan surrendered its claims to Sakhalin in exchange for the Kuril Islands—concern over the fate of Sakhalin colored the way Soejima viewed the Korea problem.

Soejima was alarmed by Russia's acquisitions of Chinese territory in 1860 and especially by the news of Korean emigration into this region. Even more troubling was the news that the Russian settlers were building houses in the southern border region.[8] He had to wonder about Russian designs regarding Korea. The de facto migration of Koreans across the Tumen River into Russia was being exploited for Russia's own gain, in order to blur the boundary between Korea and Russia. More worrisome, the scenario appeared to be a replay of the Sakhalin situation, where, in this case, the intermingling of Russian exiles with the native Ainu population was pursued to eventually annex the entire island. Concern about Sakhalin's fate led some Japanese leaders to believe that Russia "is now harboring a strong appetite toward Korea."[9]

Soejima believed that Japan must continue to push to establish diplomatic relations with Korea not only for the sake of national prestige but also for vital reasons of national security. When another Japanese mission to Korea in 1872 was again rebuffed, Soejima decided to raise the issue directly with the Qing. If Japan were to undertake a war to punish Korea, he had to make sure that China would not intervene. In March 1873, Soejima embarked for the Chinese capital.

In many ways Soejima was the ideal candidate to lead such a diplomatic mission. A master calligrapher and composer of Chinese verse whose bearing exuded both dignity and humility, Soejima was the perfect picture of the cultivated Confucian gentleman and a brilliant counterpart to the finest official the Manchu court had to offer.[10] Among these, Li Hongzhang, viceroy of Zhili Province, was considered China's best. Li had been the protégé of the great military general Zeng Guofan. During the outbreak of the Taiping Rebellion in 1850, Zeng directed Li to organize his own regional fighting force drawn from his native Anhui Province.[11] It was during this period that Li met Brevet Major Charles Gordon ("Chinese Gordon"), a British army officer and consummate player of the Great Game, and made him commander of the newly created Ever Victorious Army. Together they achieved a great victory over the rebel forces.[12] With the final defeat of the Taiping Rebellion in 1864, Li's reputation as a great military commander was sealed.

Li's role in the suppression of the Taiping brought him more than military accolades, however. Faced with the existential threat to its rule, the Qing court had provided huge financial and military resources to local military governors for suppressing the rebellion. This led them to assume enormous power after the conflict. The process of decentralization continued into the decade of the 1860s, which according to the historian Pamela Crossley "marked the period when political and economic initiatives swung permanently away from the Qing court."[13] The largest, richest, and most influential of the para-governmental organizations that appeared was the Northern (Beiyang) Intendancy, whose headquarters was located in the coastal city of Tianjin, less than a hundred miles from Beijing. Although the facade of the imperial government persisted, the provincial governors—Li Hongzhang being the most prominent among them—became the real power behind Qing domestic and foreign policy. Over six feet tall, with searching eyes and "a quick vibratory way of moving his head which suggested mental alertness," Li was an imposing figure. "He was ready in conversation to a remarkable degree," recalled

George Frederick Seward, America's minister to China, "He was never ill-tempered. He was positive in what he said, and met an issue squarely."[14]

The ostensible reason for Soejima's trip to China was to ratify the Sino-Japanese Treaty, which had been negotiated two years earlier in 1871 with the help of Yanagihara Zenko, a young diplomat assigned as first secretary of the embassy. Soejima met Li several times over the course of his visit in Tianjin, but it was during his second meeting with Li, on May 1, that Soejima broached the topic of Korea. The Japanese envoy complained about Korea's insulting behavior toward Japan, adding that his government's only interest was to establish diplomatic relations with Korea. Li expressed sympathy for Japan's plight but told Soejima that Korea did not always follow China's advice. The Korean court, he admitted, often behaved rudely to the Chinese as well.[15] He admitted that China had no jurisdiction over Korea and that, although the king of Korea received investiture from the emperor of China, the country's internal administration remained solely in the hands of the Koreans.[16] These admissions were in line with the often-repeated line by the Chinese Office of Foreign Affairs, the Zongli Yamen: "Korea, though a dependency of China, is completely autonomous in her politics, religion, prohibitions, and orders. China has never interfered into it."[17] Li told the Japanese ambassador that Korea was undergoing many difficulties and that neighboring countries "should work hard to preserve peaceful relationship with her."[18]

Despite Soejima's resolve to find a solution to the Korea problem, the issue that dominated the meetings was whether he would perform the traditional kowtow. Soejima arrived in Beijing on May 8, and for the next several weeks the etiquette of the imperial audience overwhelmed the discussion, with Soejima declaring that he categorically would not perform the kowtow but would instead follow the international standard of three bows. Chinese officials also debated such matters as what dress should be worn by Soejima and whether it was proper etiquette for the Japanese ambassador to hand his message from the Japanese emperor directly to the Chinese emperor or to place it on a side table.[19]

It fell upon the youthful Yanagihara and his interpreter, Tei Ei-nei, to meet with two ministers of the Zongli Yamen, Mao Changxi, and Dong Xun, to discuss the all-important Korean question. On June 21 Yanagihara was allowed to explore the issue of Korean sovereignty as well as the limits of Qing's authority over Korea.[20] Thus, while negotiations over audience protocol and obtaining an audience with the Chinese emperor consumed Soejima and Chinese officials, the essential work of resolving the Korea problem and ascertaining China's views about a potential Chinese intervention in a military dispute between Korea and Japan was being conducted, almost in secret, by Yanagihara.

The first order of business was to clarify the relationship between Korea and China. It had always been China's contention that China should not be held responsible for the consequences of the actions of the king of Korea despite China's claim of Korea's suzerain status. Yet the Chinese also claimed that Korea was China's "dependent territory" (shubang), according to the terms of the 1871 Sino-Japanese Treaty.[21] Obviously, the object of the Yanagihara-Yamen negotiation was for the former to extract a promise from the Manchu court that the Chinese had no right to intervene in a potential dispute between Korea and Japan because Korea was not China's dependency but instead an independent nation following new Western international norms and laws.

Yanagihara had come to the meeting fully prepared. Fortuitously, just days before his scheduled meeting Soejima received valuable information from Frederick Low, the American minister to China, concerning a letter Low had received from the Manchu court regarding the nature of China's tributary relations with Korea. The Americans wanted to open up diplomatic relations with Korea and, naturally having been rebuffed, had requested China's help in the matter. The Chinese demurred, stating that "all of Korea's diplomatic as well as domestic administrative actions are being conducted with the due authority of the king of that country in which China is unable to intervene, and hence, China should not be held responsible for the consequences of the actions by the king of Korea." Low had interpreted the statement to mean that despite Korea's status as a dependency of China, the Korean king was "free to act on his own in areas of government, religion, and intercourse with foreign powers."[22] Yanagihara had prepared for the meeting with this vital communication in mind.

"Korea lies between your country and ours," he began, "and has a long history of interactions with both our countries. Last year, the American General Counsel [Low] . . . entrusted you with a letter addressed to Korea and requested your help to have it delivered. At the time, it is our understanding that you responded to this request by stating that the Qing government would not interfere in that country's exercise of internal polities and regulations even though you referred to Korea as a 'dependent territory' [shubang]. Is this a correct understanding of the event?"

Both Mao and Dong concurred. "Using the expression 'dependent territory' was a traditional practice of the zongfan [tributary] protocol."

Yanagihara responded, "If so, then does this mean that your government will not intervene in the [internal] affairs of a dependent territory even when they relate to matters of war and peace?"

"Certainly not," the Chinese responded.[23]

Yanagihara reported the breakthrough news to Soejima, who concluded that Korea's status as an "independent" nation had finally been confirmed.[24] He jubilantly reported in a letter to the president of the Imperial Council, Sanjō Sanetomi, on June 29, that he had successfully completed the tasks he had been assigned, conveying that the Chinese government had acknowledged that it had no direct control over the political affairs of the Korean Peninsula.[25] That same day Soejima had also succeeded in being received by the Chinese emperor on his own terms, a triumphant diplomatic coup. Through erudition, cunning, and patience, Soejima became the first representative of a nontributary foreign state to be received by the Chinese sovereign in almost eighty years. He was not required to kowtow, only to bow three times. And he was dressed in a Western-styled attire along with a sword at his side.[26]

It was a diplomatic triumph and Soejima was lavishly praised. "The Japanese Ambassador proved to be a man of no ordinary ability," the American minister Low gushed, "he exhibited talent of a high order, combining rare tact and discretion."[27] Having succeeded in obtaining diplomatic recognition for his country on equal terms with China and now armed with an implicit assurance that China would not intervene in a potential confrontation between Japan and Korea, Soejima returned to Tokyo.

"A COUNTRY WITHOUT LAWS"

Soejima's arrival could not have come at a more opportune time. During his trip to China, the Koreans had allegedly committed "fresh and unspeakable outrages" against the Japanese community in the Wakan. Some Japanese merchants who did not belong to the Tsushima domain had secretly slipped in and out of the Japanese outpost, and the Koreans had responded by denouncing the violations and erecting signs at the gates of the Wakan forbidding Korean and Japanese contact. The Koreans had also belittled the Western appearance of these Japanese—criticizing their hairstyle and Western clothes—and had disparaged Japan as "a country without laws," which in the parlance of the diplomatic language of the Far East essentially meant that the Japanese were no better than Western barbarians.[28] Meiji leaders were furious.

Members of the Imperial Council met to discuss the matter. As president of the Council, Sanjō Sanetomi set out to recount the humiliating indignities the Japanese had suffered at the hands of the Koreans. "Since the onset of the Meiji era, our attitude has been to uphold a long-held friendly relationship between the two nations," he declared. "In spite of these efforts, Korea has shown no thread of understanding at all, but instead grew more arrogant and finally came to commit the offensive insults we see now."[29] Sanjō presented two courses of action: a military expedition or a diplomatic mission. Thus ensued the famous debate in the Japanese Imperial Council of State, the so-called Seikanron (literally meaning "the argument" [ron]) over whether Japan should inflict righteous punishment (for an insult) by conquering Korea (Seikan).[30]

Itagaki Taisuke, a principal member of the Imperial Council, took the lead in the June 1873 meeting by pressing for immediate punitive actions against Korea. He argued that it was incumbent upon the Japanese government to protect the lives of Japanese nationals at the Wakan, and that Japan should "dispatch one battalion of troops to Pusan and pursue negotiations with Korea for a treaty."[31] Saigō Takamori, another key member of the Imperial Council, also urged retaliation although he was opposed to sending troops. Believing that a war with Korea without sufficient provocation would alienate world opinion, he proposed a plan to send an envoy with full plenipotentiary powers to Korea, in an effort to make peaceful negotiations with the Korean government. He was convinced, however, that the mission would fail and that the envoy would be killed. This would give Japan a *casus belli* for sending an army to punish the crime. Saigō proposed that he be sent to Korea as the sacrificial envoy. "If we fail this chance to bring us into war," he explained, "it will be very difficult to find another. By enticing the Koreans with such a gentle approach, we will certainly cause them to furnish us with an opportunity for war."[32]

Others, however, were skeptical of Saigō's plans. This is because, at the time of the June meeting, several key members of the Imperial Council were on a trip abroad. Iwakura Tomomi, a prominent architect of the modern Japanese state and a close advisor to Emperor Meiji, was leading a delegation of government leaders on an extended journey to the United States and Europe to learn firsthand about the Western powers and their "secrets" of success.[33] Members of the official delegation included some fifty emissaries and about sixty linguists and interpreters. They had set sail from Yokohama in December 1871, arriving in San Francisco on January 15,

1872. On the eve of the mission's departure, the caretaker government had signed a pledge that it would communicate regularly with the mission members. They also promised to refrain as much as possible from making any major decisions or abrupt changes in official policy. Key decisions in policy were to be avoided or postponed until the mission's returning councilor members could offer their advice and input. The mission was still overseas during the June 1873 meeting.

The caretaker government did not abide by this promise, however. Not only were major laws enacted in 1871–1873, council members also convened on August 17, 1873, to make Saigō an ambassador to Korea. Soejima, who had put himself forward to lead the diplomatic mission, also backed the punitive expedition. His assurances that China would not intervene in a conflict between Korea and Japan had helped to convince council members to vote to send Saigō to Korea even though they all knew perfectly well that this would very likely excite hostilities and precipitate a war.[34]

Emperor Meiji was informed of the decision by the council's president, Sanjō Sanetomi, who had reluctantly agreed to the arrangement. Perhaps sensing Sanjō's hesitation, the emperor reiterated the condition for final approval of the mission: "The formal recommendation concerning the dispatch of Saigō Takamori to Korea as an envoy should only be made after consultation with Iwakura Tomomi pending his return."[35]

As expected, Iwakura Tomomi's return to Tokyo on September 13, 1873, put a damper on Saigō's plans. To Iwakura, like the rest of his entourage, Saigō's Seikan mission was foolhardy and dangerous, the most ill-conceived plan the caretaker government had put forward during the mission's twenty-one months abroad. Iwakura argued forcefully that a war with Korea would set back Japan's modernizing reforms. Speaking from his knowledge of the international situation, he asserted that the primary task at hand was to strengthen the country internally before embarking on a war with Korea.

TO KOREA?

Iwakura sought out Ōkubo Toshimichi, finance minister from the early 1870s, to join him in an antiwar coalition. The quick-witted and articulate former samurai from Satsuma and boyhood friend of Saigō had accompanied Iwakura on his mission abroad and agreed with Iwakura that sending Saigō to Korea was dangerous. Ōkubo was particularly concerned about the increased taxation that a war in Korea would incur on the Japanese people. "To launch a meaningless war now and waste the government's efforts and attention needlessly, increase expenditures to enormous figures, suffer the loss of countless lives, and add to the suffering of the people so as to allow no time for other matters will lead to the abandonment of the government's undertakings before their completion." He also worried about the war's impact on Japan's security, especially regarding Russia. "Russia, situated in the north, could send its troops southward to Sakhalin and could, with one blow, strike south . . . Thus, if we crossed with Korea and became like the two water birds fighting over fish, Russia would be the fisherman standing to snare the fish."[36]

The concern with Russia was shared by Iwakura and the rest of the antiwar faction. Reports in 1873 that Russia had attacked Japanese settlements in Sakhalin led Japanese leaders to ponder whether troops should be dispatched north to protect them. Kuroda Kiyotaka, the colonization commissioner of the northern territories, was enraged by reports of violence against Japanese nationals and demanded that the Meiji government do something about it.[37] The Sakhalin issue with Russia, not a conflict with Korea, he argued, was the most pressing problem because actual Japanese blood had been spilled.[38] Moreover, to invade Korea at this time was to invite intervention by Russia into Korea. If Saigō was so eager to avenge insults to Japan, why did he not advocate an expedition to Sakhalin, where Japanese subjects had been murdered and their property destroyed? The Koreans were behaving like children, not responsible adults. Was it right to go after children while ignoring the Russian bully?[39]

Saigō nevertheless continued to insist that he be dispatched as an ambassador to Korea. Iwakura, meanwhile, worked furiously behind the scenes to thwart a future conflict with Korea, but he also tried to come up with a compromise solution with Sanjō by putting forth a plan to delay Saigō's departure. Iwakura's "reform first" compromise plan was defeated, however, when the Imperial Council members met on October 15 and voted to send Saigō to Korea anyway, against Iwakura's strenuous opposition.[40] During the meeting, Sanjō had reluctantly announced his support of the pro-war faction but then wrote later to Iwakura that he had changed his mind. The strain caused Sanjō to have a nervous breakdown.[41]

Leading the antiwar faction, Iwakura moved swiftly against Saigō's group. With Sanjō incapacitated, Iwakura, as vice president of the council, took charge and assumed the role of acting president. At the last dramatic council meeting, on October 22, Iwakura announced that he would be meeting with the emperor the next day.[42] Saigō demanded that the decision reached by the council members on October 15 be put into effect, but Iwakura refused, saying, "Until my eyes are black [dead] I will not allow you to carry out your idea."[43]

During his audience with the emperor, Iwakura argued forcefully that a war with Korea would be a huge mistake. "In my in-depth evaluation, a mere four to five years have elapsed since the inauguration of the Meiji era; the nation's foundations are yet to become solid, and the system of government is yet to be consolidated," he argued. He warned that should the Koreans act inappropriately toward a Japanese emissary, the "onset of military conflict would be unavoidable."[44] Iwakura also focused on the potential conflict with Russia, arguing that Japan was not ready to embark upon a war with Korea. "At this moment, incidents frequently occur in Sakhalin. This is an emergency confronting us right now," he emphasized. "It should receive our full attention."[45] The emperor received Iwakura's memorial and explanations gravely and said that he would notify Iwakura of his decision the following day.

On October 24 Emperor Meiji issued an imperial edict against the punitive mission to Korea. Upon receiving the news, Saigō and his allies, including Soejima and Itagaki, immediately submitted their resignations.[46] Sanjō remained the nominal head of the Imperial Council, but responsibility for implementing major reforms of the Meiji government now passed into the hands of the oligarchy centered around Iwakura, Ōkubo, and Kido, the victors of the Seikanron controversy.

But the controversy was far from quelled. On the evening of January 13, 1874, Iwakura was attacked in a failed assassination attempt as he was returning home from the palace where he had dined with the emperor.[47] The assailants were all former samurai who were enraged that Iwakura had thwarted the pro-war party's plan to punish Korea. In February, Etō Shimpei, the former minister of justice who was responsible for drafting Japan's first modern penal code (the Kaitei Ritsurei) for the Meiji government, led an unsuccessful rebellion in his native Saga. He was captured and sentenced to death by decapitation. Photographs of Etō's decapitated head were for a time on sale in Tokyo, and it was rumored that Ōkubo, embittered by Etō's betrayal, hung one such photo in his reception room at the Interior Ministry.[48]

Iwakura's peace party had avoided war, but they knew full well that the fury expressed in the drive to uphold Japan's honor in Korea had hardly been quelled. Determined to force the Korean government to resolve the impasse diplomatically, they took a page from Perry's gunboat diplomacy, thus paving the way for a diplomatic solution to Japan's Korea problem. The question was whether the Koreans would be amenable to this new arrangement.

CHAPTER THREE

THE OPENING OF KOREA

Kyŏngbok Palace (Palace Blessed by Heaven) is situated in the center of Seoul near the base of Pugak Mountain, which rises like a jagged-edged crown behind the palace's rear wall. King T'aejo first began work on the palace complex in 1395, three years after he founded the Chosŏn dynasty (1392–1910), and over the next three hundred years the complex steadily expanded before it was burned to the ground by the Japanese in 1592. The burned remnants of the palace remained until 1865, when the Taewŏn'gun began an expensive reconstruction project to restore the royal residence to its former glory.

It was originally planned that the reconstruction would be financed through voluntary contributions, but these were not sufficient, so the government was obliged to raise taxes and turn to corvée labor. Carpenters from all over the country were called to the capital. Over thirty thousand men were mobilized for the construction project, much of it "donated" labor.[1] The rebuilding of Kyŏngbok Palace took seven years and five months to complete. It was one of the most ambitious projects ever undertaken during the five hundred years of the dynasty's existence. "It is an immense place," George C. Foulk, the American chargé d'affaires, wrote in 1884, "covering about sixty acres of ground, all walled in. There are probably 200 separate buildings within the palace walls . . . In the palace building and grounds are 8,000 gates so you can imagine what a tangled-up place it must be."[2]

The Taewŏn'gun had undertaken the project as a symbolic act of dynastic restoration. When Kojong ascended the throne in 1864, the Taewŏn'gun had made it his mission to restore prestige to the royal house and reinvigorate the kingly authority and power that had been weakened by the succession of child-monarchs and domination by consort clans since the 1800s. But the cost had been exorbitant, depleting the nation's treasury. Heavy taxes were imposed on the population. Corvée labor had committed thousands of people to work on the project, thwarting their ability to pursue other productive endeavors. The government resorted to minting new money. The consequence was runaway inflation that wreaked havoc on Korea's fragile economy.[3]

The other controversial act the Taewŏn'gun undertook as regent was the abolishment of private Confucian academies, or *sŏwŏns*. The emergence of these academies during the late sixteenth century was part of a system of education whereby certain eminent Confucian figures were honored after their death by having an academy established in their name. The Uam Sŏwŏn was one such academy, established after the death of the famous scholar Song Si-yŏl (penname Uam) in the late seventeenth century. Another famous sŏwŏn, the Mandongmyo, was founded in 1704 in memory of the Chinese emperor Wanli who sent troops to aid Korea against Hideyoshi's invasions during the Ming dynasty.[4] These sŏwŏns had traditionally been residences for local scholars seeking solace from the vicissitudes of the real world, and they served as centers of learning and contemplation. The state had granted them autonomy over their own internal affairs, including legal, economic, and administrative control of their students, land, and income. This effectively meant that they were exempted from taxes and their members exempted from national military service.

Despite their desire to disassociate themselves from politics, however, sŏwŏn members often engaged in criticism of the government. "If one scholar cried for or against something or other," wrote the chronicler Pak Che-gyŏng, "then all the rest would echo his views in one voice and issue an edict." Thus, if an appointment was made for an official who was deemed unqualified, the scholars from various sŏwŏns would speak up, acting as a check on royal authority. Such acts were called *ch'ŏng-ŭi* or "clean criticism," and many a state minister and royal household member "trembled in fear should they become targets of clean criticism."[5]

In time, many sŏwŏns became quite powerful. It is estimated that by 1807, private academies and shrines held anywhere from 7 to 10 percent of the total taxable land in the entire country, which the private academies paid no taxes on.[6] Not only did such large landholdings deprive the central government of needed tax revenue, the sŏwŏns effectively became fiefdoms existing outside of state control. They also functioned outside the law. Members of a sŏwŏn frequently preyed on local farmers, exacting from them corvée labor or grain without payment. Although provincial governors and magistrates were supposed to investigate such cases of extortion and intimidation of local farmers, the officials often joined with the sŏwŏns to cover up the wrongdoings and in some cases participated in the extortion.[7]

To make matters even worse, scholars and their descendants, or yangban, who were affiliated with these local academies were granted all sorts of privileges. Traditionally the bureaucratic position awarded to a yangban scholar was based on his ability to pass a state-sponsored civil service examination, but because yangban status was de facto hereditary, the descendants of an officeholder retained the privileges of his ancestor, whether he was qualified or not. "Even though they could hardly read or write prose or poetry, these yangban strutted in the streets or wandered about the villages to squeeze the rich farmers and lead a comfortable life for themselves without work," observed Pak. "If someone offended these yangban, that person was arrested . . . and was dragged into the courtyard and forced to submit to one of the five punishments (flogging, clubbing, detaining, exile, and/or death) yet the government authorities just looked the other way." He concluded: "These were long-standing evils [in Korea] that cannot be found in any place else on earth."[8]

The sŏwŏns were also hotbeds of political intrigues. Members of a powerful sŏwŏn would "attack members of other sŏwŏns, openly or underhandedly for selfish reasons and private enmity." Factional divisions among competing sŏwŏns led to fierce political struggles. For example, it was customary not to criticize members of one's own faction. Song Si-yŏl was the patriarch of the Noron (Patriarch) faction, and there were many sŏwŏns where religious rites were conducted in honor of his departed spirit. But "clean criticism" of these sŏwŏns and of the Noron Confucian officials at the court, including these officials' families, was not permitted by followers of the same Noron faction. This effectively meant that "clean criticism" was not so clean after all.[9]

In 1865 the Taewŏn'gun issued an order to abolish the sŏwŏn Mandongmyo, and between 1868 and 1871 he took steps to eliminate all private academies—an audacious act.[10] This was in keeping with his desire to restore royal authority and centralize power. The move proved extremely controversial (and was ultimately unsuccessful), not only because the ruling elite and local yangban were firmly invested in the sŏwŏns, but because the personages for whom these academies had been built to honor were all revered individuals; dismantling a holy shrine erected to honor the Ming emperors, for example, was deemed not only deeply disrespectful but even sacrilegious.

By the end of the first year of his regency, the Taewŏn'gun faced a widespread revolt as renowned Confucian literati as well as local yangban "marched to the palace gate by the hundreds and thousands and cried loudly to the king for redress." But the Taewŏn'gun stood his ground. According to Pak Che-gyŏng's colorful retelling, the Taewŏn'gun retorted: "I will never pardon anyone who harms the people even though Confucius himself is reborn again and walks the earth. I would not wink at a single scholar who has made a thieves-den of a sŏwŏn."[11]

In taking on the sŏwŏns, the Taewŏn'gun became a popular figure among the common people. His populist appeal was also helped by his purportedly irreverent behavior. He was fond of making jokes and gave everyone around him a nickname, "such as those which aptly reflected the individual's physical appearances and personal characters." Thus, for example, Minister Kim Sae-kyun was referred to as "p'yŏndae" or "flatfish" due to his flat round nose. Minister Cho Yŏng-ha was called "changdae" because he was a very tall man, and Minister Yi Ton-yŏng was given the title "hansusŏk, or "coldwater stone," because he was a "cold-hearted person." Whenever officials came to call upon the Taewŏn'gun, they were announced by their nicknames instead of their official titles, which infuriated the officials but left others "splitting their sides with laughter."[12] Because officials were not accustomed to being treated with such indignity, the Taewŏn'gun quickly made enemies.

In 1865 the Confucian scholar Yi Hang-no composed a memorial that galvanized Korea's literati and put the Taewŏn'gun on notice. Yi was a man of towering influence whose reputation for Confucian learning and integrity was celebrated throughout the nation.[13] Instead of directly attacking the Taewŏn'gun over the abolishment of private academies, Yi cleverly remonstrated against the regent's palace renovation project, which could rightly be seen as an exploitation of the people. "Put a stop to construction projects," Yi demanded in a memorial to the Korean court. "Put an end to a government which exact taxes from the people, abandon the habits of luxury and extravagance; make the palace humble and partake simply and sparingly of food and drink; shun fancy clothes and devote all the efforts to the welfare of the people."[14] Although Yi's remonstrance weighed heavily on the Taewŏn'gun, he was saved by outside events. The Catholic purge of 1866 and the subsequent French attack came just in time, and the Taewŏn'gun was able to garner enough support for his reform policies due to the shock of war and the immense pride Koreans had accumulated by their "victory" over the French.

Yet for all the authority the Taewŏn'gun yielded, his power was hampered by the weakness of his institutional position. When Queen Dowager Cho relinquished her regency in 1866, Kojong was just fourteen years old and theoretically assumed personal rule at that time. Nevertheless, the king's father continued to exercise independent authority and acted like a "shadow" king, often behaving as if he were above the monarch. He arbitrarily made decisions without consulting with Kojong and issued orders in complete disregard of procedural regulations.

The only source of the Taewŏn'gun's legitimacy derived from being the king's father. Filial piety was a revered virtue in Korea's orthodox Confucian society, and thus it was natural for the young king to defer to his father in all matters. The Taewŏn'gun's power was based on a single prop, the moral principle of filial piety, and most officials were reluctant to take issue with Kojong's obligation to show his father the proper respect of a dutiful and filial son.[15]

What complicated the relationship between Kojong and his father as regent, however, was that the son was also his father's sovereign, and hence his superior. When criticism began to mount against the Taewŏn'gun's domestic policies, it was precisely this institutional anomaly—Korea's "two king" problem—that became the main focus of attack.[16]

Among the critics, none was bolder than Ch'oe Ik-hyŏn, a disciple of Yi Hang-no who had served in some minor posts in the capital but was later promoted by Kojong, against the wishes of his father, to the high post of Royal Secretariat. On December 22, 1873, Ch'oe submitted a memorial that directly challenged the authority of the Taewŏn'gun. He leveled sharp criticisms against the Taewŏn'gun's "public works" and specifically criticized the vastly expensive reconstruction of Kyŏngbok Palace. Because "the Taewŏn'gun was neither king nor bureaucrat," Ch'oe opined, he "had no proper role to play in government affairs." The best way to resolve Korea's "two king problem" was for Kojong to accord the respect due to his father as a son, but to "prevent him [the Taewŏn'gun] from interfering in government."[17]

Ch'oe's memorial was ferociously attacked by the Taewǒn'gun's supporters, who urged Kojong to censure the memorialist. Kojong, however,
refused. He defended Ch'oe's right of remonstrance. When Ch'oe's critics
deigned to impugn the integrity of the king himself, however, Kojong recognized that they had gone too far. On December 31, 1873, Kojong at
last asserted his authority, punished his father's defenders, and forced the
Taewǒn'gun from power. The following year, in a move meant to signal
independence from his father, Kojong rebuilt the Mandongmyo, which
the Taewǒn'gun had destroyed just a few years earlier.

KOJONG AND JAPAN

The announcement that Kojong would take state affairs under his personal
rule was due to the confluence of many events. Rumors that the Japanese
were debating whether to launch an invasion of Korea during the fall of
1873 alarmed Kojong, who began to have serious doubts about the sagacity
of his father's foreign policy. Kojong's teacher and close adviser, Pak
Kyu-su, confided his fears to the young ruler that the Korean people
were unprepared for war with Japan. Pak had been sent to China as
vice-ambassador in 1861 and had seen firsthand the destruction wrought
there by Anglo-French forces.[18] Pak believed his country needed to seek a
rapprochement with Japan.

The anti-Taewǒn'gun coalition also included Kojong's wife, Queen
Min, and her family, the Min clan. In selecting the fifteen-year-old as a
wife for his son, the Taewǒn'gun had settled upon an orphan girl from
his own wife's lineage, the Yŏhǔng Min clan. The girl's close family ties,
and the fact that she was an orphan, were seen as desirable qualities, for
he wanted a daughter-in-law who was both obedient and loyal.[19] But the
choice was unfortunate for the Taewǒn'gun; conflict between the new
queen and her father-in-law began almost immediately. "The Taewǒn'gun
found the new Queen to be extremely sharp—intelligent, handsome,
and aggressive—like a heroine who outshines any man with her mas-
culine characteristics, so he looked at her with evil eyes from the
beginning," observed Pak Che-gyǒng. "When the new Queen sent a
formal letter of greetings to the Taewǒn'gun sometime later, he was astonished by her wide knowledge and called her a show-off with much
displeasure. For this reason, the two of them disliked each other from
the beginning, and a wide gulf of hatred deepened as the days went
by."[20]

45

In 1868, two years after her investiture as queen, one of the palace concubines and a favorite of Kojong, gave birth to a son, Prince Wanhwa. This posed a significant danger for the queen, as the child could potentially be named heir to the throne. Three years later, in 1871, Queen Min gave birth to her own son, but the child lived only for a few days. Queen Min was convinced he had been poisoned by the Taewŏn'gun, who had given her infant some ginseng palliative. From that day forward, "Queen Min's antipathy toward her father-in-law transformed into blind hatred."[21] Meanwhile, the queen and her relatives began plotting the Taewŏn'gun's ouster. Her position was strengthened when she gave birth to a second son, in March 1874, and by Kojong's decision to seek from Beijing investiture of the infant prince as heir to the throne.

Thus, the forces that led to the forced retirement of the Taewŏn'gun involved various groups, each with its own particular reasons for opposing the regent, each playing a different role in the final outcome. By the time Japan's Seikanron debate had been resolved in favor of peace in October 1873, the Koreans had undergone a dramatic political upheaval of their own.

Of the many items on the agenda of Kojong's new government, the most pressing was the review of Korea's Japan policy. On August 4, 1874, Kojong received a communication from the Zongli Yamen in Beijing notifying him of Japan's recent expedition to Taiwan. The Yamen relayed fears that Japan might collude with Britain and France against Korea and urged Korea to sign treaties with these countries to check Japanese ambitions. "France and America still have unsolved conflicts with Korea, so they will certainly send their troops to help Japan. Korea can't win against these countries. If China can help set up treaties between Korea, France, and America, then Japan will be isolated. The Japanese will not easily attack Korea, and the Korean people will be safe."[22]

Kojong conferred with his two most trusted ministers, Pak Kyu-su and Yi Yu-wŏn, about what should be done. Yi strenuously opposed entering into relations with Western powers, stating that Korea's Catholic "traitors" would use the alliance to undermine Confucian morality and spread their heterodox faith, just as they had done during the period that led up to the French invasion of 1866.[23] Pak agreed that the news from China was troubling, but suggested that instead of forming an alliance with Western powers, which was unthinkable, Korea should form an alliance with Japan, for Western powers could not be trusted. He had not forgotten what the Anglo-French forces had done to the Summer Palace in 1860.

46

On August 9 Kojong sent his reply to Beijing. His government rejected out of hand the Zongli Yamen's advice about entering treaty relations with France and the United States. Instead, Korea was open to pursuing new relations with Japan. To make good on this promise, leading members of the Taewŏn'gun's inner circle were purged. Among these was An Dong-jun, who had been in charge of Korean-Japanese relations. On August 11 Yi Yu-wŏn submitted a memorial to the king criticizing An for "wrecking" Korea's relations with Japan and suggested that a Korean envoy be sent immediately to Japan to help repair the damage An had caused. "Japan had relations with Korea for three hundred years without any major conflicts . . . All of a sudden, three years ago, for no reason at all, our relations started to go sour. Today, it almost seems as if we are cut off from our relations with Japan entirely." The blame for this situation lay directly at the feet of An Dong-jun. "[The government] had only trusted the word of one man, the *pyŏlch'a* [charged with interpreting dispatches to the *waegwan*] and he did as he pleased."[24] Pak agreed with Yi and both men recommended harsh punishment. An was sentenced to death and beheaded on April 9, 1875.[25]

Clearly, An was scapegoated by the new government in the hope that his execution might mollify the Japanese. But this did not prevent a fierce debate among Kojong's officials about whether the government should receive Japanese communications. There were still those who objected to the fact that Japan had used the terms "Great Nation of Japan" (*taeilbon*) and "emperor" (*hwangche*) as the title for its sovereign. They also objected to Japanese officials' use of steamed-powered ships and their wearing Western-style attire in meeting Korea's Tongnae provincial officials. Pak Kyu-su and Yi Yu-wŏn, however, strenuously argued that given that the Qing emperor himself had received the Japanese ambassadors in 1871, why should "our low-level provincial officials object?"[26]

During a tense conference on June 13, 1875, Pak argued that continued refusal to receive Japanese communications would mean certain war. "We will not have another opportunity [to receive the official letter from Japan]," he decried. "If we receive an official letter after cannons have been fired, we will already have been disgraced!"[27] A survey of opinions revealed that the court continued to be split on the issue. Pak advised that Kojong make the decision, but Kojong refused, stating that he would leave the decision up to his ministers.[28]

Meanwhile, the new developments in Korea, and especially news of the execution of An Dong-jun in April, led Meiji leaders to believe that Kojong's government might be susceptible to intimidation.[29] They would open Korea "peacefully" by imposing Western-style "gunboat" diplomacy, the same kind of pressure used on Japan by Commodore Perry twenty years earlier. The timing seemed propitious for such a move. In May 1875, Japan had signed the Treaty of Saint Petersburg, settling the question of Sakhalin and dispelling Japan's fears that Russia might intervene in its actions to open Korea. China, too, was embroiled in a new dispute with Britain over the murder of British vice-consul Augustus Raymond Margary in February of that year, lessening the likelihood of Chinese interference. Emboldened by these events, Iwakura approved the dispatch of the gunboat *Un'yō* to provoke a violent Korean response that would serve as a raison d'être and leverage to force Korea's hand. This was done on conditions of great secrecy. "Only a very few even among the ministers knew of it."[30] Iwakura wanted to prevent any excitement of the conquer Korea advocates. He still had to be cautious.

According to the Japanese version of events, the *Un'yō* was on a mission to survey Korea's coastal waters when a party of sailors landed on Kanghwa to seek food and water. The landing, which took place on September 20, provoked a response from Korean shore batteries, which opened fire on the *Un'yō*. The *Un'yō* retaliated by bombarding the Korean fort and landing a force that engaged the Koreans. Armed with modern rifles, the Japanese made short order of the small Korean force. "Most of the garrison were shot or drowned, the fort dismantled, and the spoil carried to the ship." The *Un'yō* then sailed for home, returning to Nagasaki on September 23.[31]

Although the *Un'yō* episode was no more than a minor clash involving a few dozen men, it provided the necessary pretext for the Meiji government to demand concessions from the Koreans. A special Court Council meeting was held in the presence of the emperor, and it was decided that two warships should be dispatched to Pusan to protect the lives of Japanese residents living in Korea. Kuroda Kiyotaka, the former director of the Hokkaidō Colonization Office, was appointed minister plenipotentiary and ordered to set sail for Korea on January 31, 1876, to demand an apology from the Korean government.[32] After obtaining an apology, he was tasked to negotiate a treaty of amity and commerce. Just a few years earlier Kuroda had opposed Saigō's request to be sent as an envoy, but the political upheavals of 1873 had altered his thinking. The *Un'yo* incident could not be ignored even if it had been manufactured and provoked by Japan, and Korea's refusal to accept Japan's terms would justify the use of military force.

MORI ARINORI GOES TO CHINA

As tensions between Japan and Korea mounted, the Meiji government appointed Mori Arinori as a special envoy to enlist Chinese help in resolving Japan-Korean tensions. Mori was known as "a Westerner born of Japan," or "Japan's Western offspring," as his intimate friend Itō Hirobumi once described him. For twenty years after the Meiji Restoration until his untimely death in 1889 by an assassin's sword, Mori had been a symbol to both Japanese and Westerners alike of his country's rapid and yet painful strides toward modernity. He was the first diplomatic envoy to America, the first to marry in the Western fashion, the first to advocate the discarding of samurai swords, the first and last and only one to recommend the abolition of the Japanese language, and, finally, the first education minister under the new cabinet system. As his biographer Ivan Parker Hall put it, "Mori had managed cautiously to amaze, to amuse, or to horrify—depending on the viewer."[33]

Unfortunately, Mori's meetings with Chinese officials went nowhere. When he met the Zongli Yamen on January 10, 1876, Mori took up the subject of the Qing-Korea suzerainty relationship that Soejima and Yanagihara had broached back in 1873. Because Korea was considered China's "tributary homeland" (*suoshu bangtu*) and thus part of China's national territory, the Zongli Yamen warned Mori that any act of aggression against Korea would be a violation of the terms of the 1871 Sino-Japanese Treaty.[34]

Such warnings were a complete about-face from the earlier Qing position regarding Korea given to Yanagihara in 1873. A frustrated Mori replied that because China had not taken responsibility for actions committed by the government of Korea, including the massacre of Christians in 1866, the term "tributary homeland" must be regarded as nothing but an "empty sound" and as such, he declared, "the stipulations in the Sino-Japanese Treaty are not relevant whatsoever." "Any nation which has the full right to exercise its domestic governance and foreign relations must be defined as an independent nation."[35]

With the negotiation at a deadlock, Mori sought out a meeting with Li Hongzhang. On January 24, after a sumptuous banquet, the two statesmen sat down to converse, writing on pieces of paper in literary Chinese (*bitan*, 筆談). "It is extremely important for Japan to be on friendly relations with Korea," Mori stated. "However, unfortunately, Korea does not agree to be friendly with Japan."

49

"It is not that Korea does not wish to be friendly with Japan," Li replied. "Korea, being a small nation, considers it important to be seriously mindful of her own self-protection . . . She takes this attitude with all foreign countries, not just toward Japan alone."

Mori countered that Korea and Japan are neighbors and hence "friendly interaction is necessary." Li responded with a jab: "Having experienced Hideyoshi's invasion, Korea's attitude is understandable."[36] (This would not be the last time that the painful memory of Japan's late sixteenth-century invasion was brought up in the context of contemporary Japan-Korea relations.)

The discussion then turned to the *Un'yō* incident and the talk of war between the two countries. "Korea justifiably opened fire," Li stated emphatically. "Japan deployed troops . . . and maimed and killed people. This is again Japan's fault."

Mori countered that if peace was to be preserved between the two nations, Korea must come to amicable terms with Japan. "The Japanese people are all indignant," he stated emphatically, "they are demanding punitive actions against Korea."[37]

Mori asked Li for his help in enlisting the cooperation of the Zongli Yamen on this issue. He wanted the Yamen to persuade the Korean government to accept Japanese overtures, intimating that should it refuse, war between Japan and Korea would be inevitable.

Li responded by saying that should Japan attack Korea, China would certainly not sit still, and neither would Russia, which "would attempt to thwart Japan's move by deploying military reinforcements in the Amur River region."

At the end of the heated discussion, Li penned a passage of eight characters, 徒傷和気、毫無利益 (*tushangheqi haowuliyi*), meaning "thoughtless disruption of the atmosphere of peace will yield no benefit whatsoever" and then underneath them added two more characters, 忠告 (*zhōnggao*, "friendly warning"), to emphasize his point.[38] He handed the paper back to Mori.

Despite the heated exchanges, and the ominous friendly warning, Li had, in fact, already acquiesced to Mori's entreaties. Five days before meeting with Mori, Li wrote a letter to the Yamen advising them to dispatch a confidential communication to the government in Seoul. The Koreans must have "forbearance and receive a Japanese envoy with proper courtesy," he wrote.[39]

JAPAN-KOREA TREATY

While Mori was finishing up negotiations with Li over the fate of Korea, General Kuroda Kiyotaka was preparing to depart for Korea. Accompanying him was Inoue Kaoru, future minister of foreign affairs, and Moriyama Shigeru, who had had participated in earlier missions to Korea and was considered a Korea specialist. When Kuroda sat down with Yun Chasǔng, the Korean official who was appointed to meet the Japanese plenipotentiaries on February 11, 1876, he warned that continued rejection of Japan's offer to sign a treaty "was causing considerable amount of hatred against your country from our people and military men." When Yun again stalled for time, Kuroda threw in the gauntlet: "We will not return to Japan until we have received an official approval from the Korean government [regarding the signing of a Japan-Korea treaty]," adding, "I can't be sure how long we will be able to appease our armies."[40]

Kojong was completely caught off guard by these developments. He had finally decided to compromise on the issue of protocol in December, believing that this might appease the Japanese, but it was now too late—the stakes had been raised much higher. Kojong thus faced a crucial question: Would he commit his nation to war with Japan or would he back down and settle for a peaceful solution?

Kojong had already received the letter from the Zongli Yamen, which reached Seoul on February 5, urging him to end the standoff with Japan peacefully. The arrival of Yi Yu-wǒn from Beijing a week later, on February 12, the day after the Japanese-Korean negotiations began on Kanghwa, only reconfirmed this view. Yi had gone to the Chinese capital to obtain an investiture of the young Crown Prince. During his sojourn there, the Zongli Yamen had made it clear to him that Korea was in no position to defend itself against a Japanese invasion.[41] Nor did the Yamen have any intention of interfering in the conflict as they believed that the issue was an internal matter and must be resolved by the Koreans themselves. Kojong understood that there would be no help forthcoming from China.

While Kojong was facing this unprecedented external crisis, a rising tide of domestic opposition to the king's leadership had begun. Korea's staunch Confucian isolationists, like Ch'oe Ik-hyǒn, who had allied with Kojong in 1873 to oust his father from power, now turned against him. Ch'oe led a group of fifty scholars to the gate of Kyǒngbok Palace demanding that the court not seek peace with Japan. They held axes in their hands symbolizing their willingness to be executed for their remonstrance. "Although they call themselves Japanese, they are really Western bandits," Ch'oe warned.[42]

At the court conference on February 14, Kojong's councilors were in turmoil. They agreed that the country was incapable of mobilizing sufficient resources for war with Japan, but they also faced adamant resistance from the conservatives if they sought to resolve the crisis peacefully.[43] In the end they decided that they had no choice but to submit to Japanese demands. Three days later, Kojong published a decree in which he banished Ch'oe Ik-hyŏn from the capital. "How do we know that the Japanese ships which have arrived on our shores will join forces with the Westerners?" Kojong declared. "Ch'oe thoughtlessly submitted a memorial in which he urged me to reject heterodoxy but he was really advocating a policy that would bring ruin upon a whole generation and [in doing] so ill-used his King recklessly."[44]

On the morning of February 27, 1876, representatives of Korea and Japan met on Kanghwa Island to sign the Japan-Korea Treaty of Amity, which declared in the first article that Korea was an independent state "which enjoys the right of equality with Japan." By emphasizing Korea's independent status, the treaty drove the first wedge between China and Korea, as Japan could now claim a legal foothold on the peninsula. The debate over Japan also split the Korean leadership, forcing Kojong to face the challenges of the next decade seriously weakened by domestic opposition. These political divisions would continue to widen, giving rise to turmoil at home and drawing foreign powers ever more deeply into the maelstrom of Korean politics.

PART TWO

CONTROLLING
BARBARIANS WITH
BARBARIANS

THE QING EMPIRE WAS convinced that threats to Korea from foreign powers could only be countered through active diplomacy. If Korea could be induced to enter into treaty relations with Western powers, and if these powers developed sufficient commercial interests in the peninsula, they might serve as a check on each other's ambitions. By adapting China's ancient principle of using "barbarians to control barbarians" yi yi zhi yi [以夷制夷] to Western principles of international relations, the Qing produced a creative new policy to deal with the new challenges.

The author of China's new Korea policy was a mid-level official serving in the Chinese embassy in Japan, Huang Zunxian. Like many Chinese officials, Huang believed that the most serious threat to Korea was not Japan, but Russia. In 1880 he produced his brainchild, a pathbreaking policy paper, "A Strategy for Korea," that clearly articulated China's view of Korea's new place in the emerging international order in East Asia. Huang proposed a "balance of power" with a familiar Chinese spin: China and Korea, as natural allies, had to remain as "close as lips and teeth." For historical and geographical reasons, Korea and Japan should also be united in friendship. Huang also encouraged Korea to form diplomatic relations with the United States. Korea would deter the Russian threat through alliances with both Japan and the United States. The

Korean-American Treaty was negotiated in China and signed in Korea in 1882.

These developments created a major backlash among the more conservative elements of Korean society. A rebellion, led by discontented soldiers, against Japanese influences erupted in Seoul in 1882. The rebels destroyed the Japanese legation and placed the Taewŏn'gun back in power. The primary question the Chinese faced was what this outbreak of violence meant for their Korea policy. China responded by sending troops to Korea. This was a significant departure in China's principle of noninterference under the traditional tributary system, and it brought about a transformation in China's relationship with Korea. The 1882 incident also led to the dispatch of Japanese troops to the peninsula for the first time since the late sixteenth century. All this had come about not by any specific design on Korea by China or Japan, but by the chaotic domestic situation on the peninsula.

China's tightening authority over Korea and the slow pace of reform led to the emergence of a new faction of radical young progressive leaders in Korea who were influenced by the revolutionary modernization program adopted by Meiji Japan. Another confrontation took place between China and Japan in 1884 when these radicals attempted a coup, with tacit Japanese support, to wrest control of the China-backed Korean government. China responded with overwhelming force, put down the coup, and forced Japan to back down. This was the second time in four years that the two powers almost came to blows in and over Korea. Although the Convention of Tianjin, signed on April 18, 1885, had temporarily settled the conflict between the two countries, its practical effect was to eliminate China's claim to exclusive influence over Korea. Japan now shared that claim.

Turmoil in Korea also led to the unexpected consequence of a resurgence of British interests in the peninsula. In 1885 the British seized Port Hamilton (Kŏmun-do) located on Korea's southern coast. This was partly due to heightened tensions between Russia and Britain over Afghanistan. As the Great Game spread from Central Asia to East Asia, the British occupied the Korean island from which to interdict Vladivostok and Russian forces in the Pacific. The British government was apprehensive of Kŏmun-do becoming a key naval coaling station for Russia.

Dramatic changes in Russia's Far Eastern policy were also oc-curring. For nearly three decades since 1860, when Russia had ac-quired the land north of the Amur and east of the Ussuri from China, the Russian Far East had been relatively quiet. In the intervening years, Russian interest and energy had been focused on Central Asia in the contest against the British. By the 1890s, however, the Central Asian khanates of Khiva, Bokhara, and Khokland had fallen to Russian control, and Russia's attention shifted back to East Asia.

Thus began Russia's second drive toward the Pacific. The pop-ulation of Russia's Far Eastern territory, the size of Germany and France combined, did not exceed one hundred thousand people in 1880. Transplanting large numbers of Russians to this desolate land and developing the area for commerce and trade posed a signifi-cant challenge, requiring the construction of a vast and extensive transportation system. The imperial project of bringing Russian power to this far-off region of the world would be an enormous undertaking, and it fell to the great empire builder of the age, Sergei Witte, to do it. The centerpiece of his economic initiatives for the Russian Far East was the Trans-Siberian Railway, which was to become a key instrument of Russian imperialism in Asia. These were ominous developments the Japanese could not ignore.

CHAPTER FOUR

CHINA'S KOREA PROBLEM

Three months after the formal signing of the Japan-Korea treaty, Kojong dispatched a "friendship envoy" to Japan. At 8 AM on May 29, 1876, Korea's first formal mission to Japan since 1811 arrived in Yokohama.[1] They marched through the streets of the city lined by crowds of curious Japanese onlookers. One Western observer described the scene:

> Two Neptune-like braves with symbols of power—huge iron tridents— led the procession, in which was a band of twenty performers on metal horns, conch-shells, flutes, whistles, cymbals, and drums. Effeminate- looking pages bore the treaty documents. The chief envoy rode on a platform covered with tiger skins, resting on the shoulders of eight men, while a servant bore the umbrella of state over his head, and four minor officials walked at his side. The remainder of the suite rode in *jin-riki shas,* and the Japanese military and civil escort completed the display ... The contrast between the old and the new was startling. The Japanese stood with all the outward signs of the Civilization that is coming in. On the other side were the representatives of the Barbarism that is going out.[2]

Many Japanese ridiculed the parade, but one Japanese newspaper warned the people not to be too proud of their modernizing accomplishments. It had been only sixteen years since the Japanese had sent their own envoys to the United States, during which time they too "were whirled past the wonders, mechanical and natural, of America."[3]

Kim Ki-su, the chief emissary, tried to maintain his dignity throughout the visit. Concerned primarily with reassuring Korean conservative officials that the new arrangements with Japan were nothing more than a continuation of the old ties that had once existed between the two countries, Kim's mission was largely symbolic.[4] Kim had no specific agenda in mind for his visit, and he evinced no particular interest or curiosity about Japan.

This was made clear as soon as he and his party arrived in Tokyo. When Kim was asked by his Japanese hosts whether he might want to stay longer, "in order to take a tour of the country," he politely declined. His Japanese hosts offered to show him the various Japanese ministries. Kim responded that he would not be able to make the visit. "I'm afraid I can't do this without our King's authorization," he replied.[5] Kim even had to be prodded to meet the Japanese emperor: "Today is a memorial day in Korea so I am not supposed to see the emperor today, let alone do any sightseeing," but he finally relented.[6] When asked whether he was bored spending most of his time at the inn and whether he might want to take a tour of Japan's new industrial and military facilities, Kim replied, "I am used to the quietness and so I don't feel bored at all," adding, "I am really not talented enough to learn quickly about these things during my visit."[7]

Kim's passivity puzzled Inoue Kaoru, Japan's future minister to Korea who would come to play a pivotal role in Japan-Korea relations. Inoue explained that Korea should adopt new weapons and train more troops to ward off the Russian threat, but Kim proudly explained that there was no need to do this because Koreans "have kept our traditions for five thousand years and are reluctant to learn new things."[8]

This attitude was deeply worrying to the Japanese. Their concern became particularly acute in late 1877 when Hanabusa Yoshitada, the future Japanese chargé d'affaires in Seoul, first expressed his concern that Russia might use the Russo-Turkish War (1877–1878) as a pretext for seizing the Gulf of Lazareff (Wŏnsan) on Korea's east coast. Similar warnings were raised by the Chinese minister in Japan, He Ruzhang. "The troubles of Korea stem not from Japan but from Russia," he observed. "If Russia were to use force, the first step would be the Hamgyŏng Province of Korea. Judging from the relative strength, Korea would not be able to defend herself. If Korea should perish . . . how could China remain at peace? . . . That Russia has the heart of a tiger and wolf is known by all under the sky."[9]

The Sino-Russian conflict over the city of Ili in the Xinjiang region in northwestern China in 1879–1880 deepened concern about Russian intentions toward the peninsula.[10] The year 1879 in particular was one of fear and anxiety for China as the threat of war over the control of the Ili River valley hung ominously in the air. Moreover, Russia's naval buildup at Vladivostok was viewed as a direct threat to Korea. In August 1879, Li Hongzhang addressed a long letter to Yi Yu-wŏn, the envoy who had been sent by King Kojong in 1876 to secure the all-important investiture for his infant son, in which he painstaking explained why Korea needed to enter into treaty relations with Western countries.[11]

Despite Yi's resistance to Chinese advice, attitudes in Korea were slowly changing. In July–August 1880, Korea sent a second mission to Japan, this time headed by Kim Hong-jip, one of the most brilliant of Kojong's reform-minded officials. Unlike Kim Ki-su, who evinced no curiosity about Japan, Kim enthusiastically toured the country and took detailed notes about all aspects of Japanese society and development. Kim was tasked during his special diplomatic mission to persuade the Japanese government to withdraw its request for opening the port of Inch'ŏn and stationing a Japanese minister in Seoul. He was also supposed to convince the Japanese to let Korea continue the collection of import duties at the port of Pusan and to keep in place the export ban on rice. But his extended conversations with the Chinese ambassador He Ruzhang and Counselor Huang Zunxian proved to be the highlight of the trip.

During his monthlong sojourn in Japan, Kim met with He and Huang six times between July 15 and August 3. During their confidential conversations, conducted on pieces of paper in literary Chinese (C. *bitan*, K. *p'ildam*), they discussed a wide range of topics, but Russia's recent incursions into the northern borders of Korea dominated the conversations. The Chinese officials sought to impress upon the young Korean envoy just how serious was the threat posed to Korea by Russia.[12] To ward off the Russian threat, He put forth a "balance of power" principle derived from Western principles of international relations recently introduced into China through W. A. P. Martin's recent Chinese translation of Henry Wheaton's *Elements of International Law*. "Nowadays western countries tend to keep their power balanced with other countries," he explained during a meeting on July 18 (lunar). "Once a country is adjacent to another powerful country, it will try and unite with other countries as a way of counterbalancing the situation."[13]

These ideas came together in a pathbreaking policy paper authored by Huang Zunxian entitled *A Strategy for Korea*. Written during his sojourn in Japan, Huang, for the first time, clearly articulated China's views of Korea's new place in the emerging international order in East Asia. Huang adapted Martin's "balance of power" principle with a familiar Chinese spin: China and Korea, as natural and close allies, had to remain "as close as lips and teeth." For historical and geographical reasons, Korea and Japan should also be united in friendship. Although wary of Japan in light of its recent acquisition of the Ryukyu Islands in 1879, Huang believed that China's need for joint cooperation against Russia should override any concern with the latent threat Japan may pose to Korea. Much like alliances that were formed during China's Warring States period, Japan and Korea, he argued, must also rely on one another. "Han, Zhao and Wei formed an alliance so the Qin dared not come down to the east, and during the Three Kingdoms period, the Wu and Shu combined with one another so the Wei dared not come south and invade." Huang suggested that Korea establish close friendly relations with Japan to "promote this grand plan" in order to ward off the greater Russian threat, the metaphorical Qin.[14]

Huang's next point emphasized the necessity of an alliance between Korea and the United States, "the only Western power that has never sought selfish gain."[15] "The whole world trusts that the Americans do not covet other people's land and populations," Huang explained.[16] Such an alliance would also serve to ward off Russia and other European powers. "Unfortunately, if Russia invades Korea, the Koreans will not be able to fend her off on their own and if that happens, Korea would most likely lose her independence. In addition, other Western powers (England, France, Germany, Italy, etc.) will not sit idly by and let Korea be monopolized by Russia . . . and Korea will fall to pieces."[17]

> Russia is attempting to expand its territory eastward as advancing westward is no longer possible. As a result within ten years, Russia was able to obtain Sakhalin from Japan and from China, the territory east of the Amur River. In addition, by stationing troops at the mouth of the Tumen River, its forces posture is as powerful as the torrent of water falling off a roof. The reason for Russia's all-out effort to expand its territory in the East is to fulfill what it was unable to achieve in Europe. *Korea's strategic position in Asia guarantees to trigger conflict. Furthermore, a threatened Korea will inevitably create a crisis in Central and East Asia.* Therefore, if Russia embarked on conquering territory it must begin with Korea. . . . *There is no greater task today than to block Russia's advance.* What strategy should Korea adopt to achieve this? The only way is to devise a plan for Korea to self-strengthen herself by having intimate relations with China, association with Japan, and an alliance with the United States.[18]

Huang's strategy for Korea—close ties with China, cooperation with Japan, and diplomatic relations with the United States—was his solution to the threat posed to Korea by Russia. Shortly before he departed for Korea, Huang presented Kim Hong-jip with the booklet that he had privately drafted. To avoid his country "being sliced up as a cucumber," Huang urged Kim to take on a leadership role in implementing this policy.

Upon his return to Korea, Kim had an audience with King Kojong. With Huang's *A Strategy for Korea* in hand, Kim sought to impress upon the young king the importance of implementing Huang's grand plan for Korea. "The most important thing with regard to making ourselves strong," Kim emphasized to Kojong, "is that we have to learn to protect ourselves and to keep the foreigners away from us."[19] Kim also presented Kojong with a detailed report about all his findings on the Japanese economy, education, navy, army, dress, and penal system. Kojong received the news of Japan's rapid progress solemnly. "Although the Japanese say they want to help us and work with us, we cannot trust them completely," Kojong declared, adding, "We must become prosperous and strong by our own efforts." Kim agreed, but said that although the "Japanese could not be fully trusted," they worried that Koreans were not "apt at managing their foreign affairs."[20]

Despite Kojong's misgivings, Huang's treatise made a profound impact on the young king. On October 11, Kojong summoned current and past ministers to the palace and told them to read the booklet. He was convinced that Korea should pursue a flexible and long-term approach to establishing relationships with Western powers and that Korea's isolationist foreign policy was no longer sustainable in the current international environment.[21]

ADMIRAL SHUFELDT TO TIANJIN

It was thus with some relief to the Chinese that an unexpected visitor made his way to Japan. The fortuitous arrival of American commodore Robert W. Shufeldt in Nagasaki during the spring of 1880 came as something of a godsend to the Chinese. Commodore Shufeldt commanded the USS *Ticonderoga* on a mission to Africa, the Middle East, and Asia in an attempt by the United States to further open those regions to American trade. The Panic of 1873 had triggered an economic depression in the United States and Europe, and the Rutherford B. Hayes administration had hoped that a successful trade mission would open new markets, including Korea, for the United States. The Shufeldt mission, organized in 1878, provided the Chinese leadership with a perfect opportunity to put Huang's "strategy for Korea" into practice.

Shufeldt's first inclination was to approach Japan to gain access to Korea. Arriving in Nagasaki on April 15, 1880, he was promptly informed by the American minister to Japan, John A. Bingham, that Inoue Kaoru, minister of foreign affairs, was willing to serve as an intermediary in establishing diplomatic contact with Korea. But the efforts proved futile. The Korean government would not accept any communication from any country transmitted through Japan.[22]

When Shufeldt's activities in Japan were reported to Li Hongzhang, the viceroy became greatly alarmed. Li had been urging the Koreans to sign a treaty with the United States, but he had no intention of letting the Koreans do so with Japanese help. Moreover, in following the basic tenets of Huang's strategy, Li had decided to use Korea's prospective treaty with the United States to protect, not weaken, China's position vis-à-vis Korea. Li Hongzhang wrote an urgent letter to Korean minister Yi Yu-wŏn, urging him to open up trade relations with the West.[23]

Li then wrote to Shufeldt, inviting him to visit him in Tianjin. The two men met on August 26, 1880. During the three-hour meeting, Shufeldt expressed hope that China "would use her influence to secure with the Corean Government a treaty of amity between Corea and the United States." They also discussed at length the strategic position of the Korean Peninsula concerning Russia, China, and Japan as well as fear of Russian encroachment into the peninsula.[24] Pleased with the result of his visit, Shufeldt departed for the United States in early September to seek further instructions from Washington.[25]

During his ocean voyage home, Shufeldt penned a revealing essay entitled "Corea and American Interests in the East," in which he reflected on his conversations with Li Hongzhang. In it, he expounded upon America's newfound role in the world in which Korea would play a key role— "another link in the chain" in America's path to global prominence. It is worth quoting at length:

> The acquisition of Alaska and the Aleutian Islands, the treaties with Japan, the Sandwich Islands and Samoa, are only corollaries to the proposition that the Pacific Ocean is to become at no distant day the commercial domain of America. The Atlantic, either by force of circumstances or national indifference, has been given over to foreign

flags, backed by the immense weight of European capital, but under natural law, the flow of Commerce—as of Emigration—is from the East towards the West and the geographical position of the U.S. in conformity with this, points to the Pacific Ocean as the main challenge of trade and our country as the source from which Oriental peoples must obtain whatever they need in the way of commercial exchange. In all probability, within the next half-century, the U.S. will find its largest market in Asia rather than in Europe. *Thus, a treaty with Corea becomes another link in the chain which binds the East with the West. . . . Corea can no longer remain secluded; Japan has already forced a treaty upon her and Russia is silently preparing to appropriate the northern parts, and if any means can now be found to get beyond the "barred gates" and to reach the central Government—I am convinced that Corea could be made to understand not only the policy of a treaty with the U.S. but its absolute necessity as a protection against the aggression of surrounding powers.* Corea would, in fact, be the battlefield of any war between China and Russia or Japan.[26]

Shufeldt believed that a treaty between the United States and Korea might prevent such a war, but he also saw his role in opening relations with Korea as no less important than what occurred in Japan thirty years earlier. "The *Ticonderoga* has inaugurated a movement in Korea as the *Columbus* under Commander Biddle did in Japan," he mused. "If the United States really wishes to extend its influence in the East" as it did under the "firmness and wisdom of Commodore Perry," it must take this opportunity, "otherwise we shall bestow upon some other nation the prestige and power which might belong to ourselves."[27]

On November 18, 1880, He Ruzhang and Huang Zunxian received word in Tokyo that the Korean government had decided to enter into treaty relations with the United States upon the recommendation of Kim Hong-jip. Kojong had also taken steps to prepare for opening relations with other Western countries. At the center of this new effort was the creation of a new office to handle the management of Korea's state affairs. The T'ongnigimu amun, or Office for the Management of State Affairs, was established in 1881 to oversee Korea's relations with Western nations and for overseeing the country's modernization efforts. As the most important institutional innovation of the late Chosŏn dynasty, the T'ongnigimu amun was conceived as a supervisory and coordinating body to oversee all national security matters. Government agencies both within the capital and in the provinces were required to report directly to the twelve departments within the T'ongnigimu amun.[28]

Other momentous changes were occurring in Korea as well. In the middle of January 1882 a royal edict ordered Min Yong-ik, the head of the Department of Military Matters and Queen Min's favorite nephew, to work out a sweeping program of military reorganization and reform.[29] The decision was also made to open the port of Inch'ŏn, which surprised many Japanese, who had expected protracted negotiations on the issue.

Kojong dispatched Kim Yun-sik and Ŏ Yun-chung to Tianjin as his secret envoy to meet with Li Hongzhang to discuss the proposed treaty. Kim and Ŏ were protégés of Pak Kyu-su, and part of the enlightenment group who advocated Korea's reformist ideas and whose views began to gain the ready ear of Kojong. When the three met in January 1882, Li instructed Kim Yun-sik to send a high-ranking official with plenipotentiary power to Tianjin as soon as possible to negotiate the terms of the US-Korean treaty.[30]

Li also wrote to Shufeldt, on February 2, inviting him to Baoding for immediate talks. It was clear from his letter, however, that he, not the Korean plenipotentiary, would be playing the leading role in the negotiations.[31] Chester Holcombe, the American chargé d'affaires in China, although pleased that Li would help to negotiate the treaty, was wary of Li's overbearing posture. "I am convinced," Holcombe confided to Shufeldt in early January, "that Li's main idea . . . is to control to a large extent the course of the negotiations and practically dictate the nature of the treaty to be made."[32]

Holcombe's suspicions proved correct. When Shufeldt and Li met in Baoding on March 25, 1882, the central problem of the negotiations turned out to be the question of Korea's political status. Li broached the topic of China's suzerainty over Korea. "Korea has been a vassal country of China since ancient times but she has maintained autonomy in her own political and diplomatic affairs," Li explained."[33] He wanted the insertion of a clause affirming that "for China, Korea is a dependent of China [*shubang*]; for all others, Korea is independent."[34]

But the real issue of Korean dependency was, of course, far more complex. Li's primary motivation for seeking a Korean-American treaty was to help garner US protection for Korea against Russian and Japanese incursions into the peninsula, not to create a wedge between Korea and China. Li sought to protect China's eastern flank, and that could only be done by strengthening Korea's security.

A TREATY OF PEACE, AMITY, COMMERCE, AND NAVIGATION

Shufeldt, however, would not agree to the dependency clause, insisting the suzerainty of China clause must "positively be omitted or there would be no treaty."[35] A heated showdown between Li and Shufeldt occurred on April 4, 1882.[36] The meeting ended in anger, with Shufeldt announcing "his intention of breaking off all negotiations" and to "leave the country at once."[37]

The next day, a chastened Li visited Shufeldt at his residence, and "agreed to all that was asked." In a final last-minute compromise, the American envoy relented to Li's persistent entreaty for the Korean king to include a separate note to the American president declaring Korea's suzerain status. The letter was never officially published in any record and was subsequently ignored by the US government.[38]

There was one more hurdle to overcome. The final treaty text was completed in late April and yet no Korean plenipotentiary had arrived. Shufeldt refused to postpone the negotiations any longer and declared that he would go to Korea, arriving in Inch'ŏn aboard the USS *Swatara* on May 11. Li selected Ma Jianzhong and Admiral Ding Ruchang, commander of the Beiyang Navy, to accompany the American commodore and to serve as mediators between Shufeldt and the two Korean officials, Kim Hong-jip and Sin Hŏn, who were charged with signing the treaty. The Koreans raised only one objection to the treaty terms. They wanted to grant the Korean king the right to temporarily prohibit the exportation of Korean grain. The matter was quickly resolved with a compromise solution that limited the prohibition to only the port of Inch'ŏn.

On May 22, 1882, the US-Korean Treaty of Amity and Commerce was signed in the presence of Shufeldt, Ma, Admiral Ding, Kim Hong-jip, and Sin Hŏn. The following day Shufeldt departed for Japan. "The event was signaled by a salute of twenty-one guns from the ships [USS *Swatara*] and everything passed off in a very friendly and harmonious matter."[39]

The conclusion of the treaty between Korea and the United States was a momentous event in East Asia, for it marked the official end of Korea's seclusion policy. Britain, Germany, and France all followed suit and signed treaties with Korea. Although China would continue to insist that Korea was still a dependency of China, the America-Korea treaty had driven a wedge between China and Korea, reinforcing Japan's earlier claims of Korean independence and discrediting China's claim to suzerainty over the peninsula.[40]

BACKLASH

News that the Korean government was negotiating a treaty with the Americans was not received well by Korea's Confucian literati. Across the country, grassroots conservative Confucian scholars and yangban, and even some officials within the king's own circle of advisers, reacted furiously against Kojong's diplomatic initiatives. Their ire was directed mainly against Japan. Hanabusa's frequent appearances in Seoul since 1877, coupled with the opening of the ports of Wŏnsan and Inchŏn under Japanese pressure, had set off rampant objections against the Korean government's modernization efforts, giving rise to a furious backlash that Kim Yun-sik described, somewhat obliquely, as an orchestrated attempt aimed to "stir up rebellion and disturb the peace."[41]

This backlash reached a fever pitch during the winter of 1880 following Kim Hong-jip's return to Seoul in early October.[42] As copies of Huang Zunxian's A Strategy for Korea began to circulate, angry petitions from Confucian scholars poured into the Korean court from around the country. The most famous of these was the Memorial by Ten Thousand Men of Kyŏngsang-do submitted in March 1881 by Yi Man-sŏn, a Confucian scholar from Kyŏngsang Province, on behalf of "ten thousand" men. It denounced Huang's A Strategy of Korea in the strongest possible terms. "We have no reason to dislike or hate the Russian barbarians," Yi stated emphatically. Moreover, if Korea makes an enemy of Russia, "will our own forces be able to hold off the Russian aggressors while we await the arrival of relief forces that are a thousand miles away?"[43]

The memorial concluded that for his role in bringing Huang's harmful book into Korea, Kim Hong-jip should be punished and the booklet burned.[44] Although the memorial only targeted Kim Hong-jip by name for censure, it greatly alarmed Kojong, who was persuaded to take a harder line."[45] Yi Man-sŏn was arrested and sentenced to house arrest in exile, but the move merely served to enrage other Confucian scholars, who began venting their anger not only at Kim Hong-jip but at the king's other close advisors.[46]

As rising discontent with Kojong's reign began to cloud his foreign policy and modernization goals, the Taewŏn'gun began secretly conspiring with disaffected Confucian scholars to plot the overthrow of his son the king from power and make his comeback. The plan called for a coup using the throng of Confucian students who were scheduled to gather in Seoul to take the government civil service examination. The leader of the attempted coup was Kojong's half-brother and the Taewŏn'gun's eldest son from a different mother, Yi Chae-sŏn, but everyone knew that the brains behind the coup was Kojong's father. In the scenario, Yi's co-conspirators were to enter the examination field disguised as students and at the proper moment, announce that the Taewŏn'gun had risen up to resume his role as Kojong's regent. But the plan never materialized. The plotters had been unable to procure a single firearm, and on the eve of the scheduled day of action one of the conspirators got cold feet and reported the entire plot to the authorities. Yi Chae-sŏn and his collaborators were promptly rounded up, tried, and condemned to death for treason.[47]

Kojong, however, spared the life of the Taewŏn'gun. Steeped as he was in Confucian morals with its ideals of virtuous leadership and filial piety, Kojong lacked the sort of merciless and cold-blooded qualities that were needed to put an end to the threat to his rule posed by his father. His short-comings due to Confucian moral restraint were compounded by Kojong's inherently timid and indecisive disposition, characteristics that, according to those who knew him, only grew more pronounced in the atmosphere of recrimination and fear that began to overwhelm his reign.[48]

1882 IMO UPRISING

Until 1882 the conflicts that arose between Korea's Confucian conservative literati and the more progressive elements of Korean society, who had pushed for Korea to make treaties with Japan and the United States, had been purely domestic affairs. The attempted coup to depose King Kojong's government in 1881 by Kojong's half-brother and father had not involved foreign powers. However, within a few weeks of the signing of the Korean-American treaty, a minor dispute between disgruntled soldiers and corrupt granary clerks in Seoul in July 1882 resulted in completely reversing Huang Zunxian's carefully crafted strategy for Korea. In the wake of the incident, and for the first time since the Hideyoshi invasions at the end of the sixteenth century, Japanese and Chinese troops were dispatched to the Korean Peninsula, setting in motion a transformation of the power dynamics in the region that would inexorably determine Korea's fate.

The crisis began with a dispute over soldiers' pay and the inadequate provision of rice. There was also growing tension between members of the old Korean army units and a newly established elite army unit equipped and trained by the Japanese, the so-called *pyŏlgigun* (Special Skill Force) that essentially served as Kojong's praetorian guard. When news that soldiers of a regular army unit, who had not been paid in months, were showing signs of protest, King Kojong ordered that a month's allowance of rice be immediately dispensed to these disgruntled troops.

The task was put into the hands of corrupt granary officials who, instead of distributing the rice fairly, stole a large portion of it, and bulked up the volume of the remainder with sand. The adulterated mixture was then "paid" to the hungry troops. Outraged, the soldiers refused to accept the inedible provisions and some of them exchanged blows with the officials of the granary agency. Upon receiving reports of the physical altercation, Min Kyŏm-ho, the queen's brother and a senior officer in the Ministry of Military Affairs, ordered the military police to arrest the men who had assaulted the officials. The localized disruption by angry soldiers erupted into a violent rampage. On July 23, 1882, the soldiers, joined by other garrison troops and ordinary people, burned down Min's house. "Righteous fury erupted among the people," the late nineteenth-century Korean chronicler Hwang Hyŏn reported. Fearing for his life, Min escaped to the king's palace.[49]

The full reality of their transgressions suddenly dawned on the crowd. Realizing that they were now doomed to a death penalty for having destroyed Min's property, the mutinous soldiers ran to the Taewŏn'gun's nearby palace, the Unhyŏn'gung, to seek his advice and plead for protection. The Taewŏn'gun seized upon this unexpected opportunity. Under his secret guidance, the soldiers came up with a plan to depose the queen, eradicate the Mins, and expel the Japanese from the peninsula.[50]

The guards manning the gate of the king's palace quickly fled at the sight of the approaching rebels, and the soldiers entered the king's palace grounds unopposed. Forewarned of the mortal danger she was facing, Queen Min made a narrow escape with the help of a loyal retainer, although at the time she was rumored to have been killed.[51] Faced with a military insurrection that had swelled to include villagers around the capital city, Kojong reinstated the Taewŏn'gun as regent, declaring on July 25 that "from now on, all official business, large or small, and all matters requiring authorization, should be submitted to the Taewŏn'gun."[52]

Other rebel soldiers launched an assault against the Japanese legation. They sought out and killed Horimoto Reizo, the drill instructor of the hated *pyŏlgigun*. By their own account, the Japanese had not suspected danger until the day of the riot when a large mob began to congregate around the legation walls, attacking with bullets, stones, and arrows. After the mob set fire to the building, the Japanese chargé d'affaires, Hanabusa, and a small group of legation personnel broke through the siege and at three o'clock in the afternoon on July 24, in pouring rain, made their narrow escape to Inch'ŏn, where they were able to board a British survey ship to Japan. At the end of the two-day rampage, Min Kyŏm-ho, Kim Po-Hyŏn, the governor of Kyŏnggi Province, and Yi Ch'oe-ŭng, the Taewŏn'gun's brother and former state councilor who had collaborated closely with the Mins, were dead. Seven Japanese lost their lives and five were wounded in the uprisings.[53] Hanabusa filed his first report of the incident when he reached Nagasaki on July 29. The Chinese learned of the uprising from their ambassador in Japan, Li Shuchang, two days later.[54]

THE KIDNAPPING

The eruption of violence in Korea had grave implications for both China and Japan. Enraged by the deaths of Japanese citizens and the burning of the Japanese legation, the Tokyo government acted quickly and decided to dispatch a force of four warships and a battalion of soldiers to Korea. News that Japan was about to send troops to the peninsula spurred the Chinese to action. Ambassador Li Shuchang in Tokyo immediately contacted Zhang Shusheng, who was at the time acting governor-general of Zhili because Li Hongzhang had been on leave since April to mourn his mother's death.[55] Zhang sent a message to the Zongli Yamen reporting the Korean incident although he still had no clear idea what the uprising was about.

Fortunately, Kim Yun-sik, who had been sent by Kojong months earlier to meet with Li Hongzhang about the Korean-American treaty, was still in Tianjin when news of the Imo Uprising reached China. Kim met with Zhou Fu, the Tianjin customs official, to impress upon him the seriousness of the situation. Zhou and other Chinese officials had been under the impression that the uprising was simply an anti-Japanese riot. Kim told him that it was not a spontaneous incident, but a planned rebellion by the Taewŏn'gun and his supporters. He also told Zhou that the incident was similar to the abortive coup led by Yi Chae-sŏn, Kojong's half-brother, the year before, and emphasized that the Taewŏn'gun had long schemed to take back power. "Having ruled for ten years, he still retains fearful power. He openly protects his numerous followers, who are disobedient to the king. He has become the enemy of the people." Kim continued: "The king saw that times had changed greatly and that it would be difficult to refuse to enter into relations with other countries. Therefore, he accepted the command of the Chinese court and concluded treaties [with Japan and America]. [This was done] to preserve the [peaceful state] of the nation and relieve the sufferings of the people. But he [the Taewŏn'gun] rejected harmony [with the foreigners] and regarded amity as selling out the country. He openly blamed [the king] and stirred up the people. This has led to today's disturbances."[56]

Kim begged the Chinese for assistance. "If we do not squash this revolt as soon as possible, I'm afraid that the Japanese will take advantage of the situation and intervene to suppress the rebellion. As a consequence, they may threaten us on other issues and go anywhere they please throughout our country. We would rather rely on China for support and mediation than let Japan meddle in our affairs."[57]

While Zhou Fu was conferring with Kim Yun-sik, Ma Jianzhong, who had helped to negotiate the Korean-American treaty in Seoul, returned to Shanghai, where he was making inquiries of his own. He wrote directly to Ŏ Yun-jung, the other Korean envoy who was still in China with Kim Yun-sik. Ŏ confirmed Kim's view that the Taewŏn'gun was behind the revolt. "The Taewŏn'gun knew that that the king [being his son] would not kill him, so he has been planning a revolt," Ŏ confided. "Today's revolt is the continuation of last year's (1881) plot." He concluded, "His reason for doing this is to drive out misgovernment and breaking off diplomatic relations with foreign governments, two positions which have won him the people's support."[58]

On August 9 Zhou received a telegram from Ambassador Li Shuchang that seemed to confirm the two Koreans' views.[59] It also stated that Kojong was unharmed but that "Queen Min along with thirteen of the king's ministers had been killed and that the Taewŏn'gun had taken power."[60] The primary question facing the Chinese was what this uprising would mean for their Korea policy. They feared that the Taewŏn'gun might abrogate the newly signed treaty with the United States, thereby frustrating China's new policy of protecting Korea through the Western treaty system. They also feared another showdown between Korea and Japan. It was uniformly agreed that King Kojong was more amenable to Chinese counsel and that their first objective must be to remove the Taewŏn'gun from power.[61] Zhang proposed that Ma Jianzhong and Admiral Ding Ruchang be quickly dispatched to Korea to ascertain the situation. On August 9, with a force of three Chinese warships and troops, Ma and Ding departed for Korea. The emperor also ordered Li Hongzhang to cut short his leave and to immediately return to Tianjin.[62] Li agreed with the plan that Ma and Ding be sent to Korea. Above all, he wanted to avoid an all-out war with Japan. "[We should] persuade the Japanese not to pick a fight [with the Koreans] by assuring them that all the rebels will be punished," he warned.[63]

Arriving at Inch'ŏn on August 11, Ma went to see Hanabusa, who had just returned to Korea with a large military force of his own to resume his duties as the Japanese chargé d'affaires.[64] At their August 12 meeting, Hanabusa told Ma that he had presented to Kojong a seven-point ultimatum that included punishment for those responsible for the attacks on the Japanese legation and the murder of its citizens, and an indemnity for destroyed property. He had not yet received a reply. Ma interjected that the king no longer had any power because the Taewŏn'gun was now in control. "Anything you discuss with Kojong is meaningless," he told him. Ma warned Hanabusa to carefully consider his actions lest the Chinese be forced to intervene in Korea, which would "considerably complicate matters for you in the future."[65]

Meanwhile, Admiral Ding had returned to Tianjin on August 14 with firsthand information about the crisis. Ma had chosen to remain in Korea to forestall Japanese action and to await Ding's return with more troops.[66] Ding reported that three Japanese ships had arrived in Korea with twelve hundred men but that they had behaved courteously toward the Chinese. He did not believe that Japan wanted to start a war with China. "They [the Japanese] will not dare to engage [China] openly in bloodshed," Ding assured him. The Chinese now faced the problem of defusing the crisis in a way that would not lead to direct conflict with Japan.[67]

A plan to kidnap the Taewŏn'gun and bring him back to China was quickly hatched. Because the Taewŏn'gun had been the leader of the rebellion, removing him from the scene and rounding up the rebels would eliminate the cause of the conflict and so prevent the Japanese from escalating the situation into war. "We will tell the Japanese that the Korean king and the ministers did not know anything about the rebels' plan," Li Hongzhang advised. "The Korean court bears no responsibility for this situation."[68] However, just in case troops were needed, he called upon General Wu Changqing, admiral of the Kwantung (Guandong) Squadron who was in charge of the (Huai) army contingents in Shandong, to accompany Ding going back to Korea.[69]

On August 20 a Chinese force of two thousand men led by Admiral Ding and Wu landed in Masan'po (Namyang) and marched to Seoul. The following day Ma received an urgent letter from the Taewŏn'gun asking for help in mediating the terms of the agreement between the Japanese and the Koreans. Kojong, paralyzed by the situation, had again refused to meet Hanabusa to discuss the seven-point ultimatum, and the Taewŏn'gun was worried what the Japanese might do next.[70] Ma quickly realized that this was the opportunity to put into action his plan for kidnapping the Taewŏn'gun. He wrote back that Chinese troops would be arriving in Seoul and that "they came solely to restrain the Japanese. There are no other intentions."[71]

The Taewŏn'gun greeted Ma, Wu, and Ding warmly when they visited his palace on August 26. Ma tried to put the Taewŏn'gun at ease, praising the Taewŏn'gun's taste in his furnishings and design.[72] As was the custom, the Taewŏn'gun returned their courtesy call that afternoon. Ma then lured him in a "conversation in writing" (*bitan*) while Chinese troops surreptitiously began arresting the Korean guards who had accompanied the regent. After some time, when all the Korean guards had been detained, Ma abruptly wrote:

"Do you know the Korean king has been invested by the Chinese emperor?"

The Taewŏn'gun looked up, startled.

"By initiating the Imo Rebellion you have usurped the king's power," Ma glared, "you have killed the kings' officials and replaced them with your followers. What you did to the king shows your disrespect for the Chinese emperor."

Realizing he had been deceived, the Taewŏn'gun sprang up from the table and saw that his guards were no longer there. Ma then forced him into a sedan chair and he was carried, in drenching rain, to a waiting ship bound for Tianjin.[73]

Korea's "two king problem" had thus been temporarily resolved, not by the Koreans themselves, but by the Chinese who abducted the Taewŏn'gun and proceeded to directly intervene in Korea's domestic affairs. It was a major departure from the tradition of noninterference under the tributary system that began a complete metamorphosis of China's relationship with Korea, marking the beginning of China's domination over the peninsula. The 1882 incident also led to a military confrontation between Japanese and Chinese troops on the Korean Peninsula. This had come about, not by China or Japan having any specific design on Korea, but by the chaotic domestic situation on the peninsula. The Chinese had realized that the policy of persuading Korea through informal advice, and restraining Western powers through skillful diplomacy, were no longer viable because of

Korea's unstable political situation and the continual threat to Kojong's legitimacy posed by his father. Thus, China quickly changed its policy by abandoning its long-standing practice of maintaining distance and noninterference in Korean affairs and tightening China's direct authority over the peninsula.[74]

The more subtle consequence of the 1882 Imo Uprising, however, was its impact on the public perception of the Korean king and the queen. Overwhelmed by events, Kojong's weaknesses and deficiencies were now exposed for all to see. However, Queen Min, believed to have been killed during the uprising, emerged from the crisis very much alive, and more powerful than ever. After a futile search for her corpse, the Taewŏn'gun had ordered that some of her clothes be placed in an empty coffin. A state funeral was announced for the deceased queen, and officials were directed to put on their mourning clothes. "The Taewŏn'gun intended to act as if she was already dead," observed Hwang Hyŏn. "His thinking was that everyone would think of her as dead even if she were, by chance, still alive."[75] But to the queen's great fortune, the Chinese had saved her from this phantom death. She returned to the palace from her hiding place in the countryside shortly after the Taewŏn'gun was whisked away to Tianjin. Following her miraculous "resurrection," the Chinese knew that they could count on her to be a staunch ally as they embarked on their dominance of the Korean Peninsula.

APOLOGY MISSION

On October 13, 1882, a Korean mission of apology arrived in Tokyo. In the wake of the Imo Uprising, the Japanese had insisted that the Korean government send the mission as a way to "repair the trust between Korea and Japan."[76] The mission had been part of the agreement signed between the two countries in August 1882, known as the Treaty of Chelmup'o. According to the text of the treaty, Korean envoys were to be sent to Japan to ratify the treaty and personally apologize for the damages incurred by the Korean uprising The plenipotentiary official responsible for this delicate task was Pak Yŏng-hyo, who was just twenty-one years old. Pak was the son of an obscure yangban scholar from Suwŏn, but because he was married to Princess Yŏnghye, the only daughter of the heirless King Ch'ŏlchong, he was given the title Prince Kŭmnŭng and henceforth became one of the ranking nobles of the Chosŏn dynasty. Although his marriage lasted just a few months, due to the early death of his wife, his marital ties to the royal family gave him a distinct advantage in his subsequent political career. For a man barely out of his teens, his selection as chief envoy to Japan was an extraordinary undertaking. The year before, in February 1881, he had been selected as a member of the "gentleman's mission" that had been organized as part of the Korean government's reform effort to study the conditions in Japan. During that visit, Pak toured Japanese military facilities, schools, factories, post offices, museums, arsenals, and hospitals. This time, he was asked to lead the mission. Throughout his two-month sojourn in Japan, Pak met with various Japanese ministers and officials, and even Emperor Meiji himself. He later confided that this youthful journey to Japan had been a turning point in his life and convinced him that Korea must follow the Meiji model for its own modernizing reforms.[77] Pak was accompanied by Kim Ok-kyun, an acquaintance of his student days. Both men had studied with Pak Kyu-su, Kojong's close advisor and the man most responsible for overseeing the Korea-Japan treaty in 1876.[78] Part of a small coterie of progressive reformers close to King Kojong, Kim was ten years older than Pak and had come from very different stock. His father held no official position of any consequence and, unlike Pak, he had not come from a prominent yangban family. But his innate intelligence more than made up for his lackluster pedigree. Kim passed the higher service examination at the relatively young age of twenty-one with the highest honors, a remarkable feat.[79] After taking up various official posts, he made the acquaintance of a Buddhist monk who changed his life by urging him to "cut off his top-knot" and to go to Tokyo.[80] Once in Japan, he struck up a friendship with Fukuzawa Yukichi, the founder of the so-called Keio School group who was active in the Jiyū minken (Freedom and Popular Rights) movement.[81] The friendship would last until Kim's death in 1894, with long-term consequences for both nations. The apology mission of 1882 was thus Kim's second trip to Japan.

Pak Yŏng-hyo and Kim Ok-kyun were accompanied by Sŏ Kwang-bŏm, another member of Korea's Enlightenment Party that had emerged in the wake of the Imo Uprising to advocate for the continuation of Kojong's reform program, which had been cut short by the crisis. They were also critical of China's increasing domination over Korea's domestic and foreign affairs. Although the purported aim of the mission was to sign the new treaty, Kojong was also keen to renegotiate the terms of the indemnity to be paid to the Japanese government for the damages that had been incurred during the Imo Uprising. The success of the mission—"to restore the trust between the two countries"—hinged on whether Pak could fulfill these two goals.

But there was also an unspoken political objective as well: to see whether the Japanese government might be inclined to support Korea's nascent progressive cause. In the aftermath of 1882, Qing officials reinforced their claims to suzerainty over the peninsula by concluding a commercial treaty with Korea that actively sought to promote Chinese commercial interests to the exclusion of other nations. The Regulations for Maritime and Overland Trade between Chinese and Korean Subjects guaranteed Chinese merchants the right to live and work in Seoul and to travel in the interior of Korea.

The Chinese were also given favorable tariff rates—5 percent for most goods. These types of unequal trading privileges had caused a great deal of resentment when they were imposed on the Qing by Western nations, and the imposition of a similar treaty on Korea reveals the Qing's rapid awakening to the realities of the "new commercial warfare."[82] The commercial agreement, as the British diplomat Harry Parkes put it, "clearly indicated that the relations between China and Corea rest on a different basis to those of Corea with [other] foreign countries; the latter being governed by international compact and the former, by conditions of dependency in which Corea stands to China. Foreign nations," he concluded, "cannot claim identical treatment with China."[83]

Japan's reaction to news of the treaty was predictably negative. The Japanese foreign minister, Inoue Kaoru, remarked that the treaty denoted China's intention "to assume great powers of control over Corea, and to secure exclusionary commercial privileges in that country," adding that he believed this was "chiefly directed against Japan."[84] Yet the Japanese government was constrained in what it could do. Meiji leaders had already concluded that an independent Korea would serve Japan's security interests better than a closed Korean tributary to China, and they had proved that commitment by forcing Koreans to sign the Kanghwa Treaty in 1876.[85] But the events of 1882 and China's increasing intervention in Korean affairs had made these claims murky. The Japanese government's main interest during the 1880s was treaty revision with the Western powers; and to the extent that its support of Korean independence and reform would allow Japan "to act and deliberate with Western Powers as an equal," Meiji leaders were perfectly willing to back Korea's progressive cause. But they were not prepared to risk war with China.[86]

KAPSIN COUP, 1884

Pak and Kim had come to Japan with the hope that they might find support for their progressive ideals, but they were sorely disappointed. Although written long after the events in question, Kim Ok-kyun's memoir is replete with resentment about China, but he also complained bitterly about the "cold" treatment he received from Japanese officials, notably Foreign Minister Inoue Kaoru, and Japan's new minister to Korea, Takezoe Shin'ichirō.[87] Kim had hoped that both men would be sympathetic to his reform efforts in Korea, but they had made it clear that no such support would be forthcoming. Rebuffed by Inoue, Kim turned to Fukuzawa Yukichi for help and advice instead.

Fukuzawa was one of the most prolific contributors to the Japanese liberal movement and perhaps the most influential man in Japan outside of government service. Like many Japanese liberals at the time, Fukuzawa was deeply invested in the cause of Korean reform. In a letter to his friend Koizumi Nobuichi, who was studying in London at the time, he fondly reminisced about how his conversations with Kim Ok-kyun had reminded him of the struggles that Japan had endured just thirty years before:

> At the beginning of this month, some Koreans came to Japan to observe the conditions in our country, and two young men among them were admitted to our group. I had them settled in my place, and I will apply myself to guide them gently. Truly, when I remember how I was more than twenty years ago, I cannot help but feel sympathy and compassion for them . . . When Koreans, elevated or humble, come to visit me, and when I am listening to them, it is the Japan of thirty years ago which reappears in front of my eyes.[88]

Through Fukuzawa, Kim made the acquaintance of Inoue Kakugorō, a former pupil. Inoue would help to establish a Korean newspaper, the *Hansŏng sunbo,* dedicated to propagating modern reform. Upon his arrival in Seoul in December 1882, Inoue quickly became swept into the cauldron of Korean politics. Inoue complained about China's commercial monopoly and the inadequate effort mounted by the Chinese to reform the Korean government. Chinese overlordship and the daily indignities suffered by the Koreans at the hands of the Chinese military also fueled his sympathies for Kim Ok-kyun and his Enlightenment Party. In February 1884 Inoue published an inflammatory account in the *Hansŏng*

Sunbo about a Chinese soldier who shot and killed a Korean shopkeeper because he had refused to give the soldier items in his store for free. This provoked a statement from Yuan Shikai, then the deputy commander of the Chinese troops stationed in Seoul, who demanded that the newspaper be suspended.[89]

The controversy forced Inoue to leave Korea. In the meantime, Kim Ok-kyun, Pak Yŏng-hyo, and other progressive leaders began plotting the removal of the pro-Qing Min faction from power in the Korean court. Inoue Kakugorō's recounting of the whole affair in his memoirs, *Kanjo no Zammu* (Memory of Seoul), reveals that he was intimately involved in the planning and execution of the conspiracy to overthrow the Min clan and drive a wedge between Korea and China. Fukuzawa was also apparently aware of the plot; Inoue later testified that Fukuzawa had "written the plot and trained the actors" in reference to the uprising. When Fukuzawa was later questioned, in March 1888, by the Japanese authorities about his role in the affair, he adamantly denied it, despite evidence that he had devised a secret telegraphic code to communicate with his former student in Korea.[90] In the end Inoue's testimony and the telegraphic code were insufficient evidence to indict Fukuzawa. Certainly Fukuzawa had far deeper misgivings about spreading "civilization" by force than did his eager disciples, but not enough, it seems, to dampen their enthusiasm for embarking upon a dangerous path that would almost bring China and Japan to the brink of war.

The idea for the coup was inspired by the Sino-French war of 1884. In August of that year, China and France became embroiled in a conflict over Annam (Indochina). The Qing government had dispatched troops to Tonkin to check the French, but the Chinese were caught unprepared and were defeated. Kim Ok-kyun, Pak Yŏng-hyo, and their friends hoped that the conflict might furnish them with an opportunity for bold action in Korea.

Japanese policy also seems to have undergone a marked change during this period. After a ten-month absence from Korea, the Japanese minister, Takezoe Shin'ichiro, returned to Seoul in late October 1884 to announce his support of the Korean reformers. With China distracted in a war with France, Takezoe was instructed to tacitly assist the Korean progressives.[91]

The plan was to seize the king and then, in his name, proclaim a new reformist government. The preliminaries would involve a fire and an uprising. A precise list of government officials who were to be killed was drawn up, and the venue for the assassinations, an inaugural dinner at the new post office, was settled upon. The date of the coup was set for the evening of December 4. Everything had gone according to plan and it appeared that the coup might succeed. The fire had erupted on time, forcing the guests to leave the building where the targeted Korean officials were killed. The insurrectionists then went straight to Ch'angdŏk Palace, where the king was staying, and using the pretext of a Chinese soldiers' riot, persuaded Kojong to leave with them to Kyŏng-u Palace, a smaller abode located in eastern Seoul. Before their hasty departure, the king, upon the insistence of both Pak and Kim, sent a note to Takezoe requesting Japanese protection. Once the party arrived at the palace, they were met by the Japanese minister along with a guard of about two hundred Japanese soldiers. The rebels then summoned seven high officials to the palace in Kojong's name and slaughtered them as they arrived for the audience with the king. A new government was forthwith proclaimed.[92]

But then the conspirators made a fatal mistake. Instead of continuing to hold Kojong hostage in the smaller and more defensible Kyŏng-u Palace, Takezoe decided that the king should return to the less defensible Ch'angdŏk Palace. This was done against the pleas of Pak Yŏng-hyo, who realized the folly of such a move.[93] But Queen Min complained that the secluded palace was damp and inhospitable, and Takezoe wanted to appear accommodating. Pak's objections were therefore overruled. It was a decision the rebel leaders would later come to regret. On the evening of December 6 the superior Chinese forces surrounded Ch'angdŏk Palace and the far-outnumbered Japanese troops quickly fell back. Despite not having received orders from his superiors, Yuan Shikai took the initiative and moved in quickly to lay siege on the palace.[94] In the commotion, the king and queen managed to slip away to the Chinese side. Without the king, the rebels knew their cause was lost.[95] The rest of the conspirators fled to the Japanese legation, where, according to Lucius Foote, the American minister in Seoul, "a great many people gathered in the vicinity [of the legation] making threats with occasional shots being fired."[96]

As news of the Japanese-aided coup attempt spread throughout Seoul, Korean mobs rose up crying "Death to the Japanese!" The Chinese joined in. "The Qing soldiers attacked the legation a couple of times," Inoue Kakugorō related. "The legation staff and I worked together and were able to fight them off." The next day the situation worsened. "I heard the news that my house had been burned down . . . in the Legation there were more than 100 staff members and merchants in addition to the soldiers numbering more than 200." Although Inoue believed that they could have defended themselves against the rioters, food was in short supply. As a result, the decision was made to escape to Inch'ŏn.[97]

On the evening of December 6, the fleeing party was attacked several times but they were able to cross the Han River. "By then the daylight had turned into night and the snow began to fall. After crossing the river, we looked backed toward the palace and saw that the Japanese legation was engulfed in flames. We became overwhelmed with emotion while we watched it burn."[98] Two harrowing days later, the exhausted party finally reached Inchŏn, where they were able to board the *Chitose maru* on December 11 and sail to exile and safety in Japan.[99]

1885 CONVENTION OF TIANJIN

Once order had been restored in Korea, the Chinese and Japanese governments were left to figure out what the crisis would mean for their relationship and policy toward Korea. Some "war hawks" in Japan's Imperial Council wanted to take advantage of the Sino-French War and the crisis in Korea to launch a war with China. But calmer voices prevailed. The statesman Itō Hirobumi would be sent to China as ambassador plenipotentiary to deal with the rift between the two countries, the second such crisis in just two years.

When Itō and Li Hongzhang sat down on April 4, 1885, Li had already decided that China would not risk war with Japan. Nevertheless, the discussions, lasting over several weeks, became bogged down over debates about the events surrounding the 1884 Kapsin coup. Li questioned the role of Japanese minister Takezoe and wondered aloud what role Japanese leaders in Tokyo had played in the events. Itō denied that the Japanese Foreign Ministry had any prior knowledge of the attempted coup.[100]

Itō had come to China with more pressing matters to discuss: to get China to agree to the withdrawal of Chinese troops from Korea and to demand punishment of Chinese military officers and reparations for injured Japanese residents. Li was prepared to negotiate on the matter of withdrawing troops, but he would not assent to the demand for punishment of Chinese officers or payment of reparations. When Enomoto Takeaki, the Japanese minister to China, pressed Li on the matter, saying that Itō would leave the negotiation table if these conditions were not met, Li became angry. "China did nothing wrong during the Kapsin Coup," he exclaimed. "It was all Takezoe's fault! If Japan wants to break relations with China [over this issue] then we will just have to prepare for war!"[101]

Itō came to the next meeting, on April 10, more conciliatory. Li proposed the simultaneous withdrawal of Chinese and Japanese troops, but he was adamant that China retain its traditional right to send troops to Korea in case of an internal Korean rebellion or a political crisis on the peninsula. He promised that Chinese troops would immediately withdraw as soon as order was restored, but he would not accept Itō's suggestion that Japan would dispatch troops, even if it was asked to do so by the Korean government. Li consented only to Japan's right to send troops in cases where Japanese officers or subjects were directly attacked by Koreans. Itō protested, and a deadlock followed.[102] Finally a compromise was reached. Li suggested that both countries withdraw their forces but that, in case of future troubles in Korea, both countries would notify the other if they dispatched troops to the peninsula. On the matter of punishment of Chinese soldiers, Li compromised slightly by agreeing to admonish the officers personally since they were all Li's subordinate officers.[103]

On April 18 Li and Itō signed the Convention of Tianjin. In article 1, China agreed to withdraw her troops to Masanp'o and Japan would withdraw its troops to Jinsen (Inch'ŏn) within four months. In article 2, Japan and China agreed to urge the military modernization of the Korean armed forces under instructors who would be neither Chinese nor Japanese nationals. Article 3, the most significant of the treaty, stated, "In case any disturbance of a grave nature in Korea which required the respective countries, or either of them to send troops to Korea, it is hereby understood that they shall give, each to the other, previous notice in writing of their intention to do so and that after the matter is settled, they shall withdraw their troops and not further station them there."[104] The Convention of Tianjin had thus temporarily settled the conflict between China and Japan. This was achieved, however, largely at China's expense. By stating that both China and Japan had the right to send troops to Korea, Japan had, in effect, secured an equal footing with China on the peninsula. Qing commanders' swift actions, particularly those led by Yuan Shikai, displayed sufficient aggressiveness to maintain China's superior position, but following Japan's own aggressive ascendency in Korea, it became readily apparent that some adjustments to the Qing's Korea policy would have to be made. These adjustments became particularly urgent in 1885 when the Great Game between Russia and Britain turned toward East Asia and the Korean Peninsula.

CHAPTER FIVE

THE OTHER GREAT GAME BEGINS

The turmoil in Korea had the unforeseen consequence of creating a resurgence of British and Russian interest in the peninsula. Three days before the Convention of Tianjin was signed, on April 18, 1885, the British took up a "temporary" position at the strategically important Port Hamilton (Kŏmun-do), located off Korea's southern coast. This was due to heightened tensions between Russia and Britain over Afghanistan.

The crisis between the two Great Powers was in many ways unexpected. Just five years earlier, it appeared that Russia might abandon its forward policies in Asia. This was good news for Britain, coming as it was at the end of the Second Afghan War in 1880. The British had just disentangled themselves from the Afghan quagmire by permitting Afghan tribes to maintain control of their own internal rule in exchange for British control over their foreign policy. With Russian inroads into Kabul now thwarted, it appeared that the Afghan problem, and with it the problem of protecting British India from Russian encroachment, had finally been settled.

Adding to British optimism was the humiliation the Russians had suffered at the Congress of Berlin. The Russo-Turkish War (1877–1878) had ended badly for Alexander II. After Turkey and Russia concluded the Treaty of San Stephano—in which the Ottomans ceded parts of Armenia and Bulgaria to the Russian Empire—Britain and Austria, fearful of Russian gains, intervened. Alexander had hoped that Otto von Bismark, Germany's charismatic chancellor who had offered to mediate a Congress in

Berlin, would help him out. But the tsar was sorely disappointed. Alexander was forced to accept a diminished Bulgaria divided between an Ottoman province in the south and an autonomous principality in the north. Serbia and Montenegro were also given full independence from Ottoman rule. As if these concessions, enforced by the Congress of Berlin in 1878, were not humiliating enough for Russia, Bismarck had seen to it that Austria would win the administration of Bosnia while Britain ended up taking Cyprus—all won with Russian blood.[1]

The wasted victory enraged the Russian Slavophiles. But the greater damage for the Romanov dynasty was that it gave rise to a "crisis for the autocracy" and the beginning of revolutionary activities in Russia. Following the Emancipation Reform of 1861, which effectively abolished serfdom in the Russian Empire, Alexander II began the task of relaxing the autocratic policies of his father, Nicholas I. Partly as a response to these new liberal conditions, the nihilist movement gained momentum, challenging the old social order and demanding change, while advocating violence to achieve these goals, if necessary.[2]

The first victim was General F. F. Trepov, the governor of Saint Petersburg, who was shot and wounded on January 24, 1878, by Vera Ivanovna Zasulich, a twenty-eight-year-old member of the new revolutionary organization Zemlya i Volya (Land and Liberty). Zasulich had attempted the assassination of Trepov in retaliation for the latter's brutal treatment of a fellow Zemlya i Volya member at a local prison.[3] Although the assassination attempt failed, Zasulich's trial and acquittal were viewed sympathetically by a large segment of Saint Petersburg society, signaling increasingly more negative attitudes toward the tsarist regime. The event also signaled a change in revolutionary tactics. By the fall of 1879 the People's Will (Narodnaya Volya), a splinter group of Land and Liberty, became the first organization in history dedicated to systematic political terrorism.[4] The organization enjoyed widespread public support, even among political moderates. Vladimir Burtsev, a historian of the Russian Revolution and a onetime member of People's Will, stated that the great majority of the Russian people actually sympathized with the terrorists: "The government . . . enjoyed no support and was estranged from the entire country. Its estrangement from society was such that even in law-abiding circles all and each derived malicious pleasure from whatever had the smallest bearing on state authority."[5] German ambassador General von Schweinitz put it more bluntly: "As the state decays more and more, nihilist sects grow bolder and discontent among all the educated classes becomes more pronounced."[6] The disappointing outcome of the war had allowed the mask of Russia's imperial authority to slip, allowing a handful of determined terrorists to threaten the regime. By the end of his reign, Alexander noted in his diary, "I find myself like a wolf tracked by hunters."[7]

But the humiliations of the Congress of Berlin and the increasingly volatile domestic situation did not completely curb Russian adventurism as the British had hoped it would. During the fall of 1880 the British government received reports of a major military campaign undertaken by the Russians in the region to the east of the Caspian—the Transcapia as it was known. The commander in charge, General Mikhail Skobelev, the hero of the Russo-Turkish war, had returned to Turkestan after the war to lead a bloody siege against the city of Geok Tepe, the decisive action in the Russian campaign to conquer the Teke Turkomans (present-day Turkmenistan). It fell on January 24, 1881, resulting in a massacre of eight thousand Turcomans.[8] Following an outcry from Europe for the bloodbath and worried about Skobelev's own aspirations for political power, Alexander relieved the general of his command; but the question on everyone's mind was whether Russia's eastward advance would stop. British Prime Minister William Ewart Gladstone and his liberal supporters were convinced that it would. "The most satisfactory feature of [Gen Skobeleff's] victory is that it affords the Russian Government to abandon the Turkoman country," wrote the *Pall Mall Gazette*. "They have vindicated their prestige, captured the stronghold of their enemies, and they can now follow our example in Afghanistan by abandoning a territory which would be even more costly to hold than to conquer."[9] Since Geok Tepe was of little strategic significance, the British government took General Skobelev's declaration at face value when he announced, "the whole of Turkoman territory was not worth buying at the cost of a single ruble."[10]

Britain's Russophobes were not so certain. Following the siege of Geok Tepe, and especially after the news that General "Chinese" Gordon had been cut down by a fanatical mob in Khartoum in January 1885, a new breed of forward-thinking commentators began to make their voices heard. Among them, Charles Marvin, whose books and pamphlets enjoyed a large popular following, was particularly influential. Fluent in Russian, Marvin was also a vivid and persuasive writer. His "Russian Advance towards India," published in 1882, put him on the proverbial Russophobe map. Marvin argued that successive British governments, especially Liberal ones, had been vacillating and spineless in their relations with Russia. What concerned Marvin after the siege of Geok Tepe was whether the

Russians might now press eastward to the city of Merv, located in southeastern Turkmenistan, from where they could easily be able to march into Afghanistan and take Herat. From there, the route to British India lay wide open.[11]

Russian foreign minister Giers, however, was quick to reassure the British ambassador, Lord Dufferin, that his country had no further ambitions in Transcaspia. "We do not intend to go to Merv nor do anything which may be interpreted as a menace to England," he stated emphatically.[12] Emperor Alexander reiterated his solemn assurances that Russia would never occupy Merv: "Not only do we not want to go there, but happily, there is nothing which can require us to go there."[13]

This conciliatory stance seemed to be reconfirmed by Russia's attitude in other parts of the world. News that the Russians had finally withdrawn from Kuldja, or Ili, as the Chinese called it, located to the northeast of Kashgar, and returned it to Chinese control, was encouraging.[14] The Treaty of Saint Petersburg (1881), which had finally settled the Ili crisis, was a triumph for China, for as the British ambassador to Russia, Lord Dufferin, put it, the Chinese had compelled Russia "to do what she has never done before—disgorge territory that she once absorbed." Apart from their sale of Alaska to the United States in 1867 for $7 million, the Russians had not been known to haul down their flag anywhere.[15]

RUSSIAN CRISIS

To Prime Minister Gladstone and his new liberal government, which was swept into power in 1880 on the strength of a strongly anti-imperial electoral campaign, this was all very encouraging news. The foreign press shared a collective sigh of relief. "Everything is full of hope for the new government," opined the *New York Times*. "Russia is to be conquered by friendship. The Czar is very poorly; but his ministers are ready to make any kind of treaty with Gladstone."[16] What Gladstone and the British public could not have known was that Alexander II would soon be dead—his legs were blown off by a terrorist's bomb on March 13 (OS March 1), 1881, while on his way back to the Winter Palace after reviewing his troops.[17]

Alexander III, the successor and son of the "Great Emancipator," thus began his reign in the midst of one of the gravest crises ever to face the Romanov dynasty. The assassination had been planned not as part of a palace coup d'état to place another member of the family on the throne but as part of a revolutionary plot to abolish autocracy in Russia altogether. Naturally, the new tsar had a grim view of his father's "martyred death."[18] "We knew that something immeasurably greater than a loving uncle and a courageous emperor had receded with him into the past," observed Alexander Mikhailovich, Alexander II's nephew. "Idyllic Russia, the country of the ruling father and obedient sons, ceased to exist on March 1, 1881."[19]

Assuming the throne stained by his father's blood, Alexander III, nicknamed "the Colossus" after his towering frame (he was six feet three inches tall), blamed most of Russia's ills on the "irresponsible liberalism" governing the nation's domestic affairs. As the autocrat who had launched the Great Emancipation Reform, Alexander II had been reluctant to ruthlessly suppress the political revolutionaries who had emerged in the new social and political climate that he had helped to create. His son harbored no such hesitation. The press was harshly restricted. "It is impossible to make a good beginning at anything until the newspapers are restrained," Konstantin Pobedonostsev, Alexander's closest advisor, wrote less than two months after the tsar's accession.[20] A fanatical believer in the autocracy and Russia's Slavophile mission, Pobedonostsev urged the new tsar to institute a series of "provisional" censorship regulations in August 1882 that would make the reign of Alexander III the most reactionary regime since the final years of Nicholas I's rule.[21]

To meet the regime's new security demands, the tsarist government established the Okhrannye otdeleniia (Okhrana), a secret service to infiltrate and destroy terrorist movements. The repressive measures paid off. With the help of Grigory Sudeikin, chief of the Saint Petersburg Okhrana, who enlisted highly placed informants within the People's Will, Pobedonostsev was able to wipe out the entire revolutionary organization.[22] Two years after his ascension to the throne, Alexander III finally felt safe enough to announce his coronation ceremony on January 25, 1883.[23]

The emperor also laid out a new direction in Russia's foreign policy. Although a staunch believer in Russia's Slavophile mission and proud "imperialist spirit," he was determined to avoid war. "Emperor Alexander III's greatest achievement," wrote his finance minister, Sergei Witte, "was that he gave Russia thirteen years of peace, not by being weak, but by being fair and unswervingly firm. He had no dreams of conquest or military laurels. Other nations knew this, but they knew too that under no circumstances would he besmirch the honor and dignity of Russia entrusted to him by God."[24] Alexander III saw his role slightly differently.

85

"We have just two allies in the world," he used to repeat to his ministers, "our army and our navy. Everybody else will turn on us at a second's notice."[25] The tsar sought to undo the humiliations suffered by Russia's war with Turkey by restoring the army after its disorganization and shoring up the country's finances. An adroit and efficient administrator, Alexander III "said little, but what he said he meant, and he never retreated from his word."[26]

Alexander III's first real foreign policy challenge occurred in March 1885. Despite his father's solemn pledge regarding the Russian annexation of Merv, he allowed an enterprising young officer, Lieutenant Alikhanov, to take the city on March 16, 1884. This action received howls of protests from Britain's Russophobes but had surprisingly little effect on the Gladstone government, which was not inclined to be pushed into precipitate action by an alarmist press. Marvin's pamphlet with the headline in all capital letters—"The annexation of Merv, being inevitably attended with the incorporation of the Sarik Turcomans, will extend Russia rule to Panjdeh, or within 140 miles of the Key of India"—was ignored. Lord Granville, the British foreign secretary, simply informed the Russian ambassador, Baron Arthur von Mohrenheim, that "the news [concerning Merv] had not been received . . . with indifference."[27]

Twelve months later Marvin's warning came true. The standoff between the two Great Powers took place at the remote oasis of Panjdeh, on the Murghab River, located halfway between Merv and Herat near the Afghan border. On March 30, 1885, an Afghan force, goaded by the calculating Alikhanov, attacked a Russian unit.[28] Using this as a pretext, General Komarov, the Russian commander, ordered a counterattack, taking Panjdeh. The arrival of the news of Russia's seizure of Panjdeh in London a week later led most people to assume that war between Russia and Britain was now inevitable. In America, the normally sober *New York Times,* blared, "England and Russia Almost Sure to Fight."[29] Gladstone, who had been made a fool of by Giers, denounced the Russian slaughter of Afghans and the Russian occupation of Panjdeh and announced that he was putting Britain on a war footing.[30]

Alexander III seemed to believe that his bold foreign policy was worth the risk. If he had hoped to wrest his country from the humiliations suffered at the Congress of Berlin and restore the Romanov autocracy to the power and glory it had known in the early nineteenth century, he was mostly successful. "The magnificent autocrat of Gachina had dealt the revolutionaries a severe blow," Alexander Mikhailovich observed.[31] The

Journal de St. Petersbourg reported: "The Tsar appeared at the theatre last evening (April 10). The audience, still enthusiastic over the news of Panjdeh on the general assumption that Komaroff's conduct had the imperial approval—arose when they saw the tsar and shook the building with an ovation of applause."[32] The contrast between the gloomy last days of Alexander II and the promise of a bolder and stronger Russia presaged by Alexander III was striking. What neither the Russians nor the British could foresee, however, was how the renewed conflict in Central Asia would affect their Far Eastern policies. In 1885 the Great Game made its way to East Asia.

PORT HAMILTON

On April 15, 1885, Vice Admiral William Dowell, stationed in Nagasaki, was instructed to set sail with three British warships and occupy Port Hamilton (Kŏmun-do), an island located on the southern coast of the Korean Peninsula, as a base for conducting a blockade operation against Vladivostok and the Russian Pacific Fleet. The British calculated that the threat of a blockade in the Far East would keep Russia from advancing into Herat, a move that Gladstone warned would be taken as a declaration of war. The intent behind occupying Port Hamilton was, in the words of one British official, "to make the dog drop his bone by squeezing his throat."[33] The British were also worried that the Russians might take advantage of the Sino-Japanese rift as an opportunity to move into the Korean Peninsula.

Although war was averted in Afghanistan—the British and the Russians were able to control the crisis by setting up a commission to work out the Afghan border—the Great Game rivalry made the situation more complicated for the Chinese and Japanese in Korea. At first the Chinese were agreeable to the British occupation of the island. On April 12, Li Hongzhang wrote to the Zongli Yamen that "British troops will be temporarily stationed at Port Hamilton to oppose the Russians. I think the situation does no harm to China or Korea." The Chinese ambassador to Britain, Zeng Jize, informed the British government that as long as the occupation did not disturb China or Korea, "the British could stay at Port Hamilton temporarily."[34]

But the Russians forcefully protested. If the British were allowed to occupy Port Hamilton, they stated, Russia would occupy other parts of Korea. Li was alarmed, and receiving no reply to his demand to the British to withdraw their troops from the island, wrote to Kojong, suggesting that he should not agree to a British occupation after all because it "will displease Russia and Japan."[35]

While Li was urging Kojong to be wary of the British, he was becoming increasingly alarmed by Russian intentions. The Russian chargé d'affaires to China, Nikolai Ladyzhensky, came to Tianjin in September 1886 to meet with Li and discuss the Port Hamilton crisis. During their conversation, Li asked Ladyzhensky point-blank about Russia's intentions toward Korea. Ladyzhensky denied that his country had any. "I can promise you that Russia has no desire to take over any part of Korean territory," he declared. Li asked whether he might put these guarantees in writing. Ladyzhensky declined, stating that an oral declaration would have to do. When Li pressed the point, they finally compromised. Ladyzhensky would write a written guarantee only to China, but it could not be shared with Britain. With this note in hand, China pressed Britain to withdraw from Port Hamilton.[36]

The British eventually withdrew in February 1887, but the lesson of the Kŏmun-do affair revealed that Li had severely miscalculated. Instead of using Britain as a bulwark against Russian incursions into Korea, Li Hongzhang had actually emboldened the Russians. Not content to play a secondary role in Korean affairs, and with Britain now out of the way, Sino-Russian competition over the peninsula began to heat up.

THE RETURN OF THE TAEWŎN'GUN

Meanwhile, Japanese and Chinese forces had withdrawn from the peninsula and, following article 2 of the Convention of Tianjin, Kojong was encouraged to hire foreign military instructors to train Korea's military force. Both Japan and China agreed that the Koreans should employ Americans for the job. However, Kojong's close advisor, Paul Georg von Möllendorff, recommended Russian instructors instead.[37] Ironically, Möllendorff had been recommended to the Korean king by Li Hongzhang in 1882 after a brief stint working at the Chinese Maritime Customs Service. Although a German national, he was strongly partial to Russia.

In February 1885 Möllendorf went to Tokyo, where he secretly met with the Russian minister, A. P. Davydov, to discuss the possibility of engaging Russian military officers to train the Korean army. Möllendorf also wanted to discuss the possibility of obtaining Russian "protection" for Korea in exchange for the cession of Port Lazareff (Wŏnsan) to Russia.[38] A "secret agreement" on these issues was allegedly concluded between

Möllendorf and Davydov, although Russian foreign minister Giers denied ever making a promise of Russian protectorship over Korea.[39] What the Russian government did promise was to send military instructors.

The news of Russian maneuverings alarmed both Tokyo and Beijing. Li Hongzhang eventually forced Möllendorff to resign on July 27 and leave the country. In the meantime, Foreign Minister Inoue Kaoru met with Xu Chengzu, the Chinese ambassador to Japan, to express his deep concerns about Russian intentions in Korea. Inoue suggested that the Chinese release the Taewǒn'gun from his three-year custody in Baoding and send him back to Seoul. The inveterate antiforeign, and particularly anti-Russian champion, would serve both countries' interests by putting a check on the Korean king and queen, who wanted to use Russia as a "wedge to undermine Chinese authority."[40] The Taewǒn'gun could be useful for blocking a possible Russo-Korean entente.

Li Hongzhang was amenable to the idea, especially as the Taewǒn'gun professed to have experienced a change of heart and pledged to cooperate with the Qing.[41] "Although Yi Ha-ǔng [the Taewǒn'gun] will be returning as an outsider to the Korean government, he is still very popular among the Korean people," he remarked. Kojong would have to think twice about taking any rash action. Li also believed that due to Kojong's filial piety, the Taewǒn'gun "may provide assistance in secret to the king and help him stand on the right side."[42] Moreover, "Yi Ha-ǔng has pledged absolute loyalty to the Qing court and, at the aged of 65, is still energetic and capable."[43]

Kojong first got wind of the rumor of his father's return in February 1885. Yun Ch'i-ho, a close adviser, told the king that he had nothing to fear. "If the Taewǒn'gun returns with the support of the Qing to retake power, the government will not accept him," Yun assured him. "The law says that there are no two sovereigns just as there are no two suns in the sky." Kojong was less optimistic, confiding that "if he returns, the country will be destroyed."[44]

Upon his father's arrival on October 5, 1885, Kojong ordered the execution of three officials close to the Taewǒn'gun. This was done at the persistent urgings of his wife, Queen Min. The doomed officials had been implicated in the 1882 Imo mutiny and the executions were to serve as a warning to Kojong's father.[45] The queen had planned a more elaborate, and gruesome, spectacle to greet her father-in-law upon his arrival, but this was foiled by Chinese authorities, who had the bloody and dismembered bodies removed from exposure in the streets.[46]

The great crowds that had come out to greet the former regent upon his return must have been disconcerting to the king and queen. "There had collected at Chelmulp'o about 8,000 people to welcome him back," wrote George Foulk, the American minister to Korea. "The streets were packed with excited people all day long . . . Although he [the Taewŏn'gun] was cruel, intriguing and blood-thirsty, he always managed to keep about him the masses of the people."[47]

Accompanying the Taewŏn'gun on the ship to Inch'ŏn was Yuan Shikai, the former commander of Chinese forces in Korea. A protégé of Li Hongzhang, Yuan embarked upon his colorful career as an officer in the Huai Army under Admiral Wu Changqing after twice failing the provincial civil service examinations. He arrived in Korea as a junior staff officer in August 1882 and distinguished himself during the campaign to suppress the major strongholds of the mutinous soldiers during the Imo Uprising. During the 1884 Kapsin coup, Yuan, who was then chief of staff of the Chinese garrison in Korea, earned Li Hongzhang's gratitude and admiration for his quick-witted handling of the affair. It was in large part to reward Yuan's courage in twice leading "soldiers to save the Korean King" that Li made him China's representative in Seoul.[48] The American missionary Horace Allen, who was called upon to give surgical assistance to the wounded soldiers of Yuan's troops during the 1884 crisis, recalled that Yuan's power was absolute. "I have seen Chinamen beheaded by his executioners on the street at the side of his Legation, in full view of the passing populace, for violation of his regulation against gambling."[49]

ARROGANT YUAN SHIKAI

Just twenty-six years old when he assumed his new post, Yuan "took to himself the title of Resident in imitation of the British representatives in India."[50] This irritated the other foreign representatives, for it made it appear as if they were sent by their governments to a Chinese vassal state overseen by its Resident and that their status was less than Yuan's. Naturally, Yuan's pretensions offended the Japanese most. "His arrogance knew no bounds," recounted Allen, who later became the US minister to Korea.[51]

Yuan also embarked upon a program of establishing control over all areas of Korean political and foreign affairs.[52] He aggressively defended and expanded Chinese concessions in Korean treaty ports where Qing subjects enjoyed extraterritorial and other unequal rights. He also played a prominent role in establishing and managing key communication infrastructures, such as overland telegraph lines, and oversaw the Maritime Customs Service.[53] "In an ostentatious display of gorgeous costume, palanquin, and retinue, he [Yuan] and his procession formed one of the notable sights in the Korean capital."[54]

Responding to what was in effect the transformation of Korea's traditional tributary ties of ritual suzerainty into a modern form of Qing imperialism, Kojong decided to make a direct appeal to Russia. Yuan Shikai received intelligence that Kojong had sent a secret letter to Alexander III. Although there is much controversy about its authenticity, the document created a tremendous stir in Chinese circles. In the extraordinary letter, the king requested the tsar's help in maintaining Korea's "independence" by becoming a protectorate of Russia. He also requested the dispatch of Russian warships to Korea.[55]

The letter was a remarkable reversal of the policy that Kojong had, just six years earlier, strenuously supported against strong domestic opposition. That policy, advocated by Kim Hong-jip in 1880 when he returned to Korea from Japan with Huang Zunxian's A Strategy for Korea, was based on countering the dangers of Russian incursion into the peninsula. Kojong's overtures to Russia turned China's policy for Korea on its head, and Yuan reacted with a mixture of surprise, indignation, and anger.[56]

On August 9, 1886, Yuan wrote to Li Hongzhang: "The king of Korea seeks protection from Western countries and is ashamed that his country is a vassal of China. In years past, the king, together with treacherous officials, caused trouble in 1884 by pursuing a policy of befriending Japan by repudiating China but they failed. Now the king repeats this policy by seeking Russian help against China." Yuan urged Li to take preemptive action to depose the king in favor of someone more pliable. "If you instruct the Taewŏn'gun to help [in this matter], order can be restored in three to five days. If we delay our actions until Russian troops arrive, I am afraid things will develop beyond our control."[57] The prospect of going to war with Russia over Korea was now so serious that Li took the matter to Prince Chun (Yixuan), the father of Emperor Guangxu. The emperor instructed Li to "strengthen our armaments . . . and to deploy warships to patrol the Korean coasts."[58]

In the end Li Hongzhang decided not to support Yuan's wild schemes, for he thought the Taewŏn'gun a poor choice for taking over the throne.

Furthermore, the Russian government vehemently denied receiving the controversial letter and promised not to accept any requests for a Russian protectorate and the dispatch of Russian warships to Korea.[59] Yuan would take the opportunity to strike fear in Kojong instead, warning him of "dire consequences for his actions." Kojong later denied that he had been involved in the conspiracy with Russia.[60]

Although Li Hongzhang did not capitalize on the king's pro-Russian schemes to remove him from power, the incident did lead to a reversal of China's previous position on Korean "independence," however tenuously that concept was defined. Huang Zunxian's *A Strategy for Korea* had encouraged Korea to enter into treaty relations with the United States, and other Western powers, to help China maintain the status quo by checking Russian aggression. But the chaotic events in Korea, Kojong's unreliability, and fear of Russian collusion led the Chinese to conclude that their interests would be better served by a wholesale drive to establish Chinese supremacy in Korea. Yuan went so far as to block the dispatch of a Korean mission to the United States in 1887 on the grounds that Korea was a vassal of China and thus had no authority to conduct its own foreign affairs. He justified his actions by stating to the resident US minister, Hugh Dinsmore, that Korea's vassalage to China had been affirmed in King Kojong's letter appended to the Korean-American treaty even though the letter was never formally recognized by the United States.

Dinsmore's successor, Augustine Heard, took an even dimmer view of China's ever-tightening control over the peninsula. "China has seized upon the customs; appropriated through the guise of an agreement, the telegraphy; forbidden the opening of new ports, and conducts herself throughout as a sovereign mistress," he complained. While he acknowledged that China's subjugation of Korea was motivated by its desire to protect the kingdom from Russian encroachment, Heard believed China was making a "fearful mistake": "No one who knows what the Chinese army and navy are, as at present organized, can participate in any such delusion, and the instant she comes in contact with Russian troops, she will herself discover her error."[61]

What was remarkable about Li Hongzhang's volte-face on Korea policy was that Russia had not yet made a formal move on Korea. The Russians did not capitalize on the chaos of the 1884 Kapsin coup. The following year, when Möllendorf, on behalf of Kojong, offered to access to Wŏnsan, an ice-free port on Korea's eastern coast, as part of the so-called secret agreement, Russia refused. The Russian government also eschewed the question of a Russian protectorate when Kojong raised it in his letter.[62] Russian foreign minister Giers noted, "Russia should not give a positive word to Korea to expect anything from Russia." In other words, despite repeated overtures made to them by the Koreans, the Russians continued to pursue a cautious policy.[63]

MAINTAINING THE STATUS QUO?

So what exactly was Russia's Korea policy? On May 8, 1888, a special conference took place to hash this out. It concluded that "the acquisition of Korea would not only not give us any advantage, but would also be accompanied by a considerable number of disadvantageous consequences." It continued: "Under certain conditions, Korea, on the flank of Manchuria, might be turned by us [Russia] into an important strategic position, but the advantages thereof lost their significance because of the inconveniences and difficulties with its defense . . . Occupation of Korea would spoil not only our relations with China but also with England, which has her own designs on that country."[64]

But then the tone shifted with regard to China, for Russia would not tolerate China annexing Korea. "In case this design should be realized at some later time, our position in South Ussuri will become extremely dangerous for instead of a weak and inoffensive neighbor on our flank, there will appear China which has various and considerable materials means at her disposal. England encourages the self-confidence and ambition of Chinese statesmen."[65]

Concerning Japan's designs on Korea, the conference noted that "Mikado [Japan] believing it unwise to exploit itself to the danger of a collision with China, not only gave up its aspirations to Korea, but for a time showed a complete indifference to the future of the latter country." Recently, however, Japan had begun to show "some anxiety about the means of securing Korea from being seized by the Chinese." Such a direction of Japanese policy, however, was "in perfect agreement with our point of view, and we must do our best to support Tokyo in this direction."[66]

Russian assessment of Japan's cautious policy toward Korea was for the most part correct. Following the settlement reached by Itō Hirobumi and Li Hongzhang in the 1885 Tianjin Convention, Meiji leaders were determined not to become embroiled in another fiasco like the Kapsin coup.[67] Takezoe's actions had been rash, and the plot to support the Korean progressives by Japanese liberals like Fukuzawa had badly backfired.[68]

What the Russians failed to perceive was that deep divisions concerning the Korea problem continued to exist in Japan. The shabby treatment that Kim Ok-kyun and other Korean exiles received at the hands of the Japanese government during their exile in Japan deeply disturbed Fukuzawa and other liberals. In June 1886 Yamagata Arimoto, minister of home affairs, notified Kim Ok-kyun that he would be expelled from Japan to the barren isle of Hachijō (Bonin Islands), the traditional banishment site for political criminals. Fukuzawa was furious, firing off an indignant missive to Yamagata for treating Kim like a "state criminal" when his only crime was "to escape the clutches of Korea's evil leadership and to breath the air of freedom in Japan." For that crime, Fukuzawa lamented, "the Japanese government feels uneasy?"[69]

The furor over the treatment of Kim Ok-kyun also raised the ire of Japanese reactionaries who supported Korean reform. Ōi Kentarō, an early advocate of Western learning and a noted expert in French law who had become a leading member of the People's Rights movement, and Kobayashi Kuzuo, secretary of the Liberal Party, had plotted to send an expedition to Korea in late 1885 to overthrow Kojong's government. They justified their actions in terms of their commitment to stand for freedom and progress everywhere.[70] Although the plan was foiled and the leaders of the "Osaka affair" were arrested, lasting divisions within Japanese society about the "Korean problem" brought reactionaries and liberals together in a common cause against the Japanese oligarchy on this issue.[71]

These tensions were kept in check as long as the status quo in Korea continued without significant disruptions. From 1885 onward, the Japanese government seemed content to leave Korean affairs under the guidance of China's strong hand as long as it could prevent other Western powers, namely Russia, from getting a foothold there.[72] However, by 1890 a new factor appeared that forced the Meiji leaders to rethink the wisdom of their foreign policy. The question they faced was whether they could afford to leave Korea's fate in China's hands or if they had to grab the reins of the peninsula's fortunes into their own.

CHAPTER SIX

RUSSIA'S RAILWAY TO THE EAST

Nearly thirty years after Nikolai Nikolaevich Muravev-Amursky announced the founding of Vladivostok—"the Ruler of the East"—in 1860 and laid Russian claim to the entire Manchurian tract eastward from the Ussuri to the seacoast and southward as far as the Korean border, the region remained a huge emptiness, with little or no agriculture, trade, roads, or people.[1] The Primorsky krai (Maritime Territory), located along the Tumen River and sharing a border with northern Korea, was estimated to have 54,082 residents in 1882; the Amur krai, located along the banks of the Amur and Zeya Rivers, had approximately 41,554 residents. For an area the size of France and Germany combined—approximately 350,000 square miles—the total population, including native inhabitants, did not exceed 100,000 people.[2]

This was not the rich acquisition Muravev-Amursky had hoped for. When he took possession of these vast lands, there was no end to the descriptions of their richness and potential. The Russian naturalist and geographer Richard Maak stressed the "most advantageous conditions for colonization" of the Amur region: "excellent climate, ease of internal movement over land and water, highly fertile soil, and finally, close proximity to the administrative center of Eastern Siberia." Russia's newly acquired lands, he exclaimed, "will become a breadbasket for all neighboring parts of Russia."[3]

These unrealistic expectations were spurred on by a New York businessman and adventurer, Perry McDonough Collins, who, after arriving in Russia in 1856, stimulated further Russian excitement by proposing various projects with official backing of the US government. Appointed by Secretary of State William L. Marcy as "Commercial Agent of the United States at the Amoor River," Collins set off for Irkutsk in December, the first American to set foot there, where he waxed about the Amur valley's potential riches for international trade. But it was during his stay in Chita, some 250 miles east of Lake Baikal, that Collins began to dream of creating a railway that would connect Siberia's hinterland to the Pacific and the outside world.[4] His grand project to organize an "Amoor River Railroad Company" was the first proposal made to build a railway through Siberia. Comparing Muravev's acquisition of the Amur to Jefferson's Louisiana Purchase, Collins predicted great things for Russia's commercial and civilizing role in the region. "The probability is that Russia will find it necessary, in order to give peace and security to trade on this important river, from her Siberian possession into the ocean, to follow our example in the acquisition of Louisiana; for the whole of Manchooria is as necessary to the undisturbed commerce of the Amoor as Louisiana was to our Mississippi."[5]

Such pronouncements proved wildly optimistic, even delusional. The mouth of the Amur proved too shallow to allow for free access by ocean-going vessels, and countless sandbars made navigation not only difficult but dangerous. D. I. Zavalishin, an implacable critic of Muravev-Amursky, noted that "not one ship has completely traveled the length of the Amur, or even covered even any significant portion of it."[6] This was because the ships kept running aground. Zavalishin considered the Amur completely unsuitable for commercial navigation. Moving inland from the coast, it also turned out that neither the climate nor the periodically inundated prairies were suitable to support large agricultural populations. The fertile Mississippi alluvial plain this certainly was not. Springtime in the Amur was dry and cold. The soil thawed slowly, preventing the rapid growth of plants. Dry winds evaporated the light spring precipitation before it could penetrate the soil, and as a result young crops suffered from drought. Summertime brought warmer weather but also abundant rain and thick fog. Frequent downpours caused rivers to overflow, washing away young crops. The high humidity made harvesting grain difficult, creating favorable conditions for parasites, rust, mold, fungi, and other diseases that ruined cultivated plants.[7] Instead of supplying the settlers with grain, the Amur valley had to import grain in large quantities.[8]

The only two fertile belts in the Russian Amur, one east of Blagovesh-chensk and another plain of much smaller dimensions on the Razdolnaya (or Suifen) River near Vladivostok, were roughly six hundred miles apart with low, marshy, unfertile hillocks in between. The result was that Vladivostok had no hinterland. It was, as Russian revolutionary Pyotr Kropotkin put it, "simply a port thrown out on the Pacific coast, very far from the regions where a thick population could ever be settled." Early in his career as an officer in the Cossack regiment in eastern Siberia, Kropotkin sent back numerous brief articles about his travels, painting a bleak picture of the region.[9] To make up for the sparse settlements along the Amur, Muravev-Amursky arranged for the release of a large number of convicts, "mostly robbers and murders who had settled as free men on the lower Amur." He soon realized that male-only settlements were worthless: "What is agriculture without a wife?"

> Whereupon Muravioff [sic] ordered the release of all the hard-labour con-
> vict women of the place—about a hundred—and offered them the choice
> of the man each of them would like to marry and to follow. However, there
> was little time to lose; the high water in the river was rapidly going
> down, the rafts had to start, and Muravioff, asking the people to stand in
> pairs on the beach, blessed them, saying: "I marry you children. Be kind
> to each other; you men, don't ill-treat your wives—and be happy!"[10]

While the "Muravioff" marriages "were not less happy than marriages on average," the number of criminals, both married and single, did little to solve the population problem.[11] Nor did they make the prospect of im-migrating to the region more attractive for the average Russian. By the mid-1870s, the Siberian towns were themselves protesting the ill effects of the exile population upon their communities. In Irkutsk, the so-called "Paris of Siberia," town members implored the state to end the exile system that had overburdened the local population. "The territory is bur-dened with taxes to support the thousands of deportations convoys," the weekly community paper *Siberia* reported. "Thousands of exiles and penal labourers swarm down the roads and before them lie defenseless Siberian towns. There are up to 30,000 vagabonds scattered across Siberia whom the peasantry has to feed under the daily threat of armed robbery, murder, and arson. Towns are awash with crime."[12]

The quality of life was also dreary for Siberia's settlers. Like so many Siberian towns, Vladivostok was permeated by a feeling of hopelessness and melancholy. With its "muddy and unpaved streets, open sewers and grim military barracks and warehouses, unpainted wooden houses," the town was far from being a bustling center of trade and commerce, being icebound for six months of the year and fogbound for several months more.[13] The cost of living alone left its inhabitants demoralized. "Everywhere there are shortages and difficulties," reported railroad engineer L. N. Liubimov. "The expenses are incredible. The reigning spirit of hard labor and exile crown the oppression, and many long intensely to get out of here simply to liberate themselves from the daily contemplation of the dark side of the human soul."[14] Moreover, because the Russian inhabitants were "almost entirely . . . officers and persons connected to the army and navy," with no merchants or farmers, the Chinese and Koreans became the provisioners. "Many thought their large numbers a hindrance to Russian progress," British explorer Henry Lansdell wrote of his travels there in 1881. "[This is because] they outbid the Russians, work cheaper and undersell them." Indeed, settlers from China and Korea made up a quarter of the urban population of the Amur by 1900.[15]

RAILROAD ACROSS THE AMUR?

After more than thirty years of Russian occupation, Gennady Ivanovich Nevelskoy, who along with Muravev-Amursky was responsible for locating a navigable channel along the Amur's southern bank in 1849, later acknowledged that his dream of discovering a "Siberian Mississippi" had been pure fantasy. "Commerce and industry, owing to the huge empty expanse [of the region], its geographical position, and its climate conditions, are unable to develop rapidly here as we have observed in the North American States," he observed. "This *krai* is in every way quite unlike America, and for this reason . . . the government should not be seduced by the illusions and the example of North America and California."[16] S. I. Korzhinsky of the Eastern Branch of the Imperial Geographical Society condemned the Amur region as "totally worthless," writing that "it is necessary to work out an entirely different system of economy and to cultivate other plants, more suitable to local climate conditions"[17] Even the revolutionary anarchist Mikhail Bakunin, a great admirer of Muravev-Amursky, was forced to admit: "In Moscow and Saint Petersburg, they claim that the Amur is a trifle, that even rowboats cannot travel it; that Blagoveshchensk and Nikolayevsk, and all the settlements and stations on the Amur only exist in Muravev's reports and imagination; that the

Amur ruined Russia; that it has swallowed up millions of roubles and thousands of people; that in a word, it has become Russia's Ulcer."[18]

Despite these failings, Alexander III was not yet ready to abandon the Amur region. Russia's major external concern between 1860 and 1885 was Central Asia, which by virtue of historical experience and geographical proximity possessed a direct and immediate significance to the Russian people that the remote and foreign Amur and Ussuri regions never had. By the 1880s, following the Second Anglo-Afghan War of 1878–1880, the annexation of Khiva, Bukhara, and Kokand by Russia, and the settlement of the Panjdeh crisis in 1885, however, the Russian government began shifting its focus eastward and there was talk again of constructing a railway across Siberia. In June 1887 Alexander III approved the decision made by the minister of communication to proceed with a survey for a trans-Siberian railroad.[19]

Two main factors lay behind the tsar's decision to build the Siberian railroad. As a wave of revolutionary fervor swept through Russia beginning in the 1840s, radical thinkers and writers, from Pyotr Kropotkin and Alexander Herzen to anarchists Mikhail Bakunin and M. V. Butashevich-Petrashevsky, were inspired by the thought of developing Siberia as a new land of freedom and opportunity separate from autocratic Russia. These regionalists strove for greater autonomy from Saint Petersburg and an end to the exile system that reduced Siberia to a Russian penal colony.[20] In 1860 Bakunin, from Irkutsk in the heart of Siberia, addressed a letter to an acquaintance in which he declared that "Siberia's secession from Russia was then just a matter of time."[21]

Muravev-Amursky's annexation of the Amur and Ussuri, combined with a desire for a rapprochement with the United States, had given these radical thinkers new ideas about building a "new America" on Russia's eastern frontier by spurring a revolutionary break from tsarist autocracy. Kropotkin recounted that Muravev-Amursky had even toyed with the idea of leading this separatist movement, of "creating an United States of Siberia."[22] "My thoughts turned more and more toward Siberia," Kropotkin reflected in his memoirs. "There is in Siberia an immense field for the application of the great reforms which have been made or are coming: the workers must be few there, and I shall find a field of action to my tastes."[23] The surge of revolutionary fervor that had led to the assassination of Alexander II in 1881 also helped shape his son's reactionary policies in the decade ahead. A transcontinental railroad that could make Siberia more "Russian," and thus strengthen the region's ties with the motherland, was viewed as a vital national priority. To defend the Russian government from the forces of radical change and radical ideas—as well as dangerous separatist aspirations—the railroad was deemed the best instrument for tightening the new tsar's grip on the expanding empire. "The entire future of Siberia lies in its close unity with Russia," wrote one observer. "Siberia is not a colony of Russia but Russia itself."[24]

But more than worries over a separate Siberia, the stark deficiencies of the Russian settlements in the Far East had forced Alexander III to confront the region's vulnerability to foreign aggression. The building of a Trans-Siberian Railway was thus taken up as a matter of strategic, not commercial, concern. Collins's dream of constructing a railway across Siberia and transforming the Russian Far East into a new El Dorado for traders from America and Europe had been dashed by the harsh reality of climate, hydrography, soil, and fauna. The new effort to revisit the railway issue grew out of more immediate strategic considerations regarding a revitalized China. Although China's military prowess had been deflated in the 1860s due to its humiliating defeats at the hands of the British and French, the settlement of the Ili Crisis in 1881 had boosted China's confidence. By forcing Russia, exhausted by the Russo-Turkish War, to return most of the Ili region to China, the Qing had reestablished its authority and prestige. Moreover, the Qing's successful suppression of the three great rebellions—the Taiping in the south, the Nian in the north, and the Muslim in the West—further boosted Qing confidence and gave the dynasty a new lease on life.[25]

Russian authorities were quick to perceive the change. The Chinese began to adopt a more belligerent tone in border disputes with the Russians. The Qing strengthened its military posture in Manchuria, especially in Jilin Province, located directly adjacent to the southern Ussuri region— the most vulnerable spot along the six-thousand-mile Russo-Chinese border and within striking distance of Vladivostok. The Qing's military readiness strained relations between the two powers. In August 1882, for example, a Qing official named Liu Tszin Iun from Jilin Province arrived in the Russian village of Savelovka and told the mostly Korean inhabitants that the village was on Chinese, not Russian, soil. The village, nestled near the Tumen River, had been inhabited by Koreans who had fled into Russian territory in 1875. After he declared that the Russian military post would have to be moved, Liu was chased out of the village by an indignant Russian officer. The issue of Savelovka's status was raised again in December by Qing authorities, this time to N. G. Matiunin, border commissar of the Southern Ussuri region. In addition to reiterating Chinese claims to Savelovka, the Qing authorities stated that the map accompanying the 1860 Peking Treaty was incorrect and had to be revised. Although a skirmish between Chinese and Russian forces was prevented by the resourceful actions of Matiunin, the Savelovka incident was an ominous indication of China's newfound aggressiveness, and an ominous prelude to what many Russian officers believed was the Qing's ultimate goal: to reestablish its authority over the Southern Ussuri region.[26]

The incident at Savelovka also revealed just how precarious Russia's hold on its Far Eastern possessions actually was. "In 1860, we obtained from China a whole region, luxuriant, abounding in both on land and sea with gifts of nature and in twenty years possession of this region we have made absolutely nothing of it," lamented V. Krestovsky, former secretary to Admiral Lesvosky, commander in chief of Russia's Pacific naval forces. "On the contrary, by our attitude towards this matter, we are promoting its impoverishment and ultimate ruin." He further bemoaned the fact that Russia had obtained "from all its riches not a single kopeck of profit" even though "millions of the state treasure [had been spent] on its supposed needs and requirements." "The region is being brutally exploited by alien [non-Russian] population," he warned, "and gradually through peaceful means is being won back from us by the Chinese."[27] Colonel Ia. F. Barabash, chief of staff of the Primorsky Maritime Territory, was even more pessimistic. After completing a secret mission to Jilin in 1882, Barabash concluded that not only was Beijing fostering emigration to the sparsely populated Southern Ussuri region, but the Chinese were also increasing their military buildup in the area.[28]

There was definitely more at work in Chinese minds than the promotion of peaceful assimilation of the region. More portentously, Barabash concluded that should the Chinese launch an offensive campaign to regain the Bay of Posyet, they could demand the revision of the Peking Treaty or the return, at the very least, of the Primorsky altogether. Reports that British engineers were working on plans with the Qing to build a railway in southern Manchuria that put it within just ninety miles of Vladivostok were even more alarming.[29] Chinese revanchism was "a black cloud on the horizon of relations with China," and Barabash warned that the Qing would quite likely receive support in this endeavor from the British as the Great Game shifted to East Asia.[30]

Despite growing apprehension about separatists in Siberia and reports of Chinese military buildup along the Russo-Chinese border, the Russian bureaucracy was slow to act on Alexander III's bold announcement in 1887 of his government's plans to build a trans-Siberian railway. Alexander had called for four special conferences in the winter of 1886–1887 to consider the numerous practical, technical, and financial challenges of building the railroad—by far the most ambitious project ever undertaken by the Russian government—but the project was hamstrung by ministerial strife. Moreover, due to the enormous costs involved, Finance Minister Ivan Vyshnegradsky opposed the project on fiscal grounds and repeatedly rejected or scaled-down requests for funding from K. N. Posyet, minister of transportation and communications.[31] The result was repeated and endless delays. It was not until Sergei Witte, a longtime railroad manager and Vyshengradsky's protégé, was appointed minister of finance in 1892 that Muravev-Amursky's exploits were redeemed and a new vision of Russia as a Far Eastern power finally began to take shape.

SERGEI WITTE

Much has been made of Sergei Yulevich Witte's meteoric rise from a mere railroad ticket clerk to minister of finance at the age of forty-three, the youngest man ever to reach such heights in Russia.[32] In reality, Witte came from noble stock; his maternal grandmother hailed from the Dolgorukis, one of the oldest and most distinguished families in Russia. Born in Tiflis (today Tbilisi, capital of Georgia) in 1849, his father was the director of the Department of State Domains of the Caucasus. After graduating from the University of Odessa, where he majored in mathematics and physics, Witte contemplated a university career but was instead persuaded by his family to enter the employ of a private railroad company. Thanks to his mother's connections, Witte started at a comfortable salary and became acquainted with all levels of railroad operations, including for a time sitting "in cashiers' officers of freight stations and ticket officers of passage offices."[33] Winning rapid promotion, Witte was named manager of the Southwestern Railroad in 1886, one of the longest lines in Russia, where he came to the attention of Vyshnegradsky, the new finance minister, who asked him for recommendations about how to reduce the huge subsidies the government was paying the privately owned railroads to cover shortfalls. Witte proposed the creation of a department of railroad affairs that would be directly supervised by the Ministry of Finance, one of many bold proposals the young manager discussed with Vyshnegradsky.[34] But it was luck, not only brains, that was to open the way for his brilliant career in the service of the Russian state.

During the summer and early fall of 1888, Alexander III made frequent trips from Saint Petersburg to Odessa. On one occasion the imperial train passed over the branch of the railroad administered by Witte's Southwestern Railroad. The train was running behind schedule but this did not prevent Witte from ordering a reduction in the train's speed. Later, within earshot of the tsar, Witte was reprimanded by Minister Posyet. The former defended himself vociferously, saying: "Your Excellency, let others do as they please, but I do not wish to break the tsar's neck."[35] Several weeks later, on October 17, 1888, Witte's concern for the tsar's safety was justified when the imperial train jumped the track near Borki, on the Kursk-Kharkov-Azov line, killing twenty-two and injuring dozens more but sparing Alexander III and his immediate family.[36] In his memoirs, Witte credited the Borki accident as the turning point of his career. The tsar remembered the words of the outspoken Witte and decided to transfer him to government service.

The first evidence of the tsar's favor came when Vyshnegradsky, following Witte's recommendations to set up a new Department of Railroad Affairs in the Ministry of Finance, named his young protégé its new director in 1889. Just three years later Witte succeeded his ailing mentor to become minister of finance. Now that the Department of Railroad Affairs was firmly under his jurisdiction, Witte had no trouble financing the Siberian Railway project, which would rank near the top of all the great infrastructure undertakings of the twentieth century.

Where would the funds for such a massive project be found? At first, Russia's enormous national debt seemed to preclude borrowing, but Witte insisted it could be financed through foreign loans. The political stability Alexander III had brought to Russia and the empire's improved relations with France helped secure the necessary funds. Nevertheless, Witte's "spend now, pay later" motto threatened to deepen the poverty of Russia's workers and peasants, who inevitably had to shoulder the financial burden with higher taxes. But Witte insisted that their burden could be minimized if the Trans-Siberian was built with materials and equipment manufactured in Russia.[37] Although Russia had toyed with laissez-faire economics and freedom of trade during the liberal regime of Alexander II, Witte reversed course by enacting a top-down, state-led capitalist policy of development in which the chief agent of the promotion of economic activity was the Russian government. While Witte was not responsible for the introduction of the protective tariff of 1891, the tariffs were further raised during his regime, so that by 1904 the average Russian import duty was 131 percent on goods from England.[38] Witte understood the abuses to which this protectionist system could and did give rise, but he foresaw the protection being withdrawn once Russia's national industries were firmly established.

The Trans-Siberian Railway would thus serve "as the flywheel for the entire economy."[39] Extensive railroad construction would stimulate national growth by increasing demand for heavy industries, coal, iron, and steel. The expansion of heavy industry would in turn stimulate the growth of light industries, especially the private companies and communities that would spring up along the railway. Through government intervention and extensive subsidies by the state, Witte believed, the Trans-Siberian Railway would ultimately raise the standard of living for the Russian people. "For the progress and successful development of industry we have to take measures which must inevitably lead to government expenditures," he wrote. "Both in single grants and constant subsidies."[40]

Endowed with rare energy and a huge capacity for work, Witte—who stood half a head taller than most other men and whose frame "suggested something that might have been shaped by the rude blows of an axe"—dominated the routine bureaucracy of the capital by his practical experience and good sense. He was not a man of learning. Unlike other members of the Russian bureaucratic elite, he spoke French badly and English not at all. It was widely rumored he was disliked in court circles, "where he was considered a plebeian." Yet in spite of his rather "shabby appearance and the awkwardness of his manner, he produced, on the whole, a great impression of force and originality."[41] He was, as historian Theodore Von Laue put it, "a man of the coming Russia which subordinated poetry to the five-year plan."[42] Witte's contemporary, the writer Peter Struve, observed something similar: "Witte did not search for answers in economic tracts written by strange hands, but in real state creations, unrestricted by doctrine. Witte's ability to understand the hardest political problems, find cunning solutions in unorthodox methods of governance, and appoint the necessary figures to necessary positions came from his being a born a politician and administrator, and not some cultivated knowledge-seeker."[43]

His ceaseless activity extended to "every ramification of the political and economic life of the country," wrote Russian diplomat Alexander

Izvolsky. Due to his "constant tendency to extend indefinitely the power of the State, one may say that for some ten years he was the real master of the 160,000,000 inhabitants of the empire."[44] Yet the real source of Witte's power lay with the tsar, to whom he was deeply devoted. "It is not enough to say that Alexander III had a noble heart," Witte later gushed. "He had a tsar's heart." "He gave Russia thirteen years of peace, not by being weak, but by being fair and unswervingly firm." The emperor, he continued approvingly, "had no dreams of military conquest or of military laurels." "Having assumed the reign of power at a time that seemed unpropitious for Russia, Alexander raised his country's prestige without having shed a drop of Russian blood."[45]

To the extent that Alexander III's major interest at the time was the construction of the transcontinental railroad meant to confer prestige and economic vitality on the Russian Empire, Witte and the emperor were wedded to a common national goal. The Trans-Siberian Railway, not military conquest, would be the prime agent of Russian expansionism and cultural imperialism. Describing the Trans-Siberian in almost religious terms, Witte believed that the project would place Russia at the center of the world: Moscow would become the "Third Rome." It "would occupy one of the first places in the ranks of the largest and most important undertakings of the nineteenth century, not only in our Motherland but also in the whole world."[46]

THE TRANS-SIBERIAN RAILWAY

The Trans-Siberian—stretching about 7,500 kilometers (4,600 miles)—still ranks as the world's longest continuous railway. Geographically, it extends from Chelyabinsk, east of the Ural Mountains on the Miass River dividing European Russia from Asia, to Vladivostok, six thousand miles from Moscow. George Kennan, the nineteenth-century journalist and explorer whose classic two-volume work *Siberia and the Exile System* helped to expose the dark side of tsarist Russia, illustrated the extreme dimension of the Trans-Siberian undertaking in starkly visual terms:

> If it were possible to move entire countries from one part of the globe to another, you could take the whole United States of America from Maine to California and from Lake Superior to the Gulf of Mexico, and set it down in the middle of Siberia, without touching anywhere the boundaries of the latter territory. You could then take Alaska and all

the States of Europe, with the single exception of Russia, and fit them into the remaining margin like the pieces of a dissected map; and after having thus accommodated all of the United States, including Alaska, all of Europe, except Russia, you would still have more than 300,000 square miles of Siberian territory to spare—or, in other words, you could still leave unoccupied in Siberia an area half as large again as the empire of Germany.[47]

In addition to the enormous size of the project, the severe geographical conditions of Siberia and the Russian Far East presented numerous challenges of engineering and design, particularly in the easternmost section of the Ussuri Railway line.[48] More than two hundred miles of track in the Trans-Baikal region, for example, had to be relaid because the original route turned out to be submerged by floodwaters nearly every spring and summer.[49] More than 230 miles of track were damaged by floods in the Ingoda and Shilka valleys. Near Sretensk a mountain landslide buried a newly laid track while "fifteen bridges vanished without a trace."[50]

Similar problems occurred on the Ussuri railroad that stretched between Vladivostok and Khabarovsk, the only part of the Maritime region track laid during this time. During the rainy season, the whole locality was transformed into an immense water basin, forcing the move of track onto higher ground, as well as extensive bridge building to accommodate the numerous tributaries.[51] There were also problems with Manchurian bandits, the honghuzi, who occasionally roamed the area, necessitating the construction of barracks at all the important stations as well as "the maintenance of more than twenty thousand guards, who are distributed along the lines for purposes of defense."[52] "Train and track are protected by an immense army of guards," one observer noted. "Every section is marked by neat cottages, the home of the guard and his family. Night and day the guard or one of his household must patrol the section."[53]

But the most persistent problem was the one Muravev-Amursky had faced when he first set foot in the Amur region in the 1850s: the chronic shortage of people. The mobilization of a labor force for the Siberian railroad proved just as challenging as when Muravev-Amursky sought to recruit Russian settlers for the region. Far Eastern Siberia's lack of skilled hands and the absence of technical equipment meant that every item essential to railway and bridge construction had to be transported by ship from European Russia.[54] In 1897 in the mid-Siberian section, nearly 40 percent of the labor, including most of the skilled hands, came from

Prisoners labor at excavation for the Trans-Siberian Railway. (*Razrabotka trudom 'arestantov' vyemki versty 516-ĭ, piket No. 2–24* [Moscow, 1908], Library of Congress)

the famine areas of European Russia. Thousands were shipped from Odessa through Suez across the Indian Ocean, making the five-week journey to Vladivostok, where they worked on the railway line on the eastern end.[55]

Working conditions were especially hard for those given the jobs involved in clearing and logging the land. Excavation work usually began in early spring, when the ground was still solid as stone. Spring brought rain, and workers were forced to stand in icy water or in mud up to their knees. "Their faces and hands turned blue and frozen," reported the *Northern Herald*. "Their exhausted bodies [could be seen] twitching with frequent convulsions and tremors." In the summer, the work was not much easier: gadflies, mosquitoes, and other blood-sucking insects "drove them crazy." "This is not a construction site," the *Vladivostok* observed. "This is a struggle, a war to the death."[56]

A quarter of the labor force in the eastern sections were foreign workers, mostly Chinese and Koreans but also Italians (some five hundred), and German and Finnish craftsmen.[57] Hired workers had come in the hope of good wages and driven by fear of famine and unemployment, but they were quickly disillusioned. Corruption was endemic. Most of the construction work was done by private contractors who made wage agreements directly with the workers. The railway administration paid the contractors according to the number and skill of their workers, the hours worked, and the tasks achieved, but only a fraction of these funds ever reached the workers themselves. This is because the system was left open to widespread abuse as the contractors sought to widen their profit margin by reducing construction costs. For example, contractors specified a long list of fines, including non-accomplishment of tasks, damage to equipment, or disorderly or disobedient behavior.[58] Workers lost a good portion of their wages to being fined arbitrarily.

Working conditions for prison laborers were far worse. The farther east the line went, the greater the difficulty of hiring local workers. In early 1891, Minister of Internal Affairs P. N. Durnovo approved the use of convicts and exiles for the Ussuri line to relieve the manpower shortage. Thirty-five percent of the labor force was made up of convicts and exiles.[59] Prisoners were often forced to work at night even after putting in a full day of labor during the day and were treated as virtual slaves. Before beating them to death, their jailers "wrestled maximum benefit out of the imprisoned workers."[60] Despite these and other abuses, Tsar Alexander was said to have been pleased by the success of using prison labor on the Siberian line. To the extent that it was later used to solve the manpower shortage on other public works projects, it became the direct antecedent of later Soviet practices.[61]

THE TSAREVICH'S FAR EASTERN TOUR

Witte could hardly have anticipated all the challenges that lay ahead when he was tasked by Alexander III to build the Trans-Siberian line. But he was savvy enough to know that if the project was to succeed, it would be wise to have Grand Duke Nicholas Alexandrovich—Alexander's son, the future Tsar Nicholas II—to be sufficiently invested in the Trans-Siberian Railway to guarantee its completion. To oversee this gargantuan task, Witte had proposed establishing the Siberian Railroad Committee, which would have decision-making power over all aspects of the railway's construction, and suggested that the tsarevich chair it.

It was an ingenious ploy, one that astonished the emperor. Alexander III had never taken his son and heir seriously. According to one account, when Nicholas tried to participate in a political discussion over dinner, "his father began throwing bread rolls at him."[62] Witte observed that "Nicholas II ascended the throne completely unprepared for the role he had to assume," which he believed was because Alexander "had not expected to die so soon." Alexander asked whether his finance minister "had ever spoken [to the heir apparent] in any serious matters." "He is nothing but a boy whose judgments are childish," the emperor declared. "How could he serve as chairman [of the Siberian Railroad Committee]?" Witte was insistent. The Grand Duke was young and unserious, he acknowledged, but if his Majesty did not "begin to train him in governmental affairs, he may never learn," adding that the opportunity to head the Committee would be his "first schooling in administration." In the end Alexander agreed. Witte's foresight in involving Nicholas in the Siberian Railway project was a reflection of his shrewdness. "I must say that the idea turned out well," Witte later mused, "because the tsarevich was entranced by his appointment and took it seriously . . . with his support, I was able to push the construction along so that within a few years St. Petersburg, or, to put it another way, Paris, had a direct link with Vladivostok."[63]

To prepare for Nicholas's appointment as chairman of the Siberian Railway Committee in January 1893, Alexander decided to send his son to the Far East "to round out his political development." The tsarevich's journey would cover approximately 32,000 miles, including 9,300 miles by rail and 14,000 by sea over 290 days. The delegation would depart from Vienna to the Greek port city of Piraeus, where Nicholas would be joined by his cousin, Prince George of Greece and Denmark. They would travel to Egypt, then India, and continue to Singapore and Japan, the last foreign stop on the "grand tour" of Asia. Nicholas would then resume his journey on Russian soil, to Vladivostok where, in a brief but solemn ceremony, he would turn the first sod that would eventually become the Ussuri Line, the last stop of the Trans-Siberian railway. From Vladivostok, he would visit Khabarovsk, Blagoveshchensk, and the Eastern Siberian cities of Nerchinsk, Chita, and Irkutsk before returning to Saint Petersburg by train via Tomsk.

Accompanying Nicholas on his grand tour was Esper Esperovich Ukhtomsky, a member of the Siberian Committee. After graduating from the University of Saint Petersburg, Ukhtomsky traveled extensively throughout eastern Siberia and developed a passionate interest in Buddhist Buriat minorities, a nomadic people living around Lake Baikal. Like Przhevalsky, Ukhtomsky adhered to the vision of Russia integrating the Central and East Asian worlds. During the 1880s he made several trips to the Russian Far East as well as to China and Mongolia.[64] On the Grand Tour, Ukhtomsky was tasked with keeping a travel log, which was eventually published as a lavishly illustrated three-volume set.

Ukhtomsky later wrote that Alexander III had erred in sending the tsarevich to the Far East rather than to the interior of Russia and to Western Europe. "It was a mistake, and a fatal one, but it would not have been a great mistake had the emperor not died prematurely."[65] The most significant aspect of the journey, which was virtually excised from Ukhtomsky's travel book due to imperial censorship, was the attempted assassination of Nicholas by a Japanese fanatic. According to Witte, the incident had produced a "painful effect" in Saint Petersburg and promoted the belief that "the Japanese are an unpleasant, contemptible, and powerless people who could be destroyed at one blow from the Russian giant."[66] Whether the roots of future Russo-Japanese conflict can be traced to the tsarevich's unfortunate visit to Japan in May 1891 is speculative at best, but it did raise anxieties within Japan about the limits of Russian aggression and the place of Japan in the family of "civilized" nations.

AN UNFORTUNATE INCIDENT

On May 11, 1891, Itō Hirobumi was resting at the Tōnosawa Onsen (hot spring) when he received an urgent telegram from Prime Minister Matsukata Masayoshi. A policeman in the town of Ōtsu had assaulted the tsarevich, injuring him in the head. Matsukata asked Itō to hurry back to the capital. "I was stunned and unable to finish the dinner," Itō recalled. "I immediately called for a rickshaw to make the trip for Tokyo."[67]

Nicholas and his cousin, Prince George, had arrived in Japan two weeks earlier. On the morning of the attack, the tsarevich and members of his party left Kyoto for Ōtsu to enjoy the sights of Lake Biwa. They were supposed to proceed on a sightseeing tour in Nara the following day before heading to Tokyo, where a large banquet with the Japanese emperor was being prepared. But those plans were cut short in Ōtsu. The first sword blow had lopped off the brim of Nicholas's hat and wounded his forehead. Before the attacker could strike a second blow, he was wrestled to the ground by George and the rickshaw drivers. The tsarevich was immediately taken back to his hotel. Early reports suggested the wound was fatal. Mary Craw-ford Fraser, the wife of the British minister, reported that the first message about the assault had simply stated "Two deep wounds on the head; recovery impossible."[68] Only later, when additional telegrams came in, was she able to report that the tsarevich was not mortally wounded.

Iwakura Tomomi met Itō at Odawara station and handed him the em-peror's personal directive to proceed directly to the palace. They reached the emperor's chambers at one o'clock in the morning. Consulting at his bedside, the three men discussed the situation and decided that the em-peror would leave for Kyoto on the next train and proceed directly to the hotel where the tsarevich was staying.[69] Itō would join the emperor later that day. In the meantime, to calm the fears of an alarmed public, the em-peror issued an Imperial Rescript that read in part:

> It is with the most profound grief and regret that, while We, with Our Government and Our subjects, have been preparing to welcome his Im-perial Highness, Our beloved and respected Crown Prince of Russia, with all the honors and hospitalities due to Our national guest, We received the most unexpected and surprising announcement that his Imperial Highness met with a deplorable accident at Otsu whilst on his journey. It is Our will that justice shall take its speedy course on the miscreant offender, to the end that Our mind may be relieved, and that Our friendly and intimate relations with Our good neighbor may be secured against disturbance.[70]

After the emperor departed from Shimbashi Station at six o'clock that morning, Itō and other cabinet ministers, including Prime Minister Mat-sukata, Communications Minister Gotō Shōjirō, and Minister of Agri-culture and Commerce Mutsu Munemitsu, met to discuss the crisis. The first item was the penalty that should be imposed on the would-be as-sassin. Nothing was yet known about the assailant or his motives except that he was a policeman and his name was Tsuda Sanzō, but it was gen-erally agreed that to avoid a diplomatic crisis with Russia, the Japanese government needed to impose a severe penalty. The question that imme-diately arose was how severe? Should the incident be treated as a trea-sonous act against the imperial family or simply as a premeditated attempt at murder? Article 116 of the Japanese criminal code stated that anyone who attempted to assassinate the emperor, empress, or crown prince would receive a death sentence. It was unclear whether this also applied regarding foreign royalty.

Rickshaw drivers Mukouhata Jisaburo (right) and Kitagaichi Ichitaro (left), who captured Tsarevich Nicholas's assailant, Tsuda Sanzō. (Wikimedia Commons)

Itō believed that article 116 should be applied in this case. "This incident is extremely grave," he declared. "And since its likely impact is unfathomably profound, the penalty should lean toward the severe side. If a multitude of conflicting judicial arguments emerged to hamper a severe verdict, I may even support the proclamation of martial law to enforce the closure. We should not hesitate to employ an emergency measure to avert peril to the nation."[71] But others were not so sure. Laws could not be adapted to suit particular political circumstances. The integrity of the Japanese justice system was at stake.

As Itō was preparing to join the emperor in Kyoto, Mutsu and Gotō caught up with him just as he was about to leave the Imperial Hotel. They conveyed their idea of how to bypass the dilemma of choosing a penalty: hire a professional assassin to kill the culprit and attribute his death to illness. "This type of ploy was known to be frequently practiced in Russia," they told him. "It would be an easy way out." Itō was appalled. "I told them this kind of damnable behavior should never be tolerated in a sovereign nation governed by the rule of law, and that one should feel too ashamed to even blurt it out."[72]

The Japanese emperor was well aware of Russia's plans for building the Trans-Siberian Railway, and he connected it with the tsarevich's Grand Tour when he received word of it in early 1891. Although the two nations had settled their dispute over Sakhalin in 1875, the Japanese remained wary of Russia. In January 1888 Yamagata Aritomo, who had by then had served twice as chief of the Imperial Japanese Army General Staff, noted the potential implications of the Trans-Siberian to Japan's national security. In a memorial to the emperor titled "Advice on Military Affairs" (*gunji iken-sho*), Yamagata pointed out that the railroad would make Vladivostok an important transportation center and naval base.[73] However, because it was frozen for part of the year, Russia would naturally look for an ice-free port as the next step and would very likely set its sights on the Bay of Yŏnghŭng, off Wŏnsan on Korea's east coast.[74] In June of that year Yamagata traveled to Europe to seek the advice of Lorenz von Stein, a professor emeritus of political economy at the University of Vienna whom Itō had consulted earlier when drafting the Japanese Constitution in 1882. Stein had stressed the importance of Korea for Japan's national security, stating that the peninsula must be defended at all costs. "Once Korea was occupied by other countries," he warned Yamagata, "the danger to Japan would be indescribable."[75] Keeping Korea out of foreign hands was key to preserving the security of the nation, and the Trans-Siberian Railway posed a threat to that security.

Tsuda Sanzō later confessed that he had been convinced the tsarevich had come to Japan in preparation for invading the country.[76] At his trial he said that he had first thought of killing the Russian prince earlier that day when Nicholas and George had visited the temple grounds of Miyukiyama or Hill of the Imperial Visit but had hesitated because he did not know which one of the young men was the Russian prince. Another opportunity arose later at Karasaki Shrine in Ōtsu, but Tsuda again hesitated. It was only when Nicholas's party was about to leave Ōtsu that Tsuda realized he would not have another opportunity and that if he failed to act, the Russian prince would return to invade Japan.[77]

If Tsuda thought he would be rewarded by his fellow countrymen for what he perceived to be a patriotic act, he was wrong. Journalist Lafcadio Hearn noted that Kyoto had shut down and everyone had behaved as if in mourning. "The theatres, usually thronged from early morning until late into the night, are all closed," he noted.[78] On May 29, 1891, a twenty-seven-year-old maid named Yuko "cut her slender throat" in front of the Government Building in Kyoto. On her body was found a letter explaining that she had committed suicide to expiate the crime committed against the nation's honored guest and to "remove the blot from the national scutcheon, and lift the burden of sorrow from the emperor's heart."[79] The Meiji educator and leader Nishimura Shigeki summed up the public reaction: "When the incident became known, the whole country shook with fear. Some said the crown prince was dead. Others said his wounds were grave and his life was in doubt. There were all kinds of rumors and the public became more and more agitated."[80]

Emperor Meiji arrived in Kyoto on the evening of May 13 and went immediately to the hotel where the crown prince was staying. He was told to return the following morning, one of the rare occasions when a request of his was refused. The following day Nicholas received the emperor cordially, assuring him that his wounds were not serious and that the incident had not changed his friendly feelings for the emperor and the Japanese people.[81]

Itō's reception was far cooler. Before joining the emperor in his Kyoto residence, Itō was met by Foreign Minister Aoki Shūzō, who told him that the tsarevich would be leaving Kyoto that morning to board the *Pamiat Azova*, standing by at the port of Kobe. The abrupt change of plans seemed to be a complete turnaround from the friendly attitude expressed by the tsarevich earlier that day. The Russian ambassador, Dmitry Yegorovich Shevich, had conveyed his deep displeasure, stating that Nicholas and his suite "were feeling as if they were living in the midst of an enemy siege" and weren't sure "whether or not the policeman and the soldiers guarding them could be trusted not to turn their firearms against the crown prince." Realizing that the tsarevich's abrupt departure from Japan would spell diplomatic disaster or worse, the alarmed emperor sent Itō to implore the Russian minister to reconsider his government's plans and to persuade the prince to remain in Japan.[82] Although these efforts proved futile, the emperor and the tsarevich did enjoy a cordial lunch together aboard the *Pamiat Azova* before the latter's departure on May 19.

While Japan's embarrassed officials were trying to make the best of a tough diplomatic situation, the new chief justice of the Supreme Court, Kojima Iken, met with Matsukata and Mutsu in Tokyo. Given the momentous importance of the incident, it was decided to transfer the Ōtsu criminal case to the jurisdiction of the Supreme Court.[83] The subject under discussion was the penalty that should be imposed on Tsuda. "The incident has jeopardized the nation's security and well-being," Matsukata began. "To satisfy the emperor and the people of Russia, what penal code is available for the crime committed?" Kojima replied that the case would most likely fall under a common-law case with a maximum penalty of life imprisonment. This was clearly laid out in the Meiji Constitution of 1890. The existence of the new constitutional government was a sign that Japan was a nation of laws equal to all other Western nations.[84] Would the Japanese government now decide to turn its back on its own Constitution for the sake of political expediency that would not only undermine its commitment to judicial independence but tarnish Japan's image as a civilized, law-abiding nation?

Matsukata vehemently disagreed with Kojima. "The prince [Nicholas] is the future emperor of Russia," the former declared. "The cabinet has just agreed that this crime was a case against our imperial families, which means the application of Article 116 (death penalty) of the Penal Code."[85] Kojima countered that article 116 applied only to the Japanese imperial family. Exasperated, the prime minister responded that he may be right, but what did such legal trifles matter when the very existence of the nation was at stake? "The nation's existence comes before that of the law," he proclaimed. "If there is no nation, there will be no law."[86]

Fear of Russian retaliation had spooked the Japanese prime minister. He believed that Japan faced a critical turning point, with war and peace hanging in the balance. On May 16, Aoki Shūzō met with Ambassador Shevich, who asked the Japanese foreign minister how his government was going to punish the culprit. Shevich made it clear that "the Russians would not be happy with anything other than the death sentence." Shevich criticized the Japanese government "for its glaring laxity in the handling of the crown prince's visit." And when Minister of Education Enomoto Takeaki broached the topic of punishment, implying that Japanese judges may decide to sentence the culprit to a life sentence, Shevich "immediately turned livid, and declared that the verdict of life sentence might lead to an unforeseen crisis in the relationship between the two countries."[87]

Clearly, Kojima and the rest of the Supreme Court justices were under intense political pressure to sentence Tsuda to death. They had also received a rescript from the emperor with cryptic guidance. "The present incident relating to the Russian crown prince is of great importance to the nation. Using care, dispose of the matter promptly." It was not clear what exactly the emperor had in mind. Some interpreted "taking care" as a warning not to provoke the Russians; others thought the emperor meant that the Japanese constitution should not be tampered with. Kojima adhered to the latter interpretation.[88]

After his conference with the prime minister on May 12, Kojima explored European and American precedents to see whether Western countries had special laws that applied solely to foreign royalty, but he could find no such examples. He pointed out that under Russian law, an attempt on the life of the sovereign of another country was dealt with far more leniently than an attempt on the life of the tsar. The German penal code stipulated merely one to ten years in prison for such an offense. Thus, Japanese law was actually far more severe than Russian or German law.[89]

But more than Western precedent, Kojima was apprehensive about the scorn Japan would receive from the international community if his government failed to uphold its own Constitution and bowed to Russian pressure. Moreover, if article 116 was interpreted to include foreign royalty and members of their families, what were the precise distinctions between Japan and other countries? "To apply 116 to the monarchs of foreign countries and their families would without a doubt be a violation of Japan's sovereignty," he opined. "It would invite the ridicule and scorn of foreigners familiar with the law and the regret of generations still to be born. [Whatever the feelings aroused by Tsuda's act] we must understand that the law is the spirit of the nation and judges must not act based on their personal feelings."[90]

On the morning of May 24, five days after the tsarevich's departure from Japan, Kojima notified the prime minister that article 116 would *not* be applied in Tsuda's case. The other Supreme Court justices sided with their chief justice. It was already clear that there would be no serious repercussions from Russia, but Matsukata and his cabinet were still taken aback by the ruling. A highly emotional Saigō Tsugumichi, the home minister, accused Kojima of "endangering the nation."[91]

Public support, however, favored the Supreme Court ruling. The perception of government "weakness," and concern that it was willing to bow to Russian pressure, fueled criticism from liberal groups, especially those headed by Fukuzawa Yukichi and Ōi Kentarō, who had already taken issue with the government's "weakness" on treaty revision, the most pressing issue of the day.[92] At the same time, members of the right-wing "patriotic societies" like the Gen'yōsha (Black Ocean Society) and its later offshoot, the Kokuryūkai (Black Dragon Society), saw themselves as "guardians of the nation's prestige." These groups emerged as a reactionary political force that challenged the government's slow progress on treaty revision by whipping up anti-Western and antigovernment sentiments.[93] Not only did the unequal treaties impose artificial restraints on Japan's judicial and economic sovereignty, but they were also daily reminders of Japan's inferior status as a "civilized" nation and a blot on Japanese national pride. Throughout the 1890s these groups became more vocal in their demand for a bolder foreign policy. The Ōtsu ruling was seen as the first step toward realizing this goal.[94] The next step, involving the new direction of Japan's Korea policy, was when things turned deadly.

PART THREE

WARS AND IMPERIALISM

THERE WAS A SHARP division of opinion in Japan about what the Trans-Siberian Railroad might mean for Japan's Korea policy. Throughout the 1880s, Yamagata Aritomo, Japan's chief architect of the Japanese Army and twice prime minister, supported a proactive, forward policy. He had argued for the expansion of Japanese military forces to maintain parity with China. Meanwhile, Itō Hirobumi, who became prime minister in 1892, and his foreign minister, Mutsu Munemitsu, were more cautious. For them, as for most Japanese at the time, the foreign policy issue of the day was still treaty revision and treaty equality. Japan's ongoing negotiations with Great Britain to achieve treaty revision and national autonomy in early 1894 was near fruition, and Mutsu did not want to do anything to upset the British for fear that any provocative action might be used as an excuse to delay the proceedings.

The outbreak of the Tonghak rebellion in southern Korea during the summer of 1894 laid these arguments to rest. Unable to suppress the rebellion, Korea's King Kojong asked China to send troops. In accordance with the 1885 Tianjin Convention, China notified Japan of its deployment, triggering Japan to dispatch its own troops in response. The two armies inevitably clashed, and soon China and Japan were engulfed in war in Korea. While Japan's stated goals for the war emphasized the restoration of order in Korea, its more important unstated goal concerned the Asian balance of power and the underlying fear that if Japan did not act, Russia would take advantage of the chaos in Korea to assert its power over the peninsula.

The conflict exacted a heavy toll on Korean society. After the main Japanese forces had advanced to pursue the Chinese in Manchuria, Tonghak rebels in the south launched a second uprising during the fall of 1894 to protest the Japanese presence and local Korean officials who enabled them. Unable to put down the rebellion, Kojong called again on Japanese forces for help. Between November 1894 and January 1895, Japanese and Korean government forces launched a scorched-earth pacification campaign with devastating effect. The Sino-Japanese War ignited a Korean civil war, and the rift in Korean society and polity would grow even wider in the next war, between Japan and Russia.

The Sino-Japanese War was also a turning point in Russo-Japanese relations. Six days after the signing of the Treaty of Shimonoseki that ended the war, in April 1895, the ministers of Russia, Germany, and France called on Japan to give up the Liaodong Peninsula and its strategically important harbor of Port Arthur, a prize of a bloody and costly war. Through this "Triple Intervention" Russia hoped a grateful China would listen sympathetically to its appeals to build a railway line across northern Manchuria as a key portion of the Trans-Siberian Railroad.

Japan now faced a new and more formidable enemy. But Japan was not alone in its fear of Russia. The British were also growing increasingly anxious over Russian incursions into Manchuria. News of a secret treaty between China and Russia signed in 1896 that allowed Russia to build a railway line across Manchuria had been received with alarm in London. Russia's occupation of Port Arthur in 1897 created further concern.

Russian actions in Manchuria similarly raised alarms for the United States. America's experience of the "long depression" of the 1870s and 1880s had led political and business leaders to embrace the view that industrial overproduction lay at the heart of the nation's ills. Economic expansion into China was seen as the most convenient outlet for America's industrial glut. The need to protect equal privileges among countries trading with China was recognized by Secretary of State John Hay, whose 1899 Open Door Notes became an explicit attack on the spheres of influence in China. By taking a leadership role on the China trade issue, Hay was proclaiming, at least on paper, that the United States was committed to the principle of the territorial integrity of China. The Spanish-American War in 1898 and subsequent annexation of the Philippines further widened the horizon of America's interests in Asia. Shared suspicion of Russia's ascendency in Manchuria and the desire to maintain the Open Door heralded a new spirit of Anglo-American-Japanese cooperation in East Asia.

The outbreak of the Boxer Uprising in 1900 added another new dimension to the relations between Britain, Japan, and the United States. With much of its military forces occupied by the Boer War (1899–1902), the British government had no choice but to defer to Japan and the United States in dealing with the crisis in China. Without congressional approval, President William McKinley ordered the dispatch of twenty-five hundred soldiers and marines from Manila to China. Japan also agreed to join with the imperialist powers in what was essentially a punitive expedition against the Qing. Its participation was another indication of Japan's rise in the unfolding drama in East Asia and its endeavor to join the ranks of the Western imperialist nations as an equal power.

Russia did not join the Western powers in the protest that the Qing government suppress the rebellion. Russians had not felt threatened by the Boxers and had believed the movement to be primarily a response to American and European missionary and commercial activities. When the unrest spread into Manchuria and threatened the railway line, however, the Boxers suddenly became a Russian problem, leading to the mobilization of Russian troops from the Amur and Maritime regions to safeguard the railways. As Russian forces advanced into Manchuria, they laid waste to hundreds of cities, towns, and villages. By August the Russians had taken all of Manchuria.

Only five years after the Triple Intervention, Russia had squandered all the goodwill it had built up with China and was diplomatically isolated by the other Great Powers. Already brewing were the stirrings of a new conflict in East Asia, one that would align British, American, and Chinese interests with a rising Japan against an increasingly isolated Russia.

CHAPTER SEVEN

PRELUDE TO WAR

The year 1894 marked a turning point in Japan's relations with the rest of the world. Public dissatisfaction with the direction of Japan's foreign policy put the new Itō government on the defensive. The Ōtsu affair had exposed the government's weakness in the face of Russian pressure, and the mood of dissatisfaction with the drift of Japan's foreign diplomacy gave way to more strident demands for a bolder foreign policy. First, there was the question of treaty revision, the most important item on Itō's foreign policy agenda. Beginning in the early 1890s, government "weakness" on treaty revision had handed nascent political parties and reactionaries an excellent target for anti-Western and antigovernment sentiments to rally the Japanese people around a popular patriotic issue and declare an end to Western privilege. Foreign Minister Mutsu Munemitsu's first order of business in 1894 was thus to undertake the delicate negotiations for treaty equality with Great Britain.[1]

There were also the fomenting problems with China over Korea. Under Yuan Shikai's tight reign, the Qing dominated all forms of Korean communications, including the vital Seoul-Pusan link. The Japanese government had no secure transmission route to its legation in Seoul. All telegrams between Japan and Korea had to go by the Chinese landlines, despite numerous Japanese protests of these violations of prior treaty rights and agreements.[2] Tensions continued to mount when the Korean government, with Yuan's support, limited rice exports to Japan. In October 1893 the Korean government reduced its rice exports by twenty-six thousand tons from the level set in 1892. The Japanese press was in an uproar over the grain reduction.[3]

This was the context in which news of the assassination of Kim Ok-kyun, the failed leader of the 1884 Kapsin Coup, was received in March 1894 by a discontented public eager for change. Kim had been living in exile in Japan ever since his escape from Korea ten years earlier, and the liberal press eagerly jumped on his death to proclaim him a martyr in the cause of "civilization and enlightenment," while condemning China for having facilitated the assassination of a political exile under Japan's protection.[4]

The irony was that Kim, who had been living in impoverished circumstances in Japan, had survived other assassination attempts on Japanese soil that the press had all but ignored. In 1885 Kojong sent assassins to hunt down the former rebel leader after the Japanese government had refused to extradite him, but the amateurish plot was easily exposed.[5] Kim was subsequently banished for a time to the Bonin Islands because he was deemed a nuisance and an obstacle to peaceful relations with Korea, but the ruling received with little protest from his so-called friends.[6] And yet by the spring of 1894 Kim had become a rallying point for popular frustration not only with the Japanese government's "weak" foreign policy but also with the arrogant attitude displayed by China and Korea, whose "contemptible" treatment of the Korean exile had purportedly offended Japan's honor. Kim's death laid the first stone in the path toward confrontation with China, with inexorable consequences for the future of East Asia.

Kim Ok-kyun was lured to his death by two Koreans, Hong Chong-u and Yi Il-sik. Yi had come to Japan in 1892 at the behest of the Korean government and succeeded in persuading Hong, an intimate of Kim, to join his plot to assassinate the Korean "traitor." Both men convinced Kim to go to Shanghai to meet with Li Jingfang, Li Hongzhang's adopted son who had recently served as the minister to Japan. The Chinese government, they said, was dissatisfied with the direction of affairs in Korea under Kojong and the Min clan and hinted that Kim might be able to play a role in Korean affairs.[7] Hong offered to accompany Kim on the trip. Arriving in Shanghai on March 28, the two men and a third companion, Wada Enjirō, who had no knowledge of the murderous plot, checked in at the Towa Yoko Ryōkan in Shanghai. While Wada was away on an errand, Hong shot Kim while the latter was napping.[8]

News of the assassination reached Seoul on March 28. A satisfied King Kojong contacted Yuan Shikai, who, with Li Hongzhang's help, arranged for Hong to be sent back to Korea along with Kim's corpse. Such a move went against established protocol, for Hong should have been handed over to the Shanghai authorities and Kim's body sent to Japan. Wada Enjirō had been granted temporary custody of the body, but he left the coffin unattended on the quay while he arranged for the body's shipment back to Japan, and it was seized by the Shanghai police. Wada boarded the ship without the body.[9] Meanwhile, Li Hongzhang ordered the police to deliver Hong and the coffin to two Korean officials who had rushed to Shanghai to claim their charge. By the time Japanese officials realized what had happened, the assassin, the body, and the two Korean officials were safely on their way to Korea aboard a Chinese warship, arriving on April 12 at Inch'ŏn. Hong was given a hero's welcome.

Prime Minister Itō was well aware of the danger this episode posed. Not only had the Qing authorities violated established protocol, they had also undermined Japan's authority. Kim, after all, had been under asylum protection of the Japanese government, and the Qing had allowed the assassin to escape unpunished. Itō also feared what the Koreans might do to Kim's body, as it was customary under Korean law to mutilate the corpses of criminals. Foreign Minister Mutsu immediately instructed the Japanese consul in Korea, Ōtori Keisuke, to organize a joint plea with other foreign diplomatic missions in Korea to dissuade the Korean government from carrying out the customary mutilation, which he warned "would provoke serious ill-feeling against Korea among the Japanese populace." Ōshima's plea fell on deaf ears. The Russian consul, Karl Weber, was particularly adamant, stating that "it was within the legitimate power of the Korean king to choose the method of punishment suited to the nation's most wayward criminals." Ōtori then brought the matter directly to a Korean foreign ministry official, Cho Byung-jik, who rejected the Japanese consul's pleas, "insisting that Korea would be following its own tradition of criminal laws." Despite Mutsu's entreaties, Kim's corpse was subjected to the traditional punishment; the head, hands, and feet were severed and hung on a pole at Yanghwajin—the place where the Taewŏn'gun had executed Korean Catholics during the purge of 1866—while his torso was left to rot in the grounds nearby.[10]

TONGHAK REBELLION

Popular backlash to these events in Japan was predictably intense. Critics accused the Itō government of allowing the Korean and Chinese authorities to humiliate Japan. At a plenary session of the Lower House of the

Sixth Preliminary Diet on May 18, 1894, Moriya Koresuke questioned the government's handling of the incident. "It is my conviction that the affair of Kim Ok-kyun, although it concerns a single individual, was, in fact, a matter of grave diplomatic importance involving three nations: Japan, China, and Korea," he declared. "The reason is this: Kim went to Shanghai on a round-trip and, once there, chose to stay in a Japanese-owned inn which implied that he wished to stay under the protection of Japan."[11] Moriya then accused the Qing government of "stealing" Kim's corpse from Wada Enjirō. "What kind of behavior is this?" he thundered. "Does this act not insult the Japanese nation? . . . It is my conviction that the words insult and disrespect are more than fitting to describe this act of outrage by the Qing government."[12]

Throughout April and May, large public rallies called on the Japanese government to respond in a "prompt and decisive" manner to punish Kim's assassins. "There must have been a thousand mourners at the memorial service for Mr. Kim," Miyazaki Tōten, the Japanese activist and acquaintance of the Korean "martyr" later recalled.[13]

In May, Ōi Kentarō and Inoue Kakugorō organized a "Friends of Mr. Kim" society, denouncing the government's conciliatory foreign policy and declaring that "what the people of this country are loudly clamoring for" was that the Japanese government demand an apology from the Korean and Chinese governments for violating Kim's political asylum.[14] On May 20 the society held a grand funeral in Kim's honor at the Aoyama cemetery. Since they had no body, they obtained a lock of Kim's hair to bury while angrily denouncing the government for its betrayal of Kim.[15] The newspaper *Jiji* carried a headline story two days later about a groundswell of support for a no-confidence vote against the Itō cabinet.[16] By the third week of May the Lower House had introduced four resolutions that severely criticized the government, including a memorial to the emperor expressing a vote of no-confidence.[17] A no-confidence motion succeeded on June 1. The Itō Cabinet responded by dissolving the Diet.

Yet, just as the crisis was reaching its peak, Foreign Minister Mutsu received some startling news that would make Itō's actions moot. On June 2 Sugimura Fukashi, the Japanese secretary in the Seoul legation and a trusted confidant of the foreign minister, notified Mutsu that the Chinese government had announced its intention to send troops to Korea to suppress a rebellion. Led by disaffected peasant farmers aggrieved by the corruption of local yangban officials, the Tonghak (Eastern Learning) Rebellion threatened to topple the inept Seoul government. The peasant revolt began in Kobu County in February 1894 and quickly engulfed all of northern Chŏlla Province. In April government forces were sent to restore order but suffered heavy losses.[18] An anxious Kojong requested China's help in putting down the rebellion. But Yuan failed to notify the Itō government that China was sending troops to Korea, as required under the terms of the 1885 Convention of Tianjin. Yuan believed the crisis was an internal Korean matter that did not concern the Japanese since Kojong had requested help directly from the Chinese government.[19] The Chinese ambassador in Tokyo, Wang Fengzao, formally but belatedly notified Mutsu on June 7 that Qing troops were on their way to Korea. This delay inadvertently worked in Japan's favor for it had given the Japanese government enough time to dispatch its own forces to the peninsula without having to justify its actions.[20]

Arriving in Seoul on June 9 to resume his post as Japanese minister to Korea, Ōtori Keisuke was immediately tasked with "maintaining a balance of strength with whatever Chinese forces might already have been sent into Korea." Two days after the Chinese troops landed on June 10 south of Seoul at Asan, five hundred Japanese marines disembarked at Inch'ŏn and marched to Seoul. By June 13 nearly one thousand additional regular troops arrived from Japan, and eight hundred marched to to the capital, relieving the marines while leaving a force of two hundred at the port.[21] As additional troops arrived, a distressed Yuan went to see Ōtori to discuss a joint withdrawal of troops. By this time, however, a truce between the Tonghak rebels and the Seoul government had been reached on June 11. With civil strife subdued, there was no apparent justification for the continued dispatch of more Japanese troops to the peninsula.[22]

Ōtori agreed to reduce Japanese forces at Inch'ŏn if Yuan would do the same for Chinese forces encamped at Asan. Western officials and merchants in Korea who were wary of Japanese motives put significant pressure on the Japanese minister to withdraw troops. Mutsu, too, was worried the escalating crisis would seriously undermine all the work that had gone into the treaty revision negotiations in London.[23]

Despite these apprehensions, the Japanese public had been roused to such a patriotic fever pitch that there was no possibility of reducing the troop strength, much less withdrawing completely from Korea, without facing a full-blown political crisis at home. The Itō government could not back down before something concrete had been achieved in Korea. Mutsu thought the opportunity was ripe to demand Qing concessions on the telegraph line between Seoul and Pusan and reverse the Korean ban on grain exports to Japan, but such crass economic stipulations would not go over well with Western countries sympathetic to China and alarmed by Japan's aggressive intentions.[24] They might even decide to intervene in Korea. "In the absence of any pressing reason to fight or even a plausible pretext for hostilities, no *casus belli* existed," reflected Mutsu. "For us to deal satisfactorily with the situation at home and in Korea, it now became essential to devise some sort of diplomatic strategy paving the way for a transformation of this state of affairs."[25]

Itō came up with a brilliant plan. Because the rebellion had already been quelled, he opined, the main issue must focus on reforming the *conditions* in Korea that had given rise to the rebellion in the first place. He proposed that Japan and China work together on the reform plan, but because the Qing was sure to reject this idea, he suggested that the Japanese government push ahead anyway and carry out the reform measures itself. Such a plan would also inoculate Japan from criticism by Western powers, since its motivations in Korea would be deemed both enlightened and noble. These "selfless" moves would also justify Japan's actions in the name of good neighborliness and Japanese security, reinforcing the idea that Korea lacked many of the essential elements of civilized society and that it was "necessary for her to fulfill her responsibilities as an independent state" if future conflict over the peninsula was to be avoided. But the most dazzling aspect of Itō's proposal was that it would also satisfy the government's domestic critics, like Ōi Kentarō and Fukuzawa Yukichi, who had made the reform issue the centerpiece of their Korea policy. "After strenuous effort and careful deliberation," Mutsu recalled, "Japan's foreign policy had now taken a momentous step forward."[26]

REFORM PROPOSAL

On June 16 Foreign Minister Mutsu and Chinese ambassador to Japan Wang Fengzao met to discuss the Korean crisis. Wang objected to the Japanese proposal to discuss Korean reform measures first before withdrawing foreign troops from Korea. After some bitter disagreements, Wang finally consented to transmit the Japanese proposal to his government.[27]

Li Hongzhang studied the proposal carefully before raising his objections. The first, predictably enough, was that the rebellion in Korea had already been quelled so there was no need for either China or Japan to intervene in Korea. And while he agreed in principle with Mutsu that Korea needed reform, it wasn't up to China or Japan to undertake this

task. Korea was, after all, an independent nation, as the Japanese themselves had often pointed out. Finally, under the terms of the 1885 Tianjin
Convention, both countries were obligated to withdraw their troops as
soon as the disturbance in Korea was put down. Japan's proposal would
be violating that agreement.[28] Mutsu, who expected that Li would reject
Japan's plan, communicated his government's determination to pursue the
reform proposals alone if necessary.[29] The impasse was on.

Predictably, the Koreans were not keen on the reform proposal either.
King Kojong echoed Li's position, and at his meeting with Ōtori on
June 26 he told the Japanese minister that while he would undertake domestic reform, he would be willing to do so only after the Japanese withdrew their troops from the peninsula. Ōtori was frustrated, but he knew he
could not push the issue. Both he and Mutsu were well aware that Japan
was constrained by international opinion and had to tread carefully.[30]

Realizing that Japan might somehow get around his objections, Li
Hongzhang worked behind the scenes to ask Western powers for help in
mediating the dispute, with the ultimate goal of forcing a Japanese withdrawal. His caution in avoiding a showdown with Japan stemmed from
his belief that China was not ready for war. A principal cause for this ill-
preparedness had to do with Empress Dowager Cixi's birthday.

Cixi, the daughter of an unremarkable Manchu official, was a complex
and intelligent woman who had been chosen as an imperial concubine of
Emperor Xianfeng in 1851 at the age of seventeen. Tough-minded and
ruthless, she was the only woman to attain a high level of political power in
China during the Qing dynasty. Her remarkable political ascent began in
1856 after she gave birth to Xianfeng's only son. As the emperor's favorite
concubine, she accompanied the emperor when he fled from Anglo-French
forces as they advanced to burn and sack the Summer Palace, Yuanmingyuan, in 1860. After Xianfeng died in 1861, Cixi's five-year-old son
became the Tongzhi emperor and she assumed the role of co-regent, ensuring her path to political power. When the young emperor died of smallpox
in 1875, Cixi arranged for his three-year-old cousin, the son of her younger
sister, to succeed him. She adopted the new emperor as the son of the late
Xianfeng, thereby precluding her sister from gaining control of the regency.
Cixi served as co-regent for her nephew from 1875 to 1889, relying on men
like Li Hongzhang to steer China on a new course. As the leader of the
Beiyang Intendancy, the most important para-governmental organization
to emerge after the suppression of the Taiping Rebellion, Li was effectively
in charge of Qing domestic and foreign policy.[31]

Cixi was due to reach the age of sixty—the most important milestone age in the Chinese zodiac calendar—on November 29, 1895. To celebrate, Cixi decided to construct for herself a new and magnificent summer palace, Yiheyuan. To cover the enormous cost, she diverted much of the nation's revenues from self-defense to the construction of the new palace, including, ironically, the building of an artificial lake and a marble boat.[32]

Li was quite aware of China's deficiencies, as well as Cixi's extravagances that undermined the nation's resources, but he thought he could bring about a peaceful resolution to the crisis. Yet he had fatally underestimated Japan's resolve. Reports from Ambassador Wang in Tokyo gave him the false impression that sharp political controversies in Japan would prevent the divided government from attempting a foreign adventure. Consequently, when Li dispatched troops to Korea in June 1894, he did not attempt to control strategic points in Seoul or along the coast. He also failed to reinforce Qing forces, even as Japan continued to send reinforcements.[33]

Li relied instead on the time-honored practice of "using barbarians to control barbarians." He counted on Russian mediation, despite suspicions of Russia's designs on Korea. On June 20 Li met with the Russian ambassador to China, A. P. Cassini, and requested assistance in forcing a Japanese withdrawal from Korea. He claimed that the British had proposed mediation, knowing this would raise alarm bells in Saint Petersburg. "The British already showed their willingness to undertake the mediation work," Li confided to Cassini, "but we believe that Russia has the privilege on this issue."[34] Skeptical, Russian foreign minister Nikolai de Giers smelled a Chinese plot to exploit Anglo-Russian rivalry. At the same time, Li also made overtures toward the British. But Britain was only willing to act in the interests of peace insofar as hostilities would adversely affect British trade. The British demurred at Japanese assurances that their action in Korea would be confined to reform and would not include territorial acquisition.[35]

Li Hongzhang was becoming desperate. Not only had he lost in his bid to obtain Russian and British mediation to remove Japanese troops from the peninsula, he was also facing increasing opposition from the Qing court. Li's passive stance infuriated Emperor Guangxu, who in 1889 had emerged from the shadow of his aunt. Guangxu saw the impending war between China and Japan as an opportunity to assert his authority by mobilizing support for war with Japan.[36]

With the encouragement of Weng Tonghe, his tutor, and Li Hongzao, Minister of Education, Guangxu gathered high-ranking court officials who opposed what they perceived to be the "weak-kneed" attitude of Li Hongzhang. Some even questioned Li's motivations for seeking Russia's support.[37] On July 16 the emperor convened an imperial conference attended by ministers of the Zongli Yamen and the Ministry of Military Affairs. Guangxu sought the adoption of an aggressive policy against Japan as well as the immediate reinforcement of Qing forces in Korea.

But the effort failed, revealing the limitations of Guangxu's power. The Zongli Yamen refused to consider a declaration of war but agreed to send Qing reinforcements to Korea. Arrangements were made to dispatch six thousand men to P'yŏngyang and two thousand men to Inch'ŏn to achieve parity with Japanese forces already in the theater. Still, Qing forces were woefully unprepared. The British ambassador to China, Nicholas O'Connor, noted that while there were as many as ten thousand Japanese soldiers in Korea by mid-July, there were only two thousand Chinese soldiers.[38] Li had been reluctant to mobilize for war lest it jeopardize chances for Britain and Russian mediation, but the delay had cost the Qing precious time, leaving it in a precarious military position.[39]

When the Qing finally began mobilizing its forces, Prime Minister Itō and his cabinet realized that a Sino-Japanese confrontation was now inevitable. Nevertheless, there was still no viable pretext to bring about the desired rupture of relations. The reform issue had taken center stage as the *casus belli* between the two countries, but the question the Japanese still faced was *how* to precipitate the necessary spark that would lead to the desired conflict. Mutsu wrote to Ōtori Keisuke, Japanese minister to Seoul, to take "whatever measures he felt appropriate in bringing about a clash between Japan and China."[40]

On July 19 Ōtori sent a letter to the Korean king in which he demanded that Kojong expel the Chinese forces, whose presence in Korea in the name of "protecting a tributary" had violated Korea's independence and therefore the terms of the 1876 Kanghwa Treaty. Three weeks earlier, on June 30, Ōtori had adroitly extracted a public statement from Kojong affirming Korea's status as an independent nation.[41] On that basis, the letter insisted the Koreans adopt a series of reform measures to guarantee Korea's "independence." The Japanese minister ended the July 19 letter with an ultimatum for a satisfactory reply by July 22.[42]

There was, of course, never any expectation that Kojong would agree to the reform proposals.[43] But to force the Koreans to accept them without

Kojong's sanction would be tantamount to overthrowing the Korean government, something the Japanese, always cautious about foreign power intervention, could not do outright. But how to implement a reform program in a country that wanted nothing to do with it? Or more precisely, how to justify the takeover of a foreign government in the name of guaranteeing its independence?

Ōtori proposed a solution to the dilemma that was at once brilliant and shortsighted. He sought to exploit Korea's familial and political divisions and proposed, of all people, the reactionary Taewŏn'gun to be the Korean face to lead the reform effort. Most crucially, the Taewŏn'gun would be a countervailing, if not destructive, force against the Min clan, who were at the root of opposition against Japan. As the July 22 deadline approached, Ōtori was under increasing pressure to get the Taewŏn'gun on board and "topple the Min oligarchy which was the root of all evil."[44] By this time Yuan Shikai had packed up his bags and left for China. "He went from Korea so rapidly as to leave his women's folk behind to the mercies of those to whom he had been so haughty," Horace Allen noted sarcastically.[45] With Yuan out of the way, putting the Taewŏn'gun back in power would be a much simpler task.

"JAPAN WILL NOT DEMAND AN INCH OF KOREAN TERRITORY"

Ōtori had established indirect contact with the Taewŏn'gun in early July 1894 through Okamoto Ryunosuke, an intimate of the late Kim Ok-kyun, to sound out the former regent's views about cooperating with Japan. Okamoto was well aware that the Taewŏn'gun loathed the queen and thought he might be able to persuade the old man to join the Japanese in ousting her and Kojong from power. But he was also aware that the Taewŏn'gun was deeply suspicious of Japan. Nevertheless, Okamoto hoped he might appeal to the Taewŏn'gun's ambition and pragmatism: work with the Japanese and secure a path to power.[46]

But the Taewŏn'gun staunchly refused. The July 22 response from Kojong was predictably unsatisfactory, and the pressure to persuade the Taewŏn'gun mounted. Some had voiced the opinion that the Japanese should simply kidnap the old man and force him to go to the palace, but Okomoto opposed the idea. The Japanese, after all, needed the Taewŏn'gun's cooperation to lead the new government and put a Korean face on the reform program. Finally, Sugimura Fukashi, the secretary at the Japanese legation, arrived to salvage the situation. He gave a long and heartfelt speech in which he appealed to the Taewŏn'gun's patriotism. If he did not act, Sugimura lamented, the Mins would surely lead his country to ruin. He also hinted that the Taewŏn'gun had nothing to fear because the queen had fled the palace and was rumored to be in Ch'unch'ŏn. "At this," Sugimura recalled, "the Taewŏn'gun's expression brightened."[47]

The Taewŏn'gun asked Sugimura whether he would promise "in the name of your emperor" that Japan "will not demand an inch of Korean territory." Sugimura told him that he was "merely the legation secretary" and could not make any promises, but that as he "represents Minister Ōtori who represents the Japanese government," he would give him his word in that capacity. The Taewŏn'gun asked for paper and a brush and wrote: "The Japanese government will not demand an inch of Korean territory" and asked Sugimura to sign.[48] With relief and some trepidation, the legation secretary carefully signed his name. Apparently satisfied, the Taewŏn'gun told Sugimura that he was now ready to accompany him and Ōtori to the palace.

It was nearly 11 AM on July 23 when Ōtori and the Taewŏn'gun arrived at Kyŏngbok Palace. At dawn Japanese troops had dispersed the Korean troops on duty in the compound before the Taewŏn'gun arrived.[49] Kojong was there to meet him. "When the Taewŏn'gun arrived at the Assembly Hall (Chŏng-chŏn), the king descended to the bottom of the stairs and greeted his father and they took each other's hands and cried," recalled Sugimura. "The Taewŏn'gun scolded the king for the state of affairs and Kojong apologized for it."[50] It was agreed that the son would not relinquish his throne. Instead, arrangements were made to allow his father to resume his role as regent. "The Taewŏn'gun informed Ōtori that he [the Taewŏn'gun] had been invested with full authority in all affairs of government and reform by the king, and he promised that he would henceforth consult with the Japanese minister on all matters."[51] It appeared that Ōtori's bold gamble had paid off.

The Chinese were not immediately informed of the events of July 23. The telegraph service was under the tight control of the Japanese, and the Chinese had no way to access detailed information about the Korean capital after Yuan's abrupt departure on July 19. The only report that reached Beijing was a dispatch from Qing general Ye Zhichao at Asan, who informed Qing authorities that Japanese forces in the Korean capital were moving south.[52] He also wrote that more Japanese troops were on their way from Japan.

On July 26, news of the Japanese coup reached the Chinese capital. Emperor Guangxu insisted on declaring war the next day, but Li Hong-zhang countered that the decision was premature.[53] By then the Japanese navy had sunk the British steamship *Kowshing* in the battle of P'ung-do on July 25, marking the first engagement of the Sino-Japanese War. The transport ship carrying eleven hundred troops had been leased to China by British merchants to transport troops to Korea. The thousand soldiers who perished were, according to many observers, the best Chinese troops in the country.[54] The opening shot of the Sino-Japanese War had been fired, although China would not officially declare war until August 1.

CHAPTER EIGHT

TRIUMPH, DEFEAT, AND A MASSACRE

The Japanese people greeted the formal declaration of war on August 1, 1894, with unbounded enthusiasm. Confronting China over
Korea once again since Hideyoshi's abortive attempt in the late sixteenth
century, the war seemed like a chance to affirm Japan's newfound confidence as a modern nation powerful enough to take on the Celestial Empire and prevail. Because the pretext for the conflict had been framed as
"reform of Korea," the struggle between a forward-looking Japan and a
backward-looking China had given the war a kind of transcendental
significance that appealed to the Japanese' view of themselves as the vanguard of civilization and progress. Fukuzawa Yukichi saw the war as
necessary for the spread of "civilization and enlightenment" in Asia. The
war was not simply a struggle between two countries over Korea; it was
"a battle for the sake of world culture."[1]

The journalist Uchimura Kanzō, later known for his deep pacifist con-
victions, wrote in August 1894 of his belief in Japan's civilizing role in an
article titled "Justification for the Korean War," in which he painted the
war as a righteous struggle. Accusing China of keeping Korea's "fifteen
million helpless souls" poor and dependent "merely to satisfy the envy of
the world's most retrogressive nation," he was proud that the Japanese
were "raising our voice against this evil." He prophesized that "Japan's
victory will mean free government, free education, free religion, and free
commerce for 600,000,000 souls that live on this side of the globe." Never
before in Japan's history "has the nation been fired with a nobler aim":

Whether on the scaffold high
Or in the battle's van
The fittest place where a man can die
Is where we can die for man.[2]

Such musings about the noble aims of the war appealed to Japan's patriotic pride and vanity, but they also reinforced its sense of national
purpose. The repeated allusions to a civilized Japan battling a backward
China became a mainstay in Japanese literary and artistic depictions of
the war, and each battlefield victory appeared to fulfill Japan's destiny as
"Asia's great hope." While Fukuzawa, Uchimura, and others were confident of Japan's victory in the righteous struggle, Japanese war planners
were not quite as optimistic. China was an enormous country with huge
resources. Its contest with Russia in 1880–1881, which ended with the
return to China of the eastern part of the Ili basin region, had restored a
measure of China's military reputation after the humiliating losses of the
Second Opium War. Furthermore, the two modern battleships of the Beiyang Squadron were considered superior to any ship possessed by the
Japanese fleet. Strategically, too, the Chinese were at a distinct advantage.
They possessed bases near the theater of war, whereas it took the Japanese
nearly twice as long to transport troops to Korea. The Japanese leadership understood the realities and difficulties of modern war far better
than did its enthusiastic supporters. The contest against China would not
be easy.

BATTLE OF SŎNGHWAN

Japan's plan entailed a naval and a land campaign. The naval campaign
called for the Imperial Fleet to establish command of the Yellow Sea between China and Korea, to ensure safe passage for Japanese troops deploying to the western coast of the Korean Peninsula while blocking the
deployment of Chinese reinforcements. The sinking of the *Kowshing* on
July 25 marked the start of this phase. The international outrage it engendered was not unexpected and was accepted as a calculated risk.[3] The
land campaign had two phases that created a pincerlike movement to seize
Manchuria and threaten Beijing. The first called for the landing of Yamagata's First Army on Korea's western coast, which would defeat Chinese
forces in Korea and advance up to the Chinese border, invade Manchuria,
and threaten Beijing from the north.[4] Once command of the sea had been

Japanese troop movements during the first weeks of the First Sino-Japanese War.

achieved, the Japanese Second Army, under the command of General Ōyama Iwao, would invade Manchuria from the south to take the naval bases on the Liaodong Peninsula. After completing the Liaodong mission, Ōyama's army would redeploy to the Shandong Peninsula to seize the main Qing naval port at Weihaiwei, home port of the Beiyang Fleet, to completely neutralize China's ability to threaten Korea from the Yellow Sea.[5]

The Ninth Infantry Brigade of the Fifth Division, under the command of Major General Ōshima Yoshimasa (Ōshima Combined Brigade), forming the vanguard of the First Army, had been deployed to the peninsula in June 1894, but supplying and reinforcing it posed the first major logistical problem for Japan. With the Yellow Sea not yet fully under Japanese control, Japanese ships would be vulnerable to attack en route to the Korean Peninsula. The Imperial General Headquarters (IGHQ), located in Hiroshima, therefore decided to land the remainder of the Fifth Division at Pusan while the First Army's Third Division would be sent to Wŏnsan, on Korea's east coast. Both ports were located far away from China's naval bases at Weihaiwei and Port Arthur. These units were to meet up with Lieutenant General Nozu Michitsura, commander of the Fifth Division, in Seoul.[6] The long trek from Pusan and Wŏnsan to the capital city was arduous, and in the end the IGHQ decided to take a risk and send the remaining troops directly to Inch'ŏn. Yamagata understood that his troops needed to strike hard and fast before additional Chinese reinforcements arrived in Korea. The plan was to press Chinese land forces northwest up the peninsula by quickly striking the Chinese base at P'yŏngyang.

But first the Chinese forces in Korea had to be neutralized. On July 28, two days before the official declaration of war, Yamagata ordered hostile operations to begin. Leaving a small force to guard the capital, Ōshima's Combined Brigade was ordered to attack the enemy in Asan, on the Yellow Sea coast south of Seoul, where the bulk of the Chinese forces were deployed. General Nie Shicheng had arrived in Asan in early June with eight hundred troops to help suppress the Tonghak rebellion. General Ye Zhichao, the overall Chinese commander in Korea with an additional two thousand troops under his command, ordered Nie to establish a defense line at the village of Sŏnghwan, about ten miles northwest of Asan. The surrounding area was more advantageous than Asan, as it was situated behind two small rivers with ridges where the Chinese troops could dig in. The ground in front, broken up by only rice paddies, was also almost entirely without cover, providing clear fields of fire.[7] While Nie's forces fortified their defensive positions at Sŏnghwan, Ye decided to position himself and his forces at Ch'ŏnan, a few miles south of the village. His forces would reinforce Nie's troops if they were forced to fall back. The total Chinese troop strength in Korea amounted to three thousand men, but only a portion would engage Japanese troops.

Shortly after midnight on July 28, Ōshima attacked Nie's forces at Sŏnghwan. Lieutenant Colonel Takeda conducted a strong diversionary attack against the Chinese left flank while Ōshima led the main attack against the flank and rear of the Chinese right.[8] But Takeda ran into trouble. His men were forced to cross the rivers, one of which formed a large pond. The muddy rice paddy fields made it difficult to maneuver. "The water was so deep that it even went up to our soldiers' waist," recalled one soldier. "Our feet became stuck in the mud so that we couldn't move."[9] Some men lost their way in the dark; forced to crowd under the enemy's fire, they were pushed forward into the pond and drowned. Despite the setback, Ōshima pressed the attack. By daybreak his men had turned the Chinese right flank. Almost encircled, the Chinese retreated in disorder. "Our Chinese troops were encircled by the enemy and not until we ran out of munitions did we break out of the encirclement and got out," recalled one Chinese soldier.[10] It was a resounding Japanese victory. An estimated five hundred Chinese soldiers were lost in the battle of Sŏnghwan while the Japanese lost just eighty-eight men.[11]

Nie's withdrew to Ch'ŏnan to join the main Chinese army. Ye was planning another stand farther south at Kongju when word reached him that the *Kowshing* had been sunk with the reinforcements he had counted on. According to some estimates, the loss of troops had been equal "to the loss of a bloody battle." Had the *Kowshing* been able to land eleven hundred fresh troops in Asan Bay, it is doubtful Ye would have given up his plans at Kongju.[12] Ye also assessed that he was significantly outnumbered by the Japanese due to faulty intelligence that greatly overestimated Japanese strength at the tens of thousands, when in fact Ōshima's brigade consisted of no more than four thousand men.[13] The next morning, July 30, the Chinese withdrew from Ch'ŏnan, escaping north by a circuitous route to join the Chinese forces in P'yŏngyang. The retreat from Sŏnghwan had disrupted the planned Chinese encirclement of Japanese forces in Seoul with an advance from P'yŏngyang in the north and Asan in the south.[14] Ye had effectively given up control of southern Korea to the Japanese.

Generals Nie and Ye's forces arrived in P'yŏngyang toward the end of August after an arduous 170-mile trek from Ch'ŏnan. Awaiting them were four other Chinese armies under the command of Generals Wei Rugui,

Ma Yukan, Zuo Baogui, and Feng Sheng. Although Ye was overall commander, each Chinese general operated semi-autonomously, violating an
essential principle of war that an army must fight under a unified single
command.[15] The Chinese understood not only that the concentration of
its forces at P'yŏngyang invited Japanese forces to attack them but that a
decisive battle for Korea and the war would be won or lost at P'yŏngyang.[16]

BATTLE OF P'YŎNGYANG

P'yŏngyang is an ancient city. Established in 108 BCE as a Han dynasty
colony, the Chinese were eventually forced out of the Korean Peninsula
in 313 CE by the Koguryŏ general Kwanggat'o, and P'yŏngyang became
the capital of his kingdom in 427. The city fell again to a combined
Tang/Silla assault in 668 and was subsequently abandoned, but following
the establishment of the Koryŏ dynasty in 918, the city was reclaimed and
served as the dynasty's western capital. The Mongols occupied the city in
1232 during their century-long domination of the Korean Peninsula in
conjunction with their control of China in the Yuan dynasty (1271–1368).
In the late sixteenth century, P'yŏngyang was captured by the Japanese
during the Imjin Wars (1592–1598) until they were defeated by a combined Ming/Chosŏn Korean assault in 1593. A few decades later, in 1627
and 1636, the city was twice occupied by a foreign force, this time by the
Manchus, an event that coincided with the founding of the Qing dynasty
in 1636 (the Qing became the imperial dynasty of China in 1644 after it
conquered the crumbling Ming). P'yŏngyang had seen war and occupation for nearly two millennia.[17]

Situated on the right bank of the Taedong River, a broad waterway
flowing into the Yellow Sea, P'yŏngyang was accessible by ship. To its
north lie many hills, the highest of which is called Moktan-tei, or "Peony
Hill," upon which the Chinese built a fort with commanding views of the
entire city and the surrounding area. The natural barriers formed by the
river and the hills meant that the terrain was open only on the southwest.
It was here that the Chinese fortified the two existing bridgeheads and
built earthworks for defense.[18]

Given P'yŏngyang's natural defenses, the battle advantage belonged to
the Chinese. The Chinese plan assumed that Japanese troop reinforcements would arrive by sea and the Taedong River, and the Chinese planned
their defenses accordingly. They also calculated that even if these reinforcements arrived early, the arrival of the Korean winter would seriously

hamper the Japanese. This plan had first been tried three hundred years earlier when Hideyoshi's men fought a combined Chinese-Korean force in 1593. Although the Japanese took the city, Korean naval forces had been able to successfully prevent Japanese ships from accessing Korea's west coast to bring in supplies and reinforcements. P'yŏngyang was isolated, and Hideyoshi's army, hunkered down in the city during the winter, was whittled away by starvation, cold, and disease.[19] Hideyoshi's failed Korea campaign taught Yamagata two vital lessons: the Japanese fleet had to make sure the sea lanes to the peninsula, and especially the west coast, remained open, and the battle for P'yŏngyang needed to be wrapped up quickly if the campaign was to succeed. Yamagata calculated that the Chinese would spend less energy fortifying the northern end of the city, already naturally protected by hills. He also correctly calculated that an all-out frontal attack would not be adequate and thus devised a plan to storm the city from four sides simultaneously.[20]

While Yamagata was planning strategy, General Ye's preparation for the upcoming battle had serious shortcomings. For example, Ye did not establish an adequate plan for continuous patrolling of key areas to provide intelligence on the Japanese. This deficiency was the result of an unfortunate friendly fire incident on August 3. Wei's and Ma's forces dispatched night patrols that got lost and, mistaking each other as Japanese, fired on each other. Many were killed and wounded. The incident led the Chinese commanders to be excessively cautious in sending out additional patrols at night. The result was that Ye and his generals had little idea of what was happening outside the city walls or what the Japanese were up to.[21]

The battle erupted just before midnight on September 14. The Japanese began the attack on the east bank of the Taedong River and from south of the city, a calculated move on Yamagata's part to conceal the real number of forces opposite them on the north.[22] These diversionary attacks were led by Lieutenant General Nozu Michitsura and Major General Ōshima Yoshimasa. Meanwhile, a detachment of the Third Division had arrived just in time from Wŏnsan to join Major General Tatsumi Naofumi's Tenth Infantry Regiment to begin bombardment of the city in the north. During the early morning hours of September 15, these two flanking columns, which had drawn a cordon around the Chinese forces on P'yŏngyang's northern end, attacked simultaneously and ferociously. By midmorning the Japanese were at Hyŏnmu (North) Gate on the north side of P'yŏngyang. Lieutenant Mimura led the way and, with just a few dozen men in pouring rain, scaled the walls to seize the gate. "The Chinese were busy firing in front, keeping the Japanese troops back, and never imagined that a handful of men would have the boldness to scale the walls under their very eyes."[23]

General Ye began to lose confidence. "The North Gate was occupied by the Japanese so we have lost our transportation path for the ammunition," he told the other generals. "If the enemy attacks us during the night, how will we defend ourselves?" He persuaded them to give up the city "temporarily" and regroup elsewhere. It was more prudent to save the army to fight another day than to be destroyed in a Japanese siege from which there seemed to be no escape.

Ye sent a local Korean official to inform General Tatsumi that Chinese troops would be willing to "surrender the city the following morning." The Japanese general assented but suspected a ruse. Fearing that the Chinese troops would try to slip away during the night, he ordered his men to be alert for runaway Chinese soldiers trying to escape the cordon. At 4:45 PM the Chinese fire ceased and Ye ordered "a white flag displayed above the castle walls."[24]

As Tatsumi anticipated, Chinese troops began to secretly withdraw from the city "wearing light packs during the night." Unfortunately, General Ye's escape order did not reach all the units. Those who did not get the word began to panic when they saw men slipping away. The pouring rain and the bad weather contributed to the chaos that ensued. Lu Shushan, an officer from Sheng's army, recalled the mayhem:

> The soldiers were so frightened that they rampaged through the city. The Japanese heard the noise and thought it was an attack, so they immediately opened fire . . . Those Chinese soldiers who were in the front were fired upon and started to retreat but those in the back wanted to rush forward. It was so dark and crowded that one could not distinguish between enemies and friends, so all the Chinese soldiers took out their weapons and began fighting each other. Those soldiers who were returning from the front were attacked from both sides . . . It was so distressing. Those who were familiar with the place found some Korean locals to guide them out of the trap. There were so many people who were so terrified that they even killed themselves out of sheer terror.[25]

P'yŏngyang was in Japanese hands in less than forty-eight hours. Entering the city the next morning, Tatsumi found "bodies of dead Chinese piled up everywhere." Fifteen thousand Chinese soldiers perished, many at the hands of their fellow soldiers; another 683 soldiers were captured.[26]

"A Gathering of Chinese Prisoners at P'yŏngyang." (Getty Research Institute)

BATTLE OF THE YELLOW SEA

The battle of P'yŏngyang was a major victory for Japan, but it did not end the war for Korea. Gaining control of the Yellow Sea remained a critical task for the Japanese. The IGHQ, the command staff for all Japanese forces, assessed that Japan had to prevent additional deployment of Chinese troops to Korea by sea to consolidate its gains on the peninsula. Chinese naval bases at Port Arthur and Weihaiwei gave China a strategic advantage, but Li Hongzhang's passive strategy failed to exploit this advantage until war broke out. Keen to capitalize on the delay, the Japanese Combined Fleet under the command of Admiral Itō Sukeyuki (also known as Itō Yūkō) saw an opportunity to draw the Beiyang Fleet into the Yellow Sea, where it could be engaged in a decisive battle. Japan's strategy depended on this critical naval engagement: control of the Yellow Sea would allow the Japanese Army to secure Korea, invade Manchuria, and threaten Beijing from the north while conducting landing operations on the Liaodong Peninsula to advance on Manchuria from the south. These operations were key to victory.[27]

Beginning in August, Itō's Combined Fleet began pursuing the Chinese fleet ferrying troops to northern Korea. For nearly two months after the sinking of the *Kowshing* on July 25, Itō fruitlessly attempted to lure the

Chinese fleet out of its base in Weihaiwei. But on September 17, 1894, one day after the fall of P'yŏngyang, Itō was finally given his chance.[28]

The Battle of the Yalu River was important not only as a significant turning point of the war but also in the annals of modern naval warfare as the first major fleet action since the Battle of Lissa (or Battle of Vis) in 1866, when Austrian ironclads had crushed an Italian fleet in the Adriatic Sea. During the twenty-eight-year interval, naval technology had undergone considerable innovations. The Yalu River battle was the first to use steel ships with large ordnance, "the weapons of the machine age."[29] Li Hongzhang had poured millions of *taels* into building the modern Beiyang Fleet, with ships built in Germany and Britain. The fleet, however, was technically a regional, not a national one, as Nanking and Canton had their own fleets but with obsolete ships.[30]

When the moment came for the fleet to demonstrate its worth, Li seemed reluctant to employ it because it was so expensive. His longtime British naval adviser, Captain William M. Lang, observed his reluctance: "My idea is that China is holding back her Navy, being unwilling to run unnecessary risks," he noted. "I don't believe Chinese ships will go out to look for Japanese war vessels but will remain quiet until the coast of China is menaced."[31] Admiral Ding Ruchang, the general officer in command of the fleet, was given strict orders to limit engagement with the Japanese.[32] By relinquishing the initiative, China had effectively given control of the sea to Japan and wasted one of its most powerful assets.[33]

Most naval experts at the time agreed that the Chinese and Japanese fleets were more or less equally matched. "They [the Chinese] are well trained, and excellent marksmen," observed Captain Lang. Each fleet possessed twelve ships.[34] The nucleus of the Chinese fleet was two powerful German-built battleships, the flagship *Dingyuan* and the *Zhenyuan*. The Japanese fleet did not possess any comparable ships, but its ships were faster and more agile, with quick-firing guns. Most of the Japanese ships were British-built except for the flagship, the *Matsushima,* and sister ship, the *Itsukushima,* which were French-built cruisers.

The Japanese fleet had also been busy transporting a large number of soldiers to Korea. On September 14, Itō's fleet arrived off the mouth of the Taedong River, where some vessels and torpedo boats detached from the main fleet to proceed up the river and assist the troops during their preparation for the battle of P'yŏngyang. Knowing that the land campaign plan was to push northward into Manchuria after the city was taken, Itō set off on September 16 to Haiyang (Ocean) Island to prevent any seaborne reinforcements or supplies reaching Chinese troops. But the Beiyang Fleet had already arrived at the Yalu River with four thousand troops. Having disembarked these troops on September 16, the fleet set off the next morning for its return trip to China. Thus, without either one being aware of the other, both fleets were destined for confrontation in the Yellow Sea—in the battle known as the Battle of the Yalu River, but that really took place in the waters around Haiyang Island.[35]

A number of foreigners were aboard the Chinese fleet as technical advisers. The most important was a former German officer, Major Constantin von Hanneken, who entered Li Hongzhang's service as his aide-de-camp in 1879 and had been aboard the *Kowshing* when it was sunk by the Japanese on July 25. He survived by swimming to a nearby island.[36] Hanneken had been entrusted by Li Hongzhang with preparing coastal defenses in North China and was aboard Admiral Ding's flagship as his personal advisor. As an ex-cavalry man, Ding did not pretend to be a professionally trained naval officer. "He was revered as a chief, respected and admired," observed British vice-admiral William Ferdinand Tyler, the other naval advisor aboard the *Dingyuan*. However, "his lack of technical knowledge of ships" made his role largely symbolic, "a sort of First Lord of the Admiralty afloat."[37] The man in charge with technical knowledge of ships was the British-trained naval officer Liu Buchan, referred to by Tyler as "the Commodore."[38]

On the morning of September 17, Japanese sailors spotted smoke in the distance from the fleet's position near Haiyang Island. About the same time, Chinese sailors detected the presence of the Japanese fleet on the horizon. By 11:30 AM the Chinese counted as many as eight Japanese warships advancing toward them.[39] As the Chinese fleet slowly steamed to meet its foe, it formed in an irregular, or indented, line formation; various accounts agreed that it was in great disorder. The battleships *Dingyuan* and *Zhenyuan* were at the center, flanked by the two most powerful cruisers, the *Laiyuan* and *Jingyuan*. The two older sloops, the *Chaoyong* and the *Yangwei*, justly considered the "lame ducks" of the fleet, were stationed on the right flank, farthest from the approaching Japanese. "The weak wing vessels, feeling the tragedy of their position, hung back, and thus our fleet assumed a crescent shape."[40]

The Japanese fleet advanced in a single column, steering for the center of the Chinese line, but gradually changed course, speeding diagonally across the enemy's northern end of the line, the weakest part of the formation. There are three potential weak positions of a line: the center and the two flanks. "If the center is pierced," observed naval strategist Alfred Thayer Mahan, "the force is divided; but the center can more easily be reinforced than either flank can be." In this situation, keeping the two strongest ships at the center was the wisest strategy, but the Chinese made the critical mistake of keeping the weakest ships on the two flanks, where they were easy prey. Had another ship been placed at the rear of either flank, they might have supported each other.[41]

There was an obvious and immediate need to alter course and change formation. But before Ding could give the order, he was knocked unconscious by the shock wave of the main gun firing without warning right below the bridge of the flagship *Dingyuan.* Commodore Liu had made the premature decision to open the battle with the first shot, but it had widely missed its mark. The intended target was the *Yoshino,* but the distance was slightly over four miles, far too great for a hit. There was now no more time for the Chinese fleet to maneuver. The *Yoshino* quickly steamed ahead and engaged the weakest ships, the *Chaoyong* and *Yangwei,* on the Chinese right flank, which burst into flames. The two ships did not sink immediately but they were effectively eliminated from the battle. Rear Admiral Tsuboi Kōzō later recalled that "the Japanese victory was due to this concentrated attack on these weak ships on the enemy's right wing."[42]

Thereafter the Chinese ships were in chaos. Admiral Ding was temporarily unconscious. Vice Admiral Tyler, who had recognized the need to alter course, was at Ding's side when the blast went off. He, too, was knocked unconscious, suffering a concussion and the rupture of both eardrums (as well as permanent deafness). "What was the explanation of the Commodore's act in opening fire while the Admiral and I were standing—well in sight—over the ten-inch guns," Tyler later fumed. "I never knew and I never heard the thing discussed. Where the Admiral fell I do not know. His leg was crushed, and of course, he was much shaken." To make matters even worse, a rain of Japanese fire hit the helm room of the *Dingyuan,* and any possibility of remedying the disorder was lost due to "the destruction of all our signaling apparatus during the first half-hour" of battle.[43]

The initial encounter put the Chinese on the defensive, and the Japanese fleet seized and retained control of the battle. The Japanese separated the two Chinese battleships from their consorts and, circling them, poured in "such a storm of projectiles that her crew seemed to fall into a state of the greatest confusion."[44] By midafternoon the Chinese fleet was in shambles. Although the Japanese were unable to disable the vital sections of the two ironclads, the rapid-fire guns had decimated the ranks of the Chinese sailors, leaving an insufficient number of men to work the ships' guns and machinery.[45]

It was at this low point for the Chinese, around three o'clock in the afternoon, when it looked as if everything was lost, that the Chinese fleet scored its first big win—the *Zhenyuan* struck the flagship *Matsushima*. It was not a mortal blow, but it was severe enough to put it out of action. "As a burst of flame arose from her, followed by a great cloud of white smoke, hiding her entirely from view, our [Chinese] gun's crew yelled their satisfaction," reported one observer. "This shell indeed wrought frightful havoc."[46]

Soon thereafter, around five o'clock, the Japanese fleet withdrew and headed toward the Korean coast. Three ships—the *Matsushima, Hiyei,* and *Akagi,* and also the merchant steamer *Saijyo Maru*—had all sustained considerable damage. But not one Japanese ship had been sunk. The Chinese, on the other hand, had lost five.[47] "No authoritative reason for this discontinuation of the battle—there was about another hour of daylight—appears to have been made known," observed Tyler, "but a reasonable supposition is that the failure of the concentrated fire of the Japanese fleet over a period of four and a half hours to disable the two battleships was a large factor in the decision."[48] The sudden and shocking crippling of the *Matsushima* may have also played a role in Itō's decision to withdraw. Itō was nothing but prudent. He also knew that if he risked the fleet, the Japanese Army would be in grave peril. "Like Admiral Sir John Jellicoe in World War One," wrote one observer, "it could be said of Itō in the Sino-Japanese War that he was the only man who could have lost the war in an afternoon."[49]

The Battle of the Yellow Sea was a turning point. Although Itō withdrew, the heavy damage inflicted on the Beiyang Fleet made it more or less ineffective, and Japan was able to establish control of the Yellow Sea. The Japanese were now ready to take the fighting directly to China. General Ōyama Iwao's Second Army (three divisions and one brigade) was ordered to land on the Liaodong Peninsula to begin the second phase of the land campaign. His object was to seize Port Arthur (Lüshun), the heavily fortified and strategically important naval base that had taken the Qing sixteen years to build. With its dry docks and modern equipment, Port Arthur was a key naval facility.[50] Once Port Arthur was taken, Ōyama was to seize China's second most important naval station, Weihaiwei on

Japanese soldiers reenact scaling the walls of Jinzhou Castle, January 3, 1895. (Photo by Kamei Koreaki, Meiji nijū nana hachi nen sen'eki shashin jō. jōkan. [Meiji 278 Campaign Photo Album, vol. 1], no. 78, National Diet Library, Japan)

the Shandong Peninsula, home base of the Beiyang Fleet, thus depriving the Chinese of any usable base in the Yellow Sea. Meanwhile, Yamagata's First Army would continue to push northward across Manchuria toward Haicheng.[51]

JAPANESE LANDINGS

On October 24, twenty-two thousand men of Ōyama's Second Army began landing at a little cove northeast of Dairen Bay, about a hundred miles north of Port Arthur. They faced no resistance. Ōyama's men came upon the first Chinese line of defenses only on November 5. These consisted of two forts built on hills flanking the road to Jinzhou, on Liaodong Bay where the peninsula narrows to an isthmus, forming a strategic bottleneck. Jinzhou fell to the Japanese the next day. On November 7, Dairen was attacked by the Japanese fleet, forcing its three thousand Chinese defenders to retreat south to Port Arthur.[52]

The rapid collapse of the Chinese at Dairen was surprising, especially because the defensive works were excellent in design. Kubota Beisen, the Japanese reporter traveling with the Second Army, recalled: "On dawn the next day [November 7] three of our ships maneuvered through the minefield and then bombarded and destroyed the east signal tower, shelling what appeared to be enemy barracks, [but] they encountered no retaliation. Since the bay was heavily fortified, second only to Weihaiwei and Port Arthur [Lüshun], a stiff resistance was awaited. It was truly surprising to face no defense."[53]

After the fall of Dairen, Captain Calder, the British harbormaster at Port Arthur, went to Tianjin to see Li Hongzhang. He wanted to enlighten Li "about the growing unruliness of the so-called defenders [of Port Arthur] and that the fabric [of order] was tottering." Calder's news left the viceroy reeling. "He began inquiring whether it was a fact that one or two forts at Dairen had been taken and when told that they were all lost, he visibly faltered and remarked that it was incredible."[54] On September 18, one day after the Battle of the Yalu, Li was stripped of his Three-Eyed Peacock Feather and Yellow Riding Jacket, honors that had been bestowed upon him the year before by the emperor.[55] On September 30 another imperial decree appointed Prince Gong to take charge of war operations in cooperation with Li.[56] Brought out of obscurity since his trying negotiations with the French and British after the sacking of the Summer Palace in 1860, the old prince proved even less effective than Li in handling the mounting crisis.

THE BATTLE OF PORT ARTHUR

The Japanese plan of attack on Port Arthur was fairly straightforward. Port Arthur, known as Ryojun-kō in Japanese, was located at the southwestern tip of the Liaodong Peninsula, which runs northwest to southwest. It was the most important of China's naval bases, earning its nickname the "Gibraltar of the East."[57] Two roads led into the city along the northern and southern shores of the peninsula. Ōyama's Second Army would advance along both routes with the First Division, commanded by Lieutenant

General Yamaji Motoharu, along the northern road to conduct the main attack into the city. The attack would be led by Major General Nogi Maresuke's First Infantry Brigade. The Twelfth Mixed Brigade, under Major General Hasegawa Yoshimichi, would conduct a supporting attack and cover the left flank by advancing along the southern road. Meanwhile, off the coast of Port Arthur, Itō's Combined Fleet completed the encirclement by blocking the port. The Qing forces would be trapped like a "rat in a bag."[58]

Accompanying the march to Port Arthur was James Creelman of the *New York World,* and Thomas Cowen, war correspondent for the London *Times.*[59] Both were traveling with the Second Army. Creelman, in particular, was impressed with what he saw. "As the splendid columns marched through the valleys and over the hills, now wading in line in the stream, and now sprawling painfully among loose, jagged rocks, or plodding heavily in the drifting sand, the wonderful discipline an endurance of the army displayed itself," he wrote. "No flags, no music, no pomp; a silent businesslike organization, magnificently offered and equipped, with one common object uniting thousands of men—the glory of Japan."[60]

Creelman left Ōyama's headquarters to ride ahead to join General Yamaji's forces preparing for an assault on Port Arthur's northwestern forts, part of the defenses protecting Port Arthur from a land attack. Before the attack began, Ōyama wrote to General Wei Rucheng, one of the four commanders in charge of Port Arthur's defense, demanding he give up the city. He reminded Wei that he was outnumbered by far-better-trained soldiers. "Your forces were defeated in the first battle at Asan," he wrote. "They were also vanquished for a second time at Ping Yang [P'yŏngyang], and for a third time at Jinzhou. Your forces were also defeated on the sea. Indeed, you have not had a [single] victory. This being the case, the will of Heaven seems to be plain."[61] Ōyama did not receive a reply.

On the afternoon of November 20, four thousand Chinese soldiers advanced on the Japanese positions. But Yamaji's First Division quickly drove them back.[62] Known as a "one-eyed demon" due to a childhood accident that left him blind in one eye, Yamaji was "a stern, silent man" who seldom spoke, even with his own officers. "I remember that the day before the battle of Port Arthur he listened to a discussion among his officers about the coming fight without saying a word until everybody had stopped talking," recalled Creelman. "And then he turned to me, through my interpreter, and said 'the forts will all be in our hands before the sun goes down tomorrow.'"[63]

The Second Infantry Regiment, Fifth Company, on Sanjiaoshan just before the attack on Port Arthur. (Photo by Kamei Koreaki, Meiji nijū nana hachi nen sen'eki shashin jō. jōkan. [Meiji 278 Campaign Photo Album, vol. 1], no. 113, National Diet Library, Japan)

The next day, at 2 AM, Japanese forces began "marching by circuitous and very difficult routes over the outlying hills into battle position." The northwestern forts of Itzushan (Chair Mountain) and Pine Tree Hill (Songshushan) were in Yamaji's hands by midmorning and the remaining forts collapsed, one by one, by midday.[64] With all the inland forts successfully captured, Ōyama ordered Yamaji to take the city.

The First Brigade's Second Infantry Regiment, under the command of Colonel Isechi Yoshinari, began the assault. Hasegawa's Twelfth Mixed Brigade engaged the northeastern forts to divert Chinese fire from Yamaji's forces in the west.[65] By 11 AM Hasegawa's forces had taken all eight northeastern forts. An eyewitness recounted, "At the ramparts not a Chinaman remained. They fled from fort to fort along the high wall, firing as they went, and making a stand at every point till too close for rifles. All over the hills, they were chased and for many miles around hardly a hundred years could be passed without sight of a Chinese corpse."[66] The scene was even more striking where Yamaji's forces were attacking. "The hill was strewn with thick coats, pouches containing cartridges, and all kinds of things the Chinese had thrown away in their flight," recalled Creelman. "The Chinese fled from the almost impregnable forts on their heights by the shore without firing a shot."[67] By the afternoon of November 21, Isechi's Second Infantry Regiment was marching through the streets of the town. Yamaji's prediction came true—the formidable fortress of Port Arthur had been taken in a single day.

The rapid collapse stunned the Chinese. General Wei Rucheng, whose division was posted in the business section of the town, had not stirred from his spot throughout the entire afternoon. "It is said that he did make a show of advancing to the aid of the other generals, but by two o'clock that afternoon nothing could be seen of him or his men at their original station." Wei later disguised himself as a common coolie and with a few servants made his escape from the harbor. "There happened to be quite a gale of wind blowing at this time, and their boat being a small one, it took them from five o'clock that afternoon to ten o'clock the same night before they could weather the mouth of the harbor," reported an eyewitness. "It took the boat four days more to get to Chefoo [Yantai]."[68] Wei Rucheng was the younger brother of Wei Rugui whose poor performance during the battle of P'yŏngyang later cost him his head. After Wei Rucheng landed in Chefoo, his head was on the chopping block as well.[69]

RYŌJUN / LÜSHUN MASSACRE

A grisly sight greeted Isechi's Second Infantry Regiment as they entered Port Arthur. Three human heads hung from a roadside willow tree. The heads had belonged to Japanese soldiers captured near the village of Tuchengzi (J. Dojōshi) on November 18. The heads had been mutilated, the noses and ears lopped off. Further into the town, two more heads were discovered hanging underneath the eaves of a house.[70] Stephen Hart, who was covering the war for Reuters on the Chinese side and was almost killed by a Japanese officer when the Second Regiment first entered the town, reported to Creelman that he had witnessed money for the heads being paid to Gong Zhaoyu, the commandant of Port Arthur.[71] (Fittingly, Gong escaped to Chefoo on the same boat as Wei Rucheng the same afternoon.)[72] Japanese officers covered the heads as they were taken away and "speedily cleared the scene and placed it off-limits to the prying eyes of the troops."[73]

Rumors circulated that Huang Shilin, one of the Chinese generals in charge of defending Port Arthur, had issued a special order directing all men over the age of fifteen to resist the Japanese from their homes.[74] "As it was impossible to tell Qing soldiers from noncombatants," went one report, "our soldiers had to search every cranny of the houses and get rid of whoever offered resistance."[75] Despite the officers' efforts, news of the mutilated heads had circulated among the Japanese troops. Angered by the mutilations and wary of reports that Chinese soldiers were donning civilian clothing, Japanese soldiers entered the town ready to exact revenge.

A huge unanticipated problem for the Japanese was the presence of Westerners who witnessed what happened. Creelman, Cowen, and two others, Stephen Hart and war artist Frederic Villiers of the *Black & White*, had not seen any Qing soldiers donning civilian clothing or shooting at Japanese troops from homes. "I swear that the people of Ryōjun did not attempt to offer any resistance against the invaders," Creelman later wrote. "The Japanese now insist that their troops had been shot at [from] the windows and doorways. But these claims are completely false."[76] Instead,

Japanese soldiers order Chinese residents to bury corpses from Port Arthur, November 24, 1894. (Photo by Kamei Koreaki, Meiji nijū nana hachi nen sen'eki shashin jō. gekan. [Meiji 278 Campaign Photo Album, vol. 2], no. 12, National Diet Library, Japàn)

the Westerners saw "Japanese march in, firing up the streets and into the houses, chasing and killing every live thing that crossed their path." "I looked hard for the cause," Cowen later recalled, "but saw none."[77]

What followed over the next three days was a massacre on a large scale. "I can say as an eye-witness that the wretched people of Port Arthur made no attempt to resist the invaders," wrote Creelman. "I saw a man begging for mercy pinned to the ground with a bayonet while his head was hacked off with a sword. Another Chinaman cowered in a corner while a squad of soldiers shot him to pieces. An old man on his knees in the street was almost cut in two," he recalled. "The town was sacked from end to end and the inhabitants were butchered in their own homes."[78]

Evidently some of the Japanese soldiers believed that they were, in fact, killing Chinese soldiers, not civilians. The war photographer Kamei Koreaki, who witnessed the massacre firsthand, wrote in his diary that "any enemy found hiding in Ryōjun was killed." The Chinese, he explained, "had commanded every man/boy above the age of 15 living near Ryōjun to resist the Japanese army. Therefore, the Japanese killed anyone who showed any resistance. In the city, there were was no place where you could not find a dead body, and these bodies were [all] covered with blood, brains, and stomach parts, emitting a foul odor."[79]

Yet, children lay among the dead. "A procession of ponies, donkeys, and camels went out of the western side of Port Arthur with swarms of terrified women and children," Creelman recalled. "The fugitives waded across a shallow inlet, shivering and stumbling in the icy water. A company of infantry was drawn up at the head of the inlet and poured a steady fire at the dropping victims but not a shot hit its mark. The last to cross the inlet were two men. One of them was leading two small children. As they staggered out on the opposite bank a squadron of cavalry rode up and cut one of the men down with their sabers. The other man and the children retreated into the water and were shot like dogs."[80]

The following morning, November 22, was excessively cold, about 20°F. Cowen and Hart woke up early to survey the ghastly scene. "Passing up the main street the sight was truly pitiable. Every few feet lay the dead bodies of citizens, bayoneted, shot, and hacked about in a manner that would delight the Bashi-Bazouk of Turkey, the Afghan fanatic, or the followers of Nana Sahib. Not in the whole course of our journey through the streets did we see a single body that could be taken for a soldier's, no weapons of any kind."[81] That morning Creelman came upon a victim "his neck ripped open by a Japanese sword and a pet dog shivering under his

"After the Bombardment of Port Arthur—Faithful unto Death."
Sketch by Frederick Villiers. (*New York World,* February 11, 1895)

arm." Villiers was with him and made a sketch. "There was a dead woman lying under a heap of slain men in every conceivable attitude of supplication," Creelman noted. "At one corner there were twenty-five corpses in a pile. The soldiers had been so close to their victims that the clothes partly caught fire and roasted the dying men . . . nowhere the sign of a weapon, nowhere the sign of war. It was a sight that would damn the fairest nation on earth."[82]

While Villiers was recording the horror of the events for posterity, at the other end of the city Lieutenant O'Brien, the American naval officer traveling with the Second Army as a foreign military observer, was fuming. "He declared that he would like to leave the Japanese Army immediately and said in the most emphatic language that if the facts were known at Washington the War Department would undoubtedly recall him."[83] Colonel Taylor, a British medical attaché and old East Indian campaigner, and Admiral Fremantle, a British naval officer, both with the Second Army as military observers, were similarly disgusted. Seeing that the killings were continuing into the second day with no sign of abating, the three military attachés, quartered in the same house with the four journalists and "freely exchanging ideas with them about the barbarities," wondered what steps might be taken to stop the killings. "It was suggested that one of the attachés should address a letter to the Field Marshall [Ōyama] protesting against a continuance of the slaughter of unarmed inhabitants," recalled Creelman. But Lieutenant O'Brien strongly objected. "He said it would be stepping outside the province of a spectator and would undoubtedly be considered an act of interference." Moreover, "the generals and their subordinates were thoroughly familiar with the details of the massacre."[84] O'Brien's reasoning was of course a convenient excuse to do nothing at all, but it was quietly accepted by the others, who had come to fear for their own safety. "What happened after Port Arthur fell to the Japanese would have been impossible, and even dangerous, to report on the spot," Cowen later admitted.[85]

Later that evening Creelman recounted that Mr. Ariga, a Japanese military correspondent attached to Ōyama's army, came to them for a talk. He was clearly uneasy. Turning to Creelman he asked:

"What do you think of what has happened?"

"It was a fine strategic move," I answered.

"No," Mr. Ariga responded. "You know what I mean. I mean the killing of the people of Port Arthur. What name would you give it? Would you call it a massacre? I want you to be plain with me."

The other correspondents looked at me nervously, fearing that I might betray my feelings and that the Japanese would not allow us to leave China, but compel us to send our despatches through the military censors, thus suppressing the details of the appalling scenes we had witnessed. I tried to evade the question, but Mr. Ariga pressed it.

"Would you call it a massacre?" he asked. "Would you call it civilized warfare? We are anxious to know what you are going to say about this."

Again, I turned the question aside. Mr. Ariga gave me up and turned to Frederic Villiers, the artist of the *Black and White,* of London, who also wriggled out of a plain answer as skillfully as he could.

Then he addressed Mr. Cowen, of the London *Times,* who told him flatly that whatever might be said of the excitement of the troops on the day of the battle itself, the killing of unarmed men on the succeeding days was an outright massacre. Mr. Ariga looked thoughtful.

"Do you think so?" he queried, turning to me.

"I certainly do," I replied. "It is the duty of a civilized nation to take prisoners."

Mr. Ariga was plainly trying to make us commit ourselves not to use the word massacre in our despatches and he fenced in the true Asiatic style.

"That is another question," he said. "If we choose to kill our prisoners that is another issue."

"But you are not killing prisoners; you are killing helpless inhabitants indiscriminately without attempting to make them prisoners."

"Ah," said Mr. Ariga, putting his thumbs together gently to aid his argument. "It amounts to the same thing. We took a few hundred prisoners at Pingyang [P'yŏngyang] and we found it very expensive and troublesome to feed and guard them. We are taking practically no prisoners here."[86]

The killings continued into the third day. On the fourth day, there was no one left to be slaughtered, but the outrages continued. "I went in company with Mr. Villiers to see a courtyard filled with mutilated corpses," Creelman recalled. "As we entered, we surprised two soldiers bending over one of the bodies. One had a knife in his hand. They had ripped open the corpse and were cutting out his heart. When they saw us they cowered and tried to hide their faces. I am satisfied that not more than one hundred Chinamen were killed in fair battle at Port Arthur and that at least 2,000 unarmed men were put to death."[87]

For an army that had been, until Port Arthur, praised for its discipline, the unwillingness of its commanders to restrain the soldiers from committing atrocities was jarring. Throughout the war Creelman and the other foreign observers had come to respect Field Marshal Ōyama, and especially General Yamaji, whose men had led the attack on Port Arthur. "I could scarcely realize that he [Yamaji] was the same man, who, only a few days before, at Talienwhan [Dairen], with his own hands, had set singing birds free from their cages in the Chinese fort to save them from being starved to death."[88]

JAPANESE CAT

The Second Army's official report informing IGHQ of the fall of Port Arthur reached Foreign Minister Mutsu's office on the afternoon of November 24. Mutsu immediately wrote a celebratory note to Emperor Meiji and instructed the Ministry to disseminate the news. By evening's end Japan's military victory at Port Arthur was known to the entire world.[89] The Japanese people did not find out that Port Arthur had fallen until November 25 because the previous day was a holiday and no newspapers were published. With an extra day to embellish, Japanese newspapers exploded with detailed accounts of the victory. "It is Here! The Great News is Here!" screamed the *Nippon Shimbun*. The *Jiyū Shimbun* was more subdued: "The Great News of the Fall of Ryōjun now reverberates like thousands of thunderclaps over our heads." The outpouring of joy among the Japanese people was tremendous. Streets throughout the country were adorned with rising-sun national flags. In Tokyo, two thousand torch-bearing students from Keio University paraded through the streets, chanting "Banzai!" in front of Nijubashi Bridge, the entryway to the Imperial Palace. The city of Nagano erupted in a "Great Celebration Rally" to commemorate the victory. In Osaka, a "City of Osaka Rally for the Celebration of Military Victory" was organized in Nakanoshima Municipal Park.

There were also celebrations in Korea. The Japanese consulate in Pusan reported that Japanese residents in the city "displayed the national flag during the day and lit lanterns during the night at every household, and made the celebration of our great military victory a city-wide affair." But while the Japanese people eagerly consumed stories of the military operations and detailed eyewitness accounts of battle actions by returning Japanese reporters, conspicuously absent were any reports on the three-day massacre in the city.[90]

The first report of the massacre was made by Thomas Cowen, correspondent for the London *Times,* who arrived in Hiroshima during the early morning hours of November 29. As luck would have it, he was able to secure an audience the next day with Foreign Minister Mutsu, who happened to be in town. Cowen stunned the foreign minister with his detailed description of the atrocities. Mutsu quickly grasped the gravity of the incident and immediately cabled his deputy minister, Hayashi Tadasu, in Tokyo, directing him to transmit urgent instructions to Japanese consuls around the world: "A European correspondent who has returned from Ryōjun tells me that the Japanese troops committed violent acts following the conquest of the area," the message went. "I have yet to receive an official report on this matter, and you shall be notified as soon as it is made available. In the meantime, you are hereby directed to report to me any and all information alluding to this matter which is likely to be mentioned in the newspapers."[91] Once the urgent dispatch was sent, Mutsu followed up with a coded message to Hayashi, giving him additional details about the massacre as related to him by Cowen:

Today I met a *Times* correspondent who has just returned from Ryōjun and was told that there were violent unruly behaviors by the Japanese troops after the victory was won, which included killing both the captured and bound enemy soldiers and the civilians, even women. These events, judging by his account, sounded to be true. He claimed that these acts of atrocity were witnessed not only by the reporters of the Western press but also by the naval officers of the Western fleet who were at the scene, even by a vice-admiral of the British navy. For this reason, the story of these alleged events is expected to spread among the newspapers in the Tokyo and Yokohama area very soon. Today, the *Times* correspondent was anxious to know countermeasures being contemplated by the Japanese government. I told him that although the events, if true as he alleged, were highly deplorable, I was not prepared to dwell on hypothetical government actions until a formal report from General Ōyama has been received. I also stressed that in light of the usual strict disciplines being practiced by the Japanese soldiers, the alleged events, even if they were true, should have had their due causes, and told him that the justifiable causes could provide mitigating influences to the negative impacts this unfortunate occurrence might entail. I advise you to uphold this official stance being taken by your foreign minister and to ensure that we absolutely should avoid taking any 'committed' positions whatsoever even after the events turned out to have been true.[92]

While this cable was being sent, Mutsu received an urgent message from Uchida Kōsai, the interim deputy consul in Britain, informing him that a brief mention of the massacre had appeared in the November 28 issue of the *Times*. A story also appeared on the same day in the *New York World,* based on Creelman's interviews with Chinese refugees arriving from Port Arthur, but the story was neither detailed nor graphic.[93] On December 8 the *Japan Weekly Mail* published a more detailed, alarming story: "There is no doubt that there was a massacre in the town that evening," it reported. "The Japanese soldiers say in excuse that those they killed were men who endeavored to resist their entry but this excuse is invalid, for the bodies that were lying about the next day in the streets of the town were slashed to pieces with sword cuts whereas men killed in the endeavor to resist the regular entry of soldiers would have shown chiefly rifle or bayonet wounds." It also reported that "the senior staff, at all events, were deeply distressed at what had occurred," and that the killings had been "the cause of deep regret."[94]

Mutsu's worst fears were being realized, but he had still not received any information directly from Ōyama confirming reports about the atrocity. Uchida's cable also mentioned that "each time inappropriate stories appeared in the newspapers, the *Chuo-Tsushinsha* (Central News Press) will always make sure to present a rebuttal." Uchida had taken the initiative, informing Mutsu that when the November 28 *Times* report stating that "Japanese troops had committed a wanton massacre of 200 Qing civilians, the *Chuo-Tsushinsha* had written a denial of this account which was published in the *Times*' November 29 issue." He further related, "I was able to suppress a Reuter's report sent from Shanghai which alleged that the Japanese forces had committed a highly barbaric atrocity at Ryōjun," and concluded the message with a request for cash.[95]

Mutsu cabled Uchida on December 1 that he was instructing Hayashi to remit the necessary funds. The next day he instructed Hayashi to appropriate ¥2,000 from the Foreign Ministry fund. A "pay for play" scheme was quickly established to influence news coverage of the massacre, by either suppressing unfavorable reports or encouraging the publication of competing reports aimed at sowing confusion over the events. This was done before Mutsu had received confirmation about the massacre from either Ōyama or the IGHQ. Cowen's report describing the killing of unarmed civilians at Ryōjun in the London *Times* on December 3 was promptly countered by another report from the Central News Agency denying it. "There was no killing of even a single Qing person other than the casualties justified under war conditions."[96]

Why had Mutsu acted so precipitously? It might have been more prudent for him to wait to receive details of what had actually happened in Ryōjun, but the timing required prompt action. The reason for the haste was the signing on November 22 of a new treaty with the United States abolishing extraterritorial privileges.[97] The new US-Japan treaty, like other similar treaties Japan had recently concluded with the European powers, marked the beginning of a new era for Japan.[98]

The specter of the massacre threatened to derail the treaty awaiting ratification by the US Senate.[99] The unbroken victories of the Sino-Japanese War had showcased Japan's progress to the world by demonstrating the nation's triumph over Chinese "barbarism." Indeed, the very purpose of waging the "enlightened" campaign was purportedly to liberate the Korean people from the shackles of Chinese backwardness and help them achieve "independence" from China through "civilization and enlightenment." Japan's barbarity at Port Arthur had the devastating potential for Western nations to question whether Japan was truly a civilized nation and cast into doubt the purported legitimacy of the war itself.

Foremost among the critics was James Creelman. After his return to Japan, he filed a scathing report about the massacre to the *New York World* on December 11. This was the most specific and damning story published about the incident, printed on the front page. It brought "a veritable seismic tremor of major magnitude." The article, entitled simply "A Japanese Massacre," accused Japanese troops of slaughtering the entire population of Port Arthur in cold blood. "The defenseless and unarmed inhabitants were butchered in their houses and their bodies were unspeakably mutilated," he wrote in horror. And he indicted Japanese troops for the "unrestrained reign of murder which continued for three days" and concluded, "The civilized world will be horrified by the details."[100]

The effect of Creelman's report in the United States and Britain was electric. In Washington the story gave American lawmakers pause on the matter of the new Japanese treaty. "That convention is founded in the belief that Japan has become a civilized nation," an editorial in the *World* headlined. "The atrocities described by Creelman compel a reconsideration of that judgment."[101] Other newspapers chimed in. A *San Francisco Chronicle* editorial argued that if the alleged incident proved true, the ratification of the treaty should be put on hold.[102] The London *Times* offered its own unique take, recalling the parable of the cat and the lady: "The cat changed by enchantment into a beautiful woman, who played her part to perfection until, in the midst of a banquet, a mouse was allowed to run across the table. The appeal to fundamental instincts proved too much for the laboriously acquired habits; the woman disappeared and the cat stood revealed."[103]

"A GROSS EXAGGERATION OF THE TRUTH"

Mutsu had worked too hard for his nation to now be cast in the role of the Japanese cat. On the day he received the full text of Creelman's report, December 14, he also received a telegram from Kurino Shin'ichirō. The Japanese envoy to the United States relayed that Secretary of State Walter Gresham had warned him that the ratification of the new treaty could face serious obstacles if the Ryōjun massacre alleged by the press proved to be true. He urgently requested more information from the Home Office about the events that had occurred in Port Arthur.[104] But Mutsu did not know. Nearly three weeks after the incident, Mutsu still did not have the details of what had really happened. "It appears that this matter has already been reported by the military attachés of various consulates," wrote Kurino. "For this reason, unless our government implements countermeasures in whatever form, it could cause an embarrassment to our nation and create difficulties in managing our diplomatic relationships." Kurino concluded the cable anxiously: "Have you received any report from General Ōyama on this matter? If you have please send expeditiously a copy of his report and any other additional material which might help shed light on this matter," adding that he would devote "his utmost efforts to overturning the attack by the *World*."[105]

Mutsu knew he had to act quickly and made his own efforts to repudiate the Creelman story. Responding to American consul Edwin Dun's inquiry in person on December 15 about Creelman's report, Mutsu denied it as "gross exaggeration of the truth, sensational in the extreme, and tending to work great injury and injustice to Japan in the eyes of the civilized world."[106] He repeated these claims to Russian envoy Mikhail Khitrovo when the latter paid a visit the same afternoon. Their "icy demeanor with ominous undertones in their speech" was the least of Mutsu's worries, however.[107] The day before, the *Jiji Shinpō* published an editorial that condoned the massacre as a justifiable act. "Should the unrepentant [Chinese] foes continue desecrating our fallen soldiers with barbarism, the resulting response might be a massacre easily surpassing body counts of mere 3,000 or 4,000," it stated defiantly. "Even a massacre of an entire army would not be out of the realm of possibility." The *Asahi Shinbum* went even further. In an editorial entitled "Let Us Not Be Misled by Fake Arguments," it argued that "Japan's grand aspiration to grab the helm of supremacy in Asia is too important to allow the meddling of foreigners." Mutsu wrote to Itō: "Should these defiant attitudes gain force, there could be an unpalatable collision between the public opinion in the Western countries and that in our country."[108] He urgently requested Itō's advice on responding to the crisis. On the evening of December 15, Mutsu received Itō's response:

> I [Itō] have referred the Ryōjun issue to the Imperial Headquarters and it has been agreed that conducting a disciplinary inquest will involve too much risk and is hence unfeasible. Therefore, the recourse left to us will be to seek exoneration through defensive arguments, rather than to address culpability. Our agents charged with overseas clandestine operations on duty here are currently in action in accordance with this strategy.[109]

Accompanying the message was Itō's eight-point argument countering the Creelman report: (1) The fleeing Qing soldiers had cast off their uniforms. (2) Those who were killed in civilian clothes at Ryōjun were mostly the Qing soldiers in disguise. (3) The inhabitants had left the city before the military engagement began. (4) A small number of inhabitants who remained in the city had been under order to use firearms and resist the invasion, and they carried out this order. (5) The Japanese troops became highly enraged at the grisly sight of atrocities against several of their captured fellow soldiers who had been burned alive, tortured, and horribly mutilated. (6) The Japanese troops conducted themselves in strict observance of military discipline. (7) The rest of the foreign war correspondents, other than Creelman, are in a shock over the Creelman report. Their reason for leaving the war theater was to fetch winter outfits back in Japan, and they plan to return to the war theater. And (8) The Qing soldiers who were captured after the fall of Ryōjun have been treated well.[110] Mutsu forwarded Itō's message to Kurino and drafted his own statement incorporating the eight points for release to news organizations.[111]

Mutsu also approached Japan's Central News Agency and the English-language newspaper *Japan Weekly Mail* to get the message out. Francis Binkley, owner of the *Japan Weekly Mail,* was offered monthly payments "of a certain fixed amount of money in the guise of a subsidy from the Japanese government" for favorable stories. Henceforth, the *Japan Weekly Mail* changed its tune.[112]

Aoki Shūzō, the Japanese minister to Britain, made his own secret set of overtures to Reuters, offering a payment of £600 in return for releasing sympathetic reports.[113] Itō's disinformation campaign began to have an effect. Prominent doubters of the massacre began to be quoted in the US press. George H. Pullman, financial secretary of the International Red Cross, was widely quoted in the *World,* saying "it is hard to believe that the soldiers of Japan would be permitted to indulge in the excesses." "I have personally been in contact with many of these very men and it would require strong evidence to convince me of their lapsing into such barbarism."[114]

A.B. Guerville, a special correspondent for the *New York Herald* who was not at Port Arthur when it was taken, filed several reports for the *San Francisco Chronicle* flatly denying accounts of a massacre. In several articles in the *New York Herald, New York Times,* and *Leslie's Weekly,* Guerville questioned Creelman's integrity, claiming he was sensationalizing the story for monetary gain.[115] The well-known American naturalist Albert S. Bickmore, founder of the American Museum of Natural History in New York City, also gave credence to the deniers. "As for all this talk of the soldiers showing their true colors, previously hidden because of the world's good opinion, it sounds rather wearisome to me," he opined. "Japan's actions in offering an explanation to the *World* speaks of regard for humanities and the entire conduct of the army up to the massacre was nothing more than what was to have been expected rather than wondered at. My sympathy is still with Japan."[116]

But the opinions that Mutsu valued most were those of Edwin Dun, the American minister to Japan, and Walter Gresham, US secretary of state. Their views would carry the most weight with Congress as it deliberated the new US-Japan treaty. Dun was unconvinced by Creelman's report, writing to Gresham on December 20 that "the account sent to the *World* by Mr. Creelman is sensational in the extreme." He enclosed a clipping from a *Japan Weekly Mail* editorial reiterating the point that "most of those found killed at Port Arthur proved to be soldiers in disguise." Japanese soldiers had "preserved discipline" despite being enraged by the sight of "fearfully mutilated bodies of their comrades who had been taken prisoners by the Chinese," and concluded that "about 355 Chinese prisoners who were taken at the fall of Port Arthur have been kindly treated."[117]

Remarkably, Dun's dispatch to Gresham was almost a word-for-word rehash of Itō's eight points. More surprising was that Lieutenant O'Brien, who had witnessed the massacre, backed these findings. He wrote a personal letter to Dun on December 28 in which he stated that although he had himself seen "a number of cases of killing of men," he denied any knowledge of the atrocities. Regarding the behavior of the Japanese troops, he wrote that "it ought to be borne in mind that such occurrences happen in all armies and it is hardly fair to expect miracles of the Japanese."[118] Apparently wanting to wash his hands of the entire affair, O'Brien concluded his extraordinary memo on a cynical note: "I have no doubt that exaggerated reports have been sent, but not having seen them I am not able to make any criticism of them." Field Marshal Ōyama and his staff, moreover, "had treated him very kindly" and he was "indebted to them for many comforts." Dun included O'Brien's testimony in his follow-up dispatch to Gresham on January 7, with the conclusion: "The impression Mr. Creelman's reports are prone to convey is a gross exaggeration of the truth."[119] O'Brien's letter proved to be the final blow to Creelman's credibility and gave credence to Mutsu's claim that the massacre had been greatly exaggerated.[120] On February 5, 1895, the new Japan-America treaty was easily ratified by Congress.

The crisis had passed. Interestingly, Chinese accounts were not even considered by American officials or the press, despite the receipt by Li Hongzhang of reports of the massacre by Chinese refugees.[121] Mutsu had successfully fought off the charge that Japan was not ready to be welcomed as an equal into the family of civilized nations. The war that had been fought in the name of "enlightenment and reform" for Korea had withstood its severest scrutiny at Port Arthur. Japan had emerged in the eyes of the world as the best hope for a renewed and modern Asia.

CHAPTER NINE

TWO-FRONT WAR

The Japanese had weathered the storm at Port Arthur. To the grudging disbelief of the Chinese and the newfound admiration of the West, they had proved to the world that Japan was now a "civilized" nation—and a power to be reckoned with. But the war was not supposed to be about territorial aggrandizement; it was for "uplifting" Korea, intending to preserve Korean independence, otherwise the Western powers would never have sanctioned it. Mutsu might have been skeptical on the issue of Korean reform, but Itō was not, declaring emphatically that "Korea's sovereign status was the principal cause of the current conflict between the Qing and Japan."[1] The decision to storm the Kyŏngbok Palace on July 23 and embark on a war with China had come after a month of strenuous negotiations that in the end boiled down to the reform issue and the nonconciliatory attitude of the Chinese.[2]

Two problems had immediately presented themselves at the onset of the war. First, implicit in the Japanese promise of reform was the need to secure a compliant and credible Korean leader, if only to give credence to Japan's vow to maintain Korea's "independence." But how to ensure Korea's independence while interfering in Korea's internal affairs? The second problem was an outgrowth of the first. For the reform effort to work, the Korean government had to be united behind it. Yet by selecting the Taewŏn'gun to lead the reform effort, the Japanese had deepened Korea's political divisions and further widened the chasm between father and son. Japan's attempts to square these circles would result in bitter acrimony, plunging Korea into further chaos that would give rise to a bloody, but largely forgotten, civil war.

The day after the palace was seized, Japanese minister Ōtori Keisuke arranged for a new government to be installed. A dozen or so pro-Japanese reformist leaders were appointed to cabinet posts, with Kim Hong-jip as prime minister. A decade earlier, Kim had persuaded King Kojong to make a treaty with the United States and begin a program of modernizing reforms, which were cut short by the 1882 Imo Uprising led by the Taewŏn'gun and his conservative Confucian followers. He was now working with the Taewŏn'gun to help implement a new reform program— the Kabo reforms, a program devised by the Japanese. A new organization, the Military Deliberative Council (Kun'guk kimuch'ŏ) was established in July 1894 and headed by Kim Hong-jip, who oversaw its sixteen to twenty members. It served as the conduit through which Japanese reform measures were given a Korean face. Kim and the other council members were able to add or modify measures as long as they met with Japanese approval. It was the highest policymaking organ in the Korean government and all resolutions adopted were reported to the Taewŏn'gun. Nominally the head of the new reformist government, the Taewŏn'gun's role was not to make policies as much as to perfunctorily review and pass them to the king. Kojong was required to "approve," in essence rubber-stamp, the new policies. Kojong would be relegated back to being a powerless boy-king.[3] The reform policymaking process was a Korean play controlled by a Japanese director.

The first issue on Ōtori's agenda was to conclude a provisional treaty between Japan and the new Korean government. What most concerned him was the possibility of foreign intervention in Korean affairs. This concern was prompted by the disclosure that the Taewŏn'gun had secretly visited Russian minister Karl Weber on August 2. The Taewŏn'gun had relayed to Weber his unhappiness with the reforms, which he deemed "too drastic." He also decried the fact that "Japan and China had gone to war against each other." He sought the minister's help in bringing the conflict to a quick end "through the good offices of the Powers."[4]

Mutsu was livid that the Taewŏn'gun had seen the Russian minister, and instructed Ōtori that "with regard to the conversation of the Taewŏn'gun with the Russian minister, expression of that sort of sentiment must be strongly reproved, because any wavering attitude of Korea will place Japan in an awkward situation and invite foreign interference." He added that "the Korean government must be thoroughly impressed that the present war is carried by Japan to secure Korea's independence from China, that Korea cannot refrain from being in actual war as the ally of Japan against China and that she must remain so until the object of war is attained by a conclusion of peace."[5] Only days into the Taewŏn'gun's tenure as nominal head of the new Korean government, suspicion and distrust had arisen between him and Ōtori.

Another more pressing issue, from the Taewŏn'gun's point of view, was to neutralize the corrupt but politically astute Queen Min. Days after installing himself in Kyŏngbok Palace, the former regent sent his favorite grandson, Yi Chun-yong, to see Ōtori with a draft of a royal edict proposing the demotion of the queen to commoner status. The twenty-five-year-old Yi had been showered with a series of appointments in the new government, including chief rector of the Royal Clan Administration and the special counselor to the queen's court. The latter position authorized him to supervise affairs pertaining to the queen while the former role secured for him a position of leadership among the Yi royal clan.[6] The demotion of the queen to commoner status would effectively mean her banishment from the court. Her removal would also ensure that her only son, Yi Ch'ŏk (later Emperor Sunjong), would be unable to inherit the throne. In anticipation, the Taewŏn'gun had made plans to force the new cabinet to take action to "ensure the nomination of his grandson Yi Chun-yong to be crowned king."[7]

But Ōtori refused to go along with the scheme. He did not want to get involved in Korean court politics, always a distraction. There were more pressing matters to consider and Japan was in the midst of a war. The Taewŏn'gun considered Ōtori's refusal a betrayal of a Japanese promise, for the legation secretary, Sugimura, had strongly hinted to the Taewŏn'gun that Queen Min was no longer a factor in court politics, as she had been seen fleeing the palace. Indeed, her apparent absence was the main reason the Taewŏn'gun had agreed to accompany Ōtori to the palace on the morning of July 23.[8] To make matters worse, the plot to demote the queen was leaked to Kojong, deepening the mutual antipathy between father and son. The leakers, Kim Ka-jin and An Kyŏng-su, were officials in the new government who opposed the Taewŏn'gun, believing he was "too old and conservative" to implement the radical reform plan, and had sought ways to undermine him.[9]

The family drama led to the emergence of two opposing political factions: a progressive faction within the Military Deliberative Council who supported the king and the queen as the best instruments to implement the reform plan, and a conservative faction who opposed the scope and pace of the reforms and saw the Taewŏn'gun as their champion. "The Taewŏn'gun was incredibly angry and disapproved of all the decisions made by the government office in charge of military and political matters," reported Sugimura. As a result, "the new [progressive] Deliberative Council members are not reporting their decisions to the Taewŏn'gun and are now directly requesting the approval of the king."[10]

The Japanese found themselves in the middle of a bitter family feud they had helped create. To get beyond this morass, on August 17 Mutsu submitted four options to Prime Minister Itō and his cabinet on Japan's future policy toward Korea: treat Korea as an independent nation; establish a Japanese semi-protectorate over Korea to directly and indirectly aid it while checking other foreign powers from compromising Korea's independence; sign a joint Sino-Japanese agreement to guarantee Korean independence; or conclude an international agreement to preserve Korean territorial integrity.

In the end the Japanese government decided to pursue the most intrusive course, a "protectorate policy." In the meantime, Ōtori concluded a provisional agreement with the new Korean government in an effort to keep the reform effort on track. In reality the agreement would pave the way for a vast expansion of Japanese political and economic penetration into Korea, including Japanese rights to construct railway and telegraph lines between Seoul and Pusan.[11] Six days later, on August 26, a military alliance between the two countries was signed, ensuring that during the war against China, "Corea will undertake to give every possible facility to Japanese soldiers regarding their movement and supply of provisions." Its true intent was to prevent the Korean government from switching sides in the middle of the war.[12]

Predictably, the Taewŏn'gun was appalled by the treaty. Opposing the war, he had refused to grant Japan authorization for its soldiers to drive Chinese troops out of Korea. He also opposed the reform bills sent to him by the pro-Japan Military Deliberative Council, simply refusing to sign them. When this proved fruitless, because the Council bypassed him and went directly to Kojong, the Taewŏn'gun engaged in clandestine anti-Japanese activities helped by his ambitious grandson, Yi Chun-yong.

Like the majority of Koreans and foreign observers, the Taewŏn'gun believed that the Chinese would prevail in the war. Acting on this assumption, he and his grandson schemed to help the Chinese by mobilizing the Tonghak movement in the south to spark a renewed rebellion against the

Japanese and the new Korean government.[13] The two also made contact with Chinese commanders in P'yŏngyang. In August the Taewŏn'gun sent a letter to General Wei Rugui asking for help against the Japanese: "Presently the dynasty confronts a perilous crisis," it read. "I have heard a large body of Chinese troops arrived in P'yŏngyang. This indeed will provide an occasion for our deliverance. I hope that the Celestial Empire will extend protection to our dynasty and court by sweeping away the traitors in the current regime who are selling the country to the Japanese."[14]

The Taewŏn'gun envisioned a grand plan to destroy the Japanese forces in Korea by having them attacked simultaneously by Tonghaks from the south and the Chinese forces from the north in a reprise of what Hideyoshi had faced three hundred years earlier during the Imjin Wars.[15] The unexpected and quick Japanese victory in P'yŏngyang in mid-September, however, quashed those plans. To make matters worse, the head of the Korean police, Yi Yun-yong, got wind of the conspiracy. The Taewŏn'gun sprang into action to silence him along with other officials he wanted to assassinate to thwart further investigation into his scheming.[16] Sugimura found out about the plot and countered the assassinations except for one, Military Deliberative Council member Kim Hak-u, the most outspoken critic of the Taewŏn'gun, who was cut down outside his home in Chŏndong on October 31.[17]

The Taewŏn'gun's opposition took a toll; Japan's reform plan was stalling. "The Taewŏn'gun is secretly opposing the reform program and is spreading his violent influence to carry out his plots. [Everyone] is trembling with fear and no one dares do the government's business."[18] Frustrated, Mutsu replaced Ōtori with "a man of great stature and tested ability," Inoue Kaoru, whose experience in and knowledge of Korea was deep and extensive, spanning several decades. He had accompanied Kuroda Kiyotaka to Seoul in 1876 as vice-plenipotentiary during the negotiations of the Treaty of Kanghwa.[19] It was hoped that Inoue could finally bring the Korean domestic situation under control.

INOUE KAORU TO KOREA

Inoue's first task upon arriving in Seoul on October 19 was to determine what to do about the Taewŏn'gun. The situation, he remarked, was "like two kings in one country," an ironic observation since it was the Japanese who had done so much to create this bifurcation. His first plan of action was to remove the influence of the Taewŏn'gun and then make a clear line of distinction between matters concerning the royal household and those under the authority of the Military Deliberative Council. Prime Minister Kim Hong-jip would be responsible for all affairs of state, with King Kojong disposing of these affairs with the assistance and advice of the prime minister. No members of the royal household were to take part in government affairs. "The queen, the Taewŏn'gun, and Yi Chun-yong are the obstacles in the way towards implementing administrative reform in Korea," Inoue wrote to Mutsu. "It is quite useless for us to set out on the reforms without restraining the influence of such obstacles."[20]

But how to go about purging the Korean government of these powerful political players? Fortune dealt Inoue a lucky card when the Taewŏn'gun's letter to General Wei Rugui fell into the hands of Yamagata after the capture of P'yŏngyang. Another letter from Yi Chun-yong to his subordinates "ordering them to send word to the leaders of the Tonghaks to prepare for an uprising" was also intercepted by the Japanese.[21] Inoue angrily confronted the Taewŏn'gun with the incriminating letters. "The Taewŏn'gun had stubbornly hidden his own crimes up until that point and showed no sign of guilt," recalled Sugimura. "But once he saw the letters, his façade soon broke down, and he apologized sincerely, saying that 'I sent these under unavoidable circumstances and now have nothing more to reveal.'"[22] On November 22 the Korean government issued a royal edict formally terminating the Taewŏn'gun's regency.[23]

This was not the end of Inoue's problems. The Tonghaks had become active again in October, responding to the Taewŏn'gun's appeal to stir up rebellion in the south. The Tonghaks had dispersed on their own accord in June, but this time, with the Taewŏn'gun's encouragement, they refused to back down. The insurgency posed a serious threat to Japanese communications and logistical lines in the south. Facing a two-front war— Chinese forces in the north and Tonghak rebels in the south—Mutsu feared that if the rebellion was not quickly suppressed, Russia might take advantage of the chaos and enter the war on China's side. On October 31 he wrote to Inoue: "As long as the scope of the Tonghak disturbances is limited to the southern part of Korea, that is, Chŏlla, Kyŏngsang, and Ch'ungch'ŏng Provinces, we do not need to worry about possible Russian intervention." But, he warned, "if this rebellion spreads to the Russo-Korean border across Hamgyŏng Province, it will provide a pretext for them [the Russians] to mobilize their troops." The result would mean that "our soldiers might end up fighting the Russian troops unexpectedly while conducting a mopping-up campaign [against the Tonghaks insurgents in the south]." Such a situation had to be avoided at all costs. "It is therefore deemed imperative," he continued, "to suppress this disturbance at the earliest possible moment before the impact of the disturbance spreads to northern Korea."[24]

Kojong, too, was growing increasingly nervous, especially because, as everyone knew, the Taewŏn'gun would have no qualms about riding the wave of rebellion back into power. But the government's forces were not strong enough to suppress the rebels on their own. On October 24 both the governor and the military commander of Ch'ungch'ŏng Province reported that they could no longer suppress the Tonghaks, and "begged that more [government] soldiers be sent to their aid as all their arms and ammunition have been seized by the rebels." Government officials in Chŏlla had been taken prisoner "and punished according to their just deserts."[25]

Inoue waited until November 8 to act. He wanted the Korean government to make the first step and appeal for Japanese intervention. It was not long in coming, as Kim Hong-jip, Foreign Minister Kim Yun-sik, and Minister of Finance Ŏ Yun-jung approached Inoue with an urgent request to suppress the rebellion. Inoue used this plea as leverage to coerce the king. Japanese troops would fight on behalf of the Korean government only if Kojong would agree to Inoue's stipulation about observing a clear line of distinction between the royal household and the Military Deliberative Council.[26] The king would have to pledge that neither he nor the queen would interfere in the affairs of state and that he would consult with his ministers in all matters.

Kojong relented. Inoue ordered Japanese troops, supported by Korean government forces, to engage the main body of the poorly armed and ill-trained Tonghak peasant army in a series of bloody battles in Chŏlla and Ch'ungch'ŏng Provinces, and the areas in and around Suwŏn, Yŏngun, and Kahŭng. These engagements turned out to be some of the bloodiest actions during the Sino-Japanese War.[27]

THE SINO-JAPANESE WAR AND KOREA

Ch'oe Che-u was thirty-six years old when he received a vision from Heaven to establish a new religion. The scholar from Kyŏngju in southeastern Korea was well educated in the Confucian classics but also deeply immersed in the study of Buddhism and Taoism. When he was twenty he left his wife and family, wandering the countryside for eleven years seeking spiritual enlightenment. He became convinced that the corruption and depravity of the Chosŏn dynasty required a spiritual renewal neither Buddhism nor Confucianism could provide. His new syncretic religion—Tonghak (Eastern Learning) would provide the answer, a new Way that would sustain the nation and provide for the people by combining the principles of Confucianism, Buddhism, and Taoism.[28] It was also conceived as an alternative to *Sŏhak* or "Western learning"—a designation for Roman Catholicism. *Sŏhak* was the adopted religion of a new generation of "enlightened" Confucian literati who came of age in the eighteenth century to promote social reform and were subjected to a series of persecutions in 1801, 1839, and 1846. Korea's Catholics prospered for a while under the rule of King Ch'ŏljong (r. 1849–1864) until they were purged again in 1866 by the Taewŏn'gun. Ch'oe and his Tonghak followers would suffer a similar draconian fate. On April 15, 1864, Ch'oe was executed by the Korean government.

Ch'oe's death did not stop, much less eliminate, the movement, as his protégé, Ch'oe Si-hyŏng, not only kept it alive but expanded it. In keeping with established Confucian principles governing relations between ruler and ruled, Ch'oe Si-hyŏng and his Tonghak followers submitted petitions to the government demanding the posthumous exoneration of their founder. The Tonghaks also expressed strong antipathy toward Japan and other foreigners. In their memorial petitions to the Korean government, they conveyed their "love for the King and loyalty to the country" but noted the chaos in the land. "Japanese and foreign rebels and thieves are now introduced into the very bowels of our land and anarchy has reached its zenith." The Tonghaks also let it be known that "most of the Japanese rebels cherish feelings of hatred towards us, and nurture within them the germs of disaster for our land which they will bring forth to hurt us." This was the same language used by the Confucian scholar Ch'oe Ik-hyŏn to oppose Kojong's signing of the Kanghwa Treaty in 1876. Similar to the earlier antiforeign Confucian literati, the Tonghaks beseeched the king to "unite in one common effort to sweep out the Japanese and foreigners."[29] The Tonghak movement was not simply a religious movement but from the very beginning had a strong political component.[30]

After the 1882 Imo Uprising and especially following the failed Kapsin coup of 1884, Ch'oe Si-hyŏng's refusal to authorize violent measures against Korean government corruption created a schism within the Tonghak movement. This split mirrored a similar divide between the Confucian conservatives and the enlightenment progressives in the 1870s and 1880s, with one major difference: whereas the conservative-progressive divide remained purely ideological, the fracture within the Tonghak movement also became geographical. Ch'oe Si-hyŏng retained effective control over a vast area known as *Pukchŏp* (literally, northern jurisdiction) or Northern Assembly, which included all Tonghak organizations in the southeastern provinces of Kyŏngsang and Kwangwŏn Provinces as well as the northern part of Ch'ungch'ŏng Province and the northwestern provinces of Hwanghae and P'yŏngan. The area known as *Namjŏp* (literally, southern jurisdiction), or Southern Assembly, comprising the southwestern province of Chŏlla and the southern part of Ch'ungch'ŏng, came under the control of Chŏn Pong-jun, a charismatic and controversial leader who gave the Tonghak movement its radical and revolutionary cast.[31]

Born in Kobu County, Chŏlla Province, in 1854 to a former administrator of a local Confucian shrine school (*suwŏn hyanggyo*), Chŏn received a classic Confucian education.[32] He also appeared to have received some military training. Few details are known about his early life, but what is clear is that his assumption of control of the militant wing of the Tonghak movement coincided with the death of his father in 1893 after the latter had been subjected to torture by the notoriously corrupt magistrate of Kobu, Cho Pyŏng-gap. By then Chŏn had been a Tonghak member for nine years, but the extreme malfeasance of the local Kobu government seemed to have transformed his thinking about the movement and its potential to bring about social and political change. During interrogation after his capture in February 1895, Chŏn documented his principal grievances against the local government. The corrupt magistrate had forced farmers to build a water reservoir and also a memorial pavilion and then, instead of rewarding them for their labor, had extracted extravagant taxes from them. Chŏn sought redress from the central government, but the royal commissioner, instead of punishing Cho Pyŏng-gap, "branded everyone who had revolted as a Tonghak, compiled a list of their names, and proceeded to arrest them and burn their homes, and seize and murder their family members." The grievance over this injustice had been the cause of the first Tonghak rebellion in the spring of 1894.[33]

Channeling the peasants' discontent against "greedy corrupt officials and unprincipled Confucian scholars [yangban]," Chŏn's rebel forces took over Kobu, although they failed to capture Cho Pyŏng-gap. With Kobu secured, Chŏn expanded his base of operations and by March he was largely in control of all of Chŏlla Province. Chŏn's men destroyed government offices, seized weapons, and burned all records connected to the traditional ruling class system, including family registrars and slave records.[34] By April approximately ten thousand men had joined the peasant army, although not all of them became Tonghak converts. When Kojong received word that the rebels had taken Chŏnju, he appealed to Qing China for help, precipitating the Sino-Japanese War.[35]

Chŏn agreed to withdraw from his strong position and reached a truce with government forces in mid-June because he feared the entrance of foreign troops into Korea. But there were other considerations as well. Chŏn knew that in order to advance north toward the capital, he would have to cross an area under the Northern Assembly's jurisdiction in northern Ch'ungch'ŏng Province. But Ch'oe Si-hyŏng, who controlled Tonghak followers there, disapproved of the Kobu peasant uprising, including Chŏn's violent tactics. He also frowned on the fact that the majority of Chŏn's peasant army were not, in fact, Tonghak members. "The local leaders called chŏpchu were all Tonghaks," Chŏn later admitted. "Many of the men in the ranks, however, were patriotic and righteous persons without Tonghak affiliation."[36] Without Ch'oe's approval, the route to the capital was effectively blocked, and Chŏn had to reconsider his options. He had thus not only precipitated an international crisis, he had engendered a crisis within the Tonghak movement itself. Ch'oe Si-hyŏng was critical of Chŏn and the Southern Assembly leadership as rebels to the state and heretics of the Tonghak faith.[37] Ch'oe's focus had always been to purge the country of Japanese and foreign influences, not to adopt an "antifeudalism" line against the yangban and Confucian and government officials.

Disagreements over whether to capitalize on the "antiheterodoxy" and anti-Japanese fervor or to adhere to the "reform of domestic affairs" line also raised uncomfortable questions for the Southern Assembly leadership. Although Chŏn would later insist that "resistance to Japan" was the central part of his revolutionary agenda, his links to Japanese right-wing "patriotic organizations" like the Gen'yōsha (Black Ocean Society) and its offshoot the Ten'yūkyō (Society for the Celestial Salvation of the Oppressed) revealed he was not opposed to soliciting Japanese help if it served his purposes. Uchida Ryōhei, Takeda Noriyuki, Tanaka Jirō, and other members of Ten'yūkyō eagerly sought out Chŏn at his headquarters in Namwŏn to offer support with weapons and funding.[38] Takeda, in particular, "praised the Tonghaks for their determination to relieve the suffering of the Korean people from the corruption of the Min oligarchy," adding that "Yuan Shikai was colluding with the Mins" and therefore

"the Qing was the ultimate cause of the suffering of the Korean people."
It was, of course, in the Ten'yūkyō's interest to stir up trouble in Korea in
order to bring about the hoped-for clash between Japan and China.[39]

Chŏn had already agreed to disperse his rebel army when Chinese
troops arrived in June, ostensibly to put them down. Chinese forces under
General Ye, therefore, regrouped at Asan and, anticipating the arrival of
the Japanese, began to fortify their positions. After Japan's preemptive
strike against the *Kowshing* on July 25 (Battle of P'ung-do), and in the
face of an aggressive Japan attack, Ye's forces abandoned Asan/Sŏnghwan
and joined the Chinese forces amassing in P'yŏngyang. This left the central and southern parts of Korea under Japanese control. Yet the Japanese presence was still tenuous, for the Japanese Army was dependent
upon a vulnerable supply line that ran the length of the peninsula from
Pusan, a line threatened by the Tonghak insurgency. To fight the Chinese,
the Japanese needed the cooperation of the Koreans.

The supply line followed the traditional invasion route, the Pusan-
Taegu-Seoul-P'yŏngyang corridor, which Hideyoshi had used in the late
sixteenth century. The Japanese victory at Sŏnghwan had been relatively
easy due to Ye's decision to abandon the field, but the scarcity of supplies
was quickly becoming a major potential problem, particularly as the Japanese began preparing for the upcoming battle of P'yŏngyang. Japanese
soldiers were forced to make the arid trek to Seoul in the scorching heat,
many without adequate drinking water. Inadequate supplies continued to
dog the Korea campaign over the sweltering summer. As long as the Beiyang Fleet controlled the Yellow Sea, Japanese supplies would have to be
transported overland. And because there were no trains or usable roads,
the transportation of food, equipment, armaments, and other supplies
would have to be carried on the backs of Japanese coolies and local
Korean laborers with livestock obtained from Korean farmers.

Ironically, the war purportedly waged in the name of Korean reform,
whose intended purpose might have garnered some tacit support among
the reformed-minded Tonghaks in the south like Chŏn Pong-jun, had
instead turned them decidedly against Japan. Even as late as August,
after the Japanese had invaded the king's palace, Chŏn had taken a wait-
and-see attitude toward the new reform plan.

But the demands of the Japanese Army spoiled any potential goodwill
between the Tonghaks and the Japanese-backed Korean government. On
August 26 Kojong reluctantly agreed to pass a protocol ensuring that
"Korea will undertake to give every possible facility to Japanese soldiers

regarding their movement and supply of provisions." Although the real purpose of the agreement was to prevent the Korean government from switching sides during the course of the war, the requisition order proved extremely unpopular.[40]

At first requisitions were made through local Korean government officials, but this simply inflamed local tensions between farmers and the officials. Japanese merchants then stepped in. The requisition order, especially of food, was initially done through Japanese merchants, but they also came under fire from the local population. On November 25, six merchants were attacked in P'yŏngan Province by the Tonghaks while trying to purchase rice and grain for military use. Two died as a result, while similar attacks against Japanese merchants began all along the supply lines. As a result, the Japanese Army took over the requisition orders.[41] But unlike Japanese merchants, the soldiers did not have access to large supplies of Korean currency, and the farmers were thus forced to accept payment in Japanese yen, which were useless in Korean markets.[42] When farmers refused the foreign currency, soldiers responded by employing more heavy-handed tactics. They simply took livestock, with the promise of future payment or with no payment at all. Moreover, Korean peasants who enlisted as laborers were often mistreated and would run away. Harsh methods were used to force them to stay. By the end of August, just as the Japanese were gearing up for the battle in P'yŏngyang, sporadic attacks against supply lines were becoming more frequent as resentment against the requisition orders grew to a fever pitch.[43] On October 13, fifteen hundred Korean farmers rose up in Miyrang, just north of Pusan, attacking the supply line. On the same day, a thousand farmers and Tonghaks gathered near Danyang in Ch'ungch'ŏng Province to attack the supply line, but they were violently suppressed by three Japanese units.[44]

Key Japanese supply routes were all located within Ch'oe Si-hyŏp's Northern Assembly. Chŏn Pong-jun's Southern Assembly, by contrast, did not include the supply lines, and consequently farmers in Chŏlla and South Ch'ungch'ŏng Provinces experienced far less harassment by Japanese soldiers. Chŏlla Province was virtually cut off from the rest of Korea as Tonghak "self-governing" organizations began to spring up there, ousting local magistrates and governors. Thus, even as the war continued through September, Chŏn continued to devote himself to the "liquidation of feudalism" and reforming the government, in contrast to Ch'oe, who was consumed with conducting attacks against the Japanese supply lines and rallying his members under the anti-Japanese banner.[45]

Following Japan's victory at P'yŏngyang in September, the fighting moved into China, leaving fewer Japanese troops on the peninsula to deal with the growing insurgency problem. Wrote one observer, "Instead of fighting the Chinese, the Japanese now have the Tonghaks to fight."[46] Upon his arrival in Korea in October, Inoue realized that the war had entered a new phase requiring a new plan of action. He telegrammed Prime Minister Itō with an urgent request for reinforcements.[47] Continued attacks against the telegraph lines and roads from Pusan, Ŭiju, to northeastern China jeopardized the communications and supply lines to Yamagata's First Army in Manchuria. There was also the problem of the rebellion spreading to Hamgyŏng Province in northeastern Korea, which sparked concern over the possibility of the Russians entering the war in support of China.

In mid-October the Tonghak rebellion underwent a major transition that increased the threat to Japan's position in Korea. On October 12 the Southern Assembly leadership announced that it would initiate a general uprising. Four days later the North Assembly joined them.[48] What had until then been a series of uncoordinated and sporadic attacks on the supply lines was morphing into a coordinated nationwide uprising. The first Tonghak rebellion in the spring of 1894 had been focused on ousting corrupt local officials and demanding reforms from the central government. The rallying cry of the new rebellion was focused on ejecting foreigners from Korea, the Japanese being the main target.

Neither Itō nor Inoue believed that the Tonghaks had the strength to pull off such a feat. What concerned them was that the Tonghak's antiforeign pronouncements might precipitate a Western response. Foreign diplomatic missions and missionaries were becoming uneasy. If the Japanese were unable to suppress the rebellion, Western powers were likely to intervene to bring the war to an end—exactly what the Chinese wanted. "At this time, the British government was again planning to have the powers unite in urging peace on the two belligerents," recalled Mutsu. "This was also a period when the Russians were intently alert for any opportunity on which to capitalize on their own interest."[49] If Japan did not get the rebellion under control, its war against China could be ended prematurely, and the sacrifices in lives and materiel would have been for naught.

Inoue and Itō might have been less anxious had they known the Tonghak movement was facing an internal crisis. Ch'oe Si-hyŏng was initially not in favor of the uprising and only reluctantly agreed to join. He criticized Chŏn's call for the uprising as self-serving, claiming that "rationalizing their actions in the name of righteous causes, those in the Southern Assembly have molested commoners and harmed our brothers' faith." Ch'oe had reason to be alarmed. Chŏn's peasant army attacked local yangban and government officials, confiscated private property, and committed atrocities. In one case, Chŏn's men "took a military commandant stationed at Kongju prisoner and then burned him to death."[50] Ch'oe feared that "his *Pukchŏp* was in danger of being wiped out by the *Namjŏp*," revealing the deep fissures between the two groups. But, under intense pressure from his followers to join the uprising, Ch'oe relented. In mid-October the combined Tonghak forces of the Northern and Southern Assemblies began attacking targets in Ch'ungch'ŏng, Kyŏngsang, Kangwŏn, and Kyŏnggi Provinces. Their targets were not only the Japanese, but also Korean government officials.[51]

CIVIL WAR

The war between Japan and China had sparked a civil war among the Koreans. Tonghak attacks against local government offices and officials were countered by Korean government troops under Japanese direction, intensifying the civil conflict. Tonghak factional dispute sometimes further complicated the situation; in some cases, local private bands with links to the Northern Assembly collaborated with Korean government forces to fight Chŏn's Southern Assembly forces.[52] "The government does not know the difference between medicine (Northern Assembly Tonghaks) and poison (Southern Assembly Tonghaks)," a distraught Ch'oe Si-hyŏng later lamented. Skeptical of Chŏn and the true purpose of the uprising, he stated, "They [Korean government troops] will burn both stone [Southern Assembly] and the jade [Northern Assembly]."[53] Ch'oe was right to be worried. The fighting between Koreans, government forces, and local militias against the Tonghak rebels was fierce and bloody. The Korean chronicler Hwang Hyŏn related in vivid detail how local government soldiers and civilian militia groups, the *minpo*, were attacked by the Tonghaks at Hadong in Kyŏngsang Province:

> In the early evening, when darkness started to set in, the bandits [Tonghaks] encircled the local government soldiers' position . . . The soldiers were in disarray and eventually started to abandon their posts. Only 35 *minpos* led by Kim Jin-ok [the governor of Hadong], kept up the line of fire. The *minpos* were excellent marksmen. Firing their weapons after

retreating three steps, the bullets came raining down upon the bandits [Tonghaks], and the entire valley was quickly filled with corpses . . . Due to the setting darkness, the bandits [Tonghaks] also could not pursue the retreating enemies. At daylight, however, the bandits mustered their men and entered Hadong, and burned down 10 civilian households, declaring that they would kill all hiding *minpo* . . . They then scattered into every direction and pillaged the nearby villages. In Hwagaedong, the bandits [Tonghaks] burned down 500 civilian households, as they considered the area to be the home base for the *minpo* and replenished their supplies through plunder.[54]

Hwang Hyŏn recounted another particularly gruesome scene. A *minpo* leader in Namwŏn by the name of Pak Pong-yang had lured several thousand Tonghak "bandits" up a mountain into a trap by disguising his men as government troops in retreat. As the Tonghaks pursued the retreating men, Pak sprung the trap as they were nearing the summit. The panicked Tonghaks cut down their own men in front and ran over their bodies to try to escape. Pak ordered his men in pursuit "to set out in pairs with one tasked with severing the heads [of the killed Tonghaks] with a scythe, and the other one carrying a basket to collect the heads." Pak and his militia "collected seven thousand severed rebel heads in this way." Hwang Hyŏn's account was no doubt greatly exaggerated, yet he revealed through this and numerous other descriptive accounts the intensity and savagery of the civil war.[55]

This was Korea's Sino-Japanese War. Before the battle of Sŏnghwan, the sporadic killing of local government magistrates and officials was not sanctioned practice. The Tonghaks' public proclamations only asked that they be relieved of oppression and that corrupt officials be removed from office. After the battle of Sŏnghwan, however, "no less than 23 Korean magistrates were killed," along with many dozens of military commandants and other government personnel.[56] The situation was particularly dire in Ch'ungch'ŏng Province, where weak local government forces were incapable of defeating Chŏn's army. Local officials "begged for the stationing of the Japanese army in their own districts" to help maintain order. In Kyŏngsang Province, the Tonghaks caused extreme confusion. The *Hansŏng Sunbo* reported that "in Songju they [the Tonghaks] burnt 600 houses and in Hadong, scattered houses over the entire province were burnt." It continued: "The innocent people who were killed are to be pitied as well as those who are yet alive."[57] The governor of Ch'ungch'ŏng

Province declared that the military commander stationed in Kongju "had taken 80 soldiers to attack the Tonghaks" but they "took him prisoner and burned him to death."[58]

In reply to Inoue's urgent request for reinforcements on October 27, Itō replied that the Nineteenth Reserve Battalion of six hundred men would be arriving on October 30. On November 12 Major Minami Koshirō, the battalion commander, set off with his men on the long march from Yongsan in Seoul toward Kongju, with two thousand Korean government soldiers in support. The plan was to carry out a scorched-earth pacification campaign, to be completed by the end of the year.[59] Kojong and his newly appointed cabinet minister under Kim Hong-jip welcomed Japan's quick decision to launch the pacification campaign.

Korean units served under the Japanese commanders, and Korean soldiers were given no freedom of action under Minami's strict orders. The Koreans also complained about receiving insufficient supplies, especially ammunition. They were mostly forced to rely on ammunition left behind by the Chinese who had retreated from Asan, Sŏnghwan, and Ch'ŏnan, but it was not enough. "We have to use them [the bullets] in a very frugal way and distribute only about one hundred at a time," one Korean soldier complained.[60]

In the meantime, Chŏn and his peasant army began their drive north from Ch'ungch'ŏng Province, reaching Kongju on November 13. There they linked up with Northern Assembly forces and laid siege to Kongju Castle. On November 20 Chŏn led his forces against Korean government and Japanese troops in the Battle of Ugŭmch'i but suffered heavy losses against the better-armed soldiers. "The chief of the rebels [Tonghaks] was riding a sedan chair with a cover and there were flags and horns all about him," reported the commander of government forces Yi Kyu-t'ae. "Our Korean soldiers then immediately advanced and shot over seventy [Tonghak] bandits and captured two live [while] none of our soldiers were injured."[61]

The Japanese employed Murata Type-18 rifles to devastating effect.[62] The modern Murata rifles were more accurate at a much longer effective range with a much higher rate of fire than the antiquated firearms used by the Tonghaks. "The Japanese rifles had an internal automatic ignition system which spared the bearer of the weapon from igniting it manually before firing," Hwang Hyŏn related. "So the Japanese were able to fire their weapons under rainy and snowy conditions. At a few hundred *po* distance, in which the Japanese considered that they were out of shooting

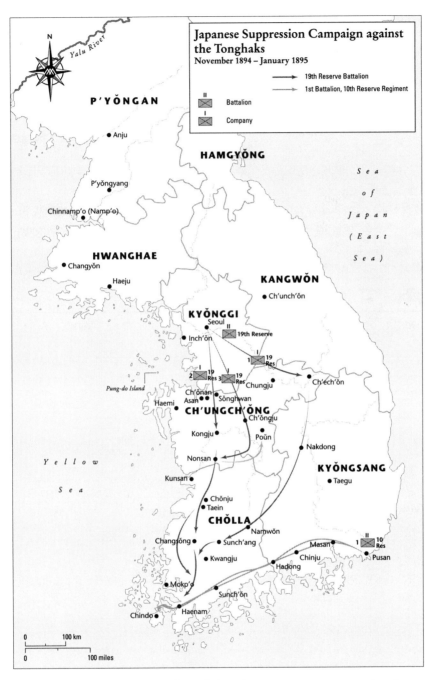

The Nineteenth Reserve Battalion advanced along three separate routes to round up the Tonghaks in southwestern Korea. The First Company of the Nineteenth Reserve Battalion took the "eastern route," toward Chech'ŏn and then proceeded south toward Nakdong; the Second Company of the Nineteenth Reserve Battalion took the "western" route toward Kongju, and the Third Company of the Nineteenth Reserve Battalion took the "central route" toward Ch'ŏngju. Finally, the First Battalion, Tenth Reserve Regiment swept westward from Pusan to round up and destroy the Tonghaks in the south.

Japanese soldiers firing Murata Type-18 rifles, 1894. Murata rifles, designed by Major Murata Tsuneoshi, were the first mass-produced Japanese-made rifles, used between 1880 and 1898. (Niday Picture Library/Alamy Stock Photo)

range of the enemy, they opened fire relentlessly" without the enemy "even firing a single shot."[63]

Tens of thousands of Tonghaks armed with bamboo spears and matchlocks were no match for the men of the Nineteenth Reserve Battalion with their superior training and advanced weapons.[64] The Tonghaks might have overcome their disadvantages by concentrating their numbers. However, in the Battle of Ugŭmch'i the Tonghaks failed to bring all their forces to bear at one place at one time. A large detachment of Northern Assembly forces in Ch'ungch'ŏng Province that could have made the difference at Ugŭmch'i was blocked by Japanese troops and was forced to fight independently, meeting defeats at Hongju, Ch'ŏngsan, and Haemi.[65]

Chŏn's ten-thousand-strong army, whose objective was to capture Seoul, was defeated by a combined Japanese and Korean government forces of fewer than three thousand men. After two unsuccessful assaults on Kongju, the Tonghaks were forced to withdraw. They were pursued and defeated at Nonsan and Ŭnjin, on December 11.[66] "I counted the number of my troops after the two battles and I found only 3000 left out of 10,000," Chŏn later recalled. These numbers were reduced further in battles at Wŏnp'yong and T'aein. "I counted the numbers again following the two additional battles and I found about 500 left," Chŏn despaired. He was able to recruit new reinforcements but "they proved ill-disciplined." Chŏn was forced to disband his army and fled to Sunch'ang, where he was eventually captured on December 27, 1894, by a local militia (*minpo*) led by a Confucian gentry, Han Sin-hyŏn.[67]

Chŏn appeared to have recognized the missteps he had made, offering a public mea culpa in an attempt to end the civil war and unite the country against the Japanese. "We Tonghaks have organized a righteous army to eliminate the Japanese enemies, suppress the reformer-officials, cleansing the courts of evil elements, and restoring security to the dynasty," he declared. "Unfortunately, however, the soldiers and officers of the government troops engaged us in battle where we proceed, without understanding our lofty, righteous cause." He regretted that Koreans had fought among themselves. "How sad it is to witness fratricidal conflict," he declared. "At the present moment, Seoul is under Japanese military occupation, and the entire country is in serious danger. And yet we continue to fight among ourselves, brother against brother."[68]

It was a stirring appeal for unity but it was too late. Kojong's harsh pronouncements against the Tonghaks were no doubt influenced by his Japanese caretakers in Seoul, but he also shared their bad opinion. Reacting to news of Tonghak excesses, he memorialized:

I cannot suppress my anger at the Tonghaks. They kill officials as well as innocent people and cause disorder in all the districts. In Seoul as well as in the country, the people are angry and all say that if they are not subdued, evil and wickedness will flourish. Now, therefore, I command that soldiers be immediately sent to the places where they [Tonghaks] are and utterly annihilate them. The leaders shall be killed and their followers dispersed. Some must be killed so that others can live.[69]

On December 11, after Chŏn's defeat at Nonsan and Ŭnjin, Minami and his men, with supporting Korean government forces, were ordered north in pursuit of the defeated army and to continue the "pacification" campaign. They forced Ch'oe's Tonghaks and the remnants of the Northern Assembly to Poŭn in Ch'ungch'ŏng Province, where the Tonghaks were defeated in the battle of Chonggok.[70]

By then the First Battalion of the Tenth Reserve Regiment near Pusan had been ordered to Chŏlla Province to surround Chŏn's army from the

Korean defense minister Cho Hŭi-yŏn (center) and his entourage visiting the Japanese Army in Jinzhou, March 19, 1895. (Getty Research Institute)

east. Two warships were deployed to block any attempts to escape to nearby islands.[71] The Tonghaks were trapped on all sides. The advance imposed violent pacification in its wake, decimating towns and villages. One Japanese soldier described how they executed captured suspected rebels at Haenam village on January 31: "Today we caught seven Tonghak peasants who were left [in the village], lined them up in the fields outside the castle, attached swords to guns and with the command of Lt. Morita, stabbed the victims at the same time. The Korean soldiers watching nearby were surprised and shocked." After capturing the village of Nanju, another Japanese soldier recalled that "you could see a small mountain of peoples' remains. They were caught either by the Korean government army or by own [Japanese] army but we [Japanese] executed them as rebels . . . the numbers of corpses we left behind reached 680."[72] Hundreds of towns and villages throughout Chŏlla Province suffered a similar fate. At the end of January 1895, with mopping-up operations completed, the Japanese and Korean government troops were ordered to return to

Seoul. A welcome parade was organized at the end of February to honor the victorious soldiers.[73]

Estimates of the number of dead in the Korean phase of the Sino-Japanese War vary, but the latest assessment put the number at thirty thousand to fifty thousand Koreans. This compares to the twenty thousand Japanese and thirty thousand Chinese who died in the formal Sino-Japanese War. The Korean figure is likely to be an underestimate, as the Tonghaks were reluctant to admit losses in order to tout their invincibility to new recruits.[74] If these numbers are correct, then, in a tragic irony, more Koreans died in the Sino-Japanese War than either the Chinese or the Japanese.

But more than the high death toll, the most consequential outcome of the Sino-Japanese War was its impact on the future stability of the Korean Peninsula. Lots of blood had been spilled, and divisions between groups had hardened. The fault line appeared not only between the Tonghak rebels and the Korean government officials and yangbans who had fought with the Japanese; deep fissures were also present within the Tonghak movement itself. Chŏn Pong-jun and other advocates of violent revolutionary tactics had split the movement by launching the Second Tonghak Uprising. Sickened and disappointed, Ch'oe Si-hyŏng, and his protégé, Son Pyŏng-hŭi, pledged that the Tonghak movement would return to its original nonviolent ways.[75] The Sino-Japanese War had thus pulled Korean society even further apart, opening up wide rifts that other Great Powers—namely, Russia—would use to their own advantage. The stage was set for increased turmoil in East Asia.

CHAPTER TEN

TRIPLE INTERVENTION

Japan's victory over the Tonghaks and triumph over the Chinese in P'yŏngyang had fulfilled the initial goal of the war to push the Chinese out of the Korean Peninsula. Japan then took the war to China, with spectacular results. With the fall of Port Arthur in late November, the Japanese were poised to take the port of Weihaiwei, the Beiyang Fleet's home port, and the last remaining Chinese base on the Yellow Sea.

Intoxicated by the victories, the Japanese celebrated. To the astonishment of the world, Japan had overturned within a few months the centuries-old Sinocentric order of the region and assumed the mantle of the new Middle Kingdom. Perception of Japan's role as the harbinger of civilization and progress in East Asia had begun appearing in 1868 with the Meiji Restoration, but that perception did not include altering the prestige of Chinese culture. Despite their aim of becoming a powerful and prosperous nation through the adoption of Western ideas and technology, Meiji leaders continued to see China as a powerful country. Chinese culture remained endemic to Japanese ways. Emperor Meiji's visits to Shintō shrines, for example, were all recorded in classical Chinese.[1] Chinese emissaries who resided in Japan prior to the Sino-Japanese War were entertained with a lavishness and familiarity impossible to replicate for Japan's European visitors, who did not share the same literary and cultural sensibilities. Knowledge of the Chinese classics was also the basic core of all Japanese educated elite, and many top-ranking Meiji officials took great pleasure in showing off their classical Chinese learning. Soejima Taneomi, for example, was a consummate scholar of the classics and thoroughly versed in the intellectual wellsprings of Chinese officialdom. Those skills served him well when he was dispatched to Beijing to finalize the first Sino-Japanese treaty in 1873.[2]

Japanese art objects and literature often depicted Chinese historical personages easily recognizable even to the less-educated public. Indeed, for most Japanese, "the image of China imprinted on our minds before the Sino-Japanese War was of a splendid, romantic and heroic country," remarked journalist and liberal philosopher Tsurumi Shunsuke. "Japan's cultural dependence on China was so great that nobody in Japan was sufficiently confident to claim that the Japanese were better than the Chinese."[3] The Sino-Japanese War, however, changed all that. "It is a melancholy fact that it took but a few months to destroy the tradition of respect built up over the centuries and turn the Japanese from friendship to contempt."[4]

The war had hardly begun when crude and unflattering commercial depictions of the Chinese began to appear. Lafcadio Hearn reported that "the announcement of each victory resulted in an enormous manufacture and sale of colored prints, rudely and cheaply executed, and mostly depicting the fancy of the artists only, but well fitted to stimulate the popular life of glory."[5] These colored woodblock prints, or *nishiki-e,* were striking for the humiliations they sought to heap upon the Chinese and for the raw violence depicted in many scenes. "The subject of the caricatures, together with the text, were of a kind to impress the reader with the idea of the superiority of the Japanese in mind and body over their enemies." Disciplined Japanese soldiers dressed in Western uniforms struck familiar poses as they dominated Chinese soldiers and prisoners, all dressed in old-fashioned garb, symbols of a backward Asia.[6] Over three thousand prints were published during the war; the most popular *nishiki-e* reputedly sold as many as one hundred thousand copies each.[7] "Every tea house has its series and all the shops in the bazaars were full of them. Wherever a poster was in sight, an admiring throng was sure to be seen."[8]

But the *nishiki-e* was just one of many objects that reshaped Japanese perceptions of China. Manufacturers of all sorts of trifles, such as hair ornaments, picture books, and toys, were quick to catch war fever and make it a profitable business. "There is a long line of mechanical toys, either of tin or wood, which, by turning a crank or by simple clockwork, are made to show Chinese combatants in a large variety of unenviable positions, sometimes pursued by infuriated Japanese troopers who make

Kiyochika Kobayashi, "The Trembling General," 1895. This
nishiki-e ridicules the fear of a Chinese general "from the tail of his
horse up to the general's own pigtails." (Library of Congress Prints and
Photographs Division, LC-DIG-jpd-00030)

terrific sweeps with sword or lances in a stately seesaw; or prisoners caught
by their queues and trying to avoid the rising and falling blades of their
captors," wrote one observer. "Clay figures representing Chinamen 'kowtowing' and pleading for mercy are used as paperweights or desk ornaments." In another instance, an elaborate toy depicting a "Japanese war-ship
gradually closing in with a Chinese vessel, the latter bearing the ideographs

Dingyuan. The Chinese ship is struck, her flag comes down with a rush, and the doomed vessel sinks with a rush, with Japanese soldiers storming it." When the mechanism was set in motion, "the Japanese leader brandishes his little tin blade, and the Chinamen on the parapet sink one after the other to the ground." This toy "is to be found in nearly every toy shop, and is very graphic though roughly executed."[9]

PEACE GESTURES

It was only natural, then, that the Japanese government sought to end the war on terms reflecting Japan's enormous sense of pride and accomplishment. Not only had the Japanese won every battle, but they had also negotiated during the conflict new and equal treaties with Britain and the United States. Thus, when the customs commissioner at Tianjin, Gustav Detring, arrived in Kōbe on November 26, 1894, with a letter from Li Hongzhang to Itō Hirobumi signaling his desire to negotiate an end to the war, the latter refused to meet him, citing Detring's lack of proper credentials.[10] Two months later, the Chinese sent another delegation to meet with Japanese representatives in Hiroshima led by Zhang Yinheng and Shao Youlian and accompanied by John W. Foster, a former US secretary of state. Months earlier, the Chinese emperor had requested Foster's "wise counsel" to act as an adviser to the Chinese peace commissioners.[11] But even before the envoys' arrival on January 31, 1895, it was apparent that Zhang and Shao were relatively minor officials.[12] More concerning was that they bore no certificate of investiture from the Qing government to negotiate a peace treaty.

As with the earlier Detring mission, the arrival of Zhang and Shao raised doubts as to the sincerity of the Chinese in wanting to negotiate an end to the war. Itō suspected that the true motivation of the Qing peace mission was to involve Western powers to intervene in the peace negotiations to make terms favorable to China.[13] The prime minister was right to be worried because almost from the start of the conflict, the Chinese had appealed directly to Western powers to bring the war to an end.[14] "It is impossible for anyone, even the wisest and experienced politicians, to predict as to what forms and degree of severity such an intervention would take, much less ensure that such an intervention can be prevented," Itō warned. "When confronted with this dilemma and to resolve the current situation with a successful outcome, it is essential that both civilian and military leadership in the service of his majesty's throne stand unified."[15]

Itō's emphasis on achieving a unity of purpose was significant. This is because two months earlier, in November, Yamagata had been recalled by the emperor for disobeying an order. After his spectacular victory in the battle of P'yŏngyang, Yamagata's First Army experienced considerable difficulties due to unexpected Chinese resistance. Many Japanese soldiers were also suffering from frostbite. Despite this, Yamagata was eager to continue his push deeper into Chinese territory. When the IGHQ refused to grant his request, Yamagata disregarded the order and attacked Haicheng, a strategic communications junction located southwest of Mukden (Shenyang). The Japanese were successful, but Chinese forces made repeated attempts to retake the city and for the first time inflicted on the Yamagata's forces what was arguably their greatest single-battle loss during the entire Manchurian campaign. Enraged, Prime Minister Itō persuaded the emperor to recall Yamagata back to Japan.[16]

The imperial rescript, issued on November 29, was deeply humiliating for the proud general. The official line was that Yamagata had suffered from a stomach ailment and was compelled to return home "in the hope of restoring his health," but the real reason was Itō's insistence that his government would not tolerate any dissension among its leaders.[17] "As long as a policy decision is achieved in harmony among his majesty's top-tier advisers on both civilian and military side, we should not be daunted by whatever dissenting opinions are voiced by the [Western] public," Itō opined.[18] To bring the war to a successful conclusion, Japanese leaders had to stand united and strong against the machinations of China and the Western powers.

THE SIEGE OF WEIHAIWEI

While Itō was contemplating the threat of Western intervention, the campaign to subdue Weihaiwei, the last stronghold of the Beiyang Fleet, was unfolding. The Weihaiwei campaign would be the last major campaign of the war and would force the Chinese government to finally take serious steps to end the conflict. The campaign would also, quite unexpectedly, rehabilitate China's damaged image in the eyes of the Japanese. Although Sino-Japanese relations would never recover, the Weihaiwei campaign restored some of the old Japanese admiration and respect for China, laying the groundwork for peace negotiations.

Situated on the northern coast of the Shandong Peninsula about fifty miles east of Yantai (Chefoo), Weihaiwei was one of the greatest of China's maritime forts and, like Port Arthur, thought to be impregnable. The strategic location at the closest point between China and Korea allowed the Beiyang Fleet to control maritime traffic between the two nations and access to the northern half of the Yellow Sea. Admiral Ding and his fleet headquarters were located on Liugongdao, a two-mile-long island at the mouth of Weihai Bay.[19] Liugong Island and a nearby islet, Ri Dao, were fortified to protect the bay and harbor where the Beiyang Fleet ships were berthed. In addition to the island defenses were massive forts located on the northeastern and southwestern ends of the harbor. The design and building of the defensive work were overseen a few years earlier by von Hammeken, the British advisor to the fleet.

Guarding the port entrance was the Beiyang Fleet. Of these, only the *Dingyuan, Jingyuan, Jiyuan,* and the *Laiyuan* were considered effective. The battleship *Zhenyuan* had recently hit a rock and, despite being patched, was not considered seaworthy.[20] Admiral Ding's fleet was too weak to take on the Japanese fleet on the open sea, but it was capable of defending the coastline against landing threats to Beijing. "If Weihaiwei held out there was also some hope for China: her battleships might still prevent the landing of troops anyway near Pekin (Beijing)," wrote one observer. "And to do them naught but justice, the Chinese themselves recognized these facts and fought with the utmost valor—at least, their fleet did."[21]

Although the odds were against him, Ding believed that Weihaiwei could be a turning point in the war. In devising his strategy, he was persuaded by his British naval adviser, William Tyler, who had distinguished himself in the Battle of the Yellow Sea, to destroy and evacuate the mainland forts before Japanese troops arrived. "I knew with certainty that the forts on the mainland would not fight," he told Ding. "They would be evacuated without a blow; and then, unless they were first destroyed, their heavy guns would be used against us."[22]

On January 20, 1895, Beiyang Fleet's headquarters received reports that Ōyama's Second Army had landed at Rongcheng Bay on the eastern coast of Shandong Peninsula, some forty miles southeast of Weihaiwei, and was rapidly advancing. Tyler immediately went to work to organize the demolition of the mainland forts.[23] For this purpose, the Chinese employed a somewhat primitive device, a joss-stick fastened to a fuse. "All joss sticks are of corresponding dimension, and every Chinaman knows pretty accurately how many minutes are absorbed in the burning of a given number of inches of them." But to use them, "coolness and deliberation are required. And the Chinese are neither cool nor deliberate under fire." The impulse to evacuate the fort without having properly lit the joss ticks, or in many cases, lighting the fuse too late, and thus allowing the enemy to extinguish the fuse before the fatal blow, often proved too tempting. "Dynamite bombs are really dangerous only in the hands of men prepared to die with those they kill—anxiety to save one's self disturbs the effectiveness of the act of destruction."[24]

The result was that all Weihaiwei's southern forts were in the possession of the Japanese by January 30. The forts were evacuated but had not been properly destroyed except for the western forts. The Japanese captured eleven serviceable artillery pieces in the eastern forts, which they promptly used to shell Liugongdao and Chinese ships in the harbor. "One crashed through the armored deck of the *Jingyuan* and sank her," Tyler recalled.[25] For most of the siege, therefore, the Chinese fleet was condemned to confine itself chiefly to the western end of the bay. As for taking the city of Weihaiwei itself, there was no struggle. "The Japanese reached the walled city and just walked in; but they found our western forts entirely demolished."[26]

The situation appeared hopeless. The Chinese were completely cut off from the outside world. On the sea, a powerful Japanese fleet prevented all escape while the Japanese Second Army blocked the landward side. Hoping to persuade the Chinese to lay down their arms and surrender the port, Vice-Admiral Itō made a direct appeal to Ding on January 25. The two men had known each other as young men. The letter was deliberately written in English to allow Ding's foreign advisers an opportunity to counsel him about the sagacity of surrender. "The vicissitudes of the times have made us enemies, yet it is our countries that are at war," Itō began his extraordinary entreaty, which deserves to be quoted in full.

> There need be no hostility between individuals. The friendship that formerly existed between you and me is as warm as ever today. Let it not be supposed that in writing you this letter I am actuated by any idle purpose of urging you to surrender. The actors in great affairs often err; the onlookers see the truth. Instead of calmly deliberating what course of procedure on his own part is best for his country, best for himself, a man sometimes allows himself to be swayed by the task in which he is actually engaged, and takes a mistaken view; it is not then the duty of his friends to advise him and to turn his thoughts to the right channel? I address myself to you from the motives of genuine friendship, and I

pray you appreciate them. What is the origin of the repeated disasters that have befallen the Chinese arms? There is, I think, little difficulty in discovering the true reason if one looks for it calmly and intelligently. Your discernment has, doubtless, shown you the cause. It is not the fault of one man that has brought China into the position she now occupies; the blames rests with the errors of the Government that has long administered her affairs . . . A country with a history running back thousands of years and territories stretching tens of thousands of miles, the oldest empire in the world, can it be an easy task to accomplish for such a country a work of restoration, replacing its foundation on a permanently solid basis? A single pillar cannot prevent the fall of a great edifice . . . To hand over squadrons to the foe, to surrender a whole army to an enemy; these are mere bagatelles compared with the fate of a country. By whatever reputation a Japanese soldier possesses in the eyes of the world, I vow that I believe your wisest course is to come to Japan and wait there until the fortunes of your country are again in the ascent, and until the time arrives when your services will be again needed. Hear these words of a true friend.

Itō concluded by appealing to Ding's role in China's future: "Will you throw in your lot with a country that you see falling to ruin [or] will you preserve the strength that remains to you and evolve another plan hereafter?"[27]

Admiral Ding did not reply. As desperate as the circumstances appeared, there was still some hope of protracted resistance. Liugongdao was beyond the reach of the shore batteries and the Ridao islet remained secure. They were also beyond the reach of the Japanese fleet. The Beiyang Fleet could lie at anchor in the harbor in security as long as supplies lasted.[28]

However, the situation changed drastically on February 1. The Japanese had repaired seven canons on the southern forts, which significantly increased their ability to shell Liugong.[29] As the new field-gun batteries fired upon the island, Ding came up with a plan to storm the Zhaobeiju fort, located at the tip of a promontory on the southeastern side of the bay. But the sailor in charge of the mission got cold feet when he spotted enemy ships.[30] Another attempt to storm the fort was planned for the following morning, February 5, but Japanese torpedo boats had slipped into the southern side of the harbor. "Shortly after the moon had set, alarm rockets had gone up from the patrol boats near Ri Dao," Tyler recalled. "Firing began again and I ran up the stand compass section erection to get a better view with my glasses. It was a torpedo boat coming end on for us on our port beam."[31] The flagship *Dingyuan* was struck.[32] Ding, who had no idea how much damage had been done, ordered the ship to proceed to the eastern entrance (southern) to block the approach of more enemy boats. But by then the *Dingyuan* was sinking. "I told the Admiral [Ding] that the ship would not float for long, and that he ought to beach her in such a way that her guns could still be used, and it should be done at once before she listed anymore," Tyler recalled. The following day, at around 4 AM, another torpedo attack took place in the darkness. Ding ordered the fleet to use searchlights to detect the Japanese gunboats, but the lights went right over their hulls and allowed the enemy to pinpoint the location of the Chinese ships instead. "Above the din of gunfire we could hear—and feel—the explosion of torpedoes, and when daylight broke, a tragic sight appeared. Capsized, with her bilge showing above the water, was the poor *Laiyuan,* and alongside the jetty, the *Weiyuan,* a lighter and steam launch were sunk."[33]

On February 8, fierce bombardment from the sea and shore sank the *Jingyuan.* Within two days, three of China's best warships were sunk. The Chinese torpedo flotilla attempted to escape to Yantai, but the thirteen boats were either captured or destroyed. The Beiyang Fleet was reduced from twenty-five ships to four battleships and five gunboats.[34] On February 11, Ding received a telegram from Li Hongzhang informing him that reinforcements could not be sent and advising the admiral and the fleet to escape to some other port. That option, was, of course, out of the question.

The following day, at 8:30 AM, the Chinese gunboat *Zhenbei* sailed toward the Japanese fleet from the southeastern part of the bay with a white flag flapping in the front. Ding had entrusted his subordinate, Cheng Biguang, to present his letter of capitulation to Admiral Itō.[35] He requested that "the lives of all persons connected with the navy and army, both Chinese and foreigners, be spared, and that they be allowed to return to their homes." Itō replied the same day, agreeing wholeheartedly to the conditions of the surrender, and repeated once again his appeal for Ding to come to Japan and to remain there until the war was over. "If you decide to offer that course," he wrote, "I offer you the strongest assurances that you shall be treated with every consideration and shall receive the fullest protection." With his reply, Itō sent two dozen bottles of wine and champagne and some dried persimmons.[36] At 8:30 AM the following morning,

Remains of the Beiyang Fleet. The vessel emitting a great quantity of black smoke on the upper left is the *Zhenyuan*. On the far left, also emitting smoke, is the *Pingyuan*. The vessel on the right is the *Jiyuan*. In the distance is Liugong Island. (Getty Research Institute)

Itō received Ding's reply. The latter told him that while he was grateful for the gifts, "the state of war existing between our countries made it difficult for me to receive them," and he relayed his regret for returning them. He also requested that Itō wait until February 16 to enter the harbor to receive the formal handover.[37] As soon as Ding had finished writing the letter, he telegrammed Li Hongzhang informing him of the surrender. He then retired to his cabin and swallowed a large dose of opium.[38]

News of Admiral Ding's suicide was shocking but not unexpected. Public disgrace, and possibly death, awaited him in Beijing, where the desperate exigencies of his situation would never have been recognized or acknowledged. Furthermore, he would have been roundly condemned for not scuttling his fleet before the act of surrender. Since further resistance could only involve the hopeless sacrifice of his men, Ding trusted Itō to spare their lives by making the ultimate sacrifice and taking his own.

When Itō was told of Ding's suicide, he was greatly moved. To honor his friend, he ordered one of the captured Chinese vessels, the *Kangji*, to be used to escort Ding's body to Yantai. "Before the ship left, the Japanese officers paid a visit to his mortal remains—the profound respect they showed greatly touched the Chinese and foreigners who beheld them."[39] As the *Kangji* left the harbor, the Japanese fleet dropped their flags to half-mast. Itō's flagship *Matsushima* fired a salute as the vessel passed by, "a testament of the bravery exhibited by the late admiral."[40]

Admiral Itō's courtesy to his fallen foe reflected his adherence to the professional military code that honored martial virtues, courage, loyalty, sacrifice, and concern for rank and file. He kept his promise to Ding and authorized the evacuation of Chinese soldiers and sailors and permitted civilians to leave Weihaiwei. "The battle for Weihaiwei had ended not only in a Japanese victory but also with a vindication of the Japanese code of the samurai after the horrors of Port Arthur."[41] Ding had been intimately involved in the buildup of tension between the two countries over the fate of Korea since the 1882 Imo Incident, which first brought the two powers to a head on the peninsula. His suicide led to a measure of restoring China's sullied military reputation and the restoration of Japan's previous veneration for China. The settlement of the Battle of Weihaiwei also led to closure on China and Japan's struggle over the fate of Korea, for not long afterward Li Hongzhang went to Japan to sue for peace.[42]

LI HONGZHANG COMES TO SHIMONOSEKI

The day after the Chinese surrender at Weihaiwei on February 17, Foreign Minister Mutsu received word that Li Hongzhang had been appointed minister plenipotentiary to negotiate the peace on behalf of the Chinese government. "It appeared that the Chinese had finally made up their minds to negotiate in good faith," recalled Mutsu, although the success of the negotiations was not ensured.[43] The Japanese laid out four demands. The first and most important stipulation was that China had to "recognize the complete and unabridged independence of Korea." Neither Mutsu nor Itō expected much pushback from Li on this point. But the second and third demands were more sensitive. Japan would require territorial concessions from China—namely, Taiwan and the southern portion of Liaoning Province (including all the islands belonging to the province in the eastern portion of Liaodong Bay). It also wanted the Chinese government to pay a hefty indemnity. The fourth stipulation, that "Japan's relations with China be on an equal footing," meant Japan would claim various Japanese rights regarding commerce and navigation, including the creation of new treaty ports and extending trade.[44] In other words, Japan demanded privileges similar to what the Western powers enjoyed in China.

On March 24 Li Hongzhang, accompanied by his adopted son and assistant, Li Jingfang, sat down with Itō Hirobumi to discuss Japan's proposal for a peace treaty. The session was a bitter reprise for Li of an encounter a decade earlier when the two men had met as equals to negotiate the Convention of Tianjin. That agreement had helped to stabilize relations between the two countries and bring them back from the brink of war, also over Korea. Now, Li represented China as a defeated nation.[45] "Ten years ago when I was at Tianjin, I talked about reform," Itō began. "Why is it that up to now not a single thing has been changed or reformed?" Reflecting on the last three decades and his role in China's self-strengthening reform, Li answered plaintively: "Affairs in my country have been so confined by tradition that I could not accomplish what I desired. Now in a twinkling of an eye ten years have gone by, and everything is still the same." Whatever hope Li had nurtured for China's modernization reforms had been dashed at Port Arthur and Weihaiwei. "I am even more regretful," he continued. "I am ashamed of having excessive wishes and lacking the power to fulfill them."[46]

Li's pitiful circumstances met a further blow when a deranged man named Koyama Toyatarō fired a pistol at Li Hongzhang as he was returning from the meeting to his lodgings, seriously wounding him in the face. A bullet entered Li's left cheek, reaching deep below his left eye.[47] The assassination attempt, reminiscent of the Ōtsu incident four years earlier, sent the Japanese public into a tailspin of anxiety.

The immediate concern was whether Li would live. Ishiguro Tadanori, surgeon inspector general of the Japanese Army, was sent to Shimonoseki with the army's chief surgeon, Satō Sasumi. The emperor had personally instructed them to oversee the medical treatment of Li due to the "grave political implications of the incident." They called first upon Mutsu, who was deeply worried. "I am in a serious predicament," he told the doctors. "First and foremost, we cannot afford to let Li Hongzhang return home at this critical moment in the negotiations." "Do not let him go home is all I want," he reiterated. "The rest is in my power to handle."[48] Mutsu was also concerned that the incident might provoke strong international criticism against Japan and sympathy for China that could lead to an intervention in the negotiations. "Throughout Japan, there seemed less concern about the attack on Li than about the international criticism people feared it would occasion," Mutsu recalled. "A nation which until yesterday had been nearly driven by delirium by the joys of military triumphs now suddenly plunged into the depths of grief."[49]

The doctors found Li lying on a sofa in the clothes he wore at the time of the attack. He was being attended by a French and a Chinese physician. Ishiguro told Li that they had been sent on the emperor's orders. "Li turned to me and asked whether the wound might cause death," Ishiguro recollected. He assured Li that the wound, if properly treated, would not be fatal. Li then requested that the Japanese doctors take charge of his care. "I will not disobey the doctors' commands but I want to make sure that not a single drop of my blood be shed," he stated emphatically. "Old men's blood cannot be restored once lost. Take extreme caution to save the blood." Ishiguro reassured him. "We will take care of you as if you were our own ailing father," he said.[50]

Li's condition improved rapidly. He spoke no more of returning to China, perhaps recognizing that his full recovery would better be ensured by staying put. The talks resumed a week later on April 1. On the first issue regarding Korean independence, Li indicated that "China had some months earlier declared her willingness to recognize the complete and unabridged independence of Korea" and was prepared to insert this in the treaty. His only condition was that Japan also recognize Korean independence as well. On the question of territorial concessions of the southern portion of Liaoning Province, Taiwan, and the Pescadores Islands, the payment of an indemnity of three hundred thousand taels, and commercial privileges, Li balked. He complained that the Japanese had publicly proclaimed at the onset of hostilities that they had "no territorial designs on China but sought only to secure the complete independence of Korea." Li pointed out that territorial concession would create permanent resentment on the part of the Chinese people. "The result could only be an eternal internecine enemy preventing mutual assistance between us, which would soon leave us both easy prey to outside aggression." As for the indemnity, Li professed that the amount demanded "far exceeded China's current financial capabilities." He added that "many valuable spoils of war had been taken by the Japanese forces in the form of Chinese warships and military supplies" and these "should be properly be deducted from the amount of the indemnity." Moreover, he pointed out the incongruity of forcing China to pay an indemnity "for the expenses of a war in which she had not been the aggressor."[51]

Neither Itō nor Mutsu were persuaded; they reminded Li that Japan, not China, was the victor. Despite his plenipotentiary powers, Li did not

want to be responsible. "Li was himself caught between his own government and the Japanese."[52] The Japanese agreed to reduce the scope
of the territorial demands.[53] Li begged Itō to reduce the indemnity
"as a parting gift to him" and the prime minister concurred. "While
such conduct was hardly worthy of a man with Li's dignity," remarked
Mutsu, "it resulted no doubt from the idea that 'the more you argued, the
more concessions you would obtain.' Whatever the case may have been,
the very fact that an old man like Li should have taken this mission to
a foreign land and met daily without showing the slightest signs of fa-
tigue must certainly inspire us with great admiration for his energy."[54]
The indemnity was reduced to two hundred thousand taels. The treaty
was signed on April 17, and Li Hongzhang departed Shimonoseki the
next day.

A farcical but potentially disastrous incident happened on the day after
the viceroy's departure. As Mutsu was making his way through the
crowded streets of Shimonoseki to board the Japanese warship *Yaeyama*
for Hiroshima, he lost his balance. Reacting reflexively to break Mutsu's
fall, his bodyguard, a police lieutenant named Matsushita, dropped into
a large puddle the wicker box containing the signed treaty documents.
Both Mutsu and the documents became soaking wet. "The documents
were to be presented to His Majesty upon arrival at Hiroshima and the
port for disembarkation was only a brief voyage away," recalled Mutsu's
aide, Nakata Takanori. "The paper used for printing the treaty was on
Chinese paper which was notoriously prone to water damage. The task
of drying this precious article took an agonizing and tender joint operation [by several aides]. This was an indelible experience which I recall as
both truly arduous yet comical."[55] Mutsu, his clothes still damp from the
accident, presented the damaged treaty to Emperor Meiji on April 18. It
was an inauspicious sign of events to come.

TRIPLE INTERVENTION

On April 23 the ministers of Russia, Germany, and France called on
Hayashi Tadasu, vice minister of foreign affairs, and lodged a serious objection to the secession of the Liaodong Peninsula in the Shimonoseki
Peace Treaty. "Their demand was that since Japan's permanent possession of the Liaodong Peninsula would threaten the Chinese capital and
make the independence of Korea merely nominal, they advised Japan to
withdraw this condition."[56]

The Triple Intervention, "which was designed to deprive Japan of the fruits of her victory," was a shock although not entirely unexpected, for during the peace talks there was suspicion that Li had come to Japan armed with "a protective guarantee from the three powers," and was secretly looking forward to the occurrence of a third-nation intervention during the talks. Nakata Takanori, a Mutsu aide, recalled, "It appears that Li Hongzhang had hoped that any one of the three powers in the alliance would make its insidious intention known while the heated negotiations for peace between the Qing and Japanese delegates were in progress. From early on, Japan, too, had feared that an intervention could be attempted by any of the Western powers. It was a pervasive feeling among the Japanese leaders that an omen of intervention was in the air although they were unsure as to whom would lead the intervention or what form it would take."[57] Fortunately for Itō, however, the intervention did not materialize during the peace negotiations. "If the demand to rescind Japan's acquisition of the Liaodong Peninsula by Russia, Germany, and France had come about in the midst of the peace talks, no doubt a great crisis could have taken place."[58]

Mutsu had no doubt that Russia was the main force behind the Triple Intervention. The Russian government had begun sending warships to Vladivostok the previous year and had maintained a strong naval force in the area.[59] Reports of Russian surveying activities in Manchuria were sources of alarm and concern. Ueno Iwataro, reporting for the newspaper *Asahi shimbun,* wrote that "it appeared that the Russians were planning to abandon the Amur line and build a railway through Manchuria."[60] Such plans would explain Russian sensitivity to Japanese control of the Liaodong Peninsula, which would threaten the Manchurian railway.

France and Germany's decision to support the Russian protest against Japan's peace terms hardened Russia's position. During a special meeting on April 11 to discuss the peace terms, Minister of War Pyotr Vannovsky stated that the Russian government must resist Japanese encroachment on Korea and should "in no way agree to the conditions Japan laid out during the peace talks which include the proposal of tearing away the Liaodong Peninsula from China."[61] Witte echoed the position and declared that "Japan's hostile activities on the continent were directed mainly against Russia" and that "the planned takeover of the southern part of Manchuria will be a threat to all of us and will probably result in all of Korea being absorbed into Japan." "If Japan could not be persuaded to relinquish its claim to the Liaodong Peninsula, Russia should begin hostile actions against the Japanese fleet, and bombard Japanese ports." Russia should advise Japan "at first amiably to give up on occupying the southern part of Manchuria," but in the event of a refusal "announce that we will begin to act in accordance with our interests."[62]

Faced with the tripartite backlash, the Imperial Council, which included Mutsu, Yamagata, and Navy Minister Saigō Tsugumichi, gathered to discuss the crisis on April 24. Itō presented the group with three options: (a) reject the demand; (b) host a conference with the three Powers along with Britain; and (c) abide by the demand as "a show of goodwill" but require "the Qing to fulfill the rest of the treaty obligations."[63]

Mutsu was keen on the second option, hoping for the possibility of a diplomatic breakthrough during a conference, but Itō refuted the idea, noting that the intentions of the powers were quite clear and there was "no need to investigate further," as it would be dangerous "to give the Three Powers the excuse to act against Japan by rejecting their recommendations without considering what might result from it."[64] Moreover, any actions involving a rupture with the Three Powers might involve Japan in another conflict, one that it could not possibly win.[65]

This was a bitter pill to swallow. The war had been a triumph of military logistical planning and execution and showcased Japan's newly developed capability and power. "It took the Chinese twenty years to fortify Port Arthur and we captured it in ten hours," Ōyama boasted.[66] The Japanese were being forced to retrocede the Liaodong Peninsula, for which they had sacrificed so much. Even more ominously, the Triple Intervention signaled a warning to Japan about its claims to Korea. "Although the pretext for the intervention was ostensibly the Liaodong Peninsula, the real reason was Russia's obsessive fear of Japan's possible takeover of Korea," recalled Itō bitterly. "Based on this reasoning, the logical interpretation of the situation is that Russia will focus first on stopping us from taking the Liaodong Peninsula, and subsequently, on undercutting our influence in Korea." He concluded darkly: "Although Russia has been cautious not to unveil the bud of its diabolical ambition in the Far East, one can readily discern that the bud has already grown ripe for action."[67] After much anguish and debate, Itō announced Japan's retrocession of the Liaodong Peninsula on May 5.

The unsatisfactory conclusion of the war notwithstanding, the conflict had done nothing to resolve the inherent contradictions of Japan's position in Korea: although the Japanese proclaimed to be acting in the name of defending Korea's independence, they continued to interfere in

Korea's internal affairs. Moreover, if the main objective had been to re-form Korea and resolve the source of unrest that had brought China and Japan into conflict in the first place, the Japanese had been unable to achieve anything of the sort. The uprisings in Ch'ungch'ŏng, Chŏlla, and Hwanghae Provinces by Tonghaks rebels throughout the fall and winter of 1894/1895 had revealed how much the Japanese had underestimated both the power of the Tonghaks and the skill of Korea's political players to resist Japan. The inevitable result was the advance of Russian power into the Korean Peninsula.

FAILED REFORM

While the Triple Intervention eroded Japan's political position in Seoul, the failure to secure reliable allies ultimately doomed its reform efforts in Korea. Following the ouster of the Taewŏn'gun in November 1894, Inoue selected Pak Yŏng-hyo, the former leader of the 1884 failed Kapsin coup who had been living in exile in Japan, to lead a new reform effort. Kim Hong-jip had not been as effective as Inoue had hoped, so the Japanese minister came up with the idea of forming a new coalition cabinet. Inoue settled on Pak not only for his "progressive" credentials but because, un-like the Taewŏn'gun, he had no other power base to rely on but the Japa-nese. Only a year earlier, Pak had been the target of an assassination plot instigated by Kojong, similar to the plot that ended Kim Ok-kyun's life in Shanghai. Now back in Korea, Pak was continually under threat. "He does not go out of the house after sunset and only during the day under the protection of a strong guard of Japanese police," reported the news-paper *Hansŏng Sunbo*. "The life of a pardoned rebel in Corea [sic] is therefore not a peaceful one. There is no doubt that he will sooner or later receive just punishment that should have been inflicted long ago. But it is only a matter of time."[68]

Pak's notoriety was an asset in Inoue's eyes and served the minister's purposes, for, as one observer put it, "he was placed in power by the Japa-nese and maintained there through their influence."[69] Naturally, Inoue expected much from him. On December 17 the Military Deliberative Council was broken up and the new cabinet was formed with Kim Hong-jip assuming the prime ministership and Pak taking on the powerful post of home minister. Sŏ Kwang-bŏm, Pak's friend and a former member of the exile group, was appointed minister of justice. The two former exiles put forward a list of radical reform proposals aimed to "sweep away the evils and abuses of the past," including the reorganization of the military.[70] New ordinances were also issued regarding the official functions of the king and the cabinet. Inoue's reform plan was to turn Korea into a quasi-constitutional monarchy with decision-making powers resting with the new coalition Korean cabinet. The separation of the king from the government replicated the Meiji government.

Pak, however, had no desire to be a Japanese puppet. "Pak was branded a traitor so for a long time he wandered from country to country," Sugimura explained. "Now he'd come home thanks to the Japanese and was promoted to the position of home minister, but even so he did not feel relieved."[71] Once in power, Pak found himself at loggerheads with Prime Minister Kim Hong-jip and his group of moderate reformers, who were in secret communications with the Taewŏn'gun.

During these political struggles Pak found an unlikely ally in Queen Min. At first, both political players found mutual interest in their shared antipathy of the Taewŏn'gun. Although ousted from office, the Taewŏn'gun and his allies in the Kim cabinet were still a force to be reckoned with. Pak was especially vulnerable, as he feared that without the political support of the queen his situation was precarious. Thus, a quiet understanding between Pak and the queen was reached. Queen Min would use Pak to help destroy the Taewŏn'gun, and Pak would use the queen to gain the political support he needed to implement his reforms.

Pak began to distance himself from Inoue and assiduously cultivate his relationship with the queen. She reciprocated the attention. It was classic Korean court power politics and Queen Min played her cards beautifully. "Pak's object is doubtless to use her as an instrument," Inoue later observed. "But she is the ablest person in Korea, and is more likely to use Pak than to be used by him."[72]

In the meantime, Inoue was still faced with the problem of Korean reform, the purported raison d'être of the war. To win Pak's cooperation, he proposed that Japan offer a financial "contribution" to Korea, a ¥3 million loan to the bankrupt Korean government. The idea was to "Egyptanize" Korea by following the British example of intervention in Egypt. Inoue, in other words, hoped to purchase the obedience of the Korean government by increasing its financial dependence on Japan.[73]

Mutsu's initial reaction to the loan idea was positive, but by the time the Japanese government had raised the loan bill in the Diet, the international situation had changed drastically. The Russian minister in Tokyo, Mikhail Khitrovo, paid a call on Mutsu on February 14, 1895, seeking clarification of Japan's Korea policy. Mutsu warned Inoue "not to indulge in any acts that would provoke Russian intervention."[74] By the time the Japanese had yielded to the demands of Triple Intervention in May, the question of the loan came under renewed scrutiny. On June 3 the Japanese cabinet decided to adopt a new policy for Korea. It would "refrain from actively interfering in Korean domestic affairs" so that Korea could stand on her own feet in the future.[75]

The psychological and diplomatic impact of the Triple Intervention on the Koreans was also enormous. It demonstrated that despite their victory over China, the Japanese still had to bend to the wishes of the Western powers. With Japan's prestige severely curtailed and the matter of the Japanese loan still unresolved, Pak decided that the time was ripe to embark on his own bold course of reform. From mid-May to early June 1895, he sought to reorganize the cabinet and implement far-reaching renovations of the military, police, judiciary, education, and local administrative systems.[76] These sweeping reforms included eighty-eight radical proposals that touched on all aspects of Koreans' military, social, political, and economic life, including the eradication of the class system, the abolishment of the concubinage system, and the end of early marriage practices, among other sweeping changes.[77] Anxious to consolidate his power, Pak also forced a confrontation between himself and Kim Hong-jip, who believed that Pak's reforms were far too radical. Prime Minister Kim and the more moderate members of his cabinet resigned en masse in protest.

Inoue placed the blame for the failure of the coalition squarely on Pak. The Japanese minister also resented Pak's loud complaints about the terms of the ¥3 million loan and his strenuous opposition to the expansion of Japanese settlements in Seoul.[78] Faced with Pak's recalcitrance and Tokyo's new caution, Inoue departed for Japan on June 7 to discuss the situation with Foreign Minister Mutsu. "He is very angry with the Koreans and especially with Pak," wrote one observer. "This individual has turned his back on the Japanese and is now smiling on the Russians or any foreigners who are willing to be pleased by his smiles."[79]

Having established himself as a "virtual dictator," Pak attempted to carve out an independent course for Korea.[80] But he was undone rather abruptly through the cunning of the queen. A plot to assassinate her was conveniently uncovered and Pak was implicated. Whether out of pity or friendship, Sugimura hid him in the Japanese legation as Korean soldiers mounted a search for his arrest. For the second time, on the early morning of July 7, Pak was forced to make another clandestine escape to Japan.[81]

Pak had no doubt he was set up and who was responsible. "As to the causes of my impeachment," he bitterly recalled, "there are many but the principal is the queen's ambition to place Korea once more under the sway of her party, namely the Mins. That ambition has always been entertained by Her Majesty and she was looking for an opportunity to carry out her scheme."[82] In just a few months Queen Min had succeeded in neutralizing her two chief rivals, the Taewŏn'gun and Pak Yŏng-hyo. Unwittingly, Pak had helped her in this endeavor. "She was too shrewd for him and the alliance did not prove satisfactory," remarked Inoue with grudging admiration.[83]

Back in Tokyo, Inoue was attempting to rehash Japan's failing Korea policy. He was nearing the end of his term in Korea and put forward his recommendation for future actions that fundamentally accepted the continuance of the cautious "hands-off" policy. Inoue recommended that Japan "purchase" its objective in Korea through conditional financing, which would both control the king and queen and put them in debt to Japan. The Japanese cabinet adopted Inoue's proposal and settled on a ¥3 million loan, this one with generous repayment terms. It would also offer the Korean government a "contribution" of ¥3 million in an attempt to preempt other countries—namely, Russia—from establishing close economic and political connections with Koreans.[84] There was one condition, however. The contribution of ¥3 million would not be made available to the Koreans until after the Imperial Diet approved it. It was a flagrant attempt at influence peddling, but Inoue saw other no option.

Returning to Korea in mid-July, Inoue was reasonably hopeful that the Diet would approve the ¥3 million "gift." Conveying the good news to the royal couple, Inoue proposed that the largest part of the contribution be used for the construction of a Seoul/Pusan railway line but also, remarkably, the construction of a new royal palace, ostensibly to build up the king's prestige and authority, but to purchase his cooperation as well.[85] "The king and queen were very happy," Sugimura recalled. "After this meeting (on July 25), the minister often went to the royal court and tried to get into the king and queen's good graces."[86] Even more extraordinary was Inoue's reversal of his opinion about the queen, for he now welcomed her to stand by the king's side in administering all state affairs. In just over six months, Inoue's Korea policy had collapsed, while Queen Min was basking in her newfound power.

In early September, acting foreign minister Saionji Kinmochi, who had replaced the ailing Mutsu (ill with tuberculosis), informed Inoue that the

Japanese Diet had turned down the ¥3 million request. Inoue was stunned. By this time Inoue's newly appointed successor, Miura Gorō, had already arrived in Korea as the new Japanese minister. News of the failed "contribution" would leave Muira "with no leg to stand on," Inoue warned.[87] The cordial relationship Inoue had tried to build up with the king and queen would collapse. Inoue departed for Tokyo, but as he had predicted, without the forthcoming "gift," relations between the king and queen and the Japanese legation quickly cooled.

RETURN OF THE TAEWŎN'GUN

Around the time of Pak Yŏng-hyo's ouster in 1895, Queen Min had confided to the Russian consul, General Karl I. Weber, that she was secretly planning to thwart Japanese inroads into Korea. She needed Russia's help. "Although Japan and Korea are neighbors, there exists an ocean between them whereas Korea and Russia share a land border and are real neighbors," the queen told him. Moreover, Japan was afraid of Russia. "This is shown by the fact that Japan was forced to return the Liaodong Peninsula this spring. Russia will never interfere with Korea's independence so if we rely on the Russians and seek their protection, we will be safe."[88]

To take advantage of the queen's outreach, and to strengthen Russia's influence in Korea, Weber maneuvered to place his in-law, Antoinette Sontag, in an official position in the Korean court.[89] The efficient housekeeper and cook at the Russian legation, Sontag was also something of a polyglot. Originally from Alsace-Lorraine, she spoke Korean fluently in addition to speaking Russian, English, and her native German and French. Officially, Sontag was tasked with establishing a handicraft school for the daughters of court families, but her frequent visits with the queen gradually deepened into a warm friendship.[90] As a result, she often knew what was happening at the court before anyone else did and would secretly pass information to Weber.

The intimacy created a dangerous situation for the queen. "If this friendship had happened at a different time and under different circumstances, namely, during a period of calm in Korea, it might have been all fine and good," recalled Russian architect Afanasy Seredin-Sabatin, who knew both Weber and Sontag. "However, from the perspective of the Japanese, Sontag was a representative of Russia, the same country that had called for Japan to restrain its ambitions and give up its dream of possessing the Liaodong Peninsula. The Japanese watched the queen gradually abandon her customary discretion to begin to act independently as if the Japanese no longer had any role to play in Korea." Nor did Sontag try to hide her contempt for Japanese officials. She criticized them openly and mockingly. "Queen Min's friendship with Ms. Sontag at such a dramatic and unsuitable time increased the ire of the Japanese and pro-Japanese Koreans to the boiling point."[91]

Alarmed by Russia's growing influence, members of the pro-Japanese Korean cabinet began to fear for their own lives. There were rumors that a plot was afoot to assassinate them and install a pro-Russian government. It had also come to their attention that the queen had secretly made a pact with Weber to lease a northern ice-free port to Russia, a long-held Russian objective. Fearful she would reassert control over the government and pave the way for Russian domination over the peninsula, disaffected officials turned once again to the Taewŏn'gun to vent their frustrations.[92]

Miura, also wary of the growing Russian hold over the queen, devised a scheme to counter it. Perhaps he could convince the Taewŏn'gun to instigate another coup and infer that Japan would support him. Sugimura was skeptical. The scheme had been tried the year before with disastrous results. "The Taewŏn'gun has a tremendous lust for power and he is very unreliable," Sugimura explained to the new Japanese minister. "It is futile to work with him." Miura, however, saw no other option. "If we just leave things the way they are, we will watch helplessly as we lose Korea to Russia," he lamented.[93]

Muira's desperation led to a fantastical plot: the assassination of Queen Min to rid Korea of the principal player in its turn toward Russia. The plan was hatched with the Taewŏn'gun's reluctant blessing. Miura called on Adachi Kenzō, owner of the Japanese-language newspaper *Kanjō shimpō,* to gather up some Japanese *sōshi* [thugs] to participate in the plot.[94] He would also rely on Japanese legation guards disguised in Korean civilian clothing "so that no foreigners would be aware of our connection with the affair." But it was the Japanese-trained Korean Army, known as the *hullyŏndae* (Drilled Troops, Jap. *kunrentai*) that would play a vanguard role by securing the palace premises.

Established during the fall of 1894 on the recommendation of Inoue, the two-thousand-strong, well-equipped *hullyŏndae* were set up as a model unit for the development of a new Korean army.[95] Under pressure from the court, however, the queen's ally, Hong Kye-hun, was appointed commander. Hong, a regimental commander during the 1882 Imo incident, had played a decisive role in aiding the queen's escape from the palace. During the Tonghak Uprising of spring 1894, he led government forces to suppress the rebellion in Chŏnju, but then negotiated an armistice with Chŏn Pong-jun's Tonghak army. Upon his return to Seoul, he was made commander of the *hullyŏndae,* but his appointment created dissension within the ranks of young Korean officers who saw his alliance with the queen as a barrier to military modernization and progress.[96] Cho Hŭi-yŏn and U Pŏm-sŏn, commanders of the First Battalion and the Second Battalion, respectively, confided to Sugimura that they had become increasingly alarmed by the precarious state of Korean affairs and were committed to backing the Taewŏn'gun. The planned coup thus involved a mutiny of what can be considered Korea's first modern army.[97]

DEATH OF QUEEN MIN

There were roughly fifteen hundred palace guards on duty during the early morning hours of October 8, 1895. They scattered once the *hullyŏndae* penetrated the northeastern wall. Alerted to the commotion, Hong Kye-hun had rushed to the palace. He told his troops to disband but "they responded that he was no longer in command and they would no longer follow his orders." Shortly thereafter, he was shot and killed, presumably by one of his subordinate officers.[98] The palace had been shorn of its defenses.[99] At that moment Japanese *sōshi,* led by Adachi, entered the palace grounds in search of the queen.

But no one had ever seen the queen in person and thus had no idea what she actually looked like. Not even the Japanese ministers, Inoue and Miura, had ever laid eyes on her despite frequent visits to the palace. "Men and women are not allowed to meet and as a result, I was not able to meet the queen in person," Miura explained.[100] A screen had always been set up between her and outside visitors. Once the plotters entered the palace grounds, a frantic search for the queen ensued.[101] Inside the royal family's dwelling, Japanese *sōshi,* numbering a dozen or more, rushed in with swords drawn to search the private rooms. "They seized all the palace women they could catch, dragging them around by the hair and beating them and demanding where the queen was."[102] The crown prince was with his father when three *sōshi* entered the family dwelling. Kojong promptly fainted. The young prince stated in his remarkable eyewitness account that a palace official ran up to the men, putting himself between the Japanese and the room where the queen was hiding. His arms were promptly sliced off as one of the *sōshi* began shouting: "Where is the

208

queen!? Where is the queen!?" "At this moment the queen tried to escape through a corridor," the crown prince recalled. "A Japanese followed her and caught her. She was pushed to the floor and then [someone] stomped on her chest three times and stabbed her."[103]

Still, it wasn't clear to the Japanese whether they had killed the queen. Only later after they returned to the scene of the crime to examine the corpses of the ladies did they positively identify her. "The Japanese soldiers received information that she had a bald spot above her temple and they found a woman with such a mark."[104] Ultimately, it was a young girl, a favorite of the queen who had visited the palace often, who identified her.[105] The queen's body was taken out the western gate to a nearby garden, where it was doused with fuel and burned.[106]

Miura arrived at the palace just as the Japanese assassins were finishing up their dirty deed. There he was joined by the Taewŏn'gun. The Japanese minister did not go to the family quarters where the terrible events had taken place but instead had an audience with the king, shaken and crying, in the adjoining Changan Pavilion. Documents were presented to Kojong for him to sign beginning with the appointment, once again, of the Taewŏn'gun as regent.[107] Two days later, on October 10, the king's decree, without his signature, announcing the queen's demotion to commoner status was published in the *Official Gazette*, signed by Kojong's ministers.[108] It read in part:

> It is now thirty-two years since We ascended the throne but Our rule has not extended wide. Queen Min introduced her relatives to the Court and place them around Our person, whereby she made dull Our senses, exposed the people to extortion, put Our government in disorder, selling offices and titles. Hence tyranny prevailed all over the country and robbers arose in all quarters. Under these circumstances, the foundation of Our dynasty was in imminent peril. We knew the extreme of her wickedness, but could not dismiss and punish her because of helplessness and fear of her party . . . We have endeavored to discover her whereabouts, but as she does not come forth and appear. We are convinced that she is not only unfit and unworthy of the Queen's rank but also that her guilt is excessive and brimful . . . So We hereby depose her from the rank of Queen and reduce her to the level of the lowest class.[109]

It was a damning document, all the more so because the Korean officials who signed it already knew the queen was dead.[110] But it also highlighted Korean complicity in the plot, which reached the highest levels. Kojong put the blame for the assassination squarely on his four top ministers, Kim Hong-jip, Yu Kil-chun, Cho Ŭi-yŏn, and Chŏng Pyŏng-ha.[111]

Reflecting on the role the Koreans had played in the coup, the newspaper *Dong-a-ilbo* later observed that although "those involved in the plot were thirty to forty Japanese, all the members of Korean enlightenment faction had, in fact, participated."[112] While none of the men had been directly involved in the murder of the queen, the Taewŏn'gun was certainly aware her death would be the inevitable result. The royal family drama had been transformed into an international drama with increasingly high stakes for the global players, embroiling not just China and Japan but also Russia in Korea's domestic affairs. As with the events of 1882, 1884, and 1894, the émeute of 1895 followed a familiar familial pattern that pitted father against son in an ever-widening struggle involving the Great Powers. The only difference this time was that Korea's central player, Queen Min, was dead.

On October 17 Miura was recalled to Japan and officially relieved of his duties. A District Court in Hiroshima would conduct a preliminary inquiry to consider charges against him while he waited in prison. But Miura remained defiant. He justified his actions by stating that the queen, working with Russia, had sought to undermine Japan's efforts "for maintaining the independence of Korea."[113] Her association with the Russians had been dangerous and foolish, creating the potential for chaos on the peninsula, a threat not only to the future independence of Korea but to the security of Japan. "The émeute [of October 1895] crushed the mischief," Miura's counsel Masujima later argued in his defense. "The form of the queen's conspiracy was criminal, and the Japanese minister was justified in preventing the execution of the criminal attempt."[114]

Forty-eight Japanese connected with the October incident were confined in Hiroshima but none of them were brought into court to face charges. By the time the trials opened on January 14, 1896, it was clear the defendants would not be punished.[115] Despite having presented evidence that Miura, Sugimura, and others were involved in the plot to assassinate the queen, the judge of the preliminary inquiry nevertheless determined there was insufficient evidence of a premeditated crime, and they were released.[116]

The irony of the émeute of October 8, 1895, was that it had paved the way for Russian domination of the peninsula, not prevented it. On February 11, 1896, Kojong, accompanied by the crown prince, took refuge in the Russian legation. From there Kojong dismissed his old pro-Japanese cabinet and appointed a new pro-Russian one. Prime Minister Kim Hong-jip and Minister of Agriculture Chŏng Pyŏng-ha were denounced as traitors, seized inside the palace, and taken to the police station, where they were decapitated. Russia's position in Korea now seemed unassailable. As for the Taewŏn'gun, his life was spared, for he was still the king's father. Retiring from politics, he never spoke about the episode again.[117] Miura's dream of "securing Korea's independence" had turned into a nightmare. With Russia's ascendency in Korea now secured, its leaders turned their gaze toward Manchuria.

CHAPTER ELEVEN

CONTINENTAL POWER

The Triple Intervention changed Russia's thinking about its plans for the Trans-Siberian Railway. Preliminary surveys of the Amur sector between Khabarovsk and Stretinsk (Sretensk) along the Amur River demonstrated the difficulties of proceeding in that direction. The vast land was covered with thick primeval coniferous forests but without an admixture of deciduous evergreen trees and shrubs, making the soil infertile.[1] The climate of the Amur was also taxing. Russians could endure the bitter winter cold, but summer brought terrible heat and humidity. Dangerous wild animals roamed the forests, including the fearsome Siberian tigers. In the 1880s, Rear Admiral Kopitov introduced the idea of building the railway through Irkutsk to Kyakhta and then through Chinese territory from Abagaytuy, Qiqihar, Jilin, and Ning'an to Nikolsk (Nikolskoye) in the Ussuri region.[2] Finance Minister Sergei Witte had been sympathetic to the idea but such a plan was fraught with difficulties. For one thing, it would mean building the railway across foreign territory. China would never agree to such a proposal. The idea of a Russo-Chinese economic alliance in 1892 was preposterous given the poisonous atmosphere that existed between the two countries in the wake of their chronic border disputes and Russian intrigues in Korea that undermined Chinese interests.

China's disastrous outcome in the Sino-Japanese War brought new opportunities for Russia, however. In the spring of 1895, while Itō and Li were discussing the terms of peace at Shimonoseki, Witte thought seriously about obviating the obstacles presented by the Amur route and striking across Manchuria. After the Triple Intervention in April, and basking in the warmth of a grateful China, Tsar Nicholas II was presented with a formal petition for authority to "reconnoiter for a Manchurian line" that foresaw saving "about 700 *versts* in length as compared with the Amur line, and 35 million rubles in expenditures."[3] Witte followed on July 6/(OS) June 24, 1895, with a plan for forming a Russian bank with French participation to "strengthen Russian economic influence in China as a counterweight to the enormous economic influence which the British had acquired there, thanks to their seizure of the administration of the Chinese maritime customs."[4] In order to make the first indemnity payment to Japan under the terms of the Shimonoseki Treaty, the Chinese needed a loan.

Witte would secure the loan for China. Working with both skill and skullduggery, the finance minister negotiated the terms of a loan with French bankers. China would receive 100 million rubles in gold guaranteed by Russia. China would make payments on the loan using revenue from its Maritime Customs Service. If it did not keep up with the payments, Russia would have the right to intervene in the Customs Service operations.[5] An agreement on the loan was reached on July 5/June 23. Witte had pulled off an impressive diplomatic feat: by guaranteeing the loan China needed in order to pay off its war indemnity to Japan, he ensured that China became indebted to Russia.[6]

Russian intrigue did not stop there. The day after the loan was signed, Witte introduced to his French counterparts a proposal "to create a Russian bank with French participation and under the protection of the Russian government." The bank would service Chinese government loans, acquire concessions for railway constructions, and set up telegraphic communications, among other projects. Its defining task, as Witte confided in his report to the tsar on July 26/14 was "to strengthen Russian economic influence which the British had acquired there, thanks in the main to their seizure of the administration of the Chinese maritime customs." The French accepted the proposal. The bank was capitalized with six million rubles, of which five-eighths were put up by French banks and the remaining three-eighths by Russia.[7] The new Russo-Chinese Bank was established on December 10/22, 1895. It was one of the largest financial institutions in East Asia. Russian diplomat Roman Rosen later labeled it no more than "a slightly disguised branch of the Russian treasury." The bank wholly served Russian national interests.[8]

In May 1895, Prince M. I. Khilkov, the future minister of ways and communications, approached the tsar for permission to begin surveying part of the railway route. In September an expedition of surveyors with translators and a security escort of Russian Cossack troops embarked for Manchuria. The survey expedition placed Arturo Cassini, the Russian ambassador to China, in an awkward position. Following the conclusion of the loan agreement in June, the Chinese became suspicious as rumors circulated that the Russians were planning on constructing a railroad along the Nerchinsk-Qiqihar-Vladivostok routes, which cut through Chinese territory in Manchuria.[9] "It looks like a bad joke," Deputy Foreign Minister V. N. Lamsdorf lamented. "While we are persistently refuting any intention to build the railway through Manchuria, our engineers are doing wide-scale research there!" S. M. Dukhovsky, governor-general of Amur Province, proposed that "the engineers pretend that they are regular travelers," but the idea was nixed by Cassini. "The job entrusted to them is too conspicuous and the Chinese workers who accompany the engineers might get the wrong idea and attach military importance to their presence, which is dangerous for China."[10]

Cassini was able to convince the Qing government that the survey party had no imperialist intentions, and, ironically, "local government officials were [eventually] ordered to protect the Russian engineers." However, Cassini was frustrated that he was not kept informed. "Repeated trips of our officers and engineers to Manchuria are starting to bother China. I ask you if it is possible to inform me about our goals so that I can express our position in communication with Chinese ministers?" What may have appeared at first to be a coordinated effort for the railway project was, in reality, rather haphazard. The decision to send the survey expedition to Manchuria in the summer of 1895 without informing the Russian ambassador, much less seek Chinese clearance, risked alienating China at a critical time. "Everyone, especially the French, has used the current situation in China for their own advantage while we continue to position ourselves as completely selfless," Cassini warned. "At the moment we enjoy great prestige in China, but the feeling of gratitude is very volatile."[11]

INTO MANCHURIA

The physical difficulties of constructing a railway line through Manchuria were formidable: 125 miles of "broad stretches of high, cold and marshy plateau" similar to those of the eastern Gobi Desert, 364 miles of mountainous terrain that rose to over three thousand feet, and 300 miles across the marshy Sungari River valley that is inundated during the monsoon

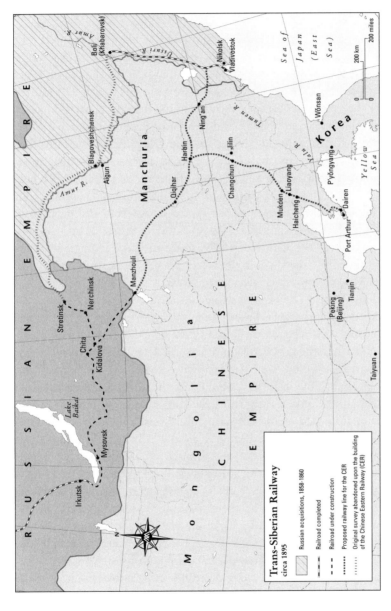

Trans-Siberian Railway
circa 1895

Russian acquisitions, 1858-1860
Railroad completed
Railroad under construction
Proposed railway line for the CER
Original survey abandoned upon the building of the Chinese Eastern Railway (CER)

The proposed new railway line through Manchuria from Nikolsk in 1895. Construction through Manchuria began in 1897 two years later, Russia extracted from China an agreement to allow an extension to Port Arthur and Dairen. The Amur Railway, abandoned for the proposed railway line, was eventually completed in 1916.

season, transforming it into "one expanse of liquid mud." The final stretch, from Ningguta (Ning'an) to Nikolsk was challenged by the "yielding character of the soil," unsuitable as a firm foundation without extensive fill.[12]

It was this final stretch of terrain that Khilkov wanted explored. The team would be led by an engineer, N. S. Sviagin. On August 30/18, 1895, they boarded the riverboat *Putyatin* at Khabarovsk on the Amur River and headed to the Ussuri River, which they followed south to Vladivostok. They then trekked on foot westward to the Russian town of Nikolsk where General Unterberger, military governor of the Primorskaya Oblast, had arranged for them to join other members of the survey team: they included Grigory Alexeevich Mosim, "a good comrade . . . with an excellent command of Chinese and of the customs of the country"; Pavel S. Tenchinsky, the team doctor who "also specialized in topography"; four Chinese soldiers; and a convoy of ten armed Cossacks.[13] From Nikolsk, the group would follow the Razdol'naya River to where it merges with the Suifen River at the Chinese border. Once in Chinese territory, they would continue to follow the river west and then trek northward, following the Mudanjiang River. They hoped to arrive in Ningguta (Ning'an), their final destination, before the winter set in.

At Nikolsk, Unterberger warned Sviagin that permission for the survey expedition had not been officially granted by the Chinese government. When they reached the border, Sviagin recalled, "the decision to cross into Chinese territory would have to be my own personal one." This was Unterberger's way to cover himself should complications arise between the Russian team and Chinese authorities. Sviagin, however, did not fear Chinese reaction so much as the constant threat posed by the fierce maundering bands of honghuzi (Red Beards) bandits. "All the merchants we met on the way [to the Chinese border] and generally all the people with means to do so, were accompanied by an armed escort," he remarked. "Using their proximity to the Russian border, the honghuzi often carried out attacks on our land; for example, in 1894, they attacked the Muravev-Amursky station, which was the final station open on the Southern Ussuri railroad. Earlier cases of armed honghuzi attacks were a regular occurrence. In 1874, the honghuzi looted and burned part of Ningguta itself."[14]

Apart from the honghuzi, Sviagin did not expect to encounter much trouble, for the region was sparsely populated. The vast emptiness of the land startled him. The group traveled for weeks without encountering a single village although "signs of erased settlements were everywhere."

Preliminary survey of engineers for the Chinese Eastern Railway (CER), led by N. S. Sviagin (center right), October 1895. (E. Kh. Nilus, *Istoricheskiĭ obzor' Kitaĭskoĭ vostochnoĭ zhelieznoĭ dorogi, 1896–1923 g.g.* [Historical survey of the Chinese Eastern Railway, 1896–1923] [Harbin, 1923], 41, 47)

Except for a few far-flung military outposts scattered along the way, the region was for the most part uninhabited. He opined that one reason may have been the Manchu invasions of the early seventeenth century. "The [Manchu] raids reached the Suifen between 1607 and 1615 and the invaders took away more than 20,000 people," he observed. "The raids destroyed the region which was quickly overtaken by forests." Moreover, the great monsoons and constant flooding may have also "coincided with the devastating Manchu invasions that led to the destruction of the culture that had once existed here." Such conditions, he surmised, "drove the population to flee to different regions, preventing the possible rebirth of the land that is now destroyed but was once cultivated."[15]

Winter was already approaching when the survey team arrived in Ningguta. Apart from a few close encounters with the honghuzi, everything had gone smoothly and according to plan. It was Sviagin's opinion that the railway could be built. He was full of praise for the Chinese officials he met along the way. "Although my traveling companions and I were private individuals with a scientific goal and without any official representation, we were met with courtesy, hospitality, and expressions of sympathy." Despite General Unterberger's warning, he had not yet encountered any difficulties with Chinese authorities. Dr. Tenchinsky was "delighted" he had managed to collect an honghuzi specimen. "Near the road, we found a human skull under a tree—a trace of the Chinese custom of putting the heads of executed criminals on display. Here they [Chinese soldiers] had executed a honghuzi and hung his head from a tree . . . [and] the doctor took it with him, being interested in Manchu skulls."[16]

A detachment of Chinese soldiers came to meet Sviagin's team as they approached Ningguta, the largest gathering of Chinese people they had met during the three-month-long journey. Mosim explained the scientific purpose of the expedition but did not mention the railway which, in any case, the soldiers would not have known anything about. The Chinese appeared satisfied and ordered the group to follow them into the town. Sviagin recalled a puzzling scene that seemed to sum up for him the meaning of Manchuria, which held "only pitiful traces of culture artificially placed there by the Chinese government." "As we entered Ningguta, the first thing I noticed was a cemetery without [individual] graves. Right alongside the roadside, in the shadow of several large trees, coffins were thrown chaotically on the open ground. Several of them were open and decaying corpses were visible; some corpses had no coffins at all." The spectacle disturbed him. "In a country with a cult of ancestors and reverence for the dead where the belief in the durable connection between the living and the deceased figured into every facet of private life and in the public order of things, such a display struck me to the core." Here was a corner of the Chinese Empire that appeared to exist apart from China.[17]

LI-WITTE MEETINGS

Would the Chinese trade away concession rights to this hinterland for better relations with Russia? While Sviagin and his team were finishing up their survey mission in Manchuria, in Saint Petersburg, Foreign Minister Aleksey Lobanov-Rostovsky, and Finance Minister Witte were discussing the issue of the Chinese Eastern Railway, the name of the line that would cut through Manchuria. Lobanov-Rostovsky wrote to Nicholas II in November that they hoped the tsar would instruct Ambassador Cassini to begin negotiations with Beijing concerning the building of the railroad through Chinese territories.[18] The decision to build the line from

Chita to Nikolsk through Manchuria was opposed by both Amur Province governor-general Dukovsky and Count Kapnist, director of the Asiatic Department at the Ministry of Foreign Affairs. Both men argued that it was wrong to consider only the lower costs of construction, because building a line through foreign territory would be impossible without coercive measures and even possibly a military occupation. It might also lead to the partition of China and the seizure by Britain "of such naval bases as might secure to her in perpetuity predominance on the Yellow Sea." Kapnist advocated for building the railway through Russian territory along the Amur. "This railway would be a bit longer," he argued, "but it would be better situated," meaning less political risk.[19]

Dukhovsky echoed Kapnist's concern that the need for substantial Russian military force would be unavoidable, as China "would otherwise have countless opportunities to interrupt the operation of the railway." If "the slightest political complication arises," he warned, "we would be forced to defend the railway line which will long be foreign to us." He considered the project to be "a great historical blunder."[20]

In the end Nicholas sided with Witte and Lobanov-Rostovsky. Preliminary studies had shown that a line along the Amur route would be beset with serious technical difficulties even greater than those facing the Manchuria route. "Much of the line would have to go through steep ridges that would mean the building of tunnel works and the construction of bridges." The bridge across the Amur to Khabarovsk would cost around 12 billion rubles. Moreover, the construction of the Amur line "would negatively influence the Amur River Russian navigation because the railway would compete with it." The Manchurian line also had the advantage of being situated "in a better climate with better soil" whose crops were in high demand. Furthermore, Vladivostok would become the main port in the Far East, linking it to Siberia and European Russia, and would create good conditions for trade "that would not only help develop the Manchurian region but the whole of China."[21]

Cassini was notified in December 1895 to begin talks with the ministers of the Zongli Yamen to secure the necessary cooperation and permission. The talks began in April 1896, and they did not go well.[22] The Zongli Yamen informed Cassini that the Chinese government had decided not to grant a concession to any foreign power or company. An angry Cassini warned that China's stance would "make a most painful" impression in Saint Petersburg and that refusal would "entail the most disastrous consequences for China."[23]

Another opportunity soon arose for Russia to pursue the railway concession. The occasion was Nicholas II's coronation in May 1896. Li Hongzhang was chosen to represent the Chinese emperor at the ceremony in Saint Petersburg.[24] Witte and Lobanov-Rostovsky arranged to meet Li ahead of the ceremony to attempt to convince the viceroy to agree to the Chinese railway concession.

Lobanov-Rostovsky and Witte sat down with Li Hongzhang in Saint Petersburg on May 3. The Russians put forth the same proposition that Cassini had discussed with the Zongli Yamen in Beijing, but this time emphasizing the security aspect. A railway from Russia across Manchuria would enable Russia to quickly come to China's aid in case of a Japanese attack.[25] Li insisted that in exchange for the railway concession, Russia must be willing to sign a mutual defense treaty.[26] He also wanted assurances of Russia's commitment to the principle of integrity of the Chinese Empire. Both Witte and Lobanov-Rostovsky reassured Li that the railroad concessions "will neither be the cause for the invasion of Chinese territory nor the violation of His Majesty the Emperor's sovereign rights." By the end of the meeting, on May 8, Li appeared to be favorably disposed. He wrote to the Zongli Yamen about the treaty the next day: "The main idea is that if anything happens to China, Russia will stand up and help us."[27]

1896 SINO-RUSSIAN SECRET TREATY

Less than a week later, Witte presented Li Hongzhang with a draft of the proposed treaty in which the Manchurian railroad would be offered as the price the Chinese would pay for Russian protection in the event of a Japanese invasion of the territory of China or Korea. It also stipulated that neither party was to conclude a separate peace agreement without the other's knowledge and that the alliance would be effective for ten years from the date the railroad began operating.[28] Lobanov-Rostovsky told Witte that he would present the draft to the tsar for approval. The following day, however, when Witte saw the draft, he was alarmed to see that the article about the defensive alliance against Japan had been changed. "In its revised form," Witte recalled, "the article stated that in the event of an attack on China, we were obliged to come to the defense of China, and that in the event of an attack on the Maritime Region, China was obliged to come to our defense." The change was a fundamental error. "There was a world of difference between a defensive alliance against Japan," he wrote "and a defensive alliance against all [third] powers." Witte told Lobanov-Rostovsky that the original wording must be restored.

Yet, to his distress, Witte discovered that on the appointed day (June 3 / May 22) to sign the treaty, the offending line had not been changed and that "we were still obligated to defend China against attack by any power." He recalled:

> I went over to Prince Lobanov-Rostovsky and told him that the article had not been changed in the way that the emperor had wanted. I thought the omission had been deliberate on the foreign minister's part, but suddenly to my surprise, he struck himself on the forehead and said "Oh my God! I forgot to tell the secretaries to rewrite this article according to the first draft." He then showed great presence of mind. He looked at his watch, which showed 12:15 PM. Then he clapped his hands and when servants appeared, he ordered them to serve lunch. (Lunch was to have been served after the signing.) Then, turning to Li Hongzhang and the others, he suggested that since it was afternoon, we should all eat lest the food be spoiled and leave the signing till later. All of us, except two secretaries went to lunch. While we were eating they recopied the treaty in the form in which I had given it to the foreign minister in Petersburg. By the time we were ready for signing, the old copies were gone and the new ones ready.[29]

As it turned out, the change was of crucial significance and would have serious consequences for China and the region. That Li Hongzhang failed to notice the restored original wording and signed the treaty without protest was a critical oversight.[30] Russia's refusal in 1897 to prevent Germany's occupation of Qingdao would reveal the dire consequence of this tragic mistake.

The key article on the railway concession in the treaty signed in Moscow on June 3 / May 22, 1896, by Witte, Lobanov-Rostovsky, and Li stated:

> Article IV: In order in the future to facilitate the rapid and safe transportation of Russian troops for opposing the enemy, and for the supply of munitions and provisions, the Chinese Government agrees to let Russia construct a railroad through the territory of Heilungkiang and Kirin to connect with Vladivostok. However, the construction of this railroad is not to be used as a pretext for the infringement of Chinese territory, or encroachment on lawful rights and privileges of His Imperial Majesty of the Emperor of China. The Chinese Government will entrust

the Russo-Chinese Bank with the management of the railroad matter. The Chinese Minister to Russia and the Bank shall consult on the spot and decide upon the terms contract.[31]

In other words, China would grant Russia concession through Chinese territory by the direct route from Chita to Vladivostok but the concession implied no territorial designs by Russia; nor did China forfeit its sovereign rights to the concession. The construction and administration of the railway were to be turned over to a private company, the Chinese Eastern Railway (CER).[32]

Witte had attained, at minimum cost, all he wanted from the treaty: the right to build the railroad through Manchuria using the CER, which, although mostly financed by French bankers, was in actuality an arm of the Russian government. Just a month after his coronation, Nicholas II was riding high on the diplomatic triumphs achieved in only a few months. Witte congratulated him heartily: "China has finally broken its century-old policy and allowed Russia to construct a railway through its most revered Manchurian province," he wrote elatedly. "This is a very important event and it has come about due to your Majesty's wisdom, vision, and perseverance. It is difficult to predict all the important consequences [that this event will yield] but I already know that it will be the subject of one of the most important pages written about Russia's history in the Far East."[33]

38TH PARALLEL

While the Russians were celebrating, the mood in Japan had turned sour. On October 28, excerpts of the document exposing the essence of the secret treaty were published even as both Witte and Li continued to publicly deny its existence. The effect was explosive and evoked fierce backlash against the alliance. Chinese provincial governors criticized the treaty for the precedent it set for other powers to seek similar territorial concessions. The revelations also had worrying implications for Japan and its interest in Korea.[34] The "secret" treaty was understood as an "anti-Japanese secret alliance."[35]

Foreign Minister Lobanov-Rostovsky understood that Japan was angry and willing to defend its interests in Korea "at all hazards, even at the risk of war."[36] Colonel Vogek, the Russian military observer in the Sino-Japanese War, was also clear on that point; neither China nor Britain, he argued, was the real threat to Russia in the Far East. "Japan is the most important and is an extremely grave factor."[37] Until the Manchurian line was up and running, Lobanov-Rostovsky counseled that the best policy was not to antagonize Japan and to come to a temporary agreement with the Japanese about Korea.

Japan's civil and military leaders Itō and Yamagata were also eager to avoid a confrontation with Russia. Arriving in Moscow during the coronation celebrations, Yamagata proposed to the Russians that Korea be divided along the 38th parallel, an eerie prelude to the same division that occurred nearly fifty years later to demarcate the American and Russian occupation zones after World War II. Lobanov-Rostovsky rejected the proposal outright but agreed to jointly recognize Korea's "independence." In June 1896 the two nations agreed to limit the number of troops they would station in Korea, help the Korean king build up his military and police force, and help manage his finances, with loans if necessary.[38] Politically, the agreement was a major setback for Japan because it recognized equal rights and status for both Russia and Japan on the peninsula. The Japanese had just concluded a war with China to win exclusive rights in Korea. Now they were forced to share equal rights with Russia.

Japan was not the only power aggrieved by Russia's moves. German Emperor Kaiser Wilhelm II also felt shortchanged. He had supported the Russian intervention against Japan with considerably more enthusiasm than the French, and yet, unlike France, Germany had not received any material benefit for backing Witte's schemes. Unlike either the British or the French, the Germans had acquired few colonial possessions befitting a true empire.

Wilhelm II settled on acquiring Qingdao on China's southern coast of the Shandong Peninsula. In 1896 Prince Radolin, Germany's ambassador to Russia, began making discreet inquiries on Qingdao with the newly appointed foreign minister, Mikhail Nikolaevich Muravev. (Lobanov-Rostovsky had died unexpectedly of heart failure while on a trip with the tsar in August 1896.) Radolin approached the subject with Muravev in July 1897. Despite this warning, Nicholas II was taken by surprise by Wilhelm's "ambush" when the two met on July 17. Wilhelm asked pointblank whether "he [Nicholas] would object if Germany should cast anchor in Kiaochow [Qingdao]." Nicholas, without thinking, replied in the negative.[39]

Nicholas regretted his words. He confided to his uncle, Grand Duke Alexei Alexandrovich, that he had been "tricked" by his German cousin.

The Grand Duke, who knew something about naval ports, replied that because Nicholas had not given Wilhelm his consent in writing, the tsar could withdraw the offer anytime. Nicholas waved him off. "No, no, I have given my word and I cannot back out. It is most vexing."[40] When Wilhelm dispatched a squadron of ships to occupy the Shandong port city of Qingdao in November 1897, using the murder of German missionaries as a pretext, the Chinese government immediately asked the Russian government for help. But Muravev, seeing an opening, used the Chinese request to justify moving into Port Arthur and Dairen instead. "Thanks to the Chinese request," Muravev argued, "we could easily explain our occupation of any location in Chinese territory by our desire to have a firm support for our squadron in case of further adverse situations for China which may occur in the Pacific Ocean."[41] Moreover, since Russia had decided to construct the Manchurian line, it was imperative to protect it from the possibility of foreign incursions into the Liaodong Peninsula.

BETRAYAL

The proper course of action would have been to compel the Germans to withdraw. When Witte heard of the plan to occupy Port Arthur and Dairen, he was bitterly opposed, insisting such an action would be contrary to the "spirit" of the secret treaty of 1896. "It is inappropriate for Russia to do what we promised to protect China from [occupation of Chinese territory]," he announced. "We should not follow the German example and we should do everything possible to dissuade Germany from occupying Qingdao."[42] Muravev responded that the treaty had obligated Russia to help China only against Japan. The German occupation of Qingdao was not viewed as falling under the terms of the treaty.[43] Nicholas at first sided with Witte, then changed his mind and backed Muravev. He was convinced by the foreign minister's report that if Russian forces did not occupy the ports, "England would."[44] Russian ships sailed into Dairen and Port Arthur during the first days of December 1897.

The Chinese were stunned. The diary of a bewildered Weng Tonghe, Emperor Guangxu's tutor, revealed the Chinese anguish. "Word was received of massive Russian troop movement at Port Arthur," Weng wrote. "We weighed the present situation. The various ministers all wiped away their tears. What sort of circumstance is this? We deeply bear the blame." The emperor was furious. On March 22 he ordered Li Hongzhang and Prince Gong to appear before him.

Emperor Guangxu became very angry and upbraided Prince Gong and Li Hongzhang to their faces, saying, "You said Russia could be depended upon and signed a treaty with her, giving her great benefit. Now, not only was she unable to prevent [Germany from taking Qingdao] but she herself revokes the treaty and demands land? You call this showing friendliness?" Gong and Li took off their caps [a sign of acknowledging fault] and kowtowed, saying, "If we give Port Arthur and Dairen to them, the secret treaty will still be as before." Guangxu shook with anger. The Empress Dowager Cixi said, "This time, then, do you want war?" Guangxu was silent.[45]

News of Russia's "temporary occupation" of Port Arthur was also greeted with anger and indignation by the Japanese, who were understandably shocked to see Russian ships at the very port from which they had been barred in 1895. Three months later, in an agreement signed between the Chinese and Russian leaders on March 27, 1898, China conferred on Russia the lease of Port Arthur and concession to build a branch line linking the Chinese Eastern Railway to the southern extremity of the Liaodong Peninsula.[46] The Japanese reacted with stunned disbelief.

The new Japanese minister to Saint Petersburg, Hayashi Tadasu, however, saw these ominous developments as an opportunity to consolidate Japan's position in Korea. In early January 1898 he approached Foreign Minister Muravev to see whether an arrangement could be reached.[47] The Japanese government had been pressing for an accord that would give Russia a free hand in Manchuria in exchange for similar freedom of action for Japan in Korea.[48] This formula would be repeatedly proposed by the Japanese and came to be known as Man-Kan kōkan, literally "the exchange of Manchuria for Korea." The Russians knew that Japan had a strong sense of grievance toward its position in China and appeared, at first, to be agreeable to the idea. Their priority lay in building the Manchurian Railway, not antagonizing Japan over Korea, which in any case Russia hoped to obtain eventually. Vice Foreign Minister Lamsdorf later noted, "The fate of Korea, as a future component of the Russian Empire, due to geographical and political considerations, was early predestined for us."[49]

The Nishi-Rosen Agreement of April 25, 1898, fell short of Japan's demand for a free hand in Korea; Russia only admitted to Japan's special commercial and industrial interest on the peninsula. It also placed Russia and Japan on an equal footing in Korea and was thus not a significant improvement over the 1896 Yamagata-Lobanov agreement. Vice minister for foreign affairs Komura Jutarō confessed later that the Nishi-Rosen Agreement amounted to "nothing at all."[50] Certainly, it was not what Hayashi had in mind when he put forth Man-Kan kōkan. But Itō Hiro-bumi, always fearful of antagonizing the Russians, had decided to back down. Japanese finances were in bad shape and military and naval prep-aration would take time. Japan was in no position to fight another war, especially if it had to deal with France and Germany as well as Russia.[51]

The Japanese were not the only ones whose suspicions were aroused by Russian actions in China. The influential *Contemporary Review* com-mented on the alarming state of affairs in the Far East: "The art of European diplomacy seems to have degenerated into the monotonous occupation of watching the progress of Russia," it warned. "To reckon up the recent triumphs of Russian diplomacy we should have to enumerate half the countries of the world. Such an enumeration, however, will do us good, for the singly reason that almost all these triumphs have been won, directly or indirectly, at British expense."[52]

After a lengthy debate in February 1898, the House of Commons passed a resolution stating that "it is of vital importance for the British commerce and influence that the independence of Chinese territory should be maintained."[53] As a countervailing move, Britain forced the Qing to lease the New Territories for ninety-nine years through the Convention for the Extension of Hong Kong Territory to ensure the security of Hong Kong. One month later, in July 1898, the British occupied Weihaiwei.

Witnessing the spectacle of Russia's "tortuous treachery," the Ameri-cans' only response was indignation. "I am thoroughly aware that since Washington's Farewell Address was uttered we have been, what we may be called, innately conservative on the question of interfering in the af-fairs of foreign powers," wrote American minister to China Charles Denby. "Still, while preserving all the sanctity of the 'Farewell Address' it is worth enquiring whether there is not some middle ground on which we may stand with advantage . . . [and] announce our disapproval of acts of brazen wrong, and spoliation, perpetrated by other nations towards China."[54] Unfortunately, the United States had not yet come up with a precise formulation of what that "middle ground" might be.

CHAPTER TWELVE

MARITIME POWER

Judging from his early career in the United States Navy, Captain Alfred Thayer Mahan did not seem destined to become one of the greatest strategists and geopolitical theorists of his day. In 1883, then in his mid-forties, Mahan was the commander of one of the worst ships in the Navy, the USS *Wachusett*. The ship had recently returned from an extended cruise in the South Pacific and was badly in need of repair. The American minister at Lima, Peru, was helping to negotiate a peace treaty in the war between Chile and Peru that was drawing to a close. Mahan's assignment was to sail between Ecuador, Peru, and Chile to protect American citizens working in those countries.[1] It was not a high-profile commission. Mahan's command of a "third-rate screw" in a dead-end assignment appeared to signal the approaching end to a relatively unremarkable naval career.[2]

Fortunately, Mahan was given the chance to change his career and life path. In 1884 he received a letter from Commodore Stephen B. Luce offering him a teaching position at the soon-to-be-established Naval War College in Newport, Rhode Island. At Luce's urging, the Navy had decided to establish a college devoted to the systematic study of naval history and strategy. Luce remembered his bright former executive officer and thought Mahan would be a good fit for the new institution. Mahan would be given wide latitude to come up with a course on naval history that would enable naval students "to group together in an intelligent manner certain classes of facts, by the generalization of which he may formulate for himself principles for his guidance as the Commander of a sea-army fleet preparatory to war."[3] It was an exciting opportunity and Mahan gladly accepted the position.

To prepare for the course, Mahan immersed himself in the study of history. At the time, he had shared the US Navy's antihistorical bias that "the naval history of the past was wholly past; of no use at all to the present." How, then, could he make the past relevant for the present day? His answer came from Callao, Peru, "as dull a coast town as one could dread to see." At the English Club library he came upon a translation of the great German historian Theodor Mommsen's three-volume *History of Rome*. The book changed his life.

Mahan was particularly struck by Mommsen's account of the third-century BCE Second Punic War between Carthage and the Roman Republic, one of the deadliest conflicts of ancient times. In describing the Carthaginian general Hannibal's invasion of Rome, Mommsen emphasized the superiority of the Roman navy in defeating Hannibal's army. "It suddenly struck me," Mahan later wrote, "whether by some chance phrase of the author I do not know, how different things might have been could Hannibal have invaded Italy by sea, as the Romans often had in Africa, instead of by the long land route; or could he, after arrival, have been in free communication with Carthage by water."[4] Hannibal eventually abandoned the struggle in Italy, putting an end to Carthage's Mediterranean empire. Hannibal's loss, Mahan concluded, ultimately came down to his inability to control the sea. His insight on the role and influence of sea power in history and, by extension, the essential nature of and conflict between continental and maritime powers, would form the nucleus of his life's work: to show how "the control of the sea, commercial and military, had been an object powerful to influence the policies of nations; and equally a mighty factor in the success or failure of those policies. This remained my guiding aim."[5]

Mahan's Naval War College lectures were eventually published in 1890 as a book, *The Influence of Sea Power upon History, 1660–1783*, his greatest achievement. It was a work of breathtaking range that reflected the conditions of the contemporary world and America's new place within it. Industrial expansion in the nineteenth century had given rise to heightened competition over markets and sources of raw material among the Great Powers that would reward those who mastered better and more efficient trade routes and highways tied to the sea.[6] Anticipating the depression-ridden years of the post-1893 period and Frederick Jackson

Turner's pronouncement that same year about the disappearance of the American frontier, Mahan believed that the United States had to choose whether it would remain a continental power or embrace its destiny as a maritime power.[7] "The internal resources are boundless as compared to with present needs; we can live off ourselves indefinitely in 'our little corner' . . . Yet should that little corner be invaded by a new commercial route through the Isthmus, the United States in her turn may have the rude awakening of those who have abandoned their share in the common birthright of all people, the sea."[8]

At the same time, Mahan was careful to distinguish American expansionism from European imperialism. Whereas Europe's leaders lusted for colonies as sources of raw materials, markets for surplus goods, and areas for settlement, Mahan stressed that the function of America's overseas possessions would be to serve as strategic bases, "stepping stones" to overseas markets in Asia and Latin America.[9] The bases would provide "resting places" where American trading ships can "coal and repair" and provide support to the Navy that protected and defended maritime commerce. "Control of the sea, by maritime commerce and naval supremacy, means predominant influence in the world," he explained. This is because "however great the wealth produced by the land, nothing facilitates the necessary exchanges as does the sea."[10]

The power of Mahan's maritime message was that it could be translated into a concrete program of action. His approach to American expansionism in the 1890s provided the intellectual justification of why and how the United States could expand beyond its continental limits.[11] Not only would it be necessary to build the Isthmian canal (Panama Canal) and join "the two Old Worlds and the two great oceans," but according to his concept of establishing "stepping stones," the annexation of the Philippines and Guam was necessary.[12] War with Spain resulted in the acquisition of these new "coaling stations" in December 1898. To these were added Hawaii, which was under de facto control of American sugar planters since 1893 and annexed in July. In 1899 the Navy took Wake Island, so a jagged line of strategic bases now extended from California to the Philippines via Hawaii, Wake, and Guam. These possessions had not come about by any prewar planning as such but were merely "an incident of the commercial expansion"—not "pieces of empire per se" but rather "stepping stones" to China.[13] "The desire of all states," Mahan reiterated, "must be to affect their commercial aims, not by show of military force, still less by violence, but by motives of advantage, mutual to themselves and

China of which commerce and its gains . . . are the most obvious and convincing expression."[14]

The focus on the China market, and on the chain of possessions that would make possible the extension of American political and commercial influence to Asia, would also justify the expansionist philosophy of prominent Americans like John Hay, William McKinley, Henry Cabot Lodge, and Theodore Roosevelt, who supported Mahan's mercantilist vision while repudiating the tenets of imperialism. Here was a doctrine of sea power that even a once stalwart anti-imperialist like Mahan himself could embrace, because the central principle was not the military acquisition of territory but the promotion of trade and commerce.[15] "The simple truth is," Theodore Roosevelt wrote defensively in 1900, "that there is nothing even remotely resembling 'imperialism' or 'militarism' involved in the present development of that policy of expansion which has been part of the history of America from the day when she became a nation."[16]

Mahan's theory of sea power was attractive for another reason. Implicit in his treatise was the view of history of human progress as a perennial struggle between maritime and continental powers. This lesson was demonstrated in Japan's recent confrontation with China. Mahan had paid little attention to the Sino-Japanese War, but the Japanese had paid a great deal of attention to Mahan, and they largely credited their victory over their continental foe by applying Mahanian principles about controlling the seas.[17] Although the Triple Intervention had forced Japanese leaders to surrender the hard-earned gains of 1894–1895, that humiliation also made them realize they needed friends if they were to thwart the rapacious threat of that other continental power, Russia. Americans' perception of the conflict was colored by how it seemed to affirm Mahan's analysis and theory. The "Korean War"—as he called it—was understood as a sign *not* of Japan's continental expansionism but rather of its readiness to work with other maritime powers to open China's vast markets and end "the folly of [China's] exclusive and conservative policy." The war had awakened the Chinese colossus, and American businesses were in a position to take advantage of Japan's good works. "The Japanese are devotedly friendly to the U.S.," Mahan confided to Roosevelt. "I am quite willing to hope it and if so it will much facilitate diplomacy."[18]

While Japan and the United States appeared to be establishing themselves as "Mahanian" maritime powers, using naval power to promote commerce, Russia was following a very different path: the conquest of territory. Witte's plea—that the Chinese Eastern Railway should merely be a peaceful instrument aimed to facilitate international trade—fell on deaf ears when the reality of his policy of *penetration pacific* resulted in what appeared to be the de facto annexation of Manchuria. For Mahan, this was Russia's predicament as a continental power that called for an American response, albeit limited, because of the threat to China. "The distribution of the Russian dominion and the concentration of its mass combined with the fact of its irremediable remoteness from an open sea, render inevitable its dependence upon land routes for the bulk of its intercourse with the debatable ground of Asia," Mahan observed.[19] No wonder Russia should be dissatisfied, and that this "dissatisfaction [should] take the form of aggression—the word most in favor with those of us who dislike all forward movement in nations." Russia's tendency "necessarily must be to advance."[20] Although it would be a mistake for the United States to observe these conflicting interests as "grounds for opposition and hostility," it nevertheless could not stand by idly when confronted "with the imminent dissolution" of those states under threat of Russian expansion.

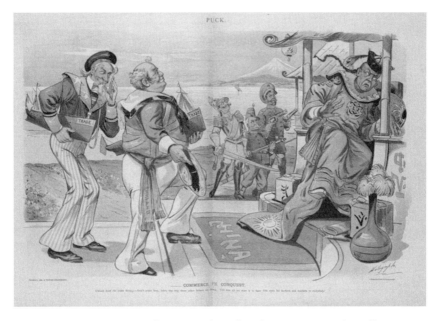

"Commerce versus Conquest," by Louis Dalrymple, February 2, 1898. John Bull "England" and Uncle Sam hold ships labeled "Trade" as they stand before the Chinese emperor, who is frightened by Germany, France, and Russia holding weapons. (Library of Congress Prints and Photographs Division, LC-DIG-ppmsca-28776)

"Such a struggle," Mahan observed, "as is implied in the phrase 'natural selection' involves conflict and suffering that might be avoided . . . by the artificial methods of counsel and agreement."[21]

What might these "artificial methods" be to thwart Russia's imperative to expand its border and prey on weaker powers—namely, China?

OPEN DOOR NOTES

Lord Charles Beresford, a member of the British Parliament and an admiral of the Royal Navy, provided one answer. During the fall of 1898 he had made a tour of China, ostensibly representing the Associated Chambers of Commerce, to investigate "matters relating to securing the trading and commercial interests" of Great Britain. Before his departure, he met with the US ambassador to Britain, John Hay, who encouraged him to meet with American business leaders in China. Returning from China by way of the United States in early 1899, Beresford told Hay that he found Americans "most sympathetic to the idea of a commercial alliance with England based on the integrity of China and the open door for all nations' trade," adding, "I have every hope that in the near future" such an alliance with reference to the open door "may become absolute fact."[22]

Beresford pitched his idea for what he called "The Open Door, or Equal Opportunity for All" to American leaders, including John Hay, who had taken up the post of US secretary of state. Beresford's book *The Break-Up of China* (1899) became one of the most influential works on China policy. "The question for the future, to my mind, is this," Beresford declared. "Are the great trading nations of the world going to allow the Powers that seek only territorial aggrandizement to blockade the wealth of China, and shut the Open Door in their faces?" The solution to the China problem must be to guarantee China's integrity and independence by strengthening the institutions responsible for external and internal security. A secure China provided the necessary foundation for all trading nations to do business with China, and this could be achieved only by instituting a "thorough reorganization of the army and police of the entire country."[23]

Beresford called for Britain to take a leadership role. "Why should not Great Britain, which has the largest vested interest in the country, lead the way, and invite the cooperation of all interested parties, in the organization of China's military and police, in the same spirit as Sir Robert Hart has organized her customs."[24] The reorganization of the military and the police meant the assignment of British and other foreign officers and advisors to essentially run them, as in the customs service Beresford compared it with. He was also sensitive to a potential criticism he perfunctorily dismissed: "If it be said that my policy for the reorganization of the Chinese army and police is a warlike policy, I reply that it is the only plan yet suggested which gives any guarantee of peace . . . without peace commerce must perish."[25]

It was a breathtaking proposal. But it was also unrealistic. While Hay was intrigued by Beresford's idea, he also knew that the US Congress would never approve such an imperial venture, much less one that would entail interfering directly in the domestic affairs of China. Nevertheless, the concept of the Open Door—minus the call for a foreign-officered Chinese army and police—was not entirely abandoned. William W. Rockhill, a close adviser of Hay on Far Eastern affairs, and Rockhill's friend Alfred E. Hippisley, a British inspector of Chinese Maritime Customs, took up Beresford's proposition and, in a furious exchange of letters throughout the summer and fall of 1899, cobbled together the main principles of what would later become known as Hay's famous Open Door Notes. It was this "masterpiece" of American diplomacy, "a double dare to play fair in China, consented to by various world powers, one by one, with Hay's coaxing," that would come to define America's policy toward Asia for generations to come. But its origins did not lie solely with Hay. As Tyler Dennett, John Hay's biographer, later put it: "The notes so long assigned to Hay and then to Rockhill, were in substance the Hippisley notes."[26]

Hippisley got directly to the point in his first letter to Rockhill, dated July 25: the United States had to take the lead in securing the open door because "action by her would be viewed with less suspicion than that of any other Power would be."[27] He believed that it was "suicidal" for the United States to sit back and do nothing, for the "Russification of Peking and of North China will proceed as rapidly . . . precisely in those districts which are the great consumers of American textile fabrics."[28]

As for Beresford's proposal, Hippisley found it completely impractical, even dangerous. Instead Hippisley proposed introducing the principles of "equality of opportunity" as regards commerce and navigation without any commitment on the part of the powers to reform China. "Of course, if the independence and integrity of China can be safeguarded, too, that can be accomplished." The most important thing was not Chinese reform but how to thwart the Russian advance in China and so prevent the partition of that country.[29] The trading powers of the world must cooperate against Russia to secure "an open market for merchandise in China and to remove dangerous sources of international conflict."[30]

Rockhill forwarded a memorandum to Hay on August 28 outlining the main principles of Hippisley's ideas, with slight changes.[31] The Open Door Notes would discourage the kind of "secret" treaties and smoke-filled backroom deals greased with million-ruble bribes such as the one that had allowed Li Hongzhang to sign over the Manchurian railway concession to the Russians. "This understanding of the various Powers," he declared, "would show China that it could not play off the interests of one foreign Power against the other."[32] Rockhill's proposal, in other words, would help save China from itself.

Hay was impressed.[33] A week later he drew up the first Open Door Notes addressed to the Great Powers. It was a direct request that the powers provide formal assurances that "they will in no way interfere with any treaty port or any vested interest within any so-called 'sphere of interest' or leased territory they may have in China."[34] The beauty of the proposal was its simplicity. No joint treaty or joint action of any sort was required. Each power was invited simply to provide formal assurances that in its sphere the trading rights outlined by the Open Door Notes would be recognized. A draft of the notes was dispatched to Britain, Russia, and Germany on September 6, and subsequently to France, Italy, and Japan.

Italy and Japan readily concurred. Britain, ironically, did not pledge Kowloon (in Hong Kong), but for Weihaiwei "and all territory in China which may hereafter be acquired by Great Britain, leased or otherwise," it had no objections.[35] Germany would agree if the others would. France came around after some quibbling over railroad rates. That left Russia.[36]

Hay knew that getting the Russians on board would be the most challenging, but without Russia's assent, the Open Door would amount to nothing. Rockhill's initial discussion with Russian ambassador Cassini in Washington went nowhere.[37] But Hay guided Rockhill to evoke a veiled threat. A negative response, Rockhill told Cassini, "would probably be misinterpreted by the [American] people and would be extremely prejudicial to the friendly relations between the two nations."[38]

In Saint Petersburg, the American ambassador to Russia, Charlemagne Tower, pressured Foreign Minister Muravev, who reluctantly signaled his general compliance to the Open Door so long as the other powers agreed to the same terms, but he would only promise that Russia would not seek "special" privileges for its own subjects to the exclusion of other foreigners.[39] This was tantamount to promising nothing. Nevertheless, Hay wanted "to give the widest possible significance to the Russian reply of which it is capable."[40]

Through perseverance and determination, Hay achieved his goal. On March 20, 1900, he announced that all the powers had assented to his proposal, and that in each case he considered the assent "final and definitive." The passage of the Open Door Notes was a masterful triumph but its real significance lay in actualizing Mahanian principles of commerce and trade as the basis for American expansionism. The timing of Mahan's treatise and Hay's Open Door Notes could not have been more prescient. Following the Spanish-American War, Americans were still grappling with the meaning of their unexpected acquisitions and traditional antipathy toward imperialism. Part of the genius of the Open Door was dispelling charges of territorial aggrandizement while justifying America's expansionism. "Even the anti-Imperialists welcome an Imperial policy which contemplates no conquests but those of commerce," the London *Times* declared.[41] Hay had turned Mahan's theory of sea power into policy and, in the process, signaled to the world the emergence of the United States as a preeminent maritime power. The dawn of the American century thus began in the shadow of China's precipitous fall.

No wonder, then, that the Chinese were furious. China had been left out of the Open Door negotiations. Wu Tingfang, the Chinese minister in Washington, did not know anything about the Open Door Notes until he read about it in the newspaper. China had been relegated to being the main course at the Great Powers diners' club, whose members promised not to eat from each other's plates but served themselves generous helpings from the Chinese trough. After losing Port Arthur, Qingdao, and Weihaiwei, Hay's Open Door Notes was another huge blow to China's pride.[42] "Empress Dowager [Cixi] has been greatly incensed by these negotiations and was endeavoring to organize a combination against the U.S. in consequence," Hippisley confided to Rockhill. "I cannot understand what is meant, or why she should be so angered by actions which is really intended to give China a breathing space in which to let her put her house in order and to introduce financial and administrative reforms, and so to strengthen her position, while there is yet time. I fear, however, whatever this may mean, China is an exemplification of the truth of the saying *quos deus vult perdere prius dementat* [Whom God wishes to destroy, he first drives mad]."[43]

Hippisley's words could not have been more prophetic.

CHAPTER THIRTEEN

BOXERS

The headwaters of the Yellow River, or Huang He (Sorrow of China), originate in the far western reaches of the Qinghai-Tibetan plateau. Cutting across the province of Gansu, the river enters Mongolia, where it forms the boundary line between Shanxi and Shaanxi at the Hukou Waterfall, the largest on the Yellow River. From there it sweeps across the southern tongue of Zhili and traverses Shandong Province. The river had two possible outlets to the sea: one north of the Shandong Peninsula into the Gulf of Zhili; the other about one hundred miles south of the peninsula. Changes in the river's course, when the Huang He would switch its outlets from one to the other, had taken place throughout China's history, usually with devastating results. In 1887 the river overtopped its dikes in Henan Province, causing huge floods that submerged hundreds of towns and villages, leaving nine hundred thousand dead and millions homeless.[1] During his travels in Tibet, William Rockhill visited the Huang He near its source, crossing the plain of Odontala in 1889. "Every year at the seventh month," Rockhill wrote, "the Chinese emperor would send an official to the river's source to sacrifice a white horse and seven or eight white sheep" in order to prevent the river from flooding.[2] The observance of these annual rites did not mean that the emperor did not recognize the need for practical solutions, however. For centuries Chinese engineers were tasked with coming up with a system to hold the river at bay and had developed an intricate network of forests and dikes.

In 1899 a young American engineer named Herbert Hoover was in China and was given an inspection tour of these networks by Qing officials. The twenty-five-year-old Hoover had come to China to start a new job as a mining consultant with the London mine management firm of Bewick, Moreing & Company. His task was to help expand a relationship the company had developed with the Kaiping Coal Mines and its manager, Chang Yanmao. Founded by Li Hongzhang and located above an immense coal reserve, the Kaiping mines were one of the most important of China's new industries. But they were in dire need of capital and Hoover was dispatched to look into the project.[3]

Chang was also the head of the Bureau of Mines, a new department created by a coalition of reformist thinkers who had gathered around Emperor Guangxu, Cixi's nephew, to implement a rigorous reform program. The twenty-seven-year-old emperor had been put on the throne at the age of four when Cixi's son, Emperor Tongzhi, died in 1875 so that Cixi could continue her rule as regent. It was only in 1889, when Guangxu had reached maturity at age eighteen, that he assumed direct rule. Guangxu decided to break sharply from the Qing establishment. In June 1898 the young emperor threw the Chinese court into turmoil when he commanded his subjects to enact sweeping changes in government and education.[4]

At first Cixi appeared to be on board with the reforms and raised no objection when Guangxu briefed her about his plans. However, by early September, opposition by Qing officials began to coalesce against the reform agenda. Word also reached Cixi that Itō Hirobumi had been summoned by Guangxu for a private conversation, which raised uncomfortable memories about the fate of Queen Min in Korea. Itō enjoyed close ties with one of Guangxu's key advisors, Kang Youwei, who had recently taken to calling Cixi the "False Empress." Kang had also been a strong advocate of reform based on the Japanese model. Reports in late September that Guangxu had summoned troops to the capital finally pushed Cixi into action. Fearing that a coup de main to eliminate her was afoot, she returned to the Forbidden City, put Guangxu under palace arrest, and announced the resumption of her regency. The brief period of imperial activism, "The Hundred Days Reform," had lasted all of 102 days.[5]

But not all the reform efforts were abandoned. Chang told Hoover, who arrived in March 1899, that although the future of China was uncertain, he believed that "the Empress Dowager's regime could yet be brought to realize China's interest in the development of its natural resources."[6]

Li Hongzhang was also anxious to meet the American engineer because he was concerned about the Yellow River. Although Li's prestige had markedly diminished since China's war with Japan, he still enjoyed the confidence of Cixi. Among his many appointments was minister of the Yellow River Conservancy. "Li said that the behavior of the river was giving him anxiety and that as I was an American engineer, he wished me to visit the flood-control works and advise him," Hoover later wrote. "I protested that I was not that kind of engineer. But all engineers were the same to him and he would have no refusal."[7]

An inspection tour was quickly arranged. Mr. Ching, "an important scholarly official," was charged with taking Hoover along the waterways by boat. He told the American engineer that for thousands of years, the Chinese had relied on a complicated system of willow beds and dikes to prevent the Yellow River from flooding. Along the banks of the river on either side, the Chinese planted forests of willows for many miles in length and width. The forests were able to flourish because while the river was in flood, it brought with it masses of fertile sediment. Over time, the river built up its bed above the surrounding land, but the floodwaters were held in check due to the planted forests of willow trees that retarded the current. "Thus, the forest automatically built itself up as a dike," Ching explained. "The job was to keep the willow forests in good condition; but beyond all this were the hundreds of miles of artificial and complicated dikes which must be kept in repair."[8]

Among the other things Ching told Hoover was that the Chinese firmly believed that "when the Yellow River broke out of its channel in one of its fatal and costly changes of mouth, it was an infallible portent of the fall of the dynasty." Ching gave corroborative instances of this claim "running thousands of years." One exception was in 1887 when the river had had its last disastrous break and the dynasty did not fall. But could it survive another such disaster? Hoover told Li that after examining the works, he was "convinced that the Chinese engineers had been capable enough and that the essential thing was to keep their works in repair." He also recommended an engineering study to see whether there was some way to relieve the pressure on the dikes. As for Ching's portentous observations about the fateful link between the river and the dynasty, Hoover concurred. "I concluded that the superstition connecting the floods with the fall of the dynasty had a sound foundation. A new dynasty meant virility in government, the renewed planting of the willows, and constant work on the dikes. As the dynasty became old and corrupt, the appropriations for works were grafted and the Chinese cut willows for fuel. Indeed, according to Mr. Ching, graft and negligence were the roots of the poor condition of the works which I found them. And the grafting had apparently been in action for a long time. The dynasty fell a few years later, according to portent."[9]

It would be simplistic to suggest that the negligence of river management was the only factor in the events that led to the collapse of the Qing dynasty in 1911, but natural disasters in 1898–1899 certainly played an important role in the dynasty's demise when poor peasants in north China began banding together in martial arts groups called the Boxers United in Righteousness.

BIG SWORD SOCIETY

The Boxer heartland stretched across the entire region south of the Yellow River, one of the more populous regions in China. But it was also one of the poorest. The main problem in the region was flooding. The rivers flowing from the mountains of Shandong all drained into this low-lying area along the southern course of the Yellow River, inundating large stretches of farmland.[10] The Shangdong-Jiangsu-Henan region was also not as politically stable as other centrally located areas. Banditry, like the kind N. S. Sviagin had described during his exploration of Manchuria, was endemic. The exigencies of the Sino-Japanese War had also depleted the area of Qing troops and the void created general lawlessness. "Highway robberies are the order of the day," wrote a missionary correspondent. "The bolder of the country folk 'taking to the road' to make up what is lacking in the field."[11] Widespread flooding in 1897 ruined crops and brought famine and increased disorder.

A major concern for farmers with property was self-defense, and unofficial armed groups were called upon to help protect villages and farms against bandits and other threats.[12] One such group was the Big Sword Society, which became active in southwestern Shandong in early 1895 to counter rampant banditry. The conditions that led to the rise of the Big Sword Society also led to the formation of other groups, which inevitably led to conflict. As historian Paul Cohen makes clear, "The same power vacuum that enabled banditry to flourish and facilitate the growth of anti-bandit Big Swords in southwestern Shandong (and northern Jiangsu) also provided an opening for an especially aggressive branch of the Catholic Church—the German Society of the Divine Word."[13] As Catholic groups like this proliferated and grew in strength, they came into conflict with the Big Sword Society.

The conflict was spurred, not by religious differences, but by something much more utilitarian: property and other legal disputes. Claiming membership in the Catholic Church often gave Chinese Christians license to act recklessly, their behavior sometimes indistinguishable from outright banditry. "It is well-known the foreign priests behave and act generally more or less in the style of native officials, and the natives know, by sad experience, that these priests represent power," wrote one Western observer. "It is perhaps due to the priest to say that at least in many cases his intentions are humane and that he is not always aware of the injustice that is done in his name by his underlings. The general principle of action seems to be, let a Chinese be but a Catholic and he shall have the protection of his foreign priest, which means foreign power."[14] This sort of situation became especially marked in Shandong. "The native province of Confucius of over two thousand years ago and now the sphere of influence of one of the Church's most energetic bishops," wrote Robert Hart, inspector general of the Chinese Maritime Customs Service. "The arrangement by which missionaries were to ride in green chairs and to be recognized as the equals of Governors and Viceroys had its special significance and underlined missionary aspirations, telling people and officials in every province what they had to expect from it."[15]

By the spring and summer of 1896, tensions between the missionaries and the Big Swords exploded when the latter attacked Christian properties along the Jiangsu-Shandong border. They were subsequently arrested and executed by Catholic friendly local authorities. In November 1897 three German missionaries were murdered by local Chinese (who may have had Big Sword involvement), giving rise to further tensions, made worse when local farmers were forced to erect a church at the villagers' expense on the site where the missionaries had been killed, as well as two other places.[16] Further fueling local resentment against the Catholics was the German seizure of the port of Jiaozhou Bay. Wilhelm II used the murder of German missionaries as the pretext for the seizure of Qingdao, which set in motion the events that would lead to Russia's subsequent occupation of Dairen and Port Arthur in 1898.

These events intensified the anger and hostility of the non-Christian Chinese toward the local Christian communities, giving rise to frequent clashes. Though Protestant converts would find themselves caught up in the growing anti-Christian movement, primary animus was directed against Catholics.[17] While these tensions mounted, a disastrous Yellow River flood wreaked havoc on Shandong. On August 9, 1898, the Yellow River broke through the banks at Shouzhang, flooding twenty-five hundred square miles of farmland. Fifteen hundred villages in thirty-four counties were flooded by "China's Sorrow," leaving over a million people homeless and hungry.[18] It was by far the most widespread and disastrous flood in living memory. Foreign travelers gave vivid accounts of the disaster. "Thousands of homes are in ruins," wrote one witness. "Furniture, winter clothing, and grain are buried beneath [the water] while that which has been rescued is only useful to people who have fallen into the depths of misery." The distress of the people was rendered even more acute due to the fact that "the region had suffered a drought during the spring and the wheat crop was a general failure," the report continued. "The flood having come before the autumn harvest was matured, only a meager portion of tall-millet has been gathered, while all low crops like cotton, beans, and small millet, are submerged and lost."[19]

Anti-Christian incidents along the northwest border area between Shandong and Zhili became more frequent as desperate refugees from the flooded areas moved toward North China to escape the destruction in the winter of 1898–1899. During this chaotic period, a mystic group called the "Spirit Boxers" became energized, taking the name "Boxers United in Righteousness."[20] Unlike the Big Swords, the Spirit Boxers frequently engaged in healing rituals. They also practiced boxing as part of their religious rituals to enable their members to claim invulnerability, the main object of spirit possession.[21] Taking up the popular slogan "Revive the Qing, Destroy the Foreign," they called on the people to "expel the foreign devils."[22]

By early 1899 disturbing news of attacks on London Missionary Society outposts in May, August, and October began causing alarm among the diplomatic community in Beijing. The shocking report that Rev. S. M. Brooks had been hacked to death while traveling between stations in a remote part of Shandong was particularly alarming, prompting Yuan Shikai, the newly appointed governor of Shandong, to wage an all-out suppression campaign against the Boxers.[23] Unlike the ineffective former governor of Shandong, Yuxian, Yuan was vehemently anti-Boxer. His suppression campaigns were the first test of his Newly Created Army (Xinjian Lujun), the modern force Yuan was tasked by the Qing court to organize in the aftermath of the Sino-Japanese War.[24] Yuan's five thousand well-trained soldiers, with the latest rapid-fire guns and heavy artillery to use against

bands of sword-carrying peasants, was reminiscent of the mismatch between the Japanese Army and the Tonghak peasant army in Korea during
1894–1895. By the early months of 1900, Yuan had effectively rid Shandong of Boxer activity.[25]

But such was not the case in the key province of Zhili, where Beijing
and its port city, Tianjin, were located. Zhili governor Yulu was unable to
control the Boxers. The situation was made more difficult because Tianjin
and Beijing held sizable foreign populations; it was natural that the
Boxer movement would thrive there. Zhili also held a large concentration of Chinese Christians, over one hundred thousand, mostly Catholic,
making it among the most highly missionized provinces in China. Brazen
acts of looting and violence had spread throughout the province by the
end of 1899.[26] The Qing court faced two bad choices for how it should react
to the upsurge of Boxer activity. "The Court appears to be in a dilemma,"
observed Robert Hart. "If the Boxers are not suppressed, the Legations
threaten to take action—if the attempt to suppress them is made, this
intensely patriotic organization will be converted into an anti-dynastic
movement. *Que faire?*"[27]

That cataclysm arrived in June 1900. Until then Boxer violence had
been directed exclusively against Chinese Christians; only one foreigner,
Reverend Brooks, had been killed. By mid-May, however, Hoover, caught
in the maelstrom, recalled that "the danger had grown so great that I
called in our geological expeditions from the interior."[28] Rumors of Boxer
attacks on missionaries "rumbled around us," as Hoover took the first
train to Tianjin. Like scores of other foreigners, he would spend the rest
of the summer holed up in the city waiting for Western forces to relieve
them. He was now convinced beyond any shadow of a doubt that the Chinese superstition linking the Yellow River flood to the fall of the dynasty
was absolutely true.[29]

CHINA RELIEF EXPEDITION

Shortly after midday on May 27, 1900, the first contingent of American
troops landed at the Dagu Forts at the mouth of the Hai (Peiho) estuary,
which emptied into the Bay of Bohai. In the early nineteenth century, the
two forts were erected on either side of the estuary to protect Tianjin and
Beijing from seaborne incursions. After China's loss in the First Opium
War (1839–1842), the number of forts was increased to six. These efforts
proved inadequate, however, for, in 1860 the forts were unable to prevent

an Anglo-French force from occupying Beijing and destroying the Summer Palace. In the decades afterward, the forts were repaired and strengthened, but the pain and shame of the humiliation of the earlier defeat remained acute.[30]

The cruiser USS *Newark*, which had seen action in the Caribbean and the Pacific during the Spanish-American War, was stationed in the Philippines as the flagship of a squadron, part of the US Asiatic Fleet, commanded by Rear Admiral Louis Kempff. In April, Kempff was ordered to proceed to Japan.[31] Upon arriving at Nagasaki, Kempff received news that trouble was brewing in North China. The American minister to China, E. H. Conger, increasingly nervous about the Qing government's lukewarm guarantee to safeguard American life and property, had requested the urgent dispatch of American forces. Although Beijing had issued a decree on May 29 directing military authorities to arrest the leaders of the Boxers and disperse their followers, Conger feared the growing turmoil. Other legations shared his anxiety and had requested help from their own nations. Kempff was ordered to immediately proceed with a contingent of troops to Dagu, where Russian and British ships had already landed.[32]

The timing of the American's arrival at Dagu was fortuitous. The Zongli Yamen had at last granted permission for a small contingent of foreign troops to go to Beijing to guard the foreign legations. On May 31 a modest force of a little more than four hundred men from eight nations departed for Beijing.[33] "There was still much difference of opinion in Tianjin as to whether there really was to be trouble," recalled one marine. "Everyday rumors indicated that the Boxers were becoming more and more active . . . However, large forces of Chinese Imperial troops were encamped nearby. It was certain that Tianjin was safe so long as the Chinese government remained friendly, and these troops remained loyal."[34] The lead element of the international forces arrived in Beijing at 8 o'clock on the evening of June 1 after a forced march of two days that, thankfully, did not encounter any resistance. The foreign community breathed a collective sigh of relief.

Meanwhile, the Boxer situation was escalating. On June 2, Governor-General Yulu telegraphed the Zongli Yamen with an urgent message that "the bandits [Boxers] have increased to such a number that they can no longer be dispersed by words of notices."[35] Yet the imperial court refused to take more drastic measures to suppress the Boxers.

On the evening of June 9, Vice Admiral Sir Edward Seymour, commander of the British fleet at Tianjin, received an urgent message from the British minister in Beijing, Claude Maxwell MacDonald: "Situation extremely tense; unless steps are made for the immediate advance on Peking, it will be too late."[36] Seymour quickly assembled an international force, this one much larger than the first, at Tianjin. Soon thereafter the telegraph line was cut, completely isolating the foreign legations.

The relief force started out for Beijing on the morning of June 10. It comprised contingents from the same eight nations as the initial force dispatched on May 31, with 736 British, 450 Germans, 100 Americans, 315 Russians, 158 French, 25 Austrians, 40 Italians, and 52 Japanese, for a total of 1,876 men, with additional Russians and French joining later.[37] It was the first time an international coalition force of such diversity and size had been assembled for a joint operation against a common foe.[38] As the senior officer, it was agreed that Seymour would take charge of the relief mission.[39]

At Yangtsun, about fifteen miles north of Tianjin, Seymour's relief mission encountered General Nie Shicheng and his government force, some four thousand men strong. The veteran general of the Sino-Japanese War had taken a harsh stance against the Boxers at first, killing many of them along the Tianjin-Beijing railroad. But he was strongly reproved for his actions by the Qing court, which still wanted to maintain a middle ground between appeasement and suppression.[40] Nie let Seymour's column pass without incident.

The first major skirmish with the Boxers occurred on June 12 in Langfang, about halfway between Tianjin and Beijing, some forty miles from the legation quarter.[41] By then additional men had joined Seymour's relief mission, bringing the total force to almost twenty one hundred men.[42] Fear gripped the Chinese residents of Beijing at the news of the approaching column, as many were led to believe they would soon be overrun by foreign troops. On June 10 the British summer legation in the Western Hills, about fifteen miles southwest of Beijing, where the legation staff spent the hot, dry months of the summer in the cool hills, was burned to the ground. The next day the Japanese secretary of legation, Sugiyama Akira, was killed at the Yongdingmen Gate. Although a decree was later published by the imperial court decrying the murder as the work of "bandits," it was "well-known throughout Beijing to have been done by regular troops."[43]

Members of the Zongli Yamen urgently called on British minister MacDonald to stop Seymour's advancing column. MacDonald would not hear of it. "The great fear has been and is that in the city it is not the Boxers only but the soldiers . . . who will attack us," wrote Robert Hart.[44] On June 13, while the foreign legations impatiently anticipated the arrival of Seymour and his men, the Boxers initiated their first attack on the legation quarter. It was the same day that they commenced a wholesale massacre of Chinese Christians. "We began to realize that the Empress had no intention of putting down the Boxers," wrote Mrs. J. Inglis of the American legation. "There was ample proof of this on the night of June 13, when Peking streets were strewn with bodies of native converts."[45] The next day the Boxers set fire to all places and things not Chinese in the capital. "Fires were started in quick succession in many parts of the city and continued to rage," recalled one witness. "Two Catholic cathedrals with their orphanages and hospitals, all the houses occupied by those in the employment of the Imperial Customs Service, the homes of professors of the Imperial University and the Imperial College, the post-office, the telegraph office, the electric light plant, the Imperial Chinese bank, the Russian bank, and all shops containing anything foreign, were consumed."[46]

The imperial court revealed its sympathies by ordering Governor-General Yulu to use force to stop the advance of Seymour's column.[47] In reality, the relief column was not advancing. It was stuck at Langfang because the railway line was by then too badly damaged to be repaired. "Lang Fang station was the farthest north we could get the trains to, the line above being badly destroyed," wrote Seymour. "We were now isolated, with no transport or means to advance, and cut off from our base behind." For five days Seymour and his men were held up at Langfang. Realizing they could not continue on, Seymour decided to turn his force around and retreat to Tianjin.[48] Meanwhile, in Beijing, impatience for the relief forces' arrival had given way to despair. "When will they reach us?" wrote a distressed Mrs. Conger. "Thus, we see that Seymour's 'coming troops' are not coming!" From then on, Admiral Seymour began to be known as Admiral "See-No-More."[49]

DECLARATION OF WAR

By the time Seymour started to make his way back to Tianjin, some twenty-seven foreign warships had arrived in the waters off the Dagu Forts. Having heard nothing from Seymour, and fearing that the Chinese might have cut them off, the allied commanders agreed to destroy the forts if the Chinese attempted to reinforce them and block the river. On the evening of June 15 they received information that the Chinese were planning to place electric mines in the Pei-Ho River and that the South Fort had received reinforcements. They issued an ultimatum to the commander of the Dagu Forts: if he did not surrender by 2 AM on June 17, the forts would be bombarded and destroyed.[50]

On June 16 the Empress Dowager summoned the Imperial Council for a crisis meeting. The Imperial Council was unaware of the surrender ultimatum and the discussion focused on what should be done about the riots breaking out all over the city. Prince Qing (Yikuang), former de facto head of the Zongli Yamen, called for suppressing the Boxers, but hardliners like the powerful Prince Duan (Zaiyi), father of the new heir apparent, Puzhuan, rebuked him. "Do you want to turn the people's hearts against us?" he said.[51] (Prince Qing was forced to resign from the council on June 10 under pressure from Prince Duan.) Prince Qing feared the reaction of the foreign powers if the court sided with the Boxers. Cixi hesitated but eventually came round to Duan's hardline position. "China is weak; the only thing we can depend on is the heart of the people. If we lose it, how can we maintain our country?"[52]

Around midnight on June 17 the forts opened fire on the international fleet.[53] The allied forces responded. For the fourth time in less than five years, the Dagu Forts had come under attack by Western powers.[54] Incredibly, the imperial court was still unaware of the Allied ultimatum issued on June 15. It was only on June 19 that Cixi received a memorial sent by Yulu from Tianjin informing her about it. Nor did Yulu mention that actual hostilities had already broken out or that the Dagu Forts had attacked the fleet first. Cixi and the imperial court thus assumed the hostilities had been started by the powers.[55]

Upon receipt of the report of the allied bombardment of Dagu Forts on June 19, the imperial court directed that all foreign legations had to depart the capital within twenty-four hours. Unaware of the Dagu incident, the German minister, Baron von Ketteler, was on his way to a meeting at the Zongli Yamen the next day when he was shot dead in the street.[56] News of the Dagu bombardment unleashed a new wave of Boxer rage that had been building up for weeks. "Precisely at 4 P.M. [on June 20] the firing began," Sir Robert Hart recalled, "and rifle bullets were whistling down the Want-ta street between Austrian Legation and Inspectorate and over the heads of the French picquet . . . By 5 o'clock, we were all quartered in the British Legation and the siege began."[57] The next day, June 21, the

Empress Dowager issued a "declaration of war" against the foreign powers which stated in part that

> for the past thirty years, [foreigners] have taken advantage of China's forbearance, to encroach on China's territory and trample on the Chinese people, and to demand China's wealth. Every concession made by China increased their reliance on violence . . . They oppressed peaceful citizens and insulted the gods and holy men, exciting the most burning indignation among the people . . . Hence the burning of the chapels by the patriotic braves [Boxers] . . . All our officials high and low are of one mind; and there have assembled without official summons several hundred thousand patriotic soldiers [I Ping—Boxers], even children carrying spears in the service of [their] country. Those others rely on crafty schemes: our trust is in Heaven's justice. They [foreigners] depend on violence; we, on humanity. Not to speak of the righteousness of our cause, our provinces number more than twenty million, our people over four hundred million and it will not be difficult to vindicate the dignity of our country.[58]

Despite the boldness of the declaration of war, a week later, on June 29, Emperor Guangxu issued a completely contradictory rescript calling for the restoration of order. He instructed "princes and high officers in command of the Boxers to arrest any brigands committing robberies" and to "execute them on the spot."[59] The officers should also make "close investigation of cases of brigands passing themselves off as soldiers, and committing acts of pillage." These so-called brigands were a far cry from the Boxers described in the June 21 declaration that had officially renamed them *yimin*, "righteous people."[60]

JAPANESE CONTINGENT

On July 3, Emperor Guangxu sent a telegram to Emperor Meiji requesting help. It was another indication of the deep division in the imperial court over the response to the crisis. Guangxu appealed to Meiji on the basis of their mutual suspicion of Western powers. "Should China be unsuccessful in opposing the West," he wrote, "Japan's independence will [also] be threatened, so China and Japan are on the same footing, and should put their differences aside to preserve their national existence." He also apologized profusely for the assassination of Legation Secretary Sugiyama. "An alliance with Japan would succeed in dispelling the present troubles and restoring order," he pleaded. "The emperor of China in all sincerity applied to the emperor of Japan for aid in restoring order."[61]

Meiji responded with a succinct note ten days later. He thanked the Chinese emperor for his regrets regarding the death of Sugiyama but was quick to point out that "the action of the insurgents [Boxers] is in complete violation of the principle of International Law." The Japanese government, he continued, will not hesitate to aid the Chinese government if it is "prompt in her efforts to suppress the rioters and relieve the ministers." Otherwise, it would have no choice but to send troops "to pacify the rebels and rescue its citizens." Meiji concluded his letter with an offer to mediate and not take sides: "Japan will not decline to use her good offices on behalf of China. If your Majesty's Government, therefore, at once suppress the insurrection and rescue the foreign Representatives, Japan will be prepared to use her influence, in eventual negotiations between Your country and foreign nations, with a view to conserve the interests of Your Empire."[62]

It was another sign that Japan had "departed Asia" even as it tried to prove itself equal to the Western powers. That anxiety was on full display during the relief expedition. Japanese officers at all levels reinforced draconian discipline on their soldiers, warning of harsh penalties for unjustified or wanton theft, arson, or violence, against the Chinese. The discipline and courage of Japanese soldiers were widely noticed. "It is impossible to express the universal feeling of admiration excited all through this campaign by the conduct of the Japanese—by their extraordinary self-restraint, as well as by their courage and military capacity," remarked one American soldier.[63] Sir Robert Hart noticed how the Japanese contingent had "won everybody's admiration," an observation keenly noted by the Japanese commanders themselves in their official dispatches from the front. "The nimbleness and courage with which our men behaved themselves," noted Rear Admiral Dewa, "has elicited the praise and admiration of the rest of the allied forces."[64]

But no amount of praise by the Western powers could calm Japanese anxieties about their self-perception as an inferior nation. Each Japanese soldier dispatched to the international force seemed to personally take responsibility for changing this perception. During the siege of Tianjin that began on July 13, Japanese soldiers sustained more than half of the allied casualties. With a strength of nearly thirteen thousand, Japan was by far the largest contingent, nearly 40 percent of the thirty-three-thousand-man allied expedition.[65] The new international relief force, consisting mainly

Japanese soldiers bringing in a prisoner during the China Relief Expedition, 1900. (CO 106/422, p. 18, National Archives, Kew, UK)

of soldiers from Japan, Russia, Britain, and the United States, set off for the capital on August 4 with the Japanese troops in the lead. "The first engagement at Beicang on August 5 was fought almost entirely by Japanese troops," recalled Captain William Crozier, a staff officer under General Chaffee's command of the American contingent. "Others would have been glad to take a more effective part, but the nerve of the Chinamen was not sufficient to provide fighting enough to go around, and the Japanese, being in advance, got it all."[66]

Reaching Beijing on August 14, Japanese troops assaulted the Dongzhi and Qihua Gates, sustaining huge losses in the process. Their actions allowed British troops, which met scarcely any resistance, to enter the city and make their way to the legations by 3 PM the next day.[67] Japanese losses accounted for two-thirds of allied losses.[68] It can rightly be said the relief of the foreign legations was in large part due to the efforts and sacrifice of the Japanese contingent.

And yet it was the German commander, Field Marshal Alfred von Waldersee, not the Japanese commander, Fukushima Yasumasa, who was selected to take control of the international force once Beijing had been captured. On August 6 the Kaiser appealed directly to Nicholas II to solicit his support for von Waldersee's nomination, even though the German contribution to the relief mission had been minimal.[69] The Germans saw the position as an opportunity to increase their country's prestige and to repay the Chinese for the murder of von Ketteler. Nicholas II backed the proposal because it meant "poking the 'modern Carthage' [Britain] in the eye with a stick."[70] Using the Russian acceptance as leverage, the Kaiser was able to obtain the reluctant approval of both Britain and France. The Japanese thus had no choice but to consent to the arrangement. Itō Hirobumi was appalled. "I was extremely shocked when I learned Emperor Meiji replied that he supported the German plan," he later recalled. "Even if the Russians had come up with this plan, they should have informed the Japanese [government] directly." He added, "We must be prepared for what might happen next. This problem has been bothering me and is keeping me awake all night."[71]

SINO-RUSSIAN WAR

Itō was right to be wary of Russia. He understood that the Russians had backed Waldersee not only to annoy the British but to check Japan's ambition, in part because the British had supported the dispatch of a large Japanese contingent to the international force.[72] British Lord Salisbury had originally proposed that Japan dispatch twenty thousand to thirty thousand troops to China because Britain was then preoccupied in the Second Boer War (1899–1902). Despite Nicholas's misgivings, the Russians acquiesced.[73]

The Japanese were suspicious of the Russians in other ways. Every action that required Russia's joint intervention in the Boxer crisis, beginning with Nicholas's decision on June 7/May 25 to deploy four thousand Russian troops from Port Arthur to Dagu, was accompanied by solemn pronouncements that Russia was somehow different from the other powers because, unlike them, the Russian people bore no ill-will toward the Chinese people and indeed, even sympathized with China's sorry predicament.[74] Nicholas set the tone early on when he blamed the Boxer crisis squarely on Western missionaries—"the root of all evil"—as well as "shameless" foreign traders, both of whom "have done more than anything else to arouse Chinese hatred of Europeans."[75] Foreign Minister Muravev also made clear that Russia's position vis-à-vis China was "far from identical with the position of other powers." "We have a common border with China for more than eight thousand miles," he opined. "We are building the Manchurian railroad on which more than 60,000 Chinese are employed. For the last two hundred years, we have enjoyed friendly relations with China."[76]

Despite these professed pronouncements of goodwill toward China, the paradox of Russia's position became obvious to everyone: How was Russia to reestablish friendly relations with China when the Chinese Eastern Railway, with its distributed guards of just forty-five hundred men, remained vulnerable to Boxer attack and thus in need of Russian military reinforcements?[77] Witte blamed Muravev directly for the Boxer crisis. "Remember, that it was you who put chestnuts in the fire with Port Arthur," he scolded him. When Muravev died suddenly the day after his conversation with Witte on June 21/8, apparently of a stroke, many thought his death was linked to the stress of the situation in China.[78] Vice Minister Vladimir Lamsdorf was selected to replace him.

Lamsdorf, the "exquisitely perfumed" and secretly gay new foreign minister, whom Nicholas nicknamed "Madame," was more circumspect than his predecessor. Reports of sporadic sabotage against the railway lines in late April 1900 led Lamsdorf to share Witte's concern regarding a Russian embroilment in China. But the attacks against Russia accelerated. Russian telegraph lines were being cut. Anonymous proclamations appeared on the walls of temples and inns fomenting violence against the "foreign devils." On May 23 a Chinese mob attacked three Cossack guards, and when the Russian officer in charge of the South Manchurian line, Konstantin Kushorov, complained to local Chinese authorities, he was warned to keep his men out of the towns and villages. The apparent impotence of Chinese officials to maintain order pushed Kushorov to request military assistance.[79]

Witte and Lamsdorf were strongly opposed. On June 14/1 Witte wrote to Admiral Y. I. Alekseev, commander of the Pacific Fleet, requesting that he not dispatch troops to Manchuria without the special permission of the Ministry of Finance. Witte emphasized to the tsar that "for the present, it would be detrimental to introduce our troops to Manchuria." He also wrote to War Minister Kuropatkin on June 29/16 warning him "not send in troops without his [Witte's] permission."[80] Kuropatkin had taken a hard-line stance on the crisis early on, hoping that troubles in China might result in Russia's outright seizure of the Liaodong Peninsula, but Witte was opposed to such a move. "Russia was not going to declare war on China," he announced. "The participation of Russian forces in the Beijing operation was aimed only to suppress the rebellion and support the legitimate Chinese government, which was not able to subdue the rebellion on its own."[81]

This fiction was exposed by Cixi's declaration of war on June 21. In the following weeks more than two hundred *versts* of railway were destroyed by Chinese government troops near Mukden (Shenyang) while the Mukden train station itself came under attack.[82] Meanwhile, Chinese troops began pouring into the villages north and south of Liaoyang. "Everywhere everything Russian was put to the torch, and up and down the railway line, as far as the Russians could see, fires lit up the sky." The Chinese were not content with simply driving out the foreigners. "Russians captured at isolated posts were ridiculed and tortured, then beheaded, their corpses thrown to the pigs. So deep was the passion aroused in the Chinese that they did not stop with the living. They dug up graves and desecrated the remains." As for the railway lines, "the Chinese burned barracks and stations and stores of wood and coal. They demolished the rolling stock and ran the expensive engines off the destroyed bridges. They dismantled the tracks, burning what could be burned and tossing the rest into the river."[83] By mid-July, Witte, under pressure, had no choice but to support the deployment of Russian reinforcements to Manchuria.

MASSACRE AT BLAGOVESHCHENSK

On July 14, 1900, the Chinese unexpectedly opened fire on the Russian steamer *Mikhail*, which was en route from Blagoveshchensk to Khabarovsk along the Amur River. The *Mikhail* was laden with guns and shells, and as it passed along the Chinese town of Aigun, just across the Amur from Blagoveshchensk, the Chinese signaled the ship to dock. The river formed the boundary line between Russia and China for hundreds of miles. Whether failing to understand the order or ignoring it, the *Mikhail* did not yield and the Chinese opened fire, boarded the ship, and arrested the captain and crew. News of the incident electrified the citizens of Blagoveshchensk.

Until this time the inhabitants of Blagoveshchensk had not thought much of the Boxer Uprising when reports reached them in June.[84] Founded as a Russian military outpost in 1856 due to its strategic location on the northern bank of the Amur, the town was renamed Blagoveshchensk (Good News Place) in 1858 to commemorate Nikolai Muravev-Amursky's announcement of Russia's annexation of the Amur region. Since then it had become a thriving commercial town. During the Manchurian gold rush of 1858, the population of Blagoveshchensk mushroomed, as did trade between Blagoveshchensk and Aigun, the latter being the main supplier of meat and produce for the Russian city.[85]

The nearly thirty-eight thousand mixed Chinese and Russian inhabitants of Blagoveshchensk had always maintained amicable relations. Leo Deich, a Blagoveshchensk-based foreign correspondent and exiled revolutionary, noted that "for decades, many Chinese citizens' lives peacefully among the Russians, being of great service to our population through their labor." Many Russian families "had young Chinese or Manchurian servants and they were accepted as part of the family."[86] Another foreigner residing in Blagoveshchensk at the time, Ishimitsu Makiyo, a Japanese military officer operating undercover in Manchuria, noted that "there were about 3,000 Chinese in the city."[87] Most of the Chinese "worked as coolies and food peddlers." Moreover, Russian and Chinese subjects "freely crossed the border, entering the neighboring country to visit each other, always showing mutual trust, with no precautions taken or passports controlled."[88]

All this changed on July 15. Ishimitsu noted that the morning had started out peacefully as the city's residents began venturing back to Blagoveshchensk after the excitement of the previous day. Around two o'clock in the afternoon, however, a ban on crossing the Amur was suddenly announced by order of the military governor of the Amur region, Governor-General K. N. Gribsky. The ferries were ordered to pull up on the Russian side of the river as Cossack cavalrymen guarded the quay. Earlier that day, Gribsky had called a special city council meeting to "deliberate on measures necessary for the defense of Blagoveshchensk itself, notably the organization of a volunteer force." When asked whether anything should be done about "the many Chinese who lived in and around the city," Gribsky replied that "special measures were neither necessary nor advisable" since no war had been declared. He also reassured a delegation of Chinese subjects, explaining that "they were under the patronage of Russian Law, and that there was no reason [for them] to feel unsafe or leave the city." Gribsky departed Blagoveshchensk to campaign against the Boxers near Aigun, "to secure navigation on the Amur River." The defense of the city was left in the hands of Police Chief Batarevich and the chairman of the Amur troops, Colonel Volkovsky.[89]

At six o'clock that evening, the Chinese began bombarding the city from across the river. The panic-stricken residents of Blagoveshchensk who had been strolling along the quay began running for cover. "Unbelievable scenes took place in the streets. People were fleeing the city shouting, crying, and cursing." Rumors that the Chinese had made a landing on the riverbank added to the panic as citizen volunteers began to take up arms. "At the city council, crowds kept struggling for hastily distributed guns, insufficient for all in need," recalled one witness. They "were about to break into shops and rob them to arm themselves properly."[90] As both sides fired at each other across the river, Russian scouts were sent along the riverbank to reconnoiter for an enemy landing. Had the Chinese decided to overrun the city at that moment, they could have done so without any difficulty. Yet, paradoxically, after just one hour of intense shooting, the Chinese guns went silent. "The Amur became unpleasantly quiet," Ishimitsu recalled. "A sense of horror gripped the city."[91]

The Chinese resumed the bombardment the following day on a much heavier scale. More ominously, on the morning of July 16, Boxer proclamations were discovered posted in the Chinese quarter of the city. "Few Russian could read them and paid no heed to them at first. But then they were translated and it was discovered—or so at least the story went among the Russian residents—that they gave notice of a Manchu landing that very night and called on the Chinese living in the city to join in the hostilities."[92] Panic now engulfed the city. The journalist L. G. Deich recalled "scenes of astonishing and brutal violence toward the unfortunate Chinese citizens who found themselves in the path of those fleeing. I myself witnessed from afar, several men, having thrown two Chinese to the ground, beat them mercilessly . . . in the evening of the same day there were several murders of entirely innocent Chinese."[93]

Police chief Batarevich solicited Gribsky's permission to begin the roundup of Chinese residents. "No matter whether they worked as a shop owner or a coolie, whether they were hired by Russians or not, the Chinese were all pulled out from their houses," recalled Ishimitsu. "The purge was ruthless and even the children were taken away."[94] Chinese from the surrounding villages were also taken from their homes. "The detainees cooperated without resistance, which quite impressed the Russian authorities. For example, a party of forty Chinese traveled fifty *versts* [33 miles] under the supervision of just three or four unarmed Russian watchmen."[95] Some Russian residents tried to shelter Chinese, hiding them in their basements, attics, and so on, "but their neighbors frequently learned what has happened and reported them to the Cossacks or the police. The Cossacks, with threats of violence, sometimes drawing out their swords, demanded that the hidden Chinese be given over."[96]

As night fell, three thousand to thirty-five hundred Chinese were huddled together in a courtyard of the Mordin Sawmill on the Zeya River.[97] "The detainees were not allowed to lay on their backs to sleep. Everyone was restless—the children were crying, some of the elderly were protesting." The Russian authorities now faced a dilemma. What were they supposed to do with the detainees? "Could we continue holding the Chinese for days without any food, bedding, or place to rest?" recalled a witness. "Someone said that it was not a big deal to starve for two or three days as long as we survived the ordeal."[98] But what would happen if the crowd became restless? The Chinese far outnumbered their Russian overseers. Moreover, the courtyard was unfenced. There was nothing to prevent the Chinese from escaping.[99]

On the morning of July 17 the Russian police officer in charge, Shabanov, rode into the crowd on horseback followed by half a dozen soldiers, and announced:

> Russia has decided to send a punitive expedition against the reckless Chinese rebels. It will be dangerous for good citizens like yourselves to stay here, so we will have to evacuate you from the city. Once the expedition is over, you will be free to go back to your original homes. Just obey our orders until then! We will have no choice but to shoot you should you try to resist or escape. We are heading for shelter at this moment. Please follow us![100]

If the Chinese believed the officer's assurances of safe passage to the other side of the river, their doubts began to grow during the six-mile trek to the village of Upper Blagoveshchensk, situated on the banks of the Amur River. It was a hot day and straining from the rapid pace, many discarded their knapsacks and pieces of clothing along the way. The elderly could not keep up. "Many collapsed or lagged far behind from heat and exhaustion," one witness reported, and "strong measures were taken." Shabanov ordered that "the stragglers be axed to death." Several dozen were killed in this way while others were shot. Ten months after the incident when investigators retraced the footsteps of this "trail of woe," large quantities of Chinese clothing and footwear were discovered, including "Chinese braids, human skulls, and entire skeletons." There was also evidence that corpses had been looted.[101]

As the party was nearing Upper Blagoveshchensk several armed Cossacks approached the Chinese to "assist the river crossing." Russians from the village witnessed the spectacle. What happened next is the subject of much controversy although the various eyewitness accounts paint a strikingly similar picture:

> A spot was chosen for the crossing—upriver from the village in a relatively narrow part of the river [about 213 meters wide and a little more than 4.5 meters deep]. Nonetheless . . . the current there is quite strong, and a strong wind blew. Having picked the location, they [the Russian and Cossack guards] decided that this was the place to make the crossing and chased the Chinese into the water and ordered them to swim. A portion of them, once in the water, began to swim but quickly went under; the others did not plunge in. The Cossacks tried to push them with their whips, and failing this, began to open fire—not only were the Cossacks firing but the villagers, including children and old men, were as well. The shooting went on for about half an hour, at which point the riverbank became strewn with a jumble of corpses. After the shooting, the commanding officer [Shabanov] gave the order to use hand weapons—the Cossacks used their sabers, and the conscripts were ordered to kill the "disobedient" Chinese with their axes. When some of the conscripts failed to lead into action immediately, the Cossacks threatened to "cut off their traitorous head." The Chinese wept; some prayed and made the sign of the Orthodox cross—but to no avail.[102]

The official investigation of the incident stated that "all eyewitnesses affirmed that the crossing was, in fact, not a crossing at all but a mass murder and drowning of the Chinese."[103] This was how the Russian conscripts understood it. Ishimitsu recalled the horror: "A mother who tried to escape while holding her child was stabbed . . . The child was thrown, stepped on, and smashed." Although there was a "mountain of dead bodies," some were discovered still alive underneath, "vomiting up blood." "Every Chinese who was still alive got tossed into the river, their shoes, hats, bags, and other things were scattered around the sea of blood on the ground."[104] Deich remembered a particularly heartbreaking scene. "A Manchu family had a child who was still breastfeeding. The mother did not want to take the child with her so she begged the many bystanders to take the baby and save his life. No one came forward. At last, she left the baby on the shore and went into the water herself. After a little while, the mother returned for her baby, and taking him in her arms went into the river again; then she went back once more and left him on the shore again. The Cossacks put an end to her hesitation by stabbing both her and her baby."[105]

The investigation findings were not made public. An anonymous article based on the "official archives" did appear ten years later in the Russian journal *Vestnik Evropy,* which attempted to reconstruct the events. But by then the massacre had been more or less forgotten. According to the author of the article, simply referred to as "V," the massacre at Upper Blagoveshchensk took place over several days. In addition to the first killings, which occurred on July 17, a second group of 84 Chinese was sent to the river. On July 19 and 21, two more groups, of 170 and 66 people, were sent to the riverbank of death. "There is little information on what happened to this [last] party and what there is, is official and one-sided," wrote V. "Suffice to say that at most twenty people successfully swam across and were saved on the other side."[106]

The Blagoveshchensk authorities did not inform the Priamur governor-general, N. I. Grodekov, about the massacre, but it was impossible to hide because thousands of bloated bodies began floating down the Amur.[107] Gribsky tried to avoid blame by placing responsibility on his chief of police, Batarevich. Subsequent investigations revealed that Colonel Volkovsky, chairman of the Amur Forces, had also played a key role in the massacre. After receiving a telegram about the arrest of 85 Chinese, he responded, "Destroy all Chinese on our side of the river. Do not ask for further instructions."[108]

On July 20 the Russian authorities seemed to realize the horror of what was happening. On that day General Gribsky received a telegram inquiry from [a low-ranking officer] Pokrovka confirming the order to expel all Chinese to the opposite bank and to "destroy them in case they resist." Horrified, Gribsky put out a stern statement that "our fight is with armed Chinese who had taken harmful action against us. Peaceful, harmless Chinese . . . have done nothing to offend us." Immediately after this message was issued, Colonel Volkovsky's orders to his subordinates changed rather abruptly. "He began sending telegrams that 'we must not touch or killed the peaceful Chinese.'" All that was necessary to stop the massacre had been a few words from Gribsky, who "until then had known and seen nothing of what was going on in front of him."[109]

The findings of the investigation were clear enough, but no trial was ever held nor was any public accounting presented. But administrative punitive measures were taken. Gribsky, accused of negligence, was quietly relieved of his command. Chief of police Batarevich was dismissed due to his "lack of diligence and misuse of power." Shabanov, the officer who had been most directly involved in the actual killings, was found responsible "for not only not preventing . . . the violence against the Chinese but giving the order to shoot at them and hacking them with axes himself." Finally, Volkovsky was relieved of his command and barred from further service "for the order and telegrams that caused so many deaths." None of the subordinates involved—Cossacks, junior leaders, and conscripts—were found to have had any responsibility for the massacre.[110]

Despite the muted ending to the affair, Gribsky and the others were disgraced. A passage from a certain General Kh's journal describing a dinner with Grodekov on September 14, 1900, revealed the discomfort the Russian authorities felt about what had taken place. He wrote: "While eating at the table with General Governor Grodekov and his staff, it is an unwritten rule not to speak of the Amur Oblast, as if it were something unsavory—but occasionally something is said to make clear that in Khabarovsk, they know about everything and do not approve . . . they related to Gribsky as to a dead man who mustn't be spoken ill of and when the conversation comes too close to these topics, they stare at their plates with embarrassment and silence reigns."[111]

BLOOD AND TREASURE

The conflict in Manchuria differed from the Boxer chaos that had unfolded in China proper. As the Boxer movement spread to China's three eastern provinces, it took on a distinctly anti-Russian, as opposed to anti-Christian, character. Regular Chinese armies joined in the struggle, threatening the CER and the Russian engineers, skilled laborers, and guards pledged to protect it. After the city of Blagoveshchensk was bombarded, the invasion of Russia by Chinese forces seemed imminent. Under these conditions, Nicholas II ordered the dispatch of Russian forces into Manchuria, marking the beginning of a brief war between Russia and China.

In late July, Russian and Cossack detachments crossed the Amur and took Aigun, burning it to ashes. The remnants of the Qing army retreated south and the Russians advanced into Manchuria, occupying all major settlements between Aigun and Qiqihar. Meanwhile, Cossack forces set off from Khabarovsk at the news that Harbin, a major railway hub on the CER, had been besieged. Their advance toward Harbin was marked by burning and looting of all Chinese settlements along the way. Starting on July 30, Huichun and then Ningguta (Ning'an) and Sanxing were successively subdued.

The Russians took Heilongjiang the next day, on July 31, and three days later the distraught general in charge of the city's defense, Shoushan,

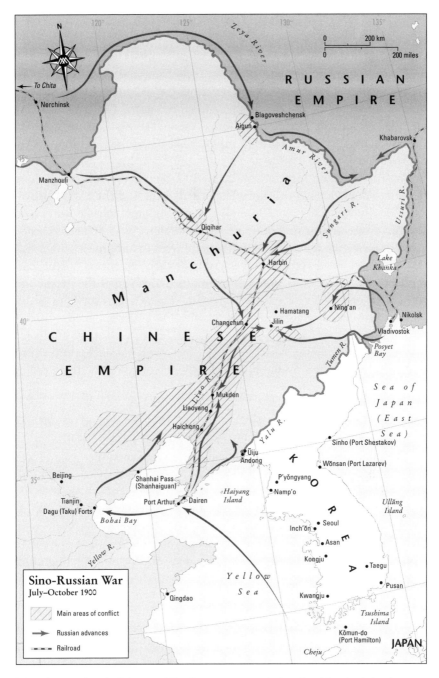

More than one hundred thousand Russian troops were deployed to Manchuria by the autumn of 1900. Most arrived by way of Siberia; smaller force came from European Russia. Adapted from Victor Zatsepine, "The Blagoveshchensk Massacre of 1900: The Sino-Russian War and Global Implication," in *Beyond Suffering: Recounting War in Modern China*, ed. James Flath and Norman Smith (Vancouver, 2011), 114.

committed suicide.[112] On August 4, Harbin, a city of over two thousand households and a population of about forty thousand, came under Russian control. "While most of the residents had escaped, quite a few of them were hiding below the floors or in storehouses. These people were all killed as soon as the Russians found them. The Russians then looted the entire city."[113] After Harbin, the Russians continued to move south, occupying Changchun, Jilin, and Kaiyuan.[114]

Another Russian force advanced north from Dairen following along the South Manchurian rail line. They easily captured the towns of Anshan, Shahe, Haicheng, and Liaoyang, near Mukden. Part of the reason the Qing were unable to mount an effective defense was that their armed forces were divided. "Occupying Russian forces did not meet unified opposition from local civilian-power groups either," historian Victor Zatsepine explained. "Local honghuzi bandits had ravaged the urban and rural areas even before the Boxers arrived." Even though the lines of differentiation between honghuzi, the regular Qing army, and the Boxers appeared indistinct from the Russian point of view, their motivations for joining the war against Russia were, in fact, quite distinct, so much so that they often ended up fighting each other. Moreover, changing policy in the Qing court confused local leaders. The day before the siege of Jilin, the military governor received orders from the Beijing government to suspend hostilities toward the Russian troops. Jilin, a fortified city of one hundred twenty thousand, was given up without a fight.[115]

The final offensive against Mukden started on September 30 and was spearheaded by Colonel Pavel Ivanovich Mishchenko's Cossack Guard Detachment. Mishchenko was a veteran of the Russo-Turkish War and was later put in charge of the security of the Manchurian railroads. He would play a key role in the battle of Mukden during Russia's war with Japan just five years later. That battle would cost the Russians more than twenty thousand dead and fifty thousand wounded, but this operation cost them a mere two hundred men.[116] By the afternoon of October 2, Mishchenko and his men were in possession of the imperial palace, birthplace of the Qing dynasty.[117]

By the middle of October, Russia's conquest of Manchuria was essentially over. Throughout the winter of 1900–1901 the Russian occupying force hunted down the bands of honghuzi who continued to pose a threat to the Russian force and the Chinese Eastern Railway. "I was told that they attacked the insufficiently prepared Russian troops and killed many soldiers, demolished parts of the railway, stealing the construction materials," wrote Ishimitsu Makiyo. "They brutally murdered all the Russian railway workers who were unable to escape."[118] The honghuzi were not a postwar phenomenon and did not emerge as a result of the Russian occupation. But they did become a major problem for the Russians, just as they had been for the Qing.

Recalling an inspection tour with Lieutenant General Grodekov, the commander of the Priamur (North Manchurian) forces, the writer A. V. Vereshchagin recalled a horrific sight at Jilin during his travels in the region shortly after the war that illustrated the difficulties the Russians now faced:

> I followed Grodekov's team out of the city. Further on, we came to a large square and stopped. Before us was a small fence which surrounded some sort of monument, and in the center [of the square] was a kind of foundation pit, enclosed with a roof. "What is that?" I thought. A Chinese policeman rode up in front of us. Grodekov went up to the hatch and shouted to the policeman. "Open it up!"
>
> The policeman stood indecisively. At last, he turned aside and with great aversion and fear lifted the lid. A terrible stench enveloped all of us. We were looking into a so-called "Honghuzi Pit." Here, two or three thousand honghuzi are executed every year. Their bodies are thrown into the pit. Their severed heads are either given to their relatives or put in cages and displayed on fences and trees . . . I looked into the pit. My God! The pit was vast, several *sazhens* across. It was terribly deep. Thousands of naked corpses lay inside. No one was clothed or had any features. All were headless. Their necks chopped like cabbage stalks. I was overtaken by horror. I hurried backward, as though I were afraid of falling in. Grodekov looked in, stepped away, and just shrugged. There was nothing else to do.[119]

The events of 1900 would force the Russians to confront a stark strategic choice: Should they remain in Manchuria and continue to fill the honghuzi pits with more headless bodies, knowing full well their presence would incur the suspicions of Japan and the other powers? Or should they withdraw their forces from Manchuria and abandon the CER to its fate? When Russian troops from Khabarovsk, Blagoveshchensk, and Nikolsk invaded Manchuria, they had no plans for its retention. But once in Manchuria, the Russians found it increasingly difficult to pull out.[120] "We had been spending hundreds of millions in providing a foreign country with railways, whilst the most crying unsatisfied need of our own country was precisely the glaring insufficiency of our own railway mileage," observed the Russian minister to Japan, Roman Rosen. "It stands to reason that such a waste of the people's treasure on helping to build the prosperity of a foreign country would be unpardonable, unless as a means to pave the way for that country's ultimate annexation."[121] Now the Manchurian railway had turned Russia's investment of treasure into one of blood as well. Every military occupation lasts too long but in the case of the Russo-Chinese War, Russia's desire to protect its railroad investment would have unforeseen consequences, not only for Russia's future relationship with China and Japan but for the future of Korea as well.

CHAPTER FOURTEEN

THE DEATH OF LI HONGZHANG

As Russian troops swept across Manchuria, William Rockhill arrived in Shanghai on August 29, 1900, and proceeded immediately to Beijing. Secretary Hay had decided to send Rockhill to China to work with E. H. Conger, the American minister in China, on the peace negotiations. Rockhill stopped over in Tokyo to see Japanese foreign minister Aoki Shūzō, who confided his concern about Russia's intentions. So long as Russian troops remained in Manchuria, Japan would not order "the withdrawal of Japanese troops from Peking," he said. Moreover, in light of "China's inability to pay a large indemnity," and the seeming "determination of many of the Powers to acquire further territory," the United States, without territorial ambitions, was the only power that could broker a credible solution to the China problem. Hay's Open Door Notes, in other words, would have to be put on the table once again.[1]

This would be a difficult task. The situation in 1900 was vastly different from when Hay first proposed the Open Door a year earlier. The Russians were now in possession of Manchuria. When peace negotiations began in October, Mikhail de Giers, the Russian minister to China, aggravated his colleagues by his reluctance to punish the Chinese. As the diplomats drew up indictments against the Chinese officials responsible for the Boxer Uprising, Giers stalled for time as Russian forces consolidated their holdings in Manchuria. Rockhill was exasperated. "Giers was perfectly willing to see negotiations drag on indefinitely, and to help waste as much time as possible over details of no special importance."[2]

263

Foreign Minister Lamsdorf had also signaled that his government would not be cooperative with the other powers on the peace negotiations. "Russia's aims in China and the Far East are in character and direction entirely different from the other powers," he declared.[3] It was obvious to everyone that Russia was attempting to restore Saint Petersburg's good standing with the Qing government. Giers's announcement in early September that Russia would be the first power to withdraw its forces from Beijing was thus not unexpected. By then it had become abundantly clear that Russia's main concern was to secure its own separate treaty with the Chinese government over Manchuria.[4]

The Qing appointed seventy-seven-year-old old Li Hongzhang as a plenipotentiary along with Prince Qing (Yikuang) to negotiate the terms of a Boxer Protocol with the powers.[5] Li had escaped the Boxer turmoil by safely ensconcing himself in the south, first in Canton and then in Shanghai, and then by refusing to obey the many imperial edicts issued by the court instructing him to return to Beijing. His calculated risk worked. Instead of Li being punished for disobeying orders, Empress Dowager Cixi welcomed his return to the capital because she realized he was the only person who could handle the diplomacy now required to settle the catastrophe she had helped create.[6]

Li's first and greatest challenge was dealing with the Russians. Russia had concluded its military operations following its final offensive against Mukden in October.[7] Despite the overwhelming victory, however, it soon became clear that military occupation alone could not ensure the security of Russia's railroads. A diplomatic solution was necessary but proved difficult. Sergei Witte argued against continued military occupation and thought the best course was to have China agree not to station forces in Manchuria that could threaten the railroads and Russian borders. War Minister Aleksei Kuropatkin, on the other hand, was against the premature withdrawal of troops, arguing that they should remain at least until the railroads were completed. He also thought Manchuria should eventually be made "dependent on Russia, following the example of Bukhara."[8]

While Saint Petersburg was trying to decide on a policy, a modus vivendi needed to be worked out between Russian and local Manchu officials in order to legitimize Russia's continued military occupation. General Zengqi, the military governor of Fengtian (Liaoning) Province, was put under enormous pressure by Admiral Alekseev, commander of the Russian Pacific Fleet, to sign an agreement that practically ceded the province to Russian control.[9] Zengqi balked, but Alekseev assured him that the agreement was only provisional and could be revised later.[10] Without formal approval from Beijing, Zengqi reluctantly signed the agreement on November 30, 1900.[11]

Unfortunately for the Russians, London *Times* correspondent George Morrison obtained a copy of the secret agreement and published its contents on January 3, 1901, with predictable outcry.[12] "The functions given to the Russian resident are similar to those of the Russian Resident in Bokhara or those of the British Residents in the native States of India," Morrison declared. "The agreement will necessarily be followed by similar agreements concerning the other two provinces [Jilin and Heilongjiang]. Then Manchuria will be a de facto Russian protectorate."[13] The *New York Times* followed up with a scathing editorial that predicted dire consequences for America's commercial situation in Manchuria.[14] Rockhill, in the midst of the Boxer Protocol negotiations—"nothing more than a miserable muddle"—wrote Hay that he had suspected Russian duplicity all along.[15] Most worrisome was that the Chinese government might be coerced into ratifying the Alekseev-Zengqi agreement. Repeating the history of the 1860 Peking Treaty, the Russians might acquire Liaoning, Jilin, and Heilongjiang Provinces—all of Manchuria—through diplomacy.

The circumstances, however, were quite different from 1860. First of all, the Chinese were no longer so gullible. Strangely, the Chinese court did not receive a copy of the Alekseev-Zengqi agreement until January 15, nearly two weeks after its contents were first published in the *Times*. Although Li Hongzhang received a copy of the provisional agreement in November, no mention was made of it in Li's correspondence for the following two months. When the agreement was finally forwarded to the Qing court, Chinese authorities were both "surprised and indignant" and simply refused to ratify it. An imperial decree to remove General Zengqi from office was also put forward but later rescinded.[16]

More critically, Russia faced a viable challenger in Japan. The Japanese were well aware of how Russia duplicitously took advantage of Chinese weakness in the Second Opium War to seize territory, and they were determined not to let history repeat itself. The situation was particularly troubling because Britain, increasingly distracted by its war in South Africa, appeared willing to simply accept Russian professions of good faith regarding its "temporary" occupation of Manchuria.[17] Meanwhile, in the United States, President McKinley was facing an election in November 1900 and was moving ahead with fulfilling his promise to withdraw American troops from Beijing despite strenuous objections from Hay and Rockhill, who argued that a withdrawal would undermine American influence at a critical moment during the peace negotiations and would show Washington's impotence to deal effectively with the Russian challenge.[18]

Japan seemed the only country willing to stand by China against Russia. Japan's motivation was not altruism but its own vital national interest to secure its influence in Korea and prevent Russia from infiltrating the peninsula from Manchuria.[19] Matters were made even worse when Foreign Minister Lamsdorf flatly denied the existence of the secret Alekseev-Zengqi agreement. Heated words were exchanged between Foreign Minister Katō Takaaki and the Russian minister to Japan, Alexander Izvolsky.[20] Relations between the two countries became extremely strained. Reports on how the Russians were trying to twist China's arm to control Manchuria at the ongoing Sino-Russian talks in Saint Petersburg merely reconfirmed Katō's grave misgivings.

SOME HELP FROM JAPAN

The Russian government suggested that talks on the future of Manchuria begin in Saint Petersburg with China's minister to Russia, Yang Ru, who had been appointed plenipotentiary. The Russians expected that the easygoing Yang would be a pushover. Sensing that Russian officials might get the best of Yang, Li limited the Chinese ambassador's plenipotentiary powers and insisted that he and Prince Qing (Yikuang) be consulted throughout the negotiations by telegraph.[21]

So what exactly were Russian objectives in Manchuria? The question seemed to confound the three Russian ministers involved in the Manchurian question—Witte, Lamsdorf, and Kuropatkin. The Manchurian issue was part of a larger question about Russia's interest encompassing the eastern part of the Russian Empire and access to the Pacific. To secure the Russian Far East (Primorsky) required securing not only Manchuria but Korea as well. Although Russia had enjoyed an ascendant position in the peninsula following the assassination of Queen Min in 1895, the tsarist regime did not capitalize on its newfound influence and instead compromised with Japan through the Nishi-Rosen agreement (1898), which in effect gave Japan equal say in the political and economic affairs of Korea. This compromise was deemed necessary because Russia's main focus at the time was on securing its gains in Port Arthur and completing the Chinese Eastern Railway. Japan, in other words, was to be placated.[22]

But the situation had changed by 1900. The CER was nearly up and running. The Russians had invested an enormous amount of the nation's treasury and blood into the railway and this investment had to be protected at all costs. Admiral P. Tyrtov, director of the naval ministry, put it this way: "The necessity of thwarting Japan's chance to acquire a dominant position in the Pacific, which would make their aggressive actions more tempting and give their action a high chance of success, demands that we control a significant point close to them—that is, in the south of Korea. We believe that this to be a necessity with Japan in the present moment, as the Japanese are strengthening themselves against us, our fleet, and our army."[23]

On December 17/4, 1900, Russia drafted a proposal for the upcoming negotiations. The key points were these: Manchuria "would remain a constituent part of the Chinese Empire and would be able to keep its civil administration but its military forces there will have to be disbanded"; local Manchu military governors (*jianjuns*) would be allowed to "keep a small police force" but it would be "up to the Russians to decide their number"; some Russian troops would remain in Manchuria to "preserve the peace"; the CER would remain under the control of Russia's Ministry of Finance; Liaoning (Fengtian) Province would be placed under the control of the Russian Kwantung military commander, Admiral E. I. Alekseev; Jilin and Heilongjiang Provinces, on the other hand, would be under the control of the Russian Amur military commander, General N. I. Grodekov; the Russian commanders "will be responsible for supervising the work of local military governors and prevent them from initiating hostile acts against Russia"; and finally, local military governors were prohibited from "increasing the number of their police force or from importing weapons."[24]

Although Witte and Kuropatkin disagreed sharply over the long-term occupation of Manchuria, they concurred that for the time being, at least, Russian forces had to stay put.[25] Negotiations began on January 4, 1901, between Witte and Yang Ru. Yang began by asking Witte how long Russian troops intended to stay in Manchuria. Witte stated matter-of-factly that Russia would keep its forces there "until such time that China had fully recovered from the Boxer chaos." "The Russian government cannot act like a child by dispatching troops one day and then withdrawing them the next." Witte perfunctorily asked that the subject of troop withdrawal not be raised again.[26]

At their third meeting, on January 17, Witte presented Yang with a thirteen-point draft proposal that covered many of the same points raised in the December 4 memorandum. Yang, unsurprisingly, was stunned and exclaimed that such an arrangement was basically "equivalent to Russia's protectorate over Bokhara."[27] Witte retorted somewhat angrily, "Russia has lost so much in Manchuria, with so many people killed. To withdraw her troops now without any precautionary measure—who in their right mind would do such an idiotic thing!?" Yang responded by saying that while "China would certainly compensate Russia for her losses," his country "would never submit to an unfair agreement."[28]

An indignant Yang reported the conversation to the Chinese government. Meanwhile, Prince Qing sought out Komura Jutarō, head of the Japanese mission in charge of negotiating the peace agreement in Beijing, to solicit his advice. Komura stressed that China must "restrict the number of Russian troops stationed in Manchuria and then set a date when they would be withdrawn." The critical task was "to not cede Manchuria to Russia and not allow them to station their troops there."[29]

Witte realized he had gone too far, and Foreign Minister Lamsdorf took over the negotiations. Over several weeks, Yang and Lamsdorf would meet thirteen times. Lamsdorf reminded Yang that Russian troops had been the first to withdraw from Beijing and Zhili, before the other powers. He also made clear that he expected China to accept the Russian proposal on Manchuria in exchange for help with the terms of the Boxer Protocol being negotiated in Beijing.

But two could play this game. Lamsdorf had expressly requested that details of the negotiations be kept confidential, but China did not oblige. On February 13 the Chinese envoy to Japan, Li Shengduo, secretly disclosed the Russian demands to the Japanese Ministry of Foreign Affairs. The Japanese informed the British about Russia's attempt to annex Manchuria. Now all the powers were aware of what the Russians were up to. "They urged us to reject the [separate] treaty and to discuss it with the other powers together," Liu Kunyi, the Viceroy of Liangguang, reported.[30] The Chinese government now had the leverage they needed to force Russia to modify its demands.

Yet, when a revised agreement was presented to Yang on February 16, the Chinese plenipotentiary hesitated.[31] Li Hongzhang was concerned that rejecting Russian demands would lead to a rupture of relations between the two countries.[32] The other powers had not offered any assurances that they would intervene on China's behalf, and even if they did, Russia could not be stopped by anything short of war. Others disagreed. Zhang Zhidong, a prominent court official, believed that going along with Russia's terms would lead other powers to believe they too could claim parts of China. "If

Russia becomes angry, we would lose only three Eastern provinces. But if all the other powers become angry, the eighteen provinces would be lost."[33]

In the end, the imperial court ordered Yang *not* to sign an agreement with Russia. On March 23 it issued an imperial decree stating that a separate agreement with Russia would be considered a "breach of the Boxer Protocol that was being negotiated with the powers in Beijing." Lamsdorf was furious. When presented with the letter of rejection, the normally taciturn minister "read it aloud, stood up for a few moments, his face turning red, and then bellowed: 'I have nothing more to say! China will suffer the consequences!'"[34]

A major concern of the imperial court was whether the Russians would try to disrupt the peace negotiations in Beijing. But this did not happen, and the Chinese breathed a sigh of relief. In this instance, Chinese officials, with Japan's assistance, had stood firm.

BOXER PROTOCOL

While the Saint Petersburg talks were taking place, the larger multinational talks were occurring in Beijing to finalize the terms of the Boxer Protocol. The issue of punishing pro-Boxer officials had been settled, and the negotiations moved on to the issue of an indemnity. The greatest difficulty was in determining the actual amount to be paid to each of the powers. Secretary of State Hay believed that an amount that impaired China's independence would ultimately be detrimental to the stability of the country and advocated the adoption of a lump sum payment not to exceed $150 million, a sum he thought was "within China's ability to pay." The idea was to divide up this payment among the powers "according to the percentage of the total loss each had suffered."[35]

Only Japan was open to the American proposal. The other powers, primarily Germany and Russia, asserted that the lump sum was far too small and insisted that the sum be raised to $333 million (450 million *taels*). Considering that the entire annual income of the Chinese government was estimated at 250 million *taels,* this was a staggering sum.[36] The Japanese representatives were taken aback. Ishii Kikujirō, who was in Beijing during the Boxer siege, was particularly scathing in his assessment of Russian behavior. Ishii was a member of the diplomatic mission in China headed by Komura Jutarō (who became minister of foreign affairs in September 1901) to negotiate the Boxer Protocol. "Russia sent her army to several strategic spots in Manchuria, but her actual relief army [in Beijing] was only half the size of Japan's," Ishii later complained. "What's more, the Russians sent their army to Manchuria out of an ambition to control the area, so they should not now require the Qing to cover the costs [of this expedition] at all."[37]

Ishii later vented his anger and frustration. "Komura Juntarō was the only one of the representatives [besides the Americans] who actually had a conscience at the time," he complained. "Compared to the amount of money each country demanded for themselves and the size of their relief force, there was an obvious contradiction. Japan requested a very fair amount; the requests of the British and the Americans were also comparatively fair." Ishii concluded bitterly that the powers had not only taken advantage of China; they had taken advantage of Japan as well. "If Japan in 1900 had been the same as France in 1919, we would have requested more than half of the total indemnity, just as France did in the Treaty of Versailles." But the Japanese lacked this kind of experience and were surrounded by a group of cunning Europeans.[38]

The Americans, too, experienced a deep sense of disappointment but for different reasons. The Protocol signed in Beijing on September 7, 1901, fell far short of the objectives Hay and Rockhill had hoped to accomplish. On July 3 Hay had introduced the second Open Door Notes proclaiming the principle of preserving the integrity of China, but it had made no impression on the other powers as a basis for an agreement. Although all the powers assented in general terms to the second Notes, "no one had cared to repeat in writing and sign the pledge about the territorial and administrative entity of China." For a few weeks the powers allowed John Hay to speak for them, "but while he talks they had their tongue in their cheeks." The published accounts passed between the European cities rarely, if ever, mentioned the Hay Notes.[39]

China, of course, was keenly disappointed by the outcome and, in particular, the actions that infringed on its sovereignty. It agreed to erect monuments to the more than two hundred Western dead, allow the stationing of heavily armed legation guards, and not to import arms for two years. It also agreed to ban all examinations for five years in cities where the atrocities had taken place.[40]

Heaped on such indignities, which led to simmering resentments, were the rampant and disgraceful lootings of China's treasures by Allied soldiers. Ernest Satow, the British representative, reported that even the Qing imperial tombs were looted. "The plague of [looting] infection has seized upon everybody though some have only mild cases."[41] General Adna R.

Chaffee, commander of the US Army China Relief Expedition, dryly described the more outrageous symptoms of this plague in a letter to a friend:

> Russia, Germany, England, perhaps France have each benefited very considerably by seizure of property of every description that could be marketed. I have been told that the item of spelter alone, sold by Germany, amounts to two and a half million max. Carloads after carloads have been shipped out and are going out still; brass gods, bronze gods, metal of all sorts seem to find ready sale. Thousands of rolls of grasscloth (much like mosquito netting) worth perhaps five cents per yard have been moved to the station in English carts on packs, and from there have disappeared in cars through the South Wall. Seemingly nothing is too insignificant in value to be overlooked if a dealer can be found who will buy; and the stuff belongs to the Chinese government. I have not been out to the Summer Palace since last fall, but from what I hear it is practically a wreck; only the walls still standing. The one-time beautiful furnishings, chairs, tables, bric-a-bracs have mostly disappeared in smoke or have been carried away. Of course, my mentioning of these matters is privately to you. If one knew that the proceedings would be accounted for to China by giving credit for the same, the seizures would not partake so much of the appearance of highway robbery.[42]

ENDGAME

On November 7, 1901, Li Hongzhang passed away. He died a broken-hearted man. A rumor that the Russian minister, P.M. Lessar, had attempted to force Li to sign the Sino-Russian agreement on his deathbed merely added to the pathos of his passing. "Poor old Li was at work thirty hours before his death," wrote Robert Hart. "Except that Russia loses her man, his disappearance will have no effect."[43] William Rockhill was more kind: "As to Li Hung Chang's part in the negotiations, he did all—absolutely all he could. Though I did not think that any of the foreign representatives—all of whom knew Li well—believed in the purity of his motives or of his patriotism, they were all convinced of his ability—quick comprehension of questions and of the great weight he still carried with his government in getting it to accept disagreeable duties or to carry out [the] most humiliating demands."[44]

Li was allegedly offered a personal bribe of three hundred thousand rubles if he would sign the Manchurian agreement. He objected vigorously

Li Hongzhang toward the end of his life, circa 1898. (Courtesy of Mrs M Nation-Dixon and SOAS Library University of London, Papers of Reginald Follett Codrington Hedgeland, SOAS reference PP MS 82/2/2)

but intimated he would ultimately go through with it. Then, at the crucial moment, he died.[45] George Morrison later wrote, "The Russian legation was very indignant because I was quoted as having stated that P.M. Lessar's attempt to force Li Hung Chang [Li Hongzhang] to sign the Manchurian Convention on his deathbed was the immediate cause of Li Hung Chang's death."[46] The obituary in the *North China Herald* summed up the general estimation of the man: "Although Li Hongzhang was not mourned by the Chinese nation, his place was a very large one and could not be easily filled."[47] Li's shortcomings and appetite for corruption were on the "hugest and unblushing scale," yet in the end the viceroy of Zhili had not given in to Russian demands. The negotiations over the fate of Manchuria would have to be postponed for another day.

PART FOUR

NEW FRIENDS,
OLD ENEMIES

AFTER OCCUPYING MANCHURIA during the summer of 1900, the Russians did not see the need to make any concession to Japan on Korea. Itō Hirobumi, who resigned as prime minister in June 1901, still hoped that some accommodation could be made with the Russians over Korea. The new prime minister, Katsura Tarō, however, initiated negotiations with the British for an alliance. Japan thus embarked upon a two-track policy in response to Russia's occupation of Manchuria: an accommodation with Russia and an alliance with Britain. The crucial point of both discussions was the fate of Korea

In 1896 Yamagata Aritomo had raised the idea of dividing Korea at the 38th parallel, which the Russians had categorically rejected. Japanese leaders then proposed an "Exchange of Manchuria for Korea" (Man-Kan kōkan), but the Russians again refused. Itō pressed for a compromise agreement on the Korea question but the talks stalled.

In London, Japanese ambassador Hayashi Tadesu's negotiations with British Foreign Secretary William Lansdowne were more productive, and the Anglo-Japanese Alliance was signed in January 1902. The treaty acknowledged Japan's interests in Korea without obligating the British to help should a conflict arise between Japan and Russia. Still, it included a provision that if a third party should join in the hostilities against the ally, "the other contracting party would be obliged to make war in common." Although the agreement was not intended to encourage Japan to resort to war with Russia, it did free the Japanese from the risk of the kind of European coalition that had deprived it of the fruits of victory in 1895.

The Russians were caught off guard by the Anglo-Japanese Alliance. They had hoped to sign a separate agreement with China to secure for Russia the concessions they wanted there. The Anglo-Japanese alliance, however, put these plans on hold. With Britain's backing, Japan put Russia on notice over its Manchurian designs. Abandoning its earlier proposal of the "Exchange of Manchuria for Korea," Japan viewed Russia's occupation of Manchuria as a direct threat to its interests in Korea.

Facing combined Anglo-Japanese pressure, Russia agreed to begin the evacuation of Russian troops from Manchuria in April 1902 and complete it by October 1903. But by the beginning of 1903, Russia reversed its pledge, and the second deadline for the evacuation passed. Meanwhile, Tsar Nicholas II created the new post of viceroy of the Russian Far East, with plenipotentiary powers to deal exclusively with the affairs of China, Korea, and Japan. A Special Committee for the Affairs of the Far East was also created in Saint Petersburg and headed by Alexander Mikhailovich Bezobrazov and Aleksei Abaza, both hard-line expansionists.

In 1898 Bezobrazov obtained a Korean lumber concession on the Yalu River. Kojong was pressed by the Japanese to declare that all ports on the Yalu be proclaimed open ports and that Russia adhere to the principles of the Open Door in Korea, a position the Americans and British supported. But due to pressure from Russian hard-liners, Kojong wavered while his government was split between pro-Japanese and pro-Russian factions.

When reports reached Japan in May 1903 that a large group of Russian soldiers disguised as laborers had been brought into the Russian concession area and that Russian troops had occupied the Korean village of Yongamp'o on the left bank of the Yalu River, Japan's reaction was swift. Without a declaration of war, Japan made a surprise attack on Port Arthur on 8–9 February 1904. Nearly simultaneously, Japanese troops began landing forces in Inch'ŏn, Korea, without incident.

For the second time in less than a decade, Japan was waging war in Korea. But this time it had British and American backing.

CHAPTER FIFTEEN

NEW AGREEMENTS

It is a curious but little-remarked irony of history that while the Boxers were rampaging against Western missionaries and their native Christian converts in north China and Manchuria in 1899–1900, Christianity was becoming more, not less, attractive to the Korean masses. Growing Catholic fervor in the northern provinces was particularly noteworthy. By the 1890s the Korean Catholic community began to grow rapidly, from twenty-six thousand members in 1895 to sixty thousand in 1904. The majority lived in Hwanghae and P'yŏngan Provinces, where Catholic authority often exceeded that of provincial officials.[1]

The explosive growth of Catholicism in Korea was largely a response to the perceived failures of the local and central governments. The year 1900 had been particularly harsh; a great deal of distress afflicted the people. Instead of finding ways to provide relief, the Korean government raised taxes and coerced payment through special inspectors, adding to the misery of the people. The governor of Hwanghae Province, Min Yŏng-ch'ŏl, reported with anxiety that an increasing number of Catholic converts in the area had simply refused to pay their taxes or to submit to local laws.[2] "It is painful to report that Catholic believers obstruct police investigations," he complained. "What is worse, they meet them with violence. We are unable to carry out administrative affairs . . . Some Catholics, in a bad slip of the tongue, declare that they are not even Koreans . . . that their loyalty is rather to the authority of the church."[3] In one case, a group of Catholics beat up local officers to protest undue tax collection.

Father Joseph Wilhelm was known for his outspoken ways and fierce protection of his Catholic congregation, which included An T'ae-hǔn and An T'ae-gǒn, father and uncle, respectively, of An Chung-gǔn, Itō Hirobumi's assassin and Korean national hero. (Maryknoll Mission Archives)

In 1899 hundreds of Catholics stormed a government hall following the arrest of four Catholics in Anak, accusing the magistrate of "false arrests and wounding several constabulary officers." The authorities suspected that these Catholics were former Tonghaks who had disguised their identities to evade punishment. Catholics were fostering "disobedient attitudes toward the government and among the people," but because they enjoyed the protection of foreign missionaries, they could not be easily disciplined, as "punishing them might lead to diplomatic trouble."[4] One such missionary, Father Joseph Wilhelm, was considered a "very fair-minded man" but was a "regular terror" to local officials. "He has been imprisoning and beating [Korean] policemen and doing other things as though he were a governor."[5]

By the fall of 1900 the Boxers had reached P'yŏngan Province bordering Manchuria along the Yalu River. Horace Allen, the American minister to Korea, reported that "800 Boxers had come to the border and tried to induce the Koreans to join" but the Koreans refused.[6] In response to the chaos, a police force was dispatched to the area, but clad in Western-style uniforms, they were mistaken for Japanese soldiers.[7] In Manchuria, disorder from the fighting between Russian and Chinese troops spread to Jiandao (Kando), the border region between China and Korea along the north bank of the Tumen River, and then to Korea's Hamgyŏng Province, where marauding bands of honghuzi bandits and Boxers found refuge.

On June 27, 1900, Kojong invited the Seoul diplomatic corps to the palace to discuss the situation. Keenly aware of his country's vulnerable position as the Boxer chaos threatened to stir up trouble in the northern provinces, he was worried Japan might be tempted to use the situation as an excuse to send troops. Kojong asked his guests for their "kind advice" on preserving order in the north. He was also concerned about the situation with Korea's Catholics. Hayashi Gonsuke, the Japanese minister, responded caustically that "all the powers are acting with complete unanimity in China and they will no doubt act the same way in Korea." Hayashi's words created a "chilling impression on Kojong." They had an equally bad effect on A. I. Pavlov, the Russian representative. He recommended that Kojong dispatch troops to the northern region as quickly as possible to maintain order.[8]

KOREAN NEUTRALITY

Nearly a year after hiding himself in the Russian legation following Queen Min's murder, Kojong returned to his palace in February 1897. A year later, the signing of the Nishi-Rosen Agreement in 1898 between Russia and Japan offered an opportunity to embark on a new program of self-strengthening and modernization. The two countries had pledged to recognize Korea's independence, and Kojong saw the agreement as his last chance to strengthen his nation before Korea slipped even further behind and became easy prey to Russian or Japanese domination. The Taewo'n'gun's death in 1898 had also relieved Kojong of the thorn that had plagued his reign since he announced his assumption of direct royal rule in 1873. In a symbolic gesture aimed to reassert Korea's independence and declare his nation an equal to Japan, Russia, and China, Kojong changed his own title from *kukwang* [國王] (king) to *hwangche* [皇帝] (emperor). (Queen Min's title was likewise posthumously changed to Empress Myŏngsŏng.) He also announced that henceforth his country would be known as the Korean Empire (*Taehan chaeguk*), literally the Great Han Empire. The Kwangmu Reforms (1897–1904), as they came to be known, were Korea's last desperate effort to change its course. But they were often enacted in a piece-meal fashion, and much of them remained on paper.[9]

The Boxer Uprising, however, threatened to undermine the reform programs before they had a chance to take off. Japan and Russia were both concerned what the Boxer chaos might mean for their position in Korea. Russian foreign minister Lamsdorf wrote to A. P. Izvolsky, Russian minister to Japan, "The most serious danger for us in the present moment is the possibility that the unrest will spread from China to the Korean Peninsula. And if that should happen, the Japanese will send significant forces to the peninsula." Izvolsky was told to remind Japanese foreign minister Aoki Shūzō of the terms of the 1898 agreement: should Japan decide to send troops to the peninsula, Russia would be within its rights to do the same.[10]

The Boxer crisis had thus raised the possibility that two foreign armies would once again clash on the Korean Peninsula. Kojong responded to the crisis by raising with Hayashi the issue of Korean neutrality. The Korean government would uphold its right to remain a neutral party should Japan and Russia come to blows. Meanwhile, in Tokyo, Izvolsky approached Itō Hirobumi, who had become prime minister in October 1900, about Kojong's neutrality proposal.

Itō flatly refused to discuss the neutrality issue as long as Russian troops remained in Manchuria. For the first time, the Manchurian and the Korean question became linked in the Russo-Japanese struggle for dominance in the region.[11] Russia was clearly unprepared and unwilling to withdraw from Manchuria. Given the new situation created in Manchuria as a result of the Boxer Uprising, Itō proposed negotiating a new pact on Korea to replace the Nishi-Rosen Agreement. But the talks were cut short when the Itō government fell in May 1901. The new cabinet, headed by Katsura Tarō, a veteran of the Sino-Japanese War, decided to take a two-track approach to the Korea problem. Japan would seek an agreement with Britain over Korea as well as pursue a separate negotiation with Russia. Having learned the bitter lessons of the Triple Intervention and the Boxer Protocol, Katsura was determined that this time it would be Russia, not Japan, that would come up short.

HAYASHI AND LANSDOWNE

Despite the unpleasantness and bickering surrounding the nearly twelve months of negotiations among the powers, the Beijing Conference (1900–1901) had led to friendship between Britain and Japan. Their collaboration was based on compatible and personal ties. The Russian presence in Manchuria aligned Japanese and British interests, and the British and Japanese representatives, Ernest Satow and Komura Jutarō, enjoyed friendly relations that predated the Beijing talks. The two men had met years earlier when Komura had been vice minister of foreign affairs and Satow was the British ambassador to Japan. Komura had earlier favored a rapprochement between Russia and Japan, but his experience dealing with the Russians in Beijing had decidedly turned him "less pro-Russian than his predecessor."[12] Komura's changed attitude toward Russia would have an important effect on Japanese-British relations. Upon his return to Tokyo in September 1901, Komura was appointed minister for foreign affairs under the first Katsura cabinet and helped to oversee an alliance between the two nations.

The idea for an Anglo-German-Japanese alliance was first hinted at in March 1901 by Hermann Freiherr von Eckardstein, first secretary at the German Embassy in London. Eckardstein worried that if Japan was left on its own, it was likely to enter into an agreement with Russia over Manchuria, and such an arrangement would spell the end of China's integrity, threatening the stability of East Asia. Eckardstein approached Hayashi Tadasu, the Japanese minister in London, with a proposal to initiate talks with the British Cabinet to form an alliance, assuring him that the German Chancellery supported the idea. He confided that Britain and Germany were at that very moment working on an agreement over Far East policy and intended to invite Japan to participate.[13]

Hayashi responded enthusiastically, as an alliance between Japan and Britain had been on his mind for some time. In 1900 he had confided to George Morrison of the London *Times,* that such an alliance would be the crowning achievement of his diplomatic career. "There was no doubt in my mind," he later wrote, "that if the British government had an intention of entering into such an alliance as the German chargé had outlined, it would prove to be a combination of the utmost advantage to Japan." Hayashi immediately sought Tokyo's permission to sound out the British government on the matter.[14]

It turned out, however, that Eckardstein was freelancing—Germany had no intention of forming an alliance with either Britain or Japan. Nor did he even have the authority to make such an overture to the Japanese ambassador.[15] But since the proposal had been put on the table, Hayashi decided to approach British foreign secretary Lord Lansdowne on his own cognizance. To his relief, he found a receptive audience. On April 17 the two men met to discuss the Far Eastern situation. "I referred to the situation in China," Hayashi later wrote, "and explained that the future of that country was a source of anxiety to myself and that I believed that it was a matter of urgent necessity for Great Britain and Japan to make a permanent agreement for the maintenance of peace in the Far East."[16] Hayashi then laid out six main principles that might form the basis for an alliance.

The third principle caught the attention of Lansdowne and subsequently became the most controversial: "That Japan, having greater interests in Korea than any other country, should be allowed freedom of action in Korea."[17] Lansdowne pointed out that this principle was very one-sided. Acceding to it was likely to lead to friction with Russia and possibly war between the two powers that would draw in Britain. "Japanese interests in Korea are very great, in fact, much greater than British interests in the Yangzte," Lansdowne explained. "Why should Britain risk a conflict with Russia when it had no stake in Korea?" Hayashi countered that having such a guarantee of British involvement was "the whole essence" of the treaty; without it there would be no point in Japan pursuing an alliance.[18] "I am afraid there will be criticism that the benefits by Japan and Britain are not proportionate," Lansdowne replied.[19] But what was the alternative for Britain? As discussions continued through the fall and winter of 1901–1902, Lansdowne would discover what that alternative might be.

TWO BRIDES TO ONE WEDDING

The death of Li Hongzhang in November 1901 created new challenges for Russian diplomats in Beijing and Saint Petersburg. Having lost their point man in China, the Russians faced an entirely new situation. The turn of the century had marked the near completion of the Trans-Siberian Railway that Witte and others had rightly trumpeted as one of the world's greatest achievements of the new century. The aftermath of the Boxer upheaval and the stalled negotiations over Manchuria threatened to undermine the whole enterprise. It was thus with a measure of relief that Witte and Lamsdorf received the news that former prime minister Itō Hirobumi was on his way to Saint Petersburg to discuss the Far Eastern situation. Witte hoped to come up with an agreement with Itō over Manchuria that gave the Russians free rein in there without Japanese interference. The question was Japan's price for such an accommodation and whether a new version of the old formula "Exchange of Korea for Manchuria" could be worked out.

Why did Prime Minister Katsura sanction Itō's trip to Saint Petersburg when talks were already under way between Hayashi and Lansdowne in London? The answer appears to be a simple one: Katsura was hedging his bets. In other words, he had decided to invite two brides to the same wedding, in case one of the brides backed out.

Negotiations in London progressed rapidly. Lansdowne handed Hayashi a first draft of the proposed treaty on November 6.[20] At this delicate moment in the negotiations, Hayashi received a telegram from Komura directing him to go to Paris and link up with Itō. At their meeting on November 14, Itō expressed surprise that the negotiations with Britain had progressed so far, but he was not convinced he should abandon talks with the Russians to come to an accommodation over Korea. "In his [Itō's] opinion it was unprofitable for Japan and Russia to continue to look at each other with 'crossed eyes' regarding Korea."[21]

Hayashi was furious, not so much at Itō as at having been kept in the dark by Tokyo about the Russian mission. "Here I was negotiating with Lord Lansdowne, getting out plenipotentiary powers from Tokyo to negotiate an alliance, and yet the Government at home had sent Itō to negotiate a convention with Russia . . . I thought that it was most inconsistent of my Government to have telegraphed accepting my views with regard to an Anglo-Japanese Alliance and then to take such a step." After "employing much persuasive oratory," Hayashi was finally assured by Itō that he would not do anything rash in Saint Petersburg that "might disturb the Anglo-Japanese negotiations."[22]

Katsura also seemed to have realized the potential harm Itō's Russian negotiations could inflict on the London negotiations. He wrote Itō in Berlin on November 22 somewhat nervously: "Please bear in mind that the negotiations for the British alliance have made such progress that they have reached a point where we cannot retract without incurring great national dishonor." In a later cable Katsura reminded Itō that he should "confine" his conversations in Saint Petersburg to "an informal exchange of views and then reiterated the point once again that the Anglo-British negotiations would have priority."[23]

Foreign Minister Komura assured Hayashi that the Japanese government was not double-dealing, and asked him to convey this message in the strongest possible terms to the British Foreign Office.[24] Relieved, Hayashi gave a rather skeptical Lansdowne his government's assurances when he returned to London on November 26. " He [Lansdowne] said that if it was the intention of the Japanese Government to negotiate a convention of agreement with Russia whilst the negotiations with Great Britain were in progress, the British government would be very angry."[25]

ITŌ IN SAINT PETERSBURG

Itō arrived in Saint Petersburg on November 26. During the first meeting with Lamsdorf on December 2, Itō stated that it was essential to clear up the misunderstanding regarding Korea. He emphasized that freedom of action in Korea "was a life and death issue for Japan." "If we do not arrive at a more permanent solution to the Korea problem, there is the danger that misunderstanding will constantly recur." Itō also reiterated that Russia should acknowledge Japan's vital interest there and rejected Lamsdorf's suggestion that the two countries work together on a joint policy in Korea. "If there is an incident, with Japan holding one view and Russia the opposite, Korea will be able to take advantage of the discord between us," Itō argued.

Lamsdorf thought that while Russia would in principle not object to "entrusting" Korea to Japan, it must have ironclad guarantees against its militarization and military use. "Russia has no ulterior motives regarding Korea," Lamsdorf stated. "But it absolutely rejects Japanese military involvement in the peninsula." Itō responded that any military activity by Japan would be to maintain internal order and would have neither intent nor capability for a military confrontation with Russia. "We simply need to be able to restore and maintain domestic order in the event of a disturbance," he said, adding that "the dispatch of troops is not tantamount to a [military] occupation." When asked whether Japan would be willing to cede to Russia a small piece of territory—namely, Masamp'o (Masan harbor) on Korea's southern coast—"while Japan had control over northern Korea," Itō strongly objected. He stated emphatically that "Japan could not agree to such a compromise for Masamp'o is the Gilbraltar of the Korean gulf; to lose it would mean losing all of Korea."[26]

The next day, December 3, Itō sat down with Witte. The finance minister claimed that "not being a diplomat," he was allowed "to speak bluntly." "Your country has always had considerable interests in Korea while mine has none," Witte told Itō. He pointed out that under the present agreement, of 1898, Japan and Russia were allowed to keep equal garrisons in Korea. "One wonders if one can avoid mutual misunderstandings if that equality is lost."[27]

Witte returned to the question of Manchuria. "I would call your attention to one point—that of our great railway in the Orient in which we have invested 300,000,000 rubles. Its benefits will be reaped by the countries of western Europe and the Far East, especially Japan. Russia must do all in its power to protect this line and obtain guarantees about its future from European countries and especially Japan." Itō countered that "it was only reasonable that measures be taken for protecting the railways. But Japan has much deeper commitments in Korea than the railway lines." His only hope was that "Korea might be entrusted to us commercially, politically and militarily." But he was quick to add: "Of course, Japan will never use Korean territory for military purposes against Russia." What might Japan expect from Russia, then, if his government gives Russia freedom of action in Manchuria? Witte answered: "Meet all our demands in Manchuria then—anything you like: *tout ce que vous voulez.*"[28]

Itō left Saint Petersburg quite optimistic. During his final meeting with Lamsdorf on December 5, the latter had promised to send along a draft of the proposed agreement to him in Berlin.[29] Itō wrote to Katsura from Berlin urging him to postpone the signing of the Anglo-Japanese Alliance.[30] "I firmly believe that signing the Russo-Japanese entente is favorable to Japan," he assured Katsura. "If we miss this opportunity to come to an agreement with Russia over Korea we will never have another such opportunity again."[31] This was quite contrary to Katsura's guidance. The British agreement was the priority.

Katsura was becoming increasingly concerned about Itō's "freelancing."[32] He was instructed to reject Lamsdorf's draft agreement, which, in any case, had pointedly excluded Japan from having any political predominance over the peninsula.[33] It took Itō six days to compose his response to Lamsdorf.[34] Privately, Itō was anguished. He understood, perhaps all too well, that without an entente the prospect of war between Russia and Japan loomed ominously.

Witte thought a momentous opportunity had been lost. "Unfortunately, Itō was received coldly," he later wrote. "And we moved slowly. Count Lamsdorf solicited opinions from the concerned ministers . . . [who] raised various objections."[35] The finance minister had been strongly in favor of a "speedy settlement" with Japan. "If Russia were to choose between a military conflict with Japan and complete cessions of Korea— the second option would still be the lesser of two evils," he wrote. "By sacrificing our interests in Korea, we would eliminate our constant mis-understanding with Japan."[36]

ANGLO-JAPANESE ALLIANCE

Itō arrived in Britain on December 24 no longer opposed to an Anglo-Japanese alliance. On January 2 he visited Lansdowne's private estate in Wiltshire. Assuming the British foreign minister knew all about his trip to Saint Petersburg, Itō made a surprising admission: "I am very anxious not to leave any misunderstanding about what I have been doing [in Russia]," he remarked remorsefully. "I have no thought of a *double jeu* [double dealing]. We never contemplated an alliance with Russia as we do with Britain."[37]

It was a face-saving measure. Still, Itō's clandestine efforts in Saint Petersburg may have helped Hayashi's negotiations in London. Itō's dealings had the effect of stimulating the British into action and hastening the conclusion of the alliance.[38] Lansdowne certainly did not push back very hard against Hayashi's demands, especially concerning article 1, which stated that Great Britain "recognizes Japan's interests in Korea" and its right to "safeguard those interests."[39] The treaty acknowledged Japanese interests in Korea without obligating Britain to help should a Russo-Japanese conflict arise except in the case that Japan becomes involved in a war with more than one power. Hayashi also refused to open up the scope of the agreement to include India. The treaty remained restricted to what the Japanese called the "Extreme East."[40]

Why did the British government concede and conclude an alliance it thought could lead to a war between Japan and Russia that might draw in Britain over a country it had little interest in? It appears the main reason was to prevent an understanding between Russia and Japan over Manchuria. Such an entente would have rendered Britain's position in East Asia "hopeless." In this sense, the alliance was more about preempting the Russians over Manchuria than gaining an ally. As historian William Langer put it, "If one looks at the [Anglo-Japanese] Alliance from this viewpoint, there will be less difficulty in seeing why the British gave the Japanese the free hand in Korea and avoided pressing too far their demand for an extension of the Alliance to India. The important thing for England was not what was *in* the Alliance, but the fact that there *was* an Alliance."[41]

Hayashi and Lansdowne signed the Anglo-Japanese Alliance on January 30, 1902. Hayashi was elated at achieving his diplomatic triumph

but he continued to nurse bitter feelings toward Itō. "It was a great pleasure for me to sign this treaty and it was a great success for Japan,"
Hayashi later wrote. "But I do not think that our Government behaved
well over it, especially in regard to sending Marquis Itō to Saint Petersburg whilst I was negotiating with Lord Lansdowne. He ought not to have
been sent whilst the negotiations with Great Britain were in progress. Besides the embarrassment which it caused me in my negotiations, as my
conversations with Lord Lansdowne showed, such a lack of faith and
breach of honour put Japan in a very bad predicament. She has indeed won
the support of Great Britain, but she lost the respect of Russia and of
other European countries."[42]

RUSSIAN MISSTEPS

Whether Japan lost the respect of the Russians is arguable, but they were
certainly surprised by Itō's abrupt rebuff. The announcement of the Anglo-
Japanese Alliance, stunned Lamsdorf and Witte. What made it all the
more troublesome was that the news came amid two other diplomatic
setbacks for Russia. Following the public disclosure of the secret Alekseev-
Zengqi Agreement, Secretary Hay sent a telegram on February 1 to China,
Russia, and the other powers, strongly objecting to the contemplated
agreement and continued Russian occupation of Manchuria. These objections would probably not have had much effect on the Russians had it
not been for the signing of the Anglo-Japanese Alliance, which gave the
impression of a new Anglo-Japanese-American bloc against Russia's Manchurian occupation. The Russians had been caught flatfooted and were
now diplomatically isolated.

Furthermore, the announcement of the alliance came on the heels of
the resumption of diplomatic negotiations over Manchuria. These talks
were not going well for Russia. News of the alliance had convinced the
Chinese to play hardball, with the result that the Russians were in the end
forced to agree to evacuate Manchuria.[43] The new Russo-Chinese agreement, signed on April 8, 1902, stipulated that Manchuria would be returned to China, which would be responsible for protecting the railway
and "all Russian subjects and their undertaking." The Russians agreed
to begin evacuating its troops from Manchuria within six months. This
evacuation would take place from April 8, 1902, to October 8, 1903.[44]
There was no doubt that the Anglo-Japanese Alliance became a major
obstacle to Russia's goals in China. The British ambassador to Russia, Sir

Charles S. Scott, observed that while Lamsdorf, Witte, and other Russian ministers "affected calm, and even indifference, as to [the alliance's] consequences, they have been greatly discomforted by it and acknowledged it as a diplomatic check, if not defeat."[45]

The alliance also had an important impact on events in Korea. "It [news of the alliance] has caused a sensation in the capital of Korea," wrote one observer, "and has come as an unexpected discovery to the Korean government."[46] The *Hwangsŏng sinmun* focused on the fundamental contradiction of the first article of the alliance that "promised Korean independence and territorial integrity" while giving "Japan the right to intervene to protect her political, industrial and commercial interests in Korea if these interests were threatened."[47]

On February 4, 1902, Kojong met with A. I. Pavlov, Russian minister to Korea. He confided that the Japanese had approached his government with a proposal to secure a new Japanese-Korean treaty that would "eliminate Russian influence in the peninsula and draw Japan and Korea close together."[48] The proposed treaty stipulated that in case of a conflict between Japan and Russia, the Koreans "must turn to Japan for aid." Moreover, in all financial matters, including the securing of loans, "the Korean government would also be obligated to turn to Japan for aid." Kojong said he had refused the Japanese request, and expected "no hostile activity from Russia."[49]

The Japanese minister to Korea, Hayashi Gonsuke, however, persisted. He forwarded a copy of the alliance to the Korean foreign minister Pak Che-sun, explaining that Britain and Japan had decided to "unite their armed forces in order to impede the existing Russian plan of aggression, first in Manchuria and then in Korea."[50] Hayashi urged Pak to sign the treaty with Japan in order to prevent any misunderstandings that could lead to a Russo-Japanese conflict over the peninsula. If war broke out between the two powers, Korea would be caught in the middle and bear a huge cost.

The Anglo-Japanese Alliance thus aggravated the struggle among Koreans over the question of the country's external orientation: Japan or Russia. Soviet historian V. I. Shipaev observed that "the [Korean] 'progressives' began, as a rule to orient themselves toward Japan and the United States, while the conservatives, to Tsarist Russia. The continuous rivalry of these two groups ('conservatives' and 'progressives') which on some level expressed the conflict between imperialist countries and their struggle to seize a dominant position on the Korean Peninsula, weakened the internal strength of the Korean nation and eventually enabled the enactment of foreign powers' plans for seizure, with imperial Japan first among them."[51]

Shipaev's observations are striking, for they show that the internal conflicts between Korean conservatives and progressives that had been waged between Kojong and his father in the 1880s and 1890s continued under a similar guise after 1900. Preoccupied with the crisis in China, Japan and Russia decided to call a truce in Korea in 1898, the same year the Taewǒn'gun died. Taking advantage of this unexpected opportunity, Kojong bolstered his imperial authority and international prestige by proclaiming himself emperor, and his country a great empire (*Taehan cheguk*). But the hollowness of these imperial epithets was exposed by the Anglo-Japanese alliance. Henceforth, Kojong was forced to rely on Russia for support, aligning himself with the erstwhile "conservative" faction while "progressive" members within his own government, including Foreign Minister Pak Che-sun, looked to Japan. The two political factions that emerged during this period of intensifying international struggle over Korea would later come into violent conflict with each other, bequeathing to posterity the basic pattern of divided politics that would continue to plague Korea's colonial and post-liberation future.

CHAPTER SIXTEEN

RUSSIA'S KOREA PROBLEM

The arrival into the circle of the tsar's intimates of Alexander Mikhailovich Bezobrazov, member of a well-known Russian noble family and a retired captain of the Chevalier Guards, had a dramatic impact on the course of Russia's Far East policy. Bezobrazov became involved in a scheme to obtain a large Korean timber concession near the Yalu River and succeeded in persuading several powerful Russian officials to support it. His persuasive powers extended to the tsar. According to Kuropatkin, Bezobrazov "made a most extraordinarily favorable impression" on Nicholas II, so much so that "in the course of just a few months, he had acquired an influence over the tsar that nothing afterward seemed to shake." An eloquent and persuasive speaker, many saw Bezobrazov's outspoken opinions as "a sign of deep conviction and even genius." Roman Rosen, Russia's ambassador to Japan, referred to him as a "celestial comet" whose "approach to our solar system" was as unexpected as it was dangerous.[1] Other opinions were less flattering; some thought him "ill-balanced—in which a strong imagination predominates—and a morbid hankering after fads."[2] Whatever his personal attributes, Bezobrazov had undeniable charisma and drew almost everyone to his venture.[3] But no one more so than his main opponent and personal enemy, Sergei Witte. The finance minister warned that Bezobrazov's Korean timber concession schemes would lead Russia to ruin and disaster.

The story of the Korean timber concession began in 1896 when Kojong agreed to sign away a large concessionary area in northern Korea to a Russian merchant from Vladivostok, Boris Yuliyevich Briner.[4] Roughly the size of Delaware, the concession encompassed timber tracts from Ullŭng Island in the East/Japan Sea to areas along the Tumen and Yalu Rivers, encompassing waterways of strategic importance to both Japan and Russia.[5] Briner secured the concession with the help of Russian minister to Korea Karl Weber when Kojong took refuge in the Russian legation in 1896–1897. Given the circumstances, it was difficult for the Korean king to refuse, but Kojong inserted an important clause: the concession expired if it was not exploited within five years.

However, Briner apparently lost interest and offered to sell the concession. Through Bezobrazov's family connections with the imperial court, the Briner concession landed on the desk of Grand Duke Alexander Mikhailovich, Nicholas II's brother-in-law and childhood friend. On May 13/April 30, Nicholas received a note from the Grand Duke: "The Briner forest concessions are extremely important, for they give us the chance to send an expedition to Korea, under the pretext of surveying its forests." The note was followed up a week later with a copy of the Briner concession, a list of people appointed for a proposed expedition, and a report on the conditions in Korea.[6]

Nicholas responded positively to the proposed enterprise. Briner would receive an initial 20,000 rubles; then, upon the expedition's return, should it prove favorable, an additional 50,000 rubles plus 80,000 rubles in company shares or in cash. The option to enact or terminate the agreement was set for February 13/1, 1899. After that, Briner would be free to offer his Korean concession to a private syndicate.[7]

A small team of surveyors was quickly organized and left for Korea on June 14, 1898. Witte was not notified of the expedition "as there were no finances required from the treasury and the success of the expedition depended upon its total secrecy to ensure success."[8] News from the expedition was encouraging. Nicholas's privy councilor, I. N. Neporozhnev, who was part of the survey team, reported that he "hoped to receive other valuable concessions [from emperor Kojong]" and requested that Foreign Minister Muravev give his support.[9] A request for permission to construct a railroad from Chinnamp'o (Namp'o) to the Russo-Korean border and the right to rent and develop new coal mines along the line was also made. The surveyors offered the possibility to create a forestry company, from the mouths of the rivers Yalu to Tumen, along with the entire extent of the Korean border from the Yellow Sea to the East/Japan Sea, "that would form a barrier between us and the Japanese who are intruding into southern Korea." Such an enterprise "would give Russia the option . . . to apply pressure to Korea and Japan in the name of defending our large commercial interests."[10]

Unfortunately, the timing of the Russian demands came at an inopportune moment for Kojong. Earlier that spring Russia's bellicose minister to Seoul, Alexey de Speyer, who had replaced Weber in January 1896, had stirred up a hornet's nest by demanding a public expression of Korea's reliance on Russia. The Independence Club, headed by a group of reform-minded officials in Seoul, organized public meetings and street demonstrations criticizing Russian meddling in Korean affairs and insisted on the dismissal of de Speyer. They also called on the Korean government to oust the government's financial adviser and military instructors. Rising Korean anti-Russianism caused concerns in Saint Petersburg, and in March 1898 de Speyer was abruptly recalled.[11] The new Russian minister, N. G. Matyunin, who replaced him in April, did not seem to understand the depth of the anti-Russian feeling, nor did he seem aware of Kojong's precarious political position.[12] The oblivious Matyunin offered Kojong a hefty bribe for his cooperation.[13]

Bezobrazov was elated, but the deal quickly fell through. On September 11, 1898, an assassination attempt was made on Kojong and the crown prince. Someone had slipped opium into the evening coffee.[14] The shaken Korean emperor told Matyunin that it was not an auspicious time to negotiate any concession deals with Russia.[15]

Meanwhile, Foreign Minister Muravev and Finance Minister Witte found out about the Korean expedition and were furious. They thought it was pure folly to antagonize Japan just at the moment when Russia was about to secure concessions over Port Arthur and Manchuria. The request for credit (the Korean "bribe") was denied. Bezobrazov complained loudly that by refusing the credit "an auspicious opportunity was being lost, perhaps irrevocably, for the establishment of our economic influence over Corea."[16]

The Korean concession story would have ended in 1899 had it not been for Bezobrazov, who persuaded Briner to cede his concession for an additional sixty-five thousand rubles with a view to eventually forming a Russian lumber company.[17] Purchasing the concession and putting it in private hands instead of abandoning it altogether seemed prudent because so much work had already gone into surveying the area. In August 1899 Nicholas was presented with an exhaustive account of the expedition, including a description of northern Korea from a military, economic, geological, and climatic point of view as well as a study of the Yalu and Tumen Rivers. The following March, Bezobrazov submitted his own detailed report outlining his concept for forming the East Asiatic Company.[18] It was to be founded as a stock company "with a capital of two million rubles at 5,000 rubles per share." Bezobrazov submitted a list of prominent people who had signaled their interest in the venture, many of whom were immensely wealthy.[19] Two hundred shares would be bought by the personal treasury of the tsar.

Nicholas weighed his options in what appeared to be a tempting proposal. It was somewhat unethical for the head of state to enter into what was essentially a promotional business venture whose fiscal outcome was not assured, but this obstacle could be easily circumvented by having the tsar's shares held in proxy by a third party. The bigger issue was that the enterprise carried great geopolitical risks. The Japanese would undoubtedly interpret a Russian venture on the Korean border as highly provocative, and it was hard to gauge how they might react. Finally, there was the question of timing. Under the original terms of the agreement between Briner and Kojong in 1896, the rights to the concession would expire after five years if the area was not exploited. That was barely a year away. The Bezobrazov group, in other words, was in a hurry. "The formation of the company hangs on your majesty's decision," Count Vorontsov-Dashkov, a Bezobrazov ally, told Nicholas. "The persons on the list in your majesty possession are going into the affair with the idea of serving you and Russia, and unless it is plain to us that we are working for you and under your patronage, very likely the majority will give up the affair." The tsar was given only days to decide the matter. "Thus a 'psychological moment' was created and the pressure produced its effect." Nicholas finally consented. He would purchase two hundred East Asiatic Company shares in the name of Bezobrazov's cousin, Captain A. M. Abaza.[20]

Nicholas had made the decision despite Witte's strenuous objections. When the proposal was first submitted to the finance minister for approval, Witte had advised the tsar to wait until "the end of the trouble in the Far East." The Manchurian problem had to be settled before such a bold venture in Korea could even be contemplated. Nicholas, in keeping with his fickle and mercurial character, agreed.[21] But the chaotic conditions in China and Manchuria during the summer and fall of 1900 had undermined Witte's standing at a critical time. Bezobrazov laid the blame for the entire Boxer catastrophe squarely at the finance minister's feet because the "whole trouble came from the Manchuria railway and in particular from the branch to Mukden and from that Polish-Jew of a right-hand man [chief railroad engineer] Alexander Yugovich who ran things there."[22] Had Russia had in its possession the telegraph and road communications in northern Korea that had been earlier proposed, "not only would Port Arthur have secure communication lines, but even more important, we should not be compelled to exert such pressure on China or to consort with Europe."[23] By the summer of 1900, as war between China and Russia raged, it was already clear Witte's days as finance minister were numbered.[24]

WARNINGS

Witte continued to preach caution, patience, and prudence on Manchuria and Korea. He warned that Russia must "eliminate our misunderstandings with Japan over Korea" otherwise "we will be under constant fear of armed conflict with this nation."[25] These were wasted words, as Witte had already lost the ear of the tsar.[26] In November 1902, Nicholas II dispatched Bezobrazov to the Far East "on a mission of very confidential nature." Once there, Bezobrazov made arrangements for the establishment of the East Asiatic Company and, responding to a rumor that "Japanese troops had already landed on the Korean banks of the Yalu and that Japanese armed boats were navigating the river," determined that "active measures [to secure] the area of the Yalu must be made."[27]

In the meantime, the deadline for the second withdrawal of Russian troops from Manchuria, on April 8, 1903, came and went.[28] "The ministers of finance, foreign affairs all recognized the danger that would threaten us if we continued to defer fulfillment of our promise to evacuate Manchuria, and, more specifically, if we failed to put an end to Bezobrazov's activities in Korea," wrote Minister of War Kuropatkin.[29] But it was too late. In May, Nicholas announced he was embarking upon a "new course." Manchuria was to be considered within Russia's sphere of exclusive political and economic interest, effectively rejecting the Open Door policy. Russia would also use its timber concession on the Yalu River "as a pretext to strengthen its position in Korea."[30]

Nicholas appointed Bezobrazov his new "state secretary to take charge of the new company and help direct Russia's new direction in policy."[31] Bezobrazov's job would be to facilitate communication between the logging company and the Russian government. In August, Nicholas appointed Admiral Alekseev to the newly created position of viceroy of the

Far East. Alekseev had been commander of the Pacific Fleet from 1895 to 1897 and now assumed supreme control over Russia's Far Eastern policy.[32] By appointing Alekseev as viceroy of the Far East, Nicholas had created what amounted to a second government whose mission would be to exclusively deal with all matters related to China, Korea, and Japan. "What I cannot understand," Count I. I. Vorontsov-Dashkov wrote in a private letter in May 1903, "is the duality of our policy in the east: the Tsar's official and the Tsar's unofficial policy, each of which has its agents, quarreling with each other."[33] Vorontsov had once been an enthusiastic member of the Bezobrazov clique.

Alekseev ordered a special military detachment under Colonel A. S. Madritov to the Yalu to defend the logging enterprise. Madritov deployed six hundred soldiers in civilian clothing, with a large mercenary detachment of three thousand honghuzi, "bandits," into Korean territory. "Since Madritov did not hope to get the support of the Chinese government, he decided to rely on the honghuzi [as mercenaries] since they could be used as an element that was in opposition to the Chinese government."[34] Alekseev also deployed four hunting squads of six hundred riflemen to form a "barricade" along the Yalu River, for "without controlling the Yalu, Russia's transport connection with Port Arthur would be endangered."[35]

Kuropatkin was appalled, warning that "our actions in the basin of the Yalu and our behavior in Manchuria have excited a feeling of hostility to us, which, upon our taking any incautious step, may lead to war [with Japan]."[36] Madritov's honghuzis could also lead to military clashes with Chinese governmental forces, which could strain Russo-Chinese relations.[37] But neither Kuropatkin nor Witte could do anything, as Madritov's action was done under the orders of Alekseev, who exercised authority in the name of the tsar.

Why had Nicholas decided on a course of action on the Yalu concession that risked conflict with China and Japan, a course that was opposed by his experienced ministers? Historian Dominic Lieven suggests that Nicholas was seduced by Bezobrazov's nationalist fervor, which fed his own patriotism in a proud and mighty Russia that took "no cheek from foreigners, especially from 'Orientals.'"[38] Frustrated by setbacks in the Far East, Bezobrazov's skepticism of the bureaucracy also reinforced Nicholas's distrust of his ministers, and above all, of Witte. Historian S. Podboltov noted how Nicholas's almost paranoid distrust of the bureaucracy extended to his own affairs. "Amazingly, the ruler of this enormous country did not even have a personal secretary; Nicholas sealed and signed his own envelops, answered endless congratulations and condolences, dealt with all sorts of minor things and endless petitions."[39] Nicholas struggled with a rapid modernization that had created "a horde of some 384,000 officials." "The unwieldy bureaucratic system suffered from a lack of coherence as the tsar jealously arranged it so that all the branches of government would have to work through him, at the expense of functionality."[40]

So what was Nicholas to do? Being a worthless strategist and administrator, it was not long before he began losing control of the bureaucratic apparatus. To compensate, he began to increasingly route the government through him, but he lacked the expertise in governance to do it properly. "The young tsar feels more and more contempt for the organs of his own power and begins to believe in the beneficial strength of his own autocracy which manifests sporadically, without preliminary discussion and without any link to the overall course of policy," observed Alexander Polovtsov, a member of the State Council.[41] The Yalu enterprise had thus come at an opportune moment for the tsar. Nicholas had always exhibited a keen interest in Russia's Far Eastern policy, an area where he thought he could excel. The Yalu venture would serve not only as a proving ground to demonstrate the tsar's ability to manage critical foreign policy but as an opportunity to consolidate the opposition against Witte, whom he had grown to loathe. In this sense, Bezobrazov's adventurous plans in Korea suited Nicholas's needs.

On August 16, 1903, Nicholas sacked Witte. Journalist S. M. Propper recalled Witte shortly after: "He was livid with anger, raised his right hand and said: 'I swear by those I hold dearest in the world, my wife and my daughter, that I will never forget what he has done to me.'"[42] Lamsdorf, however, continued as foreign minister. Witte later wrote, "Count Lamsdorf did not have the courage to leave on his own accord, and there were no grounds for dismissing him because although he expressed his views, he did not fight for them."[43]

Could a more courageous and forceful stance have forestalled the collision course between Russia and Japan? Witte seemed to think so, no doubt because he was trying to portray himself in the best possible light. But it is hard to imagine how courage or lack thereof at this late date could have had any real bearing on the events that followed. Perhaps humility and a sense of moderation might have been warranted back in 1898 when a more permanent solution to the Korean problem could have been reached, but these were qualities Witte himself also lacked.

"THE JAPANESE ARE PLAYING OUR GAME"

It was no secret that President Theodore Roosevelt favored the Japanese in the coming conflict with Russia. During the three years since he assumed the presidency after William McKinley's death by an assassin's bullet in September 1901, Roosevelt had become increasingly disillusioned with Russia. After a landslide victory in 1904 made him president in his own right, his antipathy toward Russia grew even stronger. "Russia for a number of years has treated the United States as badly as she has treated England, and almost as badly as Japan," he wrote to his close friend, British diplomat Cecil Spring-Rice. "Her diplomatists lied to us with brazen and contemptuous effrontery, and showed with cynical indifference their intention to organize China against our interests." By contrast, his admiration for Japan had no bounds. "The Japanese, as a government, treated us well, and they contended for was what all civilized powers in the East were contending for."[44] Although Roosevelt had no illusions about Japanese ambition, he believed that a rising Japan could be incorporated into a coalition of modern maritime states, along with Britain, whose main task would be to defend the principles of the Open Door in Asia.

Until 1904 Roosevelt had left the conduct of his East Asia policy largely under the control of John Hay, who had backed away from an earlier goal of preserving China's integrity and instead advocated for the more limited aim of preserving equality of commercial opportunity. Russia's refusal to continue its evacuation of Manchuria forced Hay to issue a series of diplomatic protests in 1902 and 1903. Realizing the futility of these gestures, Roosevelt sought to create a more vigorous response to Russian recalcitrance: an informal coalition with Britain and Japan to establish a check on the Russia menace.[45] But Roosevelt was limited by the constraints of the American foreign policy process. As Hay continually reminded the president, "public opinion of this country would not support such a course [of action]."[46] Though Roosevelt accepted Hay's advice, he chafed at being restrained and spoke of "going to extremes with Russia." The president seemed to believe that the American public might support a more robust defense of American interests in China, but before he had a chance to act on these views Japan stepped forward just in time to take up the challenge.[47]

Here was the solution Roosevelt had been looking for. Japan could serve as a balance against Russian power and thus protect the Open Door principles. "The one hopeful symptom is that they [the Russians] are really afraid of Japan," observed Roosevelt. "They know perfectly well that there is nothing in the situation which we would consider as justifying us in a resort to arms, but they know that it would require the very least encouragement on the part of the United States or England to induce Japan to seek a violent solution of the question." The Japanese, Roosevelt boasted "were playing our game."[48] The president would later come to regret his faith in Japan's commitment to the Open Door, but for now, he gladly gave the Japanese his full support.

By the spring of 1903, the British and American legations in Seoul were well aware of the Russian Yalu River lumber concessions. "Rumors are circulating here about the appearance of a Russian logging party accompanied by armed Chinese guards on the left [south] bank of the Yalu in Korean territory [the village of Yongamp'o]," reported Russian ambassador Roman Rosen from Tokyo. "This news is aggravating even without the excitement here concerning the Manchurian question."[49] The British minister to Korea, John Jordon, observed with rising concern that "there is a feeling of restlessness and anxiety in the attitude of the Japanese legation which I have never noticed in such a marked degree before."[50]

Hayashi Gonsuke, Japanese minister to Korea, felt this anxiety keenly, but he was not known for acting precipitously and his sanguine response to the Russian threat revealed his coolness under fire. He did not think a direct confrontation with Russia was warranted and advised Tokyo to pressure Seoul, with British and American support, to open up the Yalu River to trade. The reasoning made to gain British and American support would be to argue that the Yalu bordered China, which meant opening the Yalu was in accordance with the Open Door. This would prevent Russia from having exclusive privileges in Yongamp'o, Ŭiju, and other ports along the Yalu, and thus thwart unilateral Russian intrusion into Korea.[51] While it was a sophisticated strategy to challenge Russia by forming an alliance with the United States and Britain and appealing to their keen interest in commercial access, it also had the unfortunate consequence of putting Korea, once again, in the middle of a Great Power struggle.

In April 1903 the Japanese government officially demanded that the Korean government open the Yalu River to trade and proclaim Yongamp'o an open port.[52] As usual, when faced with a difficult decision, Kojong hesitated and then procrastinated. He replied that a definitive response would take a while because surveys had to be done. Even as the surveys were being planned, Hayashi received a report from a staff member that a Korean source had informed him that the Russians, unsurprisingly, were against the opening of the Yalu ports and had advised the Koreans to resist Japanese and Western pressure regarding them.[53]

On May 29 Lamsdorf reported to Nicholas II that the activities of the timber company "were being noticed and that this was being met with hostility on the part of foreign powers." The tsar was not deterred. On June 3 he directed Lamsdorf to telegraph Ambassador Rosen in Tokyo to convey to the Japanese that Russia "did not have any aggressive intentions toward Korea." But "this did not preclude the right of Russian entrepreneurs to use their land concessions however they saw fit, and this included the forest concession on the Yalu River."[54]

THE SEVEN PROFESSORS

As tension mounted between Japan and Russia, the debate over the opening of Yongamp'o and Ŭiju, and Japan's Korea policy more generally, was creating deep fissures in Japan, especially among the prowar faction associated with the Tōa Dōbunkai (East Asia Common Culture Society), a vocal pan-Asianist group founded by Konoe Atsumaro in 1898 with links to extreme right-wing Kokuryūkai (Black Dragon Society) activist Uchida Ryōhei.[55] Konoe would later establish the Anti-Russia Society (Tairo Dōshikai), which pushed for a hard-line policy toward the Russian Empire as a threat not only to Japan but to China and Korea as well.[56] In June 1903 seven Japanese professors with links to the Tōa Dōbunkai presented to Foreign Minister Komura a document entitled "A Memorandum Concerning the Manchuria Problem Representing the Opinion of Seven Doctors of Jurisprudence" in which they argued, among other things, that Japan had the right to wage war on Russia.[57] This right, they argued, did not come from any legitimate claim Japan had to control Korean territory but was based on Japan's right to defend the principles of the Open Door policy for Korea and Manchuria.[58] Their legal case against Russia based on principles of international order and diplomacy echoed the position taken by the prominent Diet leader Ogawa Heikichi, a member of the Anti-Russian Society and critic of Japan's "soft" foreign policy. For Ogawa, Japan's coming conflict with Russia boiled down to the simple fact that Japan was being denied open access to trade. "Since America, England, and countries throughout the world have expressed approval of the Manchurian open-door policy, Japan should take the necessary steps to open up Manchuria to development as quickly as possible."[59]

NEW FRIENDS, OLD ENEMIES

Ogawa's and the professors' logic was a variation of the "reform and civilization" argument that Foreign Minister Mutsu Munemitsu had made in 1894 to justify the Sino-Japanese War. As historian Katō Yoko explained, "rather than promoting war with Russia, [they] blamed Russia for the crime of breaking international law." Yoshino Sakuzō, a famous Taishō-era intellectual, expressed his support for the war in a similar way: "I see no reason that Japan should oppose Russia for territorial expansion in itself," he explained. "Our opposition is only that without fail Russia's territorial expansion policy is always accompanied by the exclusion of foreign trade and I consider this be uncivilized. For this reason, in order to defend ourselves, Japan must oppose this expansion with all our might."[60]

The publication of the seven professors' essay in the influential Korean newspaper *Hwangsŏng sinmun* (Imperial Gazette) in July created a sensation. As the leading organ of Korea's reformists, the *Hwangsŏng shinmun* was a powerful proponent of Korea's self-strengthening movement aimed to promote reform and capitalist development. It also reflected a strong anti-Russian bias.[61] The letters and editorials that followed agreed with the essay, arguing that Yongamp'o and Ŭiju must be opened as Japan had demanded. Ŭiju, in particular, was a strategic location for trade and commerce and the *Hwangsŏng sinmun* argued that "much could be gained in terms of the area's development should we open it up to trade." Moreover, "should foreign powers begin to enter to ports for trade purposes, we will not only be able to significantly curtail the incidents of piracy in this area but also assure that no one country gain a monopoly in terms of concessions." Although many Koreans opposed Russia's intervention on nationalist grounds, the editors of the *Hwangsŏng sinmun* based their resistance to Russia on commercial grounds as well. The best means of strengthening the nation was to have "the main economic actors, namely the people, accumulate wealth."[62] And there was no better way to do that than to promote free trade and commerce, which was championed by Japan, not Russia.[63]

The pro-Japanese views expressed by business leaders like Han Sangryŏng, vice-director of the Hansŏng bank, contrasted starkly with the pro-Russian leanings of the Korean court.[64] Han saw an alliance with Japan as a necessary compromise to allow capitalism to take root in Korea. Regarding the opening of Yongamp'o, the Korean foreign minister, Yi To-jae, complained that although he too favored the Open Door policy, his hands were tied. "The Korean foreign minister believed that the opening will not happen because of several opponents in the court, the anti-opening campaign of the Russian minister, and the uncertainty of the emperor Kojong's position," an exasperated Hayashi reported to Komura.[65] Koreans who supported the opening of the Yalu ports were in the minority in the government, their influence with the emperor limited. Hayashi advised stronger action to counter Kojong's resistance. "Japan has no influence in the Korean court," he complained. "At this time, I believe there is no other way than . . . to counter Russia's maneuvers, regardless of our agreement with Korea."[66]

KOJONG'S CHOICE

Kojong was now between a rock and a hard place. Japan and Russia were squeezing him on the Yalu ports issue while his government was split between pro-Japanese and pro-Russian factions. Making matters even worse, Russian incursions around the port of Yongamp'o in June and July led to clamoring by local leaders for the government to take action. They were especially aggrieved by the destruction of ancestral tombs by the Russians during construction.

Countering those who backed the opening of the ports to limit Russian incursions, the pro-Russian faction led by Yi Yong-ik, the emperor's "favorite," argued that the opening of Yongamp'o and Ŭiju would lead to an inevitable clash between Russian and Japanese forces along the Yalu that would turn Korea into a battlefield.[67] The disputes between the two factions came to a head in June when an assassination attempt was made on Yi Yong-ik's life. A bomb was planted in his hospital room where he was recovering from an illness. There was little damage and Yi was uninjured but the assassination attempt had sent a clear message that the pro-Russian faction was vulnerable.[68]

The Japanese government continued to press its demand for the Yalu port openings. Of particular concern to Hayashi was a July 20 report that the Korean government had negotiated a provisional lease agreement with Russia for concessions in Yongamp'o. The agreement would give the Russian company control over a large territory on the Korean side of the Yalu River that was not included in the original Briner concession.[69] With approval from Tokyo, Hayashi told Kojong, who had not yet approved the agreement, that if the lease agreement was signed allowing further concessions to Russia in the Yongamp'o area, Japan would have no choice but to occupy the same area, and threatened to dispatch forty-five thousand troops to the Korean side of the Yalu River.[70]

Deeply disturbed and worried, Kojong secretly informed Russian minister Pavlov of Japan's threat to deploy troops. The Japanese also maneuvered to strengthen their hands by getting the British to side with them.[71] "The prospect of getting a port opened on the Yalu does not seem bright," British minister to Korea John Jordon admitted. "But the Japanese are in earnest about the matter and we shall keep hammering away."[72] Jordon noted that the Korean emperor was playing with fire. "If the Coreans sign the [lease] agreement [with the Russians] and decline to open the Yalu, they may find that that they have made a mistake, but the emperor appears to think that Russia has the bigger battalions and wishes to be on the safe side in case of trouble. Whatever happened, he will probably have to reckon with Japan in the end."[73]

British pressure seemed to work. When G. G. Ginsberg, a representative for the Russian timber company, arrived in Seoul in August to finalize the lease agreement, Kojong told Pavlov he was not yet ready to sign.[74] Instead of outright canceling the agreement, Kojong, in characteristic fashion, demurred and informed Pavlov that a final decision on the agreement would have to be postponed. It was yet another ploy to gain time.

Kojong was desperate at being caught between Russian and Japan. Yi Yong-ik went to see Hayashi on October 7, imploring him to understand the situation from Kojong's point of view. "Given that the Korean court sees the opening of Yongamp'o as disadvantageous, nothing can be done [about the port openings] without Russia's approval."[75] The question had now become: Would Japan risk war with Russia over the opening of the Yalu ports?

BUILDUP TO WAR

On August 12, 1903, the Japanese envoy extraordinary and minister plenipotentiary to Russia, Kurino Shin'ichirō, submitted a proposal to Lamsdorf laying out Japan's terms for an agreement. It would acknowledge Russia's railway interests in Manchuria for Japan's unrestricted activity in Korea, including access to the Yalu ports. It was essentially a variation of the proposal Itō had laid out in Saint Petersburg in December 1901—Russia's recognition of Japan's preponderant interests in Korea in exchange for Japan's recognition of those same interests in Manchuria.[76] Lamsdorf was open to the proposal, but he had been sidelined on Far Eastern issues since the appointment of Alekseev as the new viceroy of the Far East. Alekseev categorically rejected any proposition that basically ceded Korea to Japan. Moreover, he rejected the notion that Japan had any interest in Manchuria, so it was not giving up anything by recognizing Russian interest there.[77]

Nicholas agreed with Alekseev that an agreement with Japan should be based on "Korean issues only."[78] Ambassador Rosen, who had departed for Port Arthur to confer with Alekseev personally, returned to Tokyo to present Russia's official reply to Komura on October 3. Russia would accede to Japan's position in southern Korea only, but the area north of the 39th parallel was to be recognized by both parties as a "neutral" zone. Such a counterproposal effectively meant Japan would be forced to cede control of northern Korea, a dire prospect. Indeed, there was no guarantee at all that Kojong would not secretly hand over control of this "neutral" zone to the Russians. The Japanese were under no illusion that a "neutral" northern Korea under the pro-Russian Kojong would fall under Russian dominance. The Russians also insisted that no part of Korea could be used for Japanese military purposes and that Manchuria and its coastal islands were to be regarded as entirely outside Japan's sphere of interest.

Foreign Minister Komura responded coolly to Rosen's October 30 proposal. He countered that Japan would agree only to set up a fifty-mile (eighty-kilometer) neutral zone on either side of the Korean-Manchurian frontier.[79] As for Manchuria, Japan "was prepared to recognize Russia's commercial rights but also insisted to have assurances about its own treaty right there."[80] This was a significant concession on Japan's part. The newspaper *Jiji shinpō* attacked the Russians, reporting that, despite the extreme patience shown by the Japanese people, "the conduct of the Russians renders amicable settlement almost impossible." The *Kokumin shinmun*, on the other hand, criticized what it saw as Japanese appeasement.[81]

In both cases the issue of war and peace was presented as a stark choice to the Japanese public: on the side of war stood the "enlightened" defender of the free market system and open trade; on the side of peace stood the "regressive" forces of closed markets and economic autarky. By touting the principles of the Open Door, and the argument made by Ogawa and the seven professors, the coming conflict with Russia was portrayed as something greater and more principled than a raw conflict for power and influence over Korea and Manchuria. "The salient facts are that Japan, the United States and Great Britain [are] all united in seeking to have Yongamp'o and Ŭiju opened and that the Korean government was on the point of acceding and that Russia's opposition frustrated the projects," went an editorial in the *Japan Weekly Mail*. "These nations have suffered a signal diplomatic defeat at Russia's hands, for even though some short-sighted publicists may urge that Yongamp'o itself is of small significance, the fact that its opening was officially pressed by the three Powers shows conclusively . . . that on the first occasion of a collision between the open-door and the exclusive policies, the former has been ignominiously defeated under the circumstances particularly favorably to its victory."[82]

In November 1903 the United States officially joined Japan and Britain to pressure the Korean government into opening the Yalu ports, but Kojong did not budge. The American minister to Korea, Horace Allen, glumly reported that Korea's new foreign minister, Yi Ha-yŏng, who had been favorably disposed toward the opening of the ports, was relieved in December.[83] Meanwhile, repeated requests from both British and Japanese representatives to discuss the Yalu port openings with Korean officials were refused. "Kojong seems to have put his faith entirely in Russian assurances that there will be no war and they [the Russian] will let no trouble come to him," a troubled Allen observed.[84]

Backed into a corner, Kojong revived an idea he had explored months earlier about seeking Korean neutrality. In August Kojong had sent out feelers to Japan and Russia regarding the neutrality proposal. He sought assurances from both countries that should their relations rupture, they would "consider Korea a neutral country" and would respect "our borders so that no armies would be marching through our land."[85] Japanese foreign minister Komura rejected the proposal outright, stating that if Kojong wanted to ease tensions between Russia and Japan, the Korean government should open up the Yalu ports for trade. The reaction from the Russians was, as expected, much more encouraging.[86] Although Russia refused to recognize Korea's neutrality, Pavlov assured Kojong that Russia would support Korean neutrality on principle.[87] Fearing that Japan was about to be outmaneuvered, Komura wrote Kojong directly: "We are aware that the Korean government has sent an agent to Russia to ask about a declaration of neutrality. Russia may make such a promise frivolously," he warned, "but it will refuse to fulfill it just as frivolously."[88]

While Kojong was pondering his next move, the Japanese finally received, on December 11, Russia's response to the proposal for a fifty-kilometer neutral zone on each side of the Yalu.[89] The Russian position repeated the proposal for a neutral zone north of the 39th parallel while rejecting Japan's compromise for a neutral zone on both sides of the river. The Manchurian issue was completely ignored.[90] The Russians expected the Japanese to compromise on the Korean issue yet would not budge on their position regarding their continued occupation of Manchuria. "The Russians," Jordon confided to the British Foreign Office, "speak of contempt of the Japanese. Mr. Pavlov says that if a war does come it will be short and decisive."[91]

The Japanese submitted their third proposal to Russia on December 21. Even as Komura was pursuing a diplomatic solution, Prime Minister Katsura began making preparations for war. Vice chief of the general staff of the army Kodama Gentarō estimated that Japan would have to send an expeditionary force to Korea before war was officially declared in order to seize Seoul, the hub of Korea's communications and logistical lines, before the Russians. In terms of strategy, the coming war would be a replay of the Sino-Japanese War of 1894–1895. Establishing control of the sea and rapid mobilization and deployment to the Korean Peninsula were essential. While mobilization of Japanese forces for the impending conflict did not commence until February 5, 1904, the groundwork began in December.

As the drums of war began beating louder, Kojong sought an opening with the Americans. "I have been approached for some days now on the subject of receiving the Korean Emperor at this Legation as a guest in case of war," Allen reported. "I have flatly and unequivocally refused."[92] Kojong made a similar appeal for refuge to the British legation. Jordon also refused, remarking that Kojong appeared to be paralyzed. "The palace is the area in which all the different parties are struggling for ascendency and is the scene of such divided counsels that it is impossible to evolve any definite idea of what is going on there."[93]

On January 6 the Russian reply to Japan's December proposal was delivered to the Japanese Foreign Ministry. The most significant change was a partial concession on the Manchurian issue: "Japan recognizes Manchuria as being outside her sphere of interest, while Russia, within limits of that province, will not impede Japan, or any other power, in the enjoyments of rights in Manchuria acquired by them under existing treaties with China, exclusive of the establishment of settlements." But on the most vital issue, Russia's insistence on a neutral zone north of the 39th parallel, there was no compromise.[94]

Katsura decided to make one last-ditch effort and instructed Kurino to present what was to be his government's final proposal to Lamsdorf on January 13. On the Korean issue, the Japanese rejected outright Russia's proposed restrictions on their country's strategic use of Korean territory and the creation of a neutral zone. The Japanese also insisted that Russia recognize the territorial integrity of Korea and China. Furthermore, Japan demanded that their rights and privileges in Manchuria, including settlement rights, be respected.[95]

The demands demonstrated a significant hardening of Japan's position since 1901 when Itō first visited Lamsdorf in Saint Petersburg. Initially the Japanese would have been content with a simple exchange of Manchuria for Korea, as Itō had proposed. By 1903, however, bolstered by the Anglo-Japanese Alliance and American and British support on the Yalu ports issue, Japan was resolute enough not only to call on Russia to withdraw its forces from Manchuria but to demand equal opportunity there.[96] Russia's failure to comprehend Japan's growing confidence and resolve can only be explained by Russian arrogance and racism. In his private correspondences and writing, Nicholas II often referred to the Japanese as "monkeys" (macaques). The depiction of the Japanese as childish and unworthy of serious consideration as a military threat was widespread.[97] What else could account for Russia's perplexing failure to react promptly to Japan's January 13 proposals amid the growing tensions? During the last weeks of January, Kurino made a series of urgent requests to the Russian government to respond to the proposals. None ever came.[98] The lack of urgency, and courtesy, by Russia in its failure to take prompt action to defuse the crisis led to the open break in Russo-Japanese relations. Horace Allen believed that Kojong and Pavlov shared much of the blame. "I felt that if the Koreans would have yielded on the request of the Japanese, British, and the Americans to open Yongamp'o and Wiju to trade, it might have relieved the situation by showing that the ports were not entirely under Russian domination."[99]

SURPRISE!

The Katsura cabinet had played its cards well. By demonstrating patience and, most importantly, by framing the confrontation with Russia in terms of defending the Open Door, the Japanese easily won over British and American support. But they also gained the support of Korea's reformers and capitalists who opposed Russian influence, especially over the Yalu ports issue. Kojong's inability to firmly take the reins of government pushed him to declare neutrality in an act of desperation. But the emptiness of the gesture, when the emperor could not even resolve the Yongamp'o issue on his own, exposed Kojong as Pavlov's puppet. The Japanese simply ignored his announcement on January 21 that "the Korean government declares that we have firmly decided to observe the strictest neutrality."[100]

On January 14 the tsar addressed members of the diplomatic corps, including the Japanese envoy to Russia, Kurino Shin'ichirō, expressing hope "that complications would be avoided and that all would be peacefully arranged." He concluded by telling Kurino, "Japan must remember that Russia was not only a country but an empire and that there was a limit to her patience." These words were commented upon by the press around the world. Delighted by this news, Nicholas asserted that "in his opinion, the danger of war was averted since he had told the Japanese minister that he did not want it."[101]

The arrogance of the tsar's declaration was answered by the Japanese government on February 4 when an imperial conference in the presence of the emperor was held and formally approved the breaking of Russo-Japanese relations. A crisis decision arrived when Komura was informed that the Russian Pacific Fleet had left Port Arthur. The Japanese counsel in Chefoo (Yantai), Mizuno Kōkichi, telegrammed that the fleet was heading in "an unknown direction." It was feared it might be heading toward Korea. The information turned out to be false, but the impact on the Japanese was electric.[102]

On February 6 Lamsdorf received a final message from Kurino, who stated that due to Russia's "successive rejections" of Japan's proposals regarding Korea, Japan had "no alternative but to terminate the present futile negotiations." Henceforth Japan reserved the right to sever diplomatic relations with Russia since these relations "ceased to possess any value." Kurino informed the Russian foreign minister that he and his staff intended to leave Saint Petersburg on February 10. The Russians did not reply.[103]

On the evening of February 8, operating under the command of a naval flotilla led by Admiral Uryū Sotokichi, three Japanese transport ships, escorted by several cruisers and torpedo boats, arrived off the port of Inch'ŏn (Chemulp'o). Within a few hours, ships carried out an efficient disembarkation of twenty-five hundred troops. As Japanese soldiers were dispatched to quietly and systematically take over Seoul, Vice Admiral Tōgō Heihachirō sent a torpedo flotilla against seven Russian battleships at Port Arthur. The surprise attack on the evening of February 8–9 was followed the next day by a brief and lopsided engagement a mile and a half offshore from Inch'ŏn. The battle of Chemulp'o and the surprise attack on the Russian naval base at Port Arthur on February 8–9 were conceived as part of Japan's grand strategic plan to seize command of the seas.

PART FIVE

THE RUSSO-JAPANESE WAR—WORLD WAR ZERO

ON THE SAME DAY the Japanese launched a surprise attack at Port Arthur, Japanese residents in Korea cheered as a Japanese naval squadron bombarded two Russian warships off Palmido Island at the mouth of Inch'ŏn Harbor. The port was under Japanese control in less than twenty-four hours. Two weeks later, on February 23, King Kojong was forced to sign a protocol, ex post facto, to permit the Japanese to undertake military operations on Korean soil. By May 1, 1904, the Japanese had advanced to the Yalu River, driven the Russians out of the peninsula, and were on their way to battle the main Russian army in Manchuria.

The land campaigns were vast and bloody. The final land battle at Mukden was an epic affair with the greatest concentration of land forces in modern history—275,000 Russians against 200,000 Japanese, part of the 1.3 million Russians and 1.2 million Japanese mobilized for the war. The massed armies, combined with advances in military technology, spelled mass killing on a scale not seen on the modern battlefield. Breech-loading rifles, machine guns, barbed wire, hand grenades, and quick-firing artillery all added to merciless, infernal conditions and destruction that foreshadowed the bloodbath of the Great War of 1914–1918.

The Russo-Japanese War was also a media war. Electrical means of communication informed and thrilled the entire world of frontline actions within days if not hours. Every Japanese victory and Russian defeat, for that was how all major encounters ended, reverberated in the capitals of Europe and America. The entire world looked on with awe at Japan's successes on the battlefield. In Russia, on the other hand, General Kuropatkin's inability to score a single victory during the entire war led to growing domestic unrest, quickening the pace of revolution at home.

For Japan the war was a turning point as it jumped into the ranks of the Great Powers. Its ability to take on and defeat the Russian goliath every time sparked renewed admiration for Japan in both Korea and China. Former Tonghaks and reform-minded Korean elites were inspired by Japan's performance and readily offered their services. Thousands of Koreans mobilized to support the Japanese war effort against Russia, either to work on the railroads, transport military goods, or serve as spies. This massive effort was spearheaded by a new reformist organization, the Ilchinhoe (Advance in Unity Society), which formed soon after the war began.

As for China, Yuan Shikai and China's other military leaders worked tirelessly for the Japanese war effort and saw in Japan's battlefield successes the basis for reforming China. Even before the war ended, Yuan presented a memorial to the Qing Court calling for the establishment of a constitutional government within twelve years.

While military success earned Japan a positive international image, the toll of the war on Japanese society was considerable. Japan's strategy for the pursuit of national greatness through wars created deeper and more divisive consequences for Japan than its leaders anticipated or appreciated at the time.

CHAPTER SEVENTEEN

WAR FOR KOREA

From the earliest days when the Japanese first began contemplating their struggle with Russia, it was recognized that the war would be won or lost in the maritime theater. In both the Sino-Japanese War and the Russo-Japanese War, the necessity of devoting the Japanese navy to secure the army's lines of communication and logistics from the home country was paramount. The close coordination between army and navy operations required the Japanese navy to extend its area of control of the Yellow Sea and the Strait of Korea.

Yet the Japanese navy could not undertake any offensive action that jeopardized its main mission to *support* army operations. "I carefully considered the nature of the theatre of war, the configuration of land and sea, and the line of operations on which the land forces would act," Admiral Tōgō later recalled. "[I] chose as the primary object of my strategy that I should confine within the Port Arthur zone the main portion of the enemy's fleet and prevent its getting away to Vladivostok."[1] Despite the initial strike against Port Arthur and Inch'ŏn on February 8–9, the navy plan did not include a purely offensive component other than preemptive and preventative measures to secure land operations. As naval historian Julian Corbett remarked: "His [Tōgō's] first consideration is the army's line of operation. Within the army lies the offensive part of the war plan, and his part is to provide the defensive support by confining the enemy's main fleet to an area from which it *cannot* interfere with the army's progress."[2]

In this connection it is helpful to consider the object of Japan's war aims and, again, the parallels between the two conflicts are instructive. In neither the Sino-Japanese War nor the Russo-Japanese War did Japan ever consider "overthrowing" the enemy; there was no plan to march on Beijing or Saint Petersburg, nor would the Japanese have even considered such a plan feasible. Rather, the main object of both wars was to secure Japan's domination over the Korean Peninsula. In the case of the Russo-Japanese War, it was necessary that Japan secure command of the seas to confine Russia to its inefficient rail lines of communication, and then to interdict those rail lines by advancing into Manchuria. Success in achieving these two military objectives would result in destroying enemy forces before they could be reinforced and resupplied from European Russia. Japan's war objective per se was not the conquest of Manchuria; instead it was to neutralize Manchuria so that it could serve as a buffer against the Russian threat to Korea.[3]

Thus, from the onset of the conflict, both sides recognized that the war would be won or lost in Manchuria even though the *object* of the war was control of Korea: for the Russians, the essential task was to rapidly build up their forces in Manchuria and avoid the decisive battle until the Russian army was ready; for the Japanese, it was to destroy the Russian army as quickly as possible by securing the sea communications upon which their land campaign depended.[4]

On May 3, 1903, Rear Admiral V. K. Vitgeft, chief of staff to viceroy of the Far East Yevgeny Alekseev, formulated the first detailed operational plan for the Pacific Squadron based at Port Arthur. Mirroring the Japanese, the Russians defined the central mission of the Pacific Squadron as the retention "of our mastery of the Yellow Sea and the Korea Bay based on Port Arthur." Rather than seeking to destroy the Japanese fleet, the aim of Russian naval forces was to prevent a Japanese Army from landing on Korea's western coast. The plan disregarded the significance of a Japanese landing on Korea's eastern coast, which "cannot have any decisive influence on the operations in Manchuria since the landing place would be too far removed for the latter [southern Manchuria] and owing to the mountainous nature of Korea, there are no suitable ways of communications for the movement of a large army with artillery and transport." Although the plan called for some Russian forces to be based in Vladivostok in order to "draw off a portion of the Japanese sea forces from the main theatre of operations, and prevent a Japanese landing near the Maritime provinces," the main object "must be to preserve our sea forces as long as possible so as to retain control of the Yellow Sea and be a constant threat to a hostile disembarkation [on the Korean Peninsula]."[5]

In late September 1903, as the possibility of hostilities increased, Alekseev and his staff drew up more detailed war plans. These were based on the assumption that no enemy landings would take place north of Chinnamp'o on Korea's western coast. The main idea was that the Pacific Squadron would force Japan to land troops in southern Korea to allow Russia maximum time to concentrate its forces in southern Manchuria.[6] Since it would take two or more months for Japanese troops to march from Pusan to Ŭiju on the Manchurian border, "the plan was to buy time until the arrival of greater strength from the center of Russia and slowing down the enemy." By January 1904 there were roughly ninety-eight thousand Russian troops in the Far East spread across a vast area, from Chita to Vladivostok and from Blagoveshchensk to Port Arthur.[7] Moreover, the capacity of the Chinese Eastern Railway was limited to no more than seven trains of all types per day. Augmenting these lines would take time. The Siberian winter added to the challenge of sending troops to the Far East.[8] In February, six hundred Russian soldiers froze to death while crossing twenty-two miles on foot across frozen Lake Baikal. They had lost their way in a snowstorm.[9]

In the face of these challenges, the passivity of Alekseev to the impending crisis was perplexing. The viceroy, ensconced in his headquarters at Port Arthur, learned of the break in relations with Japan on the morning of February 7, but instead of acting on the stunning news, he kept the information to himself.[10] Presumably, he was going to notify his staff during a meeting he had summoned for February 9, but by then it was too late. Moreover, he denied permission for the Port Arthur newspaper, *Novi Krai,* to publish a telegram describing the break in relations, stating that "he did not want to disrupt society."[11] He did not cancel a planned ball for the evening of February 8. Nor did he take any precautions to secure the Russian Pacific Squadron that lay in harbor, despite warnings from its commander, Vice Admiral Stepan Makarov, that the fleet was vulnerable to attack.[12]

The same kind of passivity marked the general Russian reaction to events in Korea. Throughout January–February 1904, Alekseev received clear indicators that something was afoot. It was reported that ships had arrived in Vladivostok to transport Japanese nationals back to their homeland. Other reports noted increased delivery of coal, rice, tents, and other materiel on Korea's southern coast, including six hundred boxes of telegraph materials at Inch'ŏn. There were also reports of increased activities of Japanese intelligence agents, "some of them dressed in Korean clothing."[13]

Alekseev requested instructions from the tsar on what to do if Japanese troops landed in southern Korea. Nicholas, still hoping war might be averted, responded: "It is to be desired that it should be the Japanese and not we who begin the hostilities. Consequently, if they do not begin operations against us, you should not oppose their landing in southern Korea or on the east coast as high as Gensan (Wŏnsan). But if their fleet, whether they land or not, should cross the 38th parallel going north on the west side of Korea, then you must attack and not wait for them to take the first shot."[14] The tsar's orders were the last Alekseev received; had they been acted upon, the war might have taken a different course.

In December 1903 three Russian vessels—the armored cruisers *Boyarin* and *Varyag,* and the gunboat *Gilyak*—were anchored at Inch'ŏn. On December 30, 1903–January 1, 1904, the *Gilyak* and *Boyarin* were recalled to Port Arthur and the gunboat *Korietz* was sent to replace them. Thus, in early January, the Russians had two warships in Inch'ŏn harbor, where they joined vessels from other nations, including the Japanese cruiser *Chiyoda,* whose mission was to help protect Japanese nationals in Seoul in response to the growing threat of war. The captain of the *Varyag,* V. F. Rudnev, was also tasked with collecting intelligence information on Japanese movements. However, wary of starting a war, Alekseev limited Rudnev's actions. In case of Japanese provocations, he was to remain alert but impassive. He was "not to prevent the landing of Japanese troops," merely to report directly if they had. He was also ordered to "support good relations with foreigners."[15]

As the situation grew more tense each day, an increasingly anxious Rudnev telegrammed Minister Pavlov in Seoul on February 5. "Have heard about the breakdown in diplomatic relations. Please send word." Pavlov responded that he could not confirm or deny the rumors. "Gossip about the break blossoms here [in Seoul] among private individuals. No serious confirmation of this gossip has yet been received." On the same day, unbeknownst to either Pavlov or Rudnev, Alekseev received a message from Saint Petersburg that the Russian army "was authorized, if necessary, to begin military action." Lamsdorf followed up this message on February 7, informing all Russian representatives abroad, including Alekseev, that Japan had broken off diplomatic relations with Russia.[16]

But the messages were not received in Seoul. On February 6–7, Pavlov sent three telegrams to Saint Petersburg inquiring about the rumors of rupture in relations. Later, on February 7, Pavlov learned that all telegraph communications between Seoul and Saint Petersburg had been cut off.[17] The telegraph line to Port Arthur was also not working properly. Pavlov immediately notified Rudnev, who came up with the plan to dispatch the *Korietz* to Port Arthur with an urgent message for the viceroy that included a note from Kojong warning him "of the arrival of the Japanese fleet at the mouth of the Yalu" that he had obtained from secret sources.[18] In the meantime, Rudnev advised Pavlov to leave Korea immediately with his staff on the *Varyag* "so as not to allow the Russian cruiser to be trapped in the foreign port in case of a declaration of war." Pavlov, however, refused, stating he had not obtained permission from Saint Petersburg. The fate of the *Varyag,* one of the best ships of the First Pacific Squadron, was sealed.

BATTLE OF CHEMULP'O BAY (INCH'ŎN)

With Pavlov unaware of the impending crisis, Captain Murayama, commander of the *Chiyoda,* was informed of the rupture of relations on February 5, 1904. He was ordered to leave the harbor and link up with Vice Admiral Uryū Sotokichi's flotilla on its way to Inch'ŏn from Sasebo. On the evening of the February 7, under cover of darkness, the *Chiyoda* quietly slipped out of the harbor to join the Japanese flotilla that had arrived unseen off the Korean coast. Uryū arrived just in time to intercept and force back the *Korietz* from sailing for Port Arthur with Kojong's message on February 8. The *Varyag* and *Korietz* were now effectively caught, "like rats in a trap."[19]

The disembarkation of twenty-five hundred Japanese soldiers of the Twelfth Division began late on the afternoon of February 8 in orderly fashion and under the watchful eyes of Russian sailors who took no action to impede it. "The landing and occupation of Chemulp'o [Inch'ŏn] were accomplished without the slightest disorder or confusion," remarked Horace Allen. "The soldiers marched in complete outfits, haversacks, canteens, water cups, blankets, and fully armed, marched up to the jetty during the night and were quartered in the houses of Japanese citizens in the Japanese settlement in a manner to excite the admiration of the foreign military officers who witnessed it."[20] The streets of the town were covered in snow while Japanese flags appeared over the doorways of shops and houses. "A noble address was sent out by all Japanese authorities, calling upon all Japanese to conduct themselves with the utmost propriety towards the Coreans and all foreigners, since Japan in this struggle is on trial before the civilized world."[21]

Around 2:30 AM on February 9, the troop disembarkation was complete. Uryū notified the commanders of *Varyag* and *Korietz* that "as hostilities exist between the government of Japan and the government of Russia" he was obliged to "attack the men-of-war of Russia stationed at present in the port of Chemulp'o [Inch'ŏn] with the force under his command."[22] He requested the Russian vessels sail out of Inch'ŏn by noon that day to engage Uryū's flotilla, otherwise they would be attacked within the harbor by 4 P.M. that afternoon.

Rudnev was faced with a stark choice. He could either enter into a suicidal battle he was bound to lose or permit the *Varyag* and *Korietz* to fall into enemy hands and allow himself and his crew to be taken prisoners of war. He chose to fight, surmising that confronting the Japanese even in a lopsided battle would be the only honorable course of action. On February 9 at approximately 11:30 AM, the *Varyag* and the *Korietz* steamed out of the harbor to face the Japanese fleet, the *Varyag* playing the Russian anthem. The battle of Chemulp'o lasted less than an hour. Rather than surrender the damaged *Varyag* and *Korietz* to the Japanese, Rudnev scuttled his ships.

The next day Hayashi went to visit Pavlov and tactfully told the Russian minister to pack his bags and immediately leave the Korean capital. Some feared that the Japanese might carry out vengeance against Russians living in Korea. "When the crash came many Russians nearly all lost their heads," recalled British minister Jordon. "The doctor on the *Varyag* [who was later rescued] became a raving lunatic after the engagement," but it turned out such fears were overblown.[23] Pavlov, his entire staff, the legation guards, and Russian residents of Seoul were put on the French cruiser *Pascal* at Inch'ŏn on the morning of February 12 and set sail for Shanghai. "The Japanese authorities even offered a guard for the protection of the Russians till they are safely out of Korean territory."[24] The defense of the Russian legation and the interests of Russian citizens who decided to stay was handed over to the French government, under the chargé d'affaires, Viscount de Fontaigne. Throughout the war, Kojong would use the French connection to secretly communicate with Pavlov and the tsarist government to actively undermine Japan's war efforts in Korea.[25]

JAPANESE LANDINGS

The Japanese plan called for landing General Kuroki Tamemoto's First Army, composed of the Twelfth, Second, and Imperial Guards Divisions at Sunchŏn Bay, on the southern coast of Korea halfway between Masan and Mokp'o, and then march up the peninsula to the Yalu by the end of April.[26] But the rapid successes at Inch'ŏn and Port Arthur advanced the timeline by over a month. This was exactly the scenario Admiral Vitgeft had warned against. Elements of the Twelfth Division proceeded to Seoul and reinforced the Japanese garrison of 250 there. The control of Inch'ŏn and Seoul allowed General Kuroki to reduce the distance his army had to travel by half, tracing the same route the Japanese Army took during the war against China a decade earlier.

Landing at Inch'ŏn faced significant difficulties, however. The tidal conditions, some of the most extreme in the world, required transport ships to weigh anchor two miles offshore so they would not be grounded on the wide mudflats twice daily. Troops and cargo had to be brought to shore on flat-bottomed wooden sampan boats, hundreds of them. "When the tide is out (maximum 36 feet), a large part of the bottom [of the harbor] is out of water," explained one observer. "The launch we started in the morning of the 17th stuck fast on a sand bar; a sampan took us off and it, in turn, was soon unable to advance or retire. A walk in mud and water brought us to another sampan which carried us back to the stone ramp which served as the Chemulp'o landing."[27] There was also the lack of preparation for feeding the unexpected influx of troops, who quickly devoured what food was available. Nakai Kitarō, head of the association of Japanese nationals residing in Korea, recalled, "There was no food in the stores in the Japanese concessionary area in Seoul. My wife and I were at a loss what to do when my children complained that they were hungry." One solution was buying rice in the Korean market but many complained about its poor quality. "There were many pebbles mixed with the [Korean] rice," wrote Nakai. "So, I cracked both my back teeth while eating the rice and consequently had trouble with a toothache for the next several years."[28]

By the end of February, the Japanese had brought to Inch'ŏn tens of thousands of men and over one hundred thousand tons of equipment and materiel of the First Army.[29] Foreign observers were impressed. "From present conditions and a careful observation of the Japanese infantry, I am disposed to believe that it will give a good or better account of itself

Sampans transferring men and supplies at Inch'ŏn, February 8, 1904. (Library of Congress Prints and Photographs Division, LC-DIG-ppmsca-08151)

in the coming campaign than could the infantry of any other country," wrote American minister Horace Allen.[30]

Japan's swift military occupation of Seoul was followed by coerced arrangements to ensure that Korea not only did not impede the war effort but supported it. On February 23, Korean acting foreign minister Yi Chiyong was pressured into signing an agreement stipulating that the Korean government accept Japanese advice and assistance in its administration. The Koreans were also obliged to provide full assistance to the Japanese Army as well as allow the occupation of their territory "as necessary for strategic reasons."[31] The protocol agreement was followed up with the "Order Regarding Captured Spies" published on February 27 in the newspaper *Cheguk sinmun*, stating that "any persons who caused damage to the Japanese army will face the death penalty in accordance with the laws and customs of Korea."[32]

Such draconian measures were meant to instill fear in the Korean population. At the same time, Japanese soldiers were constantly reminded by their superiors to observe strict military discipline. Japanese troops were also furnished with coolie labor and mules so they would not have to completely depend on Koreans for transport. Two thousand Japanese coolies landed in Inchon on February 13.[33] The new arrangements worked, and Japanese soldiers generally behaved themselves. Korean chronicler Hwang Hyŏn noted that "during the advance, there were few instances of pillaging the nearby villages," and for the most part the Japanese also paid for everything they took.[34]

The Japanese had learned from their experiences in the Sino-Japanese War and made a concerted effort to maintain troop discipline and prevent abuse of the local population. A noteworthy feature of the Japanese supply system was that Japanese soldiers "drew practically nothing from a country abounding in resources" during the first weeks of the war. "Although there was plenty of *kaoling* [Chinese style sorghum liquor] millet, and bean cake [in Korea], barley was religiously transported from Japan as the principal food for their ponies, eked out with the small qualities of compressed hay or fodder from Australia or America." Provisioning supplies from Japan may have been a sound decision politically, but it put a severe strain on the logistical system, with a consequent impact on mobility.[35]

By mid-February, elements of the Twelfth Division had already reached P'yŏngyang. To speed up the landings and commit the maximum number of troops in the shortest possible time, Army Vice Chief of Staff Kodama Gentarō landed the Guards Division at Chinnamp'o (Namp'o) on March 13, about forty miles from P'yŏngyang. The Second Division would follow on March 29 and march north up the coast, thus raising the fighting force to roughly forty-five thousand men. The landings at Chinnamp'o would save the 120-mile trek over rugged terrain from Inch'ŏn and had the added advantage of a direct road to Anju, about fifty miles north of P'yŏngyang, the meeting point of all three divisions of the First Army.[36]

Despite the significant change in plans, everything had gone smoothly. Some Japanese officials could not contain their euphoria about Japan's rapid success and prospects nor suppress their scorn at Russia's seeming incompetence. "Russia appears to be less prepared than was China in 1894–5," Hayashi Tadasu remarked. "I believe that only three trains a day can be run through Manchuria. Supposing these are equally divided between troops and supplies, as would be necessary, Russia could not perceptibly strengthen her land forces before April. Japan's naval coup has been so unexpectedly successful that I rather think our troops will take their time."[37] Reports from the field by foreign military observers all shared the same observation about Russia's "inexplicable" policy. "With

Japanese march through P'yŏngyang by Taedongmun, the eastern gate on the Taedong River, March 1904. (JLP 532 LA 1 #11805, Jack London Photographs and Negatives, Huntington Library, San Marino, California)

such a liberal supply of cavalry as Russia has at her disposition in Manchuria and Korea," wrote General Henry T. Allen, the American observer, "the advance of the Japanese should be seriously delayed, at every important river and pass. Anju, Pakchŏn, and the T'aeryong Rivers must be bridged; and the following passes (Kasan, Chongju, Koksan, and the three considerable hills this side of Ŭiju, etc.), if only half defended, it would at least have caused the Japanese forces to deploy. These passes are all on the main road and are four to eight hundred feet above normal level of the surrounding country. There are also passes on the side roads. In fact, the country lends itself admirably for a role the Russians should play, in not only retarding the Japanese advance, but also inflicting severe losses."[38]

But the Russians remained passive. Russian plans had always been predicated on the availability of time to mobilize sufficient forces for an offensive action in Korea, but these plans were dashed after Japan's surprise

attack on Port Arthur and Inch'ŏn. The Russians, therefore, had to im-
provise until reinforcements arrived from European Russia by rail.
Available Russian forces in the Far East numbered almost one hundred
thousand men in the Priamursky and Siberian Military Districts and the
Liaodong region in Manchuria.[39] A Frontier Guards force of another
twenty-four thousand provided security for the Chinese Eastern Railway.
This force was scattered over the vast expanse of the eastern Trans-Baikal
(Harbin-Vladivostok) to the southern (Harbin-Port Arthur) branches of
the Manchurian railway lines.

COMMAND CONFLICTS

The Cossacks and officer volunteers who made up the cadre of the frontier guards were tough warriors and fierce horsemen, "the strongest supporters of the tsar the Russian empire has got."[40] They had originally been
subordinated to the Ministry of Finance under Sergei Witte and enjoyed
the patronage and a higher salary scale than the army. However, following
Witte's ouster in 1903, they came under the control of Admiral Alekseev,
who had assumed command of all Russian land and naval forces in the
Far East. At the start of the Russo-Japanese War, these forces were renamed the Trans-Amur Region Frontier Guards and were attached to the
Russian Manchurian Army under General Kuropatkin, the war minister
appointed to command Russian land forces in Manchuria.[41]

Conflict soon arose between Kuropatkin and Alekseev due to the highly
irregular structure of the Russian Far Eastern forces.[42] Kuropatkin was
nominally subordinate to Alekseev, but the two men held widely diver-
gent views on overall strategy. Kuropatkin's concept for the first phase of
the campaign was to "prevent the destruction of our forces in detail,"
which meant that holding a position with insufficient forces was not as
important as saving them from destruction to fight another day. "While
gradually growing in numbers and preparing to take the offensive," wrote
Kuropatkin, "we should only move forward when sufficiently strong, and
when supplied with everything necessary for an uninterrupted advance
lasting over a fairly long period."[43] Alekseev, however, pushed for a more
proactive stance; for him, securing a position—like Port Arthur—was
worth the risk of incurring significant Russian losses. In large measure,
the Russian fortunes of the war would depend on Kuropatkin's resolve
to preserve his forces and trade space for time against Alekseev's increasing
calls to take offensive action before the Manchurian Army was ready.[44]

In mid-March 1904 Kuropatkin arrived in Liaoyang. He split his army into Southern and Eastern detachments. The Southern Detachment, made up primarily of the First Siberian Army Corps, was under the command of Lieutenant General G. K. Stackelberg. It was positioned along the Yingkou-Dashiqiao-Haicheng-Kaiping line with the mission to resist a Japanese landing on the Liaodong Peninsula. The Eastern detachment was deployed around Fengcheng in southeast Liaoning near the Korean border. Commanded by Lieutenant General M. I. Zasulich, it was tasked with delaying the Japanese from crossing the Yalu into Manchuria. Kuropatkin warned Zasulich not to actively engage the enemy.[45] "Use the local situation to complicate the enemy's crossing of the Yalu and stall his further offensives across the Hushanzhen mountain range," he told him. Zasulich was also to "clarify the strength, composition, and direction of movement of the Japanese Army sent against us." In keeping with the overall intent to preserve his forces until his army was sufficiently built up to undertake offensive operations, Kuropatkin wanted the Eastern detachment "to avoid a decisive battle."[46]

The Eastern detachment was joined by Major General P. I. Mishchenko's Cossack Brigade, which was dispatched to Korea to keep an eye on the Japanese forces.[47] Mishchenko was an experienced veteran of the Boxer Uprising and Russo-Chinese War who repeatedly demonstrated his bravery and audacity. In the Battle of Baitouzi, an outpost of Russian guards near Liaoyang, during the hot days of July 1900, he repulsed an enemy force of three thousand with just two hundred men.[48] At the battle of Haicheng in August, he overran a four-thousand-strong Chinese force with a much smaller force.[49] In October, the ancient imperial city of Mukden fell under his control in less than forty-eight hours. Clearly a man of action, he was this time ordered not to engage the enemy. Mishchenko's mission was to cross the Yalu and track the Japanese in Korea, going all the way to P'yŏngyang, if possible.[50]

The first confrontation between Russian and Japanese forces in Korea was a skirmish rather than a battle. On March 28 two cavalry squadrons from the Japanese Imperial Guards Divisions clashed with Mishchenko's First Chita and First Argun Trans-Baikal Cossack Regiments at Chŏngju, about forty miles north of P'yŏngyang. Heeding orders, Mishchenko did not actively engage the Japanese. He could have frustrated the Japanese advance and delayed Kuroki's First Army for weeks but did not. This action set the tone for the entire war.

BATTLE OF THE YALU RIVER

Japanese patrols from Kuroki's First Army reached the Yalu River near at Ŭiju (Wiju) on April 4 and found it nearly impassable, turbulent and filled with large chunks of ice. The Yalu at this point is about seven hundred yards wide and broken up by low sandy islands that are occasionally submerged when the river runs high. Between Ŭiju and Jiuliancheng, located across the Chinese side of the river, were two large islands known as Kintei (K: Kŭmchŏng-do) and Chukodai (K: Chŭngsŏng-do) Islands. While the channel between Ŭiju and Kintei was relatively shallow, the main channel between Kintei and Chukodai was wide, about seven hundred to a thousand feet, and deep. Chukodai was also larger than Kintei and lay where the Ai River, a tributary flowing from Manchuria, met the Yalu. Overlooking the wide flat Yalu valley at this confluence was a rocky outcrop known as Tiger Hill (Hushan), so named by the Chinese for resembling a crouching tiger looking down upon the rivers. Anyone here would have a clear view of the entire valley area between Ŭiju and Jiuliancheng; whoever possessed it would dominate the area.

Downstream from Ŭiju on the Manchurian side lies the town of Andong, where the water is deeper and wider. Further downriver is the town of Yŏngamp'o on the Korean side, and beyond lies the mouth of the river and the Yellow Sea. Zasulich's orders were to delay Kuroki's army to buy time for Kuropatkin to build up his forces. Convinced the Japanese would cross at Andong, Zasulich had deployed the bulk of his forces—sixteen thousand infantry and three thousand cavalry—along the river north and south of Andong. The area from Jiuliancheng and along the Ai River, covered by heavy brush shrouded by willow growth and jagged hills, was defended by a much smaller force. It was patrolled dutifully but disinterestedly. A more inquisitive mind might have guessed that such a landscape could make a perfect concealment for a large force, but Zasulich did not think the Japanese would risk crossing at Jiuliancheng when Andong offered a more direct and less arduous route.[51] This was the Russians' first mistake.

The second mistake was giving up Ŭiju without a fight. Kuroki ordered Japanese patrols to reconnoiter the area around Ŭiju in early April. An advance guard quickly followed up with an order to take the town. This relatively small force arrived at Ŭiju on April 8. With no other troops in supporting distance, they were highly vulnerable. The distance from Anju,

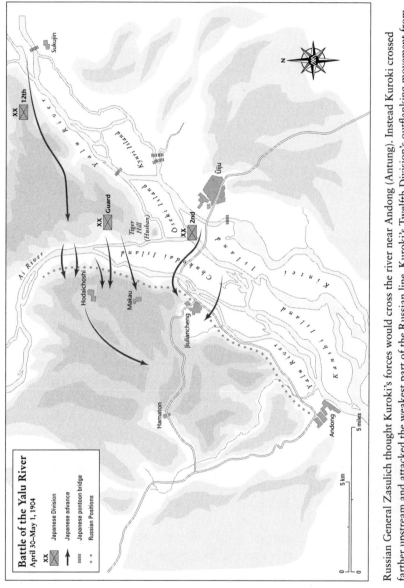

Battle of the Yalu River
April 30–May 1, 1904

XX Japanese Division
↑ Japanese advance
▦ Japanese pontoon bridge
⋯ Russian Positions

Russian General Zasulich thought Kuroki's forces would cross the river near Andong (Antung). Instead Kuroki crossed farther upstream and attacked the weakest part of the Russian line. Kuroki's Twelfth Division's outflanking movement from the north and the Second Division's breakthrough at Jiulianzheng collapsed the Russian defenses, forcing them to precipitously fall back to Hamaton (Hamatanzhen) and subsequently withdraw north to Liaoyang.

where the bulk of the First Army was located, to Ŭiju was more than a hundred miles of wild forests and rough terrain, and it would take days for supporting troops to arrive. The wisdom of this risky advance was hotly debated at Japanese headquarters, and Kuroki was well aware of the danger. It was known the Russians had boats on the Yalu and reinforcements could arrive within a matter of hours. Would the Japanese be tempting fate by pushing a weak detachment into the jaws of a powerful enemy? On the other hand, the Russian performance at Chŏngju gave them hope. Kuroki decided to take the risk because his plan for pushing the Russians out of Korea hinged on taking Ŭiju quickly.[52]

The Japanese gamble paid off. On April 8 the advance guard entered the town. American medical missionary A. M. Sharrock, living with his family near Ŭiju, witnessed the fighting, the only Western observer to do so. He estimated there were about six hundred Russians in the town facing the smaller Japanese force: "The Russians took the high ground at the north end of the town which was very steep and covered with a pine forest which also gave them [the Japanese] cover," he recounted. "Here is where the main fighting [took] place. The Japanese charged up the hill and were successful in driving out the Russians who took to their horses and left in great haste. The Japanese followed some fifteen *li* to a high pass where the Russians turned on them and made a little stand." Sharrock expected this would be the moment for the Russian attack:

> The [Russian] troops lined the ridges where rifles pits had formally been dug. . . . We [Sharrock and his family] sat on our front porch as it commands a view of the town and with field glasses in hand and awaited developments. For three hours we expected any moment to be the first foreigners treated to a view of a battle. At about 4 o'clock the situation loosened and at 5 o'clock the [Russian] troops began to move off. This was the last we saw of them in any numbers and in a couple of days, the country was entirely given over to the Japanese. . . . The present condition is simply this: not a single Russian on this [Korean] side of the Yalu.[53]

With Ŭiju under control, Kuroki was prepared for the next phase. As Japanese reinforcements began to arrive, Zasulich realized the tremendous advantage they had lost in surrendering the town. He might still have retaken it, as the Japanese force was small. But by the time Zasulich decided to take action, it was already too late. "Not until April 12th—four days, that is to say, after the Japanese advance guard had begun to come in Wiju [Ŭiju]—did the Russians make even a semblance of an attempt to grasp the initiative, which was slipping hourly away through their fingers," observed Sir Ian Hamilton, the British military attaché serving with the Japanese Army in Manchuria. "A party of some fifty of their men came close up to the town and tried to cross by boat. One company of Japanese infantry drove them off easily, killing an officer and a private soldier. The officer was Lieutenant Demidrovitch, of the 12th Regiment, and on him was found a written order telling him to pass through the Japanese outpost line and reconnoiter south of Wiju. My Japanese friends tell me that everyone felt sorry for the poor fellow, ordered to undertake with 50 men a duty which his General had hesitated to carry out with 600."[54]

On April 20 the entire First Army had completed its concentration around Ŭiju. Although the danger of a Russian attack had passed, it was important to prevent Russian forces from gathering opposite the town. "The Japanese wanted a full ten days to complete all the arrangements before delivering their blow," wrote Hamilton. "Nothing was to be left to chance."[55]

Why was taking Ŭiju so important? And why did Kuroki want to move into the area so quickly, risking his advance guard to take the town without proper reinforcements? The answer lay in the operational objective of the First Army in support of the Japanese grand strategic plan for the war. "The aim of sending the Japanese First Army to Korea is to invade Manchuria from P'yŏngan Province and to attack the Russian Manchurian Army," wrote Tani Hisao, who served as a second lieutenant in the Guard's First Infantry Battalion and later wrote an account of his wartime experiences.[56] Securing Ŭiju and its environs was necessary to advance into Manchuria, and Kuroki's crossing at the Yalu was the strategic trigger that set the rest of the Japanese land campaign in motion. Kuroki's success in Korea would determine when the Second Army, under General Oku Yasukata, would land at Pitzuwo on the Liaodong Peninsula and advance toward Liaoyang to link up with the First Army. It was also thought that Kuroki's campaign would force Kuropatkin to divert some forces from Stackelberg's Southern Detachment in the Liaodong Peninsula. The weakening of the Southern Detachment would be a signal for the Fourth Army under General Nozu Michitsura to land in Takushan (Dagushan) on the coast of Bohai Bay to cover Kuroki's left in a general advance toward Liaoyang. Finally, with Tōgō's Combined Fleet containing the Russian Pacific Squadron at Port Arthur, the Third Army under General Nogi Maresuke would land on the Liaodong Peninsula to take the fort by land and then

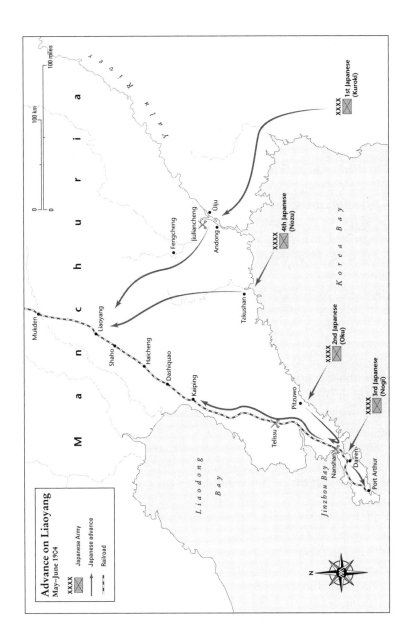

Advance on Liaoyang
May–June 1904

XXXX [Japanese Army]
Japanese advance
Railroad

100 miles
100 km

Manchuria

Yalu River

Mukden
Liaoyang
Shaho
Haicheng
Dashiqiao
Kaiping
Telissu
Nanshan
Dairen
Port Arthur

Fengcheng
Jiuliancheng
Andong
Uiju

Takushan

Pitzuwo

1st Japanese (Kuroki) XXXX
4th Japanese (Nozu) XXXX
2nd Japanese (Oku) XXXX
3rd Japanese (Nogi) XXXX

Korea Bay

Liaodong Bay

Jinzhou Bay

N

link up with Oku, Nozu, and Kuroki's armies to destroy the Russian Manchurian Army before significant reinforcements could arrive.

It all hinged on the success of the First Army and how quickly it could break through Zasulich's forces. Kuroki anticipated that the Russians expected him to cross at Andong, and set actions to confirm that expectation, but the actual crossings were planned farther upriver near Ŭiju. Everything would depend on deceiving Zasulich and achieving surprise. The battle plan was simple: the First Army would concentrate its entire force against the weak Russian northern flank with the Guard and Second Divisions crossing in front of Jiuliancheng and the Twelfth Division attached to their right against the extreme northern end of the Russian line after making a daring, wide flanking maneuver from the north.

Over the following two weeks, Kuroki worked furiously to prepare the ground for the upcoming battle. At Ŭiju, and all along the road leading to the town and at various strategic points north of the river, elaborate screens made of straw and branches were built to conceal the movement of troops and weapons. "Viewed from a distance, the road disappeared from sight, and then there was only a ravine covered with an abundant growth of foliage," wrote one observer. "Thus the Japanese were able to concentrate, without the Russians' slightest idea of its strength."[57]

This was not the case on the Russian side, where Zasulich's men took few precautions to conceal their position. "So little did the Russians trouble themselves about concealment, that they even permitted their men to water the horses in the Ai River between 2 and 4 P.M. and to exercise them on the sandy flats which extend between the north bank of that river and the Russian position at the base of the hills," wrote Hamilton. "All this was highly tantalizing to the Japanese artillery, who lay under cover watching their enemies play about within range of their guns, like a fox terrier forbidden to bark at the rabbits lest it should prematurely frighten the careless gamboling before all the nets are in position."[58]

The prelude to the main attack took place on April 25, when Japanese torpedo boats and two gunboats entered the mouth of the Yalu and fired on Russian positions. This was to give the Russians the impression that a fresh landing of Japanese troops at the mouth of the Yalu was in the works.[59] Meanwhile, on the night of April 25–26, detachments of the Twelfth Division seized and occupied the islands of Kyuri, Oseki, and Kintei. Army engineers began building a bridge to Kintei directly in front of Ŭiju, which drew the first Russian artillery shelling. The bridge construction was a deliberate ruse "to draw the artillery of the Russians, disclose the position of their guns, and obtain an advance sample of their weapons."[60]

The bridge at Ŭiju might have made Zasulich think his presupposition of a Japanese crossing at Andong was perhaps wrong, but he made no changes to the disposition of his forces. Meanwhile, with Russians distracted by the bridge ruse, the Japanese built ten other bridges to facilitate crossing the Yalu to Chukodai Island for the final assault. Japanese preparations were helped by the Russian failure to recognize the importance of Tiger Hill, the possession of which could have allowed the Russians to seriously hamper Japanese operations. Shortly after daybreak on April 27, the Guards Division seized Kyuri Island (Kuri-do) and advanced on Tiger Hill where, after a sharp engagement, the Russians fell back and the hill was seized.[61] Belatedly recognizing its tactical value, the Russians tried retaking it two days later but were repulsed.

Preparations were also made to provide close and accurate artillery support by positioning newly acquired German Krupp howitzers and artillery of the Guards and Second Divisions on Kintei's soft sandy soil.[62] Remarkably, the Russians were oblivious to the activity. "Every advantage was taken of the natural lay of the ground, and much artifice was employed to conceal the position from the Russian gunners. Trees were transplanted a short distance in front of the batteries to hide the tell-tale flash of discharge. . . . Thus the next morning the landscape appeared unchanged from the Russian side of the river."[63]

Kuroki issued orders at 10 AM of April 28 for the general attack to begin the next night.[64] At dawn on April 29 the Twelfth Division began to cross the Yalu at Sukujin in boats. The Russians put up only feeble resistance and the bridging of the river began at 2 PM that afternoon. At 3:00 AM the next day, twenty thousand men began crossing the bridge.[65] Had the Russians shown more vigor, they might have seriously upset Kuroki's timetable. Clearly, Zasulich had not learned from history, or he would have known that a successful Japanese crossing of the Yalu at Sukujin would lead to a heavy flank attack against the Russian position at Jiuliancheng, which was exactly the Japanese maneuver in October 1894 when they crossed the Yalu at this same location to catch the Chinese off guard. By the morning of April 30 the Twelfth Division had assembled on the Manchurian side of the Yalu and was on its way to the Ai River.[66] That evening, Zasulich received an alarming report about wheels heard on the islands, but he made no move to shift his main forces from Andong. In the early morning hours of May 1, as the morning fog lifted, one can only imagine Zasulich's horror when he saw before him the forty-five thousand men of Kuroki's First Army across the shallow Ai River. The three divisions—the Second and Guard Divisions on Chukodai, and the Twelfth Division on the river's eastern bank, were ready to unleash their final assault.[67]

At 5:20 AM Japanese artillery pounded the Russian positions in and around Jiuliancheng. At 7:30 AM the Japanese infantry began their advance but did not draw fire. Fearing perhaps the Russians were drawing them into a trap, the Japanese hesitated. Then, at last, the tension was broken by fire from a Russian artillery battery, promptly silenced by counterfire from the Guards Division. The Second Division advanced rapidly, overwhelming the Russian defenses at Jiuliancheng, and the town was in Japanese hands by 9:00 AM. By noon the forces around Jiuliancheng had pulled back to Hamaton.[68] As the Japanese pursued, confused columns of men, guns, and horses crowded the steep path of the Russian retreat. Some of the severest fighting took place when the Russians counterattacked during their harried retreat.[69]

By 5:30 PM, on May 1, the Japanese were in possession of the Russian positions on the western bank of the Yalu, and Zasulich's command was in full retreat. Losses, in comparison to what was to come, were relatively modest, with 1,036 Japanese and 2,700 Russian casualties.[70] Far greater than the cost in men and materiel was the psychological effect of the Yalu River battle on both sides. Kuroki's decisive victory shocked everyone. Some had thought the Japanese might be able to put up a good fight, but no one imagined Russia would lose so badly. "The slower the Russian sense of superiority dies the better it will be for Japan," remarked British journalist Alfred Stead. "An army was thrown out unsupported in a magnificent defensible position to hold back the Japanese. The mere fact that there was a Russian army there was apparently supposed to prevent a Japanese attack."[71] The battle of the Yalu had achieved Japan's primary objective of the war—to push the Russians out of the peninsula.

Less than forty-eight hours after Kuroki had reported his victory to Tokyo, General Oku's Second Army, waiting aboard seventy transports in the P'yŏngyang inlet, received orders to prepare to depart immediately for the Liaodong Peninsula. Having been held back until the First Army's crossing into Manchuria was accomplished in the event it might require assistance, the Second Army began landing at Pitzuwo on the night of May 4–5. Port Arthur was now under threat of being cut off and isolated.

Japanese military police officers (*kenpeitai*) and Korean farmers watch the Yalu River battle. (JLP 532 LA 1 #11732, Jack London Photographs and Negatives, Huntington Library, San Marino, California)

INDEPENDENCE CLUB

It was widely known that Kojong secretly supported the Russians and was convinced Russia would win the war. Before Pavlov's departure on February 12, Kojong sent him a note to "affirm his active cooperation toward Russia" and "express his hope for a quick return of the Russian mission to Seoul."[72] For the rest of the war, Pavlov remained in Shanghai as "Russian minister in Seoul, temporarily located outside of Korea" where he oversaw an intelligence network set up on the initiative of Alekseev to collect information on Japanese forces in Korea and Manchuria. The organization drew its informants from "patriotically-inclined" Koreans, be they Korean or Russian subjects, committed to helping Russia's war against Japan.[73] Astonishingly, Kojong himself was an "agent" and received encryption codes from Pavlov so he could communicate with Saint Petersburg.[74]

Matvei Ivanovich, a translator for the Russian mission in Shanghai, was put in charge of intelligence operation communications, establishing contact between Korean authorities in Seoul and secret agents on the peninsula and in Manchuria.[75] In early March 1904, a partisan detachment

331

of a thousand men was organized by Yi Pǒm-yun, the former surveil-lance commissioner of Kando, near the Russian border in Hamgyǒng Province. Alekseev ordered the First Nerchinsk Cossack Regiment, with three thousand Cossack cavalrymen, to support the Korean partisan group there. The commander of the regiment, Lieutenant Colonel I. D. Pavlov, reported that Kojong had secretly dispatched a trusted Korean officer who would be "giving Russian command intelligence data about the movement of Japanese troops," and according to local sources, "it was well-known that Kojong had given orders to local government sol-diers not to shoot at the Russians and to help them secure supplies and rations, and to show them the roads."[76]

Not all Koreans supported the Russians, however. In 1896, largely in response to the preponderant Russian influence in the Korean court, re-formists like Sǒ Chae'il (Philip Jaisohn) and Yun Ch'i-ho formed the In-dependence Club, a loose band of mostly Christian, Western-educated elites.[77] Club members had harshly criticized Kojong's yearlong stay in the Russian mission, declaring that no head of a state should hide in an-other country's legation. They also attacked unscrupulous state officials who abetted Russia's schemes. "We believe," they declared, "that for a nation to be a nation, it must be independent without needing to rely on other countries."[78] To them, Russia was a dangerous, backward autoc-racy and a predacious power, not unlike Huang Zunxian's perception of the White barbarian and "predatory wolf" shared by many Korean poli-cymakers in the 1880s.[79] Kojong's response was to disband the Indepen-dence Club in 1898.

The negative perception of Russia also reinforced the idea that Japan, not Russia, was the model for modernizing the Korean nation under the rubric of "civilization and enlightenment."[80] The newspaper *Hwangsǒng sinmun* actively debated the theme of a Russian threat after the Sino-Japanese War, and wariness of its northern neighbor markedly increased after Russia's occupation of Manchuria and the Yalu concession in northern Korea in 1900.[81] Moreover, the reformers' call for "civilization and enlightenment" went hand in hand with their advocacy for coopera-tion with Japan in the belief that Korean modernization should follow the Japanese model. It was in that spirit that the Independence Club harshly denounced outmoded Confucian norms and practices.[82]

Fear of Russia overrode any skepticism about Japan's motives for the war and instead led to acquiescence and even support for Japan's war against Russia. In the northwest provinces of Hwanghae and P'yǒngan, traditional loci of antigovernment activity and the region that had been crossed by the First Army on its way to the Manchurian border, no serious attempts were made to sabotage the Japanese war effort. The Russians received little or no information from local Koreans about the First Army's activities before the battle of the Yalu, for example. Nor were there attempts to disrupt Japanese supply lines or stage guerrilla attacks against the First Army when Kuroki's forces were particularly vulnerable. Sabotage of roads and telegraph wires during the early months of the war were almost unknown. The *Hwangsŏng sinmun* summed up the general attitude when it declared on February 20 that "Japan should be supported in its righteous war to defend Korean and Chinese territory from the Russians."[83] Japan's successive victories in Manchuria during the summer and fall of 1904 only seemed to back the claim that betting on a rising Japan against an ossified Russia had been the correct choice.

Koreans were thus not unified in their response to the war, and Japan's wartime policies often exacerbated domestic tensions. This was especially true with regard to the sensitive issue of military requisitions of labor, land, and materiel from the countryside. Instead of direct requisitions, which had proven so unpopular during the Sino-Japanese War, the requisitioning of land for military use was negotiated indirectly, through local Korean government officials who would act as a go-between for a fee. "When the people asked for payment [for land use], they were told to go to local government officials," wrote one observer.[84] A similar indirect payment system was set up to solicit Korean coolie labor for military transportation.

But such a system was ripe for abuse and corruption by local officials. "Through the government, the Japanese ordered the areas of Hwanghae-do and P'yŏngan-do to employ manual laborers who were paid 7 *nyang* a day," reported the chronicler Hwang Hyŏn. "The Japanese only employed volunteers and did not force these areas to hire people, but the local government officials tricked the people and caused great disorder."[85] A widely reported case of such disorder occurred at Sihŭng, a few miles south of Seoul. On September 20 several hundred Korean villagers burned to death their county magistrate, Pak U-yang, and his son. Pak had been accused of receiving payment from the Japanese for coolie transportation work done by the villagers and then pocketing the money for himself.[86]

By late summer and early fall 1904, the Tonghaks began resurfacing in large numbers in Hwanghae and P'yŏngan Provinces and restarting political mobilization efforts. Hayashi reported cautiously that Tonghak ire appeared to be directed at local Korean officials, not against the Japanese. "The Tonghak parties that gathered in P'yŏngan-do seem to have been people from the countryside who have been suffering from the tyranny of local government officials," he wrote. Their aim is to "improve the government" and they "criticized the corruption of the central and provincial government officials and emphasized the need for change."[87] According to the historian Yumi Moon, popular riots in the northwest began appearing due to the destabilizing effects of the war and the loss of the government's grip on power. The Tonghaks had been in hiding since their defeat during the Sino-Japanese War, but war conditions gave them an opening to reappear, "infiltrating the villages that the Japanese had passed through and provoked popular unrest there."[88]

On September 17 the local governor of P'yŏngan Province wrote that several thousand Tonghaks had convened in front of the country district office in Sunch'ŏn, the largest assembly yet. "There was an attempt to persuade them to disperse but the Tonghaks said that they would continue to rebel," reported the governor. "Officers have been sent to try and persuade the rebels, but if they disperse in one area, they end up gathering in another; instability is growing by the day," he confided. "I am growing deeply worried."[89] The main concern for the Japanese was the impact revived Tonghak activity might have on the war effort against Russia. The answer was as unexpected as it was surprising.

ILCHINHOE

After the Tonghak defeat at Kongju in December 1894, the combined Korean government and Japanese forces targeted the main Tonghak stronghold in Chŏlla and southern Ch'ungch'ŏn Provinces, the main locus of Chŏn Pong-jun's Southern Assembly (Namjŏp) and the core of Tonghak strength. The subsequent slaughter of Tonghak believers along with the arrest and execution of its most prominent leaders, including Chŏn, shattered the Southern Assembly's religious and military organization. After 1894 there was very little, if anything, left.[90]

This was not true of the Northern Assembly (Pukchŏp), however. Its leader, Ch'oe Si-hyŏng, managed to flee north with a handful of trusted lieutenants and remained underground but active, with a secret following of about four hundred thousand people.[91] Between 1896 and 1898, Ch'oe worked on reorganizing the Tonghaks, focusing on the northwest provinces of Hwanghae and P'yŏngan.[92] In July 1898 Ch'oe was captured and executed. But one of his disciples, Son Pyŏng-hŭi, escaped. After several years on the run, Son turned up mysteriously in Osaka in 1901, where he came into frequent contact with exiled Korean reform leaders and the "enlightenment and civilization" ideals they espoused. These men were all considered traitors by the Korean government. Two of them, Cho Hŭi-yŏn and Kwŏn Tong-jun, who later joined the Tonghaks, had been involved in the murder of Queen Min in 1895. While in Japan, Son began scheming to return to Korea with an eye to overthrowing the Korean monarchy.[93]

In 1903 Son dispatched his chief deputy, Yi Yong-gu, to Korea to secretly begin organizing the Tonghaks just as Japan began gearing up for war with Russia. Very little was known about Son Pyŏng-hŭi and Yi Yong-gu at the time.[94] All the Japanese knew was that Son had a large following, estimated to be around eighty thousand, and that he had "donated 10,000 won to the Japanese war fund and 3,000 won to the Japanese Red Cross."[95] Son had apparently sent Yi back to Korea in order for him to take advantage of the new political environment. "Following Japan's successive victories, the absence of Russian soldiers in Korea . . . [and] with the Chosŏn Peninsula under the sway of Japanese influence, many [exiled] Koreans believed that they could use this opportunity to send exiled leaders back to Korea to reform the government."[96] With this goal in mind, in September 1904 Yi founded an organization called the Chinbohoe (Progress Society), with Tonghak branches "in the eight provinces." But some members also began referring to themselves as Ilchinhoe (Advance in Unity Society). This latter group was made of up reform-minded intellectuals and elites, many of whom had been members of the now-defunct Independence Club. One distinctive feature of both organizations was that they all "cut their hair short" as a sign of their "civilized status."[97]

Japanese minister to Korea Hayashi Gonsuke was curious about these organizations. Who were they and what did they want? Most importantly, did they pose a threat to the Japanese in Korea? Reports of their early activities proved reassuring. Ochiai Toyosaburō chief of staff of the Korea Garrison Army, reported in November 1904 that the Chinbohoe and the Ilchinhoe were, in fact, one and the same organization. As for their stance toward Japan, "While the Chinbohoe/Ilchinhoe had the intention of defying Japan in the beginning, they do not show signs of it now. Sometimes, its members even make an effort to get on the good side of the Japanese soldiers." Ochiai reported that they had even offered to work on construction projects for the railway and refused payment for the wages offered.[98]

Approximately one hundred fifty thousand Ilchinhoe members participated in railroad construction in October 1904. Yi Yong-gu personally
led three thousand Ilchinhoe members to Hamgyŏng-do to help with the
railway construction. According to another account, "Ilchinhoe members
carried sacks of rice on their backs to Munsan. Since the Japanese soldiers were all hungry, the Ilchinhoe cooked rice for them."[99]

Why would the Ilchinhoe members go out of their way to help the
Japanese? Someya Nariaki, vice consul at Chinnamp'o, speculated it was
because "the organization is very invested in the reform movement." And
the war provided an opportunity "to get on Japan's good side." Moreover, because "railroads are part of the civilizing reform, the organization
is trying to help the war effort in any way they can so that the Japanese
government will be grateful to them."[100] Song Pyŏng-jun, one of the Ilchinhoe's founders, who also served as an interpreter for Japanese Army
headquarters in Seoul, wrote to Yasuharu Matsuishi, deputy chief of staff
of the First Army, touting their shared common goals:

> The Ilchinhoe is flourishing despite the continuing tyrannical pressure
> imposed upon it from the Korean government. . . . Members residing
> in Hwanghae and P'yŏngando which is where the Kyŏngui Seoul-Ŭiju
> railway line passes through, are claiming that words are not enough to
> demonstrate their support and trust in the Japanese. They have requested
> permission from the [Japanese] military headquarters and railroad of-
> fice to volunteer to provide free labor to work on the railroads [for
> Japan]. However, because Japanese law prohibits unpaid labor, they are
> still receiving significant pay. . . . Of the payment received, we Ilchinhoe
> members have agreed to collectively save our pay, and whatever amount
> is left over after we deduct the money for food and other necessities, we
> will donate to the Japanese government as "war funds" to punish the
> vicious Russians.[101]

This, then, was the crux of the matter. The Ilchinhoe would make strategic use of Japanese power to further its aims to reform Korea's "tyrannical government." At the same time, by offering to aid the Japanese
against Russia, Song and others believed the Ilchinhoe would eventually
be able to "share" in the victory and secure the nation's independence.
Similar ideas were articulated earlier in the war by Son Pyŏng-hŭi. At the
start of the conflict, he summoned forty Tonghak leaders to Tokyo, where
he laid out his vision of Tonghak aims summarized in three main points:
(1) establish civilization; (2) overthrow the evil Korean officials; and

Japanese soldiers with Korean laborers helping the war effort, 1904. (H. W. Wilson, *Japan's Fight for Freedom* [London: Amalgamated Press, 1904–1906], 1:300)

(3) help the [Japanese] become the victor in war.[102] According to a report published in October 1904, between 260,000 to 270,000 Ilchinhoe members participated in either railroad works or the transportation of military goods from Hwanghae and P'yŏngan Provinces. Others volunteered to work as spies.[103]

On October 23 American Minister Horace Allen received a report that included a letter from an undisclosed Ilchinhoe leader to General Hasegawa Yoshimichi, commander of the Korean Garrison Army.[104] Allen was shocked to read that Ilchinhoe leaders were plotting to assassinate members of the Korean government: "It is the intention of these radicals to resort to the common Korean method of assassination to rid the country of officials who are opposed to the Japanese reforms or who are in secret sympathy with the Russians."[105]

The Ilchinhoe's plot was in retaliation for the violent methods government officials were using to suppress their members. On September 20, 1904, Kojong ordered provincial governors and army commanders to arrest local Ilchinhoe followers and execute their leaders. In early October the Korean government permitted local governors "to shoot" the leaders of assembled members. These bloody reprisals were denounced by the Ilchinhoe as "tyrannical acts of a despotic government." The question for

An injured Japanese soldier evacuated by Ilchinhoe members, 1904. (JPL 532 LA 1 #11716, Jack London Photographs and Negatives, Huntington Library, San Marino, California)

the Japanese was where they stood with regard to their support of the Ilchinhoe, given that the Korean government was cracking down on them.[106]

Hasegawa was wary of backing the Ilchinhoe.[107] Foreign Minister Komura shared Hasegawa's concerns. He was well aware the Ilchinhoe organization "was growing rapidly" and seemed to have a much "deeper base than previously thought" but he was suspicious of their motives. "They claim to support similar ideas . . . and are striving to win the sympathy of our military through their clever talk," he wrote to Hayashi. "But we cannot know for sure whether they are actually trying to use us to achieve their leaders' own ambitions. In general, it would be advantageous [to use them] to gain the support of the Korean people, but these people forming such [political] parties may ultimately be detrimental for us."[108]

Hayashi, however, was more sanguine, advising a wait-and-see approach. "I sense that the situation has the potential to turn bad and have contemplated appropriate measures," he wrote Komura. "While it is not necessary to disband the organization at the moment, I have determined to dissolve it immediately if they start to become a threat to public order." For the time being, however, it was beneficial to keep them around. "They have wholeheartedly offered to help our soldiers and supply us with laborers whom we do not have to pay," he wrote. "When the Ilchinhoe proclaimed the establishment of their organization . . . many people who had been under the tyranny of the Korean government even before the war agreed with their ideas. The Korean Court believes that the organization has ties with the Japanese and thus is [now] too scared to do much about it."[109] Furthermore, the Ilchinhoe could be useful in putting pressure on Kojong to go along with Japan's reform measures. By targeting the "predators of the people," and publicly denouncing the personal corruption of local Korean government officials, the Ilchinhoe might boost Japan's overall popularity.

While Hasegawa and Komura were hesitant to embrace the Ilchinhoe too closely, Hayashi ultimately saw the benefits. "The Ilchinhoe principles not only coincide with our policies," he wrote Komura, "but the people all over the countryside also approve and support this organization."[110] This was not completely true but it cannot be denied that the Ilchinhoe played an important role in garnering popular support for the war effort so that the Japanese could concentrate their main energy on fighting in Manchuria.[111]

CHAPTER EIGHTEEN

WAR IN MANCHURIA

The Battle of the Yalu was a rude awakening for the Russians. It dashed the perception that Russia would easily win in a short war against an "inferior" enemy. The next shock came a few days later on May 5 when General Oku's Second Army began landing its three divisions, the First, Third, and Fourth, with thirty-nine thousand men, at Pitzuwo on the east coast of the Liaodong Peninsula. They met no resistance and the landing proceeded without interruptions.[1]

No one was more surprised by the sudden turn of events than Colonel Nikolai Alexandrovitch Tretyakov, commanding officer of the Fifth East Siberian Rifle Regiment, which had been providing security for the Manchurian Railway on the peninsula since 1903. Tretyakov had been aware of the growing tension between Russia and Japan, but like most Russian officers he had not given serious thought to the possibility of a war. It was only on February 9, when news arrived that Port Arthur had been attacked, that the daunting task ahead dawned on him. He and his three thousand men would be called upon to help defend the Liaodong Peninsula and Port Arthur. Tretyakov's situation was rather desperate for his modest regiment was quite inadequate to defend the peninsula against any concerted attack. "To oppose a landing is a very difficult business and here the rugged coast added considerably to the difficulties of the defender." His request for reinforcement was repeatedly denied by General Alexander Fok, his superior and the commander of the Fourth East Siberian Rifle Division. Tretyakov decided to establish his main defenses along the isthmus near Dairen where, during the Boxer Uprising, he had overseen the construction of a fortified line anchored on Nanshan Hill. It was the only place that would give him a fighting chance of holding back a Japanese advance on Port Arthur.[2]

About forty miles from Port Arthur an isthmus joins the southern part of the Liaodong peninsula to the mainland. This narrowest part of the peninsula was less than three miles wide, an area of deep ravines and hills dominated by Nanshan Hill. About two and a half miles to the north of Nanshan is the ancient walled town of Jinzhou (Chinchou), which the Japanese had taken in early November 1894 on their way to capture Port Arthur. Tretyakov fortified Jinzhou as a strong outpost to hinder an assault on Nanshan. Intense effort was also made to restore the main fortifications at Nanshan, which had fallen into disrepair.[3] The Fifth Siberians would soon be right in the Japanese path, for the Second Army's immediate objective was to advance through Jinzhou, penetrate the isthmian defenses anchored by Nanshan, and seize Dairen as a base to capture Port Arthur.

On May 8 Tretyakov was ordered to make a reconnaissance of the Japanese landing. The mission was plagued by difficulties from the start. "All our maps had the names of the villages defaced, the contours were scarcely marked, [and] none of the heights of the various hills were given." To make matters worse, the Russians could not hire local guides. "No amount of money could buy them," Tretyakov fumed.[4] After wandering around aimlessly, the detachment returned to Nanshan without a clear picture of what they were facing. Poor battlefield intelligence, first seen at Yalu, would plague the Russians for the rest of the war.

The Japanese were better prepared. Oku had the services of Major Ishimitsu Makiyo, the Japanese intelligence officer at Blagoveshchensk who had witnessed the terrible massacre there in July 1900. He had been operating in Manchuria before the war using a photography studio in Harbin as his cover. When Kuropatkin visited various military sites in Manchuria, the unsuspecting general had hired Ishimitsu as a photographer. Ishimitsu's knowledge was thus of tremendous value to Oku, as he was one of the few Japanese who had recent knowledge of the area.[5]

By May 24 the First, Third, and Fourth Divisions were positioned to assault Jinzhou and the Nanshan defenses. Instead of waiting for the arrival of his heavy guns, which would have taken several weeks, Oku decided to attack immediately to prevent the Russians from further strengthening their defenses. Tretyakov had already restored the fortifications that had

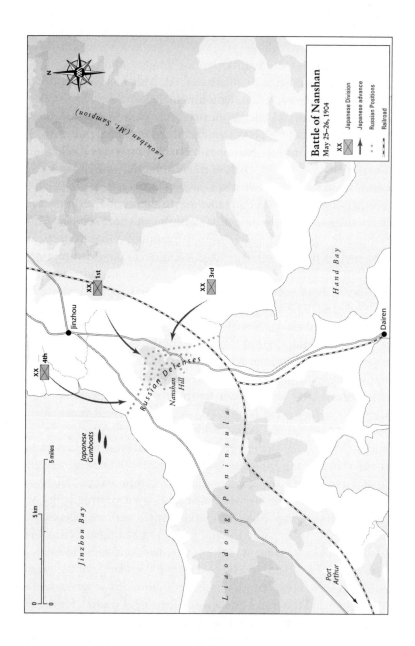

Battle of Nanshan
May 25–26, 1904

XX Japanese Division
→   Japanese advance
     Russian Positions
     Railroad

Laoshan (Mt. Sampson)

Hand Bay

XX 1st

XX 3rd

Jinzhou

Dairen

Russian Defenses

Nanshan Hill

XX 4th

Liaodong Peninsula

Japanese Gunboats

Jinzhou Bay

0   5 km
0   5 miles

Port Arthur

N

fallen into disrepair, dug new trenches, and set up new minefields and barbed wire covered by machine guns. It was the first time barbed wire was used to turn a large area into a killing zone for machine gun fire, a technique employed with increasingly devastating effects that would be perfected in the killing fields of World War I.[6]

At daylight on the morning of May 25 the Japanese began bombarding the Russian positions. The Fourth Division led the attack, pushing the Russian outpost inside Jinzhou, which was assaulted without success.[7] The promised support by gunboats from Jinzhou Bay was foiled by a storm, and Oku put off the main attack until the next day. What lay ahead appeared foreboding. "While the hills were gentle," recalled Ishimitsu, "they were covered heavily by a metal [barbed wire] net; we could see more than twenty fortresses on these hills. The tops of the hills were also fortified with more than seventy canons pointing to us. We did not have artillery that was strong enough to fight against the enemy and open a path for us. Neither did we have much ammunition."[8]

The next morning Oku's troops began the main assault. "As I observed the battlefield with a telescope, the dreadful scenes happening before me made me want to close my eyes," Ishimitsu recalled. "While our cannon fire supported the suicidal missions to march forward, the soldiers were struck down one by one by the constant shooting of machine-gun fire: none of them were able to stand up again and move forward. This was the first time our army encountered this new weapon called the machine gun." Japanese troops became hopelessly entangled in the wire, mowed down by Russian machine guns, as the next wave of soldiers scrambled over their dead comrades to advance the attack inch by inch.[9] There was almost no progress, and "the dead bodies kept piling up alongside Nanshan Hill, their blood dripping."[10] Reports from the front were growing desperate. "While Oku repeatedly ordered the launching of renewed attacks, all the reports we were getting back was that an entire company had perished." Ishimitsu was called upon to deliver a personal message from Oku to Lieutenant General Fushiminomiya Sadanaru, the First Division commander. It said simply: "Attack. Expect that all the soldiers will die."[11]

That afternoon, Oku assembled his staff and asked for their opinions. They decided to pause until nightfall and try again. The Japanese had tried nine times to take Nanshan Hill and each time had been driven back. With his men exhausted and shocked by the high casualties, Oku knew he could not afford to sustain a protracted assault. The Second Army would make a general effort all along the front, with the First and Third Divisions conducting attacks from the east to draw Russian attention while the Fourth Division made a daring enveloping attack by wading through the waist-deep water of Jinzhou Bay along the coast to outflank the Russian line.[12]

At 6:50 PM that evening, "when shadows were cast on the mountain of dead bodies," the Fourth Division moved forward with support from a flotilla of gunboats in Jinzhou Bay.[13] After a mile, the soldiers climbed onto land and turned on the Russian flank. Tretyakov ordered his troops to fall back to a second defense line but then learned that General Fok, who had taken over command of the defenses, had prematurely ordered a full-scale retreat, causing confusion. "I galloped after the retreating soldiers and made myself hoarse shouting, 'Stop, stop, my men!' But they in their turn shouted back to me: 'Your Excellency, we have been ordered to retreat!'" Tretyakov was blindsided. As soon as his troops caught sight of the Japanese, who "began to open a terrific shrapnel fire," panic ensued and it became impossible to stop his men from fleeing.[14]

Nanshan was taken on the tenth assault, at bayonet point. "Surprisingly, it took only thirty minutes for the Japanese flag to fly on Nanshan," Ishimitsu wrote. "The fortune of war is inscrutable. When we tried our best to attack, the enemy also strived to defend its position and did not retreat, and we ended up suffering huge losses. Yet, when we decided to take a break, and waited for the enemy to react, they withdrew from the battlefield."[15]

The incompetence of Russian generalship would be one of the hallmark features of the war. General Fok had an entire regiment in reserve to reinforce the line at Nanshan. He not only failed to send them in to run the tide of battle but ensured the collapse of the Russian line with his untimely withdrawal order. Fok feared being surrounded and cut off by a Japanese landing behind him, despite having no evidence that such an operation was in the offing. Tretyakov rejected Fok's precautions as preposterous.[16]

The capture of Nanshan had cut the rail line northward, isolating Dairen and Port Arthur. By the evening of May 26, throngs of panic-stricken Russian civilians began leaving Dairen in droves. The day after the battle, Ishimitsu arrived undercover in Dairen to survey the city. From the look of things, "it did not appear that the Russians had expected to lose the battle at Nanshan," he wrote. So hasty was the exodus from the city that dishes were left on tables and meals were left uneaten. The Japanese took control of the strategic port without a fight.[17] As Russian soldiers and civilians mingled together on their flight to Port Arthur, reaching

On the summit of Nanshan Hill. (COPY 1 482/201–450, p. 25, National Archives, Kew, UK)

the outskirt of the fortress two days later, they brought a large herd of cattle, snatched from local farmers, amounting to about two hundred head.[18] This food stock, and anything else the refugees had managed to carry with them, would have to last for the many months ahead as the fortress was now cut off from the outside. The siege of Port Arthur had begun.

For Oku's soldiers, left with the gruesome task of burying their dead at Nanshan, the scale of the carnage was shocking. The Japanese had 739 killed, and 5,459 wounded. This figure is compared to the 1,418 soldiers who died in combat during the entire course of Japan's 1894–1895 war

345

with China.[19] Even more shocking was that the Japanese had expended more ammunition at Nanshan than during the entire Sino-Japanese War.[20] Russian losses were comparatively light, 450 men killed, wounded, or missing, but an additional 650 were lost during the chaotic retreat.[21]

Surveying the battlefield, Sakurai Tadayoshi, whose war memoir, *Human Bullets,* became an international best-seller, reflected: "It is not pleasant to see even a piece of a blood-stained bandage. It is shocking to see dead bodies piled up in this valley or near that rock, dyed with dark purple blood, their faces blue their eyelids swollen, their hair clotted with blood and dust, their white teeth biting their lips, the red of their uniforms alone remaining unchanged. . . . Everywhere were scattered blood-covered gaiters, pieces of uniforms and underwear, caps, and so on; everywhere were loathsome smells and ghastly sights."[22] Nanshan illustrated the dramatic change that had taken place in land warfare in the great disparity in casualties between attacker and defender in an assault against a well-defended position covered by effective obstacles (mines and barbed wire) and rapid-fire weapons. This kind of warfare would be magnified to horrendous levels in World War I. The battle of Nanshan was a foreboding of the carnage to come.

DIVIDED COMMAND

On May 27, as Tretyakov's command retreated from Nanshan, Kuropatkin headed for Mukden for a conference with Alekseev at his new headquarters. A week earlier Alekseev's chief of staff, Major-General Yakov Zhilinsky, had handed Kuropatkin a note from the viceroy stating that "the time had come for the Manchurian Army to take the offensive."[23] Alekseev, who had previously boasted about Port Arthur's impenetrable defenses, now argued its relief to be absolutely essential, for "Port Arthur held symbolic importance for both countries and its loss would damage Russian prestige."[24]

But Kuropatkin thought it premature to mount an offensive, especially one that would divide his forces. He wanted to wait until additional reinforcements had arrived from European Russia. Both men appealed to the tsar to resolve their disagreement.[25] Nicholas took Alekseev's side, swayed by the argument that Port Arthur must be secured for prestige, morale, and strategic reasons. Lieutenant General G. K. Stackelberg, commander of the Eastern Detachment, was placed in command of the operations for the relief of Port Arthur.

On May 19 the Japanese Fourth Army had disembarked on the Manchurian coast at Takushan under the command of General Nozu Michitsura, another veteran of the Sino-Japanese War. The Fifth, Sixth, and Tenth Divisions, a total of sixty thousand men, once again landed unopposed, just as at Inch'ŏn and Pitzuwo. The landing place was chosen to round up Russian forces from the south.[26] The three-pronged Japanese advance to force a decisive battle for Manchuria was now in full motion. The three armies would converge at Liaoyang, where the Manchurian Army was concentrated. Oku's Second Army advanced up the Liaodong Peninsula while Kuroki's First Army advanced from the east and Nozu's Fourth Army moved northward from the center. Meanwhile, the newly formed Third Army, under General Nogi Maresuke, arrived at Dairen in mid-June to move south and seize Port Arthur.

During Japan's war with China, Nogi had been commander of the First Infantry Brigade, which had led the assault on Port Arthur. The capture of the fortress in a single day on November 21, 1894, transformed him from an obscure brigade-level officer to a national hero. It was hoped such an astonishing victory could be replicated, but as Oku and others had discovered at Nanshan, the Russians were not the Chinese of 1894, and mass infantry assaults against entrenched Russian positions were extremely costly.[27]

On May 28 Kuropatkin reluctantly headed to Stackelberg's headquarters at Haicheng, a railway town about forty miles south of Liaoyang, to confer on the campaign plan. Stackelberg had a force of about thirty-five thousand infantry, of which the First Siberian Army Corps constituted the bulk, along with thirty-five hundred cavalry. He would establish a defense at Telissu, about eighty miles north of Port Arthur on the South Manchurian Railroad. The position had good defensive terrain, and with the railway available to run supplies, Stackelberg was confident he could set up adequate defenses in time to halt Oku's advance.

At this time, however, the Russians were in the dark about where all the Japanese forces actually were. The position of only two Japanese armies had been fixed—Kuroki's First Army and Oku's Second Army. Almost nothing was known about Nozu's Fourth Army, which had landed at Takushan in late May. Moreover, information about the size of Nogi's Third Army was also scanty. Kuropatkin was furious. "Consequently, we did not know the destination of one-half of the enemy's army, and thus were not in possession of two important pieces of knowledge which were necessary before any operations of a decisive character could be

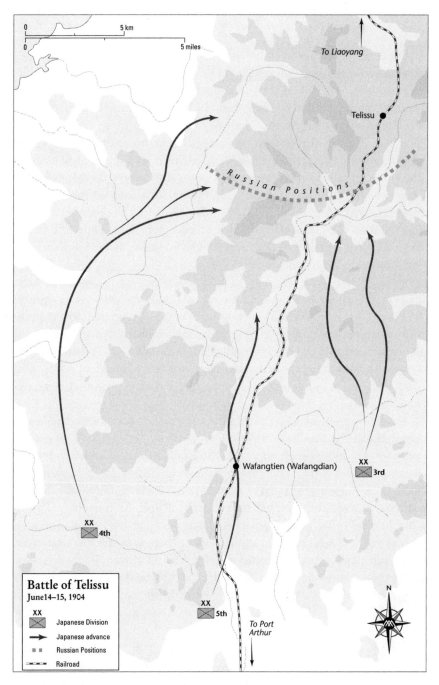

The Battle of Telissu, also called the Battle of Wafangou.

undertaken—namely, the position of the enemy's main forces and their probable plan of operations."[28] Lack of basic intelligence about the Japanese location and movement would plague the Russians throughout the war. It cost them at Telissu.

The battle of Telissu jumped off on the morning of June 14, lasting until the next day. Japanese intelligence brought information to General Oku that Stackelberg's forces were deployed south of Telissu, with its main force in the center. Approaching Telissu, Oku divided his forces into three columns—the Fourth Division on the left (west), the Fifth Division in the center, and the Third Division on the right (east)—to make a wide enveloping movement with the Fourth Division on the Russian right while the other two divisions advanced in front of the Russian line in a feint. Stackelberg, however, ignored or discredited reports that a large formation of Japanese forces was moving around the Russian line to his right. By dawn the next day, Stackelberg realized too late that the Russian main body was receiving enfilading artillery bombardment from the west. The Japanese Fourth Division had turned Stackelberg's right flank, and the devastating fire down his line caused his men to begin to lose heart. The Japanese Fifth Division in the center then mounted a resolute attack that broke through, forcing the Russians to retreat. Many of the Russian officers, disgusted at the performance of their troops, called their actions in the face of the Japanese attacks "scandalous."[29] It was a costly defeat. Official losses were more than double the casualties suffered at Nanshan—3,413 killed and wounded, although the numbers were probably much higher. Japanese losses were heavy—1,163 killed and wounded—but less than half of the Russian losses.[30]

The third land campaign of the war had resulted, once again, in a humiliating defeat for Russia. "Had the railway only been ready at the beginning of hostilities, even to run only six military trains, we should have had three army corps at Telissu," Kuropatkin later fumed. "The issue of this battle would have been different, and this would undoubtedly have affected the whole course of the campaign, for we should have secured the initiative."[31] As overall commander in charge of naval and army preparations before the war, the responsibility for the debacle clearly fell on the viceroy's shoulders. While the finger-pointing and bickering between Alekseev and Kuropatkin intensified, the people on whose territory the war was being waged began to choose sides. The Chinese people had been told Russia would win the war without question, but the impressive Japanese performance cast those prognostications into doubt.

CHINESE NEUTRALITY

In the wake of the Russian disaster at Telissu, Alekseev issued a public proclamation on June 15 urging the Chinese people to "continue your usual avocations without interruption." If they "remain quiet, there was no need to fear Russian ill-treatment." In particular, he warned of dire consequences if any vital railroads were damaged.[32] It was an ill-advised move, and Alekseev had severely miscalculated the mood of the Chinese. "Even the most cynical could not repress a smile about a threat so cruel that we cannot doubt that it will be repudiated at once," wrote one observer. "How, indeed, could the viceroy call upon disarmed country farmers, and their women and children, to protect the railway and prevent the Japanese or the honghuzi from destroying it? The chief result of such a proclamation must be made to make the people pray for the final success of the Japanese, and that the Russians will never come back to carry out their threats."[33]

Four days before the start of the war, China proclaimed its neutrality. The United States, Britain, France, Germany, and Italy, all neutral powers, jointly petitioned Russia and Japan to avoid sending troops to Zhili Province, where Beijing was located, to prevent the Chinese imperial government from fleeing Beijing once again.[34] Secretary Hay circulated a note to the powers expressing his government's "sincere desire to preserve China's neutrality." Both Russia and Japan responded positively, with Komura following up with a declaration that "the Japanese Government is prepared to promise to respect the neutrality of China outside of the regions occupied by Russia, on condition that Russia undertakes a similar obligation and adheres to it in good faith."[35] Komura never had any intention of keeping his promise, however. While the Japanese government kept its word about limiting the fighting to Manchuria, it nevertheless vigorously courted Chinese officials to take Japan's side. An active network of ties between Chinese and Japanese scholars, bureaucrats, and military personnel had already been firmly established before the war, so it was reasonable to expect China's tacit cooperation on some issues.[36]

Four Japanese officers were key in soliciting Chinese support and played prominent roles during the Russo-Japanese War: General Fukushima Yasumasa, Colonel Aoki Nobuzumi, Major Banzai Rihachirō, and Major General Senba Tarō.[37] All four men were deeply knowledgeable about China and had established strong ties to Yuan Shikai and other military reformers before the war. Fukushima, in particular, had been active in the China field since his posting to China as a young attaché. Before the outbreak of the Sino-Japanese War, he had arranged for many scouting expeditions in China and Korea, and eventually landed the job as chief of staff of the First Army during the 1894–1895 war.[38] Fukushima later led the Japanese contingent of the Chinese Relief Expedition during the Boxer Uprising in 1900; his performance had so impressed the French, British, and Americans that Yuan could not help but be dazzled too.[39]

Aoki first became acquainted with Yuan in 1897. He later served as an instructor in China's New Army established by the Qing in the aftermath of Japan's war with China.[40] Banzai, another close acquaintance, later served as Yuan's advisor when the latter became president of the Republic of China in 1912. As for Lieutenant General Senba, he became acquainted with Yuan during his time as commander of Japan's China Garrison (Shina Chutongun), also known as the Tianjin Garrison Army. Under the terms of the Boxer Protocol, the Japanese were allowed to maintain a military force to protect its embassy, concession, and other Japanese-controlled locations, but Senba's main task was to keep a close watch on the Russians and "to change the attitudes of the Chinese officials in the three Northeastern Provinces so that that they would be favorably disposed towards the Japanese."[41]

In November 1903, Kodama Gentarō, then vice chief of the Army General Staff, asked Aoki to try to secure Yuan's support for Japan's war efforts against Russia. Specifically, Kodama wanted Yuan's help in coordinating Chinese and Japanese espionage activities in Manchuria; he also wanted Chinese aid in sabotaging Russia's transportation network in Manchuria and mobilizing the honghuzi against Russian troops. Yuan agreed to all three requests. "As for collecting information about the Russians," he assured Aoki, "I have [already] sent dozens of agents from Port Arthur to Manchuria. I will share every report from them with Japan." Regarding the use of the honghuzi in the war effort, Yuan told Aoki that "the Chinese government will assist the Japanese to help mobilize and recruit honghuzi [for your purpose]." Yuan confided that "the war would not only have an immense impact on Japan but would also determine the fate of China; the future of East Asia will be affected by the war as well." He concluded: "If Japan is defeated, China might also be threatened, and for this reason, China will do everything to help Japan no matter the cost."[42]

It was well known that Yuan Shikai's rise to power had come about through an act of betrayal to the reform party during the Hundred Days'

Reform (1898), but it was also conceded by many in sympathy with the reformers that at the time of the 1898 coup d'état, the revolutionary platform was unlikely to produce practical results. Yuan supported less visionary reforms but this did not mean he did not actively seek a reformist agenda. Having gained a firm footing with Empress Dowager Cixi for his reforms, Yuan set about training and equipping his army, for one of his maxims was that "policy without force is useless." "He is regarded by his countrymen as their only hope in the future," wrote A. R. Colquhoun, "and Europeans who know him speak in the highest terms of his character and capacity." Moreover, although he was known to have close ties with Japanese military officers and had assiduously adopted their methods for modernizing his army, "Yuan is not, as is sometimes represented, a Japanese tool." On the contrary, his motto was always "China for the Chinese."[43] Bitter memories of the Sino-Russian War and Alekseev's order that "all Chinese harboring honghuzi will be shot, and their villages burnt" did little to rally Yuan, or the Chinese people, to the Russian cause. "The worm has raised its head," wrote one observer about China's new attitude. "It is now trying to bite the heel of the Cossacks who have so long trodden it in the dust."[44]

P. M. Lessar, the Russian minister to China, was alarmed. In a March 7, 1904, dispatch to Chinese officials complaining bitterly that the honghuzi were disrupting Russia's telegraph wires and railways, he demanded that the governor of Mukden, General Tsung, take action to suppress the bandits. Failure to do so would mean that "China's declaration of neutrality was a farce." China's reply was simple: the Russians had first employed the honghuzi and compelled many Chinese to join them to suppress the Boxers during the Russo-Chinese War. "Now that Russia is troubled with these bandits, she wants to suppress them with the aid of Chinese troops?" When the question was raised about Chinese neutrality from other nations—namely, the United States—the Chinese government once again denied it had violated its neutrality agreement. It rebuffed accusations that it had offered the service of mounted bandits to Japan, stating emphatically that "the use of the honghuzi by a foreign army was first initiated by a Russian officer, Lt Col. Madritov," whom Alekseev dispatched to northern Korea in 1903 in order to secure Russia's timber enterprise.[45] Russians' past transgressions had now come back to bite them.

Yuan helped the Japanese in other ways. He made sure that Chinese officials in Mukden, Liaodong, Haicheng, and Dashiqiao were all favorably disposed toward the Japanese. For example, when Aoki expressed

Honghuzi heads hung in wooden boxes, circa 1904. They were allegedly beheaded by the Russians for trying to derail a train between Harbin and Mukden. (De Agostini-Biblioteca Ambrosiana/De Agostinia Editore/agefotostock)

reservations about the appointment of a certain Chinese official in Mukden, Yuan assured him the official was "pro-Japanese."[46] Through secret channels, Yuan supplied the Japanese Army with more than two hundred thousand sets of winter clothing and boots, as well as rations through Tianjin and the Shanhai pass, and facilitated the conscription of many horses from Mongolia.[47] One source stated that "two special trains from Shanhai pass made up of 20 freight cars of 10 horses each (200 horses per train)" were smuggled to the Japanese Army at the end of 1904 as well as a large number of cows, pigs, and vegetables.[48] When the Russian consul in Tianjin found out about the smuggling scheme, he protested loudly enough to have the shipments temporarily suspended.[49] By the end of 1904 the Russians had apparently had enough. They hatched a plot to assassinate Yuan, but the attempt was foiled by Senba.[50]

JAPANESE INTELLIGENCE

Even more impressive than the Japanese ability to secure cooperation from the top was the information they were able to gather from the bottom rung of Chinese society. This was made possible by a sophisticated intelligence operation that had begun to take form during the Sino-Japanese War. Resources were poured into establishing a comprehensive covert network of sources. Japan had entered that conflict unsure of its ability to prevail, and to maximize its warmaking capacity it established a top-notch intelligence operation. Then chief of staff of the First Army, Fukushima Yasumasa demanded a detailed assessment of China's weaknesses and vulnerabilities that led to the creation of a network of informants that could provide Japan with vital information.[51]

After the Boxer Uprising, Japanese intelligence was extended to tracking Russian activities in Asia and Europe. At the European end, Japan supported independence movements in Poland and Finland against Russia. Colonel Akashi Motojirō, the military attaché in Saint Petersburg, was in charge of this effort, which he continued from Stockholm after the Japanese legation was evacuated at the start of the war.[52] Akashi's skills were so impressive that by March 1904 he had been able to obtain the cooperation of Polish Socialist Party members to lead an effort to "circulate propaganda pamphlets urging Polish soldiers in Manchuria to desert the Russian army." The Poles also promised to help sabotage "iron bridges and railways in Eastern Russia and Siberia."[53] This bold initiative to attack the "flabby underbelly" of Russia became most effective during the second year of the war, when domestic frustrations boiled over into rising revolutionary fervor, culminating in the Russian Revolution of 1905.[54]

In Manchuria, Major Ishimitsu Makiyo had worked undercover as part of a highly sophisticated spy network from Port Arthur to Vladivostok. He continued with his espionage activities until the eve of the war, when he was abruptly recalled to Japan in late January 1904. According to A. Votinov, who published a detailed report on Japan's espionage activities during the Russo-Japanese War, local Japanese intelligence officers in Manchuria ran a network of agents and informants of various nationalities— Chinese, Korean, Manchu, and Mongolian—who collected critical information on Russian activities, especially the railway. "The penetration of Japanese spies into railway construction was made easier by the fact that beginning in 1899, the tsarist government ordered tens of thousands of Chinese from Tianjin and Yantai into the railway construction, with the cities still being centers of Japanese espionage. Naturally, among these groups of workers, there were Japanese spies."[55]

Japanese intelligence officers sent detailed reports to their superiors in Japan, where they would be verified and supplemented with reports from military attachés and consulates. The result was impressive. Votinov wrote, with some sense of admiration, that "General Fukushima's declaration before the war that the Japanese knew Russia's military mobilization capabilities better than the Russians themselves have a certain factual basis."[56]

After fleeing Blagoveshchensk in August 1900, Ishimitsu arrived in Khabarovsk via the Nikolsk and Ussuri line, where "the honghuzi were making a fuss along the Chinese Eastern Railway."[57] From his base in Harbin, Ishimitsu was able to gather intelligence about the CER, then in the advanced stages of construction.[58] Having obtained sufficient intelligence about the railway, Ishimitsu headed for Vladivostok at the end of 1900 to report his findings to Major Mutō Nobuyoshi, the Japanese military attaché there. (Mutō later was the commander in chief of the Kwangtung Army in 1926–1927 and again in 1932–1933 while simultaneously holding the positions of commander of the Manchukuo Imperial Army and governor of the Kwantung Leased Territory.)[59] On December 28 Ishimitsu and Mutō received orders to proceed together to Harbin, where they would assume false identities and businesses, Mutō as a grocer and Ishimitsu as a photographer.[60]

Ishimitsu's photography studio turned out to be an unexpected bonanza, as "the Russian military and the railway company usually ordered full-sized photographs," he wrote. "When we received orders from the Russians or the railway company to take pictures of construction sites of the Chinese Eastern Railway or some important bridges, there were usually a lot of restrictions. We were required to develop all the photos in the darkroom in the railway office in the presence of the Russian staff [officers], and to submit the original negative plate to the office." Ishimitsu found an ingenious way to circumvent these strict controls:

> We employed a trick when we printed photos in these conditions: we intentionally spoiled some photos. These photos were blurred with a certain technique, and we were able to restore the images after we took them back [to our studio]. This process costs quite a lot of money. . . . In addition, we also made a lot of copies of Japanese prostitutes or Russian beauties and sent them to the Russian staff and military personnel to please them. In this way, we gradually gained their trust and were asked to take all the photographs that the Russian troops used to report their progress of various military construction sites, from Manchuria to the central region.[61]

The professional photographer turned out to be an especially effective cover. In Vladivostok, a photographer agent specialized in group portraits, especially of Russian officers. "Two weeks before the start of the war this photographer vanished from Vladivostok, having secured accurate information of the officers on the Tsarist border regions, and in some of the photographs he took with him, there were even images of the unfortunate officers, charmed by his delicate words and masterful work. As a result, the Japanese General Staff possessed precise data, confirmed by the photographer, on the makeup of the command of the tsarist border forces stationed in Vladivostok."[62]

If the Russians were oblivious about these espionage activities before the war, they were equally blind to them during the conflict. In the Russian army's rear areas, the Japanese employed Chinese for reconnaissance missions. This was not an especially difficult task, as the Russians were cooperative targets. In villages occupied by Russian troops, signs on houses clearly provided not only the names of the occupants but their unit affiliation. An agent had absolutely "no trouble compiling reports on the troops located in one region or another, for which they only needed to walk around and write down everything he saw on the signs." The reports from the three hundred to four hundred spies employed by the Japanese provided an accurate picture of the Russian units, their commanders, locations, and activities.[63]

General Kuropatkin later lamented the advantage the Japanese had due to their superior intelligence. "Having been preparing for war for ten years, the Japanese had not only studied the country but had sown it with agents, who were of immense service to them," he later wrote. "In spite of their severe, almost cruel attitude, the Chinese population assisted them greatly in their operations; and notwithstanding our superiority in cavalry, they generally had good information as to our strength and dispositions. We, on the contrary, often operated in the dark."[64]

Part of the problem was that the Russians had little or no regard for maintaining secrecy. In one instance, a Chinese entertainer came into a Russian encampment.

> In one settlement where the Nth regiment was quartered, there arrived a Chinese conjurer who turned out to be a master of his trade. He was paid generously for his tricks. However, before his departure, he modestly asked for a certificate from the regimental commander, stating that he had performed artfully; the "conjurer" explained that he needed a recommendation to prove his skills. His request was approved. Gradually, he moved from one military encampment to another, wherever Russian troops were stationed and received a certificate for his performances. As a result of such a "tour," this exceptionally disguised Japanese spy had compiled documentary information on the position of a series of military encampments of the Russian Army—information that was supported by actual certificates.[65]

Eventually the conjurer was detained during his second "tour" by a suspicious Russian official, but by then he had already passed on the critical information to his superiors. Traveling with Kuroki's First Army, American correspondent Frederick Palmer identified the crux of the matter—that the "Russians had reaped what they had sowed":

> It is too late now for the Russians to make friends with the Chinese; the first seeds were sown in the brutalities of the Boxer rebellion—I have seen them brain children in cold blood—and now they reap the harvest not only of these, but of years of occupation which have been years of fear for every peasant woman in Manchuria.[66]

SIEGE OF PORT ARTHUR

On August 10, as General Nogi's Third Army began closing in around Port Arthur, the Pacific Squadron made its attempt to break through the Japanese blockade. The sortie was the brainchild of Alekseev, who wanted the squadron to link up with the Vladivostok Squadron in a force that could challenge the Japanese fleet. But Admiral Vitgeft, commander of the Pacific Squadron, believed that the best course of action was for his ships to remain in the harbor until naval reinforcements arrived and, in the meantime, act as floating artillery for the coming siege. He was overruled. The ensuing seven-hour battle of the Yellow Sea was a close call for Admiral Tōgō and the Combined Fleet, but in the end he prevailed when Vitgeft was killed. The bridge of his flagship, the *Tsarevich,* was hit by two 12-inch shells fired by Tōgō's flagship, the *Mikasa.*[67] It immediately turned the battle against the Russians, as the loss of command and the failure to reestablish it rapidly scattered the squadron.

The severely damaged *Tsarevich,* with a few destroyers, was able to escape to Qingdao, where they were interned by the Germans. A cruiser and a destroyer made it to Shanghai, and another cruiser reached Saigon, where they were interned by the Chinese and the French, respectively. The light cruiser *Novik* made it as far as the East Sea but had to be scuttled before it could reach Vladivostok.[68] Four days later, on August 14, the Japanese Second Fleet under Admiral Kamimura Hikonojō intercepted the Vladivostok Cruiser Squadron, commanded by Rear Admiral Karl Jessen, in the Korean Strait off the coast of Ulsan. Jessen's squadron had steamed from Vladivostok to link up with the Pacific Squadron but turned around when it failed to show up. At this vulnerable moment, far from home base, they ran into Kamimura's cruisers at dawn on August 14. The one-sided battle lasted six hours, leaving the Russian cruiser *Rurik* so damaged it was scuttled by the crew while two others, although making it back to Vladivostok, were too damaged to be repaired.

The two naval defeats were a staggering blow for Russia, effectively neutralizing the Russian Pacific Fleet and leaving Japan in complete control of the seas. Kuropatkin and his staff took measures to delay the news of the disaster from reaching the rank and file lest it affect their morale. "The official reports were so arranged that it required thirteen days to make known the fact that a sea-fight had occurred near the coast of Korea, and the army was only beginning to realize that there had been another disaster [at sea]."[69] Alekseev's immediate reaction was a call to relieve Port Arthur, even if "just a demonstration towards Haicheng," but Kuropatkin insisted that nothing should be done to "prevent our concentration in strength at Liaoyang."[70]

Following Japan's victories at sea, Nogi's Third Army initiated the first of three general assaults to seize the heavily fortified Port Arthur. The assault, begun on August 19, would cost the Japanese a staggering eighteen thousand casualties. Two additional attempts to storm the fortress would follow in October and late November, when the Japanese infantry were once again turned into "human bullets" advancing into barbed wire entanglements against devastating artillery and machine-gun fire.[71]

Why was Port Arthur so important that the Japanese were willing to sacrifice so much blood? Port Arthur was originally not a main objective of the land campaign. General Kodama had envisioned containing the port with a "bamboo palisade," by which he meant "a relatively small and light equipped force sufficient to prevent a Russian break-out."[72] Two developments changed the plan, however. One was the news in May 1904 that a new Russian fleet was assembling in the Baltic to reinforce the Pacific Squadron. This made taking Port Arthur imperative. The other development was the realization that with each passing day, more troops and materiel were arriving from European Russia to reinforce Kuropatkin's army. The sooner Port Arthur could be captured, the sooner Nogi's Third Army could join the First, Second, and Fourth Armies to destroy the Russian Manchurian Army in Liaoyang. Time was against Japan, and the earliest possible subjugation of Port Arthur was key to securing both land and sea campaigns.[73]

Generals Kuroki, Oku, and Nozu were also under time pressure to engage Kuropatkin's army before it became too strong. By contemporary standards, Kuropatkin had assembled a considerable force of two European and five Siberian army corps, totaling fourteen divisions with 158,000 men (128,000 infantry and 30,000 cavalry) and supported by 609 guns. Opposing him was Ōyama's First, Second, and Fourth Armies, with 125,000 men (about 115,000 infantry and 10,000 cavalry) and supported by 170 guns. The combined total of forces confronting each other was nearly 300,000, one of the largest forces facing each other in modern history. Only at Sedan, when the Germans overwhelmed the French during the Franco-Prussian War in 1870, were more men involved.[74]

359

BATTLE OF LIAOYANG

Liaoyang is one of the oldest cities in northeast China and during the Han dynasty became part of the northern boundary of the ancient Korean kingdom of Koguryŏ (AD 300–700).[75] During the Liao dynasty (916–1125), Liaoyang became one of the five capital cities of the conquering Khitans. The streets were laid out in the traditional Chinese pattern of a square with neat grids of streets and surrounded by massive protective walls. These walls, with their outer gates, were extensively rebuilt during the early Ming dynasty (1368–1644), but the basic outlay of the city remained unchanged. At the north end of the city flows the Taizi (Taitzu) River, which is rapid and deep, with few fords. As the river approaches Liaoyang from the east, it begins to bend to the northwest, almost touching the imposing northern city walls.

In the years since Russia's occupation of Manchuria, Liaoyang had transformed to resemble a provincial European city, with a railway station, a church, various trading houses, a locomotive yard, and a Russian settlement filled with brick-style houses. General Kuropatkin's headquarters were located near the railway station on the west end of the city.

By early August, Field Marshal Ōyama Iwao and his chief of staff, Kodama Gentarō, relocated their headquarters with Oku's headquarters, and despite Kuropatkin's desperate attempts to delay the Japanese advances, the Second, Fourth and First Armies, arrayed west to east, were positioned south of Liaoyang for what they hoped would be the decisive battle to destroy the Russian army.[76] The land campaign entered an extended pause, stymied by the weather. "As Manchuria entered the rainy season during that time, the mud was literally knee-deep," recalled Ishimitsu. "Many soldiers, horses, and the laborers who pushed carts died in the heavy rain . . . These carts were loaded with military supplies and they sank in the mud and couldn't be moved."[77]

Bad weather was not the only problem Ōyama faced. The advance on Liaoyang had stalled because the Japanese Army was facing a critical shortage of ammunition. Army planners had severely underestimated the amount that would be needed. It was simply inconceivable to them that the rate of consumption in one battle alone might be equal to that expended during the entire Sino-Japanese War.[78] Making matters worse was Nogi's failure to take Port Arthur in August. It seemed unlikely he would be able to join the other armies at Liaoyang. Ōyama would have to take

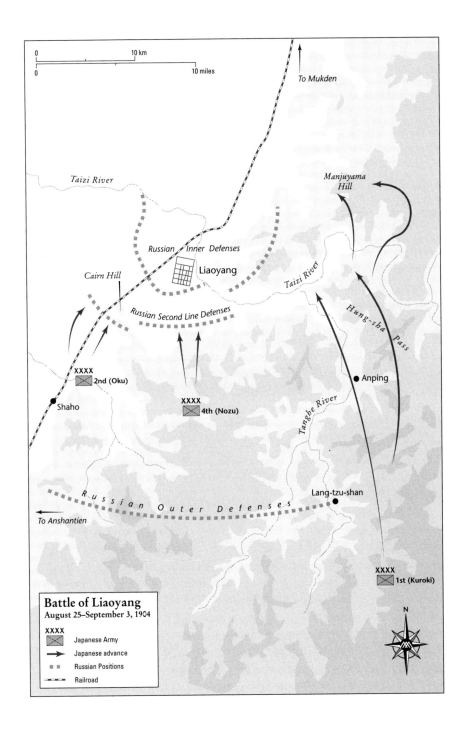

Battle of Liaoyang
August 25–September 3, 1904

| XXXX | Japanese Army |
| Japanese advance |
| Russian Positions |
| Railroad |

To Mukden

Taizi River

Russian Inner Defenses

Liaoyang

Cairn Hill

Russian Second Line Defenses

Taizi River

Manjuyama Hill

Hung-sha Pass

XXXX
2nd (Oku)

Shaho

XXXX
4th (Nozu)

Anping

Tanghe River

Russian Outer Defenses

Lang-tzu-shan

To Anshantien

XXXX
1st (Kuroki)

N

0   10 km
0   10 miles

on Kuropatkin's forces with fewer troops than desired. Port Arthur would be consuming still more lives and munitions.

As he waited for the approaching Japanese armies, Kuropatkin was receiving intelligence reports that made the Japanese seem far stronger than his own forces when, in fact, the opposite was true.[79] Once again, poor battlefield intelligence worked fatally against the Russians, as did Kuropatkin's wholly defensive mindset. He was relying on Liaoyang's three layers of defenses—an outer line some fifteen to twenty miles south of the city, the main defense line about five miles south and anchored by Cairn Hill on its western end, and the city itself, which was fortified. A strong reserve was formed to respond to the main Japanese attack. The prepared positions in the main defense line were impressive.[80] The redoubts were dug deep and turfed in front, intended to shelter the infantry. In front of the redoubts were pits, row upon row, each containing "a sharp stake at the bottom to impale living men who might fall into it." If a soldier was lucky enough not to fall into one of these pits, he would still be forced to maneuver the open ground which was covered with mines and barbed wire that were "almost impassable tangles firmly planted with excellent support" and in some places, charged with electrical currents. The redoubts defending the city itself were even more elaborate. "In addition to the honeycomb of pits with sharp stakes and the tangle of barbed wire and live wires, were deep moats or ditches, with sides so steep that they could not be climbed." These obstacles were covered with machine guns, and the whole complex was christened "little Port Arthur" for its alleged impregnability.[81]

The formidable Russian defense would be an immense challenge for the Japanese, but Ōyama's plan was simple. Oku's Second Army in the west, on the Russian right, would launch a frontal attack. Nozu's Fourth Army in the center would then draw the Russian reserves while Kuroki's First Army would swing around the Russian left on the east, cross the Taizi River, and head toward the railway line north of Liaoyang to surround the Russian army. The whole maneuver to turn the enemy's left flank was a replay of the Yalu River battle on a grander scale.

On August 26 Kuroki's First Army skirmished with the outer defense line, prompting Kuropatkin to order a general withdrawal from the entire outer defense line. This precipitous move showed Kuropatkin's frame of mind. Unlike other Russian generals, he had never underestimated the Japanese. On August 28 Oku's Second Army engaged the eastern end of the main defense line at Cairn Hill where they encountered an extremely stubborn defense by Stackelberg's First Siberian Army Corps. The Japanese assaults were repeatedly driven back. "They went down in threes and fours, but the unwounded still advanced. One hundred and fifty men had fallen to 20 before the entanglements were gained, yet that party of 20 perished almost to a man in their grapple with the barbed wire."[82] Oku tried again on August 31, but the Russians continued to put up an impenetrable defense. The carnage, however, did not seem to reduce the will of the Japanese soldiers to prevail. Ishimitsu recalled:

> We couldn't take care of the dead and the injured. Soldiers who could use their sabers or guns as walking sticks managed to come to the medical camp. Those who couldn't move lay in the blazing sun with the dead and waited for their own death. Some brave soldiers covered by blood fainted and fell over on their way to the medical camp; they were lying here and there. However, other soldiers were not allowed to help them. "Today is special. Do not stop even when your comrades fall down. Step over their bodies and move forward."[83]

Meanwhile, Kuroki's First Army was moving around the Russian left. "As ever in the First Army's career, we were in the valley and the Russians were on the hills which we must take. In front of the Second [defense line], northeast by southwest, ran one long and intact ridge of the height of a thousand feet or more."[84] The hill was taken by nightfall. On August 28 Ōyama ordered Kuroki's First Army to cross the Taizi River, which they did on the night of August 30. General Ian Hamilton, the British military observer, was shocked to discover that the Russians just let them do it. "Under the most elementary system, there should have been no difficulty in obtaining information of the Japanese crossing the moment it began; indeed, I have it on sure authority that the movement was not conducted with any exceptional secrecy or silence." Although the Russians might not have been able to arrest the progress of Kuroki's Division, "they could most certainly have seriously harassed and delayed its advance."[85]

Kuroki's threat against Kuropatkin's rear that would cut off his forces from Mukden forty miles up the rail line, the very thing Kuropatkin had feared the most, set off a chain of disastrous decisions that sealed the Russian Army's fate. In reality, Kuroki's relatively small force could have been destroyed had Kuropatkin reacted swiftly and dispassionately. On the morning of August 31 he ordered a withdrawal from the main line to reposition his forces to meet the new threat to the rear. Oku and Nozu lost no time in setting up artillery on Cairn Hill to shell Liaoyang itself. By September 3, after an abortive counterattack on the left against Kuroki, Kuropatkin ordered a general retreat to Mukden. The Japanese were too exhausted to pursue, which could have ended the war right there and then. Kuropatkin later admitted that the decision to retire from Liaoyang had hurt morale, but he justified it later as the only course of action: "The abandonment of Liaoyang could not fail both to depress the troops who had so gallantly defended it . . . but, on the other hand, we should be extricated by such a retirement from a situation in which we were threatened in front and flank."[86] "Kuropatkin may be a great organizer," wrote General Fujii Shigeta, Kuroki's chief of staff. "But in the field, he is not to be feared."[87] The battle for Liaoyang was the bloodiest yet, attesting to the new form of warfare that exacted a heavy toll. The Japanese lost 5,537 killed and 18,063 wounded. Russian losses were fewer, reinforcing the lesson that the new warfare exacted a greater cost on the attacker: 3,611 killed and missing and 14,301 wounded.[88]

SETBACKS AND SACRIFICES

The Liaoyang disaster led to an attempt to streamline the Russian command structure, starting with the removal of Viceroy Alekseev as supreme commander on October 26. For better or worse, he was replaced by Kuropatkin. At the end of October, Alekseev boarded a special train and disappeared into semi-obscurity, a precipitous fall for a man who had, just a year earlier, wielded supreme powers.[89]

The Russian Manchurian Army under Kuropatkin was reorganized into three new armies; First Army (eastern) under General Nikolai Petrovich Linievich; Second Army (western) under General Oskar Ferdinand Grippenberg; and Third Army (central), headed by General Aleksandr Kaulbars.[90] All three had served with Kuropatkin in the Russo-Turkish War of 1877–1878, but only Linievich had had long-term experience in Asia. He remained in China after serving as commander of the Russian forces during the Eight-Nation Relief Expedition to Beijing in 1900 and in 1903 was appointed governor-general and commander in chief of the Priamur region. Liaoyang had been a cruel setback, but Linievich still believed things could be turned around.

At Ōyama's headquarters in Fenshan, Ian Hamilton went to pay his respects. Ōyama's chief of staff, Kodama, as well as General Fukushima, were also present. Hamilton asked Ōyama whether he was pleased with

Japanese soldiers advancing through a millet field to prepare for their advance against Port Arthur. (COPY 1/485 1–250, p. 16, National Archives, Kew, UK)

the results of the operations. "Moderately," the Japanese general replied. "The Russians have managed their retreat too cleverly." Ōyama understood well enough that Liaoyang was no Sedan. "We must crack the next one at Mukden!" The mood was cheerful. "No one could have been brighter or cheerier than the redoubtable trio," remarked Hamilton. "I did not know till I got back here again that General Fukushima had lost his son in the battle."[91] Nogi had also lost his two sons in the war, his eldest at Jinzhou. Such sacrifices began to weigh heavily on the Japanese back home. There was growing concern that the amount of blood being spilled was excessive. Concerned about the impact on public opinion and support for the war, letters from the front began to be censored.[92]

Ishimitsu, too, was becoming agitated. He recalled coming across an article published in the newspaper *Jiji Shinpō* about the battle of Liaoyang by Ukita Kazutami, a prominent professor and legal scholar. "We have sacrificed too much for the Liaoyang battle," Ukita wrote. "Are we not wasting the lives of our promising officers and soldiers?" Ishimitsu was deeply offended and dashed off a response to Ukita. "Fighting in a battle is not the same as doing office work," he wrote derisively. "In the face of the large numbers of soldiers who have unfortunately died [on the battle-field], how can you possibly suggest that they died because they sacrificed more than they should have? Who [among us] would ever willingly seek death?" Many others agreed with Ishimitsu, but doubts were growing.[93]

FALL OF PORT ARTHUR

Specifically, there was increasing frustration at General Nogi's lack of pro-gress in taking Port Arthur. Weighing heavily on the Japanese leadership was Nogi's seemingly futile strategy of hurling soldiers in repeated sui-cidal assaults with no discernable progress made. Nogi calculated that with the probable sacrifice of a division of infantry, the port could be taken by a direct assault without a preliminary siege, as had been done during the Sino-Japanese War. One observer recalled Nogi's thinking: "After an extended bombardment with siege cannon, the obstacle would certainly no present a harder task than Nanshan."[94] The attack plan called for taking two redoubts known as Big and Little Orphan followed by the capture of the old forts along the Chinese Wall. The road to the port would then be wide open.[95]

But much had changed in the intervening years. The Russians had put a significant amount of work into fortifying Little and Big Orphan Hills. These hills, which had been quite vulnerable in the Sino-Japanese War, had been turned into daunting redoubts bristling with the new tools of war: barbed wire, machine guns, and land mines. "All the hills in our signs, large and small nigh or low, were wrapped up with these horrible things," re-called Sakurai Tadayoshi. Many of the wires were, moreover, charged with electricity and if touched by ordinary pliers would kill soldiers instantly. The forts were also protected by mines buried everywhere. Engineers had to be sent in before an attack to defuse the mines. "Until the very day of our attack, we could see through our field glasses groups of Russians at work here and there, burying these explosives in the ground with picks. We marked those places on our maps . . . and remembered everything we could."[96]

Nogi nevertheless believed that the overwhelming power of "human wave attacks" could overcome these obstacles. The battles at the Yalu and

366

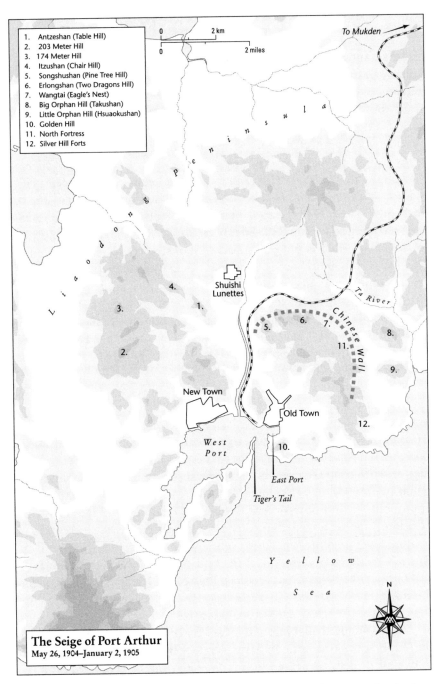

1. Antzeshan (Table Hill)
2. 203 Meter Hill
3. 174 Meter Hill
4. Itzushan (Chair Hill)
5. Songshushan (Pine Tree Hill)
6. Erlongshan (Two Dragons Hill)
7. Wangtai (Eagle's Nest)
8. Big Orphan Hill (Takushan)
9. Little Orphan Hill (Hsuaokushan)
10. Golden Hill
11. North Fortress
12. Silver Hill Forts

0   2 km
0   2 miles

To Mukden

L i a o d o n g   P e n i n s u l a

Shuishi
Lunettes

Ta River

Chinese Wall

4.

3.   1.

5.   6.   7.

8.

11.

2.   9.

New Town

Old Town

12.

West
Port

10.

East Port

Tiger's Tail

Y e l l o w

S e a

N

The Seige of Port Arthur
May 26, 1904–January 2, 1905

The Siege of Port Arthur. Big Orphan Hill (8) and Little Orphan Hill (9) were taken by the Japanese during the Battle of Takushan, August 7–9. The key to the fall of Port Arthur would turn out to be 203 Meter Hill (2).

Nanshan appeared to affirm his view that the Russians "were taught to believe in retreat," whereas the Japanese only advanced. "Every time we fought we won, because we did not believe in retreating," recalled Sakurai.[97] But advancing in the face of continuous machine gun fire, land mines, and barbed wire resulted in enormous casualties. Little and Big Orphan were captured on August 7–9 but at a huge cost of 3,000 casualties.[98] Nogi paused to prepare for the next attack, against the Chinese Wall forts and 174 Meter Hill in the west. The capture of 174 Meter Hill did not offset the failure to take the Chinese Wall forts during an attack on August 19–24, with the appalling loss of 18,000 men.[99] Russian losses were also large. Colonel P. V. Efimovich wrote in a letter: "We managed to survive those days but paid dearly. Almost 50 officers lay at Eagle's Nest (Wangtai) and about 2,500 from the marksmen, artillery . . . were killed. Some companies lost up to 80% of their men, and the 10th company of the 16th regiment . . . has been decimated and both its commanders killed." In addition, the hot Manchurian summer made the stench of rotting corpses almost unbearable. Russian soldiers complained bitterly that "one could only stand to walk around if you stuffed your nose with rope soaked with kerosene."[100]

After the failure of the first general assault in August, a meeting was held at Third Army headquarters, where Nogi reiterated his view that Port Arthur could captured by a frontal assault, despite the huge losses. "The Russians do not have any ways to replenish their manpower or munitions," Nogi declared. "With every soldier or bullet they lose, the weaker they grow. In contrast, even though our army is short of supplies and ammunition, we can always replenish them. Therefore, a direct assault is appropriate."[101] In other words, Nogi's approach was to fight a war of attrition.[102] What he failed to consider was that the Japanese Army was fighting a war against time; capturing Port Arthur before the arrival of Russia's Baltic Fleet was vital. Prior to the start of the war, Nicholas II had ordered the Baltic Fleet, renamed the Second Pacific Squadron under the command of Admiral Rozhestvensky, to East Asia to protect Port Arthur. But it was unclear when it would arrive.

Tokyo was alarmed. Nogi and his staff seemed to be out of touch with the sensibilities at the front. In particular, Ijichi Kōsuke, who was in charge of overall strategy, appeared to be completely out of his depth. As a result, General Tsukushi Kumashichi was dispatched from Tokyo to Third Army Headquarters to find out what was going on. On October 22, just before Nogi launched a second general assault, the vice chief of the general staff, General Nagaoka Gaishi, wrote to Tsukushi to solicit his support in redirecting the Third Army to take 203-Meter Hill, located in the northwest and of a height that commanded the view of the city and the entire harbor. Nagaoka pointed out that 203-Meter Hill could serve as an artillery observation point to direct fire on the city, and more importantly, on the Russian fleet in the harbor. It was the linchpin to neutralizing and capturing Port Arthur.[103] Time was running out as the rate of reinforcements from European Russia was increasing daily and the Third Army was needed against Kuropatkin's force in Mukden. Port Arthur might not surrender right away but taking 203-Meter Hill would effectively reduce the urgency of outright capture by wreaking havoc on the Pacific Squadron.[104]

Nogi rejected the revised strategy outright. He considered 203-Meter Hill of secondary importance, a diversion from the main assault taking place in the east. After the failure of the second general assault in late October, a frustrated Nagaoka consulted his friend Samejima Shigeo, commander of the newly formed Eleventh Division that would later join Nogi's army. Samejima told Nagaoka that no one in the Third Army Staff would agree to the proposal. "No matter what happens, the Third Army headquarters is determined to stick to the frontal assault strategy [against the northeastern forts]," he complained. Nagaoka contacted General Iguchi Shōgo, the senior General Staff officer attached to the Manchurian Army. After his exchange with Samejima, Nagaoka was more convinced than ever that it was time Ōyama intervene before it was too late. The Third Army Staff needed to be "shaken up" and Chief of Staff Ijichi needed to be replaced.[105]

Yet nothing happened. Ōyama would not get on board with the new plan. Like Nogi, he continued to insist that taking 203-Meter Hill "was not key to seizing Port Arthur." "The hill could serve as nothing more than a place for observing and firing at the Russian fleet," and concluded that "occupying 203-Meter Hill would make no difference." Launching a "quick and massive assault on Port Arthur would be much more efficient."[106] Fresh troops of the Seventh Division had just arrived from Japan to reinforce Nogi's Third Army, and Ōyama was hopeful it would make a difference.

The day after Nogi launched his third general assault on November 26 with no new discernable results, Nagaoka vented his fury in a scathing memorandum criticizing the Third Army for its failure of leadership. The initial attack had cost some 4,500 lives.[107] "The headquarters of the Third

Army is in a state of disintegration," he raged. "Division commanders no longer respect the main headquarters [staff]. Even the soldiers have lost their respect. In the field hospitals, the soldiers are saying 'our Chief of Staff [Ijichi] is useless.'" Nagaoka also wanted to know when the shake-up of Third Army Headquarters was going to take place. "If we do not do anything about reconfiguring Third Army Staff [now] we will be wasting our reserve troops for nothing! This would be extremely distressing," he fumed.[108] The response from Ōyama's headquarters was short and to the point: "After the capture of Port Arthur, we will withdraw the Third Army headquarters to Japan and disband it."[109] Kodama had gotten on board with the idea that a shake-up was necessary, but only after Port Arthur was captured.

The opening of the third assault at the end of November left outside observers horrified. David James, a reporter for the *Daily Telegraph,* was aghast at what he was witnessing. "The former assaults by comparison [to the third] were skirmishes, merely preludes to this tragedy," he wrote.[110] The assault party wore white scarfs tied over their uniforms so they could distinguish one another in the dark. A Russian officer, Captain Schwindt, noted in his journal, "after the night storm on the slope of Kurgan battery, the corpses of the Japanese were like flies on a sheet of tanglefoot paper."[111]

In the face of yet another disaster, Kodama decided he had no choice but to directly intervene. Ōyama also realized that the Third Army's debacle was putting the entire Manchurian campaign at risk. The two men hatched a plan of action. Ōyama agreed to allow Kodama to temporarily take over Nogi's command and oversee the Third Army's operations in taking 203-Meter Hill. This was a highly delicate matter. In case Nogi refused, Ōyama gave Kodama a secret letter instructing Nogi to hand over his command to Kodama.[112]

Kodama departed his field quarters in Liaoyang for Port Arthur on November 29. With extreme delicacy and tact, Kodama told the proud general that he simply wanted to assume the command temporarily, in effect "borrowing" the Third Army so that he might direct it to seize 203-Meter Hill. Kodama was also careful not to invoke Ōyama's name. He was prepared to show Ōyama's order to Nogi if he had to, but the two men were childhood friends and Kodama wanted to spare him any unnecessary humiliation. Kodama also understood that the shame of losing his command might drive Nogi to take his own life.[113]

To Kodama's relief, Nogi did not protest. Exhausted and frustrated, the stoic commander was at a loss what to do. Under Kodama's direction, the Third Army quickly revamped its strategy. The powerful 28-centimeter howitzers, which had arrived in mid-November, were used to reduce the fortifications on 203-Meter Hill, followed by continued infantry assaults. For nearly a week the Russians put up a valiant resistance, but on December 5, 1904, the Japanese finally took the hill.[114] The Third Army could now direct artillery on the Pacific Squadron and the town below. Within two days, three battleships and two cruisers were sunk and by early January the entire fleet was destroyed. Three weeks later, on January 2, 1905, General Stoessel formally surrendered Port Arthur. Total losses for the Japanese Third Army were 93,000 men, with 15,400 dead, 44,000 wounded, and 34,000 sick, a toll, once again, much higher than the Russian total of 31,306, of whom 12,660 were killed and missing, the rest wounded and captured.[115]

After the fall of Port Arthur, there were discussions on whether Nogi and his staff should be relieved, but in the end the old general kept his post and was later lauded as a national hero.[116] Kodama's delicate maneuvering had saved the day as well as Nogi's honor and reputation. Kodama had allowed Nogi to take credit for the seizure of Port Arthur because he understood that much greater things were at stake.

STOESSEL'S SURRENDER

But what of General Stoessel? What calculations had led him to surrender the fortress? What of his famous dictum, "I shall die in the last ditch"?

A week before the capitulation, Stoessel was hailed a hero, a sentiment that changed the instant the capitulation was announced. "Nothing was more remarkable in the whole course of the war than the sudden revulsion of feeling against General Stoessel and his garrison which followed the surrender of Port Arthur," wrote British war correspondent Ellis Ashmead-Bartlett, who was with the Russians during the siege.[117] The revulsion can be partly explained by the sacred duty of all Russian soldiers to never surrender a Russian fortress, a creed epitomized by Tsar Nicholas I's rallying cry of 1850: "Where a Russian flag was raised once, it should never be taken down." Also, the majority of the garrison officers had been against capitulation. Moreover, when it was later revealed that Port Arthur had a plentiful stockpile of food, ammunition, and supplies to support its fighting force, the revulsion turned to outrage.[118] Stoessel was denounced as a fop and a traitor. Demands for his court-martial and then his head were loud and furious. In one fell swoop, he went from being one of the most revered fighting heroes of the war to the most hated man in Russia.

So why did Stoessel surrender? One of the first things he asked after his capitulation was, "Where is Kuropatkin?" The last time Stoessel had heard from him had been on October 6 when Kuropatkin had assured him help was on the way. Stoessel then asked, "Where is the Baltic Fleet?" Neither General Nogi nor his staff could answer either question precisely. Their best guess was that Kuropatkin was in Mukden and the Baltic Fleet was somewhere near the Cape of Good Hope, but they could not know for certain.[119]

Until the Japanese seizure of 203-Meter Hill, the defense of the garrison can only be described as heroic. "The manner in which the Russian infantry stood over and over again for hours under concentrated shell fire, the equal of which has never been seen in war, will always form on of the brightest pages in Russian military annals."[120] In particular General Roman Kondratenko, "the flower of the Russian officers," was a towering figure who commanded great respect from his men. He effectively functioned as third in command of Port Arthur.[121] Under Kondratenko's leadership, the Port Arthur garrison displayed unusual bravery; with a force of 34,000 men, the Russians repeatedly repulsed fierce attacks by the Japanese for 233 days, holding off 70,000–80,000 men, not counting reinforcements.[122] Kondratenko was in the bowels of Fort Chikuanshan when a Japanese shell exploded. In mid-December, the Manchurian winter winds carried poisonous fumes to Fort Chikuanshan. "The Japanese burnt a material soaked in arsenic," wrote one Russian officer. "The men were stifled by the fumes and the sentries on the breastworks had to be relieved every few minutes." The Japanese "had tried to smoke us out . . . by using arsenic gas. . . . These were the first instances in the war that poison gas was used." Arriving that evening to see the critical situation for himself, General Kondratenko was killed when a 28-centimeter shell exploded in the casement where his council was meeting.[123] His death, on December 15, "had made a lasting impression on the garrison; everyone lost heart since we knew there was no one to take his place," Tretyakov later recalled.[124]

Other officers had been just as dedicated to the fight. Colonel Illeman made his men sit for hours under massive shell fire to defend 203-Meter hill. It took the Japanese ten days to finally knock the Russians off it.

"That night [of December 31] we were all very depressed," Tretyakov reported. "Everyone discussed plans for continuing the defense . . . this was the universal wish, and could certainly have been realized."[125]

But Stoessel had come to other conclusions. When the start of the siege commenced on August 1, he was faced with two main problems: to preserve the fortress until its relief from Kuropatkin's army from the north; and to protect the Pacific Squadron from destruction. News of the Russian army's defeat at Liaoyang had dashed the promise of a quick rescue, but Kuropatkin's October 6 letter had temporarily revived Stoessel's spirits. And then, silence. When the Pacific Squadron set out for Vladivostok on August 10, a great burden of responsibility had been lifted from his shoulders, for he was sure Admiral Vitgeft would reach his destination. However, when the shell-shocked Squadron came limping back into the harbor the next day, without its damaged flagship, the *Tsarevich*, Stoessel realized the Pacific Squadron would never venture out into the open sea again.[126] The battle of the Yellow Sea had turned the Pacific Squadron, or what was left of it, into "an immobile fleet." The only hope of relief now lay in the arrival of the Baltic Fleet. But it was slow in coming. "What on earth can they be doing?" he once cried in frustration.[127]

On November 26, at the start of Nogi's third general assault, the Port Arthur garrison put up a tremendous and most determined resistance. Then the Japanese changed strategy and concentrated on taking 203-Meter Hill. When the hill was finally captured on December 5, the town and the harbor were mercilessly bombarded.[128] On December 29 Stoessel called a Council of War. While the majority, including Smirnov, insisted on holding out, a few voted for capitulation.[129] General Fok, who had played such an ignominious role in the retreat from Nanshan, believed that the fortress could not hold out and compared the besieged city to "an organism succumbing to gangrene."[130] Most of the other officers, however, voted to continue the defense of Port Arthur. Stoessel said he would concur with the majority opinion. "Well, gentleman, I see that almost all of you are in favor of further defense, and we will accordingly carry on."[131] What he did not tell the officers was that the decision to give up the fortress had already been made. On that day Stoessel had sent a telegram to Tsar Nicholas informing him that "the fortress could not possibly hold out more than a few days." Simultaneously, Rear-Admiral R. N. Viren, commanding officer of the Pacific Squadron, received a letter from Stoessel's chief of staff informing him that a letter had been sent "from General Stoessel to General Baron Nogi proposing to begin negotiations for a capitulation; there is, therefore, only tonight for you to do what you consider necessary to your ships."[132]

Admiral Viren was stunned. So were the officers of the Council of War, which met again on January 2. "General Stoessel told them that he had given all instructions and full authority for the conclusion of capitulation." Many of the officers protested but they were cut short. "They [the Japanese] are the victors; we must submit to their demands," they were told.[133] Some openly wept. To Nicholas, Stoessel telegraphed, "Great Sovereign! Forgive us; we have done everything possible. Be merciful in your judgment upon us. The constant struggle for eleven months has worn down our strength. Three-quarters of the garrison are in the hospitals or the cemeteries . . . The men are shadows."[134] This was a lie but Stoessel had nothing else to offer.

Colonel Tretyakov and the other officers gathered at Signal Hill near Takhe Bay when they heard the news. "Suddenly an officer came galloping out of the town and informed us that he had seen two officers riding out beyond our lines with a white flag," Tretyakov recalled, "My heart froze at this news. There was tremendous commotion at the receipt of this news," he continued. "The majority had no wish to surrender and vehemently attacked our seniors for surrendering the fortress without the consent of all the officers. . . . When the surrender of Port Arthur became an acknowledged fact, we had great difficulty in preserving order in the fortress."[135]

No doubt Stoessel had ample excuses for the surrender, but he apparently had not considered what effect it might have on the rest of the Manchurian campaign. He did not seem to have taken into account that continuing the defense of the fortress would keep Nogi's Third Army from being used against Kuropatkin, which could give him the edge he needed. That Kuropatkin realized the importance of keeping this force occupied is apparent, for immediately after the fall of the fortress he assumed the offensive, to gain, if possible, a success before Nogi's troops could arrive in the north.[136] The surrender of Port Arthur released an army of one hundred thousand soldiers, buoyed by victory, to join the rest of the Japanese Army to confront Kuropatkin's army in Manchuria.

REVOLUTION OF 1905

"As the year 1904 drew to a close, rebellion was on the mind of all levels of Russian society," Witte recalled. "The mood became even more intense at the news of such shameful disasters as the surrender of Port Arthur."[137]

The war with Japan had greatly worsened the domestic political crisis in Russia. The most egregious offense in the eyes of the Russian public was not that Kuropatkin had failed to score a single victory, it was what the defeats revealed about the incompetence of the ruling elite. "The Generals and regimental commanders have shown [their] mediocrity and worthlessness," Vladimir Lenin wrote at the time. "The civil and military bureaucracy have proved themselves to be as parasitic and corrupt as they were in the time of the peasantry. The officeriat is formless, underdeveloped, unprepared, lacks close connection to the soldier, and has not earned their trust."[138] Lenin's newspaper, *Vpered,* on January 4 announced that the hour of reckoning was approaching. There was a "ten-fold increase of unrest, discontent, and rebellion." It asked its readers to prepare for this moment "with all energy."[139]

That moment arrived on January 16 when the Putilov ironworks in Saint Petersburg went on strike. The leader behind the strikes was Father Georgy Gapon, who the year before the war had organized a labor society, the Assembly of Saint Petersburg Factory Workers.[140] The strike triggered nearly one hundred sixty thousand workers to seize Saint Petersburg's

Russian prisoners of war after the siege of Port Arthur embarking at Dairen for Japan.
(H. W. Wilson, *Japan's Fight for Freedom* [London: Amalgamated Press, 1904–1906], 3:1243)

Warsaw and Baltic railway stations, paralyzing the city. Gapon, meanwhile, was putting final touches on his plan to have tens of thousands of workers and their families march to the Winter Palace on Sunday, January 22. The idea was to bow to the emperor, hand him the petition, and then quietly disperse. It is difficult to say whether Gapon and the organizers expected bloodshed. The petition certainly hinted that they did.[141]

Pyotr Sviatopolk-Mirsky, Russia's new minister of interior, and Saint Petersburg city governor Ivan Fullon, along with other members of the tsar's government, met on the evening of January 21 to discuss what to do. They decided that the workers must be prevented from reaching the Winter Palace. The plan was to intercept the procession along the way, at designated points. They hoped the crowd would disperse once people saw armed troops. The question of what to do if the protesters did not was apparently not even discussed.[142]

The procession started at ten o'clock in the morning. According to local reports, a detachment of Cossacks cut into the crowd, brandishing their swords. Soon thereafter, the troops open fire. Witte recalled the scene from his apartment window: "I got to the balcony just in time to hear shots, a few of which whizzed close by. One of these killed a porter at nearby Tsarskoe Selo Lycée. Then came a series of salvoes. Within minutes a large crowd came running back, some of them carrying dead and wounded, among them children."[143]

The people of Saint Petersburg reacted to Bloody Sunday by turning the city into an embattled zone as police and troops worked to prevent demonstrations and protect government property. On February 2, 1905, the universities of Kiev, Warsaw, Kharkov, and Kazan were closed by authorities. On February 17 a social revolutionary named I. P. Kalyaev threw a bomb into the carriage of Grand Duke Sergei Alexandrovich, killing him instantly. The governor-general of Moscow was on his way home from lunch at the Nicholas Palace when the terrorist's bomb struck, scattering his remains over the bloodstained snow. In March, police headquarters in Chiaturi, Georgia, was sacked by demonstrators. A general railroad strike broke out in the Caucasus in April. In June, a mutiny of the armored cruiser *Potemkin* occurred in Odessa when the 763 crew sailors threw their officers overboard into the Black Sea. The mutiny became immortalized by Sergei Eisenstein in his 1925 film *Battleship Potemkin,* in which the maggots in the sailor's meat came to stand for the rottenness of the tsarist system.[144] This was the first phase of the Russian Revolution of 1905, and it set the stage for Nicholas's October 30 manifesto in which he formally surrendered his autocratic powers, granting basic civil rights, freedom of conscience, speech, assembly, and association. A new legislative body, the State Duma, was forthwith established to guarantee these rights, providing "the opportunity of real participation in control over the legality of actions the authorities appointed by us."[145]

KOREAN GUERRILLAS

All these events had a profound impact on Korean resistance to Japan. Many Korean émigrés living in the Russian Far East saw Bloody Sunday and the revolutionary fervor that followed as inspiration for their own "revolutionary" struggle against Japanese rule. Korean laborers who had been involved with their Russian comrades in the strike movements in the gold and coal mining industries between 1901 and 1904, for example, were inspired by the 1905 Russian Revolution.[146] According to Aleksandr Somov, Russia's general counsel in Seoul, these Koreans "looked to Vladivostok as the last bastion of their complete independence [from Japan] whose fall would mean the loss of all hope for salvation." It was, he remarked, the city where "progressive actors studied revolutionary theory and created patriotic national organizations." The events of Bloody Sunday had whipped up their revolutionary fervor.[147] As the Russian official at the Ministry of Foreign Affairs, V. Gravye observed: "Vladivostok and the Korean enclave there is now the center around which gather those dissatisfied by the regime in Korea, by political emigrants and generally those for whom remaining in their homeland represents a threat to their life."[148]

After initially withdrawing from their positions in northern Korea in the fall of 1904, the Russian command once again took up the offensive there beginning in January 1905.[149] They did so with the cooperation of anti-Japanese Korean guerrillas, known as the ŭibyŏng (Righteous Army). Although bands of ŭibyŏng fighters first rose up in 1895 to avenge the death of Queen Min, it was not until the Russo-Japanese War that they became organized as a modern fighting force under Russian tutelage. The initiative was first taken up by Victor Kim (Kim In-soo) in cooperation with Capt. N. N. Biriukov in November 1904. Biriukov and other Russian officers expected that the militia would garner especially strong support from Korea's conservative faction because "they were known to be fiercely loyal to the Korean monarchy."[150]

In Jiandao (Kando), the historic border region between China and Korea, Yi Pŏm-yun, the former governor-inspector of Jiandao turned "Righteous Army" leader, organized a large guerrilla force during the fall of 1904 under Russian auspices using the Korean emperor's seal (*map'ae*, literally, horse pass) to requisition men and supplies from the local population.[151] In the aftermath of the Russian Revolution in March 1905, fierce clashes between Russian, Korean, and Japanese forces took place near the city of Kilju in North Hamgyŏng Province. These battles continued along the Russo-Korean-Manchurian border with a new Korean division of guerrilla fighters formed under the command of Major General A. D. Anisimov. Yi Pŏm-yun's "volunteer squad" of Righteous Army fighters joined the Korean division in military operations against the Japanese.[152] Frustrated by this unrest, the Japanese plotted to transfer Kojong to Japan but were thwarted by the energetic actions of Russian diplomats.[153]

Russia's support of Korean guerrillas and their anti-Japanese activities and militia raids along Korea's northeastern border would become of increasing concern for Japan and Korea's pro-Japanese promoters.

CHAPTER NINETEEN

MUKDEN

The fall of Port Arthur on January 2, 1904, changed the dynamic of the war, as Kuropatkin could no longer afford to wait for replacements and reinforcements to arrive from European Russia. Finally freed from Port Arthur, Nogi's Third Army would be able to march north to join the Manchurian campaign. Kuropatkin decided he had better strike before Nogi arrived.[1] To buy time, Kuropatkin ordered General Mishchenko's cavalry of some seventy-five hundred to conduct behind-the-lines raids to destroy the railway line in order to delay the Third Army while he ascertained its whereabouts.

Mishchenko's raid proved useless, not because of a fault in the intent and mission of the operation, but because it was ineptly executed. The cavalry, as an arm of battle, is supposed to be capable of rapid movement; a behind-the-line raid is a classic cavalry mission. But Mishchenko's Cossacks were burdened by large pack trains that forced them to move at a pace barely above that of a column of marching soldiers. There was a shortage of adequate maps, a chronic situation that affected the Russian army for the duration of the war. Most critically, the operation was widely anticipated, as it had been the subject of gossip in every "café and barbershop" in Mukden for months. The Japanese expected it.[2] The result was predictably a fiasco of epic proportions. Most of the cavalry sent ahead to destroy the rail line could not find it. The critical rail bridge at Kaizhou remained elusive. The few that found the line improperly prepared charges that failed to explode.[3] The raid barely affected the Japanese operations.

379

Another raid in March by a smaller force of about four hundred inflicted perfunctory damages that were repaired within hours.[4]

THE BATTLE OF SANDEPU / HEIKOUTAI

The fall of Port Arthur prompted Kuropatkin to gather his three army commanders to discuss future operations, especially regarding the question of whether to go on the offensive before Nogi arrived. General Linievich, newly arrived from Vladivostok to take command of the First Manchurian Army, was a bit old at sixty-seven but a dependable "warhorse" known as "the Siberian wolf." Commanding the Second Manchurian Army was General Grippenberg, "deaf, aged, and jittery." The Third Manchurian Army was led by General Kaulbars, "vain and blustery" but reliable. Kuropatkin had reasons to question the overall competency of his army commanders, except perhaps Linievich, but he sought their views. The meeting in January resulted in a decision, if not with full enthusiasm given that the prospect of Nogi's arrival filled them with gloom, to attack.[5]

The objective was to push the Japanese back to Liaoyang, and the plan of attack issued by Kuropatkin on January 19 was simple. Grippenberg's Second Army would make the main attack on the western end of the line to turn the Japanese flank anchored at the village of Heikoutai on the Sha River.[6] Kaulbars's Third Army and Linievich's First Army east of Grippenberg would hold the line and be prepared to advance once the Second Army successfully turned the Japanese flank.[7] Kuropatkin had under his command one of the largest forces Russia had ever fielded under one command, about three hundred thousand men, growing daily with reinforcements arriving from European Russia.[8]

The Japanese Manchurian Army under Ōyama was not significantly smaller. The Japanese Army Staff in Tokyo had been optimistic, estimating that the force of about two hundred thousand would be sufficient to hold the Russian Army at bay until Nogi's Third Army raised the strength close to three hundred thousand. The resulting parity in force would allow the Japanese Army to go on the offensive by mid-February. The Japanese did not expect a Russian offensive earlier, certainly not in the middle of the harsh Manchurian winter. At Ōyama's headquarters, staff officer Matsukawa Toshitane firmly rejected the possibility of a Russian offensive in January, and Chief of Staff Kodama, who trusted Matsukawa's judgment, agreed.[9] Kuropatkin thus had a chance of having the benefit of surprise in throwing Ōyama's army back, or even destroying it.

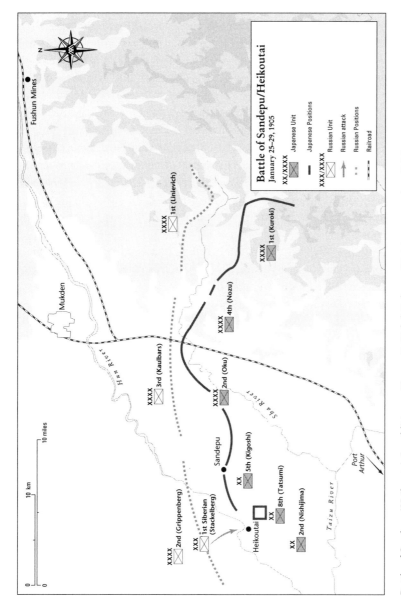

Battle of Sandepu/Heikoutai

January 25–29, 1905

XX/XXXX ☒ Japanese Unit

▮ Japanese Positions

XXX/XXXX ☒ Russian Unit

↑ Russian attack

▦ Russian Positions

▦ Railroad

N

Fushun Mines

1st (Linievich)

1st (Kuroki)

4th (Nozu)

Mukden

3rd (Kaulbars)

2nd (Oku)

Hun River

Sha River

Sandepu

5th (Kigoshi)

2nd (Grippenberg)

1st Siberian (Stackelberg)

8th (Tatsumi)

Heikoutai

2nd (Nishijima)

Port Arthur

Taizu River

0   10 km

0   10 miles

Battle of Sandepu/Heikoutai. In addition to Tatsumi's Eighth Infantry Division, two other divisions were sent as reinforcements. Such a large force needed a single leader; Tatsumi became official commander of "Tatsumi's provisional army."

Grippenberg's plan to turn the Japanese flank began with the Second Army crossing the Hun River (Hunhe) and then capturing the village of Heikoutai, the outermost position on the Japanese Army's extreme left (west). After its capture, Grippenberg's forces would take the village of Sandepu, a few miles northeast of Heikoutai about ten miles west of the railway. By tearing open the Japanese extreme left, the way would be open for his army to push toward the railway, which would either force the entire Japanese line, under pressure from the Kaulbars's Third and Linievich's First Army, to fall back toward Liaoyang or, if the Japanese did nothing, be encircled and destroyed in place.

Kuropatkin, however, was cautious. He still had no idea where Nogi's Third Army was and he did not trust his army commanders, especially Grippenberg. He wanted to see how Grippenberg's offensive developed before ordering Kaulbars and Linievich forward. In effect, his attitude was, "You attack first and if all goes well, we will follow." It was not an inspiring position to take. "Kuropatkin did not want a long or deep bypass of the enemy [southwest], but to limit things to a smaller attack," noted Linievich in his diary.[10] "My son, who visited Grippenberg's headquarters told me that Grippenberg and his whole staff are very dissatisfied with Kuropatkin. [They say that] Kuropatkin interferes in everything and very often gives orders in person, even to minor army commanders, by bypassing Grippenberg and only telling him later what order he had given."[11]

The battle jumped off on the morning of January 25 when General Stackelberg's First Siberian Corps (of Grippenberg's Second Army) attacked Heikoutai, where the Japanese had an outpost, advancing from the west.[12] The open snow-covered ground highlighted the attacking troops, who suffered frightful losses before driving the two Japanese battalions from Heikoutai.[13]

Taking Sandepu proved more difficult. Now that it was clear that Russian forces wanted to turn the flank, Sandepu had to be held at all costs. Stackelberg's advancing forces were met with "sheets of steel" from the entrenched Japanese. A furious battle for Sandepu ensued on the night of January 25. The next morning Grippenberg received the welcomed news that "Sandaepu had been taken by storm." Overjoyed, he "smothered in kisses the messenger who had brought the happy news and reported it to Kuropatkin."[14]

Grippenberg's euphoria was short-lived, however. It turned out that Stackelberg's forces had taken the wrong village, one of no consequence, taken in a bayonet attack costing the First Siberian Rifle Corps six thousand men.[15] Kuropatkin was furious. "There had been no significant reconnoiter before the storm of Sandepu—not only did Grippenberg and his staff know next to nothing about Sandepu, but literally no one knew that there was a redoubt on the eastern side of the village, secured by several rows of barbed wire, with an esplanade of more than 500 steps."[16] Linievich also was livid. "The advance of the First Siberian Rifle Corps, which took place inexplicitly without reconnaissance, was an almost criminal move on the part of Stackelberg and when we consider that he had put 300 officers and nearly 8,000 lower officers into this move, then the crime becomes even greater."[17]

In the end the Japanese held on to Sandepu, but their forces were weakened.[18] On January 27, fresh troops arrived to support the retaking of Heikoutai. Ōyama had quickly created a "provisional army" under General Tatsumi Naofumi that was actually a reserve division, the Eighth Infantry Division, to secure the Japanese extreme left flank.[19] It would be up to Tatsumi's severely undermanned and overextended forces to hold the flank against the weight of Grippenberg's entire Second Army.

Both sides were also battling extreme cold. On January 23, the temperature suddenly fell as a cold Siberian wind blew in from the north. On the night of January 27, the temperature plummeted to −20°C (−4°F); fires could not be lit lest the troops give away their position, and many men succumbed to frostbite. The bitter cold also affected the soldiers' eyesight, with some suffering night blindness. Food and water froze, rendering it impossible for the soldiers to eat or drink.[20]

But it was the wounded who suffered the most. "For hours they lay on the field unattended . . . in the meantime, the frost and snow to which the men were exposed increased the agony caused by their wounds," recalled Lord Brooke, the war correspondent for Reuter's. "Indeed, the tortures endured by these men are beyond description—many a soldier who would have recovered in the summer now died of frost-bite."[21] Most simply froze to death.

While Grippenberg's army struggled, Kuropatkin remained inexplicably inert and neither Kaulbaus nor Linievich did anything to assist. Taken aback by the Sandepu fiasco, Kuropatkin hesitated. "Impatiently we awaited orders to begin the offensive," wrote one Russian officer. "And we waited. As January 26, 27, and 28 went by, we were perplexed."[22] Kuropatkin had lost all confidence in Grippenberg at a critical moment. Kaulbars and Linievich were in strong positions, ready to strike the Japanese army at its center and right, but Kuropatkin still held back. Ōyama's decision to order a tactical diversion against the Russian Army's center to hide the Japanese's Army vulnerabilities on its left flank may have given Kuropatkin pause. This feint was so small it should not have even mattered, but coming after Stackelberg's debacle at Sandepu, the move appeared to have made an indelible impact on Kuropatkin's fragile nerves.[23]

When Grippenberg ordered the attack to resume on January 29, Kuropatkin decided to abandon the entire operation altogether and had the Second Army pull back to its former positions. Grippenberg was stunned. That morning the Japanese reoccupied Heikoutai, and by evening "the Russian were everywhere in retreat, and hotly pursued by their foe." The Russians had suffered yet another ignominious setback. The battle of Sandepu/Heikoutai had been initiated by the Russians, but with victory almost within grasp, they retreated. "General Khakevich told me that the whole 2nd Army curses Kuropatkin, especially for his orders which bypassed Grippenberg to retreat the entire 2nd Army to their former position," wrote Linievich in his diary. "The entire 2nd Army believes that if there had not been such an order, we would have won the whole conflict."[24] Lord Brooke summed up the general feeling:

> Grippenberg's army was very sore over its defeat, every man in it felt that they had been badly "left" by the rest of the Russian forces. Neither Kaulbars nor Linievich had moved a man or fired a gun to relieve the pressure on the 2nd Army, if we except a slight and ineffectual artillery demonstration by Kaulbars on the opening day of the battle. Grippenberg had been allowed to fight a lone hand, and this fact struck every one of us as most extraordinary. Fully 20,000 men out of a force of about 85,000 had been killed or wounded; and when it was known throughout the army that these casualties had been incurred in a battle fought and lost by the right wing, absolutely unsupported, a very painful feeling was created. For Stackelberg's Corps much commiseration was expressed; "that unfortunate 1st Siberian Army Corps" was the universal remark.[25]

The next day, January 30, Grippenberg sent a telegram to War Minister Viktor Sakharov requesting permission to return to Russia "because of illness." It was an extraordinary move for a general officer to essentially desert his army in the middle of a war. Although many blamed Kuropatkin for Grippenberg's abrupt departure, Linievich thought Kuropatkin had been justified in ordering the retreat. "Kuropatkin is depressed by recent events and by Grippenberg's flight to Russia although there is nothing to regret about that," Linievich noted. "Grippenberg's beginning action at Sandepu, being extremely unlucky, unplanned, not thought through, and thus doomed by the second day, shows that he is not only not gifted and lacks foresight, but is simply incapable as well, and sick, too, as it turns out."[26]

Later evidence would show that the battle of Sandepu/Heikoutai could have been a turning point in the war because of Japanese vulnerability, but neither Kuropatkin nor Linievich had any clue just how vulnerable the Japanese actually were. Indeed, Kuropatkin had thought himself the inferior force since Liaoyang when in fact the opposite was true. Had Grippenberg been allowed to continue the fight just one more day, he might have crushed Tatsumi's division. A coordinated attack by Russian forces at the Japanese center and right flank would have had a good chance at breaking through the thinly stretch Japanese lines. Kuropatkin's caution based on his belief in his inferior forces was reinforced by his concern over the arrival of Nogi's Third Army, whose position he did not know.

Kuropatkin appointed Kaulbars to take over Grippenberg's Second Army. General Bilderling was brought in to be the new Third Army commander. All told, Russian casualties in this short battle were over twelve thousand killed, wounded, and missing, seven thousand of which came from Stackelberg's First Siberian Corps. Stackelberg was relieved for incompetence. Japanese losses were nine thousand killed and wounded.[27] The Russians had once again snatched defeat from the jaws of victory.

BATTLE OF MUKDEN

Kuropatkin was in an agitated state as he was about to engage in the largest land battle of the war. Mukden would involve over half a million combatants (nearly three hundred thousand Russians and more than two hundred thousand Japanese), the largest land force ever assembled in the history of warfare.[28] Kuropatkin understood that the coming battle would decide the fate of the Russian Manchurian Army, the war, and possibly the Russian nation. The string of defeats could no longer continue. The revolutionary mood at home demanded results and Kuropatkin saw Mukden as the place to defeat Japan. But he was beset with doubts. For one thing, he still did not know where Nogi's Third Army was located.

The failure of Russian intelligence was crippling. Kuropatkin's faith in his commanders remained low. "Their most pronounced weak points," he later said, "were their lack of initiative, their ignorance of the method in which an attack should be conducted, and their want of determination."[29] Finally, Grippenberg's departure had a debilitating effect on morale. "It set a fatal example both to those under him and to the rest of the army, and was most harmful to all discipline," he recollected.[30] In short, Kuropatkin was quite pessimistic. "I went to check up on the commander-in-chief and found him very dejected," Linievich noted in his diary on February 16, just days before the battle was to begin. "He's grown emaciated and grey-haired . . . Grippenberg destroyed much of his spirited vitality by leaving. He has somehow shrunk into himself; lost his control, and now all his hopes lie with Kaulbars who is acting on the right flank against Sandepu."[31]

Soldiers of the Russian Manchurian Army passing through the gates of Mukden, 1905. (Library of Congress, LC-USZ62-103623)

Facing Kuropatkin was Ōyama, who saw Mukden as his chance to bring the war to an end. He had thus far allowed the Russian Army to slip away only to have to fight them again. Time was against him and soon Kuropatkin would grow too strong. Ōyama needed to deal a crushing blow. His intent for the coming battle was reflected in his orders: "The object of the battle is to decide the issue of the war. The question is not one, therefore, of occupying certain points or seizing tracts of territory. It is essential that the enemy should be dealt a heavy blow."[32]

Mukden was to be a titanic contest of will between two commanders who saw the battle as the one that would decide the war. Kuropatkin and Ōyama both prepared plans for their offensives to prevail. The only question that remained was not who would make the first move but who would seize the initiative and drive the direction and pace of the battle. In this sense, Mukden was no different from any other battle where the first to take action seizes the initiative. Then the question becomes whether the initiative will remain or change hands. In the case of Mukden, Japan moved first, seized the initiative, and never lost it.

By mid-February Ōyama's army was moving into final positions and included a new formation, the Fifth Army, also known as the Army of the Yalu, consisting of the First Reserve Division and the Eleventh Division detached from Nogi's Third Army.[33] Its commander, Kawamura Kagaeki, was ordered to marched swiftly into position on the Japanese extreme right (east). On the line next to the Fifth Army, from east to west were: the First Army (Kuroki), Fourth Army (Nozu), Second Army (Oku), and Third Army (Nogi), which was marching northward to assemble just west of Liaoyang. Ōyama did not want to waste time and called for the offensive to start as soon as Nogi's army was in position. Ōyama's plan called for a feint on the right by the Army of the Yalu and the First Army to draw Russian reserves eastward. He would then send Nogi's Third Army in a wide flanking maneuver on the opposite end around the Russian western flank to threaten the rail line north of Mukden. If the Russians were deceived into thinking that the Japanese main attack was in the east, the First and Fourth Army were to break through east of Mukden to meet the Third Army north of the city to trap the bulk of the Russian force. The plan was a classic double envelopment devised by Ōyama's brilliant chief of staff, Kodama.

It was an ambitious and audacious plan considering that Kuropatkin's army was bigger and Ōyama still had doubts about Nogi's competence. But several things worked in Ōyama's favor, including Russian incompetence

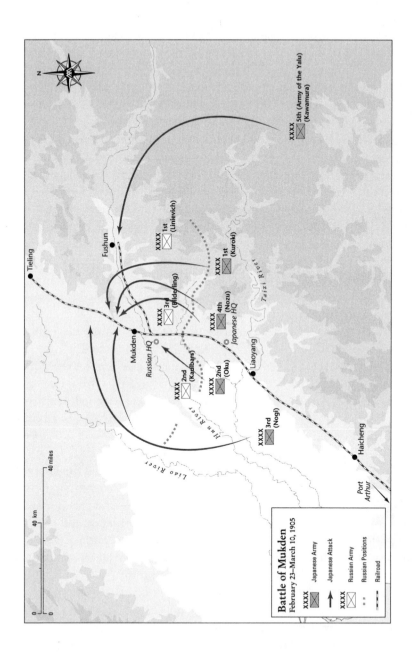

Battle of Mukden
February 23–March 10, 1905

XXXX Japanese Army

Japanese Attack

XXXX Russian Army

Russian Positions

Railroad

XXXX 5th (Army of the Yalu) (Kawamura)

XXXX 1st (Linievich)

XXXX 1st (Kuroki)

XXXX 3rd (Bilderling)

XXXX 4th (Nozu)

Japanese HQ

Russian HQ

XXXX 2nd (Kaulbars)

XXXX 2nd (Oku)

XXXX 3rd (Nogi)

Tieling

Fushun

Mukden

Liaoyang

Haicheng

Port Arthur

Taizi River

Hun River

Liao River

40 km

40 miles

and bad luck. For example, Kuropatkin had only a vague knowledge of the newly formed Fifth Army but believed it was a small force consisting of a standby division of reservists and nothing more. The attachment of Nogi's Eleventh Division had the fortunate effect of deceiving Kuropatkin into thinking that Nogi's army was in the east. These developments also led Kuropatkin to dissipate his resources by shoring up the defenses of Vladivostok. "The rumors that we heard at this time of a landing of a large Japanese force in Northern Korea (assumed to be in connection with the liberation of Nogi's army by the surrender of Port Arthur), compelled me to take a hand in the strengthening of our forces in the Primorsky district, and of the Vladivostok garrison in particular."[34]

Meanwhile, Ōyama took every precaution to conceal the Third Army's location. Cossacks, who had so far proved nearly useless, continued their dismal record by failing to locate Nogi's forces, reconnoitering just a few miles from their encampment west of Liaoyang. Kuropatkin was convinced that the main strike would come in the east.[35]

Kodama's decision not to relieve Nogi of his command, or to disclose the truth about the latter's incompetence at Port Arthur, also worked in favor of the Japanese. To the Russians, Nogi had become a legendary figure. "The name of Nogi was to the Russians something of what that of Achilles must have been to the defenders of Troy," observed American war correspondent Frederick McCormick, who was with the Russian Army. "Ever since the fall of Port Arthur, they tried to trace and locate him. Each of the three Russian armies had stood in equal dread of him, of his eleven-inch guns, and of his invincible, bandy-legged, 203 Meter-Hill conquerors."[36] The Japanese would be able to exploit that fear when the time came for the surprise attack on the Russian right.

Kuropatkin had issued orders for his own offensive to begin on February 24. It was a replay of the Sandepu operations, calling for Kaulbars's Second Army on the western end of the line to break through the Japanese western flank held by Oku's Second Army, then to envelop the Japanese line followed by frontal attacks by Linievich's First and Bilderling's Third Army. But Ōyama seized the initiative by launching the Army of the Yalu against Linievich's First Army on the Russian eastern flank on February 23. Anticipating Ōyama's orders, Kawamura had already made contact with Linievich's forces a few days earlier and had been skirmishing for several days.[37] Kuropatkin's spirits were high, for the Japanese were acting as he had anticipated "He [Kuropatkin] told me on the telephone . . . that he had lunch with 80 officers on the field and added that the spirit of the troops is unmatched. And he has high hopes for them," Linievich confided.[38]

Kawamura's attack began in earnest on February 23 and Kuropatkin sent his entire reserve to reinforce Linievich to meet the "main" Japanese attack. Word that the Japanese Eleventh Division (previously of Nogi's Third and now part of the Fifth Army) had launched an attack against Taling (Motien) Pass, just south of Fushun, convinced Kuropatkin that the main thrust would be against Russia's left (east). Securing the pass was critical in case a retreat of Linievich First Army was necessary. To meet this "grave" threat, Kuropatkin doubled down on his mistake and pulled the First Siberian Corps, now commanded by General Aleksandr Gerngross, who had replaced the disgraced Stackelberg, from Kaulbars's Second Army and sent it east to shore up Linievich's First Army. The Sixteenth Army Corps, which formed the reserve of the whole army, was also moved east.

Kuropatkin now wondered whether to launch his own offensive planned for the next day by Kaulbars's Second Army. Kaulbars asked for reinforcements before he attacked, but Kuropatkin had none to give. The attack was stillborn and Kuropatkin lost his chance to seize the initiative.[39] "This Kuropatkin is an unbelievable guy," Linievich confided. "He's afraid of everything, and he sent me orders through everyone, even my subordinates and he is afraid of any workaround. You can't win a war if you think like that! This wouldn't be so bad on its own, but his fear for the flank and the path of retreat are contagious and get passed on to his subordinates. We've all become afraid of something, especially concerning the flank and the path of retreat. Consequently, we are in a position where there are a significant number of troops with which we might beat back the enemy that could be placed on the front line, but we insist on keeping them to the back."[40]

General Kuroki, who had marched his First Army through difficult mountainous terrain to the left of the Fifth Army, received word of the rapid success. Despite being a supporting feint, the attack against the Russian left was unexpectedly going well. "In four days, the Japanese advanced twenty miles on the east, pushing the left flank back to the nest of mountains which constituted the Russian eastern barrier and took the past 'Taling' [Motien] which opened to them the direct road to Fushun and Tieling."[41] The state of affairs was becoming critical. "Kuroki and Kawamura were rolling back the Russian left with such rapidity and violence that General Kuropatkin could be excused for believing that the principal Japanese attack was to come from that queue."[42] Kuropatkin hurriedly wrote to Linievich, "Today I'm giving the order to look overall routes to Tieling in case of retreat."[43]

On February 28 the Japanese began bombarding the Russian positions in the center occupied by Bilderling's Third Army with the 28-centimeter (11-inch) howitzers that had had such a devastating psychological impact at Port Arthur. This caught Kuropatkin by surprise. "I do not believe it is an exaggeration to say that the hearts of serious commanders there sunk to the lowest ebb . . . If the Japanese expected some effective moral damage from opening fire with their Port Arthur siege guns, they were not disappointed."[44] Kuropatkin was now under the impression that the main attack would come from the center.

Then came the greatest shock of all. Kaulbars realized that a large unforeseen buildup of forces had appeared, seemingly out of nowhere, on the Russian right (west). As early as February 27, Cossacks on the Russian extreme right flank noticed a large force moving north. This was Nogi's Third Army. A great panic ensued. Kuropatkin had no reserve to send to reinforce Kaulbars or to establish new defenses. Gerngross's First Siberian Army Corps, which had hastily been sent to shore up Linievich's First Army, was immediately ordered to return. During the battle, the First Siberian Army Corps had marched east and then west, hardly firing a shot, wasting time and exhausting the men.[45] It was a frightful waste of a formidable fighting force, but due to Kuropatkin's vacillation and loss of nerve, Gerngross's reputation as a skilled commander was never actually tested.

On March 1 Kuropatkin contemplated a full-scale retreat. "Today the commander-in-chief ordered that all supply stores between the main position and Mukden be withdrawn to Tieling or further," Linievich noted. "I think it is safe to say that he probably intends for the entire army to retreat. If that happens, I can imagine how happy Grippenberg will be, since he insisted on a retreat to Harbin, and only got a spiteful laughter from Kuropatkin in response."[46] Writing about the war in his enormously popular historical novel *Saka no Ue no Kumo* [Clouds Above the Hill], Shiba Ryōtarō, a keen student of the conflict with an eye for psychological detail, believed that "Kuropatkin was ultimately defeated by himself [at Mukden]."[47] Shiba is partially correct; the Russian commander seemed to have only followed the Japanese lead, having no offensive plan of his own, "wandering first left then right in response to each enemy moves as if he had been a general hired by Japan for that purpose."[48] But Shiba failed to consider Kuropatkin's larger strategic goals. Kuropatkin had taken to heart the lessons of Borodino that winning tactical victories, even a string of them, did not guarantee victory in war. Kuropatkin was still trading space for time. The main problem he faced was not that his strategy of attrition was flawed, but that it was not well suited to the times. Revolutionary conditions in Russia demanded victory, even if it was just a tactical win.[49]

Between March 2 and 8, furious fighting continued. Oku's Second Army was ordered to frontally assault Kaulbars's Second Army to prevent him from redeploying forces against Nogi's Third Army, which could complete the envelopment north of Mukden. Ishimitsu recalled:

> The Russian and Japanese armies . . . turned into miserable demons and fought a battle in the boundless wilderness. The soldiers fought in a melee: hand-to-hand fights were taking place everywhere. Neither messages nor supplies could reach the battlefield. Even when an order from headquarters managed to reach a division, the division was unable to pass it on to the soldiers fighting at the front. The units were simply unable to carry out orders as they were scattered everywhere; whenever they encountered the enemy, they just shot at one another. When they ran out of bullets, they just held up rifles and leaped toward the enemy to fight him hand-to-hand. No one was providing any orders or leading the fight. There was only the enemy and us.[50]

A particularly gruesome action took place on March 7 when Colonel Yoshioka Tomoyashi, commander of the Thirty-Third Infantry Regiment (Nagoya) in Oku's Second Army, found himself surrounded by Russian troops. "The men ran out of bullets and began to fight hand to hand; the soldiers didn't stop fighting until their swords were broken and they ran out of strength." The entire regiment was destroyed. Ishimitsu recalled visiting the site after the battle. "The rifles, bullets, packages, and water bottles were abandoned by the dead and the severely injured soldiers were scattered everywhere and buried by the yellow dust in the field, which looked like a desert. The soldiers had dug holes with their shovels to hide their heads from the incoming machine-gun fire; now, though half-covered by the dust, these holes still left traces all over the landscape. Seeing such a dreadful spectacle that took so many soldiers' young lives, I felt a constriction in my heart as I was riding through the remnants of the battle on horseback."[51]

Such terrible sacrifices, however, had allowed Nogi's forces to advance and threaten the railway line north of Mukden. At the first report of Japanese soldiers on the line, a small scouting party, Kuropatkin sent a dramatic message to Saint Petersburg: "I am surrounded!" This was an exaggeration, but it was only a matter of time before Nogi's force would cut the line.[52] To Linievich, Kuropatkin seemed to have lost all hope. "Things are not easy for him," he observed. "He meant to attack the Japanese with his 2nd Army today [March 6] but when I asked him what was going on our western front, he replied 'bad' and ended the conversation . . . He spoke to me curtly, scattered, and without interest in how things were going for the First Army. It's clear that he's extremely agitated by something. In our conversation, yesterday, he was more loquacious and cheerful." Kuropatkin had not yet shared the alarming news that Nogi's army had turned.[53]

In the east, Linievich could not believe the tenacity of the Japanese troops. "They climbed out of their trenches and attack over and over again, day and night; our people are worn out," he noted incredulously. "The surprises the Japanese come up with—and how fearless they do it! They aren't even afraid of sending three regiments north, 60 *versts* to Taling [Motien] to destroy the road and take it over. We'd be scared to do something like that."[54] On March 6 Kuropatkin ordered the First and Third Armies to pull back, and Linievich was ordered to retreat beyond the Hun River.[55]

Learning that the Russians were quietly retreating, Ōyama sent new orders to his armies at midnight, March 7: "I intend to pursue in earnest and to turn the enemy's retreat into a rout."[56] The time had finally arrived to destroy Kuropatkin's army. On the morning of March 8 all the Japanese armies would launch forward in pursuit of the enemy.

The Japanese were helped by an unusual meteorological phenomenon. A dust storm blew up out of nowhere, making visibility practically impossible. This southerly wind, recorded by Japanese soldiers as *kamikaze* (divine winds) for intervening on behalf of the Japanese Army, worked in favor of the Japanese forces, intensifying the chaos and confusion now permeating the Russians as they tried to pull out.[57] On March 9 news that Oku's forces had broken through created a wave of panic as thousands of Russian soldiers threw down their weapons and fled.[58]

The feared Japanese pursuit across the Manchurian plains did not materialize and the Russian army, though defeated and demoralized, was not destroyed. Ōyama's armies were simply too exhausted to continue.[59]

"We pressed the attack regardless of heavy losses and drove the enemy from his position at Mukden," Ōyama wrote to the emperor after the battle. "But we have not yet succeeded in accomplishing our aim."[60] Ishi-mitsu lamented that the situation was still so precarious after everything the Japanese had sacrificed. "The Japanese army had reached its limit," he wrote. "If Russians take control of the seas, the Japanese Army will be crushed. The Russians could then invade the Japanese mainland and that would be the end of our country."[61] The enormous losses befit the largest battle in history. Kuropatkin lost a third of his army—more than 20,000 killed or missing, 50,000 wounded, and 20,000 taken prisoner. The Japanese lost 16,000 dead and 60,000 wounded.[62]

On March 15 Kuropatkin was relieved of command and Linievich was selected to replace him. Not wanting to return to Saint Petersburg in disgrace, Kuropatkin pleaded with the tsar to appoint him to take over Linievich's command of the First Army. "I may not be a good general," he said, "but I am at least as good as some of my corps commanders."[63]

As for Linievich, he decided to dig in, and so Mukden became the last major land battle of the war. Linievich's caution in renewing the offensive was due to lack of confidence in its feasibility. He also wanted to wait for more reinforcements. At the same time, before considering another land campaign, Linievich was keen to wait until he heard about the arrival of the Second and Third Pacific Squadrons that had departed Russia in October.[64] If Admiral Rozhestvensky was successful in destroying Tōgō's Combined Fleet, it would just be a matter of time before Ōyama's armies would be forced to retreat from Manchuria.

On the other side of the world, President Theodore Roosevelt was following the Manchurian campaigns with keen interest. After the battle of Mukden, he sat down with the Japanese ambassador, Takahira Kogorō. The president broached the idea that Japanese leaders might consider a peace initiative. It would be impossible for Japan to prolong the war, the president said. Why not end the conflict while Japan was ahead? But Takahira demurred. "If we reveal our terms of peace to the public now, the Russians would take advantage of it. They are not serious about negotiating a peace treaty yet."[65] Roosevelt felt a duty and a necessity to convince Japan and Russia that a peaceful settlement was in both parties' interest. But mostly, he wanted a quick settlement of the war to further American interests. Roosevelt wished, above all else, to safeguard the principles of the Open Door in Manchuria. He said nothing, however, about extending those same principles to the Korean Peninsula.

PART SIX

NEW EAST ASIAN ORDER

IN THE EARLY DAYS of the Russo-Japanese War, President Theodore Roosevelt welcomed Japan's string of victories as a counter to his concerns over Russian expansion in Asia. Nevertheless, he pushed hard to reach a settlement between the two adversaries to maintain a balance of power in the region. But for such an arrangement to succeed, the Korean problem had to be resolved. Left to its own devices, he argued, Korea would inevitably become, again, the object of great power rivalry and regional instability. Thus, without formal protest from the United States or any other Western power, the Japan-Korea Treaty was concluded on November 17, 1905. It deprived Korea of its diplomatic sovereignty and made it a protectorate of Japan.

These events led to a complete reversal in the Asian balance of power in Japan's favor. But instead of resolving the problem of Korean instability, the war created an even greater challenge: an increasingly unstable China. The thousands of Chinese students who had flocked to Japan before and during the war were inspired by Japan. In 1905 the Qing court agreed to abolish the traditional Confucian examination system by which candidates were selected for government appointments. New options appeared for China's youth, and the gateway to a profitable academic or intellectual career was thrown wide open. Among their energetic ranks, Sun

Yat-sen, the future provisional president of the Republic of China, found ready recruits for his anti-Qing reformist organization, the Revolutionary Alliance.

While the Qing government was attempting to rally its dynastic forces, Japan's response to China's predicaments was decidedly mixed. Up to and including the Russo-Japanese War, the principal goal of Japan's national security policy was clear—to prevent Korea from falling into the hands of a Western power. The Katsura cabinet had accepted the Open Door policy as the logical extension of the argument about commercial rather than military penetration of the continent. But the blood and treasure spilled in the hills and valleys of Manchuria had changed all that. Army leaders like Generals Kodama Gentarō and Yamagata Aritomo were adamant that Japan had to secure some profit from these terrible sacrifices. The Russo-Japanese War thus became a turning point, setting the groundwork for the ensuing domestic conflicts over the direction of Japan's foreign policy. Subsequent conflicts arose not only between army and navy leaders but also between army and civilian leaders like Itō Hirobumi, who wanted Japan to pursue a maritime route to Great Power status along with cooperative relations with China and United States.

In large part these conflicts over policy arose out of Japan's deep disappointments at Portsmouth. The end of the Russo-Japanese War had not been a cause for celebration in Japan. Instead the war reinforced the old perception from the First Sino-Japanese War that the generals had won the battle but the civilians had lost the peace. Such resentments soured Japan's relations with China. If Yuan Shikai had expected his wartime collaboration would be rewarded with the coming of peace, he was gravely mistaken. Embittered by the outcome of the war, Japanese Foreign Minister Komura Jutarō traveled to Beijing to win new Chinese concessions and rights for Japan in Manchuria.

In Korea, Yi Yong-gu and Son Pyŏng-hŭi as well as other members of the Ilchinhoe were even more disillusioned. By aiding Japan in its war effort against Russia, they had hoped to secure the former's help in Korea's development and reform. Instead, they had facilitated their nation's colonization. Meanwhile, other conservative groups, including former Confucian officials, joined up with the "Righteous Army" (ŭibyŏng), anti-Japanese guerrilla groups that had formed after 1895 to avenge the death of Empress Myŏngsong. Many of these same agents after the war settled in the Russian Far East, where they organized armed raids against the Japanese in Korea. The Russian Revolution of 1905 and later Lenin's advocacy of national self-determination, inspired ŭibyŏng guerrillas to take up arms against Japan.

In the years 1906–1910, Japan thus became increasingly embroiled in fighting Korean guerrillas along the Russo-Korean border. Japan's encroachment into Manchuria also stirred anti-Japanese feelings in China. Under these conditions, Japan concluded it had to come to some sort of an agreement with Russia to stem the tide of rising Chinese and Korean anti-Japanese nationalism. In particular, the Japanese needed Russia's help in cracking down on Korean guerrillas operating in the Russian Far East. In 1910 the two countries agreed to safeguard their respective spheres of influence; Japan would get exclusive rights in southern Manchuria and Korea, and Russia would have rights in northern Manchuria and Outer Mongolia. With Russia's cooperation secured, Japan succeeded in formally annexing the Korean Peninsula in 1910. A year later, the 250-year-old Qing dynasty collapsed.

The long journey Japan had taken to usurp China's place as the dominant power in East Asia was complete. Japan's new self-confidence against an increasingly unstable China would be tested in the next decade with the rise of the other non-European great power, the United States. Its emergence from the bloodbath of World War I would challenge Japan's supremacy in East Asia. But it was the Other Great Game that set the stage for the ensuing struggles between these two powers to come.

CHAPTER TWENTY

THE PORTSMOUTH TREATY AND KOREA

The fate of the Korean Peninsula did not figure into Theodore Roosevelt's thinking when the subject of peace negotiations was first raised in early March by War Minister Terauchi Masatake. Terauchi had approached Lloyd C. Griscom, the American minister to Japan, to probe the administration's views about ending the war, but Korea never came up.[1] As far as Roosevelt was concerned, the Korean problem had been resolved. "Of course the military situation may alter," he later wrote. "But if peace should come now, Japan ought to have a protectorate over Korea (which has shown its utter inability to stand by itself) and ought to succeed to Russia's rights in Port Arthur, while I should hope to see Manchuria restored to China."[2]

The irony of these pronouncements is poignant. It was, after all, Japan's use of the Open Door principle to protest Russia's occupation of northern Korea that had partly justified going to war. Furthermore, the Japanese leaders had made use of the "Open Door" rhetoric to solicit American and British support for the war. Komura and others continued to publicly declare, until 1905, their nation's adherence to the Open Door in Manchuria, but nothing of the sort was ever alluded to again regarding Korea.[3] Nor did the Americans ever insist on it. When it came to claims that Korea was an independent state, Roosevelt weighed acquiescence of an injustice inflicted on a weak country against his greater concern with preserving the balance of power and stability in East Asia. "The choice, unless an American protectorate were to be established over Korea—a chimerical and quixotic alternative—was between Korea as a source of strength to Japan, or as a part of Russia."[4] Such was the cold hard reality of Great Power politics.

The most pressing problem for Japan after Mukden was how to bring the conflict to an end. Nagaoka was still keen to continue the advance to Tieling. He also wanted to take the war to Vladivostok, the refuge port for the approaching Baltic Fleet.[5] This was to be achieved through the creation of a new North Korean Army, consisting of two to three divisions with members of the Fifth Army (Yalu River).[6] Both Ōyama and Yamagata however, had second thoughts. Writing to Prime Minister Katsura on March 23, Yamagata addressed his concerns about continuing the war: "The planning of great operations should always be in harmony with national [foreign] policy. If there is any discrepancy between them, victories on the battlefield would not promote the national interest."[7] Furthermore, Japan would have to increase its army by six more divisions and prepare a war chest of one billion yen to take on Linievich's Army, anticipated at three times the size of Ōyama's forces. "While the enemy still has powerful forces in its home country, we have already exhausted ours," he observed. "Our military operation in the third period of the war is of greatest significance, and should we make a mistake, our glorious victory thus far would be nullified. We must now be prudent."[8]

Kodama repeated Yamagata's main argument. He wanted the Japanese government to make peace overtures. Nagaoka, however, remained unconvinced, insisting that Vladivostok and the surrounding area must be seized. "Maintaining peace by driving back the Russian forces in northern Korea is an obligation of the Japanese empire as stated in the Japan-Korea treaty of 1904," he said. "Vladivostok is the only naval port in the [Russian] Far East, so occupying Vladivostok means to deter Russia permanently."[9] The port city was also the center of Korean resistance; occupying it would remove a potential trouble spot. But Kodama had grave misgivings about taking the war to Vladivostok. When Kodama met Nagaoka at the Shimbashi Station on the morning of March 28, he is said to have reprimanded the vice chief of the Army General Staff as soon as he got off the train. "Nagaoka! Don't be stupid. If one has started a fire, he must put it out. Have you forgotten this?" Nagaoka was apparently so incensed that he stormed off the platform.[10]

The idea of occupying Vladivostok was eventually dropped, but control of Sakhalin was identified as desirable.[11] On April 17 the *genrō* and cabinet members sat down to deliberate on how to pursue peace negotiations.[12]

They decided to approach Roosevelt to serve as mediator. In the meantime they began formulating the conditions on which Japan would seek peace. Russia's acknowledgment of Japan's right of complete freedom of action in Korea, the withdrawal of Russian troops from Manchuria, and control of Port Arthur and Dairen were non-negotiable items. Less important were the issues of war indemnity, the secession of Sakhalin, Japanese fishing rights along the Maritime Province, and Japanese claim to Russian ships interned in neutral ports. Indemnity from Russia was originally a high-priority issue for Komura and Katsura, whereas the military leaders viewed it as much lower priority.[13] In the end, all agreed that indemnity was not an indispensable item.[14] The emperor concurred when the terms of peace were presented to him. Roosevelt also thought a war indemnity was far too optimistic when he first got wind of it.[15]

While the Japanese were debating peace terms, Nicholas had not even begun to contemplate the possibility of ending the war, causing Roosevelt to exclaim in exasperation: "The Czar is a preposterous little creature as the absolute autocrat of 150,000,000 people. He has been unable to make war, and he is now unable to make peace."[16] Nicholas had been urged before the outcome of the battle of Mukden to begin making gestures toward peace, but he expressed no interest. Nor did he seem to grasp the mood of the country. The French ambassador to Russia, Maurice Bompard, alarmingly confided to a friend that "the war is getting more and more unpopular with the masses in Russia . . . In many villages, the departure of reservists has been accompanied by riots."[17] Threats of mutiny appeared in the army. In Moscow "a thousand reservists, after insulting and beating their officers, refused to leave for Manchuria [and] Cossacks had to charge before the mutiny was quelled."[18] The *Osvobozhdenie* [Liberation] put it bluntly: "The war drags on only because a victory is needed, desperately needed, to save autocracy."[19]

Those close to the tsar tried to awaken him to these realities. His mother, Empress Maria Fedorovna, enlisted the aid of the French government, Russia's ostensible ally. Through Grand Duke Paul, she implored French foreign minister Théophile Declassé to appeal to Nicholas to open peace negotiations.[20] In February the empress was shaken by a petition she had received from "the women of Russia," who implored her "to use her powers to end the war."[21] Declassé drafted a letter to the tsar but apparently thought the better of it, fearing perhaps that Russia would blame France for any unfavorable peace that resulted. He was nevertheless in full sympathy with the empress and told the Japanese minister in Paris that continuing the war was utterly "useless."[22] In March, Nicholas received the startling news that French bankers had broken off negotiations on a six-hundred-million-franc loan. That failure, coming after the defeat of Mukden, "brought the first break in the tsar's determination to go on with the war."[23]

Despite the mounting pressures to sue for peace, Nicholas was buoyed by the news that the Baltic Fleet was entering the South China Sea. Ambassador Takahira wrote to Komura on May 13 that, according to sources in Washington, the Russian people appeared to be "in high spirits because the Baltic Fleet has appeared in the waters near China."[24] Then came news of Tōgō's tremendous naval victory in the battle of Tsushima in May, when the Baltic Fleet had been annihilated. The reaction throughout Russia was profound disbelief and grief. "The appalling disaster at Tsushima has released a torrent of national fury," wrote the French diplomat Maurice Paléologue. Nicholas wrote resignedly in his diary, "Now finally the awfulness about the destruction of almost the entire squadron in the two-day battle has been confirmed."[25]

Major Ishimitsu Makiyo, still with the Second Army, received the news of Tsushima with a mixture of joy and relief. "Just like when we received the news of the fall of Port Arthur, the Second Army headquarters threw a big party . . . We all realized that there was indeed a possibility that we might return home alive but then suddenly a new kind of anxiety took hold of us. We asked ourselves, 'will the negotiations go smoothly,' and 'what if they fail?'"[26]

Japanese leaders shared the anxiety. The truth was that Tōgō had simply given Japan a reprieve. All that was accomplished by his victory was the opportunity for the Japanese to initiate peace negotiations, nothing more. For no matter how many battles Ōyama's army might win in the future, it was becoming clear that Japan would lose the war of attrition.

Upon receiving Japan's official request for assistance in starting peace negotiations from Ambassador Takahira on May 31, Roosevelt arranged to meet with the Russian ambassador, Arturo Cassini. On June 2 Roosevelt told Cassini that the war was hopeless for Russia and the Russians should look for a way to end the conflict. If national pride prevented Russia from taking the first step, he was willing to serve as the intermediary to set up talks.[27] Even before Cassini's report reached the tsar, Kaiser Wilhelm II was urging his cousin to seek peace, arguing that the naval defeat had put an end to any chance of a Russian victory, and Nicholas should seek Roosevelt's help.[28] To Charlemagne Tower, the American ambassador to Germany, Wilhelm was more blunt: "Unless peace is made, they will kill the Tsar!" he exclaimed. What he feared above all was revolutionary Russia.

Nicholas did not share the Kaiser's panic but agreed to raise the issue of negotiations with his war council, which he convened on May 25.[29] Admiral Alekseev was there, demonstrating that he still held some sway with the emperor. Both War Minister Sakharov and Admiral F. V. Dubasov, chairman of the Naval Technical Committee of the Russian Admiralty, came out vigorously against peace negotiations, arguing that Russia would be disgraced to seek an end to the war without having achieved a single battle victory. On the opposing side, Alekseev and Grand Duke Vladimir Alexandrovich argued forcefully for opening negotiations; if peace terms were unacceptable, the tsar could always back out and continue the war. The peace negotiations would give time for Linievich to build up his army should the talks fail.[30]

Nicholas weighed his options and finally decided to proceed with opening peace talks. The fundamental basis for his reasoning was the fact that not "one inch of Russian territory had yet fallen to the enemy." The Japanese had not yet made a move on Sakhalin, but he reasoned it was only a matter of time, and without a fleet, it could not be defended. He had to act quickly, for "tomorrow the situation may change," he said.[31]

The following day American ambassador George von Lengerke Meyer was given an audience with the tsar. Meyer brought with him a personal message from President Roosevelt. He stressed that he and President Roosevelt knew Russia would "never accept peace at any price" and that "if Japan demanded absolutely unreasonable term or excessive indemnity, His Majesty would have almost a united Russia behind him." What seemed to sway Nicholas was not anything Meyer said, but something the tsar himself had brought up the day before at the war council: "You [Meyer] have come at a psychological moment, as yet no foot has been placed on Russian soil, but I realize that at almost any moment they can make an attack on Sakhalin. Therefore it is important that the meeting should take place before that occurs."[32] What might have been the response had Nagaoka's plan to occupy Vladivostok been realized? It seems fairly certain that Nicholas would never have agreed to the negotiations and the war would have continued, with unforeseen consequences for both Russia and Japan.

TO PORTSMOUTH

Washington, D.C., was originally selected as the site for the peace negotiations to begin, but owing to the humid summer climate Roosevelt moved it to Portsmouth, New Hampshire. Given the distance both delegations would have to travel, the peace conference was set to begin in early August.

Appointing the chief negotiator for the peace talks became a significant problem for Nicholas II, for the first three candidates he had selected—A. I. Nelidov, A. Izvolsky, N. V. Muravev, ambassadors to France, Denmark, and Italy, respectively—declined the thankless task. The tsar was thus forced to settle on Sergei Witte, his last choice, despite his personal loathing. Lamsdorf reminded the tsar that there was no one more knowledgeable about Far Eastern affairs. "Knowing the character of our gentle, delicate Emperor," Witte later reflected sarcastically, "I could understand that after everything that had happened, His Majesty would not find it very pleasant to bring me close to him once more by appointing me chief plenipotentiary."[33]

Witte's instructions were simple and straightforward. Should Japan present demands that might in any way "tarnish the honor and reputation of Russia," he should not hesitate to stop the negotiations. Specifically, there was to be no payment of an indemnity and no loss of Russian territory. Witte publicly backed his sovereign's position if for no other reason than it was prudent politics. When he met with French premier Maurice Rouvier in Paris on his way to the conference, he was told that France would not be able to give Russia another loan until peace negotiations were concluded. Rouvier even offered to put up the money for an indemnity if needed. Witte replied that although he was "unreservedly in favor of peace," he would never agree "for us to pay as much as a *sou* because Russia had never paid and would never pay an indemnity." Rouvier pointed out that after the Franco-Prussian War, France had paid an indemnity without injury to its honor. "My [Witte] response was that if the Japanese army reached Moscow, we might reconsider."[34]

Accompanying Witte were Friedrich Martens, professor of international law at Saint Petersburg University, "a fine man . . . but a limited person in a number of respects [and] afflicted with pathological vanity"; G. A. Planson, "a typical obsequious bureaucrat" who had served under Viceroy Alekseev "as a servile executor of a policy that had led us into this war," and his secretary, D. Nabokov, the uncle of then six-year-old novelist Vladimir Nabokov; D. Pokotilov, "a very intelligent and gifted man . . . who had been opposed to the war from the beginning"; Baron Rosen, "a gentleman of average intelligence of a logical Baltic German"; and finally D. N. Shipov, a "very able man," but who likes, as the French say, "*manger à deux râteliers.*" "He is always subservient to his superiors, praises them to the skies but when they lose power, he gradually disassociated himself from them." Also included in this group was Witte's "talented" private secretary, Vladimir Korostovets, who at Witte's request kept a detailed record of events.[35] Witte clearly believed that of all his associates, he, Witte, was, in character, intelligence, and temperament, head and shoulders above the rest.

The Japanese delegation was headed by Foreign Minister Komura. Itō Hirobumi had been the obvious choice, but he declined. "One must harvest the result of what one has sown," he is reported to have said. "I started the Sino-Japanese War, and therefore I naturally concluded it. I consider it in order that the present war be concluded by Katsura himself."[36] Katsura was under pressure to take the position, but he thought it a thankless mission and was deeply grateful when Komura stepped forward to lead it.

In contrast to the acerbic and flamboyant Witte, Komura made a far less dramatic impression. Yet beneath his unprepossessing appearance lay a steely intelligence and prickly pride. As a young man Komura had been a student in America, during which time he became deeply conscious of his national identity and his pride as a Japanese. He remained throughout his life "scornful of foreignism and internationalism."[37]After graduating from Harvard Law School, Komura returned to Japan openly professing that he was a new *joi* (antiforeign) activist; no nation, he said, "could maintain its independence without a strong *joi* spirit." He impressed everyone with his nativist values by proudly wearing a cotton kimono and wooden clogs despite years of study abroad.[38] He also accepted uncritically the idea that Japanese expansion into the continent was indispensable for strengthening the nation and was keenly aware of the threat posed to Japan by Western powers. Not surprisingly, the group he selected to assist him and Takahira during the peace negotiations all shared Komura's hard-line nationalist views.[39]

On their departure on July 8, Komura and his party were treated to a festive sendoff at the Shimbashi railway station in Tokyo, where five thousand people gathered with shouts of "Banzai!" Komura whispered to Shidehara Kijūrō, the future prime minister. "When I return, these people will turn into unruly mobs that will attack me with mud pies or pistols. So I had better enjoy their *banzai*'s now."[40]

TRIUMPHS AND DISAPPOINTMENTS

It became clear in the talks that compromise was required from Russia on the Sakhalin and indemnity issues, particularly because the Japanese had already taken possession of the island. On July 7, 1905, Japanese troops landed in the town of Korsakov and took over the Russian garrison there without difficulty. By July 31, Russian forces, some seventy officers and thirty-two hundred rank and file, became Japanese POWs, and Sakhalin came under Japanese control.[41] Komura was hard-pressed to give up Sakhalin without some kind of compensation. He also refused to budge on the indemnity issue even though it had been low on the original list of priorities agreed to in April. The payment of an indemnity was also vigorously demanded by the Japanese public, which Komura was keenly aware of.[42]

On August 15 Witte wrote to Lamsdorf: "I think instructions from His Majesty would be in order, don't you?" But the tsar remained adamant, writing on the text of Witte's telegram: "On the loss of Sakhalin, there cannot be any talk. The Russian people would not forgive me for giving one inch of our land to any enemy and my own conscience would not allow it either."[43] Witte's heart sank. "The day before we were to resume negotiations [on August 23] was a very tense one for me," he later wrote. "I knew that peace was indispensable for us, and without it, we would be threatened with new troubles, with the prospect of the fall of the dynasty, to which I was devoted with every fiber of my being."[44] With the negotiations stalled over the indemnity and Sakhalin, Lamsdorf telegraphed Witte on August 21 to expect final instructions for ending the conference the following day.[45]

Roosevelt decided to intervene, sending a personal appeal to the tsar not to break off the talks and to consider accepting a compromise—the return of the northern half of Sakhalin, which was already in Japanese hands, to Russia in exchange for Russian payment of an indemnity. "So long as Japan returns [the northern] half of Sakhalin, there should be no reason why Russia should not pay compensation for it to Japan," the president opined. Roosevelt had cleverly forwarded a copy of this dispatch to Witte, who discounted the final instructions from Lamsdorf and informed the foreign minister that it would not be advisable to break off negotiations until the tsar had responded to the president's appeal.[46]

On August 23 at 3:50 PM, Ambassador Meyer arrived at the tsar's villa to deliver the president's message. Nicholas told him that "he would only sign an honorable peace, and an indemnity in any form was out of the question." The two men then discussed Sakhalin. Meyer pointed out that the southern half of Sakhalin had been Japanese territory prior to 1875, whereas the Russians had only recently acquired it. "Sakhalin was not *really* Russian territory any more than Port Arthur is," Meyer emphasized. "Why should it not go to the Japanese?" Meyer warned that if the war continued because Russia did not compromise on southern Sakhalin, Russia was in danger of losing Vladivostok. "If the Russian army is beaten, you will lose Vladivostok, the whole of Sakhalin, and probably all of eastern Siberia; what then?" After continuing in this vein for about two hours, Nicholas finally relented. He would agree to give up southern Sakhalin to the Japanese, but he would not, under any circumstances, pay an indemnity.[47]

While Meyer was pleading with the tsar, Roosevelt took the case for peace directly to the Japanese emperor. Through his friend and former classmate Kaneko Kentarō, a Harvard-educated lawyer and member of the House of Peers, the president applied subtle pressure on Japan to forgo an indemnity: "The civilized world looks to Japan to make the nations believe in her, let her show her leadership in matters ethical no less than in matters military."[48] What Roosevelt had failed to mention to either Kaneko or the emperor was that the tsar had agreed to give up southern Sakhalin. This vital piece of information had also been inexplicably withheld from the Japanese delegation.[49]

Despite the increasing pressure from Roosevelt, Komura wrote to Katsura on August 26 that the situation was hopeless. "We think that the Czar, influenced by the reports from General Linievich and others, has come to believe firmly that the Russian army in Manchuria is superior and can change the tide of the war. It appears that he has no intention of making peace at this time." Komura argued that there was no other alternative but to terminate the negotiations. "The responsibility for the continuation of the war rests solely with Russia," he continued. "As there is no way of further continuing the conference, we will leave here immediately when its breakdown takes place."[50]

Komura's telegram on the likelihood of the talks breaking down was unwelcome news in Tokyo. On August 25 the American financier Jacob Schiff, who had helped secure Japan's war loans, notified Ambassador Takahira that "the markets of the United States, England and Germany will . . . no longer be prepared to finance Japan's requirements to any great extent," which meant that Japan would not have the finances to continue the war.[51] Schiff urged the Japanese to settle. Katsura instructed Komura to postpone the final meeting for another twenty-four hours to give the cabinet time to deliberate. Meanwhile, Katsura, Itō, Yamagata, Terauchi, and the rest of the Japanese cabinet spent an agonizing day discussing what to do. In the end, given Japan's exhaustion and accepting the reality of its inability to continue the war, they saw no option but to give up the demand for both Sakhalin and the indemnity.[52] Komura received his instructions on the afternoon of August 28 to first withdraw his demand for an indemnity but to insist upon the cession of Sakhalin. However, if Witte rejected the proposal, Komura would withdraw the Sakhalin demand too. The decision amounted to a complete capitulation on both issues.[53]

The Japanese delegation was stunned. Komura took the news stoically, merely saying, "I was expecting this kind of decision."[54] Honda Kumatarō, secretary of the delegation, recalls that his colleagues began openly weeping. Komura sought to bolster the spirits of the delegation by reminding them of Kusunoki Masashige, the tragic war hero and loyalist of Kamakura Japan who had fought for Emperor Go-Daigo and lost a decisive battle in the Battle of Minatogawa in 1336. "Today is Minatogawa," he declared solemnly.[55]

That evening a number of remarkable things happened. After the final instructions to Komura had been sent, the director of the foreign ministry's commerce bureau, Ishii Kikujirō, decided to call on the British minister, Claude MacDonald. At the impromptu meeting, Ishii was flabbergasted to discover that the tsar had agreed to the cession of the southern half of Sakhalin at his meeting with Ambassador Meyer on August 23.[56] MacDonald had received this surprising news from London. Ishii immediately went to see Katsura, who telegrammed Komura to hold out for southern Sakhalin. Unaware of the reasons behind the volte-face, Komura was doubtful that Witte would agree. It was a high-stakes gamble because if MacDonald's information proved to be incorrect—Katsura had no time to verify the claim—the entire peace process would be jeopardized.

And indeed, it might have been had it not been for the courage of Witte. As Komura was gathering his wits, Witte received a telegram from the tsar via Lamsdorf late on the evening of August 28: "Send Witte the order to end discussions no matter what," Nicholas wrote. "I don't want to wait [any longer] for the kind concessions from Japan." This was in response to the Japanese request for a twenty-four-hour postponement. Witte, however, ignored the order. "His response was that if we end the discussion without hearing the new Japanese proposal, then we will be accused of wanting to continue the war no matter what, and it was his duty to the Motherland to listen to the new conditions," wrote Korostovets.[57] Witte was wracked by the enormity of what he had done. In defying Nicholas' instructions, he risked the emperor's wrath. "When I went to bed that night my soul was torn," he later wrote. "On the one hand reason and conscience told me that if peace arrived the following day, it would be cause for rejoicing. But then a voice inside me would whisper: 'How much happier you would be if fate kept you from signing a peace treaty, for if you do sign, you will be blamed for everything, since no one, not even a Russian Tsar, particularly a Russian Tsar like Nicholas II, is willing to admit his sins toward God and the fatherland.' I spent a restless, nightmarish night sobbing and praying."[58]

The plenipotentiaries of Japan and Russia held their final meeting on Tuesday, August 29. Before the formal session, Komura invited Witte and Rosen to join him in the private session. "Absolute silence reigned for a few seconds . . . at last Komura, in a controlled voice, said that the Japanese Government, having for its aim the restoration of peace . . . expressed its consent to Russia's proposal to divide Sakhalin in two, without an indemnity being paid. Witte calmly replied that the Japanese proposal was accepted and that the line of the demarcation of Sakhalin would be reckoned the fiftieth degree."[59]

The meeting ended at 11:00 AM. "When Witte came out of the meeting hall, he was blushing and smiling," recalled Korostovets. "Then stopping in the middle of the room, he said in an excited voice: 'Well, gentlemen, we have peace! Congratulations! The Japanese have conceded to everything.' These words burst open the dam of social felicitations. Everyone began speaking at once, interrupting one another, shaking hands, embracing. Witte kissed me and several of my companions. Everyone was satisfied, even Baron Rosen . . . who lost his unusual dispassion and smiled, saying: Excellent work! Sergei Yulyevich! The lively discussion continued for ten minutes longer, after which Witte sent a telegram to Count Lamsdorf to be passed on to the tsar telling him of the news."[60]

Komura and the rest of the Japanese delegation felt they had little reason to celebrate. Komura, in particular, knew that trouble was brewing at home. News reports of the peace agreement were already painting it as a Russian victory. Claude MacDonald wrote to his friend Sir Arthur

Sergei Witte (right) and Baron Rosen at the Wentworth Hotel, Portsmouth, New Hampshire, 1905. (Library of Congress, Prints and Photographs Division, LC-DIG-ppmsca-08801)

Hardinge at the Foreign Office: "There is no doubt that the R[ussian]s have jockeyed our little Allies pretty severely over these peace terms."[61] The papers solidified this impression. Throughout his stay in Portsmouth, Witte had assiduously cultivated good relations with the American reporters, and now that he had succeeded, he reveled in his success. "They gathered in the hotel to congratulate Witte and thank him for his kind relations to them," wrote Korostovets. "The general tone has been kind to us. Russia had achieved shining diplomatic victory, and Japan is allegedly depressed."[62]

The tsar was stunned by the news. Witte's telegram notifying him of the peace agreement left him reeling, as if, he later wrote, he were "in a trance." He was not sure whether he should be happy or angry. The British diplomat Cecil Spring-Rice heard from several people that Nicholas described himself as being "tricked" into the peace.[63] Witte had disobeyed a direct order, after all. "It was only after he had received congratulations from all over the world, including an enthusiastic communication from Emperor Wilhelm, that he sent me a telegram expressing thanks," Witte rather bitterly reflected. Witte's flaunting of his success, and of Russia's "victory" into the face of the Japanese, was conduct unbecoming of his dignity, especially when both parties had undergone such an arduous process. But Witte, blinded by his antipathy for the tsar and the need to prove his worth, behaved tactlessly and crudely toward the Japanese, and especially toward Komura. "The Russians feel themselves to be the victors—the heroes of the day," wrote Korostovets. "At the [hotel] buffet, people raised toasts to Russia and to the United States. The state governor, the kind Maclean, occupied a table on the terrace and offered champagne to all—he was very joyful and expressed his love to Russia. . . . The Japanese took a backseat, not wishing to disturb the Russo-American outpouring."[64]

It was all a very bitter pill for Komura to swallow. This proud man, whose country had spilled so much blood and treasure to take on the Russian Goliath, and prevailed every single time, felt little satisfaction at Portsmouth. "I am exceedingly sorry for Komura," Eki Hioki, Japan's chargé d'affaires at the Japanese legation in Washington, confided to a friend: "It is sad that the victor was actually dictated the terms by the vanquished."[65] Komura had predicted that he would not receive a warm welcome upon his return from the talks, but he did not anticipate the Japanese depth of anger and sense of humiliation that the agreement did not include an indemnity. Komura appealed to their sense of higher purpose for the nation:

> The Japanese race is penetrated by the spirit of *bushido* and the honor of the samurai. The honor of our country is both personally and nationally more important to us than money. . . . Is this not more important than whether or not we received an indemnity? Through our strategy and tactics, our armaments, and the command of our fleet, we have amazed the people of the world. Is this not the true essence of our victory? Russia wanted an honorable peace. We stood for an equal one. We have achieved this, and what we give to humanity, civilization, and the whole world is something more significant than whether or not we received an indemnity.[66]

Komura and others may have harbored a sense of betrayal over Roosevelt withholding the critical information on the tsar's concession of southern Sakhalin. There is no evidence to suggest that the president did so intentionally or for political gain.[67] But it was one more ax to grind in a long list of grievances Japan had experienced at the hands of Western powers.

KOREAN INTRIGUES

Despite bitter feelings, Komura did succeed in reaching an agreement on all non-negotiable items, including Russian recognition of Japan's rights and interests in Korea, the evacuation of Russian forces from Manchuria, and Japanese control of the southern branch of the Chinese Eastern Railway. In Korea, meanwhile, Kojong was well aware of what was happening at Portsmouth and tried his best to influence the proceedings. In September he wrote to Foreign Minister Lamsdorf that "the conclusion of peace between Russia and Japan would create such conditions that Korea would lose her last hope" and asked what help Korea might expect from Russia to secure Korea's independence. Lamsdorf assured him that "the Russian emperor held close to his heart the interests of the neighboring Korean empire, and that preserving the territorial integrity of Korea was the object of his tireless effort."[68]

Kojong was not going to rely solely on Russia to secure Korea's independence, however. In August 1904, with the war clearly going against Russia, Kojong pulled out of prison a young, plucky, missionary-educated reformist named Yi Sŭng-man, whose name became better known as Syngman Rhee. Rhee had been jailed and tortured for his antigovernment activities as well as his association with the now-defunct Independence Club.[69] Due to his missionary education, Rhee spoke fluent English, and Kojong decided to send him to the United States to plead Korea's case with American officials. Rhee would stay on after his mission to earn a bachelor's degree at George Washington University and a doctorate from Princeton, returning to Korea only to flee back to the United States in 1912 to escape Japanese colonial authorities. He spent the following three decades lobbying the United States and European powers on behalf of Korea's independence. In 1945 he returned, under the auspices of the American occupation government, to lead South Korea, becoming the first president of the newly established country.[70]

Somewhat curiously, the Japanese did not hinder Kojong's plan or Rhee's journey to America.[71] In February 1905 Rhee managed to secure a meeting with Secretary of State John Hay, who was sympathetic but knew that Roosevelt would not intercede on Korea's behalf. Earlier in January the president had written to him: "We cannot possibly interfere for the Koreans against Japan. They couldn't strike one blow in their own defense."[72]

Kojong was undeterred and continued his efforts to get the Americans to intercede. In June 1905 he met with A. W. Lucci, an official at the US legation. Kojong pressed him on whether he could count on America exercising its "good offices" in accordance with the US-Korea Treaty of 1882, should the occasion arise. Lucci was blunt. He explained that although Roosevelt had pursued peace negotiations, "the United States had bound itself not to interfere in the negotiations themselves, and had thereby set an example which would prevent other powers from interfering." When Kojong confided that he had hoped to enter into secret negotiations with the United States, Lucci pointed out that "any such efforts would certainly elicit an energetic protest from Japan and the world would regard Japan as justified in taking strong measures." He then warned the emperor, "After all the blood and treasure the war has cost Japan, she would not brook the interference of any third power or permit Korea herself to endanger the fruits of victory."[73]

Russia had anticipated that Japan would demand complete freedom of action over the Korean Peninsula. Nevertheless, Nicholas still wanted a clause in the peace treaty to include Japan's acceptance of Korean independence. He also considered it essential "to include in the treaty a clause forbidding Japan from building forts in the southern coast of Korea, in order to preserve freedom of passage through the Korean gulf."[74] But the tsar was quickly disabused of these ideas since, as he was reminded by both Witte and Lamsdorf, Korea was not Russian territory and thus not an issue subject to compromise.

The Korean issue, as the principal reason for the war and Japan's primary objective of the talks, was a central focus in the early part of the negotiations. Witte's position was that "Russia would agree to Japan's complete freedom of action in Korea," but he insisted Japan not impair the rights of the Korean nation and that it refrain from measures that might menace the security of Russia's border territory while guaranteeing that Russian citizens enjoy the same rights and privileges in Korea as other foreign nationals.[75]

Komura accepted it all except the question of Korean sovereignty, on which he adroitly asserted that Japan could not allow such a formulation because Korean independence had already been lost. The issue at hand was exclusively about whether Russia "would accept full Japanese freedom of action in Korea." Witte and Komura compromised; Korean independence would not be mentioned in the text of the agreement. Instead, the following caveat would be added to the minutes of the meeting: "Japanese officials declare it has been agreed here that measures Japan finds essential to take in Korea in the future, which may threaten the sovereignty of the country, will be taken solely with the agreement of the Korean government."[76] It was an empty phrase, but it satisfied both parties.

Witte was aware that the other powers—namely, the United States and Britain—did not support Korean sovereignty. An understanding between Japan and the United States had been worked out in July while Secretary of War William Taft was visiting Tokyo on his way to the Philippines. Meeting Katsura on July 27, Taft made it clear that he concurred with the Japanese prime minister's views of the Korea problem. Taft stated that "in his personal opinion, the establishment by Japanese troops of a suzerainty over Korea . . . was the logical result of the present war and would directly contribute to the permanent peace in the East."[77] His remarks expressed "the spirit as well as the letter of Roosevelt's policy."[78] Around the same time, British foreign minister Lansdowne and Ambassador Hayashi Tadasu were finalizing the renewal of the Anglo-Japanese alliance agreement in which Britain implicitly sanctioned Japan's takeover of Korea.[79]

ITŌ AND KOJONG MEETING

News of the signing of the Portsmouth Treaty on September 5, 1905, was thus ominously received in Seoul. Because article 2 stated that Russia would not interfere with Japan's supervision of Korea, Kojong had anticipated that a protectorate treaty was on the horizon. The problem was whether he would be able to whittle away some small concessions from the Japanese that might make the signing of the treaty more palatable.

Itō Hirobumi was dispatched by Emperor Meiji to Korea to negotiate the new treaty. He arrived in Seoul on November 9 and presented Meiji's letter to Kojong the next day. The first formal meeting between them took place on November 15 at 3 PM. A detailed record of their extraordinary conversation was chronicled in *Meiji Tenno Ki* [The record of Emperor Meiji] and is worth recounting at length.[80]

Itō got down to business at once. He told Kojong that "the Japanese government would like to take charge of Korea's foreign policy although Your Majesty will still retain control over domestic affairs." Itō proposed a Japanese protectorate over Korea as a way to maintain the peace and stability of East Asia "since Korea's situation is closely connected to the security of East Asia as a whole." Itō reminded Kojong of the current international situation. "We very much hope to have your consent for the protectorateship now."

414

"There is, of course, no way for me to reject your proposal," Kojong replied, but he had one request: "When authorizing Japan to take charge of Korea's foreign policy, I hope to retain nominal power."

"What do you mean by 'nominal'?" Itō asked.

"For example, the exchange of ambassadors," Kojong replied.

Itō was firm. "It is impossible to separate 'nominal' with 'actuality' in any kind of diplomatic relationship. If Japan allows Korea to continue its current foreign policy [in name only], Korea will once again become involved in conflicts regarding its territorial sovereignty and such conflicts will certainly threaten to destabilize East Asia [once again]. As Japan will not tolerate another conflict [like the one that just occurred], we hope to take charge of Korea's foreign policy. We made this decision based on careful considerations and the lesson we learned from the past. We must adhere to this principle."

Kojong insisted that his government at least "preserve *the appearance* of having control over its foreign policy" and asked whether the Japanese government might reconsider. "I'm concerned that Korea will fall into the same status as Hungary in the Austria-Hungarian Empire, or with various African countries."

"The Hungarian emperor no longer exists," Itō replied dryly. "That situation is completely incompatible with the relationship between Japan and Korea, both of whom still retain their own emperors and independent status. It is also inappropriate to make the comparison with Africa, where no country exists as an independent state. As I mentioned before, this treaty between Japan and Korea is meant to help prevent potential future conflicts from happening again in East Asia. Japan would like only to be authorized to oversee Korea's foreign policy and the Korean government will reserve the right to oversee its own domestic affairs."

Kojong persisted, asking Itō whether Emperor Meiji might reconsider the issue. "Perhaps there is a chance he may change his mind?"

Itō responded sternly: "The Japanese government has already fully thought out this matter and will not make even a small change regarding it." He then threatened: "The point of my coming today is to obtain your consent. And if Your Majesty refuses to consent, the Japanese government has already made up its mind anyway, and it will be hard to predict how things will turn out for you. Please do not waffle anymore and agree to sign the treaty."

Kojong then pleaded for more time. "I cannot make this decision by myself. I must consult with my ministers and survey public opinion."

This last request appears to have angered Itō. "It is perfectly reasonable that Your Majesty may find it necessary to consult your ministers. . . . Nonetheless, I suspect that your concern about public opinion is just a pretext. Your true intention is to provoke public unrest against Japan's proposals. If this is indeed the case, in the future Your Majesty will be held responsible for the consequences." Itō then went on to explain that the public had no understanding of the issues. "The Korean people still lack the knowledge about foreign relations and are ignorant of the current international situation. If you consult with them on this matter of crucial national significance, you will achieve nothing besides stirring up public anger."

Taken aback, Kojong denied trying to stir up public opinion against Japan. He merely wanted to consult with his ministers.

Itō replied that Kojong may consult with them, "but," he added, "you must promise me first that Korea will accept our proposal at the end." He feared that Kojong would procrastinate on the decision, and then blame his ministers. "The issue cannot be delayed any longer," Itō blurted and demanded that Kojong call a meeting with his ministers that evening. "Please waste no more time," Itō said with exasperation.

Kojong agreed, but once again raised the issue of retaining "nominal" authority over Korea's foreign affairs and his request to appeal to the Japanese emperor.

This time Itō lost his patience and abruptly told Kojong "to give up on such thoughts." The meeting had lasted four hours, ending at 7 PM.

THE SIGNING OF THE PROTECTORATE TREATY

Kojong's plea to survey public opinion was indeed a ploy for time, as he knew that many groups, particularly local Confucian scholars and yangban, were aware of the precarious political situation and were already opposing Japan. The *Taehan maeil sinbo,* the stridently anti-Japanese Korean daily newspaper run by British journalist Ernest Thomas Bethell, began stirring up anti-Japanese feelings as soon as the Portsmouth Treaty was made public. "Confucian scholars who have recently gathered downtown are buying copies of the *Taehan maeil sinbo* and are mocking Japan," wrote one Japanese legation official. These scholars were "also putting pressure on Korea's ministers like Yi Chi-yong, Yi Kŭn-t'aek, and Yi Ha-yŏng, calling them traitors and rebellious subjects . . . That these scholars have been acting in opposition to Japan and their influence is becoming impossible to ignore."[81]

Rumors circulated that Japan's decision to back down on the indemnity issue revealed that it was not such a powerful country after all. A Japanese police report noted: "The Confucian scholars are harshly mocking Japan for being weak, with some saying that Komura . . . probably received a large bribe from Russia and finally signed the peace treaty despite its disadvantage to Japan."[82] There was a brief hope that, as with the aftermath of the 1895 Triple Intervention when Japan's reputation took a hit, the Portsmouth Treaty would severely undermine Japan's standing in the world, particularly as the Hibiya anti-peace riots were rocking Tokyo, and, somehow, that Korea could benefit from the unrest. But Itō's arrival in Seoul burst that hopeful fantasy. As Kojong's ministers gathered for a final showdown with the Japanese, it was becoming clear that the dreaded day of reckoning, now nearly two decades in the making, had finally arrived.

At 11 AM on November 17, Minister Hayashi met with Korean ministers Yi Chi-yong (interior minister), Yi Wan-yong (minister of education), Pak Che-sun (minister of foreign affairs), Yi Kŭn-t'aek (army minister), and Kwon Chung-hyŏn (agricultural, commerce and industry minister), later to be infamously known as the "Five Eulsa Traitors," at the Japanese legation to discuss the Protectorate Teaty. After the meeting, the entire party went to the palace to see Kojong.[83] The meeting did not go well, and Hayashi called on Itō, who was staying at General Hasegawa's house, to help move the negotiations along. Itō and Hasegawa arrived at the palace around eight o'clock in the evening as Japanese troops and police surrounded the palace.[84]

What happened next is unclear. Kojong refused to put his imperial seal on the document and Itō began to berate him. Seeing he was getting nowhere, Itō called on Pak Che-sun, the foreign minister, and declared: "This is a matter dealing with foreign affairs so Pak can use the imperial seal." Deputy prime minister Han Kyu-sŏl refused to go along, telling Itō, "I have decided that I will die a martyr for my country so what will you say to that?" Furious, Itō called him a "disloyal subject," but the other ministers declared, "Han's approval is irrelevant; the other high-ranking government officials just need to stamp their seals of approval." At 1:00 AM on November 18, the treaty was sealed and signed by the "Five Eulsa Traitors." Shortly thereafter, Itō and Hasegawa left the palace.

Immediately after Itō and Hasegawa departed, Pak Che-sun began weeping, but Han rebuked him harshly. "You said this morning [during the meeting with Hayashi] that you opposed the treaty. You said that because you knew you would be threatened into signing the treaty, you wanted to throw the imperial seal into the pond. Why didn't you do that?" Han then convened a number of lower-ranking officials to draft an appeal to the emperor requesting the expulsion of the signers of the protectorate treaty.[85]

The first reporting on the events was published in the *China Gazette* on November 23. It quoted a long description, most likely written by Ernest Bethell, that contained many discrepancies. According to this version, Itō, Hasegawa, and Hayashi arrived together at the palace on the evening of November 17, bringing Japanese soldiers and policemen to physically threaten the emperor. It also reported that Numano Yasutarō, Japanese adviser to Korea's Ministry of Foreign Affairs, had stolen the imperial seal and used it to sign the document himself. While these reports cannot be verified, there is no question that the treaty was signed under duress.[86]

The Japanese government published an edict on the Korean protectorate treaty on November 20 to explain the action to the world. It lamented the "unwise and imprudent actions of Korea more especially in the domain of her international concerns [which had] been the most fruitful source of complications." Moreover, "to permit the present unsatisfactory condition of things to continue unrestrained and unregulated would be to invite fresh difficulties." Japan, therefore, "must take the steps necessary to put an end once and for all to this dangerous situation." With this objective in mind, the Meiji government was resolved to assume control over Korea's foreign policy to ensure "the peace and stability of Asia." It concluded:

> In bringing this agreement to the notice of the powers having treaties with Corea the Japanese Imperial Government declares that in assuming charge of the foreign relations of Corea and undertaking the duty of watching over the execution of the existing treaties of that country, Japan will see to it that those treaties are maintained and respected and that Japan will act without prejudice in any way regarding the legitimate commercial and industrial interests of those powers.[87]

It was an extraordinary document. By framing the signing of the protectorate treaty in terms of ensuring the "eternal peace and stability of

Asia," the Japanese justified their takeover of Korea by claiming that since its opening in 1876, the peninsula had been the site of continual strife and conflict in the region. In late October 1905, a few weeks before Itō's arrival in Seoul, Kojong asked his trusted American confidant Homer Hulbert to carry a letter to Roosevelt. The lengthy voyage meant that Hulbert was unable to deliver the letter until a few days after the protectorate treaty was signed. Kojong's main point was Japan's unjust treatment of Korea, and he called upon the "good offices" of the United States in accordance with the Treaty of 1882 to intercede with Japan to protect Korea's sovereignty. This was precisely the kind of Korean "meddling" that Japan's proclamation had warned the Americans against and could lead to "international complications." On November 21 Hulbert handed the letter to Secretary of State Elihu Root, who simply remarked: "Do you want us to get in trouble with Japan?"[88]

In a secret meeting in Beijing on November 21, Komura told the American minister to China, William W. Rockhill, that in view of Kojong's hope of Roosevelt's intervention on Korea's behalf, "it would be pleasing to Japan if the United States should be the first nation to close its legation in Seoul, as the moral effect upon the Koreans would be great."[89] Three days later, on November 24, Root instructed Edwin Morgan, the American minister to Korea, to withdraw the American legation from Seoul. Soon other governments followed suit. One American official in Seoul likened the exodus of foreign diplomats from the Korean capital to "a stampede of rats leaving a sinking ship."[90]

A wave of fury swept through Seoul, and memorials from angry Confucian literati poured into the palace calling on Kojong to execute the "Five Traitors" and annul the treaty.[91] The Confucian scholar Ch'oe Ik-hyŏn declared that Pak Che-sun "deserved a punishment worse than *nŭngji* torture [death by a thousand cuts]."[92] His petition to Emperor Kojong is worth quoting at length:

> How many times were we guaranteed the independence of our nation and the integrity of our lands? And how many times were we cheated by Japan in the name of friendship? They've tricked us so many times, and it is impossible for us to trust them. They now claim that they will make sure that the integrity of the Korean royal family remains intact. Your Majesty, how can you believe them? Luckily, for now, at least, the king has not yet been dethroned; the people have not yet been eliminated, and the foreign ambassadors have not yet been recalled. All the

Japanese have in their possession [for the moment] is nothing but a meaningless piece of paper signed by lowly traitors. We should first decapitate Pak Che-sun and the four other [traitors] who followed him as punishments for their crimes. Then, we should select someone in the foreign ministry to contact the Japanese government immediately. We shall coerce Japan to hand over or destroy the Eulsa [Protectorate] Treaty . . . Meanwhile, we shall contact the embassies of the foreign countries and hold a meeting with them, announcing the crime Japan has committed [against us] and how it has abused its power against a weaker country. Your Majesty's will and our people's will can finally be heard by the entire world. If the nations around the world can learn about our [nation's] spirit, the people all around the world will rise up and support us . . . Whenever I imagine the grim future of our country, I can't hold back my tears. I hope your Majesty will heed my words even though they come from a man on his death bed. I hope you can do what is necessary to remedy this situation: punish the Five Traitors and annul the protectorate treaty![93]

Strikingly, Ch'oe's memorial made no mention of Japan's victory over Russia. This galvanizing event appeared to vindicate Korean reformers' argument that Meiji Japan was the model for Korea to follow, but Ch'oe did not address the significance for Korea of Japan's victory.[94] Nor did he seem to understand the realpolitik predicament of Korea's situation, which pointed to the futility of appealing to the United States, and its "abandonment" of Korea to maintain "peace and order" in Asia.[95] Ultimately, Roosevelt's aim in concluding the Portsmouth Treaty was to establish a new Japan-centric regional order based on the shared principles of the Open Door. Such realpolitik calculations were lost on Ch'oe.

On November 30 Min Yŏng-kwan, a cousin of Empress Myŏngsong, cut his own throat as a final act of remonstrance. Six suicide notes were found in his pocket, all signed in blood, each addressed to the representatives of the United States, France, Great Britain, Germany, and China, imploring them "to assist our people's freedom and independence." A separate letter was addressed to his countrymen, offering "his sincere apology" for "the nation's shame and peoples' disgrace."[96] Other suicides followed. Also on November 30 the Confucian scholar Cho Pyŏng-se chose death by poison. On December 6, Kim Pong-hak, commander of the army's Changsangdae unit based in P'yŏngyang, killed himself by falling on his sword. Another Confucian scholar, Song Pyŏng-sŏn, also committed suicide by drinking poison, leaving a note that "if the treaty is not annulled the country will cease to exist."[97]

Following these rash of suicides, a group of yangban and officials entered the palace on December 3 to appeal directly to Kojong. "The land of Korea and its 20 million people was not created by you, but was passed down to you from your ancestors," they said. "The past kings and our people cannot help but be enraged by the fact that this country has been reduced to such a situation [under your rule]." They demanded he annul the treaty and then apologize to the Korean people.[98]

Those who saw Japan in a more positive light took the news in stride. Yun Ch'i-ho, former leader of the Independence Club, thought the officials' reactions too extreme. Yun had begun his career in the Reform Party (Kaehwadang) in the early 1880s. In 1895–1896 he served as vice minister of foreign affairs and acting minister of education. "Koreans believed that [the Protectorate Treaty] would arouse such a storm of indignation among the powers that Japan would be compelled to cancel it," he wrote mockingly in his diary. "In the first place, which of the powers is righteous enough to throw the first stone at Japan? Secondly, what has Korea done during the last twenty years of independent relations with the powers to deserve sympathy, much less the help of the world? God himself will not help those who don't help themselves . . . What power will risk the displeasure of the conqueror Japan just for the sake of Koreans, who are in the last state of putrefaction?"[99]

EXODUS AND REDEMPTION

In 1906 there began an exodus of Koreans to the Primorskaya oblast in the Russian Far East.[100] That same year Ch'oe Chae-hyŏng (Pyotr Semyonvich Tsoi) and Yi Pŏm-yun established a volunteer group of anti-Japanese Righteous Army (ŭibyŏng) fighters in the Posyet region.[101] Both men had been active during the Russo-Japanese War and subsequently began leading regular raids against Japanese garrisons in northern Korea.[102]

For those Koreans who had supported Japan's war, its victory over Russia seemed to vindicate the argument that Meiji Japan was indeed a country to be emulated. The island nation had been able to transform itself and through its military and economic prowess had beaten the Russian Bear. "The war is thus definitely ended," Yun Ch'i-ho remarked cynically. "Russia got the lesson of it; Japan, the glory of it; Korea the worst of it. Under the galling slavery of Japan, Koreans will learn that despotism of their own rulers has been the stepping stone to the despotism of alien masters."[103]

Song Pyŏng-jun, leader of the Ilchinhoe, was more optimistic about Korea's future, believing that continued cooperation with Japan would be beneficial. Japan's victory in the war had allowed him and his followers to reap the benefit of their cooperation with the Japanese, which they hoped would translate into Japan's help in reforming Korea's decrepit institutions.[104] On that basis, he believed that the protectorate treaty was merely a temporary measure to put Korea on the path to "progress and civilization" and eventual independence. The Ilchinhoe welcomed the opportunity to work under Japan's "guidance" as a friendly ally in order to make progress toward the attainment of "true" independence "in substance," not in name.[105] He declared that

> we of the Ilchinhoe did our utmost [to help Japan], and sacrificed the lives of a few hundreds of our followers in building railroads and transporting military provisions. Thus we suffered for our devotion to Japan, the most advanced nation in the East, [and for] our belief in the righteousness of her cause and our appreciation of her friendship for Korea as shown by her alliance with us. But the corrupt Koreans called us traitors, blind to our true purpose; we regret this although we do not fear their malediction.[106]

It was a striking contrast to Ch'oe Ik-hyŏn's memorial. One school harkened back to moralistic arguments and atavistic pride based on the idea of protecting Korea's identity and culture from threats to the nation's "Koreanness"; the other advocated a model of development for Korea based on cooperation with Japan, giving rise to all sorts of questions about the core meaning of Korean sovereignty and identity. The settlement of the Russo-Japanese War thus bequeathed to Korea striking political divisions that would continue to be felt well into the twentieth century.

CHAPTER TWENTY-ONE

"ETERNAL PEACE AND SECURITY IN ASIA"

In June 1904, Suematsu Kenchō, Japan's former home minister and the son-in-law of Itō Hirobumi, gave a public address calculated to counteract anti-Japanese fears and ease European and American leaders stunned by Japan's recent successes in the war. He said: "No matter how successful Japan may be in the war now in progress, this will make no difference to her well-defined policy regarding Korea and Manchuria or China generally, and Europe need have no apprehension on the subject. First may be laid down that under no conceivable circumstances will Russia be permitted to have the least political or territorial hold in Korea. This is absolutely certain." In the matter of Manchuria, he continued, "Japan desires no rights there other than those enjoyed in common by all the Powers. Manchuria will be given back to China, but such measures will have to be taken as to render impossible for the future any return to the conditions existing before the war."[1]

American politicians and business leaders were glad to hear these reassurances. E. H. Harriman, the railroad magnate and head of the Union Pacific and Southern Pacific Railroads (and father of statesman W. Averell Harriman) was particularly keen about keeping Manchuria open for commerce and trade. In the spring of 1905, Lloyd C. Griscom, the American minister to Japan, wrote Harriman a note urging that he visit Japan. Japanese leaders were then coming to the painful realization that their country was broke. The war had cost ¥1.7 billion, and as the annual national income was a little more than ¥2 billion, the financial burden was tremendous, and Griscom explained the need for foreign loans totaling some ¥700 million.[2]

Japan's dire financial situation also had important implications for its postwar reconstruction plans in Manchuria. In particular, the Chinese Eastern Railway (CER), parts of which Japan obtained from Russia in the treaty, was in urgent need of repair. Not a single passenger car or locomotive was left, and only a few freight cars were still in service. Many railroad bridges had been destroyed. New coaches and locomotives, other railroad equipment, and bridge repairs would be needed to make the line operational.[3] Griscom thought Harriman and the Japanese could strike a deal that would help advance both countries' interests: American capital for shared railroad rights in Manchuria.

Harriman was perfectly suited for such a grand venture, given his close association with Jacob Schiff, whose bank had helped Japan finance the war.[4] "It is important," he replied to Griscom, "to save the commercial interests of the United States from being entirely wiped from the Pacific Ocean in the future . . . and the way to find out what is best to do is to start something."[5]

E. H. HARRIMAN'S GRAND VISION

What Harriman had in mind "by starting something" was a breathtaking plan to connect the globe. His vision was to build an around-the-world transportation corridor to connect Asia, Europe, and the United States. It would be a grand commercial trunk linking the world's industrial and commercial centers with the largest markets. More importantly, it would enable the United States to take a commanding position in the Far East. "It'll be the most marvelous transportation in the world. We'll girdle the earth," he boasted. "From the lips of anybody else such a scheme would have been pipe dream," Griscom reported. "But as Mr. Harriman put it into words, it sounded quite feasible."[6] The CER would be a vital component in Harriman's visionary project to link together the grand transportation projects of the era: the Suez Canal (1859–1869), the US transcontinental railroad (1863–1869), the Panama Canal (1881–1914), and the Trans-Siberian Railroad (1891–1904).

Harriman arrived with great fanfare in Yokohama on the evening of August 31, 1905. At a banquet hosted in his honor by Griscom, he presented a toast calling for a future of shared interest, common endeavor, and joint prosperity between the United States and Japan: "You have made great strides in the art of war; but you must look to the arts of peace for those greater achievements which mean prosperity, contentment, and happiness. I hope the day may not be far distant when Japanese businessmen and American businessmen, realizing their interests are common, may be brought into a closer relationship."[7]

Over the next few days Harriman made the acquaintance of several *genrō*, including Itō Hirobumi and Inoue Kaoru, but also Soyeda Juichi, president of the Japanese Industrial Bank, and cabinet ministers. Harriman presented a bold proposal of forming a Japanese-American syndicate to provide capital and manage the southern branch of the CER—officially renamed the Japanese South Manchurian Railway (SMR) in 1906. He and his associates would put up the money for the purchase in exchange for part ownership and control of the railroad.[8] Such a partnership would save the Japanese government the tremendous expense of getting the railroad up and running while also putting needed cash in Japanese coffers. Moreover, the Japanese could trust the Americans since Harriman and his business associates were after profit, not territory.

Unfortunately, the timing of the proposal came at a tumultuous moment. News of the terms of the Portsmouth Treaty had just reached Tokyo, sparking riots on September 5. The Japanese were angered by the treaty terms. Many blamed the United States. Some even burned President Roosevelt in effigy.[9] As the riots continued over the next few days, Harriman decided to leave Tokyo for China and Korea, and return when the situation had calmed down. In the meantime, Griscom continued to lobby Japanese officials and promote Harriman's plans. "I was surprised to meet no deep-lying objections," Griscom wrote. "Count Katsura, never an easy person to convince, admitted he was favorably disposed. So did Vice Minister of Finance Saketani; and finally, Count Inoue himself said: 'We would be foolish to let such a chance slip.'"[10] Industrialist Shibusawa Eiichi was also on board, bringing tremendous influence in the business community.

Two factors swayed the Japanese to support Harriman's proposal. The first was Japan's dire financial situation, which would be strained even further to repair and operate the railroad. There was doubt that the government could manage the railroad efficiently. Harriman's deep experience and expertise as a railway man would provide assurances that it would be properly managed, perhaps even profitable. The second major consideration was strategic—Japan's national security concerns regarding Russia. Inoue, the most senior *genrō*, was particularly concerned that a defeated Russia might restart a war to seek vengeance. The railroad being under joint American and Japanese control would force Russia to think twice about starting a conflict that could embroil the United States.[11]

Harriman returned from his sojourn to China and Korea on October 8 and was pleased to learn of the positive receptive his proposal had received. Four days later a memorandum of "Preliminary Understanding" was drawn up between Katsura and Harriman, agreeing to the formation of a syndicate of investors under Harriman's leadership that would provide capital for "the purchase of the CER, acquired by the Japanese Government, and its appurtenances; the rehabilitation, equipment, reconstruction, and extension of the same, and the completion and improvement of the terminals of Dairen (Dalny)." The two parties also agreed to have "joint and equal" ownership of the railway. The corporation was to be organized under Japanese law, as a Japanese company. Furthermore "in case of war between Japan and China, or Japan and Russia," the railroad was to be operated under Japanese control and under instructions of the Japanese government "in the matter of the conveyance of troops and war materials."[12] It was a good deal for Japan since the entire burden of financing the project was left to Harriman and his associates; they would take all the financial risks and the Japanese would share in the profits.

The day before the agreement was to be signed, however, Ōura Kanetake, minister of communications, came out strongly against it, stating that Komura, who was on his way back to Japan from Portsmouth, should be consulted first. But Ōura had a more fundamental concern. The agreement could further inflame the volatile public by selling Japan's rights to the railway that had been "bought" with Japanese blood and treasure. Harriman was informed that the signing should be postponed until a more opportune time. With the unsigned memorandum in hand, Harriman sailed for San Francisco on October 13, disappointed but still hopeful that his grand project would be approved once Komura returned to Tokyo.

Troubles were brewing in the United States while Harriman was at sea. In early September, Kaneko Kentarō, who had served as an important liaison between Roosevelt and Komura during the negotiations and was preparing to return to Japan, received an unexpected visit from Samuel Montgomery Roosevelt, a businessman and cousin of the president, who informed him about Harriman's railroad project. Samuel Roosevelt expressed strong reservations about the joint project, as he believed that Japan's railway rights were "the essence of the current peace treaty." He told Kaneko he could make suitable arrangements and come up with a loan of "¥40–50 million at 5% interest."[13] It would be a cleaner financial arrangement than the one Harriman had proposed, and ownership would remain wholly with Japan. There is no evidence to suggest that President Roosevelt, through his cousin, actively sought to sabotage Harriman's plans, but the complicated relations between Harriman and Roosevelt were well known.[14]

Komura and Kaneko set sail for Japan on October 2. Komura fretted that he would be met by angry mobs throwing "bombs" at him upon his arrival at Yokohama. The fact that he had been unable to exact an indemnity from Russia highlighted the importance of Japan's rights to the southern branch of the CER for Japan's future interest in Manchuria.[15] Komura was therefore elated when Kaneko told him about Harriman's plan and Samuel Roosevelt's offer to help with financing the railway. "I did my utmost [at the peace conference] to insist on the railway and obtained it for Japan," he confided. Now he was determined to make the most of it.[16]

Komura and Kaneko arrived in Japan on October 16 intent on recommending the rejection of Harriman's plans. Komura brushed aside the deterrent value of a joint US-Japan railroad against a Russian threat. After his humiliation at Portsmouth, he was not about to relinquish what he perceived as his one major triumph of the negotiations: rights to the southern branch of the Chinese Eastern Railway that would open the way to Japan's future position in southern Manchuria. Article 6 of the treaty had stipulated that Russian railway rights be transferred to Japan subject to agreement by China.[17] Komura also wanted to spare the Japanese people the further humiliation of Japan's hard-won railway rights being sold to the highest bidder. As journalist George Kennan put it: "To have made peace without an indemnity was bad enough; to sell more than half the fruits of their victory to the Americans, and thus throw open to foreign competition the commercial field which they had bought with their treasure and blood would seem intolerable to them." When Harriman arrived in New York in early November, he received a cable from Soyeda informing him the memorandum of October 12 was canceled.[18]

Interestingly, the Japanese found themselves in almost exactly the same situation in 1905 as the Russians had been in 1900. In both cases, blood and treasure had been expended in Manchuria, and the evacuation and return of Manchuria to China proved difficult. Every military occupation lasts too long, but for Japan the staggering sacrifices and the unsatisfying end to the war convinced Komura, and others, that Japan had to take advantage of its victory to expand its own rights and interests. On November 6 Komura left for Beijing to negotiate a new agreement on Japan's postwar position in Manchuria.[19]

AWAKENING CHINA

Japan's victory was a watershed event for China, for it exposed the myth of Western powers' invincibility while showing that reform was still a possibility, even for China. The end of the war capped what had been an extraordinary period of change since 1900—including a complete revamping of the educational system, an extensive administrative and military reorganization, a more effective military training system, and an attempted centralization of financial institutions.[20] These reforms had a direct impact on Sino-Japanese relations. The abrupt decision in September 1905 to abolish the traditional Confucian examination system for government posts opened the floodgates for thousands of China's youths seeking new knowledge in Japan, the destination of choice for many future political and cultural leaders. With encouragement from the Qing government, Chinese students were promised good positions upon their return from their studies abroad. They found Japanese universities fertile ground for intellectual exploration; many for the first time enjoyed exposure to exciting new ideas and freedom from supervision.

One such student was Zhou Shuren, who later became China's most famous writer, poet, translator and literary critic, better know by his pen name Lu Xun. Initially educated at a local Confucian school, Lu went to Japan to become a doctor. One day in class, while watching a propaganda slide show of triumphant Japanese executing an alleged Chinese spy during the Russo-Japanese War, Lu experienced an epiphany. The alleged spy was surrounded by a large, passive crowd of Chinese onlookers. In his countrymen's reaction to the execution of one of their own, Lu saw the spiritual sickness of a people too apathetic and weak to save either themselves or their country. He decided at that moment to abandon his medical studies for literature, to heal the Chinese people's souls instead of their bodies. He later wrote, "I reinvented myself as a crusader for cultural reform."[21]

Thousands of Chinese students like Lu Xun organized to condemn outmoded Confucian thought and promote a New China. Their watchword was nationalism, and three principal goals motivated their call to action. The first was to reclaim everything China had lost to foreign imperial powers. This anti-imperialist sentiment was different from the xenophobia of the Boxers, who were allied with the Qing and wanted China to return to what had been the status quo before the arrival of Western powers. For the young new nationalists, the main idea was the recovery of sovereign rights and the push to make China an equal in the community of nations. Second was a call for the organization of a modern and centralized nation-state capable of defending its sovereign rights against the imperialist powers by engaging in Great Power diplomacy on an equal footing. Finally, to achieve these goals, the overthrow of the Qing dynasty was necessary. The recovery of national rights meant not only reclaiming everything the Qing had lost to foreigners but reclaiming China itself from the Manchus, who were also deemed foreign.[22]

In sharp contrast with China's earlier 1898 reformers like Kang Youwei, who supported a constitutional monarchy and opposed the overthrow of the Qing, the New China reformers engaged in explicitly anti-Qing activities. In early 1903 the first avowedly anti-Manchu organization, Qingnian hui (Youth Association), was established in Japan but with only a few members.[23] Following the influx of Chinese students flocking to Japan after the war, however, the number of anti-Qing groups grew rapidly. In 1905 Sun Yat-sen, a missionary-educated revolutionary, established the "Revolutionary Alliance" (Tongmenghui), dedicated to the overthrow of the Qing dynasty and the establishment of a new republican form of government.[24] Its ideology was a mixture of Sun's republican ideas developed during his study of "Western learning" and socialist theories. Finding support among restless overseas Chinese who felt little allegiance to the Qing, Sun found ready recruits for his revolutionary organization. His bold call for action to save China by instituting drastic social and political reforms attracted many more followers than the more cautious and conservative Kang Youwei.[25]

Nationalist stirrings and anti-Qing feelings were evident within China as well. In May 1905 the Shanghai Chamber of Commerce passed a resolution urging all Chinese in Shanghai to boycott American goods. The Chinese were angered by American exclusionary laws that discriminated against Chinese students and merchants in the United States. In October 1902, 250 Chinese immigrants were arrested by Boston immigration officials without warrants. One of the victims, Feng Xiawei, later returned to China and committed suicide in front of the American Consulate in Shanghai to protest the treatment of Chinese immigrants in America.[26] Thousands of Chinese joined in demonstrations to commemorate Feng's martyrdom. Soon merchants in Canton, Xiamen, Tianjin, and elsewhere joined in the boycott of American goods. Due to the lack of coordination among the boycott leaders and Qing pressure to end the movement, the boycott did not last long, and trade eventually returned to normal. But the action marked a new kind of popular movement in China, one that attempted to respond to national humiliation through a coordinated economic campaign, revealing the depth of Chinese frustrations.[27]

KOMURA-YUAN NEGOTIATIONS IN BEIJING

Upon his arrival in Beijing on November 12, 1905, Komura was greeted by Uchida Kōsai, the Japanese minister to China. The first formal session of the Sino-Japanese conference was held five days later with the Chinese plenipotentiaries Prince Qing, chief grand councilor and presiding minister of foreign affairs, and Yuan Shikai, viceroy of Zhili. In view of the Qing decision to implement sweeping reform measures, the Chinese plenipotentiaries were not inclined to give away further concessions to foreign powers.[28] Earlier, in December 1904, Itō Hirobumi had reaffirmed Japan's position regarding China. "Japan neither wanted Manchuria nor was she strong enough to maintain a large garrison indefinitely on the remote borders of that province," Itō said. "[Japan] had already made explicit declarations that she would respect the integrity of China . . . and considers that integrity to be of utmost importance . . . provided that it was always accompanied by the policy of the Open Door."[29]

Yuan Shikai and Prince Qing thus expected that an amicable agreement between the two countries could be reached. But their expectations were quickly dashed. Komura made a short opening speech that set the tone for the entire negotiations. He began by describing the origins of the Russo-Japanese War and emphasized how much Japan had sacrificed, not only for its own self-defense but for the general "peace and security" of East Asia. "The Chinese government should consider how China might have been negatively affected had Japan not chosen to fight a war against Russia and how many sacrifices the Japanese have made on China's behalf." He wanted to obtain assurances from China that it would "eliminate every factor that could cause future international conflict in Manchuria."[30] Finally, Komura laid out a plan for Japan to develop trade and commerce in Manchuria.[31] He also explained that a major Japanese concern was Russian revanchism. If Russia renewed its aggression against Manchuria, Japan must have the right to deploy railway guards along the southern branch of the CER.[32]

Prince Qing and Yuan Shikai acquiesced to Komura's demand for the transfer of rights to the southern branch of the railway and the leased territory, with conditions.[33] They explained that China intended to form a genuine partnership with Japan, yet they were emphatic that "Manchuria is still Chinese territory."[34] Yuan thus forcefully called for the complete withdrawal of all foreign forces from Manchuria, the prohibition of any foreign officials bearing the title of military governor, and finally, a guarantee for the use of Dairen solely as a commercial port "with an office to monitor the movement of Japanese military forces into and out of the leased territory of Liaodong [Kwantung]."[35]

Komura and Uchida responded brusquely and unsympathetically. Japan had risked its national existence to force the withdrawal of Russian forces from Manchuria, they argued, so it was not unreasonable to expect Japan to be fully compensated for the blood and treasure it had expended for China's benefit.[36] Regarding the withdrawal of Japanese troops, Komura stated that Japan would remove its guards from Manchuria simultaneously with Russia "if the restoration of civil order was achieved there." What Komura neglected to tell his Chinese counterparts was that he had learned from Witte at Portsmouth that Russia had no intention of ever removing its railway guards in northern Manchuria.[37]

Komura then pressured Yuan to agree to a series of "secret protocols," some of which were a clear violation of China's sovereignty. For example, according to the third protocol, the Chinese government could not engage in any railway construction of its own accord because any branch line might be "prejudicial to the interest of the above-mentioned railway (CER)." Item 8 was more egregious, stipulating that "the regulations respecting the places to be opened [for commerce] in Manchuria shall be made by China herself, but the Japanese minister in Peking must be previously consulted in the matter." According to item 13, local Chinese authorities were not allowed to dispatch troops to subdue native bandits without first consulting the commander of the Japanese troops stationed in those regions.[38]

These protocols clearly infringed on China's sovereignty, but Komura went even further. Following the completion of the Seoul-Ŭiju line in Korea, he was keen to have rights over the Mukden-Andong line so that the two lines could be eventually joined. (Andong and Ŭiju were across from each other on the Yalu River.)[39] Yuan was strongly opposed, but Uchida retorted: "If China owns the railway, what happens if Russia takes over Manchuria [again] in the near future?"[40] Eventually a compromise

Komura Jutarō (center) and Uchida Kōsai with Yuan Shikai after the signing of the Sino-Japanese Treaty, December 22, 1905. (De Agostini-Biblioteca Ambrosiana/De Agostinia Editore/agefotostock)

of sorts was made: Japan would have rights to the Mukden-Andong line, but only for a fixed period, until 1924.[41]

The Sino-Japanese Treaty was signed on December 22, 1905, marking the beginning of a new era in the history of East Asia and a turning point in Japan's foreign policy. The issues raised by the settlement of the war opened a wide rift in Japan on a broad range of questions about Japan's position in Manchuria, and opinions varied greatly about the immediate course to take. Hard-liners like Komura wanted Japan to pursue its political and commercial interests there regardless of the cost to its international standing or its relationship with China. Hard-liners who shared such views included Ōshima Yoshimasa, the new viceroy of the Kwangtung Leased Territory, who had replaced Ōyama as commander of all Japanese forces in Manchuria. But more far-seeing Japanese statesmen, like Itō Hirobumi, saw serious difficulties with this position. For one thing, Japan's pursuit of its Asian continental ambitions would put it on a collision course with the United States and most certainly would isolate Japan in the international community. Even more critically, the pursuit of a hard-line policy would cause anti-Japanese agitation in China.

These differences of opinion led to the fall of the Katsura cabinet in January 1906. The new Saionji Kinmochi government was supposed to be a compromise between the extreme hard-line factions and the anti-hard-line factions.[42] Following his visit to Manchuria in early 1906, Prime Minister Saionji returned to Japan with Ōshima's resignation letter in hand. Ōshima had threatened to resign unless his views on Manchuria were partly met. A compromise was apparently reached. Ōshima's headquarters was moved from Liaoyang to Port Arthur, and his title changed from viceroy to governor-general. It was also announced that the Kwantung Leased Territory would be under the administrative control of the Foreign Office, not the army.[43] While this move appeared to be a defeat for the hard-liners, in reality, Manchuria still remained in the hands of Japanese military administrators.

SHOWDOWN

During the early months of 1906, doubts began to stir about Japan's pledge to uphold the integrity of China and defend "the eternal peace and security of Asia." "The Japanese are playing a big game before the world," wrote Ambassador George Von Lengerke Meyer to President Roosevelt in January, quoting his conversation with journalist Stanley Washburn, who had spent months on the front line with the Japanese Army. "They [the Japanese] at heart do not care for any whites, nor even for the English or Americans, who are useful to them now and are working them for all they can. They laugh in their sleeves about the Open Door in Manchuria, for when the time comes they can beat us in manufacturing, due to cheap labor, and there get the trade."[44]

Similar observations were made by J. Gordon Smith, another war correspondent, who wrote that "Japanese traders had already begun to rush into Manchuria behind the Japanese armies, although all other foreign merchants were excluded by the Japanese Government."[45] Meanwhile, Chinese authorities waited impatiently for Japan to notify them when they could resume control, in accordance with article 3 of the "Additional Agreement" of the Sino-Japanese Treaty. In March 1906, Britain and the United States officially protested to Japan, demanding an Open Door policy for Manchuria.[46]

As pressure mounted to "open" Manchuria, Chinese officials joined the chorus to express their frustrations with Japan, especially when they realized that they could do nothing of substance without "consulting" the Japanese first. It appeared to the Chinese that nothing had really changed; the Japanese had simply replaced the Russians. "There is at the present time a very strong anti-concession wave sweeping over China," the American diplomat H. W. Denison reported to Griscom in January. "The [Chinese] Government are endeavoring by hook or by crook, to get back the grants already made. They cancel concessions in case of default in any direction, and then buy back the grants if no grounds of cancellation exist."[47] The rising wave of nationalism, of which anti-concessionism was but one symptom, collided with the hard realities of Japanese military occupation of Manchuria. The Saionji cabinet's initial response was to continue to reassure China, and the world, that its withdrawal would soon be forthcoming. As long as actual conditions in Manchuria remained unchanged, Japan's hard-liners continued to be assuaged. But the withdrawal from Manchuria could not be postponed indefinitely.

A joint meeting of the Saionji cabinet, military leaders, and the *genrō* was held on May 22, 1906, to discuss the Manchurian question. Itō opened with a speech. "I heard from Foreign Minister Katō Takaaki that we have received quite a few inquiries from other countries with regard to the Manchurian problem, and need to reply to them," he said. Itō then summarized a message he had received from Ambassador Claude Mac-Donald in March warning him that Britain was losing patience. Japan's position was "alienating all those countries which had once sympathized with Japan during the war." The situation for Japan, the ambassador confided to Itō, "was suicidal."[48]

Itō told the assembled leaders that MacDonald's message hit him like "a bolt of lightning from the sky." Furthermore, "European media has been suggesting that Japan is preparing for another war with Russia and that Japan perceived the Portsmouth Treaty not as a peace treaty but as a truce." Itō was concerned that such rumors may have actually originated in Japan and that doubts about Japan's Manchurian policy were creating an unstable domestic situation. Moreover, "reports from China reveal that Yuan Shikai is also unhappy," signaling further trouble ahead. Itō warned that "the whole of China could rise up against Japan." "The Qing is in a state of turbulence. Many Chinese are advocating to reassert their country's sovereignty and we should not overlook what they are capable of doing." Itō noted that another uprising might take place, similar to the Boxers, which would undoubtedly bring in Russian forces. If Japan did not want to fight another war with Russia, "we must do everything [in our power] to maintain the peace and tranquility of China"—and for this reason it was imperative for Japan to "respect the Chinese people's demands regarding Manchuria."[49]

Itō then accused the Japanese military administration in Manchuria of acting like the Russians. "The guidelines for the military administration do not leave the Chinese with any room for action," he complained.[50]

General Kodama, the newly appointed chief of the Imperial Japanese Army General Staff, denied that other countries were as concerned about Japan's administrative control of Manchuria as Itō had laid out. Japan was simply taking time to sort out the situation there, implying that much of the confusion in policy was due to military administrators being hampered by the Foreign Ministry and consulates. There was no clear line of authority between military and civilian authorities.[51]

This observation appeared to have made Itō very angry. He said that "he would like to remind Kodama that the outline for the military administration in Manchuria" was laid out in the "The Outline of Implementing Military Administration in Manchuria" that was created in April 1906. That document stipulated that the army's role was limited to three main functions and nothing more. "The main duty of the military administration is to mediate the relationship between the Japanese army and the Chinese government and people." It was not the function of the military administration "to interfere with the operation of Japanese consuls." Moreover, it was the duty of the military administration to "delegate power to the local Chinese authorities" so that they could carry out the proper function of governance over its own people. Finally, the main task of the Japanese military administration was "to protect the safety of Japanese residents within its jurisdiction" and to "oversee their commercial activities and travels." Itō accused the military of overstepping its role, and snapped, "The military seems to consider Manchuria as a new territory of Japan." After a heated exchange over the restoration of administrative rights to Fengtian [Mukden] and Andong to Qing control, Kodama proposed appointing one person, a kind of viceroy, to oversee all matters relating to Manchuria. "This person can deal with all the bureaucratic procedures that I just mentioned all at once and establish a new institution that oversees everything."[52]

Itō was furious. He condemned the Japanese Army for continuing to remain in Manchuria and criticized army officers and merchants who talked presumptuously of "running Manchuria" as if it were part of Japan. "You [Kodama]," he said "have misunderstood Japan's status in Manchuria. Japan's rights in Manchuria include nothing more than rights that we take over from Russia, namely the concessions in the Liaodong Peninsula and the railways. The phrase 'management of Manchuria' [*Manshū keiei*] was used first by the Japanese people during the war, and then by our [military] administrators. But Manchuria is by no means a territory of Japan! It belongs to the Qing! It's unreasonable for Japan to wield its sovereign power over a land that does not belong to us. There's also no need to build and run colonial institutions there. We should let the Qing government take the responsibilities for Manchuria."[53]

Katsura sided with Itō while Terauchi tried to find a middle ground, proposing to keep military and consular functions separate. In the end they reached a compromise of sorts. The Japanese government would work to reduce the number of military administrative officers, "thus removing the high-handed proceedings of the military men." At the same time, the South Manchurian Railway Company, or Mantetsu, would be established as a semiprivate company under the direction of General Kodama, who, during the war, recognized the importance of the railway. This semigovernmental project would become the backbone of Japan's commercial expansion into Manchuria. After Kodama's sudden death in July 1906, General Terauchi replaced him as Army chief of staff, while Gotō Shinpei, Kodama's deputy during the war and the former chief of civil affairs in Taiwan, was named the company's first president.[54] Gotō's motto was "Military preparedness in civilian garb," meaning that the Japanese had to coexist peacefully with the Chinese.[55] A fine balance was struck between Itō's efforts to maintain the integrity of China and uphold Japan's international standing, and Gotō's headlong push toward colonization in Manchuria.[56]

In the immediate aftermath of the war, Japanese leaders thus found themselves at a crossroads: What kind of expansionism should the nation follow? What form should it assume—continental or maritime?[57] Up to and including the Russo-Japanese War, the main principle and goal of Japan's national security policy was clear—to prevent Korea from falling into the hands of another power. Although the two continental wars against China and Russia pulled Japan's focus and power to the Asian continent, this did not mean that Japanese leaders had abandoned the notion of Japan as a maritime nation altogether.[58] The large debt incurred from the war meant that military expenditures had to be kept in check.[59] There were also great risks in becoming a continental power, which required maintaining a large standing army, not an ideal situation for an island nation. Nor could Japan afford to antagonize its Western allies completely.

But events in Korea once again changed the calculus, upending the precarious internal compromise reached by Japanese leaders in 1906. By the end of 1907 it was clear which side had come out on top. Thomas Millard, an astute American journalist and observer of East Asian affairs, noticed the stark transformation. "On my second visit to Manchuria since the war ended [in early 1907], I could notice slight alterations of the general political status, although the situation is constantly being modified by the course of events, and outward evidence of Japanese occupation was less conspicuous. Japanese troops in the country had been reduced. The garrisons which when I was last there, eighteen months before, were maintained at Moukden, Liaoyang, Newchang, Tieling, Tsinmintun, and Kirin had been withdrawn. Moukden was the last important place evacuated, the troops being withdrawn from the city in 1907. As the Japanese military grip was relaxed, Chinese administrative process gradually resumed their functions throughout the country with some limitations and exceptions." By late 1907, however, that grip had returned and Millard now complained loudly that "the restoration of Chinese autonomy is a fiction . . . The real authority in southern Manchuria does not now lie with China, but with Japan."[60] What had precipitated this change?

TO KOREA

In March 1906 Itō Hirobumi took up his duties as Korea's first resident-general. His main task, as he had reiterated many times, was to bring about "a fundamental institutional and economic reform of that country."

To make sure that he would be able to manage his resident-generalship free from interference from Tokyo, and especially from the army, Itō insisted he have sole command over all military forces in Korea. General Kodama was strongly opposed because, as one of his staff officers, Iguchi Shōgo, noted, it would set a bad precedent for a civilian to lead the Korean Garrison Army. Yamagata opposed Itō's demands as a violation of the army's right to have direct access to the emperor.[61]

But Itō was stubborn. "If I do not have control over the army, I will not assume the post of resident-general," he declared flatly. He wanted power "equivalent to that of a field marshal." An exception was inevitable, for "no one had the same trust from the emperor" as Itō did, and it was vital that someone of his experience and stature assume the position of resident-general.[62] Itō's reason for wanting this power had to do with the governing apparatus in Korea, which had become highly militarized as a consequence of the war. By January 1905, Japan's Korean Garrison Army [Kankoku Chusatsugun], established the year before to protect the Japanese embassy and civilians, had assumed control over all police operations in Seoul and the surrounding areas, including martial law, even after the Russo-Japanese War officially ended.[63] The same draconian edict on punishment for destroying Japanese railway and telegraph lines was kept in place after the war. Between July 1904 and October 1906, 257 Koreans from Kyŏngsang and P'yŏngan Provinces were punished, including thirty-five executions for violating or disturbing these railways.[64] Itō believed that bringing the military under his control and demilitarizing the Japanese presence was vital for him to exercise his authority as resident-general and obtain Korean cooperation.

Another compelling factor was the extremely unruly Japanese behavior in Korea, which had enormous potential to undermine his authority and legitimacy. "There is a wholesale system of exploitation that focuses every side of Korean life," wrote one observer. "Concessions are granted to Japanese, contracts are given on the most generous terms to Japanese, and emigration laws, land laws, and general administrative measures are made solely with regard to Japanese interests." Koreans were also routinely swindled. "Act after act has revealed that the Japanese consider Korea and all in it belongs to them. Do they want a thing? Then let them take it, and woe be to the man who dares hinder them!"[65] Homer Hulbert observed that while "unlawful actions by a Japanese soldier was almost unknown," the "influx of low-class Japanese" that followed the army caused endless trouble. "When these Japanese, on the strength of the prowess of

Japanese arms, began to treat the Koreans as the very scum of the earth and to perpetrate all sorts of outrages, it was inevitable that a mighty reaction should take place."[66]

By early 1906, reports that local Ilchinhoe members were coming under increasingly violent attack from local Korean militia groups (*chiwidae*) and others were giving the Japanese some concern. The Ilchinhoe, which had enjoyed widespread influence during the war, had become deeply unpopular.[67] In Kanglŭlkun County, for example, it was reported that "hundreds of people had wreaked havoc there, beating Ilchinhoe members and destroying their homes." In the village of Koksan, "groups of villagers destroyed the Ilchinhoe's office, injuring 5 people." Ŭibyŏng [Righteous Army] members in the village of Hamyŏl "brandished their bayonets and attacked the Ilchinhoe officer there, injuring 40 members."[68] These assaults represented a startling reversal of the Ilchinhoe's standing and did not bode well for the stability of the peninsula.

During this time, Kojong was secretly soliciting Russia's help. In January 1906, G. A. Planson, the new Russian minister, was instructed to establish a general consulate in Korea. Instead of negotiating the terms directly with Itō, Planson argued that he should be allowed to do so directly with the Korean government. He insisted that the Portsmouth Treaty in no way annulled Korean independence, nor did the treaty invalidate the previous Russo-Korean agreement of 1884. The Russians insisted their assets that had been seized by the Japanese during the war should be returned, including the Briner concession along the Yalu River, which had been the cause of the war. Itō had earlier demanded that the Japanese be given logging rights there, but Kojong refused, saying that it belonged to the Russians.[69]

Serious complications thus emerged again between Russia and Japan over Korea. Fortunately, Russia's new foreign minister, Alexander Izvolsky, who succeeded Lamsdorf after the latter's unexpected death in May 1906, decided to follow an entirely new course. Izvolsky had been critical of Russia's reckless expansion into the Far East, as he believed that Russia's primary interest lay in Europe.[70] He thus set about to improve relations not only with Britain but also with its ally, Japan. New instructions were sent to Planson that, because Korea was a "sore spot" for Japan, he should avoid any entanglements with Kojong.[71]

In view of Russia's new stance, Itō began to exercise stronger constraints on the personal life of the emperor. In July 1906 Kojong's palace guards were withdrawn and the emperor was made "a virtual prisoner" in his own palace. "Police officers were posted at each gate, and no one was allowed in or out without a permit from a Japanese-nominated official."[72] In desperation, Kojong managed to sneak a message to Planson that "he continued to count on Russian help" and hoped "to retain his last shred of independence." The Russian minister was no longer encouraging, advising him that Korea "should make peace with her position, however difficult, and await for better day," since "every attempt to resist will only worsen her position."[73] Kojong was thus left out in the cold, but Itō had underestimated the Korean emperor. Despite his attempts to box Kojong in, the Japanese resident-general "struck against a vein of obstinacy and determination that he could scarce have reckoned with."[74]

THE HAGUE CONFERENCE AND THE 1907 RUSSO-JAPANESE CONVENTION

On July 3 a telegram dated July 1 was received in Seoul announcing the arrival of three Koreans at the 1907 Second Hague Conference, an international forum to address the conduct of warfare and settlements of international disputes. The officials had brought with them an open letter addressed to the delegates attending. The letter stated, in essence, that the Protectorate Treaty had been signed under duress, that the Japanese "had used threats in violation of all international norms," and that, as a sovereign, Kojong had been "deprived of the right to direct communications with friendly countries." Refusing to accept this state of affairs, Kojong had therefore appointed the delegates "in order to notify the other powers about Japan's infringements of my [Kojong's] rights" and to restore direct communication between Korea and other powers, "which was Korea's right as an independent country."[75]

Contrary to their expectations, the Korean delegates received an icy reception. When Izvolsky heard rumors that the mission was on its way, he sent an urgent message to A. I. Nelidov, the Russian ambassador in Paris and president of the Second Hague Conference, instructing him to "refrain from reacting with the delegates in case they really do go to The Hague and petition for your cooperation." Izvolsky was in the middle of tough negotiations with Motono Ichirō, Japanese minister to Russia, over the fate of Manchuria, Korea, and Outer Mongolia and wanted to avoid complications with the Japanese. Similar fears of unnecessary entanglements with Japan had prompted the other powers to give the Koreans the cold shoulder. The Dutch minister of foreign affairs, Jonkheer van Tets van Goudriaan, refused to admit them into the conference. Representatives of Russia, Britain, France, the United States, and Germany also refused to meet them.[76]

Although Itō was relieved by news of the Korean delegates' failure to gain admittance to the conference, he was furious at Kojong for the embarrassment he had caused.[77] The story of The Hague Korean emissaries became a media sensation. The *Herald Paris,* for example, recounted in salacious detail all the terrible conditions under which Kojong was forced to live, like "a virtual prisoner and in constant fear for his life." The paper also repeated the story that Kojong had been forced to sign the Protectorate Treaty under duress.[78]

The news from The Hague also prompted a lively debate in Tokyo. Inoue Kaoru suggested that Kojong be brought to Japan to observe all the wonderful things Japan had accomplished so that he might understand "what Japan wished to do for Korea."[79] But that idea was quickly dropped, for it would certainly be viewed as a kidnapping. Instead they decided to force Kojong to abdicate.[80] Foreign Minister Hayashi arrived in Korea on July 18 to consult with Itō, but on that very day Itō was informed that the Korean cabinet was meeting with Kojong to resolve the situation by themselves. Fearful of what the Japanese might do, Kojong's ministers had taken matters into their own hands and forced Kojong to abdicate in favor of his son, Sunjong. Events moved quickly. "The emperor's abdication edict was published at 3 AM on July 19, and the enthronement ceremony was held at 8 AM on the same day. At 2:30 PM, July 20, the new emperor [Sunjong] held his first meeting with all the ministers and officially announced his enthronement."[81] In less than twenty-four hours, Korea had a new emperor.

The timing could not have been more fortuitous. Ten days after Sunjong became emperor, Izvolsky and Motono had finally concluded their negotiations, and the Russo-Japanese Convention of 1907 was signed on July 30. Manchuria was to be divided into two spheres of influence, with Russia in the north and Japan in the south. While most accounts of the convention saw American maneuvers to preserve the Open Door in Manchuria as the primary reason behind Russo-Japanese rapprochement, in reality the status of Korea and Outer Mongolia, not Manchuria, was the primary focus of the negotiations.[82] What Hayashi wanted above all from Izvolsky was a firm assurance that Russia would not interfere in Japan's relations with Korea. For this pledge, Japan was willing to supply "a fair measure of guarantee" not to interfere with Russia's rights and privileges in Mongolia. Itō heartily approved of the quid pro quo.

Itō might have also thought that a Russo-Japanese agreement would resolve the Manchurian issue as well, since Kodama's—and the army's—main argument for keeping troops in Manchuria would have been muted. Russia no longer posed a security threat and Japanese forces could therefore be withdrawn. But just the opposite turned out to be true. With the spheres of influence now clearly defined in Manchuria, Korea, and Outer Mongolia, Japan lost the incentive to follow the Open Door and uphold the integrity of China. The old arguments about Japan having sacrificed so much blood and treasure in the hills and plains of Manchuria had won out. The Russo-Japanese Convention of 1907 settled the debate in the army's favor.

EMPEROR SUNJONG

The convention also settled the Korea problem. Diplomatically isolated, Kojong no longer had any cards left to play.[83] Sunjong, the new emperor, was much more to Itō's taste. It is not known to what degree the Korean people were aware of the limited mental acuity their thirty-three-year-old new emperor, but foreign observers were certainly mindful of his mental deficiencies and freely discussed them. John A. Cockerill, an American journalist, reported that Sunjong was "mentally flabby." Alice Graham, sister-in-law of John M. B. Sill, the American minister to Korea in 1894, wrote that "the crown prince looks quite like an imbecile [and] it is said that his looks do not belie him." Some have surmised that his condition was due to the residual effects of a coffee poisoning incident in 1898. Others attributed it to the psychological trauma surrounding his mother's death. A biography of Empress Myŏngsŏng, written from a stridently Korean nationalistic viewpoint, reported that Sunjong's mental weakness and impotence were symptoms of an opium addiction encouraged by his Japanese handlers.[84] Whatever the causes of his fragile mental state, Sunjong was far more pliable than Kojong had ever been.

On July 24, 1907, only five days after assuming the throne, Sunjong approved a new treaty giving Japan control of his nation's internal affairs, including control of the royal household treasury Kojong had used to fund his pet projects, such as The Hague emissary fiasco. Among the secret provisions of the new treaty was an agreement to disband the Korean Army. This would eliminate any possibility of organized resistance to Japanese rule by the Korean military.[85] But Itō had severely underestimated the reaction of the Korean people. Kojong's abdication followed

Sunjong, known also as Emperor Yonghŭi (1874–1926), was the second and final emperor of Korea, ruling from 1907 until 1910. He is seated second from right. Next to him is Prince Yoshihito (middle), the future emperor Taishō. The young boy on the far right is Crown Prince Yi Ŭn, Sunjong's half-brother. The photo was taken in Korea sometime in 1907. (World History Archive/Image Asset Management/agefotostock)

by the disbandment of the Korean Army caused an uproar. Disbanded soldiers filled the ranks of rebel forces by joining up with the Righteous Army. After July 1907, Itō faced the largest insurrection Japan had experienced since 1894, requiring Japan to mobilize six army divisions.[86] These developments aggravated already existing tensions in Japan between the army and navy, as army leaders such as Yamagata called for a moratorium on naval spending to accommodate the army's mobilization.[87] Meanwhile, in Manchuria, despite the transfer of the Japanese administration to the Foreign Ministry in 1906, followed by the withdrawal of troops, Japan continued to maintain its military capabilities in southern Manchuria. It did this by placing under control of the governor-general of Kwantung Leased Territories, General Ōshima in Port Arthur, a division and six additional battalions including a new battalion unit of reserve soldiers by spring of 1907.[88]

Having thus embarked upon a continental path to achieve Great Power status, Japan now faced the problems common to all continental powers:

443

the search for national security through the absorption of territory and domination of the local population. This was not the vision of Japan's maritime expansionists when they embarked upon the war with Russia.[89] Before the war, the Katsura cabinet and the *genrō* had agreed with Alfred Thayer Mahan's view of Japan as a maritime power and accepted the Open Door policy as the logical extension of his argument about commercial rather than military penetration of the continent. But the terrible sacrifices of the war, the unsatisfying conclusion at Portsmouth, fear of Russian revanchism in Manchuria, and the violent developments in Korea had changed the calculus of power. More forebodingly, though not yet understood nor realized, was that Japan's continental expansionism put it on the path to confrontation with its old friend and ally, the United States. Japan's promise to maintain "eternal peace and security in Asia" turned out to be something quite different altogether.

CHAPTER TWENTY-TWO

ANNEXATION

Following the signing of the Russo-Japanese Convention of 1907, Foreign Minister Alexander Izvolsky instructed the Russian consul in Seoul to observe extreme caution, "and to give no grounds for suspicion of anti-Japanese activity." Members of the consulate were to bear in mind that Russia's overall political goal was "to preserve stable relations with Japan."[1] If Kojong was still banking on Russia's intervention on his nation's behalf, Izvolsky made it clear this would not happen.

Rising tensions between Japan and the United States, however, offered some faint hope that Korea might be able to capitalize on the fallout between the two countries. The Japanese government was infuriated by a series of incidents in the United States in 1906 and 1907, which began with a decision by the San Francisco school board. On October 11, 1906, the school board passed a resolution to direct all Chinese, Japanese, and Korean children to separate "Oriental public schools," located in earthquake-devastated Chinatown. Active anti-Japanese agitation had been roused by the San Francisco earthquake in April, and Japanese businesses and persons became the victims of violence. At issue were the traditional arguments against immigration, centered on racism. Disputes over the Roosevelt administration's handling of the influx of Japanese immigrants incited anti-Japanese hostility on the West Coast, as it was widely seen that unless the tide was checked, or preferably stopped, amicable relations with Japan would not be possible.[2]

445

Anti-Japanese agitation in San Francisco was in large part due to the machinations of powerful local labor groups. It became a popular pastime of California politicians seeking to capitalize on fear of the Yellow Peril. Suspicions of Japanese expansionism in Manchuria and the closing of the Open Door there only added fuel to the anti-immigration fire. John Holladay Latane's *America as a World Power,* published in 1907, was typical of the kind of anxiety expressed over Japanese expansionism in Asia and the Pacific and the repercussions for American interests. He warned that America "can no longer pose as a disinterested spectator of political changes" in the Far East and that "strained relations with Japan have already resulted." He concluded: "In the reshaping of the Far East, the United States has interests that it must protect and a well-formulated policy that it cannot afford to renounce."[3]

The San Francisco decision thus arose out of a complex of factors, not least of which were Japanese military designs on Manchuria. It also gave rise to a backlash in Japan. One of the more jingoistic of the Tokyo dailies, *Mainichi shinbun,* stated on October 21 that Japan should send its navy to chastise the Americans. Meanwhile, former prime minister Ōkuma Shigenobu, founder of the Progressive Party (Shimpotō), sought to have the government recall Japan's ambassador to the United States, Aoki Shūzō, and demand an apology from as well as an indemnity for the "alleged acts of violence against Japanese subjects residing in San Francisco." Ōkuma also demanded that the school order be rescinded.[4] Rumors circulated in January 1907 that thousands of Japanese veterans of the Russo-Japanese War were "fomenting a movement in secret to organize military units on American soil." Ambassador Aoki insisted that the US government "grant all rights granted to citizens or subjects of the most favored nations [to Japanese residents in the United States], which included the privilege of Japanese children to attend public schools."[5]

Roosevelt did his best to diffuse the situation by threatening to sue the San Francisco Board of Education. Addressing Congress on December 3, he announced that "anti-Japanese hostility is most discreditable to us as a people and maybe fraught with the gravest consequences to the nation . . . To shut them out from the public schools is a wicked absurdity."[6] Nevertheless, the president feared that should his administration win a lawsuit in California, "there would be such a protest on the [West] Coast as to precipitate a war."[7] Itō and Ambassador Aoki were so alarmed by the California crisis, they recommended that an "explicit understanding with the United States" be arrived at so as to avoid a diplomatic rupture.[8]

Prime Minister Saionji also did his best to calm things down, reminding the Japanese people in a speech in January 1908 that "there should still continue to exist the anti-Japanese agitations in San Francisco . . . is a circumstance regretted alike by both countries."[9] Although the school order was amended to apply only to Chinese and Korean children, the aura of mutual suspicion and anger never quite went away.[10]

Korean immigrants in the United States experienced the same discrimination as their Japanese and Chinese counterparts, although their numbers were relatively small. Between 1889 and 1910, the total immigrant entries by group were approximately 148,000 Japanese, 22,400 Chinese, and just 8,300 Koreans.[11] Higher Korean emigration to the United States and its territories only began in 1903, when many immigrants were recruited to work in Hawaiian sugar plantations.[12] But there also existed a smaller group of Korean students who were encouraged by American missionaries in Korea to study in American colleges. Included in this group was Syngman Rhee; his close associate Pak Yong-nam, who had shared a prison cell with him when they were incarcerated for antigovernment activities; and An Chang-ho, who had arrived a few years earlier, in 1902. Pak attended Hastings College in Nebraska; An was a missionary-educated Korean Christian. Following the outbreak of the Russo-Japanese War, a number of Korean organizations began to appear in the United States to advocate for Korean independence in anticipation of Japan's victory. The Mutual Assistance Society (MAS) (Kongnip hyŏphoe) based in San Francisco, was the most far-reaching. Established by An Chang-ho in 1905, its newsletter, *Kongnip sinmun,* was distributed twice a month to the Korean diaspora in places as far away as Vladivostok, Honolulu, and even Harbin.[13] The organization's primary task was to promote public awareness of Korea's plight and to raise money for Korean independence.

Although the Mutual Assistance Society worked through nonviolent means, it did not disown political violence. For example, one of its members, Chŏn Myŏng-un, was involved in the assassination of the former American adviser to Japan, Durham Stevens, in San Francisco in March 1908. When the assassins were charged, the Mutual Assistance Society rallied behind them, hiring lawyers, soliciting defense funds, and providing interpreters.[14] The Stevens case provided an occasion for Koreans in the United States to unite around a shared nationalist cause, but a greater opportunity was provided by the ongoing diplomatic crisis between the United States and Japan. The *Kongnip sinmun* reported that "a Japanese-American war was inevitable" and would provide the perfect opportunity for Korea to regain its independence. "If the two countries go to war, Japan will no longer be able to influence Korea . . . Japan does not stand a chance against America."[15]

In August 1908 the Mutual Assistance Society sent a delegation to the Democratic National Convention in Denver.[16] The delegates included Syngman Rhee and Yi Sang-sŏl, one of the three delegates on the failed mission to The Hague. Their aim was to leverage Japanese-American acrimony for Korea's benefit. The Koreans hoped to capitalize on the anti-Japanese sentiment contained in a plank in the Democratic platform calling for "the exclusion of Asiatic laborers from the United States," which was directed specifically at Japan.[17] Although nothing came of these efforts, the Stevens assassination and the Democratic Convention did succeed in bringing the Korean American community together. In February 1909 An Chang-ho established the Korean National Association (KNA) (Taehanin kungminhoe), whose purpose was "to unite overseas Koreans into one organization" with the overall goal of achieving Korean independence.[18] Although the KNA began with two regional headquarters in Hawaii and San Francisco, it soon branched out, establishing regional headquarters and local chapters in California, Hawaii, the Russian Far East, and Manchuria.[19] Over the next decade Koreans in these places became all loosely connected. Although their methods for achieving independence varied greatly, for the first time Koreans outside the peninsula came together in the shared cause of gaining their nation's full sovereignty.[20] Hoping to capitalize on the growing acrimonious relations between the United States and Japan, Syngman Rhee actively sought American help in this endeavor.

RIGHTEOUS ARMY

Inside Korea, Itō worked diligently to assume all levers of power in the Korean government. A key provision of the 1907 Japan-Korea Treaty was the secret agreement to disband the Korean Army. The idea was not simply a response to The Hague mission fiasco; it had been considered as early as November 1905 when the Protectorate Treaty was signed. A major question facing Japan after the war with Russia was whether Korea should revert to civilian control. Earlier in 1904 the Japanese military attaché in Korea, Ijichi Kōsuke, had submitted a proposal to General Headquarters strongly advocating direct military supervision of the peninsula, a plan endorsed by the Korean Garrison Army General Staff.[21] They based their arguments partly on past precedent. A major failing by Inoue Kaoru as minister to Korea after the Sino-Japanese War was the precipitous withdrawal of Japanese troops and reliance on the Korean emperor to get things done. Itō was persuaded, and endorsed continuing Japan's military control of Korea, despite his opposition to a similar arrangement in Manchuria.[22]

On the evening of July 31, barely a week after the 1907 treaty was signed, the order to disband the Korean Army was issued. The following morning at 7 AM, General Hasegawa Yoshimichi summoned all Korean commanding officers to his headquarters to deliver the orders to their units.[23] Itō and Hasegawa understood the move was controversial, but they also believed it was necessary.[24] Maintaining an organized force of armed Korean soldiers with questionable loyalty was neither wise nor viable at a time when the resident-general was consolidating his power over the peninsula. Hasegawa ordered two squadrons of cavalry to accompany the Korean commanding officers back to their units as they disbanded and ordered them "to use military force if deemed necessary."[25]

The Korean soldiers were, predictably, outraged. Major Pak Se-han, who belonged to a unit in Seoul, committed suicide in protest, which incited a mutiny.[26] Provincial units also resisted the disbandment order. The outpost in Kanghwa mutinied on August 11 but was quickly suppressed. The Wŏnsan Regiment, however, was able to escape with all its munitions before it was formally disbanded.[27]

As the disbandment proceeded, the Japanese suddenly faced an unanticipated danger as thousands of disaffected soldiers joined the ranks of the rebel Righteous Army and took up arms against the Japanese. By the end of August the Japanese faced the largest Korean insurgency since the suppression campaigns of 1894. Estimates vary on the strength of the Righteous Army, but the best estimate is that by the end of 1907 there were approximately fifty thousand members waging guerrilla warfare; the numbers swelled to seventy thousand in 1908. As the scale and effectiveness of the Japanese counter operations intensified, the ranks of the Righteous Army rapidly decreased to twenty-eight thousand in 1909 and nineteen thousand in 1910.[28]

The Japanese faced a situation in 1907–1910 that differed greatly in many important ways from the suppression campaigns waged in 1894–1895. First was the geographical scope of the campaign. The suppression campaigns against the Tonghaks had largely been fought in the populated south and northwest.[29] This time, most of the intense fighting was waged in the more sparsely populated northeast. Another important contrast was the role of the Korean government and people. In 1894 Korean government troops and private militia groups had fought alongside the Japanese to crush the Tonghaks. This time the Japanese faced the rebel forces alone. These two factors logically resulted in the exertion of much greater effort over a longer period of time to suppress the Righteous Army. The 1894–1895 suppression campaigns were wrapped up quickly, within a matter of months, while fighting the Righteous Army dragged on for three years.

The Righteous Army was also a far more cohesive and effective force than the peasant armies of 1894–1895 had ever been. One reason was the injection of professional soldiers into its ranks. Many Righteous Army commanders, like Yi Pŏm-yun and Ch'oe Chae-hyŏng, had fought alongside the Russians during the Russo-Japanese War and received training and equipment from Russian officers. Others had served in the Korean Army and had been trained by the Japanese. In January 1908, Kim In-su, captain of Kojong's Imperial Guards, arrived in Khabarovsk, and three months later Yi Sang-sŏl and Yi Wi-jŏng (Yi Pŏm-jin's son, also known by his Russian name, Vladimir Sergeevich Lee) arrived. Both men had been sent to the Hague Conference the year before.[30] With the support of the ethnic Korean communities in Primorskaya and Manchuria, Righteous Army detachments near the border of Korea and Manchuria and the South Ussuri Krai were able to conduct a series of successful military operations beginning in the summer of 1907 against Japanese garrisons in Kyŏnghŭng, Hoeryŏng, and Myŏngch'ŏn, inflicting serious casualties.[31]

On May 15, 1908, the border commissar of South Ussuri Krai, E. Smirnov, reported that "Koreans are donating weapons to the [Righteous] volunteer army all over Russian Far East." He also stated that in areas where ethnic Koreans had settled along the border areas of Korea and Manchuria, the honghuzi were helping them. "These Korean villages are not under Chinese control and are ruled by self-governing bandits in the areas of the eastern Russia-China borderland," he reported. "The area is comprised of villages surrounded by mountains and forests, so it is a convenient location for the Koreans . . . The Korean political exiles are acting in areas in Manchuria under the silent support of the Chinese; Chinese residents in these areas who are hostile toward the Japanese are sympathetic with the Koreans' anti-Japanese activities in Manchuria." He added, "The anti-Japanese struggle that unfolded in Korea is successfully progressing in the regions of the Tumen and Yalu rivers. Three weeks ago, Japanese soldiers near Musan were annihilated; the city itself has been seized by armed Koreans and 150 Japanese were annihilated near Samsun."[32]

The Koreans also received tacit support from local Russian authorities, who were "well aware that Korean volunteer armies are forming into Korea from Russia." Smirnov reported in April 1908 that "the nest of Korean political emigrants in Novokievskiy has been stirred up under the command of Yi Pŏm-yun, Ch'oe Chae-hyŏng and Yi Wi-jŏng (Vladimir Sergeevich Lee)." A Righteous Army detachment of seven hundred men under the command of Hong Pŏm-do seized the cities of Sansa, Kapsan, and Ch'ŏngjin, destroying their Japanese garrisons. By the end of the month, "nearly 1,000 rebels had gone from Russian territory to North Korea," Smirnov reported. He believed that "with the onset of summer, a bloody drama will be playing out in the eastern and northern regions of Korea, and the upper regions of the Yalu and Tuman Rivers."[33]

By June 1908 the Japanese were experiencing severe disruptions in their communications. Smirnov reported in July that "telegraph poles and lines of communication between Kyŏnghŭng, Kaebong, and Hoeryŏng have been suspended due to the armed attacks of the Korean political exiled." Moreover, "Japanese garrison bases and smaller units [located] downstream of the Tumen River were being annihilated." The Japanese attempted to stem the tide of the attacks by employing the Ilchinhoe as spies to get advance warnings, but they were "were being ruthlessly hunted down and executed by the Korean patriots [rebels]."[34] Support for the Righteous Army surged.[35]

In northwest P'yŏngan Province, several cities came under rebel occupation. The district of Musan was in rebel hands in June 1908. "All this is lifting up the Koreans' spirits, and in Manchuria, and in our country, the Korean people are raising money and buying weapons."[36] On July 10 Smirnov reported that "one Japanese company suffered a crushing defeat after being besieged near Unsŏngsan, about 25 kilometers from Hoeryŏng. Sixty-four Japanese soldiers were killed and 30 were injured. The rebels had no fatalities and only four of them were injured."[37]

Vasily Flug, military governor of the Primorskaya Oblast, was becoming increasingly wary of rebel activity.[38] In April 1908 he requested instructions from the Ministry of Foreign Affairs on handling the Korean rebels, as "this business is related to the purview of higher politics." He was also nervous "not to make any political mistakes or tactless errors in our relations with the Japanese." Smirnov was informed that Yi Pŏm-yun had transported weapons from Vladivostok to Novokievsky, and was "preparing to cross the border into Korea," but he was alarmed to find out that twenty Russians were in this group. "From my perspective," he wrote, "I [Smirnov] having no prior knowledge of the action of the No-vokievskiy immigrants, must watch them through my fingers." However, Smirnov did not think it prudent for Russians to get directly involved with the Korean insurgency, as doing so might heighten tensions with Japan. Flug shared Smirnov's concerns. They agreed that while not "specifically showing official support, we must also not obstruct their [the Korean rebels'] activities, as long as they do not violate our laws."[39]

Russia's hands-off policy was not enough for Japan. It wanted the Russian government to actively intervene to suppress the rebels. The Russian Foreign Ministry demurred. In late July 1908 a confidential memo from Russian ambassador to Tokyo, Malevsky-Malevich, informed P. F. Unterberger, the Priamursky governor-general, that "the Russian government is interested in eliminating even the slightest suspicion of [our] supporting the insurgency in Korea." He instructed Unterberger to "take active measures to disarm the [Korean] conspirators and to prevent Russian participation in the conspiracy," adding, "If Yi Pŏm-yun is not a Russian citizen, then exile him from the empire."[40] Unterberger thus began a crackdown on Korean ŭibyŏng activities in the Priamursky Oblast. Yi Pŏm-yun was given notice to leave Novokievsky; Russian citizens were also instructed to no longer cooperate with the Koreans, tacitly or otherwise.[41]

In Manchuria, too, Korean rebels were coming under increasing pressure from local Chinese authorities. On the basis of the 1907 Korea-Japan Treaty, Japan claimed jurisdiction over Korean subjects in Kando (Jiandao), the ethnic Korean enclave on the border along the north bank of the Tumen River (located in modern-day Jilin Province), and moved into the territory in force in August 1907. By August 1908 Smirnov reported that "following the Chinese government's yielding of Jiandao," the Japanese were "reinforcing their positions" and hunting down the rebels. "Thanks to China, [Japan's] vigorous efforts in quietly executing Koreans is being kept secret."[42] Meanwhile, A. S. Somov, the Russian consul in Seoul, was instructed "to observe extreme caution in his relations with Koreans," and to quickly "squash all undesirable gossip about our potential aid that might arise," since "in refraining from encouraging Koreans toward any attempt at struggle, we are in fact doing them a service, since we are depriving Japan of an essential weapon—the justification for spreading and strengthening their supremacy."[43]

As the Righteous Army was being squeezed from their bases of support in Russia and Manchuria, the Japanese launched a scorched-earth campaign meant to put pressure on the rebels fighting inside Korea. F. A. McKenzie, a correspondent for the *Daily Mail,* was the only Western reporter to witness the fighting directly. According to him, the favorite tactic employed by Japanese soldiers was to terrorize Korean farmers—to prevent them from giving aid and succor to the rebels by burning their villages to the ground.[44]

Japanese soldiers were also accused of committing unheard-of outrages and atrocities. The rape of Korean women, in particular, produced a terrifying reaction from the local population.[45] The Japanese apparently executed rebels who surrendered as well as anyone suspected of assisting them. "When describing these executions to me, the Koreans always finished up by mentioning how, after the volley had been fired, the Japanese officer in command of the firing party went up to the corpse and plunged his sword into it or hacked it."[46] To McKenzie, the Korean rebels were patriotic yet ill-fated heroes. "A pitiful group they seemed—men already doomed to certain death, fighting an absolutely hopeless cause . . . [yet] at least they were showing their countrymen an example of patriotism, however mistaken their methods of displaying it might be."[47]

Not every Westerner saw the Righteous Army in such a positive light. American missionary Charlie Clark, who spent much of 1907 traveling east of Seoul in Kyŏnggi and Kangwŏn Provinces, recalled the destruction wrought by both sides. "I saw the ruins of hundreds of houses burned either by the Japanese or the 'euibyong' for both are in the business. At Yanggeun, 300 houses, at Tuksoo, 80, Yongmoon, 80 and so on. These were the largest towns but every day we passed isolated houses and small villagers burned in whole or in part. Hundreds are living in caves . . . The Japanese have been very cruel, in some places, but on the whole, no worse than the other side."

The "euibyong" are the real oppressors of the poor. Some months ago, there was a faint spark of patriotism in this movement and it no doubt lingers in some individuals, but my conclusion, from what I saw, is that 90% of them are in it for Number One and not for the sake of the country. They have never, so far as I could find, sought the Japanese to fight them. From the beginning, they have gone around in bands of 30 to 1500 men, going from village to village, summoning the leaders of the town, and demanding great sums of money. Whenever they refused, they murdered or tortured without limit. In Hong Sung Eup alone, they have squeezed a total in money and goods of 46,000 *nyang,* or over ¥5000, as the exchange is now. They have actually taken the clothes off the backs of the poor, where no money was available. When the Japanese appear, they scatter and run.[48]

Smirnov confirmed some of Clark's observations. In June 1908 he confronted Ch'oe Chae-hyŏng over the "fraudulent" activities of "receiving money and using his army for his own profit."[49] Yi Pŏm-yun was also quick to condemn Ch'oe and his men, accusing them "of acting more like robbers and not like patriots."[50]

By 1909 the number of battles fought between *ŭibyŏng* and Japanese troops had decreased rapidly. This was due in large part to Russia's crackdowns on Righteous Army activity within its borders but also because as the *ŭibyŏng* became increasingly reluctant to take on the Japanese. In February 1909 Smirnov reported that Yi Pŏm-yun was experiencing significant difficulties due to a lack of funding and other problems. Soon thereafter Yi was forced to disband his army and went into hiding. "The Japanese sent in spies to find and kill Yi and all his close associates. We [Russians] obtained information that anyone who succeeded in this mission (to assassinate) Yi would receive a reward of 10,000 rubles."[51]

The situation was similarly going poorly for the Righteous Army in the south, the most fertile and populous in Korea. A Russian report published in 1906 noted that the southern provinces of Chŏlla and Ch'ungch'ŏng were the most fully exploited by the Japanese and accounted for nearly 65 percent of the entire Korean population. Its economy was also almost completely dependent on Japan, its main export of rice going nearly exclusively to that country. Most Japanese established their residences along the railroad line, especially near the Taegu, Taejŏn, and Pusan stations, and in port cities such as Chinhae. Thus, when the Japanese launched "the great southern pacification campaign" in the fall of 1909, the rebels found it much harder to organize and to hide than did their counterparts in the north. Nor were they as well trained. Of the three local organized Righteous Army bands in the south, two were led by former high Confucian officials, Min Chong-sik and Ch'oe Ik-hyŏn, while the other army was led by a minor government official, Sin Ŭl-sŏk. Min led a force of about 500 *ŭibyŏng* rebels in Ch'ungch'ŏng Province. Ch'oe's force consisted of about 450 rebels and was located in Chŏlla. Sin's force, located in north

Kyŏngsang Province, was larger, about a thousand men strong. These poorly equipped, poorly trained peasant armies, similar in force to what the Japanese had faced in 1894, were no match for the two Japanese modern battalions employed to destroy them.[52]

THE KOREAN REVIVAL MOVEMENT, 1907

The northwest provinces of Hwanghae and P'yŏngan were also affected by these upheavals, but unlike the other provinces, in this region the North American Presbyterian Mission and the North American Methodist Episcopal Mission were firmly rooted. Both provinces also had a history of strong Christian presence, particularly in P'yŏngan. The presence of these foreign missionaries frequently served as a kind of protective buffer for their congregations against abuses by local officials or the Japanese. Uchida Ryōhei, a close advisor of the Ilchinhoe, reported that "more than half of the population of P'yŏngyang was Christian in 1907." "In P'yŏngyang there are the Minkai [K. Minhoe, or Peoples Council], the Self-Strengthening Society and Youth Associations . . . Everything is being run by Christians." The collapse of Ilchinhoe had strengthened the Christian communities in this region by allowing them to seize the Ilchinhoe's reformist message for themselves. Uchida explained that

> P'yŏngyang is called the "den of Christianity" . . . Ever since the Ilchinhoe began acting as an intermediary between the government officials and the Korean people to "protect lives and wealth," each church began openly declaring that it would also protect those who wish to enter the church in order to recruit new followers. The Ilchinhoe were unable to do anything about Japanese troops; the Christians on the other hand were taken seriously by the Japanese and thus were believed by their followers to have great influence and power. In addition, as Japanese military presence became more widespread, Christian pastors nursed their followers—as a mother would nurse her child—and awaited the right opportunity. Taking advantage of the Ilchinhoe's activities, the Christians now make strenuous efforts to declare their independence, saying that being anti-Japanese meant being anti-Ilchinhoe.[53]

This area had been a stronghold of the Ilchinhoe during the war. It also had a long history of antigovernment activity and civil unrest since the late 1890s.[54] The growth of Christianity owed much to the weakness of the Korean state and the willingness of Christian missionaries to use their power to protect, and sometimes aggressively assert, the interests of their converts.

Taking advantage of antigovernment fervor, the Ilchinhoe initially made strong inroads in this area with its pro-Japanese reformist message.[55] Missionary William N. Blair recalled how the Koreans in Anju, in south P'yŏngan Province, took up arms on behalf of the Japanese against the Russians.[56] The end of the war and the signing of the Korea-Japan Protectorate Treaty in November 1905, however, resulted in deep disillusionment with Japan. Ilchinhoe membership in the region subsequently plummeted as attacks against them increased. Membership in Christian churches, on the other hand, surged.

In August 1906 Methodist and Presbyterian missionaries in P'yŏngyang organized a Bible study and prayer conference that set the stage for a national phenomenon of unparalleled religious and national significance in Korea. Presbyterian minister George S. McCune recalled, "After Christmas [of 1906], the missionaries began praying for God's power . . . We began the meeting by confessions among ourselves . . . so that we might have the blessings we were praying for."[57] Many confessions were taken up by those seeking redemption for "the sins of hating the Japanese." Blair noted, "We felt that the Korean Church needed not only to repent of hating the Japanese but a clearer vision of all sin against God." He continued: "We felt that the whole Church, to become holy, needed a vision of God's holiness, that embittered souls needed to have their thoughts taken away from the national situation to their own personal relations with the Master."[58]

The Great Protestant Revival of 1907 spread across the country from P'yŏngyang, and thousands of Koreans gathered for fervent, even frenzied, praying, "confessing their sins and begging forgiveness both from God and from those they had wronged."[59] "The prayer sounded to me like the falling of many waters, an ocean of prayer beating against God's throne," recalled Blair. "As the prayer continued, a spirit of heaviness and sorrow for sin came down upon the audience. Over on one side, someone began to weep, and in a moment the whole audience was weeping."[60]

The missionaries were amazed at what was taking place. The revival movement "awed" Charlie Clark, who in his country travels visited many villages where local churches were filled with villagers praying and weeping. "Every day we saw them with tears confessing one to the other and begging forgiveness . . . As in P'yŏngyang, prayer aloud went on all

Weekly prayer meeting in P'yŏngyang with children, probably 1907 or 1908. The enthusiastic response of the northwest provinces to the Protestant message is indicated not only by the large membership in the region but also by the number of children enrolled in missionary schools. (Methodist Episcopal Church/Wikimedia Commons)

the time with 300 to 500 people praying aloud at once."[61] The message of repentance and redemption in the face of the collapse of the nation's autonomy and independence seemed to have contributed to Koreans' receptiveness to the Protestant message. But instead of focusing on the abject conditions of their nation, the Great Revival of 1907 promoted a reformist message that was uniquely personal. Although Koreans Protestants had not given up on attaining the independence of their country, they saw the regeneration of Korean society as starting from their own individual and personal spiritual redemption, which took precedence over political agitation.

The psychological development of the people as "modern and enlightened" citizens was to become one of the major tenets of cultural nationalism that took root during the second decade of the twentieth century. The most famous proponent of this national movement was Yun Ch'i-ho, a key member of the defunct Independence Club. During the Great Revival,

Yun helped to establish a number of new organizations, the most prominent of which were the New Citizens Society (Sinminhoe) and the Youth Student Fraternity (Ch'ŏngnyŏn hak'hoe), both with the purpose of promoting the spiritual and moral growth of the Korean people through education, commerce, and industry. "To all who desire reform of corrupt old customs and are willing to cultivate true public virtues we declare that this cannot be achieved by academic ability or fine writing and rhetoric alone," he declared. "It will be attained by forming a grand spiritual organization of young men of one mind; by the mutual exchange and application of knowledge; by formulating forward-looking policies, despising backwardness and danger; by stemming the angry tide of convention regardless of the cost; and by making your youthful renewal in pursuit of the way of happiness the pivotal point of our [national] re-revival."[62]

In April 1907 Yun envisioned establishing "a model Christian settlement" with other Christian leaders—including Syngman Rhee, who had briefly returned to Korea in 1910 to head the Seoul YMCA—as its version of utopia, "a visible alternative to the [violent] methods of the patriotic Righteous Army guerrillas."[63] The 1907 Protestant revivalist message of "national uplift" based on principles of individual self-development and Christian teachings continued to find a receptive audience in many sectors of Korean society. Their beliefs and hopes for Korea began to diverge sharply from those harbored by Righteous Army leaders like Yi Pŏm-yun and Ch'oe Chae-hyŏng. Although all these groups had been connected through their association with the Korean National Association (KNA), by 1913 noticeable divisions were already becoming apparent. That same year, An Chang-ho founded the Hŭngsadan [Young Korean Society] in San Francisco to prepare not only for Korea's eventual liberation from Japan but for Korea's modernization through the cultivation of an "enlightened" and democratic citizenry. As Soviet historian Boris Pak observed, "It soon became clear that part of the KNA leadership had fallen under the influence of American missionaries, and, in guiding things towards a more pro-American politics, this group had begun to deploy not just anti-Japanese but also anti-Russian propaganda."[64]

Two main political groups thus began to emerge during this period. One group, populated by Christians and capitalists, espoused an outwardly oriented nationalism with a developmental agenda aimed at reforming the nation and integrating it within the wider world order. The other, essentially in opposition to the first, was followed by reformed Confucianists and Righteous Army followers and was inwardly oriented, pursuing a defensive nationalism premised on the idea that the purity of the nation must be preserved and protected from external "contamination." Vladimir Lenin's advocacy of national self-determination and anticolonial revolution would later inspire a number of these nationalists to channel their anti-Japanese sentiments into a revolutionary project to defend Korea from foreign encroachment and the capitalist West. Eventually these two strands of modern Korean nationalism became the foundational basis for capitalist South Korea and communist North Korea. The division of the peninsula, though crudely drawn at the 38th parallel by the United States and the Soviet Union in 1945, actually traces its origins to the years following the Russo-Japanese War or even earlier.

EMPEROR SUNJONG'S INSPECTION TOUR

Itō's sense of frustration was palpable when he resigned his post as resident-general in June 1909. He had been unable to implement his reformist agenda, and unrest throughout the country amplified voices within the Japanese government that now called for the annexation of Korea. Itō had never entirely ruled out annexation as a solution to the Korea problem, but he had always held out hope it might be avoided. Yet by the end of his residency, he believed the time was right for his successor, Sone Arasuke, to move Japan and Korea beyond "trivial arguments" and "work together to unite the two countries."[65] What had led to his change of heart?

During the winter of 1908 Itō proposed a major propaganda offensive. As Emperor Meiji had done in the early days of the Meiji Restoration, he believed that a series of imperial tours by Emperor Sunjong might help buoy a sense of national belonging and unify the country through the symbol of the royal family. The hope was that the Korean people might rally around their new emperor, encouraging the acceptance of unsettling reforms while also abandoning their resistance to Japanese-Korean unity.[66] The itinerary included overnight visits to Taegu, Pusan, and Masan, and several stops along the Seoul-Pusan line. It was to be a short trip, January 7–11, 1909.

The travel entourage, consisting of Emperor Sunjong, Itō, Prime Minister Yi Wan-yong, Crown Prince Yi Ŭn (Sungjong's younger half-brother), Home Minister Song Pyŏng-jun, and a retinue of other officials, set off from Seoul station on the morning of January 7. Every leg of the journey was highly scripted, but the "tens of thousands" of Koreans and Japanese who lined the streets to welcome them seemed to exhibit genuine enthusiasm.

The many Japanese made their reception especially warm. At Pusan, Sunjong toured the Chamber of Commerce and then boarded the cruiser *Azuma*, flagship of the Second Squadron, to observe a demonstration of fleet maneuvering and other tactical exercises.[67] Writing from Masan on January 11, Itō was delighted to report to his friend Kaneko Kentarō that "the dispatch of the fleet has been the most profitable event of the tour and the emperor is greatly impressed by it."[68] The entourage was warmly received everywhere the party went and there were no serious incidents. The Japanese press also appeared satisfied. The *Tokyo Asahi* reported approvingly, "It was but a short time ago that Japanese emperors themselves were influenced by the Chinese example of shutting themselves within the palace gates, and if ever they went out, staying within a single province of Yamashiro. A Chinese tributary [state] until only recent times, Korea had completely followed this [same] Chinese example, and the present trip through a part of the country is really an unprecedented event." It continued, "The paper reflects credit on Prince Itō for the happy idea and its successful execution."[69]

The apparent success of the imperial tour prompted Itō to consider doing another one, this time to the northwest provinces. This would prove to be a huge mistake. Pusan and Masan were largely Japanese cities, but few Japanese lived north of Seoul, and the Koreans who lived in Hwanghae and P'yŏngan Provinces were not inclined to be friendly.[70] Nevertheless, Itō decided to proceed, using the Seoul-Ŭiju rail line with stops at Kaesŏng, P'yŏngyang, Chŏngju, and Sinŭiju on the Manchurian border.

On January 27 the imperial party set off. The *Keijo Shimpo* reported that "the Resident-General received in northern Korea a very chilly reception from the Koreans."[71] At Kaesŏng, young students from a local missionary school who had come to greet the imperial train only waved Korean flags, not Japanese ones, reflecting, as one observer noted, "the anti-Japanese feeling among them." Education Minister Yi Che-gŏn, who had been responsible for organizing the welcome, defended the flag bearers, saying that as an attendant to the Korean emperor, Itō deserved neither public salutes nor flag-waving receptions.[72] Home Minister Song Pyŏng-jun, apparently frustrated by the affront to Itō, got into a brawl with one of the emperor's aides-de-camp.[73] But the most unfortunate result of the tour occurred after the emperor's return to Seoul on February 3. Song was interviewed by *Asahi Shimbun* about the tour, and in published remarks on February 16 he lashed out against the Korean Christian community and American missionaries: "The most serious question relates to the native Christians, numbering about 350,000, whose affiliations are of questionable nature," he declared. "They are united in the common object of opposing the present administration and resort to underhanded methods." Song then dropped a bombshell. "I am going to adopt drastic steps and annihilate them as soon as they take up armed insurrection. Of course, they are backed by a group of American missionaries. This will likely become one of the most important questions in Korea."[74]

The American ambassador to Japan, Thomas O'Brien, was appalled and demanded an explanation from Itō. The matter was real cause for alarm, as it threatened to rupture Japan's already tense relationship with the United States. Itō responded defensively that "Minister Song has not yet mastered the Japanese language and is, therefore, unable to express himself satisfactorily in that language." He assured O'Brien that he supported the American missionaries in Korea. "Christians in Korea will continue to receive equal treatment with other subjects and to be dealt with only in case of a distinct violation of the laws of the country. It may be true that among many Korean Christians not a few are attempting to make use of that religion for inspiring the idea of independence. This fact, however, cannot be regarded as due to the instigation of the American missionaries."[75]

While Itō went into damage control, Song was forced to resign.[76] Itō replaced him with Pak Che-jun, a political adversary of Song and an ally of Prime Minister Yi Wan-yong. Song, whose ongoing conflicts with Yi had been bothersome but tolerable, went too far in his outburst against American missionaries, which threatened to undermine Itō's position as Japanese resident-general. He had to be replaced.

On April 10 Itō received Katsura and Komura at his residence. They had come prepared to discuss the annexation question. Knowing Itō's feelings on the subject, they brought with them "detailed reports to answer any question Itō might ask." Both were stunned at how easily Itō yielded on the annexation issue. His chief of foreign affairs, Komatsu Midori, recalled: "Itō listened to their words while smoking and then finally replied, 'Well, [I suppose] there is no other way' . . . Katsura and Komura were prepared to have a big argument with Itō . . . and they were very pleased to discover Itō's unexpected attitude."[77] The disappointing results of Sunjong's imperial tour, the cold reception they had received in Hwanghae and P'yŏngan Provinces, and Song's bitter remarks about Korean Christians and American missionaries had convinced Itō that the status quo could not continue. But questions still remained: How was annexation to be achieved? What steps would be necessary for its imple-mentation? How long would the process take? And most importantly, how would the other powers respond to Japan's annexation of Korea?

ITŌ'S LAST TRIP

In June 1909 Sone Arasuke was appointed the second resident-general of Korea. Itō, meanwhile, was spending his time as the self-appointed royal tutor to Korean crown prince Yi Ŭn. A matter of considerable controversy at the time, the position had allowed him to remove the eleven-year-old prince from his family in Korea and bring him up as a member of the Japanese royal family (Yi Ŭn later married the Japanese princess Masako of Nashimoto).[78] That summer Itō ran into Gotō Shinpei. Before becoming president of the South Manchurian Railway Company (SMRC), Gotō had served as the civil administrator of Taiwan. His mentor, Kodama Gentarō, the fourth governor-general, had selected Gotō to help him administer the island in 1898. Gotō was able to implement rigorous reform programs that transformed Taiwan into a successful modern Japanese colony. By the time Gotō left in 1906 to take over the SMRC, the colony was eco-nomically self-supporting, a "model" achievement compared to Itō's frus-trated efforts in Korea.[79] When Katsura became prime minister again in July 1908, Gotō became minister of communications and head of the Railway Bureau.

Gotō urged Itō to make a voyage to China and the Russian Far East to help handle anti-Japanese troubles brewing in China and to smooth things over with Russia on the Korean annexation issue. At the time, China was in turmoil following the death of both Empress Dowager Cixi in November 1908 and Emperor Guangxu, who passed away just one day before Cixi, of poisoning. "With the death of Empress Dowager Cixi, China has been weakened and it is now possible to begin establishing a new order in the East," Gotō informed Itō. More urgently, "the principal power of the Peking Court will hereafter be placed in the hands of Zai-feng (Prince Chun) [and] he is not interested in being a friend of Japan."[80] Although the Qing would reluctantly come around to signing a new agree-ment with Japan over the disputed territory of Kando (Jiandao) in September 1909, the situation had created a new wave of anti-Japanese resentment in China.[81] To Sun Yat-sen and his anti-Qing followers, the Jiandao agreement was another indication that the Qing could not be trusted to protect China from rapacious encroachments of foreign powers. Gotō told

Itō that he would help arrange a meeting between Itō and Russian finance minister Vladimir Kokovtsov to come to an understanding over Far Eastern affairs. It was also imperative to finally settle the Korean annexation issue. "Itō's driving force in making the voyage," Gotō later confided, "was the wish to complete the annexation of Korea and to seek Russia's and China's understanding [in that endeavor]."[82]

Kokovtsov set out for Harbin on the first week of October, reaching the city on the evening of October 25, in time to prepare for Itō's arrival the next day.[83] What the Russian finance minister did not know was that another person was waiting for Itō in Harbin. An Chung-gǔn was a Catholic from Hwanghae Province whose family had been harassed for decades for antigovernment activities. In 1907 An left his home in northern Korea for Vladivostok in an act of self-exile over Kojong's forced abdication, which, he later wrote, "outraged not just me but all the citizens of the Korean emperor, and all of them developed one tortuous wish—to revive Korean power."[84] In Vladivostok he met up with Ch'oe Chae-hyǒng and Yi Pǒm-yun, both key leaders in the Righteous Army. He also became friendly with Chǒn Myǒng-un, one of the two conspirators involved in Durham Stevens's assassination in March 1908. The Russian ambassador to Japan, Nikolai Malevsky-Malevich, later remarked that behind Prince Itō's assassination stood a circle of Korean revolutionaries "from Vladivostok to San Francisco."[85]

By seven o'clock on the morning of October 26, a large crowd had already gathered for Itō's 9 AM arrival. Japanese consul-general Kawakami Toshitsune, who oversaw the security arrangements, had decided as a safety measure to forgo inviting guests and holding a welcoming ceremony and to only admit to the train platform Japanese who were known to him and his staff personally.[86] "The train pulled in exactly on time," Kokovtsov recalled. "I immediately entered the Prince's car, where he welcomed me and conveyed to me the greetings of his government." Traveling with Itō was Secretary Mori Yasujirō and Tanaka Seijirō, director of the South Manchurian Railway. "After their [Itō's and Kokovtsov's] conversation, Itō followed the Russian minister onto the platform, passing some Russian soldiers who were all lined up to greet Itō," Kawakami later recalled. "Suddenly, a Korean man in a suit emerged from the line of [Russian] soldiers and shot Itō three times with a revolver." According to some witnesses, he shouted "Banzai Korea!" Although An was immediately seized by the neck and arm by nearby officers, he managed to get off another three shots. One bullet hit Kawakami, injuring his right arm. Mori and Tanaka were spared and suffered only minor injuries.[87] An made no attempt to escape, and along with three accomplices was arrested by Chinese authorities and delivered to the Japanese moments after the incident.[88] According to Murota Yoshifumi, a member of Itō's entourage, the dying man had asked who had attacked him, and when he was told that it was a Korean, the sixty-nine-year-old Itō had murmured, "What a fool!" These were his last words.[89]

The shock of Itō's untimely death by a Korean assassin's hand convinced the Japanese government of the necessity to formally annex Korea as soon as possible.[90] "He had gone on his Far Eastern tour to make the case for Korean annexation. His untimely death ironically made it for him," remarked Komatsu. The assassination also made Kokovtsov realize how urgent the Korean problem had become for Japan. "The incident not only showed the Russians, but also the entire world, that Japan's handling of Korea was understandable. Although Itō's death impeded the establishment of a new East Asian policy, he actually contributed to the immediate mission—obtaining Russian support for the annexation of Korea."[91]

This support was premised on coming to some sort of permanent agreement with Japan on Manchuria. American maneuvers to preserve the Open Door had once again threatened Russian interests there. In 1908 an investment banker, Willard Straight, offered yet another plan to pour American capital into Manchuria with the aim of internationalizing the Manchurian railways. Straight received permission from Secretary of State Elihu Root to draft an agreement between Tang Shaoyi, governor of Fengtian (Liaoning) Province, and Xu Shichang, viceroy of Manchuria, and a group of American investors for the financing, construction, and operation of a railway from Jinzhou to Aigun. The project was backed by Philander Chase Knox, who had just been appointed as the new secretary of state in March 1909 in the incoming William Howard Taft administration. Like Roosevelt, Taft desired to continue the Open Door policy under a new "dollar diplomacy" aimed to encourage and protect US investments abroad. Knox put forward his "neutralization plan" for China, which he hoped could be presented to Russia and Japan as a fait accompli. A preliminary agreement was signed on October 2, 1909.[92] In the fall of 1909 the Russians were therefore under pressure to act with Japan to secure their holdings in Manchuria.

Japan was likewise under pressure to come to an agreement with Russia on Korea. The assassination of Itō had energized the Korean insurgency, "raising the spirits of Korean patriots," according to Smirnov. "The assassin [An Chung-gŭn] is considered a national hero . . . all the Koreans glorify him." Donations were pouring in from Vladivostok, Nikolsk, and the other Korean settlements in the Russian Far East to "establish assassination squads with the aim of killing Japanese officials and their supporters." In November 1909 an armed crowd unexpectedly attacked the railway station near the South Gate, which Japanese gendarmes had great difficulty handling. "The Japanese were so disturbed by these demonstrations," noted an observer, "that they even feared a general uprising was beginning in Korea." Japan now realized that to bring the situation under control, they would have to eliminate the main nexus of the rebel movement in the north, especially in the Russian Far East, and annex Korea as expeditiously as possible. And to do this, they urgently needed Russian support.[93]

At the end of December, Malevsky-Malevich sat down to discuss the "notorious American [railway] project" with Japanese ambassador Motono. A treaty signed on July 4, 1910, in Saint Petersburg by Foreign Minister Izvolsky and Motono stipulated that the two countries would

Yi Pŏm-yun's Northern Kando Righteous Army. In July 1910, Yi Pŏm-yun with Yu Yin-sŏk and Han Ban-do established the Chanykhve (Military Organization) in Vladivostok. The society aimed to coordinate the efforts of the various units of the Righteous Armies to attack Japanese garrisons in northern Korea and to unite all Koreans in the struggle against Japan. (*Kyonggi sinmun*)

465

refrain from all political activity within the other party's sphere of interest. Although Korea was not specifically mentioned in the agreement, it was implicit in Russia's promise "not to hinder in any way the consolidation and any further development of the special interests of the other Party," which meant Japanese freedom of action in Korea, including annexation.[94] The Russians also promised to stop any aid or succor to Korean rebels and the Righteous Army.[95] Primorskaya Oblast governor-general Unterberger ordered Smirnov "not to let any former Korean volunteer soldiers [ŭibyŏng], under any circumstances, to go back to Korea." He wanted them sent to Manchuria instead. In October 1910, Yi Pŏm-yun was arrested by Russian police.[96]

Meanwhile, the Knox project fell through. Russia had succeeded, with Japan's cooperation, in preventing the entry of American capital into Manchuria by placing tremendous pressure on China not to go along with the agreement.[97] Katsura was later quoted in the *New York Times* as saying that the July 1910 Russo-Japanese Treaty had not been influenced by the Knox proposal "nor was it directly or indirectly intended as an answer to the United States."[98] This was partly true. Although the Japanese were worried about American encroachment into Manchuria, they were far more concerned about the turmoil in Korea.[99] With the Russians now on board, Japanese plans for the annexation of Korea could proceed quickly.

JAPAN-KOREA ANNEXATION TREATY

Sensing that the time for the "Japan-Korean union" was close at hand, Ilchinhoe president Yi Yong-gu put forth his own annexation proposal, hoping that its members might still retain some power in the new arrangement. Claiming to represent one million Ilchinhoe members and twenty million Koreans, Yi submitted an annexation petition to Resident-General Sone and Emperor Sunjong on December 4, 1909. It read in part:

> This country is blessed and so rich in resources, but 20 million people here are desperate and could not evolve into a civilized country—why is this the case? This is because Korea has not established a foundation for the country nor settled any general principles to manage to country; [the government] constantly relies on strong neighbors and never comes up with a sustainable plan to help its people—how foolish this is! If it were not for the kindness of the Japanese emperor, the corrupted Korean

466

leaders would have never been where they are today, nor had any hopes for turning Korea into a civilized country in the future. Now the system of protectorate is established. Korea and Japan now share the exact same interests. If Japan and Korea can no longer protect each other, the current situation will not be sustained. Therefore we should lay an unshakable foundation for the "union of Japan and Korea" [J. *Nikkangappō;* K. *Ilhanhyŏpbang*]. This is the only way for Korea to protect itself, as well as the only way for Japan to defend itself. It not only allows Japan to defend itself but also enables Japan to support East Asia on the one hand and sustain the peace of the world on the other.[100]

Why had the Ilchinhoe put forth such a petition, knowing the backlash it would receive? One reason was simple political maneuvering by both Yi Yong-gu and Song Pyŏng-jun, who returned as a senior leader in the Ilchinhoe, as they engaged in a fierce political struggle against the Korean prime minister, Yi Wan-yong. Yi Yong-gu and Song believed that under Japanese pressure, the prime minister would eventually have to yield to Japan on the annexation issue. But instead of simply "throwing away" Korea's independence without retaining anything in return, the Ilchinhoe leadership wanted to retain some control over Korea's domestic policy.[101] As historian Sŏ Yŏng-hŭi explained, the goal of the *Nikkangappō* idea was not to bring about Korea's absorption by Japan as a colony per se but to establish a kind of "federation" in which the Ilchinhoe would still be nominally in charge of Korea's local governmental affairs.[102] "Koreans will therefore no longer be deemed citizens of a protectorate of an inferior country," Yi Yong-gu declared. "We will become part of a new union and a first ranked peoples of the world [*segyeiltŭngminjok*]."[103] By getting out ahead of the annexation issue, Yi Yong-gu and Song Pyŏng-jun intended, according to Acting British Council in Seoul Arthur Hyde Lay, "to pre-empt any unilateral move that would leave Korea in servitude."[104]

It was an intriguing idea. Both Yi Yong-gu and Yi Wan-yong had by then accepted the fact that Japan's greater military strength left Korea powerless and that it was unlikely that Korea would regain its independence, despite the efforts of the Righteous Army. Nor did they wish the *ŭibyŏng* guerrillas to succeed in this endeavor, as their own heads would be on the chopping block if they did. Prime Minister Yi Wan-yong had recently survived an assassination attempt in December, so he was acutely aware of the precariousness of his position. Nevertheless, he believed that Yi Yong-gu's annexation petition was premature. Hoping to capitalize on the unpopular proposal, he requested Japanese resident-general Sone to punish Yi Yong-gu and disband the Ilchinhoe.[105]

The Japanese were also reluctant to accept Yi Yong-gu's proposal, but for different reasons. They were hesitant about embracing any proposal that left the Ilchinhoe with any supervisory authority over affairs of state, local or otherwise. Nor could they allow the Ilchinhoe to have even nominal jurisdiction over local governments; to do so would not solve the Korean problem but merely perpetuate it.

In the middle of this crisis, Sone was diagnosed with stomach cancer and on May 13, 1910, Army Minister Terauchi Masatake was appointed to replace him as resident-general.[106] By this time the international situation had changed drastically. The 1910 Russo-Japanese agreement was moving toward completion and Prime Minister Katsura had decided that annexation must take place as soon as possible. Terauchi was therefore instructed to move ahead and appoint a committee to prepare for annexation.[107]

Upon his arrival in Seoul on July 24, Terauchi moved to freeze the Ilchinhoe out of the annexation discussions and to work directly with Yi Wan-yong and his cabinet.[108] The Korean prime minister was deemed far more pliable. There was always the possibility that Yi would refuse to work with Terauchi, but then he would have to worry that the Japanese would set up a cabinet with Ilchinhoe leaders Yi Yong-gu or Song Pyŏng-jun. With the Ilchinhoe in power, there was no telling what they might do. "If Song ever became prime minister, it is hard to predict what would happen to Yi Wan-yong, Song's lifelong enemy," remarked Komatsu, who remained as foreign affairs chief on the resident-general's staff. "If Prime Minister Yi Wan-yong escapes, he will be criticized by the Koreans as a treacherous minister and he will also be abandoned by the Japanese. He won't be welcomed anywhere in the world. Yi is a smart person and he certainly understands this."[109] In other words, Yi Wan-yong and his cabinet ministers would all be dead men walking. Terauchi had Yi exactly where he wanted him.

Yi Wan-yong's main concern, besides saving his own life, was the treatment of the royal family. "Yi said that as long as the emperor does not have to abdicate" he would cooperate. "Yi seemed really upset and even shed tears when he said this," Komatsu confided. "I could barely look him in the face." Yi was also worried about the fate of his ministers. Komatsu offered assurances of generous treatment; the Korean emperor and his family would become part of the Japanese imperial family. "Japan will treat the Korean royal family and high-ranking officers (like yourself) well and never hurt them. I can promise you that," he told Yi.[110]

Yi accepted these assurances, and events moved quickly from there. On August 17, Yi received a draft treaty from Terauchi and discussed it with his cabinet the next day. As Komatsu had promised, assurances were given for the Korean royal family to be treated generously. Wide-ranging compensation for Korean statesmen and nobles would be provided. The treaty also promised to employ Koreans in official positions as long as they accepted the annexation. While Yi Wan-yong was pondering the treaty, he received word that Song Pyŏng-jun had suddenly turned up Seoul. This was all it took for the prime minister to accept the treaty.

The final step was for Emperor Sunjong to give his approval, which he did without complaint. On August 22, 1910, at four o'clock in the afternoon, the Japan-Korea annexation treaty was signed. During the reception that took place afterward, Emperor Sunjong, who did not attend, sent this message to Terauchi: "I have always believed that our problem [Japan and Korea] would be solved. Now has come the time to do so, and I have therefore given the complete power of attorney to Prime Minister Yi Wan-yong [to accomplish this task] . . . I will not participate in any state affairs from now on, and will only focus on taking care of my family." The emperor's only request was to limit layoffs of his imperial staff. "I will be ashamed and the people's feelings will be hurt." But he was also quick to add, "I truly appreciate that the Japanese emperor has kindly agreed to provide us the same living stipend as before."[111]

So, with these few simple and self-deprecating words, without protest or fanfare, five hundred years of Korea's dynastic history was brought to a close. The unceasing struggles over the peninsula that had begun in the 1870s with China's fight to retain Korea's status as a Chinese dependency ended in 1910 with the final incorporation of Korea into the Japanese Empire. One year later, the Qing dynasty, which had lasted more than two and a half centuries, collapsed. The long-range goals of the revolutionaries who overthrew the Manchu state were to "avenge the national disgrace" and to "restore the Chinese."[112] In these goals, China and Korea shared a similar worldview, setting the stage for a new order in East Asia that was no less bloody, or dramatic.

EPILOGUE

LEGACIES

What did the Other Great Game bequeath to East Asia and how did it define the future of the region and the world?

One major outcome was widespread regional violence and instability that occurred as a result of Japan's rise as the new imperial power in Asia. The historian Richard Overy observed something similar when he noted that the struggle for empire in the late nineteenth century helped give rise to the crisis of the 1930s and the coming war. We don't usually consider the colonial dimensions of World War II, but that's only when we focus on Germany's invasion of Poland in 1939 and not Japan's invasion of Manchuria in 1931. Most histories of the war have preferred to view the Second World War as Winston Churchill did—as a titanic struggle between liberty-loving nations and ruthless dictatorships. But this view falters in the Pacific. This is because the Pacific War was transparently a clash over colonies. Japan succeeded in merging the war in the Pacific with the war in Europe when it attacked the British Empire in Asia. The United States was then dragged into the war after Japan bombed Pearl Harbor on December 7, 1941, making it a truly global event. But it wasn't just the sinking of American battleships that the Japanese were after. They made a blitzkrieg dash for American possessions in Guam, the Philippines, Midway, and Wake Island as well as British and French possessions in Malaya, Singapore, Hong Kong, and Indochina. And when the Japanese Empire collapsed in 1945, the Allies rushed to reclaim their lost colonies. Overy is certainly correct to argue that the Second World War is better

471

understood as a conflict over empire, not an Armageddon-style struggle between good and evil. "The long roots of the global violence, which ended in the 1940s and 1950s with the collapse of territorial empire, were to be found in the last decades of the nineteenth century, where the pace of economic and political modernization quickened across the developing world."[1] The focus on 1914 as the "end of peace" is thus misleading. The world was *already* destabilized by large-scale conflicts well before the Great War. Nor did the reversal of the Asian balance of power in Japan's favor ever diminish the fight over territory.

For Japan, the annexation of Korea in 1910 was the culmination of an ongoing struggle since the 1880s to control the Korean Peninsula. Although the Japan-Korea Treaty of 1910 had finally settled the question of Korea's status, it did not address the problem of maintaining China's territorial integrity.[2] In July 1910, Russia and Japan signed a new treaty of friendship that pushed the 1907 entente a step further. The two powers pledged to take common action to support the defense of each other's respective spheres of interest through "whatever measures" at their disposal.

After the fall of the Qing dynasty in 1911, pro-Army members of the Japanese Diet, led by Yamagata Aritomo, hoped to mediate a settlement of the Chinese Revolution and send troops to the continent, but Prime Minister Saionji Kinmochi refused. Conflict over Japan's China policy, however, was quickly resolved following the outbreak of World War I in Europe. Taking advantage of the life-and-death struggle in Europe, the new government of Prime Minister Ōkuma Shigenobu, a Yamagata ally, swiftly moved to seize German colonies in the Asia-Pacific region, including Shandong, which the Germans had taken in 1898. Geography had blessed Japan with the opportunity to pursue a maritime route to power, but in the end the Japanese elite chose to make Japan a continental power instead.

This was not the vision of Japan's expansionists when they embarked on war against Russia. Before the war the Katsura cabinet and the *genrō* accepted the Open Door policy as the logical extension of the Mahanian argument about commercial rather than military penetration of the continent. But the blood and treasure sacrificed in the war, the unsatisfying conclusion at Portsmouth, and violent developments in Korea changed all that.

The failure to draw proper lessons from the Russo-Japanese War and to assess the viability of Japan as a continental power led to future disasters.[3] The Bolshevik Revolution prompted Home Minister Gotō Shinpei to call for one million troops to occupy Russia east of Lake Baikal. Japan's pursuit of continental Great Power status would now extend, it seems, beyond Korea and China into Russia.[4] Although Prime Minister Hamaguchi Osachi fought hard to steer his nation toward a different course, he was shot in November 1930 by a right-wing ultranationalist youth in Tokyo and subsequently died of his wounds in August 1931. The collapse of the world economy in the Great Depression and the domestic tribulations Japan suffered, along with the rise of militant Japanese nationalism, eventually led a cabal of Japanese Army officers in Mukden to set off an explosion on a stretch of tracks on the South Manchurian Railway on the night of September 18, 1931. By year's end, Manchuria was under Japanese control and Japan was on its way to war with China and the United States.

What of China? The Sino-Japanese secret treaty of December 22, 1905, like earlier precedents, was an attempt to preempt through alliance any aggression China could not handle alone. The time-worn strategy of "controlling barbarians with barbarians" proved ineffective in this case. As in the past, such a stratagem resulted in an even greater threat to China's integrity, but not enough to convince the Qing government that the way to preserve China was to try and recover rights lost and not to parcel them out.

The new postimperial Chinese state under Yuan Shikai, titular head of the Republic of China, was weak and vulnerable, subject to exploitation by the Great Powers just as the Qing had been. Yuan gave in to Japan's Twenty-One Demands to acquire German rights in Shandong and economic control of Fujian Province in 1915. Threatened and undermined by his detractors, Yuan was gone by 1916.[5]

China's inability to resolve the Shandong question at the 1919 Versailles Peace Conference and the disappointments surrounding Wilson's Fourteen Points led many Chinese to conclude that the antidote to China's centuries-long decline and humiliation lay with Bolshevism and Marxism. Just four weeks after the signing of the Paris Peace Treaty in June 1919, L. M. Karakhan, deputy commissar for foreign affairs, announced that Soviet Russia would voluntarily relinquish its special rights in Manchuria, including that it would return the Chinese Eastern Railway to Chinese control without compensation. The Soviets also promised to cancel all tsarist secret treaties with China and renounce all further indemnities due from the Boxer Uprising. Although the Soviets later reneged on the promise to return the railways, the Chinese were deeply impressed by the announcement, which seemed to offer an alternative to the failed promises of Wilsonianism. The early death of Sun Yat-sen in March 1925

473

saw his protégé, Chiang Kai-shek [Jiang Jieshi], rise as the new leader of the Guomindang (Nationalist Party), and until the Nationalist unification of China in 1928 under Chiang, Sun's message of anti-imperialism became the ideological force that bound all Chinese together.[6]

The main lesson of the Other Great Game for China was not just the embrace of anti-imperialism as an antidote to national humiliation, but the vital link it made between feelings of humiliation and the loss of China's territorial integrity. One can say that China's tortuous developmental story is one long quest for territorial recovery and national unity. This is the crux of the story of China's unraveling in the nineteenth century—not simply the relentless humiliation, but the slow and steady crumbling of its empire, which accelerated after its conflict with Japan over control of the Korean Peninsula. Beijing's quest to reclaim all territories it regards as its historical possessions is related to its effort to efface China's national humiliation and restore China to its former greatness. Certainly, there is little that would signal more forcefully to its own citizens about China's new global standing in the world than to bring Taiwan back into Beijing's fold, thus closing the most contentious, and bitter, chapter of the Other Great Game.

What about Russia? The outbreak of World War I forced the tsarist regime to draw back from intrigues in the Far East as Russia waged a life-and-death struggle. In the end it was the Great War, not the Russo-Japanese War, that administered the coup de grace that ended the Romanov dynasty. Soon after the 1917 Revolution, Russia, now under the Bolsheviks, once again found itself in a struggle over control of the Far East as an international expeditionary force, including seventy-three thousand Japanese, landed in Vladivostok to support the Whites in the Russian civil war. Korean partisans and *ŭibyŏng* leaders, previously hunted down by the tsarist regime, now joined hands with the Bolsheviks to fight a proxy war against a common enemy.[7] In November 1922, a month after the last Japanese soldier left Vladivostok, the Bolsheviks claimed victory in the Russian Far East.

Russia had thus suffered its share of humiliating setbacks during its story of the Other Great Game, but in contrast to China it had not lost any territory but added a great new swath of land that pushed its boundary to the Pacific. After 1918, moreover, the Bolsheviks gained influence and power in East Asia. With the end of the Russian civil war in 1922, the Soviets allied themselves with Sun Yat-sen and his Nationalist Party. Desperate for funds, Sun turned to the Soviet Union and, in exchange for aid, agreed to allow Communists into the Guomindang Party. The conclusion of the 1924 Guomindang-Communist alliance at Guangzhou, later known as the First United Front, stunned the Japanese, who quickly established relations with the Soviet Union the following year.

The Soviets continued to expand their influence in East Asia after World War II, recovering the rights Russia had lost in the Russo-Japanese War. Furthermore, Stalin created a satellite buffer state in the northern half of Korea, fulfilling Nicholas II's objective half a century earlier. Is it any wonder, then, that today's Russia looks east to Asia as Vladimir Putin seeks to recapture the glories of his country's imperial past?[8] As Fyodor Dostoevsky put it in 1881: "In Europe we are canaille, but in Asia we are a great power."[9]

For Korea, the main question after annexation became one of survival— that is, how the nation's independence, its "Koreanness" might best be preserved. How that question was answered determined everything, from resistance struggles *against* Japan to varieties of accommodation and collaboration with Tokyo.

After 1910 the tsarist regime began to reverse its support of Korean partisans, initiating a harsh crackdown on Korean anti-Japanese activity in the Russian Far East, including the widespread arrests of *ŭibyŏng* leaders. This was especially true after the outbreak of World War I, when Russia sought to strengthen its ties with Japan and to act against a common enemy.

The October Revolution of 1917, however, changed all this. Reversing tsarist policy, the new Bolshevik government cut its ties to Japan and gave support to Korean anti-Japanese organizations. Lenin's anti-imperialist narrative also appealed to many Korean groups, including reformist Confucians, whose desire to defend the nation from Japan was channeled into a new revolutionary project, this one appealing directly to anti-imperialist nationalism.

The outbreak of the Russian civil war in 1918 provided the occasion for the Russians and Koreans to work together again in the Russian Far East. The Bolsheviks needed allies, and Korean militants helped them mount a second front against the Siberian Expedition (1918–1922), to which Japan contributed a large force. For the second time since the Russo-Japanese War, the Russians and Koreans were engaged in fighting a war against Japan.

Emigration to the Russian Far East greatly increased during the 1920s and 1930s, with the large majority of Koreans concentrated in Vladivostok, where they formed about one-quarter of the population.[10] But relations between the Soviets and the Koreans, never easy, took a drastic turn for the worse in 1937 following the forced deportation of ethnic Koreans from the Russian Far East to the Central Asian states of Uzbekistan and Kazakhstan as part of Stalin's Great Terror (1936–1938).[11] One result of Stalin's policy was that it forced Korean partisans to move their base for anti-Japanese activities to eastern Manchuria. As the strength of the Communist guerrillas operating there intensified, Korean guerrillas increasingly drew the attention of Japanese authorities. The harsh crackdowns eventually forced the guerrillas to give up operations in Manchuria and seek refuge in the Soviet Union in 1940. Among them was a young Communist leader named Kim Il Sung.[12]

Other Koreans sought a different path to ensure their nation's survival. In 1919 Korean émigrés from Hawaii, Vladivostok, San Francisco, and Seoul came together in Shanghai to establish a united front of all Korean nationalists, forming the so-called Korean Provisional Government (KPG) under the leadership of its first president, Syngman Rhee. From its founding in 1919 until Japan's surrender in 1945, the Provisional Government aimed to secure support for Korean independence at international conferences, while other like-minded Korean moderates worked within the colony to focus on national "self-strengthening." They were willing to collaborate with the colonial regime rather than oppose it as long as colonialism served Korea's "developmental" goal and was seen as an agent of civilization.

Following the end of the Second World War and the occupation of the peninsula by Soviet and American forces in 1945, these two main Korean groups vied for power. The history of the 38th parallel forced the spatial separation of Koreans according to ideological alliances. Northern Koreans who went south during the unsettled period between liberation in 1945 and 1948 played an integral role in resisting the North Korean revolution and also had a profound impact on the formation of postwar South Korea as they became incorporated into the conservative nationalist politics of the Syngman Rhee regime (1948–1960).[13] In fact, a large proportion of the northern refugees came from P'yŏngan and Hwanghae Provinces, traditional centers of Christianity, and had experienced firsthand persecution and oppression by the Soviet-backed leadership in the north that turned them into visceral anticommunists.

The division of the peninsula thus reinforced a divide that had *already* grown in Korea under the stresses of Japanese colonial occupation and created two partisan camps with the support of two rival patrons, the Soviet Union and the United States. Their diverging visions of Korea's future exploded into war in June 1950, as two antagonistic regimes each tried to achieve its dream of reunifying the Korean Peninsula under its own rule.

As for the United States, the Other Great Game gave both America and Japan the opening to become the two non-European Great Powers that would dominate the Asia-Pacific region. World War II destroyed Japan's position, but the United States used the stage constructed during the Other Great Game to emerge as a preeminent Asia-Pacific power. After the Sino-Japanese War of 1894–1895 for Japan, and the Spanish-American War of 1898 for the United States, expanding overseas presence and spheres of influence played major roles in both nations' self-conceptions. Japan would eventually choose to become a continental power and attempt to control the Asian mainland. The United States focused less on territorial acquisitions and more on expanding its trade and commerce.[14] Inasmuch as the United States was separated from most of the world by two oceans, such an aim necessitated that it become a maritime power.

By 1905 the United States and Japan were seemingly moving in opposite directions. Whereas Japan secured its occupation of Korea and the Liaodong Peninsula as prerequisites for attaining status as a continental power, the United States, in accordance with the commercial focus of Mahanian principles and the Open Door, continued on as a maritime power, making the case that wealth and power came from commerce and free trade.

Paradoxically, their contrasting conception of national power and interest—continental focus to secure national security versus maritime focus to secure commerce—placed the United States and Japan on a collision course. Following the signing of the Russo-Japanese Agreement in July 1910, talk of a coming conflict between the United States and Japan became more frequent. But it was the Great War in Europe that put the United States on notice. The opportunity to expand imperial gains had temporarily united disparate voices in Japan as Japan's elder statesmen, generals, and politicians all hailed the war as "the divine aid of the new Taisho era for the development of the destiny of Japan."[15]

Under these chaotic circumstances, and to fill the void the European powers left behind, the United States emerged as the only power capable of moderating Japan's acrimonious relations with China. US entry into World War I in April 1917 further hardened President Woodrow Wilson's commitment to China, and to the principles of the Open Door. Wilson stood firmly against the old imperialist practice of diplomacy that would rob China of its sovereignty. Although it would not be until January 1918 that Wilson articulated his vision of the postwar order—introducing such concepts as autonomous development and free trade—it is clear that he entered the war already harboring these idealistic principles.

Although Wilson did not fulfill his promises to China at the Versailles Conference—Japan flatly refused to give up Shandong—the Washington Conference of 1921–1922 offered another opportunity for the United States to reaffirm its commitment to international agreements, trade, and the Open Door. The architects of postwar American policy recognized the necessity of restoring equilibrium in East Asia through a new framework of cooperation and stability, but they were also responding to global pressures for military disarmament. In the aftermath of the war to end all wars, military spending, which had taken up so many resources in the past, could now be more constructively spent on economic development.[16]

The American plan also envisioned providing developmental loans to Japan from a new international banking consortium in exchange for its pledge to honor the Open Door principles in China (except for Manchuria).[17] Cash-strapped Japan seemed amenable, as the trend toward accommodation with China had already been in the works for a number of years. Historian Frederick Dickinson noted that the year 1919 was celebrated in Japan "not as the year of Versailles, but as the first year of Japan's true party government."[18] Prime Minister Hara Takashi led and oversaw the expansion of a truly representative government, aided by a postwar economic boom and privatization of state enterprises. In March 1919, some fifty thousand students and clerical and factory workers gathered at Tokyo's Hibiya Park calling for universal suffrage. At the same time the March First movement in Korea, which brought tens of thousands of Koreans to the streets demanding independence and self-determination, created opportunities for administrative reform in the Korean colony. In response, Hara called for the liberalization of colonial administration in all of Japan's overseas possessions. Tokyo's pledge to adhere to a new framework of international relations and economic interdependence thus gave rise to a new hope that Hay's and Mahan's vision might finally be realized in East Asia.

The United States also offered its good offices for the Japanese and Chinese delegates to settle the Shandong question, whereby Japan agreed to return Shandong to China. China's full sovereign rights were not restored, but Japan backed off from the Twenty-One Demands of 1915 and agreed to reinstate to China management rights of the Qingdao-Jinan Railway.

But then came the stock market crash of 1929. The collapse of the world economy during the Great Depression laid bare the failed promises of the Washington system and immediately affected trade patterns. The contraction of the American market for Japanese goods due to a radical decline in American purchasing power meant that Japanese imports fell to one-fourth of what they had been before the crash.[19] Japanese leaders, who had bet their economy and foreign policy on US trade, turned against the liberal capitalist system and economic internationalism that had flourished during the 1920s. By 1932 Manchuria was under Japan's control. Five years later Japan invaded China proper and the United States and Japan were on their way to war.

The bombing of the US naval base at Pearl Harbor, Hawaii, on December 7, 1941, was thus the culmination of a clash between two nations that had been moving along opposing paths since the conclusion of the Russo-Japanese in 1905. And yet, following the disastrous end to Japan's continental ambitions at the end of World War II, it managed to successfully reintegrate into an American-led global system as Washington's East Asian hub. Soon after the end of the Second World War, Japan once again emerged as a stalwart of the new maritime order against the ambition and drive of the old Russian continental power as the dawn of the Cold War was breaking.[20]

• • •

When the Cold War in Europe ended in 1989, the notion that the course of human history had come to an end in the triumph of capitalist liberal democracy became fashionable. Francis Fukuyama's famous formulation that the end of the Cold War meant the end of history appeared to portend that not only was humanity's ideological struggle over but that geopolitics itself had come to a permanent end.[21] Closed Communist societies like China and Russia were too uncreative to compete economically with the West, so the only remaining dangers would come from rogue states like Communist North Korea. It would only take a little bit of prodding, the thinking went, for these states to jump on the modernization bandwagon and become liberal open societies, simulacrums of America.

That, of course, did not happen. Instead many of the same voices who declared that history ended in 1989 are now proclaiming that the Cold

479

War is back.[22] The idea of Cold War II not only implies a new US confrontation with Russia and China but also includes the one that has never ended on the Korean Peninsula, where North and South Korea *still* face each other across the demilitarized zone. One observer has even suggested that the war in Ukraine is analogous to the Korean War, another "hot" opening salvo in a new Cold War pitting Washington and its democratic allies against a powerful bloc of dictatorships.[23]

Focus on the Cold War, however, can obfuscate contemporary challenges as much as it can elucidate them. If Americans had expected traditional geopolitical rivalries to go away once the Cold War ended, this is because they misread what the Cold War settlement meant for China and Russia: It was *not* the triumph of American-style liberal capitalist democracy over Communism, but the return of revanchism and good old-fashioned Great Power politics.[24] The invasion of Ukraine on February 24, 2022, showed Russia behaving like a classic imperial power. As Russian poet Alexander Pushkin astutely reminds us, we have seen this type of war before. During the Russo-Polish War when Russian troops were laying siege to Warsaw in 1831, Pushkin wrote his famous patriotic ode "To the Slanderers of Russia," addressing the political leaders in Europe:

> This is a strife of Slavs among themselves,
> An old domestic strife, already weighed by fate,
> An issue not to be resolved by you.
> Leave us alone . . .
> To you is unintelligible, to you is alien
> This family feud.[25]

Pushkin's defiant poem justifying Russia's imperial war against Poland contains all the basic features that would later come to characterize Russia's relationship to its Slavic borderlands, including Ukraine in 2022.[26]

Something similar can be said about the Asia-Pacific region, which is arguably less stable now than it was at the start of the twenty-first century and for reasons that echo this past. For example, the various contested claims by China and Japan in the East China Sea go back to the Sino-Japanese War of 1894–1895, when Tokyo took control of the Chinese territory of Taiwan, including the now disputed Senkaku/Diaoyu Islands.[27] China's ongoing support for North Korea reflects a deeper desire to revive elements of the Sinocentric order that prevailed in East Asia before the arrival of Westerners and the ascent of Meiji Japan, when Korea's rulers paid annual tribute to the Chinese court. The Korean Peninsula continues to be a destabilizing presence in the region, mainly due to factors to which most policymakers have paid the least attention—namely, issues of Korean identity, legitimacy, and nationalism that trace their origins back to the late nineteenth century. Finally, the age-old dispute between Russia and Japan over the status of the Kuril Islands finds its origins as far back as the 1873 Seikanron debate. The Treaty of Saint Petersburg in 1875 had settled the conflict until the islands were ambiguously ceded to Russia at the end of World War II.[28] Nearly eighty years after the end of the Second World War, Japan and Russia have yet to sign a formal peace treaty. Putin's revision of the Russian Constitution in 2020, in which he explicitly banned the ceding of Russian territory to another nation, means the dispute between Russia and Japan will likely continue.[29]

Thus, far from being a replay of the Cold War, the new era of Great Power politics is about the settling of old scores. For Vladimir Putin, this has entailed the creation of an entirely *new* narrative of Russia's imperial history as continuous, and one without *any* discernible legal change after the Bolshevik Revolution of 1917 when the empire technically ceased to exist. By insisting that Russia has been a unitary empire all along and that the legal foundations upon which the USSR was established were illegitimate, Putin has not only refused to recognize the dissolution of the Soviet Union; he has reserved the right to claim *any* land that belonged to the former tsarist empire, including Ukraine.[30]

Putin's watershed invasion of that country has thus steered history in a new direction. Not only has the crisis put a question mark behind Swiss neutrality and German pacifism; it has also opened up a large gap between the West and the rest of the world that threatens to hand the revisionist powers major opportunities in the years to come. While enthusiastic Western democracies have welcomed the imposition of draconian sanctions on Russia, many non-Western countries, including the world's two most populous states, China and India, fear the consequences of Western responses to Russian behavior more than they fear Russia itself. For one thing, the invasion of Ukraine has sped up China's medium imperative of "decoupling" the global economy into Chinese and Western spheres of influence. In 2020, Chinese president Xi Jinping put forth an economic paradigm of "dual circulation," which laid out a vision of a largely self-sufficient Chinese economy that would continue to engage with the international economy through exports but keep the manufacturing and consumption of critical goods within its own domestic economy.[31] Confronted by the West's willingness to confiscate Russia's assets, Chinese nationalists around

President Xi appear to be even more motivated to realize this goal.[32] Meanwhile, the Chinese leader has spent much of his rule building a Sinocentric economic order through his Belt and Road Initiative, China's colossal infrastructure investments sometimes referred to as the New Silk Road.[33] Further initiatives to "decouple" China from the global economy have taken on more urgency after Ukraine.[34]

The trend of geopolitics is thus moving against globalization and in favor of a multipolar world dominated by two or three great trading blocs, similar to what existed in the late nineteenth century.[35] As the Bulgarian writer Ivan Krastev astutely observed: "We used to be in a postwar world, now we are in a prewar world. That is the change."[36]

The story of the Other Great Game is thus as relevant today as it was in the late nineteenth century, not just because of the lessons it offers about the potential for war and violence in the region but for what it can teach us about our contemporary moment: The origins and legacy of Korea's bifurcated identity and perennial instability in the region; China's revanchist territorial ambitions and efforts to reassert its old position as the Middle Kingdom; Japan's role as a model of developmental modernization and, equally, the object of loathing; finally, Russia's nostalgic (and now shattered) dreams to recover a bygone imperial era when it was a preeminent power in Asia.

It is my hope that this chronicle of the Other Great Game, which can sometimes appear fragmented and opaque to the Western reader, will impart a sense of coherence and wonder to a region of the world that now holds the key to all our global futures.

ABBREVIATIONS

NOTES

ACKNOWLEDGMENTS

INDEX

ABBREVIATIONS

CHKSR   Sugimura Fukashi, "Chaehan koshim rok," [Contemplations from Korea] in *Sŏulae namgyŏdun kkum* [Dreams from Seoul], ed. and trans. Han Sang-il (Seoul, 1993)

CIK   Chuhan ilbonsa kongsagwan [Records of the Japanese Legation in Korea], https://db.history.go.kr/item/level.do?itemId=jh

CJCC   Shao Xun Zheng, ed., *Zhong Ri Zhan Zheng* (Chung-Jih chan-cheng) [Sino-Japanese War], vol. 2 (Shanghai, 1956)

CRNJR   *Correspondence regarding the Negotiations between Japan and Russia* (Tokyo, 1904)

DPEC   *Diary of the Principal Events in China during the Boxer Insurrection, 1900*, National Archives, Kew, UK, CAB 3Y/53/62 1900

ERJW   US War Department General Staff, *Epitome of the Russo-Japanese War*, pt. 2 (Washington, DC, 1907)

FRUS   *Papers Relating to the Foreign Relations of the United States, 1850–1899* and *1900–1919* (Washington, DC, Government Printing Office 1915–1935), https://www.archives.gov/research/alic/reference/foreign-relations/about-frus.html

IHH   Itō Hirobumi, *Itō Hirobumi hiroku* [The Confidential Papers of Itō Hirobumi], ed. Atsushi Hiratsuka, 2 vols. (Tokyo, 1929–1930)

KA   Louise Boutelle and Gordon W. Thayer, eds., *A Digest of the Krasnyi Arkiv (Red Archives): A Historical Journal of the Central Archive Department of the USSR* (Cleveland, 1947)

KDC   Sergei Witte, *Koreyskoye delo 1 chast'. Ekspeditsiya v Severnuyu Koreyu. 1898–1899 gg.* [The Korean case, pt.1. The expedition to

North Korea, 1898–1899], Boris Yeltsin Library, https://www.prlib
.ru/en/node/337637

KJSL Kojong sillok [Veritable records of King Kojong], https://sillok
.history.go.kr/search/inspectionMonthList.do

KNKK Tabohashi Kiyoshi, *Kindai Nissen kankei no kenkyū* [Japan-Korea
relations in the modern era], vols. 1–2 (Seoul, 2002)

LD V. N. Lamzdorf, *Dnevnik, 1894–1896* [Diary, 1894–1896]
(Moscow, 1991)

LOC Library of Congress, Washington, DC

LZR Wang Yusheng, *Liu shi nian lai Zhongguo yu Riben* [Sixty years of
relations between China and Japan], vols. 1–4 (Tianjin, 1932)

MSC Kim Yŏng-su, *Myŏngsŏnghwanghu ch'oehuǔi nal: sŏyangin
sabatchini mŏkkyŏkh'an ŭlmisabyŏn, kŭ haruǔi kiŏk* [The last
moments of Empress Myŏngsong: The recollections of the Westerner Sabatin] (Seoul, 2014)

MSRP Yi Yŏng-suk, ed., *Myŏngsŏnghwanghu sihae sakŏn rŏsia
pimilmunsŏ* [Secret Russian documents on Empress Myŏngsŏng's
assassination] (Seoul 2005)

NA National Archives, Kew, UK

NARA National Archives and Records Administration, College Park, MD

NGB *Nihon Gaikō Bunsho* [Documents on Japanese Foreign Policy]
(Tokyo, 1938–1963)

PORKMK N.S. Sviagin, *Po russkoi i kitaskoi Man'chzhurii ot Khabarovska
do Ninguty: vpechatleniia i nabliudeniia* [Through Russian and
Chinese Manchuria from Khabarovsk to Ninguta: Impressions and
observations] (Saint Petersburg, 1897)

PRI B. B. Glinsky, *Prolog Russko-Iaponskoi voiny: materialy iz arkhiva
Grafa S. Iu. Vitte* [Prologue to the Russo-Japanese War: Materials
from the archive of Count S. Iu. Witte] (Saint Petersburg, 1916)

RICKH ROK Ministry of National Defense, *Rŏsiawa ilbonŭi chŏnjaeng
kŭrigo hanbando* [The Russo-Japanese War and the Korean Peninsula],
vols. 1–2 (Seoul, 2004, 2012)

WWRP William Woodville Rockhill Papers, Houghton Library, Harvard
University

NOTES

PROLOGUE

1. Although this bloody description of the Mongol siege is often quoted, its source is elusive. Howorth attributes it to the "Chronicle of Kostroma" (Henry H. Howorth, *History of the Mongols,* vol. 1 [London, 1876], 1:139), but other scholars dispute it. See J. J. Saunders, *The History of the Mongol Conquests* (Philadelphia, 1971), 82. For a description of the capture of Kiev, see Howorth, *History of the Mongols,* 1:141. Quotes about the massacre are from Howorth, *History of the Mongols,*139. On the Tatar siege of Russian cities, especially Ryazan and Vladimir, see Robert Michell, ed., *The Chronicles of Novgorod, 1016–1472* (London, 1914).

2. The Mongol impact on Russian history, society, and politics continues to be one of the most hotly debated subjects among historians of Russia. See Thomas T. Allsen, *Mongol Imperialism: The Politics of the Grand Qan Möngke in China, Russia, and Islamic Lands, 1251–1259* (Berkeley, 1987); Timothy May, *The Mongol Conquest in World History* (London, 2021); Marie Favereau, *The Horde: How Mongols Changed the World* (Cambridge, MA, 2021); Donald Ostrowsky, *Muscovy and the Mongols: Cross-Cultural Influences on the Steppe Frontier, 1304–1589* (Cambridge, 1998); Charles J. Halperin, *Russia and the Golden Horde: Mongol Impact on Medieval Russian History* (Bloomington, IN, 1987).

3. The conflict was caused by Ivan III's refusal to pay annual tribute to his oppressor. See Michael T. Florinsky, *Russia: A History and Interpretation,* vol. 1 (New York, 1953); Michael Khodarkovsky, *Russia's Steppe Frontier: The Making of a Colonial Empire, 1500–1800* (Bloomington, IN, 2002).

4. The border along the Stanovoy Mountains and the Argun (Amur) River (Treaty of Nerchinsk, 1689) was the officially recognized border between China and Russia until Russia's annexation in 1860. Leo Pasvolsky, *Russia in the Far East* (New York, 1922); James Forsyth, *A History of the Peoples of Siberia: Russia's North Asian Colony, 1581–1990* (Cambridge, 1992).

5. Peter Hopkirk, *The Great Game: The Struggle for Empire in Central Asia* (Tokyo, 1992), 4.

6. Pasvolsky, *Russia in the Far East,* 12.

7. Vladimir [pseud.] [Z. Volpicelli], *Russia on the Pacific and the Siberian Railway* (London, 1899), 178–179.

8. G. I. Nevelskoy, *Podvigi russkikh morskikh ofitserov na krainem Vostoke Rossii, 1849–1855 g, Pri-Amurskiy i Pri-Ussuriyskiy krai: Posmertnyya zapiski Admirala Nevel'skogo* [The exploits of Russian naval officers in the Russian Far East, 1849–1855: Priamursky and Priussuriysky krai: Posthumous notes of Admiral Nevelskoy] (Saint Petersburg, 1897), 95–97. See also George Alexander Lensen, *The Russian Push toward Japan: Russo-Japanese Relations, 1697–1875* (Princeton, NJ, 1959), 277–278.

9. Ivan Barsukov, ed., *Graf Nikolai Nikolaevich Muraviev-Amursky: Iograficheskie materialy po ego pis'mam, ofitsial'nym dokumentam, rasskazam sovremenikov i pechatnym istochnikam* [Count Nikolai Nikolaevich Muravev-Amursky: Materials on his letters, official documents, stories of contemporaries and printed sources],vol. 2 (Khabarvosk, 2009), 46–48.

10. Lensen, *The Russian Push*, 278.

11. David Schimmelpenninck van der Oye, *Russian Orientalism: Asia in the Russian Mind from Peter the Great to the Emigration* (New Haven, CT, 2010), 229.

12. Orlando Figes, *Natasha's Dance: A Cultural History of Russia* (New York, 2002), 380.

13. Martin Malia, *Russia under Western Eyes: From Bronze Horseman to the Lenin Mausoleum* (Cambridge, MA, 2000), 20.

14. Marquis de Custine, *Empire of the Czar: A Journey through Eternal Russia* (New York, 1989), 214, 230.

15. Figes, *Natasha's Dance*, 380.

16. Figes, *Natasha's Dance*, 369.

17. Peter Waldron, "Przheval'skii, Asia and Empire," *Slavonic and East European Review* 88, no. 1–2 (January–April 2010): 314. See also Katya Hokanson, *Writing at Russia's Border* (Toronto, 2008).

18. Waldron, "Przheval'skii, Asia and Empire," 314; Katya Holanson, "Literary Imperialism, Narodnost' and Pushkin's Invention of the Caucasus," *Russian Review* 53, no. 3 (July 1994): 314–342. A *sarafan* is the traditional folk Russian jumper dress worn by women and girls.

19. Waldron, "Przheval'skii, Asia and Empire," 318; Schimmelpenninck van Oye, *Russian Orientalism*, 156–157; Bassin, *Imperial Visions*, 42. For a description of Uvarov's policies, see Martin Malia, *Alexander Herzen and the Birth of Russian Socialism* (New York, 1965); Simon Sebag Montefiore, *Romanovs, 1613–1918* (New York, 2016), 370–371.

20. Schimmelpenninck van Oye, *Russian Orientalism*, 229.

21. Sarah Crosby Mallory Paine, "A History of the Sino-Soviet Border, 1858–1924" (PhD diss., Columbia University, 1993), 103. There was a discrepancy between the Russian and Chinese versions of the treaty. Either Nevelskoy's memory failed him or Muravev deliberately drew up a Russian text that gave the maritime area to Russia. See also R. K. I. Quested, *The Expansion of Russia in East Asia, 1857–1860* (Singapore, 1968), 150–152.

22. David J. Dallin, *The Rise of Russia* (New Haven, CT, 1949), 19. See also Hugh Seton-Watson, *The Russian Empire* (Oxford, 1967), 438–445.

23. Jonathan Spence, *The Search for Modern China* (New York, 1990), 181.

24. Orville Schell and John Delury, *Wealth and Power: China's Long March to the Twenty-First Century* (New York, 2013), 39; Douglas Hurd, *The Arrow War: An Anglo-Chinese Confusion, 1856–1860* (New York, 1967), 221–222.

25. PRO, 20/22 (49), Lord Thomas Elgin to Lord John Russell, October 27, 1860, NA; Orville and Delury, *Wealth and Power*, 9.

26. A. Buksgevden, *Russkii Kitaii: ocherki diplomaticheskikh snoshenii Rossii s Kitayem. t. 1. Pekinskii dogovor, 1860 g* [Russian China: An outline of Russia's diplomatic relations with

China—Vol. 1. Treaty of Peking, 1860] (Port Arthur, China, 1902), 53–57. For a translation of these documents, see T. G. Tsiang, "China, England and Russia in 1860," *Cambridge Historical Journal* 3, no. 1 (1929): 115–121.

27. Buksgevden, *Russkii Kitai*, 76–78.

28. Barsukov, *Graf Nikolai Nikolaevich Muravev-Amursky*, 2:315–317.

29. Dallin, *Rise of Russia*, 23; Donald W. Treadgold, "Russia and the Far East," in *Russian Foreign Policy: Essays in Historical Perspective*, ed. Ivo J. Lederer (New Haven, CT, 1962), 540–541.

1. KOREA'S PYRRHIC VICTORY

1. Yuangchong Wang, "Provincializing Korea: The Construction of the Chinese Empire in the Borderland and the Rise of the Modern Chinese State," *T'oung Pao* 105 (2019): 128–182; Carl F. Bartz, "The Korean Seclusion Policy, 1860–1876" (PhD diss., University of California, 1952), 2–3; Mary C Wright, "The Adaptability of Ch'ing Diplomacy: The Case of Korea," *Journal of Asian Studies* 17, no. 3 (May 1958): 364.

2. Bartz, "Korean Seclusion Policy," 2.

3. Samuel Hawley, *The Imjin War: Japan's Sixteenth-Century Invasion of Korea and Attempts to Conquer China* (Lexington, KY, 2014), 564. See also G. H. Jones, "The Japanese Invasion," *Korean Repository* 1 (1892): 308–311.

4. Bartz, "Korean Seclusion Policy," 7–8.

5. This was known as the *zongfan* system. Most histories on it state that the Qing simply adopted the Ming tributary system. After 1637 the new Chosŏn-Qing relationship actually became quite coercive, and Manchu rule was resented by many Koreans. Kirk W. Larsen, "Comforting Fictions: The Tribute System—The Westphalian Order, and Sino-Korean Relations," *Journal of East Asian Studies* 13 (2013): 233–257. See also Yuanchong Wang, "Claiming Centrality in the Chinese World: Manchu-Chosŏn Relations and the Making of the Qing's 'Zhongguo' Identity, 1616–43," *Chinese Historical Review* 22, no. 2 (2015): 95–119; Wang, "Recasting the Chinese Empire: Qing China and Chŏson Korea, 1610s–1910" (PhD diss., Cornell University, 2014). Contact between the two nations varied. From 1637 to 1643, the Qing sent 12 missions and 28 emissaries to Chosŏn Korea, an average of 1.5 missions per year, while Chosŏn sent 56 missions and 102 emissaries over the same period, an average of 7 missions a year. See Wang, "Recasting the Chinese Empire," 100–101.

6. A Qing official described the eastern line thus: "The Willow Palisade divides [the inner land] from the Mongols. It reaches the Chosŏn in the south and the Shanhai Mountains in the west. Illegal intruders beyond the [palisade] are severely punished. . . . Within the preserve, barren mountains bar the passage, so that the roads are decayed and closed." See Seomin Kim, *Ginseng and Borderland: Territorial Boundaries and Political Relations between Qing China and Chosŏn Korea, 1636–1912* (Oakland, 2017): 82; 88–92. Bartz, "Korean Seclusion Policy," 27; Mary C. Wright, The Adaptability of Ch'ing Diplomacy: The Case of Korea," *Journal of Asian Studies* 17, no. 3 (May 1958): 366; Niansheng Song, *Making Borders in Modern East Asia: The Tumen River Demarcation, 1881–1919* (Cambridge, 2019), 16–53; Alyssa Park, *Sovereignty Experiments: Korean Migrants and the Building of Borders in Northeast Asia, 1860–1945* (Ithaca, NY, 2019), 30–38.

7. KJSL, May 15, 1864 (lunar), http://sillok.history.go.kr/id/kza_10105015_006; Takemichi Hara, "Korea, China, and Western Barbarians: Diplomacy in Early Nineteenth-Century Korea," *Modern Asian Studies* 32, no. 2 (May 1998): 396.

8. David J. Dillon, *The Rise of Asia* (London, 1950), 23.

9. B. D. Pak, *Koreitsy v Rossiiskoi imperii (Dal'nevostochnyi period)* [Koreans in the Russian Empire (The Far East period)] (Moscow, 1993), 19–20.

10. N. M. Przhevalsky, *Puteshestvie v Ussuriiskom krae, 1867–1869 gg* [Travels in Ussuri Krai, 1867–1869] (Moscow, 1947), 97. Przhevalsky was a renowned explorer of Central Asia and East Asia. In 1867 he embarked on an expedition of the Ussuri Krai and even went into northern Korea.

11. Pak, *Koreitsy v Rossiiskoi Imperii*, 24–25.

12. Pak, *Koreitsy v Rossiiskoi Imperii*, 20–21.

13. Similar conflict between Korea and China over the Yalu border region was ever present. Hwang Chong-hyŏn, governor of P'yŏngan Province, often complained about the smuggling activities occurring along the border region. KJSL, 11 kwan, January 28, 1874, http://sillok.history.go.kr/id/kza_11101028_001.

14. Przhevalsky, *Puteshestvie*, 97.

15. King Ch'ŏlchong died in December 1863, so Kojong ascended the throne in December when his reign technically began. In 1864, the Taewŏn'gun and the Dowager Queen became co-regents.

16. Pak Chae-gyŏng, *Kŭnse Chosŏn Chŏnggam* [Treatise on early Korean politics] (Seoul, 1975) (hereafter cited as *Chŏnggam*), 42–47. The *Chŏnggam* was originally written in Chinese and published in Tokyo in 1886. The primary author is not known. While the title page lists Pak Chae-hyŏng as the author, the preface of the book refers to I-sun as the book's author. I-sun was the penname of Pak Chae-gyŏng. See Kenneth Quinones, "The Kunse Chosŏn Chŏnggam and Modern Korean Historiography," *Harvard Journal of Asiatic Studies* 40, no. 2 (December 1980): 507–548.

17. *Chŏnggam*, 26.

18. Samuel Hawley, ed., *America's Man in Korea: The Private Letters of George C. Foulk, 1884–1887* (Lanham, MD, 2008), 132.

19. King Ch'ŏlchong was the grandson of King Chŏngjo's (r. 1776–1800) illegitimate brother, who was killed during the Catholic Persecution of 1801. See Kang Jae-eun, *Land of Scholars: Two Thousand Years of Korean Confucianism*, trans. Suzanne Lee (New Jersey, 2003), 422–423.

20. Missions étrangères de Paris, *The Catholic Church in Korea* (Hong Kong, 1924), 39. By the end of Ch'ŏlchong's reign it was said that there were twelve French missionaries and nearly twenty thousand converts in the country. See Ch'oe Ching-young "The Decade of the Taewŏn'gun: Reform, Seclusion and Disaster" (PhD diss., Harvard University, 1960), 262.

21. William Elliot Griffis, *Corea: The Hermit Nation* (New York, 1904), 372–373. Other sources say the number of Catholics more than doubled, from eleven thousand in 1850 to twenty-three thousand in 1865. Jai-Keun Choi, *The Origins of the Roman Catholic Church in Korea: An Examination of Popular and Governmental Responses to Catholic Missions in the Late Chosôn Dynasty* (Norwalk, 2006), 165.

22. Cho Kwang, "Kojong hwangjewa Mwit'el chugyo" [Emperor Kojong and Bishop Mutel], *Kyŏnghyangjapchi* 96 (March 2004): 62–65. See also Cho Kwang, "Wangŭi ŏmŏniŭi yŏngse" [The King's mother's baptism], *Kyŏnghyangjapchi* 96 (June 2004): 62–65; Frederick Pichon, *The Life of Monseigneur Berneux, Bishop of Capse, Vicar-Apostolic of Corea* (London, 1872), 156–157; Charles Dallet, *Histoire de l'Église de Corée*, vol. 2 (Paris, 1874), 502–503.

23. Niansheng Song, *Making Borders*, 16–53.

24. B. D. Pak, *Rossiia i Koreia* [Russia and Korea] (Moscow, 2004), 58. Przhevalsky said that when his expedition crossed the Tumen River, the Koreans were afraid to meet him for fear of getting "their heads chopped off." Przhevalsky, *Puteshestvie, 1867–1869*, 102–103.

25. According to Pak Che-gyŏng, the Taewŏn'gun did in fact meet with Nam and approved the plan to use the French missionaries to prevent a Russian invasion. However, it appears that Bishop Berneux did not respond in time to the Taewŏn'gun's inquiries. *Chŏnggam*,

53–54; Dallet, *Histoire de l'Église de Corée*, 2:522–523; Yi Sŏn-gŭn, *Han'guksa ch'oegunse p'yŏn* [History of Korea: The modern period] (Seoul 1962), 229–240.

26. Cho Kwang, "Kojong hwangjewa Mwitel chugyo," 62–65. See also Cho Kwang, "Wangŭi ŏmŏniŭi yŏngsae," 62–65; Pichon, *Life of Monseigneur Berneux*,156–157; *KNKK*, 55–57.

27. Missions étrangères de Paris, *Catholic Church in Korea*, 40.

28. Missions étrangères de Paris, *Catholic Church in Korea*, 40.

29. Bishop Berneux made Father Daveluy a coadjutor bishop as soon as he arrived in Korea in 1856. He was consecrated bishop in a private house on March 25, 1857. See "The Lives of the 103 Korean Martyr Saints: Bishop Marie Nicholas Antoine Daveluy (1818–1866)," *Catholic Bishops' Conference of Korea Newsletter*, no. 47, Summer 2004, http://www .cbck.or.kr/bbs/enewsletter.asp?board_id=E5100&bid=13001534.

30. Missions étrangères de Paris, *Catholic Church in Korea*, 40; Dallet, *Histories de l'Église Corée*, 2:512–513.

31. Griffis, *Corea*, 374.

32. Vladimir [pseud.] [Z. Volpicelli], *Russia on the Pacific and the Siberian Railroad* (London, 1899), 267–269.

33. Pak, *Koreitsy v Rossiiskoi Imperii*, 24–26.

34. Kang, Sang-kyu, *Chosŏn chŏngch'isa ŭi palgyŏn: Chosŏn ŭi chŏngch'i chihyŏng kwa munmyŏng chŏnhwan ŭi wigi* [Discovering Chosŏn's political history: The political topography of Chosŏn and the crisis of civilizational transformation] (Seoul, 2013), 358. On January 20, 1866, the Korean State Tribunal condemned Nam Chong-sam and Hong Pong-ju and had them executed for treason. KJSL, January 20, 1866 (lunar), http://sillok.history.go .kr/id/kza_10301020_002.

35. Pichon, *Life of Monseigneur Berneux*, 158–159. Pak wrote that "a wholesale arrest was made of all Catholics. The Taewŏn'gun ordered them all to be killed, except for the children, to whom he gave special pardon. Outside of the Sugumun [Sugu Gate] were the corpses of these faithful believers piled up mountains high in the open air. All the people trembled at this dreadful sight and feared the Taewŏn'gun's tigerish might." Nam Chong-sam and Yi Sin-kyu, another Catholic convert, suffered death by dismemberment outside the West Gate. *Chŏnggam*, 56–57.

36. Daniel C. Kane, "Bellonet and Roze: Overzealous Servants of Empire and the 1866 French Attack on Korea," *Korean Studies* 23 (1999): 23.

37. Kane, "Bellonet and Roze," 6.

38. Kane, "Bellonet and Roze," 9.

39. Pichon, *Life of Monseigneur Berneux*, 158; Griffis, *Corea*, 377.

40. KJSL, July 8, 1866, http://sillok.history.go.kr/id/kza_10307008_004.

41. *Chŏnggam*, 73.

42. Griffis, *Corea*, 381. Daniel Kane notes that the Roze mission consisted of nine hundred men. See Kane, "Bellonet and Roze," 23.

43. Daniel Kane, "A Forgotten Firsthand Account of the *Pyŏng'in yangyo* (1866): An Annotated Translation of the Narrative of G. Pradier," *Seoul Journal of Korean Studies* 21, no. 1 (June 2008): 70.

44. See Lee Kyong-hee, "Joseon Royal Books Return Home after 145 years in France," *Koreana: A Quarterly on Korean Art and Culture*, http://www.koreana.or.kr/months/news _view.asp?b_idx=1576&lang=en&page_type=list; and Jean-Marie Thiébaud, *La présence française en Corée de la fin du XVIIIe siècle à nos jours* (Paris, 2005).

45. *Chŏnggam*, 74.

46. For an excellent summary of these events, see Daniel C. Kane, "Heroic Defense of the Hermit Kingdom," *MHQ: The Quarterly Journal of Military History* 12, no. 4 (Summer 2000): 38–47.

47. Griffis, *Corea*, 386.

48. Missions étrangères de Paris, *Catholic Church in Korea*, 50; *Chŏnggam*, 78–79.

49. Carter Eckert, ed., *Korea Old and New: A History* (Seoul, 1990), 197.

50. Months before the French campaign, in August 1866, the American merchant ship *General Sherman* disappeared off the coast of Korea. In June 1871 a fleet of five US warships with five hundred men arrived at Kanghwa to investigate. A brief battle ensued, after which the US commander of the fleet, Rear Admiral John Rodgers, withdrew to China. The Taewŏn'gun hailed this second great "victory" against a Western power as added proof of the wisdom of his seclusion policy. Tyler Dennett, "Seward's Far Eastern Policy," *American Historical Review* 28, no. 1 (October 1922): 54–60.

2. JAPAN'S KOREA PROBLEM

1. "Memorial of Okubo Ichizo, of the Satsuma Clan," extract from newspaper published in *Yeddo*, April 10, 1868, *British Documents on Foreign Affairs, Part 1 Series E* (Asia, 1860–1914) (Bethesda, 2012), 189.

2. Hilary Conroy, *The Japanese Seizure of Korea, 1868–1910: A Study of Realism and Idealism in International Relations* (Philadelphia, 1960), 18–19; Marius Jansen, *The Making of Modern Japan* (Cambridge, MA, 2000), 333–364; E. H. Norman, *The Origins of the Modern Japanese State: Selected Writings of E. H. Norman* (New York, 1975), 192–195; Norman, *Japan's Emergence as a Modern State* (New York, 1940), 85–91.

3. Conroy, *Japanese Seizure of Korea, 1868–1910*, 18.

4. James Lewis, *Frontier Contact between Choson Korea and Tokugawa Japan* (New York, 2003), 146–176.

5. Joseph H. Longford, "Japan's Relations with Korea," *Nineteenth Century* 5 (1904): 210.

6. Tabohashi Kiyoshi, *Kindai Nissen kankei no kenkyū*, [Study of Japan and Korea relations in the modern era], vol. 1 (Seoul, 2002), 301.

7. Marlene Mayo, "The Korean Crisis of 1873 and Early Meiji Foreign Policy," *Journal of Asian Studies* 31, no. 4 (August 1972): 800. See George Alexander Lensen, *The Russian Push toward Japan: Russo-Japanese Relations, 1697–1875* (Princeton, NJ, 1959), 271–307.

8. Shinichi Fumoto, "Russia's Expansion to the Far East and Its Impact on Early Meiji Policy," in *Russia and Its Northeast Asian Neighbors: China, Japan and Korea, 1858–1945*, ed. Kimitaka Matsuzato (Lanham, MD, 2017), 3–4.

9. Fumoto, "Russia's Expansion," 8–10; Tabohashi, *Kindai Nissen kankei no kenkyū*, 1:304–305.

10. Wayne C. McWilliams, "East Meets East: The Soejima Mission to China, 1873," *Monumenta Nipponica* 30, no. 3 (Autumn 1975): 245.

11. Jonathan Spence, *God's Chinese Son: The Taiping Rebellion and the Western Powers* (New York, 1996); Stephen R. Platt, *Autumn in the Heavenly Kingdom: China, the West and the Epic Story of the Taiping Civil War* (New York, 2012).

12. James A. Gao, *Historical Dictionary of Modern China, 1800–1849* (Lanham, MD, 2009), 7.

13. Pamela Kyle Crossley, *The Wobbling Pivot: China since 1800* (London, 2010), 118. See also Albert Feuerwerker, *China's Early Industrialization: Sheng Hsuan-huai (1844–1916) and the Mandarin Enterprise* (Cambridge, MA, 1958); Stanley Spector, *Li Hung Chang and the Huai Army: A Study of Nineteenth Century Chinese Regionalism* (Seattle, 1964).

14. Seward, "Li Hung Chang," *Chinese Recorder and Missionary Journal* 25, no. 12 (December 1894): 584–585.

15. Mayo, "Korean Crisis," 808; McWilliams, "East Meets East," 249–251. See also, Wayne C. McWilliams, "Soejima Taneomi: Statesman of Early Meiji Japan, 1868–1874" (PhD diss., University of Michigan, 1973), 273–274.

16. Mayo, "Korean Crisis," 810.

17. Frederick Foo Chien, *The Opening of Korea: A Study of Chinese Diplomacy* (New York, 1967), 16.

18. T. C. Lin, "Li Hung-chang: His Korean Policies, 1870–1885," *Chinese Social and Political Science Review* 19 (1935–1936): 211–212; McWilliams, "East Meets East," 250–251.

19. McWilliams, "East Meets East," 259–260.

20. McWilliams, "East Meets East," 263.

21. In article 1 of the finalized 1871 Sino-Japanese Treaty, one finds the phrase *suoshu bangtu* (tributary homeland). This phrase was used with the initial intention of identifying Korea as China's "dependency" (*shubang*). When referencing the treaty, however, the Qing used the term *shubang* to refer to Korea. See Okamoto Takashi, "Internalzing 'Territory': How the 'Territory' Concept Became Part of China's Contemporary Apparatus," in *A World History of Suzerainty: A Modern History of East and West Asia and Translated Concept*, ed. Okamoto Takashi (Tokyo 2019), 221–223; T. F. Tiang, "Sino-Japanese Diplomatic Relations, 1870–1984," *Chinese Social and Political Science Review* 28 (April 1933): 17. Disagreements between China and Japan over what exactly was meant by *suoshu bangtu* and *shubang* continued throughout the 1870s; the phrases came to encompass much more than just Korea and were also used in reference to Taiwan and the Ryukyus. See Tabohashi, *Kindai Nissen kankei no kenkyū*, 1:531–533.

22. Tabohashi, *Kindai Nissen kankei no kenkyū*, 315–316.

23. Tabohashi, *Kindai Nissen kankei no kenkyū*, 318.

24. Tabohashi, *Kindai Nissen kankei no kenkyū*, 318–319.

25. Soejima was head of the Imperial Council of State (*Daijō-kan*, or Great Council of the State). His position was formally called "Imperial Councilor of the State" or "Imperial Minister of the State" (*Daijō-daijin*). Under the Meiji Constitution, he was appointed to this position in 1871; the office was abolished in 1885 in favor of the newly created office of prime minister. See McWilliams, "East Meets East," 264–267; Tabohashi, *Kindai Nissen kankei no kenkyū*, 319; Tsiang "Sino-Japanese Diplomatic Relations, 1870–1894," 17. The standard English translation of the Japanese record of the Yanagihara-Yamen dialogue is that given by Nagao Ariga, which appears in Alfread Stead, ed., *Japan by the Japanese* (London, 1904), 161–163.

26. McWilliams, "East Meets East," 269.

27. McWilliams, "East Meets East," 270.

28. On the Korean poster was written: "[The Japanese] do not feel shame in adopting the system from foreigners and changed their appearance as well as their customs. We should not consider them 'Japanese' any more nor should they be allowed to cross into our land. Judging from how the Japanese have behaved recently, we may call [Japan] a lawless country." Tabohashi, *Kindai Nissen kankei no kenkyū*, 320. See also *Meiji Tennō Ki* [Record of the Emperor Meiji], vol. 3 (Tokyo, 1968), 115. It is not clear that the poster on the guardhouse wall was even put up by Tongnae officials. Korean historian Yi Son-gun has argued that it was not, stating that "there is no record in the Korean annals concerning these secret instructions [to insult the Japanese]." See Yi, "Some Lesser Known Facts about the Taewongun and His Foreign Policy," *Transactions of the Korean Branch of the Royal Asiatic Society* 39 (1962): 41–42.

29. Tabohashi, *Kindai Nissen kankei no kenkyū*, 320; *Meiji Tennō Ki*, 3:116–117.

30. Peter Duus, *The Abacus and the Sword: The Japanese Penetration of Korea, 1895–1910* (Berkeley, 1995), 32.

31. Ben Limb, "Sei-Kan Ron: A Study in the Evolution of Expansionism in Modern Japan, 1869–1973" (PhD diss., St. John's University, 1979), 141.

32. Wm. Theodore de Bary, ed., *Sources of Japanese Tradition,* vol. 2 (New York, 2005), 684; *Meiji Tennō Ki,* 3, 117–118.

33. The Iwakura Mission was a large government delegation sent around the world from December 1871 to September 1873. Its progress was meticulously recorded by Kumi Kunitake, who later published an account in *Account of Travel to America and Europe.* See Marius Jensen, *The Making of Modern Japan* (London, 2000), 355–361; Ian Nish, *The Iwakura Mission in America and Europe: A New Assessment* (Tokyo, 1998).

34. Mayo, "Korean Crisis," 794–795.

35. Tabohashi, *Kindai Nissen kankei no kenkyū,* 322–323; *Meiji Tennō Ki,* 3:119–120.

36. De Bary, *Sources of Japanese Tradition,* 686.

37. Mayo, "Korean Crisis," 798.

38. On May 7, 1875, the Sakhalin-Kuril Treaty was signed. Both parties agreed to recognize the entire island of Sakhalin as Russian and the entire Kuril Archipelago as Japanese. See Lensen, *The Russian Push,* 441–443.

39. Mayo, "Korean Crisis," 813; *Meiji Tennō Ki,* 3:140–141.

40. The October 15 meeting of the Supreme Council was attended by Imperial Council members. At the meeting Saigō motioned that a vote be taken to finalize the appointment of the head of the diplomatic mission in accordance with the council decision of August 17. *Meiji Tennō Ki,* 3:143–147.

41. Tabohashi, *Kindai Nissen kankei no kenkyū,* 326.

42. Tabohashi, *Kindai Nissen kankei no kenkyū,* 326.

43. Conroy, *Japanese Seizure of Korea,* 45–47. See also Tabohashi, *Kindai Nissen kankei no kenkyū,* 319–327.

44. *Meiji Tennō Ki,* 3:148–149. From "Memorial concerning the Korea Question," in *Iwakura Tomomi kankei Monjo* [Papers of Iwakura Tomomi], ed. Takematsu Ōtsuka (Tokyo, 1927–1935), 1:363–366; Limb, *Sei-Kan Ron,* 197–198.

45. *Meiji Tennō Ki,* 3:148–149; Tabohashi, *Kindai Nissen kankei no kenkyū,* 327; Limb, *Sei-Kan Ron,* 198.

46. Saigō had already tendered his resignation on October 23; all former members of his pro-war camp—Itagaki, Gotō, Etō, and Soejima—resigned the following day. Tabohashi, *Kindai Nissen Kankei no Kenkyū,* 328; *Meiji Tennō Ki,* 3:150–151.

47. John Russell Young, a member of General Ulysses S. Grant's party who met Iwakura in 1879 during the latter's travel to Japan, recalled, "He has a striking face with lines showing firmness and decision, and you saw the scar which marked the attempt of an assassin to cut him down and slay him." John Russell Young, *Around the World with General Grant,* vol. 2 (New York, 1879), 527. See also Richard T. Chang, "General Grant's 1879 Visit to Japan," *Monumenta Nipponica* 24, no. 4 (1969): 373–392.

48. Keene, *Emperor of Japan,* 244.

3. THE OPENING OF KOREA

1. James Palais, *Politics and Policy in Traditional Korea* (Cambridge, MA, 1975), 39; Pak Chae-gyŏng, *Kŭnse Chosŏn Chŏnggam* [Treatise on early Korean politics] (Seoul, 1975) (hereafter cited as *Chŏnggam*), 49–50.

2. George C. Foulk, *America's Man in Korea: The Private Letters of George C. Foulk, 1884–1887* (Plymouth, 2008), 49.

3. Palais, *Politics and Policy*, 202–219; *Chŏnggam*, 50–53.

4. Song Si-yŏl (1607–1687, pen name Uam) was a renowned seventeenth-century scholar. See Palais, *Politics and Policy*, 113–119.

5. *Chŏnggam*, 98. The term *ch'ŏng-ŭi* [清議] is literally translated as "clean criticism or pure critique."

6. Palais, *Politics and Policy*, 115–127.

7. *Chŏnggam*, 99–100.

8. *Chŏnggam*, 99–100.

9. *Cho'nggam*, 99–101; Palais, *Politics and Policy*, 47, 121–122. See also Key-huik Kim, *The Last Phase of the East Asian World Order* (Berkeley, 1980), 31–32; Munsang Seoh, "The Ultimate Concern of Yi Korean Confucians: An Analysis of the i-ki Debates," *Occasional Papers on Korea* 5 (March 1977): 41.

10. Palais, *Politics and Policy*, 119. Private academies were not eliminated completely.

11. *Chŏnggam*, 101, 102.

12. *Chŏnggam*, 110.

13. Ching Young Choe, "The Decade of the Taewŏn'gun: Reform, Seclusion and Disaster" (PhD diss., Harvard University, 1960), 488–489.

14. Palais, *Politics and Policy*, 181. Choe, "Decade of the Taewongun," 493.

15. Palais, *Politics and Policy*, 28. This was essentially the argument that was made to Queen Dowager Cho by her ministers, who advocated that the Taewŏn'gun be accorded a ceremonial role with respect to Kojong but not hold real power. *Chŏnggam*, 41–42.

16. Palais, *Politics and Policy*, 176–201. Pak Chae-gyŏng also notes the Taewŏn'gun's crackdown on local corruption, especially regarding the grain storage problem, which made him very popular. See *Chŏnggam*, 104–105.

17. Palais, *Politics and Policy*, 191–192.

18. Kang Jae-eun, *The Land of Scholars: Two Thousand Years of Korean Confucianism*, trans. Suzanne Lee (Paramus, NJ, 2006), 445.

19. The queen consort of Kojong was the sister (by adoption) of Min Sung-ho, the brother of the Taewŏn'gun's wife. *Chŏnggam*, 69–70.

20. *Chŏnggam*, 70.

21. Ch'oe Mun-hyŏng, *Myŏngsŏnghwanghu sihaeŭi chinsirŭl palk'inda* [Revealing the truth behind Empress Myŏngsŏng's assassination] (Seoul, 2006), 70.

22. This advice was also proffered by Prosper Marie-Giquel, a French naval officer who played an important role in coordinating the French and English campaigns to drive the Taiping rebels out of Shanghai. KJSL, June 24, 1874 (lunar), http://sillok.history.go.kr/id/kza_11106024_001. See also T. C. Lin, "Li Hung Chang: His Korea Policies, 1870–1885," *Chinese Social and Political Science Review* 19, no. 2 (July 1935): 213.

23. Yi Yu-wŏn rejected China's help out of hand. KJSL, June 25, 1874 (lunar), http://sillok.history.go.kr/id/kza_11106025_002.

24. "The destruction of relations between us and Japan is the fault of this official [An Dong-jun]," Yi concluded. "Therefore I suggest that we should immediately investigate and punish him." KJSL, June 29, 1874 (lunar), http://sillok.history.go.kr/id/kza_11106029_001.

25. Pak Kyu-su, accusing An of exaggerating Japan's political changes and being overly critical of its official usage of the term *hwangche* (emperor), faulted An for refusing to accept the Japanese documents. KJSL, June 29, 1874 (lunar), http://sillok.history.go.kr/id/kza_11106029_001. See also Choe, "Decade of the Taewongun," 518–520.

26. KNKK, 549. See also KJSL, September 20, 1874 (lunar), http://sillok.history.go.kr/id/kza_11109020_001.

27. Kang Sang-kyu, *Chosŏn chŏngch'isaŭi palgyŏn* [Discovering Chosŏn's political history], 436; James B. Palais, "Korea on the Eve of the Kanghwa Treaty, 1873–1876" (PhD diss., Harvard University 1968), 621.

28. Palais, *Politics and Policy,* 290.

29. Palais, *Politics and Policy,* 255.

30. Hilary Conroy, *The Japanese Seizure of Korea, 1868–1910: A Study of Realism and Idealism in International Relations* (Philadelphia, 1960), 61.

31. William Elliot Griffis, *Corea: The Hermit Nation* (New York, 1904), 422.

32. Donald Keene, *Emperor of Japan: Meiji and His World, 1852–1912* (New York, 2002), 256. Keene notes the day Kuroda set sail as January 6. He meant January 31; January 6 is the lunar date.

33. Ivan Parker Hall, *Mori Arinori* (Cambridge, MA, 1973), 1.

34. The phrase in the 1871 Sino-Japanese treaty that was signed in Chinese and Japanese is *suoshu bangtu. Suoshu* [所属] means "belong to"; *bangtu* [邦土] is too vague to be exactly defined. *Bang* [邦] means "country," and *tu* [土] means "land." But *bangtu* can also mean "country," "land," or "territorial possessions," which is how it is translated in the English version of the treaty. However, the more literal translation of the *suoshu bangtu* is "tributary homeland"—because the implication is that the land/territory/country "belongs to" China. See Yuanchong Wang, "Provincializing Korea: The Construction of the Chinese Empire in the Borderland and the Rise of the Modern Chinese State," *T'ong Pao* 105 (2019): 165–166; Wang, "Recasting the Chinese Empire: Qing China and Chosŏn Korea, 1610s–1910s" (PhD diss., Cornell University, 2014), 225–226.

35. *KNKK,* 532.

36. *KNKK,* 537–539; T. F. Tsiang, "Sino-Japanese Diplomatic Relations, 1870–1894," *Chinese Social and Political Science Review* 17, no. 1 (April 1933): 59–60; *LZR,* 1:122–127.

37. *KNKK,* 539.

38. *KNKK,* 542–543.

39. Cited in Carl Bartz, "The Korean Seclusion Policy, 1860–1976" (PhD diss., University of California, 1952), 164.

40. KJSL, January 20, 1876 (lunar), http://sillok.history.go.kr/id/kza_11301020_001.

41. Kim, *The Last Phase,* 241; *KNKK,* 549–553.

42. Palais, "Korea on the Eve," 743; Peter Lee et al., eds., *Sourcebook of Korean Civilization,* vol. 2 (New York, 2000), 240–241.

43. Palais, *Politics and Policy,* 263.

44. KJSL, January 27, 1876 (lunar), http://sillok.history.go.kr/id/kza_11301027_001#.

4. CHINA'S KOREA PROBLEM

1. From 1607 to 1811 the Korean embassy visited Japan twelve times, but the last embassy (1811) only went as far as Tsushima. See James Lewis, *Frontier Contact between Chosŏn Korea and Tokugawa* (London, 2003), 7–8.

2. William Elliot Griffis, *Corea: The Hermit Nation* (New York, 1904), 423–424.

3. Thomas Bailey, *A Diplomatic History of the American People* (New York, 1950), 334; Pow-key Sohn, "The Opening of Korea: A Conflict of Tradition," *Transactions of the Korea Branch of the Royal Asiatic Society* 36 (1960): 102.

4. Key-Huik Kim, *The Last Phase of East Asian World Order: Korea, Japan and the Chinese Empire, 1860–1882* (Berkeley, 1980), 258.

5. Kim Ki-su, Kim Hong-jip, and Pak Yŏng-hyo, *Susinsa kirok* [Collection of records of envoys] (Seoul, 1971), 116.

6. Kim Ki-su et al., *Susinsa kirok,* 118.

7. Kim Ki-su et al., *Susinsa kirok*, 119–120.

8. Kim Ki-su et al., *Susinsa kirok*, 122; *KNKK*, 740.

9. Frederick Foo Chien, *The Opening of Korea: A Study of Chinese Diplomacy* (New York, 1967), 57–58.

10. Immanuel C. Y. Hsu, *The Ili Crisis: A Study of Sino-Russian Diplomacy, 1871–1881* (Oxford, 1965).

11. In his letter of August 26, 1879, Li explains why opening trade relations with Western countries was so critical to Korea's security: "Britain, France, Germany and the US are all tens of thousands of miles away from Korea." The only dangerous country is Russia, "because it shares a border with Korea on the north. If Korea trades with Western countries, it can prevent harassment from Russia." KJSL, July 9, 1879 (lunar), http://sillok.history.go.kr/id/kza_11607009_001. See also Key-Huik Kim, *The Last Phase*, 284–285.

12. Huang Zunxian, *Chosŏn ch'aekryak* [A strategy for Korea], ed. Kim Sung-il (Seoul, 2011), 39–40.

13. Kim Ki-su et al., *Susinsa Kirok*, 176; Henry Wheaton, *Elements of International Law, with a Sketch of the History of Science* (Philadelphia, 1836). William Alexander Parsons Martin was an American Presbyterian missionary to China.

14. Huang, *Chosŏn ch'aekryak*, 72.

15. Key-Huik Kim, *The Last Phase*, 295.

16. Huang, *Chosŏn ch'aekryak*, 81–82.

17. Huang, *Chosŏn ch'aekryak*, 87–88.

18. Huang, *Chosŏn ch'aekryak*, 68–69. Emphasis is mine.

19. Kim Ki-su et al., *Susinsa kirok*, 155–158.

20. Kim Ki-su et al., *Susinsa Kirok*, 158–159. See also KJSL, August 28, 1880 (lunar), http://sillok.history.go.kr/id/kza_11708028_001#.

21. At the court conference on September 8, 1880 (lunar), State Councilor Yi Ch'oe-ŭng tried to persuade Kojong of the merits of Huang's treatise: "Indeed. If Russia invades Korea, Japan will also be in danger. We cannot take it for granted that Russia will not invade Korea while paying its attention to Japan. Our city guards and armies never took the threat seriously, and they never made any preparation for this [potential] war." KJSL, September 8, 1880 (lunar), http://sillok.history.go.kr/id/kza_11709008_001.

22. Key-Huik Kim, *The Last Phase*, 304; Charles Oscar Paullin, "The Opening of Korea by Commodore Shufeldt," *Political Science Quarterly* 25, no. 3 (September 1910): 478–479.

23. *LZR*, 1:142–143.

24. Shufeldt to R. W. Thompson, August 30, 1880, Shufeldt Papers, box 24, LOC.

25. Key-Huik Kim, *The Last Phase*, 305.

26. Shufeldt, "Corea and American Interests in the East," October 13, 1880, Shufeldt Papers, box 24, LOC. Emphasis is mine.

27. Shufeldt, "Corea and American Interests."

28. Martina Deuchler, *Confucian Gentlemen and Barbarian Envoys, 1875–1885* (Seattle, 1977), 92–98; *KNKK*, 751–752.

29. Deuchler, *Confucian Gentlemen*, 103.

30. Kim Yun-se, *Ŭmch'ŏng-sa* [Kim yun-sik's diary] (Seoul, 1958), 45–46. It is unclear whether Ŏ was at this meeting. He is not mentioned by Kim, but presumably they were together.

31. Li to Shufeldt, February 6, 1882, Shufeldt Papers, box 24, LOC.

32. Chester Holcombe to Shufeldt, January 3, 1882, Shufeldt Papers, box 24, LOC.

33. *LZR*, 1:195–196.

34. Kim Yun-se, *Ŭmch'ŏng-sa*, 111–112; Deuchler, *Confucian Gentlemen*, 119.

35. Halcombe to Shufeldt, April 6, 1882, Shufeldt Papers, box 24, LOC.

36. Although a date is not specified, it seems that the meeting took place on April 4. See Kim Yun-se, *Ŭmch'ŏng-sa*, 200.

37. Shufeldt, "The Treaty with Korea," Shufeldt Papers, box 28, LOC. Shufeldt gives no date for this interview, but based on other sources it most likely occurred on April 4, 1882.

38. In a letter of April 22 to Prime Minister Yi Ch'ae-ŭng, Li assured his Korean friends of their continued security: "If you establish treaty relations with the United States, not only will you be free from Japan's covetous advances, you can also have a model treaty for other Western countries which will come to Korea to conclude similar treaties with Korea." See Kim Yun-se, *Ŭmch'ŏng-sa*, 201.

39. Deuchler, *Confucian Gentlemen*, 121–122.

40. Like the Korea-American counterpart, the Korean-British Treaty and the Korean-German Treaty were negotiated though the good offices of Chinese official Ma Jiangzhong. The provisions of these treaties were virtually indistinguishable from the American version. See Kirk W. Larsen, *Tradition, Treaties and Trade: Qing Imperialism and Chosŏn Korea, 1850–1910* (Cambridge, MA, 2008), 79–80; Huajeong Seok, "International Rivalry in Korea and Russia's East Asian Policy in the Late 19th Century," *Korea Journal* 50, no. 3 (Autumn 2010): 182.

41. *KNKK*, 752.

42. Key-Huik Kim, *The Last Phase*, 297.

43. KJSL, February 26, 1881 (lunar), http://sillok.history.go.kr/id/kza_11802026_004. See also Peter H. Lee, ed., *Sourcebook of Korean Civilization*, vol. 1 (New York, 1996), 335–336.

44. *KNKK*, 752–753.

45. KJSL, February 26, 1881 (lunar), http://sillok.history.go.kr/id/kza_11802026_004.

46. For example, in a memorial submitted by the scholar Sin-sŏp, from Kyonggi-do, on July 31, 1881, Sin singles out Yi Yu-wŏn and Kim Hong-jip for treason: "They intend to put the country into chaos. Why does your Majesty believe these traitors and reject the sincere advice of righteous people?" KJSL, July 6, 1881 (lunar), http://sillok.history.go.kr/id/kza_11807106_005.

47. The entire conspiracy is covered in depth in Tabohashi Kiyoshi, *Kindai Nissen kankei no kenkyū*, [Study of Japan and Korea relations in the modern era], vol. 1 (Seoul, 2002), 758–762. See also Griffis, *Corea*, 433; Key-Huik Kim, *The Last Phase*, 310; Homer Hulbert, *Hulbert's History of Korea*, ed. Clarence Weems (New York, 1962), 222–224.

48. Hwang Hyŏn, *Maech'ŏn yarok* [Memoirs of Hwang Hyŏn], vol. 1 (Seoul, 2005), 277.

49. Hwang, *Maech'ŏn yarok*, 165–166; *KNKK*, 772.

50. Hwang's portrayal of the Taewŏn'gun as a reluctant participant is very different from the account given by Tabohashi, who wrote that from the moment the mutinous soldiers sought his help, the Taewŏn'gun took charge of plans to depose the queen, attack the Japanese legation, and expel the Japanese. See *KNKK*, 772–773.

51. The Taewŏn'gun's wife rescued the queen by leading her to her own private carriage and hiding her there. At the moment when her hiding place was discovered, a quick-thinking officer loyal to the queen pronounced that the woman in the carriage was his sister and carried her out of the palace; she was then moved to a safe house in the countryside. *KNKK*, 774–775.

52. *KNKK*, 780. Min Kyŏm-ho, the main culprit in the events that had led to the political upheaval, threw himself on the mercy of the Taewŏn'gun, who refused to help. Hwang, *Maech'ŏn yarok*, 167–168.

53. Hwang, *Maech'ŏn yarok*, 165–166. Tabohashi writes that all twenty-eight Japanese legation personnel managed to escape alive, with only three sustaining light wounds during the ordeal. The fact that there were no women or children among them "provided a feeling of relief." See *KNKK*, 778.

54. Kim Yun-se, *Ŭmch'ŏng-sa*, 177–178; Key-Huik Kim, *The Last Phase*, 318.

55. Key-Huik Kim, *The Last Phase*, 318.

56. Dong Jae Yim, "The Abduction of the Taewŏn'gun: 1882," in *Papers on China*, vol. 21 (Cambridge, MA, February 1968), 106–107; Hwang, *Maech'ŏn yarok*, 167; Kim Yun-se, *Ŭmch'ŏng-sa*, 181.

57. Kim Yun-se, *Ŭmch'ŏng-sa*, 178–179.

58. Ma Jianzhong, *Dong xing san lu* [Three journals of the journey to the East], pt. 1 (Taipei, 1967), 56–57.

59. Dong, "The Abduction," 108.

60. Kim Yun-se, *Ŭmch'ŏng-sa*, 183–184; Dong, "The Abduction," 108.

61. Ma, *Dong xing san lu*, 58–60.

62. Li received a telegram from Zhang Shusheng on July 19 (lunar) informing him that "Ma Jianzhong and others had managed to trap the Taewŏn'gun and send him to Tianjin under escort." See *CJCC*, 18. See also Key-Huik Kim, *The Last Phase*, 319; Ma, *Dong xing san lu*, 70–72.

63. *CJCC*, 1–2 (Li's letter to Zhang Zhixuan, June 30, 1882 [lunar]). Li wrote to Zhang that he wanted to avoid at all costs fighting a war with Japan in Korea.

64. Kim Yun-sik wrote that the Chinese arrived on August 11 (lunar June 29). Kim Yun-se, *Ŭmch'ŏng-sa*, 187. Other sources put the date of arrival in Korea at August 10. Key-Huik Kim, *The Last Phase*, 321.

65. Ma, *Dong xing san lu*, 71–72; Dong, "The Abduction," 116.

66. Dong, "The Abduction," 112.

67. *CJCC*, 1–2 (Li's letter to Zhang Zhixuan, June 30, 1882 [lunar]).

68. *CJCC*, 1–2 (Li's letter to Zhang Zhixuan, June 30, 1882 [lunar], August 13 [solar]).

69. According to Kim Yun-sik, thirteen Chinese war vessels and four thousand men were deployed to Korea. Kim Hong-jip and Ŏ Yun-jung served as guides for the journey. See Kim Yun-se, *Ŭmch'ŏngsa*, 185–186.

70. Ma, *Dong xing san lu*, 70–72. This implies that the August 21 letter that Ma received from the Taewŏn'gun was his second letter, as Ma arrived in Inch'ŏn on or about August 11. It is assumed, therefore, that Japan's seven-point ultimatum was discussed earlier, during Ma's first meeting with the Taewŏn'gun.

71. Dong, "The Abduction," 117.

72. Ma, *Dong xing san lu*, 73.

73. Dong, "The Abduction," 119; Hwang *Maech'ŏn yarok*, 179–180; Ma, *Dong xing san lu*, 73.

74. Ma arranged for the Japanese and the Koreans to work out an indemnity agreement. Japan was also allowed to station Japanese troops in Korea to guard the Japanese legation. The treaty further mandated the destruction of all anti-foreign tablets that had been erected by the Taewŏn'gun. See Larsen, *Tradition, Treaties and Trade*, 88; Hwang, *Maech'ŏn yarok*, 185.

75. Hwang, *Maech'ŏn yarok*, 173. Preparations for the state funeral for the deceased queen diverted major government resources from the substantial work of actual governing. *KNKK*, 785.

76. Kim Ki-su et al., *Susina kirok*, 195.

77. Young I. Lew, "The Reform Efforts and Ideas of Pak Yŏng-hyo, 1894–1895," *Korean Studies* 1 (1977): 22.

78. Andre Schmid, *Korea between Empires, 1895–1919* (New York, 2002), 30.

79. Harold F. Cook, *Korea's 1884 Incident and Kim Ok-kyun's Elusive Dream* (Seoul, 1972), 22.

80. Ishikawa Mikiaki, *Fukuzawa Yukichi Den* [The life of Fukuzawa Yukichi] (Tokyo, 1932), 285–289.

81. Hilary Conroy, *The Japanese Seizure of Korea, 1868–1910: A Study of Realism and Idealism in International Relations* (Philadelphia, 1960), 127–140.

82. Larsen, *Tradition, Treaties and Trade*, 89–90.

83. H. Parkes to Earl Granville, December 21, 1882, *British Documents on Foreign Affairs*, pt. 1, ser. E, Asia, 1860–1914, vol. 2, ed. Ian Nish (Bethesda, MD, 2012), 105.

84. H. Parkes to Earl Granville, 104; Larsen, *Tradition, Treaties and Trade*, 91–92.

85. Marlene J. Mayo, "The Korean Crisis of 1873 and Early Meiji Foreign Policy," *Journal of Asian Studies* 31, no. 4 (August 1972): 817.

86. Conroy, *Japanese Seizure of Korea*, 135.

87. Inoue officially became the Japanese foreign min 1885. Kim Ok-kyun, *Kapsin illok* [Kapsin diary] (Seoul, 1977), 30–31, 36–41, 63–65. "Kapsin" refers to the year 1884 in the traditional Korean calendar.

88. Ishikawa, *Fukuzawa Yukichi Den*, 288.

89. Inoue Kakugorō, *Kanjo no zanmu* [K. *Sŏul namgyŏdun kkum*, Memory of Seoul] (1891), trans. Han Sang-il (Seoul, 1993), 41.

90. Ishikawa, *Fukuzawa Yukichi Den*, 363–379. The police interrogation of Fukuzawa was conducted on March 15, 1888. Inoue Kakugorō had been arrested in January 1888. See also Cook, *Korea's 1884 Incident*, 160.

91. Chien, *The Opening of Korea*, 149–150. Kim Ok-kyun, *Kapsin illok*, 63–65; Deuchler, *Confucian Gentlemen*, 206. The incident is known in Korea as the *kaspin chŏngbyŏn*, the political disturbance of the year *kapsin* (1884).

92. *LZR*, 1:219.

93. Inoue, *Kanjo no zanmu*, 50–51.

94. *LZR*, 1:219–221. See also Jerome Ch'en, *Yuan Shih-K'ai, 1856–1916: Brutus Assumes the Purple* (Stanford, 1961), 26–30.

95. The fate of the coup leaders and their families was tragic. Hong Yŏng-sik was killed by Qing soldiers; his family committed suicide. Pak Yŏng-hyo's two brothers were also killed during the uprising; his father later starved himself to death. Kim Ok-kyun's father, older brother, wife, and children were all put to death after the Kapsin coup. The families of Sŏ Kwang-bŏm and Sŏ Jae-p'il were also killed. Inoue, *Kanjo no zanmu*, 55–56.

96. George M. McCune and John A. Harrison, *Korean-American Relations: Documents Pertaining to the Far Eastern Diplomacy of the United States*, vol. 1, *Initial Period, 1883–1886* (Berkeley, 1951), 96–97.

97. Inoue, *Kanjo no zanmu*, 55.

98. Inoue, *Kanjo no zanmu*, 55.

99. Inoue, *Kanjo no zanmu*, 56.

100. *LZR*, 1:269–272.

101. *LZR*, 1:272–273.

102. T. C. Lin, "Li Hung-Chang: His Korea Policies, 1870–1885," *Chinese Social and Political Science Review* 19, no. 2 (July 1935): 231.

103. *LZR*, 1:279.

104. Lin, "Li Hung-Chang," 231.

5. THE OTHER GREAT GAME BEGINS

1. Simon Sebag Montefiore, *The Romanovs, 1613–1918* (New York, 2016), 432.

2. Russian anarchist Pyotr Kropotkin defined it as a struggle against all forms of tyranny, hypocrisy, and artificiality, which he linked to the mores and values of Saint Petersburg

society and the repressive Russian state. P. Kropotkin, *Memoirs of a Revolutionist* (London, 1899), 182–183.

3. Samuel Kucherov, "The Case of Vera Zasulich," *Russian Review* 11, no. 2 (April 1952): 86–87. See also Jay Bergman, *Vera Zasulich: A Biography* (Stanford, CA, 1983).

4. E. Belfer, "Zemlya vs. Volya from Narodnichestvo to Marxism," *Soviet Studies* 30, no. 3 (July 1978): 301–302. See also Richard Pipes, *The Degaev Affair: Terror and Treason in Tsarist Russia* (New Haven, CT, 2003), 10; Pipes, "The Trial of Vera Z," *Russian History* 37, no. 1 (2010): 33–50.

5. Cited in Pipes, *The Degaev Affair*, 19–22. Pipes notes that Ivan Turgenev was so impressed by Vera Zasulich that he glorified her in *Senilia*, his "Poems in Prose," in a sketch called "Threshold." Even the archreactionary Fyodor Dostoevsky confessed that if he accidentally overheard a discussion among revolutionaries plotting a terrorist act, he would not report them to the authorities.

6. Dietrich Geyer, *Russian Imperialism: Interaction of Domestic and Foreign Policy, 1960–1914* (New Haven, CT, 1987), 83–84.

7. Montefiore, *The Romanovs*, 435.

8. Charles Marvin describes the siege of Geok Tepe in vivid detail. Marvin, "The Russians at the Gates of Herat," *Harper's Franklin Square Library*, April 24, 1885.

9. "Russia's Campaign in Asia," *New York Times*, February 13, 1881.

10. "Russia's Campaign in Asia."

11. Marvin, "Russians at the Gates," 3. Another prominent writer on the Russian peril was Arminius Vambery. In his first English-language introductory travel book, *Travels in Central Asia* (London, 1864), and in his *Coming Struggle for India* (London, 1865), Vambery devotes considerable space to the Russian menace to British interests in Central Asia. Peter Hopkirk, *The Great Game: The Struggle for Empire in Central Asia* (Tokyo, 1992), 418–419; David Mandler, "Introduction to Arminius Vambery," *Shofar* 25, no. 3 (Spring 2007): 1–31.

12. "England and Russia," *New York Times*, February 8, 1879.

13. J. H. Rose, *Development of the European Nations, 1870–1914*, vol. 2 (New York, 1905), 127–128. As late as April 1882, M. de Giers assured Edward Thornton, the ambassador at Constantinople, "not once, but several times, . . . that Russia had no intention whatever at present of advancing towards Sarakhs or Merv, or of occupying with her forces any territory in that region beyond what was already in her possession" (Thorton to Granville, April 29, 1882, in *Parliamentary Papers*,1884, vol. 87, *Central Asia*, no. 1, 13, NA. Within three months, however, British agents were in possession of documents showing that the Russians were seeking to obtain the submission of the Merv chiefs. See William Habberton, *Anglo-Russian Relations concerning Afghanistan, 1837–1907*, monograph, *Illinois Studies in the Social Sciences* 21, no. 4 (1937): 49–50, n. 6.

14. Immanuel C. Y. Hsu, *The Ili Crisis: A Study of Sino-Russian Diplomacy, 1878–1881* (Oxford, 1965).

15. Hopkirk, *The Great Game*, 409–410.

16. "The Rout of the Jingoes: Mr. Gladstone's Triumph over His Political Rival," *New York Times*, April 19, 1880.

17. Hopkirk, *The Great Game*, 409; Alexander Mikhailovich, *Once a Grand Duke* (London, 1932), 450–454.

18. W. Bruce Lincoln, *The Romanovs: Autocrats of All the Russians* (New York, 1981), 601; W. T. Stead, ed., *The M.P. for Russia: Reminiscences and Correspondence of Madame Olga Novikoff* (New York, 1909), 126.

19. Mikhailovich, *Once a Grand Duke*, 63.

20. Lincoln, *The Romanovs*, 590.

21. Frederic S. Zuckerman, *The Tsarist Secret Police in Russian Society, 1880–1917* (New York, 1996), 2; Montefiore, *The Romanovs,* 465.

22. *Okhrana* typically appears as the designation for the tsarist secret police, from *Okhrannoe otdeleniye* (Guard Department). Frederic S. Zuckerman, *The Tsarist Secret Police in Russian Society, 1880–1917* (New York, 1996), 465–466.

23. Pipes, *The Degaev Affair,* 88. See also Michael Aronson, "Geographical and Socioeconomic Factors in the 1881 Anti-Jewish Pogroms in Russia," *Russian Review* 39, no. 1 (January 1980): 18–31; Montefiore, *The Romanovs,* 463–464; Lincoln, *The Romanovs,* 591–593.

24. Sergei Witte, *The Memoirs of Sergei Witte,* trans. Sidney Harcave (New York, 1990), 173.

25. Mikhailovich, *Once a Grand Duke,* 67.

26. Witte, *Memoirs,* 173.

27. Habberton, "Anglo-Russian Relations," 50.

28. "The Muscovite Advance," *New York Times,* April 30, 1885; Hopkirk, *The Great Game,* 427.

29. "A Conflict Inevitable: England and Russia Almost Sure to Fight," *New York Times,* April 24, 1885.

30. Habberton, "Anglo-Russian Relations," 54.

31. Mikhailovich, *Once a Grand Duke,* 69.

32. "England's War Fever," *New York Times,* April 12, 1885.

33. George Alexander Lensen, *Balance of Intrigue: International Rivalry in Korea and Manchuria, 1884–1899,* vol. 1 (Tallahassee, 1982), 55.

34. *LZR,* 1:297.

35. *LZR,* 1:298; KJSL, March 22, 1885 (lunar), http://sillok.history.go.kr/id/kza _12203020_007.

36. On October 1, as promised, Ladyzhensky sent the written declaration to Li. It included the promise "not to occupy Korean territory," but it suggested that Russia still maintained the right to interfere in Korea's internal affairs. After a series of frustrating negotiations, Li had to finally accept an ambiguously written statement, dated October 6, that made it clear that while Russia had no intention of occupying any part of the peninsula, it would not abandon its interests in the peninsula altogether. *LZR,* 1:299–306.

37. Yur-bok Lee, *West Goes East: Paul Georg Von Mollendorff and Great Power Imperialism in Late Yi Korea* (Honolulu, 1988), 89. Möllendorf also objected to the British occupation of Port Hamilton. KJSL, April 3, 1885 (lunar calendar), http://sillok.history.go.kr /id/kza_12204003_002. The British occupation of the island thus set up the context for Möllendorf's strong-arm policy in Korea regarding military advisers. Li responded by writing to the Zongli Yamen requesting that troops be deployed to Korea on September 27, 1885 (lunar) and that Möllendorf be recalled.

38. Yur-bok Lee, *Diplomatic Relations between the United States and Korea, 1866–1887* (New York, 1970), 98–99.

39. Lee, *Diplomatic Relations,* 111; Huangjeong Seok, "International Rivalry in Korea and Russia's East Asian Policy in the Late Nineteenth Century," *Korea Journal* 30, no. 30 (Autumn 2010): 184.

40. *LZR,* 1:312–315; Young Ick Lew, "Yüan Shih-k'ai's Residency and the Korean Enlightenment Movement (1885–94)," *Journal of Korean Studies* 5 (1984): 69. On June 19, 1885 (lunar calendar) (July 30 solar), Li met with the Taewŏn'gun, who said he wanted to return to Korea, promising to "step back and never interfere in government affairs again." See *CJCC,* 31–32.

41. Li Honghang wrote: "Because the incident [the 1884 Kapsin coup] came about out of the blue, at the moment we really have no other better way than to place our hope on Yi

Ha-ŭng. It seems that Yi Ha-ŭng is desirous to devote himself to protecting and saving his country . . . After going through so many [personal] upheavals, I can see him calming down. So if we send him back to Korea, [I think] he would feel so appreciative toward us that he will seek to repay his debt of gratitude [by being loyal to us]." See *CJCC*, 23-24.

42. *CJCC*, 31-32. See also F. Tsiang, "Sino-Japanese Diplomatic Relations," *Chinese Social and Political Review* 27 (1933): 92; Lew, "Yüan Shih-k'ai's Residency," 70.

43. *CJCC*, 23-24.

44. Song Pyŏng-gi, ed., *Yun Ch'i-ho ilgi* [Diary of Ilchin-ho], vol. 1 (Yonsei Taehakkyo ch'ulp'ansa, 2011), 84. See also Shin Myŏng-ho, *Kojongkwa maeichiŭi sidae* (Seoul, 2014), 365-356.

45. Tsiang, "Sino-Japanese Diplomatic Relations," 93; Hwang Hyŏn, *Maech'ŏn yarok* [Memoirs of Hwang Hyŏn], vol. 1 (Seoul, 2005), 230-231.

46. Kirk W. Larsen, *Tradition, Treaties and Trade: Qing Imperialism and Choson Korea, 1850-1910* (Cambridge, MA, 2008), 129.

47. Samuel Hawley, *America's Man in Korea: The Private Letters of George C. Foulk, 1884-1887* (Lanham, MD, 2008), 132. Hwang Hyŏn also described the jubilation of "tradespeople, soldiers, wives, and children" who greeted the Taewŏn'gun enthusiastically upon his arrival. See Hwang, *Maech'ŏn yarok*, 230-231.

48. Tiang, "Sino-Japanese Diplomatic Relations," 93.

49. Horace Allen, "An Acquaintance with Yuan Shi Kai," *North American Review* 196, no. 680 (July 1912): 112. See also Larsen, *Tradition, Treaties and Trade*, 130; Lew, "Yüan Shih-k'ai's Residency," 73-74; Arthur W. Hummel, ed., *Eminent Chinese of the Ch'ing Period (1644-1912)*, vol. 2 (Washington, DC, 1944), 950-951.

50. Allen, "An Acquaintance," 113.

51. Allen, "An Acquaintance," 113-114.

52. In his letter to Kojong on October 2 (lunar) (November 8 solar), 1885, Li Hong-zhang wrote ominously: "From now on, for anything that relates to the domestic or foreign affairs of Korea, I [Li Hongzhang] hope you will be open and honest with Yuan Shikai and discuss with him all the important issues, which I believe will be beneficial to both you and your country." As for Möllendorf, "he has already been dismissed from his post and will have nothing more to do with Korea." *CJCC*, 50.

53. Larsen, *Tradition, Treaties and Trade*, 16.

54. William Elliot Griffis, *Corea: The Hermit Nation* (New York, 1904), 471.

55. Lew, "Yüan Shih-k'ai's Residency," 81; see also Lee, *West Goes East*, 159; S. C. M. Paine, *The Sino-Japanese War of 1894-1895: Perceptions, Power, and Primacy* (Cambridge, 2006), 76.

56. Although some historians believe that the letter was a forgery, an examination based on Russian archival materials confirms that Weber, at the king's request, did indeed send the proposal to his superiors in Saint Petersburg. Lee, *West Goes East*, 159.

57. *LZR*, 1:319-320. The letter is also cited in Lew, "Yuan Shi-kai's Residency," 83. See also Lee, *West Goes East*, 159-160.

58. *LZR*, 1:322-323.

59. Liu Ruifen, the Chinese minister to Russia, wrote to Li on August 22: "I [Ruifen Liu] asked Giers whether or not he had ever heard about the fact that Korean officials had sent a secret message to Russia to ask for their assistance. I [Liu] also told him [Giers] that Korea is a vassal of China, so Russia should not accept any such request from Korea. Giers said that he never heard about the matter at all." *LZR*, 1:325-326. See also Lee, *West Goes East*, 161.

60. The Taewŏn'gun later reported to Yuan that when he went to see Kojong in the palace, "everyone was crying, which made the king and his mother cry too." *LZR*, 1:324-325.

61. Cited in Lensen, *Balance of Intrigue,* 90.

62. Cited in Lensen, *Balance of Intrigue,* 34–35.

63. Huanjeong Seok, "International Rivalry in Korea and Russia's East Asian Policy in the Late Nineteenth Century," 184; See also Seung-kwon Synn, "The Russo-Korean Relations in the 1880s," *Korea Journal* 20, no. 9 (September 1980): 26–39; Lensen, *Balance of Intrigue,* 34–35.

64. Krasny Archiv, "First Steps of Russian Imperialism in Far East (1888–1903)," *Chinese Social and Political Science Review* 28, no. 2 (July 1934): 236–251. See also Synn, "Russo-Korean Relations," 36.

65. Krasny Archiv, "First Steps," 238–239.

66. Krasny Archiv, "First Steps," 238–239.

67. Hilary Conroy, *The Japanese Seizure of Korea, 1868–1910: A Study of Realism and Idealism in International Relations* (Philadelphia, 1960), 161.

68. Kakugorō Inoue, *Kanjo no zanmu* [K. Hansŏngji chanmong, Memory of Seoul] (1891), in *Sŏul e namgyŏdun kkum* [Dreams of Seoul], trans. Han Sang-il (Seoul, 1993), 56.

69. Ichikawa Mikiakira, *Fukuzawa Yukichi Den* [The Life of Fukuzawa Yukichi], vol. 3 (Tokyo, 1932–1933), 354.

70. Robert Scalapino, *Democracy and the Party Movement in Prewar Japan: The Failure of the First Attempt* (Berkeley, 1953), 107; Hilary Conroy, "Chōsen Mondai: The Korean Problem in Meiji Japan," *Proceedings of the American Philosophical Society* 100, no. 5 (October 1956): 446. Ōi Kentarō is probably best known for his role in the attempt to invade Korea, known as the Osaka Incident. The plot was foiled, and on November 23, 1885, the police rounded up 130 adventurers and accomplices. See Marius B. Jansen, "Ōi Kentarō: Radicalism and Chauvinism," *Far Eastern Quarterly Review* 2, no. 3 (May 1952): 305–316; Conroy, *Japanese Seizure of Korea,* 167–168.

71. Conroy, *Japanese Seizure of Korea,* 218–220; Jansen, "Ōi Kentarō," 310. See also Marius Jansen's classic work *The Japanese and Sun Yat-sen* (Stanford, CA, 1954).

72. Tsiang, "Sino-Japanese Diplomatic Relations," 106.

6. RUSSIA'S RAILWAY TO THE EAST

1. The actual Russian occupation of Vladivostok was effected on May 20, 1860, when the warship *Manchur* arrived with a crew of forty soldiers. In 1864, 157 settlers arrived from Nikolaevsk; two years later the town was connected with Khabarovsk by telegraph for the first time. See A. I. Dmitriev-Mámonov and A. F. Zdziárski, *Guide to the Great Siberian Railway,* trans. K. Kukol-Yasnopolsky (Saint Petersburg, 1900), 466. Nikolai Muravev was granted the title Count Muravev-Amursky in recognition of his role in expanding Russia's territory in Siberia in 1858–1860.

2. According to David J. Dallin, the population of the Russian Far East amounted to 11,850 in 1861; by 1897 it was 310,000. See Dallin, *The Rise of Russia in Asia* (London, 1950), 23–25; Andrew Malozemoff, *Russian Far Eastern Policy, 1881–1904* (New York, 1958), 1–19; Steven G. Marks, *Road to Power: The Trans-Siberian Railroad and the Colonization of Asian Russia, 1850–1917* (Ithaca, NY, 1991), 14–15; Ernest George Ravenstein, *The Russians on the Amur: Its Discovery, Conquest, and Colonization* (London, 1861), 154–155.

3. Mark Bassin, "A Russian Mississippi? A Political-Geographical Inquiry into the Vision of Russia on the Pacific, 1840–1865" (PhD diss., University of California, Berkeley, 1983), 199.

4. W. Bruce Lincoln, *The Conquest of a Continent: Siberia and the Russians* (New York, 1994), 194; Christian Wolmar, *To the Edge of the World: The Story of the Trans-Siberian*

Express, the World's Greatest Railroad (New York, 2013), 33; Harmon Tupper, *To the Great Ocean: Siberia and the Trans-Siberian Railway* (Boston, 1965), 47–61.

5. Perry McDonough Collins, *Siberian Journey: Down the Amur to the Pacific, 1856–1857,* ed. Charles Vevier (Madison, WI, 1962), 95.

6. Zavalishin, a Decembrist and a severe critic of Muravev, believed that articles about the Amur appearing in the press were completely misleading, even dishonest. D. I. Zavalishin, "Po povodu statei ob Amure" [Concerning articles about the Amur], *Morskoi Sbornik* (Naval Digest) 38, no. 11 (November 1858): 31–36.

7. S. P. Suslov, *Physical Geography of Asiatic Russia,* trans. Noah D. Gershevsky (London, 1961), 333–337.

8. Malozemoff, *Russian Far Eastern Policy,* 3.

9. Bassin, *Russian Mississippi?,* 277–278.

10. P. Kropotkin, *Memoirs of a Revolutionist,* vol. 2 (London, 1899), 215–217.

11. Beginning in 1879, more than thirty thousand convicts were sent to Siberia to solve the problem of underpopulation of the Russian Far East. Malozemoff, *Russian Far Eastern Policy,* 11.

12. Cited in Daniel Beer, *House of the Dead: Siberian Exile under the Tsars* (New York, 2017), 335.

13. Malozemoff, *Russian Far Eastern Policy,* 5.

14. Charles A. Conant, "The Russians in Manchuria," *Forum* 31, no. 3 (May 1901): 6.

15. Henry Lansdell, *Through Siberia* (London, 1882), 713.

16. Bassin, *Russian Mississippi?,* 241; G. I. Nevelskoy, *Podvigi russkikh morskikh ofitserov na Kraynem vostoke Rossii 1849–55 g. Pri-Amurskii i Pri-Ussuriiskii krai: Posmertnyia zapiski Admirala Nevel'skogo* [The exploits of Russian naval officers in the Russian Far East, 1849–1855: Priamursky and Priussuriysky krai: Posthumous notes of Admiral Nevelskoy] (Saint Petersburg, 1897), 365–367.

17. Cited in Malozemoff, *Russian Far Eastern Policy,* 4.

18. M. A. Bakunin, *Pis'ma M. A. Bakunina k A. I. Gertsenu i N. P. Ogarevu/ s biogr. vved. i obyasn. primech. M. P. Dragomanova* [The letters to M. A. Bakunin to A. I. Herzen and N. P. Ogarev; with a biographical introduction and explanatory notes by M. P. Dragomanov) (The Hague, 1968), 120–121.

19. Malozemoff, *Russian Far Eastern Policy,* 39; *Times* (London), June 25, 1887.

20. Beer, *House of the Dead,* 335. Herzen also especially admired Muravev-Amursky. See M. A. Kakunin to A. Herzen, November 7, 1860 (OS), in Bakunin, *Pis'ma M. A. Bakunina,*118–119.

21. Cited in Victor L. Mote, *Siberia: Worlds Apart* (Colorado, 1998), 64.

22. Bassin, *Russian Mississippi?,* 122–123. Herzen also saw Russia's destiny in Siberia as linked to the United States. See A. I. Herzen, "Amerika i Sibir'" [America and Siberia], *Kolokol* [The Bell], December 28, 1858, 233–234. See also Mark Bassin, *Imperial Visions: Nationalist Imagination and Geographical Expansion in the Russian Far East, 1840–1865* (Cambridge, 1999), 160–173.

23. Kropotkin, *Memoirs,* 182.

24. A similar view was expressed by E. V. Bogdanovich, who had been charged with investigating the cause of the famine in Viatka and Perm' provinces in 1866: "Siberia is no longer. Henceforth this is Russia." See Lincoln, *Conquest of a Continent,* 225; Marks, *Road to Power,* 7.

25. Immanuel C. Y. Hsü, *Ili Crisis: A Study of Sino-Russian Diplomacy, 1871–1881* (Oxford, 1965), 189–196.

26. Edwin G. Bilof, "China in Imperial Russian Military Planning, 1881–1887," *Military Affairs,* April 1, 1882, 7–9. Savelovka was known as Hŭkjŏngja to Koreans. See Alyssa

Park, *Sovereignty Experiments: Korean Migrants and the Building of Borders in Northeast Asia, 1860–1945* (Ithaca, NY, 2019), 55–56.

27. Cited in Bilof, "China in Imperial Russian Military Planning," 16.

28. Bilof, "China in Imperial Russian Military Planning," 32; David Scott, *China and the International System, 1849–1949: Power, Presence and Perceptions in a Century of Humiliation* (New York, 2008), 104–105.

29. Theodore H. Von Laue, *Sergei Witte and the Industrialization of Russia* (New York, 1974), 81.

30. Edwin G. Bilaf, "China in Imperial Russian Military Planning," 70–72; Marks, *Road to Power,* 38–39.

31. Marks, *Road to Power,* 96

32. Sidney Harcave, *Count Sergei Witte and the Twilight of Imperial Russia* (Armonk, 2004), 40.

33. Sergei Witte, *The Memoirs of Count Witte,* trans. Sidney Harcave (Armonk, 1990), 42.

34. Witte boosted the efficiency of the Russian railway system. See von Laue, *Sergei Witte* (New York, 1974).

35. Witte, *Memoirs,* 93.

36. Harcave, *Count Sergei Witte,* 29.

37. Lincoln, *Conquest of a Continent,* 232; von Laue, *Sergei Witte,* 76–77.

38. Stuart R. Tompkins "Witte as Foreign Minister, 1892–1903," *Slavonic and East European Review* 11, no. 33 (April 1933): 604–605; T. H. Von Laue, "A Secret Memorandum of Sergei Witte on the Industrialization of Imperial Russia," *Journal of Modern History* 26, no. 1 (March 1954): 60–74. See also Von Laue, "The Industrialization of Russia in the Writing of Sergei Witte," *American Slavic and East European Review* 10, no. 3 (October 1951): 177–190; Von Laue, "The High Cost and the Gamble of the Witte System: A Chapter in the Industrialization of Russia," *Journal of Economic History* 13, no. 4 (Autumn 1953): 425–448.

39. Von Laue, *Sergei Witte,* 77; Tompkins, "Witte as Foreign Minister," 5.

40. Cited in Von Laue, *Sergei Witte,* 76. According to Von Laue, by 1900 the Trans-Siberian Railway would become the largest single industry in Russia, employing four hundred thousand workers, 78–79.

41. Alexander Isvolsky, *The Memoirs of Alexander Iswolsky, Formerly Russian Minister of Foreign Affairs and Ambassador to France,* trans. Charles Louis Seeger (London, 1920), 114.

42. Von Laue, *Sergei Witte,* 38.

43. Peter Struve, "Graf S. Yu. Vitte: Opyt' Kharakteristiki" [Graf S. Yu. Witte: A character study], in *Russkaya mysl',* vol. 3 (1915), 129.

44. Isvolsky, *Memoirs,* 118–119.

45. Witte, *Memoirs,* 172–173.

46. Marks, *Road to Power,* 126; Marlene Laruelle, "'The White Tsar': Romantic Imperialism in Russia's Legitimizing of Conquering the Far East," *Acta Slavica Iaponica* 25 (2008): 113–134.

47. George Kennan, *Siberia and the Exile System,* vol. 1 (New York, 1970), 56–57.

48. Marks, *Road to Power,* 174.

49. Lincoln, *Conquest of a Continent,* 233.

50. Tupper, *To the Great Ocean,* 189–190.

51. Dmitriev-Mámonov and Zdziárski, *Guide,* 456.

52. James W. Davidson, "The Great Siberian Railway: From Recent Investigation," *Century Illustrated Magazine,* April 1904, 940.

53. William Turban, "The Trans-Siberian Railway," *Contemporary Review,* July 1, 1899, 266.

54. Harmon, *To the Great Ocean,* 169–170.

55. Hilda Hookham, "Builders of Trans-Siberian Railway," *History Today,* August 1, 1966, 530.

56. V. F. Borzunov, *Proletariat Sibiri i Dal'nego Vostoka nakanune pervoi russkoi revo-liutsii (po materialam stroitel'stva Transsibirskoi magistrali, 1891–1904 gg)* [The proletariat of Siberia and the Far East on the eve of the first Russian Revolution (based on the construction of the Trans-Siberian Railway, 1891–1894)] (Moscow 1965), 91–92, 90.

57. Hookham, "Builders," 530.

58. Borzunov, *Proletariat Sibiri,* 99.

59. Hookham, "Builders," 530–532.

60. Borzunov, *Proletariat Sibiri,* 94.

61. Marks, *Road to Power,* 181–183. See also Beer, *House of the Dead,* 376.

62. Mikhail Zygar, *The Empire Must Die: Russia's Revolutionary Collapse, 1900–1917* (New York, 2017), 50.

63. Witte, *Memoirs,* 91, 125, 126.

64. Laruelle, "'The White Tsar,'" 123.

65. Prince E. E. Ukhtomsky, *Travels in the East of Nicholas II, Emperor of Russia, When Cesarewitch, 1890–1891,* trans. R. Goodlet (London, 1900), 127.

66. Witte, *Memoirs,* 126–127.

67. *IHH,* 1:250.

68. Mary Crawford Fisher, *A Diplomat's Wife in Japan: Sketches at the Turn of the Century,* ed. Hugh Cortazzi (New York, 1983), 281; see also Donald Keene, *Emperor of Japan: Meiji and His World, 1852–1912* (New York, 2002), 443–458.

69. *IHH,* 1:250–251.

70. Cited in Fisher, *Diplomat's Wife,* 286.

71. *IHH,* 1:251.

72. *IHH,* 1:251–252.

73. Katō Yoko, *Sensō no nihon kin-gendaishi: Seikanron kara Taiheiyō sensō made* [History of wars in modern-era Japan: From Seikanron to the Pacific War] (Tokyo, 2002), 86; Robert Britton Valliant, "Japan and the Trans-Siberian Railroad, 1885–1905" (PhD diss., University of Hawai'i, 1974), 47–48.

74. Katō, *Sensō no nihon kin-gendaisi,* 99. Gotō Shōjirō, a founder of the Liberal Party (Jiyūto), also warned in July 1888, "The Trans-Siberian Railway . . . will reach Vladivostok in four or five years' time." If that happened, "the Russian fleet will be able to deploy its troops to Sakata Port [located at the mouth of the Mogami River in northern Honshu]." See Ōmachi Keigetsu, *Hakushaku Gotō Shōjirō* [Biography: Count Gotō Shōjirō] (Tokyo, 1914), 611–618.

75. Katō, *Senso-no nihon kin gendaisi,* 91.

76. Tsuda also told interrogators that he had tried to kill the tsarevich because of the latter's discourtesy in not visiting the emperor first before going to Kagoshima and Otsu. See Peter Yongshik Shin, "The Otsu Incident: Japan's Hidden History of the Attempted Assassination of the Future Emperor Nicholas II of Russia in the Town of Otsu, Japan, May 11, 1891, and Its Implication for Historical Analysis" (PhD diss., University of Pennsylvania, 1989); George Alexander Lensen, "The Attempt on the Life of Nicholas in Japan," *Russian Review* 20, no. 2 (July 1961): 232–253.

77. Keene, *Emperor of Japan,* 455.

78. Lafcadio Hearn, *Out of the East* (Boston, 1896), 331.

79. Arthur Diósy, *The New Far East* (London, 1905), 258; Hearn, *Out of the East,* 331–341; Fraser, *Diplomat's Wife,* 288. See also Keene, *Emperor of Japan,* 453–454.

80. Barbara Teters, "The Otsu Affair: The Formation of Japan's Judicial Conscience," in *Meiji Japan's Centennial,* ed. David Wurfel (Lawrence, KS, 1971), 54.

81. Keene, *Emperor of Japan,* 451–452.

82. *IHH*, 1:252–253.

83. Teters, "Otsu Affair,"39.

84. Cited in Shin, "Otsu Incident," 147–148. Shin provides a translated abridged diary of Chief Justice Kojima.

85. Cited in Shin, "Otsu Incident," 148.

86. Teters, "Otsu Affair,"" 47–48.

87. *IHH*, 1:256–257.

88. Keene, *Emperor of Japan,* 456.

89. Keene, *Emperor of Japan,* 456; Teters, "Otsu Affair," 52.

90. Teters, "Otsu Affair," 53.

91. Cited in Teters, "Otsu Affair," 57–58; Shin, "Otsu Incident," 157; Keene, *Emperor of Japan,* 457.

92. William P. Ker, "Treaty Revision in Japan: A Survey of the Steps by Which the Abolition of Foreign Privilege Was Accomplished in the Island Empire," *Pacific Affairs* 1, no. 6 (November 1928): 1–10; Louis Perez, *Japan Comes of Age: Mutsu Munemitsu and the Revision of Unequal Treaties* (Madison, WI, 1999); Ozaki Yukio, *The Autobiography of Ozaki Yukio: The Struggle for Constitutional Government in Japan,* trans. Fukiko Hara (Princeton, NJ, 2001).

93. Sven Saaler, "The Kokuryūkai (Black Dragon Society) and the Rise of Nationalism, Pan-Asianism, and Militarism in Japan, 1901–1925, *International Journal of Asian Studies* 11, no. 2 (2014): 125–160; Gen'yōsha, *Gen'yōsha shasi* [History of the Gen'yōsha] (Tokyo, 2016). Gen'yōsha members closely followed events in Korea. They were particularly dissatisfied with Itō's signing of the 1885 Tianjin Convention and believed Japan could not rely on so weak a diplomat (*Gen'yōsha shasi,* 244–245). They also supported the reform efforts of Korean exiles Kim Ok-kyun and Pak Yŏng-hyo (*Gen'yōsha shasi,* 244–245). See also E. Herbert Norman, "The Genyōsha: A Study in the Origins of Japanese Imperialism," *Pacific Affairs* 17, no. 3 (September 1944): 261–284; *Gen'yōsha shasi,* 244–248.

94. Tsuda was sentenced to life imprisonment and incarcerated in a Hokkaidō prison, where he died of pneumonia on September 30, 1891, six months after his trial. See also *IHH,* 1:276.

7. PRELUDE TO WAR

1. Hilary Conroy, *The Japanese Seizure of Korea, 1868–1910: A Study of Realism and Idealism in International Relations* (Philadelphia, 1960), 222; Louis G. Perez, *Japan Comes of Age: Mutsu Munemitsu and the Revision of the Unequal Treaties* (Cranbury, 1999).

2. "The Impending War," *North-China Herald* (Shanghai), June 19, 1894, 1010.

3. S. C. M. Paine, *The Sino-Japanese War of 1894–1895: Perceptions, Power and Primacy* (Cambridge, 2003), 96.

4. Conroy, *Japanese Seizure of Korea,* 223.

5. Ishikawa Mikiaki, *Fukuzawa Den* [The life of Fukuzawa] (Tokyo, 1932), 353.

6. While in exile for ten years in Japan, Kim had parted ways with former political comrade Pak Yŏng-hyo and lost the sympathy of Japanese officials and friends alike. Only Fukuzawa Yukichi remained Kim's stalwart supporter. Ishikawa, *Fukuzawa Den,* 353–356.

7. Ishikawa, *Fukuzawa Den,* 351–363. Contrary to most standard Japanese interpretations of Kim Ok-kyun's assassination, the Korean Confucian scholar-turned-nationalist Chŏng Kyo (1856–1925) believed it was the Japanese, not the Koreans, who had enlisted Hong to assassinate Kim. See *Taehan kyenyŏnsa* [The history of the final years of the Great

Korean Empire] (Seoul, 1957), 73. Chŏng later became a member of Sŏ Chae-pil and Yun Ch'i-ho's Independence Club until it was forcibly dissolved in 1898.

8. *Japan Mail Weekly*, April 7, 1894. Cai Er-kang, editor of a Shanghai newspaper, published a detailed account of Kim's murder. See *LZR*, 2:13.

9. *KNKK*, 185-187.

10. *KNKK*, 189, 190, 191.

11. *KNKK*, 205. Itō shared Mutsu's skepticism and took a far more balanced view of the situation, conceding that blame lay on both sides. See *IHH*, 1:141.

12. Cited in *KNKK*, 206-207. Mutsu blamed Wada for leaving the corpse unattended, failing to retrieve it through due process, and coming to Japan without the body. When members of the Diet heard Mutsu reply, they "erupted with loud outrage." *KNKK*, 208.

13. Miyazaki Tōten, *My Thirty Years' Dream*, trans. Etō Shinkichi and Marius B. Jansen (New Jersey, 1982), 58.

14. Louis G. Perez, "Mutsu Munemitsu and the Revision of the 'Unequal Treaties'" (PhD diss., University of Michigan, 1986), 290-292.

15. *Tokyo Nichi Shimbun*, April 22, 1894. Also, *KNKK*, 204-205; Bonnie Oh, "The Background of Chinese Foreign Policy in the Sino-Japanese War" (PhD diss., University of Chicago, 1974), 211-212. Tributes to Kim appearing in *Chūō Shinbun* and *Jiji Shinpō*, as well as other Tokyo newspapers, launched a fund drive in memory of the Korean martyr. Ishikawa, *Fukuzawa Den*, 380-398; Conroy, *Japanese Seizure of Korea*, 226-227; *Japan Mail*, May 12, 1894.

16. Conroy, *Japanese Seizure of Korea*, 228.

17. Perez, *Japan Comes of Age*, 151; *Japan Mail*, June 2, 1894; George Akita, *Foundations of Constitutional Government in Modern Japan, 1868-1900* (Cambridge, MA, 1967), 114; Conroy, *Japanese Seizure of Korea*, 228.

18. Yukkun Sagwan Hakkyo Han'guk Kunsa Yŏng'gusil, *Han'guk kunjesa* [History of the military system in Korea], vol. 2 (Seoul, 1968-1977), 337-338. The Korean government dispatched eight hundred soldiers, headed by Hong Gye-hun, to put down the rebellion, but they were defeated.

19. *LZR*, 2:23-24. In Yuan's letter of June 1 to Li Hongzhang, he urged the Zongli Yamen to dispatch troops to Korea as quickly as possible. However, it was only on June 3 that Kojong, under pressure from Yuan, sent an official request for military support.

20. Sugimura notes in his diary that when Yuan came to the legation on June 15 and brought up the issue of a simultaneous withdrawal of troops with Ōtori, the latter made it clear that Chinese troops would have to be withdrawn first before the Japanese would consider withdrawing theirs. See CHKSR, 95-96; Horace Allen, "An Acquaintance with Yuan Shi Kai," *North American Review* 196, no. 680 (July 1912): 115.

21. Allen, "Acquaintance with Yuan Shi Kai," 115.

22. *LZR*, 2:31. After signing the truce with the Korean government, the Tonghaks retreated to Chonju, and Kojong sent a letter to Yuan asking him to withdraw Chinese troops so the Japanese would also have no reason to stay in Korea. Cited in Morinosuke Kojima, *The Diplomacy of Japan, 1894-1922*, vol. 1 (Tokyo, 1978), 38.

23. Mutsu Munemitsu, *Kenkenroku: A Diplomatic Record of the Sino-Japanese War, 1894-1895*, ed. and trans. Gordon Mark Berger (Tokyo, 1982), 67.

24. Sugimura noted that Mutsu wrote Ōtori several telegrams over June 16-20 relating his concern that some concrete diplomatic victory should be achieved before Japan withdrew its troops. See CHKSR, 97-98; Mutsu, *Kenkenroku*, 21.

25. Mutsu, *Kenkenroku*, 20.

26. Mutsu, *Kenkenroku*, 23.

27. Mutsu, *Kenkenroku*, 24.

28. *LZR*, 2:35–37; Mutsu, *Kenkenroku*, 24.

29. Mutsu, *Kenkenroku*, 26; Edmund Fung, "The Peace Efforts of Li Hung-chang on the Eve of the Sino-Japanese War," *Papers on Far Eastern History* 3 (March 1971): 135; Kojima, *Diplomacy of Japan*, 40; *NGB*, vol. 27, bk. 1, no. 384, Mutsu to Wang, June–22, 1894; *NGB*, vol. 27, bk.1, no. 370, Mutsu to Ōtori, June 22, 1894.

30. *LZR*, 2:38–39; Mutsu, *Kenkenroku*, 36–37, 30.

31. Pamela Kyle Crossley, *The Wobbling Pivot: China since 1800* (London, 2010), 118–119; Jonathan Spence, *The Search for Modern China* (New York, 1990), 216–224.

32. Tabohashi Kiyoshi, *Nisshin seneki gaikōshi no kenkyū* [Study of the diplomatic history of the Sino-Japanese War] (Tokyo, 1951), 266–267; Orville Schell and John Delury, *Wealth and Power: China's Long March to the Twenty-First Century* (New York, 2013), 70.

33. Fung, "Peace Efforts, 136.

34. *LZR*, 2:43–44; Fung, "Peace Efforts," 143; CHKSR, 113.

35. Fung, "Peace Efforts," 145.

36. Luke S. K. Kwong, *A Mosaic of the Hundred Days: Personalities, Politics and Ideas of 1898* (Cambridge, MA, 1984), 74–75; Tabohashi, *Nisshin seneki gaikōshi no kenkyū*, 267–268; Crossley, *Wobbling Pivot*, 123–124.

37. In his July 12 memorial, Wen Tingshi, a National Academy scholar, presented a unique argument against Li's diplomatic approach, which he stressed was misplaced, even dangerous. See Tabohashi, *Nisshin seneki gaikōshi no kenkyū*, 274–275.

38. Allen Fung, "Testing Self-Strengthening: The Chinese Army in the Sino-Japanese War of 1894–1895," *Modern Asian Studies* 30, no. 4 (October 1996): 1014.

39. William Ferdinand Tyler, *Pulling Strings in China* (London, 1929), 43.

40. Mutsu, *Kenkenroku*, 82. See also Kojima, *Diplomacy of Japan*, 59–61.

41. Donald Keene, *Emperor of Japan: Meiji and His World, 1852–1912* (New York, 2002), 479.

42. Mutsu, *Kenkenroku*, 82–83; Kojima, *Diplomacy of Japan*, 62–63.

43. The Korean government agreed in principle to reform but demanded Japan withdraw its troops first. CHKSR, 113–114.

44. CHKSR, 121–122.

45. Allen, "Acquaintance with Yuan Shi Kai," 116. Yuan secretly left Korea on July 19. Kojima, *Diplomacy of Japan*, 62–63; *LZR*, 2:69.

46. The Japanese began enlisting the Taewŏn'gun's help during a series of secret meetings in early June. Young I. Lew, "Korean-Japanese Politics behind the Kabo-Ŭlmi Reform Movement, 1894–1896," *Journal of Korean Studies* 3 (1981): 48.

47. CHKSR, 127.

48. CHKSR, 128.

49. *NGB*, vol. 27, bk. 1, no. 419, cited in Kajima, *Diplomacy of Japan*, 65. The official Korean version of events is described in KJSL in *Chosŏn wangjo sillhok* [Annals of the Chosŏn dynasty], June 21, 1894 (solar), http://sillok.history.go.kr/id/kza_13106021_001. Distinct from other accounts, it says that when Korean soldiers began firing on the invading Japanese troops, Kojong ordered them to stop. It also mentions that the weapons taken by Japanese troops were returned to the Korean soldiers later.

50. CHKSR, 129.

51. Mutsu, *Kenkenroku*, 83; KJSL, June 21, 1894 (lunar), http://sillok.history.go.kr/id/kza_13106021_003.

52. See Tabohashi, *Nisshin seneki gaikōshi no kenkyū*, 282–283.

53. According to the diary of Weng Tonghe, on July 27 Emperor Guangxu had again insisted on declaring war on Japan. However, up to the very last moment Li Hongzhang

"refused to lose faith in the success of the mediation efforts made by Britain to help avert the breakdown of Qing-Japan diplomatic relations." Tabohashi, *Nisshin seneki gaikōshi no kenkyū*, 282–283.

54. On board were eight Europeans and a thousand Chinese troops. See Fung, "Testing Self-Strengthening," 1015. A full eyewitness account of the sinking, by Von Hanneken, who was aboard, is in "The War: Mr. Von Hanneken's Report," *North China Herald*, August 10, 1894, 216, 236. Chief Officer Lewes Henry Tamplin also offered a detailed as account in "The Sinking of the *Kowshing*: The Chief Officer's Account," *North China Herald*, August 10, 1894, 236

8. TRIUMPH, DEFEAT, AND A MASSACRE

1. Donald Keene, *Landscapes and Portraits: Appreciations of Japanese Culture* (Tokyo, 1971), 263.

2. *Japan Weekly Mail*, August 11, 1894. According to John F. Howles, "no single item in Uchimura's corpus has damaged his reputation more than this "justification." Howles, *Japan's Modern Prophet: Uchimura Kanzō, 1861–1930* (Toronto, 2005), 128.

3. Douglas Howard, "The Sinking of the S.S. *Kowshing*: International Law, Diplomacy, and the Sino-Japanese War," *Modern Asian Studies* 42, no. 4 (July 2008): 673–703.

4. The goal of taking of Beijing was eventually dropped as Itō and others recognized that it would be diplomatic suicide for Japan. See Stewart Lone, *Japan's First Modern War: Army and Society in the Conflict with China, 1894–5* (New York, 1994), 40.

5. See S. C. M. Paine, *The Sino-Japanese War of 1894–1895: Perceptions, Power and Primacy* (Cambridge, 2003), 225–226; Lone, *Japan's First Modern War*, 39–40.

6. Lone, *Japan's First Modern War*, 34–35.

7. LZR, 2:79–80. Vladimir [pseud.] [Z. Volpicelli], *The China-Japan War: Compiled from Japanese, Chinese and Foreign Sources* (London, 1896), 106.

8. Vladimir, *China-Japan War*, 107.

9. Qi Qizhang, *Jia wu zhan zheng shi* [History of the Sino-Japanese War] (Shanghai, 2005), 67–68.

10. Qi, *Jia wu zhan zheng shi*, 70.

11. Vladimir, *China-Japan War*, 103.

12. Vladimir, *China-Japan War*, 103.

13. Qi, *Jia wu zhan zheng shi*, 66.

14. Paine, *Sino-Japanese War*, 159.

15. General Nie and his men were in such bad shape when they arrived in P'yŏngyang that Nie departed almost immediately for Tianjin on an unsuccessful mission to request reinforcements. When the Japanese Army attacked P'yŏngyang on September 15, only Zuo Baogui resisted; he was killed in action. Ye fled, as did Wei. See LZR, 2:97–99; Arthur W. Hummel, *Eminent Chinese of the Ch'ing Period (1644–1912)* (Washington, DC, 1944), 2:687. Despite setbacks on the field, Ye continued to send positive reports to Li Hongzhang. See LZR, 2:81.

16. Qi, *Jia wu zhan zheng shi*, 83–84.

17. For an account of the Manchu invasion of Korea, see Na Man'gap, *The Diary of 1636: The Second Invasion of Korea*, trans. George Kallander (New York, 2020).

18. Warrington Eastlake and Yamada Yoshiaki, *Heroic Japan: A History of the War between China and Japan* (London, 1897), 28–29; Vladimir, *China-Japan War*, 32.

19. The plight of the Japanese at P'yŏngyang in the winter of 1593 was but a microcosm of the problem Hideyoshi faced in his campaign to conquer Korea. See Samuel Hawley, *The Imjin Wars: Japan's Sixteenth Invasion of Korea and Attempt to Conquer China* (London, 2014).

20. Eastlake and Yamada, *Heroic Japan*, 28–29; Vladimir, *China-Japan War*, 120–131.

21. *LZR*, 2:98.

22. Trumbull White, *The War in the East: Japan, China and Corea: A Complete History of the War* (Philadelphia, 1895), 483–484. The Chinese commanders apparently did not realize they were surrounded.

23. Vladimir, *China-Japan War*, 157.

24. White, *War in the East*, 484; Eastlake and Yamada, *Heroic Japan*, 38; *LZR*, 2:100–102.

25. Cited in Qi, *Jia wu zhan zheng shi*, 108–109.

26. Qi, *Jia wu zhan zheng shi*, 109. This figure is contested. According to other accounts, the number of Chinese dead was much higher—about two thousand dead and twelve hundred captured, a third of whom were allegedly executed by the Japanese. See Ōe Shinobu, *Heishitachi no nichiro sensō: 500-tsu o gunji yubin kara* [Soldiers of the Russo-Japanese War: Through 500 military letters] (Tokyo, 1988), 238–239. Japanese losses were comparatively light: 102 killed, 410 wounded, and 33 missing. See also Inoue Jukichi, *A Concise History of the War between Japan and China* (Tokyo, 1895), 36.

27. David C. Evans and Mark R. Peattie, *Kaigun: Strategy, Tactics and Technology in the Imperial Japanese Navy, 1887–1941* (Annapolis, MD, 1997), 40–41.

28. Lone, *Japan's First Modern War*, 37. With roughly thirteen thousand Chinese and fourteen thousand Japanese, the force distribution was relatively equal; the Chinese should have been able to hold the city for more than a day. See Paine, *Sino-Japanese War*, 167–168; Vladimir, *China-Japan War*, 129; Eastlake and Yamada, *Heroic Japan*, 32.

29. J. C. Perry, "The Battle of Tayang, September 17, 1894," *Mariner's Mirror* 50 (November 1964): 244.

30. Li wanted to purchase four armored ships but because of the price tag had to settle for two. David Pong, "Keeping the Foochow Navy Yard Afloat: Government Finance and China's Early Modern Defense Industry, 1866–85," *Modern Asian Studies* 21, no. 1 (1987): 121–152.

31. "The Chinese Navy: Interview with a Naval Expert," *North China Herald*, September 21, 1894.

32. Alfred Thayer Mahan, "Lessons from the Yalu Fight," *Century Illustrated Magazine*, August 1895, 629.

33. Evans and Peattie, *Kaigun*, 40.

34. Some accounts state there were ten vessels. The most accurate figure can be found in Secretary of the Navy Hilary A. Herbert's description of both fleets; he puts the number at twelve, figures based on the US Office of Naval Intelligence. See Hilary A. Herbert, "The Fight off the Yalu River," *North American Review*, November 1894, 513–529; John Rawlinson, *China's Struggle for Naval Development, 1839–1895* (Cambridge, MA, 1967); Philo N. McGiffin, "The Battle of the Yalu: Personal Recollections by the Commander of the Chinese Ironclad 'Chen Yuen,'" *Century Illustrated Magazine*, August 1895, 585–604; William Ferdinand Tyler, *Pulling Strings in China* (New York, 1929).

35. It is also called the Battle of Dagushan/Takushan or the Battle of Haiyang Island. G. A. Ballard, *The Influence of the Sea on the Political History of Japan* (New York, 1921), 146–147; Vladimir, *China-Japan War*, 164–165.

36. Von Hanneken, "The War: Mr. Von Hannekan's Report," *North China Herald*, August 10, 1894.

37. Tyler, *Pulling Strings*, 47.

38. Tyler, *Pulling Strings*, 51, 47.

39. Perry, "Battle of Tayang," 251.

40. Tyler, *Pulling Strings*, 49.

41. Alfred Thayer Mahan, "Lesson from the Yalu Fight," *Century Illustrated Magazine*, August 1895, 631.

42. Perry, "Battle of Tayang," 252.

43. Tyler, *Pulling Strings,* 51–52.

44. Ensign Frank Marble, "The Battle of the Yalu," *Naval Institute Proceedings* 21/3/75 (1895): 484.

45. Perry, "Battle of Tayang," 254. Chinese casualty figures vary, but it is generally agreed the Chinese suffered fifteen hundred casualties altogether, including men who went down with their ships. The Japanese losses were far lower. According to the highest figures of any report, the loss was just 254, the greatest occurring aboard the *Matsushima.* See Marble, "Battle of the Yalu," 493.

46. McGiffin, "Battle of the Yalu," 601.

47. Marble, "Battle of the Yalu," 492. For Vice Admiral Itō Sukeyuki's brief overview of the battle, see "The Naval Fight," *Japan Weekly Mail,* October 13, 1894.

48. Tyler, *Pulling Strings,* 51.

49. Perry, "Battle of Tayang," 257.

50. Paine, *Sino-Japanese War,* 198.

51. The march on Beijing was eventually abandoned, and Yamagata was recalled. See Lone, *Japan's First Modern War,* 40–41; Paine, *Sino-Japanese War,* 197–198.

52. Robert John Perrins, "Great Connections: The Creation of a City, Dalian, 1905–1931: China and Japan on the Liaodong Peninsula" (PhD diss., York University, 1997), 63–64.

53. Cited in Okamoto Shumpei, *Impressions of the Front: Woodcuts of the Sino-Japanese War, 1894–5* (Philadelphia, 1983), 35; Perrins, "Great Connections," 64.

54. "The Chino-Japanese War," *London and China Telegraph,* January 14, 1895, 40.

55. Denby to Gresham, September 18, 1895, no. 52, *FRUS,* 53rd Congress, 3rd sess., House of Representatives, vol. 1, ser. 3292 (Washington, DC, 1895), 60.

56. White, *War in the East,* 516.

57. The port took its English name from British Royal Navy lieutenant William C. Arthur, who surveyed it in August 1860. See Eastlake and Yamada, *Heroic Japan,* 152; White, *War in the East,* 583; James Allan, *Under the Dragon Flag* (New York, 1898), 31.

58. Inoue Haruki, *Ryōjun gyakusatsu jiken* [Ryōjun massacre] (Tokyo, 1995), 143; White, *War in the East,* 584–585; James Creelman, "Massacre at Port Arthur," *New York World,* December 20, 1894.

59. "Port Arthur Atrocities," *Japan Weekly Mail,* December 22, 1894, 702.

60. Creelman, "Massacre at Port Arthur."

61. James Creelman, *On the Great Highway: The Wanderings and Adventures of a Special Correspondent* (Boston, 1901), 113–114.

62. Eastlake and Yamada, *Heroic Japan,* 154.

63. James Creelman, "The Extraordinary General Yamaji," *New York World,* February 11, 1895.

64. White, *War in the East,* 584; Vladimir, *China-Japan War,* 225–228; Eastlake and Yamada, *Heroic Japan,* 157.

65. White, *War in the East,* 588. Isechi Yoshinari is also known as Tomonari Ise.

66. White, *War in the East,* 591; Eastlake and Yamada, *Heroic Japan,* 157.

67. *New York World,* January 20, 1895; White, *War in the East,* 593–594.

68. *North China Herald,* December 21, 1894. On November 25, Li Hongzhang wrote an official report to the Yamen based on what he knew at the time. He stated that Wei Rucheng escaped Port Arthur after putting up a good fight. Li blamed Jinzhou's poor defenses and lack of manpower, not the competence of his generals. See *LZR,* 2:140–141.

69. *North China Herald,* February 8, 1895. Wei Rucheng was never captured and his fate is unknown.

70. Along the route from Dojōshi to Port Arthur, Qing soldiers savagely violated the dead bodies, "slicing their abdomen and stuffing their bodies with rocks" and in some cases "even removed their testicles." Inoue Haruki, *Ryojun gyakusatsu jiken,* 147.

71. Inoue, *Ryōjun gyakusatsu jiken,* 147.

72. "The Fall of Port Arthur," *North China Herald,* December 21, 1894.

73. Inoue, *Ryōjun gyakusatsu jiken,* 147.

74. According to Japanese newspaper reports, this situation must have contributed to the difficulty of distinguishing between civilians and soldiers. Japanese soldiers, therefore, were compelled to "storm into the civilian houses and drag out males of a likely age to be a soldier and kill them." (Ko Hidesuke, "Second Army War Correspondent's Notebook," *Tokyo Nichinichi Shimbun,* December 19, 1894). Inoue, *Ryōjun gyakusatsu jiken,* 147–148.

75. *Chūō Shimbun,* December 8, 1894; Inoue, *Ryōjun gyakusatsu jiken,* 147.

76. Creelman, "Massacre at Port Arthur." The lack of any meaningful treatment of the Ryōjun massacre in Tabohashi Kiyoshi's study on the Sino-Japanese War is remarkable. See his *Nisshin sen'eki gaikōshi no kenkyū* [Study of the diplomatic history of the Sino-Japanese War] (Tokyo, 1951), 350.

77. Thomas Cowen, "Port Arthur Atrocities," *London and China Telegram,* January 14, 1895, 40.

78. James Creelman, "Massacre at Port Arthur." Cowen recalled that "every home was entered and searched . . . I saw bodies under the beds having bullet wounds upon them— evidently the poor creatures had tried to hide themselves under the beds. Some corpses I saw were in a kneeling position—they had evidently been killed while kowtowing" (*Japan Daily Mail,* December 22, 1894).

79. Kamei Koreaki, *Nisshin Sensō jūgun shashinchō: Hakushaku Kamei Koreaki no nikki* [Sino-Japanese War Service photo album: Count Kamei Koreki's diary] (Tokyo, 1992), 199.

80. Creelman, "Massacre at Port Arthur." Cowen recalled that he saw "several women killed and a few children," but also "a rather large number of women—some scores—whom the Japanese left unhurt." *Japan Weekly Mail,* December 22, 1894, 702.

81. "In China," *London and China Telegraph,* January 14, 1895, 39.

82. Creelman, "Massacre at Port Arthur."

83. *New York World,* December 23, 1894.

84. "The Horrors of Port Arthur Massacre," *New York World,* February 11, 1895.

85. "Port Arthur Atrocities," *London and China Telegraph,* January 14, 1895, 41.

86. Creelman, "Massacre at Port Arthur." A similar description can be found in "Port Arthur Atrocities," *London and China Telegraph,* January 14, 1895, 42

87. Creelman, "Massacre at Port Arthur."

88. "Horrors of Port Arthur Massacre," *New York World,* February 11, 1895.

89. Inoue, *Ryōjun gyakusatsu jiken,* 21–22.

90. Inoue, *Ryōjun gyakusatsu jiken,* 23–24.

91. Inoue, *Ryōjun gyakusatsu jiken,* 24.

92. Inoue, *Ryōjun gyakusatsu jiken,* 25–26.

93. Inoue, *Ryōjun gyakusatsu jiken,* 27.

94. *Japan Daily Mail,* December 8, 1894.

95. Inoue, *Ryōjun gyakusatsu jiken,* 28–29.

96. Inoue, *Ryōjun gyakusatsu jiken,* 28–30.

97. See William Ker, "Treaty Revision in Japan: A Survey of the Steps by Which the Abolition of Foreign Privilege Was Accomplished in the Island Empire," *Pacific Affairs* 1, no. 6 (November 1928): 1–10.

98. The countries with which Japan signed new, equal treaties included, among others: Great Britain, July 16, 1894; Italy, December 1, 1894; Peru, March 20, 1895; Russia, June 8,

1895; Germany, April 4, 1896; and France, August 4, 1896. See "The New Japanese Treaty of Commerce and Navigation," *American Journal of Law* 5, no. 2 (April 1911): 444.

99. The *World* reported that the US Congress declined to ratify the treaty until after the massacre was investigated. *New York World*, December 16, 1894.

100. *New York World*, December 12, 1894.

101. *New York World*, December 13, 1894.

102. Inoue, *Ryōjun gyakusatsu jiken*, 55.

103. "Port Arthur Atrocities," *London and China Telegraph*, January 14, 1895.

104. Inoue, *Ryōjun gyakusatsu jiken*, 55.

105. On December 12, Japanese consul general Hashiguchi Naoyemon stormed into the offices of the *New York World* and "accused the persons present for acting disrespectfully to Japan by printing a report which bordered on fabrication and fancy." *New York World*, December 21, 1894. See also Inoue, *Ryōjun gyakusatsu jiken*, 60–62.

106. Dun to Gresham, January 11, 1895, no. 88, 85, *FRUS*, 53rd Congress, 3rd sess., vol. 1, ser. 3292 (Washington, DC, 1895).

107. Inoue, *Ryōjun gyakusatsu jiken*, 61.

108. Inoue, *Ryōjun gyakusatsu jiken*, 61–62.

109. Inoue, *Ryōjun gyakusatsu jiken*, 63.

110. Inoue, *Ryōjun gyakusatsu jiken*, 63–64.

111. Writing for the *New York Tribune*, House signaled his strong sympathy for the Meiji leadership. See Inoue, *Ryōjun gyakusatsu jiken*, 65. See also James L. Huffman, *A Yankee in Meiji Japan: The Crusading Journalist Edward H. House* (New York, 2003).

112. It claimed that all four journalists, with the exception of Villiers, had "never before seen anything of war and even its most ordinary incidents must have been shocking to them" and suggested that more value should be focused on the testimony of the military attaché who accompanied the Second Army. *Japan Weekly Mail*, December 22, 1894.

113. Inoue, *Ryōjun gyakusatsu jiken*, 31.

114. *New York World*, December 21, 1894.

115. Creelman wrote: "I am now the general target for abuse in Japan simply because I have told the truth about Port Arthur." Creelman to wife, December 21, 1895, box 1, folders 1–6, SPEC.CMS 19, Ohio State University, Special Collections, Thompson Library. Regarding Guerville's claims about Creelman's sensationalism, the two journalists' mutual antipathy was well known. "He is a cold-blooded villain," Creelman wrote of Guerville. Creelman to wife, November 1, 1894, box 1, folders 1–6, SPEC.CMS 19.

116. *New York World*, December 21, 1894. Thomas L. Hardin notes that "many Americans accepted and even justified the act [massacre]." The *New York Herald* in particular downplayed the atrocities stories. See Hardin's "American Press and Public Opinion in the First Sino-Japanese War," *Journalism Quarterly* (Spring 1973): 57.

117. Dun to Gresham, December 20, 1894, enclosure 88, 86, *FRUS*, 53rd Congress, 3rd sess., vol. 1, ser. 3292 (Washington, DC 1895), 85–87.

118. Dun to Gresham, January 7, 1895, enclosure 90, 89, *FRUS*, 53rd Congress, 3rd sess., vol. 1, ser. 3292 (Washington, DC 1895), 85–87.

119. Dun to Gresham, January 7, 1895, 89.

120. Inoue, *Ryōjun gyakusatsu jiken*, 70. The memo did not mention either Cowen or Villers. Although Cowen had published early reports about the incident, he admitted afterward that "he and other correspondents were afraid to write or cable the facts when Creelman sent them to the *World*." *New York World*, January 9, 1895.

121. On January 9, 1895, for example, Li Hongzhang forwarded a telegram to the Zongli Yamen, received from customs official Liu Hanfang, relating the dire situation in Lushun. *LZR*, 2:137–138.

9. TWO-FRONT WAR

1. *IHH*, vol. 1; Mutsu Munemitsu, *Kenkenroku: A Diplomatic Record of the Sino-Japanese War*, ed. and trans. Gordon Mark Berger (Tokyo, 1982), 29–30.

2. Edmund Fung, "The Peace Efforts of Li Hung-chang on the Eve of the Sino-Japanese War," in *Papers on Far Eastern History*, ed. Department of Far Eastern History, Australian National University, vol. 3 (Canberra, March 1971), 154.

3. The Military Deliberative Council was established in July 1894 and dismantled that December. Two royal edits promulgated on July 24 reestablished the Taewŏn'gun as regent and supreme decision-maker on military affairs. KJSL, 31 kwan, June 22, 1894 (lunar), http://sillok.history.go.kr/id/kza_13106022_003. An interesting insight into Kojong's character was how easily he accepted the reform measures proposed by the Japanese. KJSL, 31 kwan, June 27, 1894 (lunar), http://sillok.history.go.kr/id/kza_13106027_001. Also see Young I. Lew, "Korean-Japanese Politics behind the Kabo-Ulmi Reform Movement, 1894 to 1896," *Journal of Korean Studies* 3 (1981): 53.

4. *NGB*, vol. 27, bk. 2, no. 700. Also Morinosuke Kajima, *The Diplomacy of Japan, 1894–1922*, vol. 1 (Tokyo, 1976), 107.

5. *NGB*, vol. 27, bk. 2, no. 700; Kajima, *Diplomacy of Japan*, 107–108; Lew, "Korean-Japanese Politics," 58.

6. Lew, "Korean-Japanese Politics," 55.

7. *Japan Weekly Mail*, October 20, 1894.

8. Sugimura, *Sŏule namkyŏdun kkum* [Memoirs of troubles while living in Seoul] (Seoul, 1993), 126–127.

9. Sugimura, *Sŏule namkyŏdun kkum*, 138.

10. Sugimura, *Sŏule namkyŏdun kkum*, 138–139.

11. The tentative compact between Korea and Japan was made on August 20. See Peter Duus, *The Abacus and the Sword: The Japanese Penetration of Korea, 1895–1910* (Berkeley, 1995), 80–81; Kajima, *Diplomacy of Japan*, 109–117; Hilary Conroy, *The Japanese Seizure of Korea, 1868–1910: A Study of Realism and Idealism in International Relations* (Philadelphia, 1960), 265–266.

12. The Korean government was also expected to help support Japanese troops in Korea. KJSL, 32 kwan, July 22, 1894, http://sillok.history.go.kr/id/kza_13107022_004. See also Kajima, *Diplomacy of Japan*, 113–114; 118; Duus, *Abacus and the Sword*, 81.

13. Chŏng Kyo, *Taehan kyenyŏn sa* (Chronological history of Taehan), vol. 1, kwan 2 (Seoul, 1957), 98; Lew Young Ick, "The Conservative Character of the 1894 Tonghak Peasant Uprising: A Reappraisal with Emphasis on Chŏn Pong-jun's Background and Motivation," *Journal of Korean Studies* 7 (1990): 149–180; Bishop Gustav Mutel, *Mwit'el chugyo ilgi* [Diaries of Bishop Mutel], vol. 1, *1890–1895* (Seoul, 2009), 373. The Japanese were also aware of the Taewŏn'gun's double dealings with the Tonghak leaders, as revealed by dispatches to Tokyo. See CIK, 5 kwan (5) [12908], no. 123, Sugimura to Mutsu, October 20, 1894, http://db.history.go.kr/id/jh_005r_0050_0070.

14. CIK, 3 kwan [12809], Otori to Komura, October 8, 1894, http://db.history.go.kr/item/level.do?setId=88&itemId=jh&synonym=off&chinessChar=on&page=1&pre_page=1&brokerPagingInfo=&position=19&levelId=jh_003r_0070_0600. The Taewŏn'gun's letter, dated August 28, was sent to the governor of P'yŏngyang, Min Pyŏng-sok. See also Lew, "Korean-Japanese Politics," 63–64.

15. The letter promised the Chinese that "on the approach of their troops to Seoul, the Taewŏn'gun would instigate the Tonghaks to rise and attack the Japanese from their rear." *Japan Weekly Mail*, December 15, 1894. Chŏng Kyo also describes the conspiracy in detail. See Chŏng Kyo, *Taehan kyenyŏn sa*, vol. 1, kwan 2, 93.

16. *NGB*, vol. 28, bk. 1, no. 226, 381; Sugimura, *Sŏule namkyŏdun kkum*, 138–139.

17. Kim, born in Vladivostok, spoke fluent Russian, Chinese, and Japanese. He was intensely pro-Japanese. See *North-China Herald*, November 16, 1894. Details of the assassination plot and the trial can be found in Inoue's long dispatch to Mutsu on May 10, 1895. *NGB*, vol. 28, bk. 1, no. 268, 403–412; *NGB*, vol. 28, bk. 1, no. 267; Sugimura, *Sŏule namkyŏdun kkum*, 142–143; Lew, "Korean-Japanese Politics," 69. See also Chŏng Kyo's *Taehan kyenyŏn sa*, vol. 1, kwan 2, 98–99.

18. Inoue's assessment shortly after he arrived in Korea. CIK, 1 kwan (49) [12810], Inoue to Ōyama, November 10, 1894, http://db.history.go.kr/item/level.do?setId=88&itemId =jh&synonym=off&chinessChar=on&page=1&pre_page=1&brokerPagingInfo=&position =45&levelId=jh_003r_0080_1940.

19. Duus, *Abacus and the Sword*, 84; Conroy, *Japanese Seizure of Korea*, 271.

20. Kajima, *Diplomacy of Japan*, 120.

21. Sugimura, *Sŏule namkyŏdun kkum*, 158–159.

22. Sugimura, *Sŏule namgyŏdun kkum*, 160; Kajima, *Diplomacy of Japan*, 122.

23. Lew Young-Ick, "The Kabo Reform Movement: Korean and Japanese Reform Efforts in Korea, 1894" (PhD diss., Harvard University, 1972), 431.

24. Nakatsuka Akira, Inoue Katsuo, and Pak Mengsu, *Tōgaku nōmin sensō to nihon: Mō hitotsu no nisshin sensō* [Tonghak peasant war and Japan: Another Sino-Japanese war] (Tokyo, 2013), 76. See also Young Ick Lew, "Minister Inoue Kaoru and the Japanese Reform Attempts in Korea during the Sino-Japanese War, 1894–1895," *Asea Yongu* 27, no. 2 (1984): 11.

25. *North-China Herald*, November 16, 1895.

26. *NBG*, vol. 28, bk. 2, no. 485; Kajima, *Diplomacy of Japan*, 123–124.

27. Lew, "Minister Inoue Kaoru," 12.

28. The Confucianism Ch'oe included in his new religion was not only the classical Confucian texts of Confucius and Mencius but also the works of Lu Xiangshan and Wang Yangming. See Shin Yong-ha, "Conjunction of Tonghak and the Peasant War of 1894," *Korea Journal* 34, no. 4 (1994): 63.

29. "Translation of Manifesto issued by Tong Hak Society," April 1893, and "Decrees, Proclamation, Order and Placards to the Koreans from Various Sources, 1882–1895," WWRP, MS 2122 (82), folder 2 of 2.

30. Sin Yong-ha, "Conjunction of Tonghak and Peasant War of 1894," 65.

31. Benjamin B. Weems, *Reform, Rebellion and the Heavenly Way* (Tucson, AZ, 1964), 37.

32. A *hyanggyo* was a government-run academy, distinguished from the private *sŏwŏns*.

33. Peter Lee, *Sourcebook of Korean Civilization*, vol. 2 (New York, 1996), 371–373. See also Lew, "Conservative Character," 155–157.

34. Suh Young-hee, "Tracing the Course of the Peasant War of 1894," *Korea Journal* 34, no. 4 (Winter 1994): 20.

35. Han'guk kŭnsa yŏn'gusil, *Taehankunchesa* [History of the Taehan army], vol. 2 (Seoul, 1968–1977), 337–338.

36. Lee, *Sourcebook of Korean Civilization*, 376.

37. Weems, *Reform, Rebellion*, 45.

38. Gen'yōsha shashi hensankai hen [Gen'yōsha History Compilation Society], *Gen'yōsha shashi* [History of the Gen'yōsha] (Tokyo, 2016), 438–441, 460–461. Following the outbreak of the Sino-Japanese War, some Ten'yūkyō members volunteered to serve in the Japanese Army as scouts and local intelligence agents. *Gen'yōsha shashi*, 499–502. See also E. Herbert Norman, "A Study in the Origins of Japanese Imperialism," *Pacific Affairs* 17, no. 3 (September 1944): 261–284.

39. *Gen'yōsha shashi,* 451–455. Anti-Qing rhetoric was used frequently by members of the Ten'yūkyō in discussions with the Tonghaks.

40. Pak Chŏng-gun, *Nisshin Sensō to Chōsen* [The first Sino-Japanese War and Korea] (Tokyo, 1982), 89–93.

41. Pak, *Nisshin Sensō to Chōsen,* 207–208.

42. Pak, *Nisshin Sensō to Chōsen,* 89–93.

43. Nakatsuka et al., *Tōgaku Nōmin Sensō to Nihon,* 57–58.

44. Pak, *Nisshin Sensō to Chōsen,* 197.

45. Nakatsuka et al., *Tōgaku Nōmin Sensō to Nihon,* 59.

46. *North China Herald,* November 2, 1894.

47. Nakatsuka et al., *Tōgaku Nōmin Sensō to Nihon,* 68.

48. Nakatsuka et al., *Tōgaku Nōmin Sensō to Nihon,* 60.

49. Mutsu, *Kenkenroku,* 109.

50. *North China Herald,* December 14, 1894.

51. Suh, "Tracing the Course," 26; Nakatsuka et al., *Tōgaku Nōmin Sensō to Nihon,* 63.

52. Private civilian armies like the Ch'angŭikun were organized to help suppress the Tonghak peasant army, which these groups condemned as "heretics and rebels." See Pak, *Nisshin Sensō to Chōsen,* 206–210; Suh, "Tracing the Course," 27.

53. This refers to the Chinese idiom 玉石俱焚 (yu shi ju fen), "burning both jade and stone"—meaning, in this context, "to destroy indiscriminately."

54. Hwang Hyŏn, *Odong namu araeesŏ yŏksarŭl kirokhada: Hwang-hyŏni pon tonghak nongminjo'njaeng* [History recorded under a pawlonia tree: The Tonghak peasant war as witnessed by Hwang Hyŏn] (Seoul, 2016), 384–387.

55. Hwang Hyŏn, *Odong namu araeesŏ yŏksarŭl kirokhada,* 463–464. Hwang refers to the Tonghaks as "tochŏk" (bandits), which reveals where his sympathies lay.

56. *North China Herald,* March 1, 1895.

57. *North China Herald,* December 7, 1894. In an after-action report on May 13, 1895, Major Minami Koshiro remarked that "the Tonghaks were indistinguishable from the rest of the population." He also noted that "when the Tonghaks were powerful, the leaders would do the Tonghaks' bidding; when our military forces arrived, they took our army's side, but when our troops left, they [grew afraid] and wanted our troops to stay on because they feared being attacked by the Tonghaks." CIK, 6 kwan [14647], Minami to Inoue, May 13, 1895, http://db.history.go.kr/item/level.do?setId=4&itemId=jh&synonym=off&chinessChar=on&page=1&pre_page=1&brokerPagingInfo=&position=3&levelId=jh_006r_0020_0030.

58. *North China Herald,* December 14, 1894. To counter the rising chaos surrounding the Tonghak rebellion, the Korean government circulated a public notice stating that "there was no reason to fear [the Japanese Army]" and that the "so-called leaders of the rebellion are just lowly scum of the earth." The notices also offered a hefty reward for the capture of the rebel leaders. See *Tonghaknan kirok* [Records of the Eastern learning], ed. Kuksa P'yŏnch'an Wiwŏnhoe, vol. 2 (Seoul, 1974), 127–128.

59. Even though the Korean troops were expected "to follow Japanese officers' commands," the Chosŏn government dispatched its own forces independently of the Japanese, although all Korean units were required to coordinate movements with the Japanese. CIK, 4 kwan, no. 174 [12557], Lieutenant Col. Itō to Inoue, November 4, 1894, http://db.history.go.kr/item/level.do?itemId=jh&levelId=jh_001r_0040_0300&types=r; CIK, 1 kwan [12557], Lieutenant Col. Itō to Inoue, November 9, 1894, http://db.history.go.kr/item/level.do?itemId=jh&levelId=jh_001r_0040_0390_0010&types=r.

60. T'aehanmyŏn'guk munkyobukuksabyŏn ch'anwiunwŏn, eds., *Tonghaknan kirok* [Records of the Eastern Learning], vol. 2 (Seoul, 1974), 280–281. There were also not enough winter coats, and Sin was afraid the troops were becoming mutinous.

61. KJSL, November 3, 1894 (lunar), http://sillok.history.go.kr/id/kza_13111003_002, CIK, 1 kwan [12538], Report of Captain Morioma, November 22, 1894, http://db.history .go.kr/item/level.do?setId=117&itemId=jh&synonym=off&chinessChar=on&page=1&pre _page=1&brokerPagingInfo=&position=13&levelId=jh_001r_0060_0070.

62. On the effects of the new magazine rifles, see George Buchanan, MD, "The Surgical Effects of Rifle Bullet," *British Medical Journal* 1, no. 1789 (April 13, 1895): 827–828. The Type-18 Murata rifle was a single-shot weapon. Some Japanese units were equipped with the Murata Type 22, a repeating rifle, but it did not become standard equipment until the Boxer Uprising. See Edward J. Drea, *Japan's Imperial Army: Its Rise and Fall, 1853–1945* (Lawrence, 2009), 74.

63. Hwang Hyŏn, *Odong namu araeesŏ yŏksarŭl kirokhada*, 441–443.

64. Nakatsuka et al., *Tōgaku nōmin sensō to nihon*, 80–81. The report sent to the government states: "The two battles were both successful. None of our soldiers were injured." KJSL, kwan 32, November 3, 1894, http://sillok.history.go.kr/id/kza_13111003_002.

65. Suh, "Tracing the Course," 26, 28.

66. CIK, 1 kwan [14647], Report of Captain Morioma, December 11, 1894, http://db .history.go.kr/item/level.do?setId=4&itemId=jh&synonym=off&chinessChar=on&page =1&pre_page=1&brokerPagingInfo=&position=1&levelId=jh_001r_0070_0080.

67. Lew, "Korean-Japanese Politics." Inoue was informed of the arrests of Chŏn Pong-jun and Kim Kim-hae on January 7, 1895; CIK, 6 kwan [12558], Infantry Captain of the Nineteenth Battalion to Inoue, January 7, 1895. http://db.history.go.kr/item/level.do?setId =18&itemId=jh&synonym=off&chinessChar=on&page=1&pre_page=1&brokerPagingInfo =&position=17&levelId=jh_006r_0010_0070.

68. The document was published on December 8. Cited in Lee, *Sourcebook of Korean Civilization*, 2:369–370; Lew, "Kabo Reform Movement," 410–411.

69. *North China Herald*, December 14, 1894. There is plenty of evidence that people were forced to join Chŏn's Tonghak army against their will. See *Tonghaknan kirok*, 127–148.

70. Nakatsuka et al., *Tōgaku nōmin sensō to Nihon*, 92.

71. Pak, *Nisshin sensō to chōsen*, 205.

72. Nakatsuka et al., *Tōgaku nōmin sensō to nihon*, 102.

73. Pak, *Nisshin sensō to chōsen*, 206.

74. Nakatsuka et al., *Tōgaku nōmin sensō to nihon*, 97; Harada Keiichi, *Nisshin ensō* [Sino-Japanese War] (Tokyo, 2008), 283. There is no reliable record to determine the exact number of casualties on the Korean side or the number of Korean civilian lives lost. One reason is that the Tonghak peasant army quickly buried fallen comrades so as to continue the myth of their invincibility to bullets. Many were unaware they had suffered heavy casualties during a battle and that government troops had suffered no major losses. Hwang Hyŏn, *Odong namu araeesŏ yŏksarŭl kirokhada*, 384.

75. Weems, *Reform, Rebellion*, 52.

10. TRIPLE INTERVENTION

1. Donald Keene, *Landscapes and Portraits: Appreciations of Japanese Culture* (Tokyo, 1971), 260.

2. Wayne C. McWilliams, "East Meets East: The Soejima Mission to China, 1893," *Monumenta Nipponica* 30, no. 3 (Autumn 1975): 245.

3. Cited in Keene, *Landscapes*, 262.

4. Keene, *Landscapes*, 263.

5. Lafcadio Hearn, *Kokoro: Hints and Echoes of Japanese Inner Life* (Leipzig, 1907), 75.

6. John Dower, "Throwing Off Asia II: Woodblock Prints of the Sino-Japanese War (1894–95)," MIT Visualizing Culture, https://visualizingcultures.mit.edu/throwing_off_asia _01/2000_380_07_l.html.

7. Keene, *Landscapes*, 268–271.

8. D. R. B Conkling, "Japanese War Posters," *Century Illustrated Magazine*, April 1896, 936.

9. *Japan Weekly Mail*, June 1, 1895. Lafcadio Hearn wrote that the storming of the defenses of Port Arthur was the subject of one ingenious mechanical toy; another, "equally clever, repeated the fight of the Matsushima with the Chinese iron-clads." Hearn, *Kokoro*, 75.

10. Li Hongzhang's letter is reprinted in the *North-China Herald*, December 28, 1894; Trumbull White, *The War in the East: Japan, China and Corea—A Complete History of the War* (Philadelphia, 1895), 612.

11. John W. Foster, *Diplomatic Memoirs*, vol. 2 (Boston, 1909), 102–103.

12. Foster, *Diplomatic Memoirs*, 113.

13. *IHH*, 1:43–45.

14. The United States firmly rejected a proposal by the British minister on October 8 that the United States, Russia, France, and Britain intervene to terminate the war on the basis of an indemnity paid by China and a multipower guarantee of Korean independence. Lawrence H. Battstini, "The Korea Problem in the Nineteenth Century," *Monumenta Nipponica* 8, no. 1–2 (1952): 63; Payson Jackson Treat, *Japan and the United States, 1853–1921* (New York, 1928), 158–160.

15. *IHH*, 1:43–45. See also Mutsu Munemitsu, *Kenkenroku: A Diplomatic Record of the Sino-Japanese War, 1894–1895*, ed. and trans. Gordon Mark Berger (Tokyo, 1982), 148–151.

16. Donald Keene, *Emperor of Japan: Meiji and His World, 1852–1912* (New York, 2002), 498. The text of the rescript is in *Meiji Tenno ki* [Chronicles of Emperor Meiji], vol. 8 (Tokyo, 1968–1977), 601–602. See also Steward Lone, *Japan's First Modern War: Army Society in the Conflict with China, 1894–5* (London, 1994), 42–44; Bruce Elleman, *Modern Chinese Warfare, 1795–1989* (New York, 2001), 109–110.

17. Keene, *Emperor of Japan*, 497–498; White, *War in the East*, 615.

18. *IHH*, 1:42–43.

19. William Ferdinand Tyler, *Pulling Strings in China* (New York, 1929), 63; White, *War in the East*, 629.

20. White, *War in the East*, 630. Tyler, *Pulling Strings*, 68. Vladimir writes that there were twenty-five vessels remaining. Vladimir [pseud.] [Z. Volpicelli], *The China-Japan War: Compiled from Japanese, Chinese and Foreign Sources* (London, 1896), 276.

21. Eastlake Warrington et al., *Heroic Japan: A History of the War between China and Japan* (London, 1897), 297.

22. Tyler, *Pulling Strings*, 67.

23. Tyler, *Pulling Strings*, 67. Admiral Ding put him in charge of the destruction of the forts.

24. Henry Davenport Northrop, *The Flowery Kingdom and the Land of Mikado; or, China, Japan and Corea; Together with a Graphic Account of the War between China and Japan, Its Causes, Land and Naval Battles, etc., etc.* (Dallas, 1894), 619.

25. Tyler, *Pulling Strings*, 70. Northrop, *Flowery Kingdom*, 619.

26. Tyler, *Pulling Strings*, 71; Qi Qizhang, *Jia wu zhan zheng shi* [History of the Sino-Japanese War] (Shanghai, 2005), 366.

27. Reprinted in Vladimir, *China-Japan War*, 380–382.

28. Vladimir, *China-Japan War*, 285.

29. Qi, *Jia wu zhan zheng shi*, 367.

30. Wang Ping was Ding's trusted subordinate. Qi Qizhang, *Jia wu zhan zheng shi,* 367.

31. Tyler, *Pulling Strings,* 74.

32. The *Dingyuan* was struck on the evening of February 4; only during daylight on February 5 was its dire situation confirmed. See Qi, *Jia wu zhan zheng shi,* 358.

33. Tyler, *Pulling Strings,* 75; Vladimir, *China-Japan War,* 293. Qi, *Jia wu zhan zheng shi,* 359.

34. *Japan Weekly Mail,* February 16, 1895; Tyler, *Pulling Strings,* 84. Other sources list four men-of-war and six gunboats out of a previous twenty-eight ships. See Elleman, *Modern Chinese Warfare,* 112.

35. Qi, *Jia wu zhan zheng shi,* 365.

36. Vladimir, *China-Japan War,* 384; Shumpei Okamoto, *Impressions from the Front: Woodcuts of the Sino-Japanese War, 1894–95* (Philadelphia, 1983), 44; Qi, *Jia wu zhan zheng shi,* 365.

37. Arthur Diósy, *The New Far East* (London, 1898), 159; Vladimir, *China-Japan War,* 380–386.

38. Chŏng Kyo chŏ, *Taehan kyenyŏnsa* [The chronological history of Great Korea], vol. 1 (Seoul, 1974), 104. See also Miyake Setsurei, *Dojidaishi* [Contemporary history], vol. 3 (Tokyo, 1967), 47.

39. Vladimir, *China-Japan War,* 299.

40. White, *War in the East,* 641; Inouye Jikichi, *The Fall of Wei-hai-wei: Compiled from Official Sources* (Yokohama, 1895), 24, https://babel.hathitrust.org/cgi/pt?id=uc2.ark:/13960/t4nk38qoh;view=1up;seq=9. Despite the honors, the Japanese were still distrustful. In order to guarantee that the *Kangji* was not used to smuggle arms, Itō ordered it to be "inspected by military officers of the Japanese Navy on the morning of February 15." Miyake Setsurei, *Dojidaishi,* 3:47.

41. Keene, *Emperor of Japan,* 501.

42. After the destruction of the Beiyang Fleet, the Japanese embarked upon the capture of the Pescadores islands—the last military operation of the war and an essential preliminary to the Japanese conquest of Taiwan (Formosa), which it justified on the basis of Japan's overall maritime expansion. J. Charles Schencking, "The Imperial Japanese Navy and the Constructed Consciousness of a South Seas Destiny, 1872–1921," *Modern Asian Studies* 33, no. 4 (October 1999): 769–796; Edward I-Te Chen, "Japan's Decision to Annex Taiwan: A Study of Itō -Mutsu Diplomacy, 1894–5," *Journal of Asian Studies* 35, no. 1 (November 1977): 61–72; David C. Evans and Mark R. Peattie, *Kaigun: Strategies, Tactics and Technology in the Imperial Japanese Navy, 1887–1941* (Annapolis, MD, 1997); G. A. Ballard, *The Influence of the Sea on the Political History of Japan* (New York, 1921).

43. Mutsu, *Kenkenroku,* 166.

44. Mutsu, *Kenkenroku,* 148, 181.

45. Orville Schnell and John Delury, *Wealth and Power: China's Long March to the Twenty-First Century* (New York, 2013), 71.

46. Ssu-Yu Teng and John K. Fairbank, *China's Response to the West: A Documentary Survey, 1839–1923* (New York, 1967), 126. The first meeting was held on March 20. China asked for an armistice at the meeting. Also see *NBG,* vol. 28, bk. 2, no. 1089; and Morinosuke Kajima, *The Diplomacy of Japan, 1894–1922: Sino-Japanese War and Triple Intervention,* vol. 1 (Tokyo, 1976), 202–203.

47. The assassin was brought down by local police. *LZR,* 2:239.

48. "Recollections by Viscount Ishiguro Tadanori, MD," in *IHH,* 1:222.

49. Mutsu, *Kenkenroku,* 175. The Zongli Yamen was also not keen on having Li return to China without having completed his mission. *LZR,* 2:240.

50. *IHH*, 1:224–226. Li did not forget the Japanese doctors' service. Upon his return he wrote to thank Dr. Satō for his care. Reprinted in *Japan Weekly Mail,* October 12, 1895, 380; *IHH*, 1:226.

51. Mutsu, *Kenkenroku,* 183–185.

52. Mutsu, *Kenkenroku,* 191.

53. Keene, *Emperor of Japan,* 505; Mutsu, *Kenkenroku,* 193.

54. Mutsu, *Kenkenroku,* 198–199.

55. *IHH*, 1:40–41. See also George Alexandre Lensen, *Balance of Intrigue: International Rivalry in Korea and Manchuria, 1884–1899,* vol. 1 (Tallahassee, 1982), 282–308; S. C. M. Paine, *The Sino-Japanese War of 1894–1895: Perceptions, Power and Primacy* (Cambridge, 2003), 247–293.

56. Kojima, *Diplomacy of Japan,* 282.

57. *IHH*, 1:40–41. China's overtures to Russia are confirmed by Deputy Foreign Minister V. N. Lamsdorf, *LD,* 144.

58. *IHH*, 1:45.

59. Kojima, *Diplomacy of Japan,* 297.

60. Robert Britton Valliant, "Japan and the Trans-Siberian Railroad, 1885–1905" (PhD diss., University of Hawai'i, 1974), 131–132.

61. B. D. Pak, *Rossiia i Koreia* [Russia and Korea] (Moscow, 2004), 216. See also William L. Langer, *The Diplomacy of Imperialism* (New York, 1935), 185.

62. Pak, *Rossiia i Koreia,* 217–218. "In case Japan refuses, Witte was ready to call Russia to threaten war with Japan," in *PRI,* 25.

63. *IHH*, 1:39; Kojima, *Diplomacy of Japan,* 298.

64. Mutsu *Kenkenroku,* 206–207; Kojima, *Diplomacy of Japan,* 299; *IHH*, 39–40.

65. Mutsu, *Kenkenroku,* 207.

66. *Japan Weekly Mail,* August 3, 1895, 120.

67. *IHH*, 1:64.

68. Extracts of the *Hansŏng Sinbo* were reprinted in the *North-China Herald,* March 1, 1895.

69. *Japan Mail Weekly,* July 20, 1895, 61.

70. Peter Duus, *The Abacus and the Sword: The Japanese Penetration of Korea, 1895–1910* (Berkeley, 1995), 87–89.

71. CHKSR, 194.

72. "Her strength lies in her power to win the confidence of everybody coming into contact with her, even men of great ability and sagacity find it very difficult to resist her power of persuasion." *Japan Weekly Mail,* July 6, 1895, 11.

73. See Duus, *Abacus and the Sword,* 92.

74. Young Ick Lew, "Minister Inoue Kaoru and the Japanese Reform Attempts in Korea during the Sino-Japanese War, 1894–1895," *Asea Yongu* 27, no. 2 (1984): 27.

75. Hilary Conroy, *The Japanese Seizure of Korea, 1868–1910: A Study of Realism and Idealism in International Relations* (Philadelphia, 1960), 299.

76. Pak "put his signature on at least 68 of 213 reform documents," according to Lew Young-ik. For a complete list of these reforms, see Lew, "The Reform Efforts and Ideas of Pak Yŏng-hyo, 1894–1895," *Korean Studies* 1 (1977): 21–61. The plan was submitted to the Diet on February 22. *IHH*, 1:330.

77. Many of his sweeping reform measures were enacted immediately. *Hansŏng Sunbo,* January 22. See *North China Herald,* March 1, 1895, 304–305.

78. Duus, *Abacus and the Sword,* 100. Sugimura notes that Pak accused Kim Hong-jip of being a "spineless" man for bowing to Inoue, so that "we absolutely can't expect him to make plans for [Korea's] self-reliance." CHKSR, 200.

79. *Japan Weekly Mail,* July 6, 1895, 15.

80. On June 7 Sill reported that the new prime minister, Pak Yŏng-hyo, was a "virtual dictator." Conroy, *Japanese Seizure of Korea*, 305.

81. Sugimura to Saionji, July 12, 1895, *NGB*, vol. 28, bk. 466, no. 336; *IHH*, 1:302.

82. *Japan Weekly Mail*, July 27, 1895, 86.

83. *Japan Weekly Mail*, July 20, 1895, 61.

84. Duus, *Abacus and the Sword*, 106.

85. Conroy, *Japanese Seizure of Korea*, 282-284.

86. CHKSR, 215-216; Lew, "Minister Inoue Kapru, 179.

87. Conroy, *Japanese Seizure of Korea*, 284. Itō did everything he could to raise private funds, even writing to Kawada Koichirō, head of the Bank of Japan. See *IHH*, 1:328-330.

88. CHKSR, 225; Conroy, *Japanese Seizure of Korea*, 313-314.

89. *MSC*, 140. See also Sylvia Braesel, "Marie Antoinette Sontag (1838-1922): Uncrowned Empress of Korea," *Transactions of the Royal Asiatic Society Korea Branch* 89 (2014): 131-143; Komatsu Midori, *Meiji Gaikō Hiwa* [The secret history of Meiji diplomacy] (Tokyo, 1966), 240-242.

90. Sabatin was the first European architect employed by the Korean government and oversaw dozens of projects. See Simbirseva Tatiana and Levvoshko Svetlana, "Russian Architect Afansasy Seredin-Sabatin (1860-1921): At the Roots of Modernity," *Okhraniaetsia gosudarstvom*, January 2018, http://ohrgos.ru/index.php/rubriki/dostoyanie/420. See also *MSRP*, 94-95.

91. *MSRP*, 94-95.

92. Both Prime Minister Kim Hong-jip and Foreign Minister Kim Yun-sik supported the coup, although it does not appear that they were aware of the planned assassination of the queen. See CHKSR, 231-234.

93. CHKSR, 227-228.

94. The *sōshi* (literally, "manly warriors") traced their ideological lineage to rebels of the 1870s such as Saigō Takamori; the term carried a negative connotation, closer to the English word *thug*. In July 1895 *Jiji Shinpō* published a series of articles calling out the bad behavior of the *sōshi* in Korea as "prone to be overbearing and rough toward Koreans." *Japan Weekly Mail*, July 20, 1895, 54.

95. The *hullyŏndae* was established in February 1894 following the arrival of Inoue Kaoru to Korea. He envisioned that the elite, Japanese-trained force would play an important role in the military reform of Korea. See Yukkun Sagwan Hakkyo Han'guk Kunsa Yŏng'gusil, *Han'guk kunjesa* [History of the military system in Korea] vol. 2 (Seoul, 1968-1977), 353-357; Carter Eckert, *Park Chung Hee and Modern Korea: The Roots of Militarism, 1866-1945* (Cambridge, MA, 2016), 39-41.

96. *MSC*, 92-93. See also O Chi-yŏng, *Tonghak sa* [History of the Tonghak] (Seoul, 1940), 138-139; Benjamin Weems, *Reform, Rebellion and the Heavenly Way* (Tucson, AZ, 1964), 40-41.

97. CHKSR, 237-238; Keene, *Emperor of Japan*, 512. See *MSC*, 92-99; CHKSR, 233.

98. *MSC*, 113-114. See also "Witness Account of Yi Hak-kyun (Commander of the First Battalion of the Palace Guards)," in *MSRP*, 38-39.

99. "Witness Account of Yi Hak-kyun," 38.

100. Kim Mun-cha, *Myŏngsŏnghwanghwu sihaewa ilbonin* [Queen Min's Assassination and the Japanese] (Seoul, 2010), 394.

101. "Testimony of Sabatin," in *MSRP*, 85-86.

102. Testimony of Sabatin," 80-85. Also "Official Report on Matters Connected with the Events of October 8th 1895 and the Death of the Queen," *Korean Repository* 3 (1896): 126.

103. "Testimony of King Kojong's Son as Told through a Court Lady to the American Minister," in *MSRP*, 36.

104. *MSC*, 208; "Official Report," 216.

105. *MSC*, 262. See also Theodore M. Critchfield, "Queen Min's Murder" (PhD diss., Indiana University, 1975), 175.

106. "Testimony of Hyŏn Hŭng-t'aek," in *MSRP*, 41. A curious report by General P. F. Unterberger, which he wrote while visiting Korea in 1897, makes the claim that the queen might not have been dead when she was burned. *MSC*, 213. See also Pak, *Rossiia i Koreia*, 233. This account was backed by A. Sontag, who told journalist George Kennan that "the Queen was not dead when the murderers poured Kerosene over her body and set fire to it. She was still moving her head from side to side." George Kennan Papers, box 22, "Diary of Japan and Korea," July 26, 1905, LOC.

107. Critchfield, *Queen Min's Murder*, 184–186.

108. "Weber's Report, II" in *MSRP*, 65.

109. "King's Royal Order without Signature or the King's Seal," in *MSRP*, 69.

110. The only person who seemed not to have known about the queen's demise was Kojong. FO/405/64, enclosure 3, no. 86, Hillier to O'Conor, October 10, 1895, NA.

111. *MSC*, 65; Pak, *Rossiia i Koreia*, 224.

112. *MSC*, 66. Kim also cites a *Dong-a-ilbo* article published on January 29, 1930, for this information. See *MSC*, 229.

113. *MSC*, 77.

114. "Russian and England in the Far East," *Fortnightly Review* 65 (Jan–June 1896), 875. "Mr. R. Masujima was professor of jurisprudence at the Imperial University in Tokyo." Also quoted in F. A. McKenzie, *The Tragedy of Korea* (London, 1908), 73.

115. Henry Chung, *The Case of Korea: A Collection of Evidence on the Japanese Domination of Korea, and on the Development of the Korean Independence Movement* (New York, 1921), 327; *North China Herald*, January 31, 1896.

116. Keene, *Emperor of Japan*, 521. See "Copy of the Decision of the Japanese Court of Preliminary Inquiries," *Korean Repository* 3 (1896): 122–125. See also Critchfield, *Queen Min's Murder*, 220. In an attempt to inoculate themselves from their involvement in the assassination plot, the Taewŏn'gun and the Korean Cabinet seized three Koreans, among them a poor soldier who happened to be passing through the grove where the queen's body was burned, for their alleged role in the conspiracy. All three were promptly executed. See "Copy of the Decision of the Japanese Court of Preliminary Inquiries," 135–142.

117. *MSC*, 62–66.

11. CONTINENTAL POWER

1. S. P. Suslov, *Physical Geography of Asiatic Russia* (London, 1961), 325.

2. *PRI*, 29. Founded as the village of Nikolskoye in 1866, it was renamed Nikolsk-Ussuriysk in 1926. Today the city is known simply as Ussuriysk.

3. The petition was presented to Nicholas on May 12, 1895. See B. A. Romanov, *Russia in Manchuria (1892–1906)* (Leningrad, 1928), 62–63.

4. Olga Crisp, "The Russo-Chinese Bank: An Episode in Franco-Russian Relations," *Slavonic and East European Review* 52, no. 127 (April 1974): 198.

5. The French bankers accepted Witte's proposals because the promise of Russian government support in the event of a Chinese default was deemed vital. Crisp, "Russo-Chinese Bank," 198; Romanov, *Russia in Manchuria*, 67.

6. For the text of this loan agreement, see John V. S. MacMurray, ed., *Treaties and Agreement with and concerning China, 1894–1919*, vol. 1 (Washington, DC, 1921), 35–27. See also Harold Perry Ford, "Russian Far Eastern Diplomacy, Count Witte, and the Penetration of China, 1895–1904" (PhD diss., University of Chicago, 1950), 125–126. Writing to

A. P. Mohrenheim, the Russian ambassador to France, Foreign Minister Lobanov-Rostovsky confided the main thrust of Witte's plan: "*For our future plans, it is also important to make China dependent on us, and to stop Britain from spreading her influence in China*" (my emphasis). See *LD*, entry May 11 (MS 23), 176.

7. Crisp "Russo-Chinese Bank," 198; Romanov, *Russia in Manchuria*, 68–69; Rosemary Quested, *The Russo-Chinese Bank: A Multi-National Financial Base of Tsarism in China* (Birmingham, UK, 1977), 3–4.

8. Baron Rosen, *My Forty Years of Diplomacy*, vol. 1 (New York, 1922), 198.

9. George Alexander Lensen, *Balance of Intrigue: International Rivalry in Korea and Manchuria*, vol. 2 (Tallahassee, 1982), 487; *LD*, 283–284.

10. *LD*, 282, 284.

11. *LD*, 284, 303.

12. Archibald Colquhoun, "The Great Trans-Siberian Manchurian Railway," *Journal of the Royal United Service Institution* 44, no. 274 (December 1900): 1419–1420; P. Kropotkin, "The Russian in Manchuria," *Forum*, May 1901, 267–274.

13. *PORKMK*, 9–10.

14. *PORKMK*, 10–11, 44, 35, 41–42.

15. *PORKMK*, 70–71.

16. *PORKMK*, 85–86, 59.

17. *PORKMK*, 87, 77–78; Owen Lattimore, *Manchuria: Cradle of Conflict* (New York, 1932); Robert H. G. Lee, *The Manchurian Frontier in Ch'ing History* (Cambridge, MA, 1970).

18. *LD*, 327.

19. *LD*, 349; Romanov, *Russia in Manchuria*, 73.

20. Romanov, *Russia in Manchuria*, 73.

21. *PRI*, 31–32.

22. Romanov, *Russia in Manchuria*, 78; Lensen, *Balance of Intrigue*, 495.

23. Cited in Marcella Bounds, "The Sino-Russian Secret Treaty of 1896," *Papers on China*, no. 23, Harvard University East Asia Center (Cambridge, MA, July 1970), 115. Lensen, *Balance of Intrigue*, 495–496. See also Auguste Gerard, *Ma mission en Chine, 1894–1897* (Paris, 1918), 137–138.

24. *Da lu Za Zhi* (The Continent), vol. 1, *Minguo* 39 (1950): 14–16. The documents were published by Li Zongtong. They appeared in the journal *Minguo* as follows: vol. 1, no. 1 (July 15), *Minguo* 39 (1950); vol. 1, no. 3 (August 15), *Minguo* 39 (1950); vol. 1, no. 4 (August 31), *Minguo* 39 (1950); vol, 1, no. 5 (September 15), *Minguo* 39 (1950); vol. 1, no. 8 (October 31), Minguo 39 (1950); vol. 25, no. 6 (September 30), *Minguo* 51 (1962); vol. 25, no. 7 (October 15), Minguo 51 (1962); vol. 25, no. 8 (October 31), *Minguo* 51 (1962). See also Bounds, "Sino-Russian Secret Treaty," 109–125.

25. *Da lu Za Zhi*, vol. 1, no. 1 (July 15), *Minguo* 39 (1950): 17.

26. Bounds, "Sino-Russian Secret Treaty," 111–112; *Da lu Za Zhi*, vol. 1, no. 1 (July 15), *Minguo* 39 (1950): 17–18. The lunar date is March 26.

27. *Da lu Za Zhi*, vol. 1, no. 1 (1950), 18; *LD*, 380. See also "Secret History of the Russo-Japanese Treaty," *Contemporary Review*, January 1, 1897, 178.

28. S. C. M. Paine, *Imperial Rivals: China, Russia, and Their Disputed Frontier* (Armonk, 1996), 186; Bounds, "Sino-Russian Secret Treaty," 118.

29. Sergei Witte, The *Memoirs of Count Witte*, trans and ed. Sidney Harcave (New York, 1990), 233–235; *Da lu Za Zhi*, vol. 25, no. 7, *Minguo* 51 (1962), 217.

30. E. J. Dillon, *The Eclipse of Russia* (New York, 1918), 264.

31. Bounds, "Sino-Russian Secret Treaty," 119.

32. The May 22, 1896, treaty signed between China and Russia also entailed a special agreement between the board of directors of the Russo-Chinese Bank dated May–18, 1896.

See Economic Bureau of CER, *North Manchuria and the Chinese Eastern Railway* (Harbin, 1924), 35.

33. S. Yu. Witte, *Zapiski po povodu zaklyuchennogo mezhdu Kitayskim Pravitel'stvom i Russko-Kitayskim bankom dogovora na postroyku i ekspluatatsiyu zheleznoye dorogi v Manchzhurii* [A note on the agreement concluded between the Chinese government and the Russian-Chinese Bank on the construction and operation of the railway in Manchuria], 1896, Russian State Historical Archives (RIGA), 4, https://www.prlib.ru/en/node/687662.

34. Howard R. Spendelow, "Russia's Lease of Port Arthur and Talien: The Failure of China's Traditional Foreign Policy," in *Papers on China*, vol. 24, Harvard University East Asia Center (Cambridge, MA, December 1971), 148.

35. Ian H. Nish, *The Anglo-Japanese Alliance: The Diplomacy of Two Island Empires, 1894–1907* (London, 2013), 41: William L. Langer, *Diplomacy of Imperialism, 1890–1902*, 2 vols. (New York, 1935), 2:460.

36. Rosen, *My Forty Years*, 125.

37. Langer, *Diplomacy of Imperialism*, 1:405.

38. Two written agreements regarding Korea were made between Japan and Russia at this time: the Komura-Weber memorandum, May 1896, and the Yamagata-Lobanov agreement, June 1896. See Langer, *Diplomacy of Imperialism*, 1:406–407; Ian Nish, *The Origins of the Russo-Japanese War* (London, 1985), 33. See also Romanov, *Russia in Manchuria*, 104–105; Shannon McCune, "The Thirty-Eighth Parallel in Korea," *World Politics* 1, no. 2 (January 1949): 225.

39. Romanov, *Russia in Manchuria*, 132.

40. Dillon, *Eclipse of Russia*, 248–249; Witte, *Memoirs*, 269.

41. *PRI*, 43.

42. *PRI*, 44–45.

43. *PRI*, 44–45; William Stead, "Count Muravieff and His Successor," *Contemporary Review*, July 1, 1900, 331.

44. *PRI*, 56.

45. Cited in Spendelow, "Russia's Lease of Port Arthur," 155.

46. The convention between Russia and China enabled Russia to obtain a lease for twenty-five years, subject to renewal by mutual consent, of Port Arthur and Darien (Dalien) with a large defensible tract of land embracing the southern extremity of the Liaodong Peninsula. Russia also obtained the right to fortify Port Arthur as a naval station. The official text of the agreement was not published by either party. https://history.state.gov/historicaldocuments /frus1945Berlinv01/d579, retrieved June 11, 2019. See also the editorial "The Integrity of China and the 'Open Door,'" *American Journal of International Law* 1, no. 4 (October 1907): 956–957.

47. Nish, *Origins of the Russo-Japanese War*, 51.

48. Langer, *Diplomacy of Imperialism*, 2:471.

49. Quoted in Ford, "Russian Far Eastern Diplomacy," 154.

50. Nish, *Origins of the Russo-Japanese War*, 60.

51. Langer, *Diplomacy of Imperialism*, 2:472.

52. Henry Norman, "Russia and England: Down the Long Avenue," *Contemporary Review*, January 1, 1897, 153.

53. R. Stanley McCordock, *British Far Eastern Policy, 1894–1900* (New York, 1931), 222; William Stead, "Russia and Mr. Chamberlain's Long Spoon," *Contemporary Review*, January 1, 1898, 761–777.

54. Cited in Alfred L. P. Dennis, *Adventures in American Diplomacy, 1896–1906* (New York, 1928), 204–205.

12. MARITIME POWER

1. Alfred Thayer Mahan, *From Sail to Steam: Recollections of Naval Life* (New York, 1968), 270; W. D. Puleston, *Mahan: The Life and Work of Captain Alfred Thayer Mahan* (New Haven, CT, 1939), 66.

2. Warren Zimmerman, *The First Great Triumph: How Five Americans Made Their Country a World Power* (New York, 2002), 85.

3. Cited in Puleston, *Mahan*, 68.

4. Mahan, *From Sail to Steam*, 277.

5. Mahan, *From Sail to Steam*, 283; see also Mahan's letter to Luce, January 33, 1886, reels 2–3, LOC. Also reprinted in Robert Seager II and Doris D. Maguire, eds., *Letters and Papers of Alfred Thayer Mahan*, 2 vols. (Annapolis, MD, 1975), 1:622–623.

6. Alfred Thayer Mahan, *The Influence of Sea Power upon History, 1660–1783* (Boston, 1895), 25–28.

7. Milton Friedman and Anna Jacobson Schwartz, *A Monetary History of the United States, 1867–1960* (New Jersey, 1963).

8. Mahan, *Influence of Sea Power*, 42.

9. Walter LaFeber, *The New Empire: An Interpretation of American Expansionism, 1860–1898* (Ithaca, NY, 1963), 91.

10. Mahan, "Possibilities of an Anglo-American Reunion," in *The Interest of America in Sea Power, Present and Future* (Port Washington, 1897), 124.

11. William E. Livezey, *Mahan on Sea Power* (Norman, OK, 1947), 85.

12. Mahan, "The United States Looking Outward," 22; Mahan, *Lessons of the War with Spain and Other Articles* (Boston, 1899), 249; see also Livezey, *Mahan on Sea Power*, 183–187; LaFeber, *New Empire*, 91–91.

13. Thomas McCormick, *China Market: America's Quest for Informal Empire, 1893–1901* (Chicago, 1967), 120–125. Also McCormick, "Insular Imperialism and the Open Door: The China Market and the Spanish-American War," *Pacific Historical Review* 32, no. 2 (May 1963): 169.

14. Mahan, *The Problem of Asia and Its Effect upon International Policies* (Boston, 1900), 163.

15. Mahan, *From Sail to Steam*, 273–274.

16. Cited in Akira Iriye, *Pacific Estrangement: Japanese and American Expansion, 1897–1911* (Cambridge, MA, 1971), 1.

17. On Mahanian ideas in Japan, see Seager and Maguire, *Letters and Papers*, 2:511; David D. Evans and Mark R. Peattie, eds., *Kaigun: Strategy, Tactics and Technology in the Imperial Japanese Navy, 887–1941* (Annapolis, MD, 1997), 24–25; Roger Dingman, "Japan and Mahan," in *The Influence of History on Mahan: The Proceedings of a Conference Marking the Century of Alfred Thayer Mahan's* The Influence of Sear Power upon History, 1660–1783, ed. John B. Hattendorf, Naval War College Historical Monograph Series, no. 9 (Annapolis, MD, 1991), 49–66.

18. John W. Foster to Charles Denby, September 26, 1894. Cited in McCormick, "Insular Imperialism," 156. See also Michael J. Green, *By More than Providence: Grand Strategy and American Power in the Asia Pacific since 1783* (New York, 2017), 82; Seager and Maguire, *Letters and Papers of Alfred Thayer Mahan*, 2:335.

19. Mahan, *Problem of Asia*, 43.

20. Mahan, *Problem of Asia*, 44.

21. Mahan, *Problem of Asia*, 46.

22. Cited in Tyler Dennett, *John Hay: From Poetry to Politics* (New York, 1933), 286.

23. Lord Charles Beresford, *The Break-Up of China: With an Account of the Present Commerce, Currency, Waterways, Armies, Railways, Politics and Future Prospects* (London, 1899), 437–445.

24. Beresford, *Break-Up of China,* 439.

25. Beresford, *Break-Up of China,* 445–446.

26. Cited in Dennett, *John Hay,* 290–291. See also John Taliaferro, *All the Great Prizes: The Life of John Hay from Lincoln to Roosevelt* (New York, 2013), 9; Paul A. Varg, *Open Door Diplomat: The Life of W. W. Rockhill* (Urbana, IL, 1952), 29; WWRP (MS Am 2121).

27. Hippisley to Rockhill, July 25, 1899, WWRP.

28. Hippisley to Rockhill, August 16, 1899, WWRP.

29. Hippisley to Rockhill, August 21, 1899, WWRP.

30. Hippisley to Rockhill, August 21, 1899, WWRP.

31. Rockhill's contribution to the memorandum was still noteworthy. Whereas Hippisley stressed preserving equal commercial opportunity, Rockhill emphasized preserving China's integrity. See Rockhill, "Policy of the Open Door in China: A Memorandum to John Hay," August 28, 1899, folder 1, MS 2122 (54), WWRP.

32. Rockhill, "Memorandum," December 19, 1899, John Hay Papers, Rockhill folder, reel 9, LOC.

33. Rockhill omitted Hippisley's name from the draft on the grounds that the latter's contributions "would require additional explanations." Both Rockhill and Hay wanted to avoid questions about the memorandum's "British origins," due to the fierce anti-British climate in Congress and the press. See Hay to John W. Foster, June 23, 1900, Tyler Dennett Papers, John Hay Correspondence, box 4, LOC.

34. Hay memorandum, September 6, 1899 (no. 927), *FRUS,* 1899, 129–130.

35. Joseph Choate to Hay, December 11, 1899, WWRP.

36. Taliaferro, *All the Great Prizes,* 362.

37. Rockhill to Hay, "Memorandum," December 19, 1899, John Hay Papers, reel 9, LOC.

38. Rockhill to Hay, "Memorandum," December 19, 1899.

39. See *FRUS,* 1899, 128–142, for replies of all the powers to the Open Door note.

40. Hay to Tower, January 22, 1900, Tyler Dennett Papers, John Hay Correspondence, box 4, LOC.

41. *Times* (London), January 6, 1900. Also cited in Alfred Dennis, *Adventures in American Diplomacy, 1896–1906* (New York, 1928), 195.

42. Taliaferro, *All the Great Prizes,* 364–365.

43. Hippisley to Rockhill, April 12, 1900, WWRP.

13. BOXERS

1. H. G. W. Woodhead and H. T. Montague Bell, *The China Year Book, 1914* (London, 1914), 11–12.

2. W. W. Rockhill, *The Land of the Lamas* (New York, 1891), 170–173.

3. Ellsworth Carlson, *The Kaiping Mines* (Cambridge, MA, 1971); George Nash, *The Life of Herbert Hoover: Engineer, 1874–1914* (New York, 1983).

4. Jonathan D. Spence, *The Search for Modern China* (New York, 1990), 229–231.

5. Orville Schell and John Delury, *Wealth and Power: China's Long March to the Twenty-First Century* (New York, 2013), 78.

6. Herbert Hoover, *The Memoirs of Herbert Hoover: Years of Adventure, 1874–1920* (New York, 1951), 37.

7. Hoover, *Memoirs,* 45.

8. Hoover, *Memoirs*, 46.

9. Hoover, *Memoirs*, 47.

10. Joseph W. Esherick, *The Origins of the Boxer Uprising* (Berkeley, 1987), 174.

11. Esherick, *Origins of the Boxer Uprising*, 174.

12. Paul A. Cohen, *History in Three Keys: The Boxers as Event, Experience and Myth* (New York, 1997), 17.

13. Cohen, *History in Three Keys*, 19.

14. *North China Herald*, January 9, 1899.

15. Sir Robert Hart, *These from the Land of Sinim: Essays on the Chinese Question* (London, 1901), 5.

16. Cohen, *History in Three Keys*, 19–21.

17. Esherick, *Origins of the Boxer Uprising*, 242.

18. *North China Herald*, December 12, 1898. Esherick notes that the banks of the Yellow River broke on August 8, not on August 9. See *Origins of the Boxer Uprising*, 177.

19. *North China Herald*, November 21, 1898.

20. Esherick, *Origins of the Boxer Uprising*, 233.

21. In the contemporary literature, the Boxers were still often referred to as The Big Sword Society. See *North China Herald*, December 1899; Cohen, *History in Three Keys*, 31.

22. Cited in Spence, *Search for Modern China*, 232.

23. John King Fairbank, Katherine Frost Bruner, and Elizabeth MacLeod Matheson, eds., *The I.G. in Peking: Letters of Robert Hart, Chinese Maritime Customs, 1868–1907*, vol. 2 (Cambridge, MA, 1976), 1224.

24. The Newly Created Army, or New Army, was initially organized by Hu Yufen, aided by German advisor Constantin von Hanneken. See Jerome Ch'en, *Yuan Shi-Kai, 1859–1916: Brutus Assumes the Purple* (Stanford, CA, 1961), 50–51; Patrick Fuliang Shan, *Yuan Shi-kai: A Reappraisal* (Toronto, 2018), 62–70.

25. Chen, *Yuan Shi-Kai*, 66–67.

26. *North China Herald*, December 27, 1899. Charles Denby Jr. published a detailed and troubling description of the looting. See Denby, "The Loot and the Man," *Harper's Weekly*, October 27, 1900, 1008; Cohen, *History in Three Keys*, 36.

27. Fairbank et al., *The I.G. in Peking*, 2:1230.

28. Hoover, *Memoirs*, 48.

29. Hoover, *Memoirs*, 46–48.

30. James L. Hevia, "Remembering the Century of Humiliation: The Yuanming Garden and Dagu Forts Museums," in *Ruptured Histories: War, Memory, and the Post–Cold War in Asia*, ed. Sheila Miyoshi Jager and Rana Mitter (Cambridge, MA, 2007), 192–232.

31. Captain J. K. Taussig, "Experiences during the Boxer Rebellion," *Proceedings of the United States Naval Institute*, April 27, 1927, 404.

32. On May 28 the Boxers attacked rail stations and railway lines between Beijing and Tianjin, and the foreign minister sent for Legation guards. *DPEC*, 4.

33. Chester M. Biggs, *The United States Marines in North China, 1894–1942* (London, 2003), 29–30. Slightly different figures are found in *DPEC*, 4. See also Chester Tan, *The Boxer Catastrophe* (New York, 1955), 64.

34. Taussig, "Experiences," 406; Tan, *Boxer Catastrophe*, 64.

35. Tan, *Boxer Catastrophe*, 66.

36. *DPEC*, 6; E. H. Seymour, *My Naval Career and Travels* (New York, 1911), 343; Peter Fleming, *The Siege at Peking* (New York, 1959), 69–71.

37. *DPEC*, 6; Biggs, *United States Marines in North China*, 34; Major E. W. M. Norie, *Official Account of the Military Operations in China, 1900–1901* (Nashville, TN, 1903), 11.

38. Umio Otsuka, "Coalition Coordination during the Boxer Rebellion," *U.S. Naval War College Review* 71, no. 4 (Autumn 2018): 111–130.

39. Seymour, *My Naval Career,* 344.

40. Tan, *Boxer Catastrophe,* 66–67.

41. Taussig, "Experiences," 412. See also Clive Bigham, *A Year in China, 1899–1900* (New York, 1901), 171–173; *North China Herald,* July 18, 1900.

42. These consisted of 915 British (62 officers, 640 seamen, and 213 Marines), 25 Austrians, 40 Italians, 100 French, 450 Germans, 54 Japanese, 112 Americans, and 112 Russians. See Norie, *Official Account,* 11.

43. Fleming, *Siege at Peking,* 91; Tan, *Boxer Catastrophe;* 71; Norie, *Official Account,* 7. The entire June 11 decree is translated and reprinted in W. A. P. Martin, *The Siege in Peking* (London, 1900), 110–112.

44. Tan, *Boxer Catastrophe,* 71; Fairbank et al., *The I.G. in Peking,* 2:1232.

45. Ada Haven Mateer, *Siege Days: Personal Experiences of American Women and Children during the Peking Siege* (New York, 1903), 87; Norie, *Official Account,* 7; Sir Robert Hart, *These from the Land of Sinim,* 24.

46. Mateer, *Siege Days,* 87.

47. Cited in Tan, *Boxer Catastrophe,* 71.

48. Seymour, *My Naval Career,* 346; *North China Herald,* July 18, 1900.

49. Fleming, *Siege at Peking,* 100–101; Sarah Pike Conger, *Letters from China: With Particular Reference to the Empress Dowager and the Women of China* (Chicago, 1909), 137.

50. Norie, *Official Account,* 1, 12.

51. *LZR,* 4:4. In 1899 Cixi designated Puzhuan heir apparent, but these plans were foiled; the son of Prince Chun (Yixuan), Puyi, was selected.

52. Cited in Tan, *Boxer Catastrophe,* 72. See also *LZR,* 4:3–5. Prince Duan was also a cousin of Emperors Tonghzi and Guangxu. See Arthur Hummel, *Eminent Chinese of the Ch'ing Period* (Washington, DC, 1944), 2:781; Sir Robert Hart, *These from the Lands of Sinim,* 21.

53. Biggs, *United States Marines in North China,* 50.

54. These were 1858, 1859 (repulsed), 1860, 1900. See Hevia, "Remembering the Century of Humiliation," 192–232. See also Martin, *Siege in Peking,* 128.

55. Tan, *Boxer Catastrophe,* 75. Only American admiral Louis Kempff had disagreed and "refused to allow the United States ships to take part in the bombardment." Although he was criticized at the time, "later events proved that Admiral Kempff was absolutely right." Taussig, "Experiences," 414.

56. To the demand that foreign ministers with their staff and families withdraw from Beijing within twenty-four hours, the ministers at first agreed. But the subsequent murder of Baron von Ketteler on June 20 laid to rest those plans, thus "avoiding certain death for themselves." See Norie, *Official Account,* 78–79.

57. Hart, *These from the Land of Sinim,* 19–20.

58. *North China Herald,* September 19, 1900. See also Tan, *Boxer Catastrophe,* 51. After declaring war against the powers on June 21, Cixi attempted to save herself if things went wrong, exclaiming to her ministers: "You all have witnessed the situation. I was compelled to fight to protect our country. If we lose in the end, you should acknowledge my efforts, and should not say that it was I alone who lost our country." *LZR,* 4:5–6.

59. *North China Herald,* September 19, 1900; Donald Keene, *Emperor of Japan: Meiji and His World, 1852–1912* (New York, 2002), 558–559.

60. Cohen, *History in Three Keys,* 51.

61. *North China Herald,* July 25, 1900. See also Keene, *Emperor of Japan,* 559; *LZR,* 4:7–8.

62. *North China Herald*, August 1, 1900; see also July 25, 1900; Keene, *Emperor of Japan*, 559; *LZR*, 4:8.

63. *North China Herald*, July 25, 1900.

64. Hart, *These from the Land of Sinim*, 10; *North China Herald*, July 25, 1900.

65. Edward J. Drea, *Japan's Imperial Army: Its Rise and Fall, 1853–1945* (Lawrence, KS, 2009), 98; Aaron Simon Daggett, *America in the China Relief Expedition* (Kansas City, 1903), 70–71.

66. William Crozier, "Some Observations on the Pekin Relief Expedition," *North American Review*, February 1901, 226; A. Henry Savage-Landor, *China and the Allies*, vol. 1 (London, 1901), 125–126.

67. Benjamin R. Beede, *The War of 1898 and U.S. Interventions, 1898–1934* (New York, 1994), 46–47. See also *Japan Weekly Mail*, August 25, 1900; H. C. Thompson, *China and the Powers: A Narrative of the Outbreak of 1900* (London, 1902), 102–106.

68. Drea, *Japan's Imperial Army*, 99.

69. *KA*, 134.

70. David Silbey, *The Boxer Rebellion and the Great Game in China* (New York, 2012), 143–144.

71. *IHH*, 1:27. Baron Kigoshi Yasutsuna, director of the Bureau of Military Affairs, was even angrier, stating that it was Yamaguchi's forces that had "successfully rescued the ambassadors in Beijing" (1:28). See also *Meiji Tennō Ki* [Record of the Emperor Meiji], vol. 9 (Tokyo, 1968–1977), 872–873.

72. *KA*, 135; see *LZR*, 4:10–11.

73. *KA*, 133–134. The Japanese were eager to deploy more troops to China but understood that the other powers might be suspicious of their intentions. *LZR*, 4:10–11.

74. David Schimmelpenninck van der Oye, *Toward the Rising Sun: Russian Ideologies and the Path to War with Japan* (Dekalb, 2006), 168.

75. *KA*, 136; B. A. Romanov, *Russia in Manchuria (1892–1906)* (Leningrad, 1928), 179.

76. *KA*, 133; *PRI*, 112.

77. Alena N. Eskridge-Kosmach, "Russia in the Boxer Rebellion," *Journal of Slavic Military Studies* 21 (2008): 48–49; George Alexander Lensen, *The Russo-Chinese War* (Tallahassee, FL, 1967), 9.

78. A. S. Suvorin, *Dnevnik* [Diary] (Moscow, 2015), 289–290. Suvorin notes rumors that Muravev may have committed suicide (290). Eugene de Schelking, former secretary of the Russian Embassy in Berlin, wrote that Muravev died in an accident. Schelking, *Recollections of a Russian Diplomat: The Suicide of Monarchies (William II and Nicholas II)* (New York, 1918), 164. See also Sidney Hardcave, ed. and trans., *The Memoirs of Count Witte* (New York, 1990), 286–287; Schimmelpenninck van der Oye, *Toward the Rising Sun*, 166–167.

79. Lensen, *Russo-Chinese War*, 9.

80. *PRI*, 112; Lensen, *Russo-Chinese War*, 10.

81. *PRI*, 112–117. See also Ralph Edward Glatfelter, "Russia in China: The Russian Reaction to the Boxer Rebellion" (PhD diss., Indiana University, 1975), 94.

82. *PRI*, 114. A Russian *verst* is roughly 0.666 mile (1.1 km).

83. Cited in Lensen, *Russo-Chinese War*, 19–20.

84. Three regiments plus an artillery brigade were stationed in Blagoveshchensk. After they were deployed to Khabarovsk, the city's inhabitants realized they were vulnerable to attack by the Chinese from Aigun. This uneasiness partly explains the events that followed. See Lev G. Deich, *Krovavye Dni: Epizod iz Russo-Kitaiskoi Voiny* [Bloody days: An episode from the Russo-Chinese War] (Saint Petersburg, 1906), 7–8.

85. Lensen, *Russo-Chinese War*, 69.

86. Deich, "Krovavye Dni," 4; Tatyana N. Sorokina, "'The Blagoveshchensk Panic' of the Year 1900: The Version of the Authorities," *Sensus Historiae* 8 (2012–2013): 98.

87. Ishimitsu Makiyo, *Kōya no Hana* (The flower of the wasteland) (Tokyo, 2017), 30–31. See also Ian Nish, *Collected Writings of Ian Nish*, pt. 2 (London, 2001), 134–135.

88. Sorokina, "'Blagoveshchensk Panic,'" 98; Ishimitsu, *Kōya no Hana*, 26. See also Deich, *Krovavye Dni*, 5–6.

89. V., "Blagoveshchenskaya 'Utopiya,'" *Vestnik Evropy* [The messenger of Europe] (Saint Petersburg) 7 (191): 237. The anonymous author based his article on "materials taken from official court records" (231). He does not explain how he gained access to the records, nor does he provide names of those involved in the massacre. Deich says he was later told by a city representative that the reason the governor believed it inappropriate to take precautionary measures toward the Chinese citizens was that "war had not formally been declared between Russia and China." Deich, *Krovavye Dni*, 9–10. See also Lensen, *Russo-Chinese War*, 76–78.

90. Sorokina, "'Blagoveshchensk Panic,'" 101; Ishimitsu, *Kōya no Hana*, 29; Deich, *Krovavye Dni*, 8–9.

91. Ishimitsu, *Kōya no Hana*, 29–30.

92. Lensen, *Russo-Chinese War*, 89; Sorokina, "'Blagoveshchensk Panic,'" 101.

93. Deich, *Krovavye Dni*, 13.

94. Ishimitsu, *Kōya no Hana* 30; 32.

95. V., "Blagoveshchenskaya 'Utopiya,'" 231–232.

96. Deich, *Krovavye Dni*, 14.

97. Reports of the number of Chinese killed at Blagoveshchensk vary from 800 to 4,000. The anonymous author for *Vestnik Evropy* writes that "the most reasonable estimate is probably 3,000 to 3,500" (232). Ishimitsu (*Kōya no Hana*, 32) puts the figure at 3,000; Sorokina ("'Blagoveshchensk Panic,'" 111) estimates 2,000.

98. Ishimitsu, *Kōya no Hana*, 33, cited in Lensen, *Russo-Chinese War*, 92.

99. V., "Blagoveshchenskaya 'Utopiya,'" 232, says that the field was unfenced.

100. Ishimitsu, *Kōya no Hana*, 33. Ishimitsu does not name the officer as Shabanov in his memoir, but in a description of a similar scene described in V., "Blagoveshchenskaya 'Utopiya,'" the officer is referred to as "Sh" (232). See Sorokina, "'Blagoveshchensk Panic,'" 105–106.

101. V., "Blagoveshchenskaya 'Utopiya,'" 233.

102. V., "Blagoveshchenskaya 'Utopiya,'" 233–234.

103. V., "Blagoveshchenskaya 'Utopiya,'" 234.

104. Ishimitsu, *Kōya no Hana*, 36.

105. Deich, *Krovavye Dni*, 16.

106. V., "Blagoveshchenskaya 'Utopiya,'" 235; Deich, *Krovavye Dni*, 17.

107. Cited in Sorokina, "'Blagoveshchensk Panic,'" 104.

108. V., "Blagoveshchenskaya 'Utopiya,'" 238.

109. V., "Blagoveshchenskaya 'Utopiya,'" 239; Lensen, *Russo-Chinese War*, 100.

110. V., "Blagoveshchenskaya 'Utopiya,'" 240–241; Lensen, *Russo-Chinese War*, 100–101. Gribsky was not dismissed. A year later, in recognition of his military service in the conflict with China, he was appointed general chief of staff.

111. V., "Blagoveshchenskaya 'Utopiya,'" 241.

112. *LZR*, 4:41–42.

113. E. H. Nilus, *Istoricheskii obzor Kitaiskoi vostochnoi zheleznoi dorogi, 1896–1923 gg* [A historical survey of the Chinese Eastern Railway, 1896–1923] (Harbin, 1923), 205; Ishimitsu, *Kōya no Hana*, 177. Lensen (*Russo-Chinese War*, 152) writes that Harbin was occupied on August 4.

114. *LZR*, 4:41–47. Despite this violence, Witte continued to insist that Russian intentions were "peaceful." Nilus, *Istoricheskii Obzor Kitaiskoi*, 222–223.

115. *LZR*, 4:43; Victor Zatsepine, "The Blagoveshchensk Massacre of 1900: The Sino-Russian War and Global Imperialism," in *Beyond Suffering: Recounting War in Modern China*, ed. Norman Smith and James Flath (Vancouver, 2011), 117.

116. David Schimmelpenninck van der Oye, "Russia's Ambivalent Response to the Boxers," *Cahier du Monde russe* 41, no. 1 (January–March 2000): 76.

117. Lensen, *Russo-Chinese War*, 229–230.

118. Ishimitsu, *Koyo no hana*, 65.

119. A. V. Vereshchagin, *Po Manchzhurii, 1900–1901: Vospominaniya i rasskazy* [Through Manchuria, 1900–1911: Memories and stories] (Saint Petersburg, 1903), 188–189. Vereshchagin visited Blagoveshchensk a few days after the massacre. See also Viktor Innokentievich Dyatlov, "'The Blagoshchensk Utopia': Historical Memory and History Responsibility," *Sensus Historiae* 8 (2012–2013): 119; Lensen, *Russo-Chinese War*, 160.

120. *PRI*, 114–115.

121. Roman Rosen, *Forty Years of Diplomacy*, vol. 1 (New York, 1922), 202.

14. THE DEATH OF LI HONGZHANG

1. Rockhill to Hay, August 26, 1900, John Hay Papers, reel 9, LOC. Rockhill appeared convinced even before negotiations began in Beijing that the Open Door would probably not survive.

2. Cited in Paul S. Varg, *Open Door Diplomat: The Life of W. W. Rockhill* (Urbana, IL, 195), 44.

3. Krasny Archiv, "First Steps of Russian Imperialism in Far East (1888–1903)," *Chinese Social and Political Science Review* 28, no. 2 (July 1934): 134. The main reason for Russian leniency was to encourage the Chinese to come to a separate agreement with the Russians "on the questions of mutual relations between neighboring states, including the question of evacuating Manchuria." E. H. Nilus, *Istoricheskii Obzor Kitaiskoi Vostochnoi Zheleznoi Dorogi, 1896–1923* [A historical survey of the Chinese Eastern Railway, 1896–1923] (Harbin, 1923), 224–225.

4. *PRI*, 144–145.

5. Prince Qing had been rehabilitated to his former position in the Zongli Yamen while his enemy Prince Duan and others were punished for their sponsorship of the Boxers. See Chan Lau Kit-Ching, "Li Hung-Chang and the Boxer Uprising," *Monumenta Serica* 32 (1976): 72; Chester Tan, *The Boxer Catastrophe* (New York, 1967), 170–171. Also *FRUS*, 1901, "Report of W. W. Rockhill, Late Commissioner to China, with Accompanying Documents" (Washington, DC, 1902), 14, 21–22, http://images.library.wisc.edu/FRUS/EFacs/1901b/reference /frus.frus1901b.i0005.pdf.

6. Chan Lau Kit-Ching, "Li Hung-Chang," 82–84; Tan, *Boxer Catastrophe*, 91.

7. George Alexander Lensen, *The Russo-Chinese War* (Tallahassee, FL, 1967), 232; *LZR*, 4:47. Zengqi's report describing the fall of Shenyang is reproduced in *LZR*, 4.

8. *PRI*, 140–141. Kuropatkin "thought that Russia should not be in such a rush to withdraw our forces from Manchuria"; he wrote that, instead, "our main goal was to complete the construction of the railroad, and after that, to concentrate our attention on the maintenance of unhindered traffic from Transbaikalia to Vladivostok and Port Arthur." See also Nilus, "Istoricheskii Obzor," 222–223.

9. The text of the agreement in English can be found in Tan, *Boxer Catastrophe*, 165–166; and John V. A. MacMurray, ed., *Treaties and Conventions with and concerning China* (New York, 1921), 1:329. An original handwritten copy can also be found in FO 233/125/53,

"Petition to Li Hung Chang [Li Hongzhang] from Chou Mien [Zhou Mian]," September 20, 1900 (lunar), November 11, 1900 (solar), NA.

10. *LZR*, 4:52–53; Tan, *Boxer Catastrophe,* 165–166; *PRI,* 143–145.

11. Tan, *Boxer Catastrophe,* 165; *LZR,* 4:53.

12. Tan, *Boxer Catastrophe,* 167.

13. *Times* (London), January 3, 1901; *New York Times,* January 3, 1901.

14. *New York Times,* January 8, 1901.

15. Cited in Varg, *Open Door Diplomat,* 43.

16. Tan, *Boxer Catastrophe,* 167–169.

17. *North China Herald,* February 27, 1901.

18. Varg, *Open Door Diplomat,* 47; Tyler Dennett, *John Hay: From Poetry to Politics* (New York, 1933), 313–317.

19. Ian Nish, *Japanese Foreign Policy, 1869–1942: Kasumigaseki to Miyakezaka* (London, 1977), 55–56. Also see Nish, "Korea, Focus of Russo-Japanese Diplomacy," *Asian Studies* 4 (1966): 77–83.

20. Cited in William L. Langer, *The Diplomacy of Imperialism, 1890–1902,* vol. 2 (New York, 1935), 716–717.

21. Tan, *Boxer Catastrophe,* 170–171.

22. M. N. Muravev, "The Tasks in the Far East," a memorandum submitted to Nicholas on January 25/February 7, 1900, in M. N. Pokrovsky, "Tsarskaia diplomatiia o zadachaiakh Rossii na Vostoke v 1900 g" [Tsarist diplomacy on Russia's tasks in the East in 1900], *Krasnyi Arkiv* 28, no. 192 (1926): 15–18.

23. Pokrovsky, *Tsarskaia Diplomatiya,* 20.

24. The December 4 memorandum laying out these provisions was entitled *Osnovanii Russkago Pravitel'stvennago Nadzora v Manchurii* [The foundations of Russian governmental supervision in Manchuria]. See Nilus, *Istoricheskii Obzor Kitaiskoi,* 225–228; *PRI,* 139; B. A. Romanov, *Russia in Manchuria (1892–1906)* (Leningrad, 1928), 198.

25. Romanov, *Russia in Manchuria,* 199.

26. *LZR,* 4:54–55; Tan, *Boxer Catastrophe,* 172–173.

27. *LZR,* 4:58. The exchange is also described in Tan, *Boxer Catastrophe,* 173–174.

28. *LZR,* 4:59; *PRI,* 143–144.

29. *LZR,* 4:60–62.

30. *LZR,* 4:91–93; *PRI,* 145. Although Itō and his cabinet still favored some kind of compromise with Russia, Katō was adamant that Japan pursue a hard line vis-à-vis Russia and secured permission to send a protest to Saint Petersburg on March 24. See Langer, *Diplomacy of Imperialism,* 2:723.

31. The proposed twelve articles can be found in Tan, *Boxer Catastrophe,* 178–179; and *LZR,* 4:112–113.

32. *LZR,* 4:107.

33. Cited in Tan, *Boxer Catastrophe,* 190. Japan warned the Chinese that if Russian terms were accepted, Japan intended to ask for extensive concessions of its own. Langer, *Diplomacy of Imperialism,* 2:724.

34. *LZR,* 4:121; Romanov, *Russia in Manchuria,* 228–229.

35. Michael Hunt, "The American Remission of the Boxer Indemnity: A Reappraisal," *Journal of Asian Studies* 31 (May 1972): 539–559. See also Tan, *Boxer Catastophe,* 178–179; Varg, *Open Door Diplomat.* Varg (p. 45) cites the amount as $200 million.

36. Jonathan D. Spence, *The Search for Modern China* (New York, 1990), 235.

37. Ishii Kikujirō, *Gaikō Yoroku* [Diplomatic commentaries] (Tokyo, 1930), 31.

38. Ishii, *Gaikō Yoroku,* 31–33.

39. Dennett, *John Hay,* 317–318. A. E. Hippisley was enraged, writing to Rockhill about the huge indemnity, estimated at £75 million, which "China cannot possibly pay." Rockhill Papers, MS AM 121, ser. 1, folder 1, Hippisley to Rockhill, March 1, 1901, WWRP.

40. Spence, *Search for Modern China,* 235.

41. Ernest Satow to Salisbury, November 8, 1900, PRO 30/33 14–11 (private letter from June 10, 1899–March 14, 1901), NA.

42. Adna R. Chaffee to Henry C. Corbin, April 10, 1901, Henry Corbin Papers, box 1, LOC.

43. John King Fairbank, Katherine Frost Bruner, and Elizabeth MacLeod Matheson, eds., *The I.G. in Peking: Letters of Robert Hart, Chinese Maritime Customs, 1868–1907* (Cambridge, MA, 1975), 1289.

44. Rockhill to Wilson James Harrison, December 2, 1901, Rockhill Papers, Ms Am 2121, ser. 1, WWRP.

45. *LZR,* 4:134. Wang also noted, "One hour before his death, a Russian messenger was still coercing him to sign the Sino-Russo agreement."

46. George Morrison, *The Correspondence of George Morrison,* vol. 1, *1895–1912* (Cambridge, 1976), 197; *LZR,* 4:134; Langer, *Diplomacy of Imperialism,* 2:751. See also *North China Herald,* November 25, 1904.

47. *North China Herald,* November 13, 1901.

15. NEW AGREEMENTS

1. Yun Kyŏng-no, "The Relationship between Korean Catholics and Korean Protestants in the Early Mission Period," in *Korea and Christianity,* ed. Chai-Sun Yu (Seoul, 1996), 17. Official sources put the number at 26,000 members in 1895, which rose to over 73,000 in 1910. See G. M. Gompertz, "Archbishop Mutel: A Biographical Sketch," *Translations of the Korea Branch of the Royal Asiatic Society* 27 (1937): 121; *Han'guk chonggyo yong'am 1993* [Yearbook of Korean religion for the year 1993] (Seoul, 1993), 122.

2. Yumi Moon, "The Populist Contest: The Ilchinhoe and the Japanese Colonization of Korea, 1896–1910" (PhD diss., Harvard University, 2005), 56; Homer Hulbert, *Hulbert's History of Korea,* ed. Clarence Weems (New York, 1962), 334.

3. Cited in Yun, "Relationship," 17. See also Mutel, *Mwit'el chungo ilgi* [Bishop Mutel's journals], vol. 3 (1901–1905) (Seoul, 1986), 103 (entry for December 9, 1901). Mutel also notes that on October 25, 1901, Kojong requested his help in preventing Catholics from joining antigovernment groups. See Mutel, *Mwit'el chungo ilgi,* 3:89 (entry for October 25, 1901).

4. Yun, "Relationship," 17; Yumi Moon, *Populist Collaborators: The Ilchinhoe and the Japanese Colonization of Korea, 1896–1910* (Ithaca, NY, 2013), 55–57. Mutel describes a similar conversation with the governor of Hwanghae, who complained that despite everything he had done for the Catholics, he was being threatened by them. See Mutel, *Mwit'el chungo ilgi,* 3:124 (entry for March 19, 1901).

5. Horace Allen, March 6, 1903, Horace Newton Allen Papers, 1883–1923, letterpress copy books no. 7–8, MNN ZZ 23704-2, New York Public Library.

6. Allen to Rockhill, July 29, 1900, Horace Allen folder, folder 1, Rockhill papers, MS Am 2121, WWRP.

7. Moon, *Populist Collaborators,* 69; Alyssa M. Park, *Sovereignty Experiments: Korean Migrants and the Building of Border in Northeast Asia, 1860–1945* (Ithaca, NY, 2019), 95.

8. Cited in B. D. Pak, *Rossiia i Koreia* [Russia and Korea] (Moscow, 2004), 326–327.

9. The Kwangmu reforms succeeded the Kabo-Ŭlmi (1894–1895) reforms to carry out sweeping economic, military, educational, agricultural, and cultural changes across society. See Andre Schmid, *Korea between Empires, 1895–1919* (New York, 2002), 74–92; Peter Duus, *The Abacus and the Sword: The Japanese Penetration of Korea, 1895–1910* (Berkeley, 1995), 127–133; Han Sang-yun, *Kojongkwa Meiji* [Kojong and Meiji] (Seoul, 2019), 158–180.

10. Pak *Rossiia i Koreia*, 327.

11. Pak, *Rossiia i Koreia*, 330. See also Ian Nish, *Japanese Foreign Policy, 1869–1942: Kasumigaseki to Miyakezaka* (London, 1977), 54–55.

12. Ernest Satow to Lansdowne, December 25, 1900, PRO 30/33, 14–11 (private letter from June 10, 1899–March 14, 1901), NA. Ian Nish identifies the joint effort in suppressing the Boxers as the real starting point of an Anglo-Japanese Alliance. Nish, "Japan's Policies toward Britain," in *Japan's Foreign Policy, 1869–1945: A Research Guide*, ed. J. W. Morely (New York, 1974).

13. Ian Nish, *The Anglo-Japanese Alliance: The Diplomacy of Two Island Empires, 1894–1907* (London, 1966), 126; Hayashi Tadasu, *The Secret Memoirs of Count Tadasu Hayashi*, ed. A. M. Pooley (London, 1915), 120; William L. Langer, *The Diplomacy of Imperialism, 1890–1902*, vol. 2 (New York, 1935), 727. See also Zara Steiner, *The Foreign Office and Foreign Policy, 1898–1914* (London, 1969).

14. Hayashi, *Secret Memoirs*, 121.

15. Nish, *Anglo Japanese Alliance*, 125–126. Langer, *Diplomacy of Imperialism*, 2:727–728.

16. Hayashi, *Secret Memoirs*, 121. See also T. G. Otte, *The China Question: Great Power Rivalry and British Isolation, 1894–1905* (Oxford, 2007), 205–216.

17. Hayashi, *Secret Memoirs*, 123. A more detailed description of the conversation between Hayashi and Lansdowne is reproduced in *IHH*, 2:9–10 (append. 6).

18. Hayashi, *Secret Memoirs*, 139. Komura, who had become foreign minister in September 1901, instructed Hayashi to emphasize that "Japan's policy in Korea is a peaceful one," and that consequently "the British government does not need to be concerned that Japan will invade Korea even if the British government approves of Japan's freedom of action there." *IHH*, 2:31–34 (append. 32).

19. Hayashi, *Secret Memoirs*, 189.

20. FO, Japan, 563, no. 110, Marquess of Lansdowne to Sir C. MacDonald, November 6, 1901, in *British Documents on the Origins of the War, 1898–1914*, vol. 2, *Anglo-Japanese Alliance and the Franco-British Entente*, ed. G. P. Gooch and Harold Temperley (London, 1927), 99.

21. Hayashi, *Secret Memoirs*, 142–144. In Paris, Hayashi handed Itō copies of the telegrams he had written to (Acting) foreign minister Sone. The telegram dated July 31 noted: "Now that our conversation has gotten to the point at which we are beginning talks regarding an agreement between Japan and Britain, it is necessary for me to know whether or not the Japanese government has the intention to sign the alliance, and if so, under what conditions." *IHH*, 2:9–10 (append. 6). Sone responded on August 8 that while "the Japanese government does not have any objections to the intent of the British government's proposal to sign a clear agreement regarding the issue of the Far East," he was "skeptical if it is actually possible to sign such an agreement." Thus, Sone was clearly not convinced an Anglo-Japanese alliance would succeed, which explains why he and Katsura sanctioned Itō's trip to Saint Petersburg. See *IHH*, 2:10–11 (append. 7).

22. Hayashi, *Secret Memoirs*, 142–144, 146.

23. Ian Nish, *Collected Writings*, pt. 1 (London, 2001), 86.

24. Nish related that Hayashi gave these assurances on November 26, most likely the first occasion in which Katsura had come to a decision on Itō's visit to Russia. By the end of

November, the Japanese cabinet was definitely committed to accepting a treaty with Britain. Nish, *Anglo-Japanese Alliance*, 187–188.

25. Hayashi, *Secret Memoirs*, 150.

26. *IHH*, 2:19–23 (append. 26). Itō ended the meeting by insinuating that Russia's actions during the Triple Intervention had been devious. A summary of appendixes 26 and 27, with selected quotations, can also be found in Ian Nish, *The History of Manchuria, 1840–1948: A Sino-Russian Triangle*, vol. 2 (Kent, 2016), 42–43; and Nish, "Korea, Focus of Russo-Japanese Diplomacy, 1898–1903," *Asian Studies* (Manila) 4, no. 1 (April 1966): 74. See also B. A. Romanov, *Russia in Manchuria (1892–1906)* (Leningrad, 1928), 235–238.

27. Witte remarked that misunderstanding between Japan and Russia could be prevented only by maintaining the terms of 1898 as the basis for a new agreement. This basically meant Witte still wanted to wait on equal rights in Korea. Sergei Witte, *The Memoirs of Sergei Witte*, trans. Sidney Harcave (New York, 1990), 24. See *IHH*, 2:23 (append. 27).

28. *IHH*, 2:23–27 (append. 27). See also Romanov, *Russia in Manchuria*, 237.

29. During their parting conversation, Itō made it clear that he very much wanted to come to a formal agreement with Russia, thus going far beyond the limits of what he was supposed to discuss with Lamsdorf and Witte. *IHH*, 2:28–31 (append. 30).

30. *IHH*, 2:39–40 (append. 48). In his telegram to Katsura, dated December 17, Itō describes his reaction to Lamsdorf's proposal (append. 51). See also Ian Nish, "Korea, Focus of Russo-Japanese Diplomacy," in *Collected Writings*, pt. 2 (London, 2001), 76; Nish, *Anglo-Japanese Alliance*, 198; Romanov, *Russia in Korea*, 237; Andrew Malozemoff, *Russian Far Eastern Policy, 1881–1904, with a Special Emphasis on the Causes of the Russo-Japanese War* (Berkeley, 1958), 172–173.

31. Lamsdorf's formal reply reached Itō in Berlin on December 17. The Russian offer boiled down to: "We take Manchuria to do anything we like with it, and give you Korea, with some restrictions." Itō wrote to Katsura the same day, saying that amendments to Lamsdorf's proposal were in order, but he nevertheless urged Katura to consider the entente "while we wait for Russia's reconsideration." *IHH*, 2:44–45 (append. 53).

32. *IHH*, 2:45–47 (append. 58). Itō wrote to Katsura that Russia's decision to exercise its own freedom of action in Manchuria was not dependent upon Japan's consent or agreement. Because China was too weak to defend itself, Russia could do what it liked. So why not officially recognize Russian rights in Manchuria if, in the process, Japan could secure its own freedom of action in Korea? *IHH*, 2:47 (append. 59).

33. In article 5 of his proposed agreement, Lamsdorf suggested creating a "neutral zone" around the Russo-Korean border where Japanese troops would be barred from entering article 6 was also problematic. Japan had to agree to Russian "control of Chinese territory along the Sino-Russian border and should give Russia freedom of action there." *IHH*, 2:44–45 (append. 53).

34. Itō replied to Lamsdorf on December 23, rejecting the proposal. See *IHH*, 2:47–49 (append. 60). See also Nish, *Collected Writings*, pt. 1, 89; Pak, *Rossiia i Koreia*, 331.

35. Witte, *Memoirs*, 303. See also Pak, *Rossiia i Koreia*, 331.

36. Witte was not quite ready to give up Korea. *PRI*, 189.

37. Cited in Ian Nish, "The First Anglo-Alliance Treaty," symposium paper, The Suntory and Toyota International Centres for Economics and Related Disciplines in association with the Japan Society, London, February 22, 2002, 7. Also see *IHH*, 2:51–54 (append. 64).

38. Langer, *Diplomacy of Imperialism*, 2:780–781. Pak believes that Itō's mission in Petersburg was "just a smokescreen to cover up talks with Britain." Pak, *Rossiia i Koreia*, 331–332.

39. Hayashi, *Secret Memoirs*, 170.

40. Hayashi, *Secret Memoirs*, 189.

41. Langer, *Diplomacy of Imperialism,* 2:783.

42. Hayashi, *Secret Memoirs,* 198–199. Katō Takaaki, foreign minister under the Itō cabinet, defended the former prime minister from newspaper reports claiming Itō had opposed the alliance. See Naraoka Sōchi, "Katō Takaaki and the Russo-Japanese War," in *Rethinking-Japanese War, 1904-5,* vol. 2, *The Nichinan Papers,* ed. John W. M. Chapman and Chiharu Inaba (Leiden, 2007), 35; *IHH,* 1:432 (chap. 8).

43. Malozemoff, *Russian Far Eastern Policy,* 173–174; Tyler Dennett, *Roosevelt and the Russo-Japanese War* (New York, 1925), 130–131. For the text of the April 8, 1902, "Convention with regard to Manchuria," see John V. A. MacMurray, ed., *Treaties and Agreements with and concerning China, 1894-1919* (Oxford, 1921), 1:326–331; Ian Nish, *The Origins of the Russo-Japanese War* (Essex, 1985), 140–141.

44. Romanov, *Russia in Manchuria,* 283; Ian Nish, "Stretching Out to the Yalu: A Contested Frontier, 1900–1903," in *The Russo-Japanese War in Global Perspective: World War Zero,* ed. John Steinberg et al. (London, 2005), 51.

45. G. P. Goch and Harold Temperley, eds., *British Documents on the Origins of the War,* vol. 2 (London, 1927), 130–131.

46. Ch'oe Tŏk-su, *Choyakŭro pon han'guk kŭndaesa* [Korean modern history through its treaties] (Seoul, 2011), 475.

47. Ch'oe, *Choyakŭro pon han'guk kŭndaesa,* 459; Morinosuke Kajima, *The Diplomacy of Japan, 1894-1922,* 2 (Tokyo, 1978), 65–66, 87.

48. Pak, *Rossiia i Koreia,* 332.

49. Pak, *Rossiia i Koreia,* 332–333.

50. Pak, *Rossiia i Koreia,* 333.

51. V. I. Shipaev, *Kolonial'noye zakabaleniye Korei yaponskim imperializamom* [The colonial enslavement of Korea by Japanese imperialism] (Moscow, 1964), 64–65.

16. RUSSIA'S KOREA PROBLEM

1. Andrew Malozemoff, *Russian Far Eastern Policy, 1881-1904, with a Special Emphasis on the Causes of the Russo-Japanese War* (Berkeley, 1958), 179; Roman Romanovich Rosen, *Forty Years of Diplomacy,* vol. 1 (New York, 1923), 209–211.

2. A. M. Vonliarliarsky, "Why Russia Went to War with Japan, 1: The Story of the Yalu Concession," *Fortnightly Review,* May 1910, 816. Published anonymously, the article was later revealed to be authored by Vonliarliarsky, an ex-officer of the Chevalier Guards Regiment.

3. General Kuropatkin, *The Russian Army and the Japanese War,* trans. Capt. A. B. Lindsay, ed. Major E. D. Winton, vol. 2 (New York, 1909), 306.

4. Boris Yuliyevich Briner was the father of Hollywood actor Yul Brynner. See Rock Brynner, *Empire and Odyssey: The Brynners in the Far East and Beyond* (Hanover, NH, 2006).

5. Sidney S. Harcave, *Count Sergei Witte and the Twilight of Imperial Russia: A Biography* (Armonk, 2004), 92; Bella Park, "Russia's Policy towards Korea during the Russo-Japanese War," *International Journal of Korean History* 7 (February 2005): 35.

6. *KDC,* 12–13. See also Vonliarliarsky, "Why Russia Went to War," 825.

7. *KDC,* 13–14; Vonliarliarsky, "Why Russia Went to War," 826; B. D. Pak, *Rossiia i Koreia* [Russia and Korea] (Moscow, 2004), 337.

8. *KDC,* 15.

9. *KDC,* 17.

10. Pak, *Rossiia i Koreia,* 338–339.

11. De Speyer aggressively promoted Russia's interests in Korea—alienating Korea's "progressives," who saw Kojong's living under the protection of the Russian legation as a

national embarrassment. Homer Hulbert, ed., *Korea Review* 4, no. 9 (September 1904): 416–422.

12. Stewart Lone, "Of Collaborators and Kings: The Ilchinhoe, Korean Court and Japanese Agricultural Demands during the Russo-Japanese War," *Papers on Far Eastern History* 38 (1988): 103–124. For a vivid description of de Speyer's abrupt departure, see *Japan Daily Mail*, April 2, 1898.

13. *KDC*, 19.

14. The incident was reported by the *Tongnip sinmun* [The Independent] September 13, 1898. For fascinating details of the plot, see Robert Neff, "September 11, Coffee and Russia in the 19th Century," *Korea Times*, September 9, 2018.

15. Vonaliarliarsky, "Why Russia Went to War," 830.

16. Vonliarliarsky, "Why Russia Went to War" 830; *KDC*, 19.

17. *PRI*, 248–249. The total cost was 85,000 rubles, which included the 20,000-ruble down payment given to Briner before the expedition began.

18. V. I. Gurko, *Features and Figures of the Past: Government and Opinion in the Reign of Nicholas II* (New York, 1970), 266–267; B. A. Romanov, *Russia in Manchuria (1892–1906)* (Leningrad, 1928), 274–275.

19. Romanov, *Russia in Manchuria,* 271.

20. Romanov, *Russia in Manchuria,* 272–273; David S. Crist, "Russia's Far Eastern Policy in the Making," *Journal of Modern History* 14, no. 3 (September 1942): 331.

21. Sergei Witte, *The Memoirs of Sergei Witte,* trans. Sidney Harcave (New York, 1990), 308.

22. E. H. Nilus, *Istoricheskii Obzor Kitaiskoi Vostochnoi Zheleznoi Dorogi, 1896–1923* [A historical survey of the Chinese Eastern Railway, 1896–1923] (Harbin, 1923), 36–37.

23. Romanov, *Russia in Manchuria,* 273.

24. Pak, *Rossiia i Koreia,* 340; Vladimir Tikhonov, "Korea in the Russian and Soviet Imagination, 1850s–1945," *Journal of Korean Studies* 21, no. 2 (Fall 2016): 393.

25. *PRI,* 242–243.

26. Cited in Crist, "Russia's Far Eastern Policy," 326.

27. *PRI,* 253–255.

28. Pak, *Rossiia i Koreia,* 348; Ian Nish, *The Origins of the Russo-Japanese War* (Essex, 1985), 140–143.

29. General Kuropatkin, "The Secret Causes of the War with Japan," *McClure's Magazine,* September 1908, 488. On the Russian withdrawal, see memorandum to Hay from Rockhill, September 16, 1903, John Hay Papers, Rockhill folder, reel 9, LOC. See also Nish, *Origins of the Russo-Japanese War,* 147–148.

30. *PRI,* 309–310.

31. *PRI,* 281–284; Park, "Russia's Policy towards Korea," 37.

32. According to Kuropatkin, Alekseev gave him "repeated assurances that he was wholly opposed to Bezobrazov's schemes, and that he was holding them back with all his strength." This was false. Kuropatkin, "Secret Causes," 498. See also S. C. M. Paine, *The Japanese Empire: Grand Strategy from Meiji Restoration to the Pacific War* (Cambridge, 2017), 58.

33. Cited in David J. Dallin, *The Rise of Russia in Asia* (Hong Kong, 2008),76.

34. *PRI,* 287–288. See also Pak, *Rossiia i Koreia,* 341; Andrew Malozemoff, "Russia's Far Eastern Policy, 1881–1904, with an emphasis on the Causes of the Russo-Japanese War" (PhD diss., University of California, Berkeley, 1952), 377.

35. *PRI,* 277.

36. Kuropatkin, "Secret Causes," 290. See also Pak, *Rossiia i Koreia,* 342. The war minister did not support the Bezobrazovites' aggressive stance in southern Manchuria and

Korea, but he continued to advocate keeping Russian forces in northern Manchuria. *PRI,* 272-273.

37. Madritov's recruitment of these "stray bandits" angered the Chinese government, and officials lodged complaints with Russia's Ministry of Foreign Affairs. *PRI,* 287-288.

38. Dominic Lieven, *Nicholas II: Emperor of All the Russians* (London, 1994), 98. Bezabrozov's national arrogance is revealed in a report he submitted on August 2/July 20, 1903, that expressed his opinion concerning the international obligations of Russia: "With regard to international agreements and treaties, they should not be an obstacle for us on our way to the realization of our historical mission in the Far East. We should not be deterred by these incidental forms of current political paperwork if we want to achieve our long overdue destiny as a nation." See *PRI,* 259.

39. S. Podbolotov, "Nikolai II kak russkii natsionalist" [Nikolai II as Russian nationalist], *Ab Imperio* 3 (2003): 204.

40. Podbolotov, "Nikolai II," 203-204.

41. Cited in Lieven, *Nicholas II,* 99.

42. Cited in Witte, *Memoirs,* 744.

43. Witte, *Memoirs,* 775. Witte is unfair to Lamsdorf, who submitted his resignation to the tsar on March 27, 1903. See Aleksandr Aleksandrovich Savinsky, *Recollections of a Russian Diplomat* (London, 1917), 47-48.

44. Elting E. Morison, ed., *The Letters of Theodore Roosevelt,* vol. 4 (Cambridge, MA, 1951), 1085.

45. Raymond Esthus, *Theodore Roosevelt and Japan* (Seattle, 1967), 11-12; Charles E. Neu, "Theodore Roosevelt and American Involvement in the Far East, 1901-1909," *Pacific Historical Review* 35, no. 4 (November 1966): 436-437.

46. Hay to Roosevelt, May 12, 1903, cited in Tyler Dennett, *John Hay: From Poetry to Politics* (New York, 1933), 405; see also Edward H. Zabriskie, *American-Russian Rivalry in the Far East: A Study in Diplomacy and Power Politics, 1895-1914* (London, 1946), 65.

47. Neu, "Theodore Roosevelt," 436.

48. Morison, *Letters of Theodore Roosevelt,* 4:724. Also cited in Dennett, *John Hay,* 405.

49. Cited in Pak, *Rossiia i Koreia,* 343.

50. Foreign Office Document (FO) 350/3: 34-36, Jordon to Campbell, June 16, 1903, Sir Newell John Jordon Papers, NA.

51. As the *Asahi Shimbun* points out, the third article of the Russo-Japanese Protocol of 1898 also stated: "Russia will not impede the development of the commercial and industrial relations between Korea and Japan." This meant "if Japan deems that the opening of Ŭiju is essential to development of relations names in the Protocol, Russia certainly is pledged not to offer any objection." Cited in *Japan Weekly Mail,* August 1, 1903. See Kato Yoko, "Japan Justifies War by Way of the 'Open Door': 1903 as Turning Point," in *The Russo-Japanese War in Global Perspective: World War Zero,* vol. 2, ed. David Wolff et al. (Leiden, 2007), 206.

52. Park, "Russia's Policy towards Korea," 38.

53. CIK, 19 kwan [12635-12641] (108), Nakamura to Seoul Japanese Embassy, May 28, 1903, http://db.history.go.kr/item/level.do?itemId=jh.

54. See Pak, *Rossiia i Koreia,* 344-345.

55. Moon, *Populist Collaborators,* 73. See also Marius Jansen, *The Japanese and Sun Yat-sen* (Cambridge, MA, 1967), 75.

56. Established in August 1903, the Tairo Dōshikai was a successor to Konoe's earlier political organization, the Kokumin Dōmeikai [National Alliance]. See Rotem Kowner, *Historical Dictionary of the Russo-Japanese War* (London, 2017), 523.

57. The incident was referred to as the "Affair of the Seven *Hakushi.*" For an English summary see *Japan Weekly Mail,* August 1, 1903. See also Bryon K. Marshall, "Professor and Politics: The Meiji Academic Elite," *Journal of Japanese Studies* 3, no. 1 (Winter 1977): 86–87; John Albert White, *Diplomacy of the Russo-Japanese War* (Princeton, NJ, 1964), 319–321.

58. *Japan Weekly Mail,* June 20, 1903.

59. Ogawa Heikichi was member of the anti-Russian Society. Andrew Gordon, *Labor and Imperial Democracy in Prewar Japan* (Berkeley, 1992), 55; Kato, "Japan Justifies War," 215.

60. Cited in Kato, "Japan Justifies War," 222.

61. Kim Yun-hee, "Direction of Public Opinion during the Taehan Empire and the People's Perception of Their Era during the Period of Russo-Japanese Conflict—With a Special Focus on the *Hwangsŏng Shinmun,*" *International Journal of Korean History* 7 (February 2005): 53–84. On the *Hwangsŏng shinmun* as popular advocate for Korean pan-Asianism, see Andre Schmid, *Korea between Empires, 1895–1919* (New York, 2002), 56–57. On anti-Russian attitudes of Korea's progressives, see Vladimir Tikhonov, "Images of Russia and the Soviet Union in Modern Korea, 1880s–1930s: An Overview," *Seoul Journal of Korean Studies* 22, no. 2 (December 2009): 215–247.

62. Kim, "Direction of Public Opinion," 58–64. For articles relating to the Open Door and the Yalu Ports, see *Hwangsŏng shinmun,* July 16, 17, September 15, 19, 22–23, 29, 30, and October 1, 2, 29. Online access: South Korea Newspaper Archives, National Library of Korea https://www.nl.go.kr/newspaper/index.do.

63. Kim Yun-hee, "Rŏil taeripki (1898–1904): Hwangsŏng shinmunŭi ijungjihyangsŏnggwa chagangnon" [The dualistic pursuit and self-strengthening theory of the *Hwangsong sinmun,* during Russo-Japanese rivalry, 1898–1904], *Hanguksa hakpo* 25 (November 2006): 327–355.

64. Kim, "Direction of Public Opinion," 71–72. Han argued that the introduction of loans from Japan would be beneficial for Korea. See Han Ik-kyo, ed., *Han Sang-nyo ŭl mal handa* [Han Sang-ryong in his own words] (Seoul, 2007). See also Carter Eckert, *Offspring of Empire: The Koch'ang Kims and the Colonial Origins of Korean Capitalism, 1876–1945* (Seattle, 1991); Chan-sup Chang and Nahn Joo Chang, *The Korean Management System: Cultural, Political, Economic Foundations* (Westport, CT, 1994). See also Kim Yun-hee, "Kyŏnginjiyŏk ch'aejabongaŭi yiyunch'uku hwaldong (1897–1905)" [Profit-seeking activities of capitalists in the Seoul-Inch'ŏn area (1897–1905)] *Kodae sahakhoe* 53 (September 2003): 27–53.

65. CIK, 19 kwan [12635–12641], 19 kwan (202), no. 181, Hayashi to Komura, June 27, 1903, http://db.history.go.kr/item/level.do?itemId=jh.

66. CIK, 19 kwan (169) [12635–12641], no. 167, Hayashi to Komura, June 20, 1903, http://db.history.go.kr/item/level.do?itemId=jh.

67. CIK, 19 kwan (349) [12635–12641], no. 345, Hayashi to Komura, October 7, 1903, http://db.history.go.kr/item/level.do?itemId=jh.

68. Gustav Mutel, *Mwit'el chukyo ilgi* [Bishop Mutel's diaries], vol. 3, *1901–1905* (Seoul, 2008), 241.

69. The agreement Hayashi was referring to was reached on July 20 between the director of Korea's forestry department, Cho Song-hyŏp, and the representative of the Russian timber company, G.G. Ginzburg. See "Yoshishū Shinjō to Hayashi," CIK, 19 kwan [12635–12641] (298), no. 24, July 20, 1903, http://db.history.go.kr/item/level.do?itemId=jh.

70. Park, "Russia's Policy towards Korea," 39. On August 12 Kojong secretly sent the contents of Hayashi's declaration to Pavlov. See Pak, *Rossiia i Koreia,* 348.

71. See *Hochi Shimbun,* October 4, 1903; *Japan Daily Mail,* October 10, 1903.

72. FO 350/3 34-37-40, Jordon to Campbell, July 8, 1903, Sir Newell John Jordon Papers, NA.

73. FO 350/3 34-37-40, Jordon to Campbell, August 20, 1903, Sir Newell John Jordon Papers, NA.

74. Park, "Russia's Policy towards Korea," 40–41.

75. CIK, 21 kwan [12820–12822] (349), no. 354, Hayashi to Mutsu, October 7, 1903, http://db.history.go.kr/item/level.do?itemId=jh.

76. This recognition included "the right of Japan to take in Corea and of Russia to take in Manchuria such measures as may be necessary for the protection of their respective interests." CRNJR, 8.

77. CRNJR, 22–23.

78. Igor V. Lukoyanov, "Russia and Japan in the Late 19th to 20th Centuries: The Road to War and Peace," in A History of Russo-Japanese Relations: Over Two Centuries of Cooperation and Competition, ed. Dmitry V. Streltsov and Shimotomai Nobuo (Leiden, 2019), 67.

79. CRNJR, 28–29.

80. Ian Nish, Origins of the Russo-Japanese War (London, 1985), 185–186; Lukoyanov, "Russia and Japan," 68. Lukoyanov states the meeting took place on October 31. I have relied on the dates presented by Nish, as they match up with newspaper sources.

81. Japan Weekly Mail, October 17, 1903.

82. Japan Weekly Mail, November 28, 1903.

83. NARA, RG 59, M-134, roll 20, Gordon Paddock [Acting Director of the U.S. Mission in Seoul] to John Hay, November 19, 1903.

84. NARA, RG 59, M-134, roll 20, Horace Allen to John Hay, January 2, 1904.

85. CIK, 21 kwan [12820–12822] (271), no. 268, Hayashi to Komura, August 26, 1903; CIK, 23 kwan [12826–12828] (56), no. 59, Hayashi to Komura, October 27, 1903, http://db .history.go.kr/item/level.do?itemId=jh.

86. CIK, 21 kwan [12820–12822] (271), no. 268, Hayashi to Komura, August 26, 1903, http://db.history.go.kr/item/level.do?itemId=jh. See also Morinosuke Kajima, The Diplomacy of Japan, 1894–1922, vol. 2 (Tokyo, 1978), 128–129.

87. Park, "Russia's Policy towards Korea," 50.

88. Cited in Pak, Rossiia i Koreia, 361. An opposite view was put forth by Allen, who wrote that "the Japanese would be glad to see the emperor take refuge in the Russian Legation, and would then declare him to have abdicated and would take over the administration of government." NARA, RG 59, M-134, roll 20, Allen to Hay, January 2, 1904.

89. Lamsdorf told Kurino on November 25 that he had been unable to see the emperor because of an apparent "inflammation of his wife's right ear," a transparent excuse that no doubt infuriated the Japanese even more. CRNJR, 37–39. See also Kobe Chronicles, A Diary of the Russo-Japanese War, pt. 5 (Kobe, 1904), 102.

90. CRNJR, 41–42.

91. FO 305/3 [December 19, 1903–December 8, 1904], Jordon to Campbell, December 19, 1903, Sir Newell John Jordon Papers, NA.

92. NARA, RG 59, M-134, roll 20, Allan to Hay, January 2, 1904.

93. FO 350/3 [December 19, 1903–December 8, 1904], Jordon to Campbell, January 1, 1904, Sir Newell John Jordon Papers, NA.

94. Komura to Kurino, December 12, 1904, no. 34, in Kobe Chronicles, Diary of the Russo-Japanese War, pt. 5, 103; White, Diplomacy, 120–121; Nish, Origins of the Russo-Japanese War, 203. See also CRNJR, 46–47.

95. CRNJR, 47–49. See also White, Diplomacy, 122–123.

96. Ian Nish, "Korea, Focus of Russo-Japanese Diplomacy," Asian Studies 4, no. 1 (April 1966): 83.

97. Paul Bushkovitch, "The Far East in the Eyes of the Russian Intelligentsia, 1830–1890," Richard Stites, "Russian Representations of the Japanese Enemy," Tatiana Filippova, "Images of the Foe in the Russian Satirical Press," and Barry P. Scherr, "The Russo-Japanese War and the Russian Literary Imagination," all in Steinberg et al., *Russia-Japanese War in Global Perspective*, 348–363, 395–410, 411–424, 425–446. See also Rosamund Barlett, "Japonism and Japanophobia: The Russo-Japanese War in Russian Cultural Consciousness," *Russian Review* 67, no. 1 (January 2008): 8–33.

98. On the final communications between Kurino and Lamsdorf before the rupture of diplomatic relations, see *CRNJR*, 55–56.

99. Horace Allen, "Resumé of Chief Events," Horace Newton Allen Papers, 1883–1923, no. 9, box 4B, New York Public Library.

100. Kojong finally resolved not to open the Yalu ports, despite British, Japanese, and American demands. Pak, *Rossiia i Koreia*, 361.

101. Savinsky, *Recollections*, 73; Bernard Pares, *The Fall of the Russian Monarchy: A Study of the Evidence* (New York, 1939), 56–57. See also Malozemoff, *Russian Far Eastern Policy*, 243.

102. Pak Chon-Khe [Pak Chonghyo], *Russko-iaponskaya voina 1904–1905 gg i Koreia* [The Russo-Japanese War of 1904–1905 and Korea] (Moscow, 1997), 158. See also J. Kefeli, B. Bock, B. Dudorov, V. Berg, et al., *Port-Artur: Vospominanii uchastnikov* [Port Arthur: Memories of the participants] (New York, 1955), 92. Nakai Kinjō, head of the Keijo/Seoul Japanese Settlers' Association, noted that when it was rumored that the Pacific Fleet had left Chefoo, there was widespread speculation it was heading to Inch'on, sparking fear that Korean soldiers might rise up against the Japanese. See Nakai Kinjō, *Nakai Chōsen kaikoroku* [Memoir of Chosen] (Tokyo, 1915), 90–92.

103. Komura sent the two telegrams to Kurino on February 5 at 2:15 PM (Tokyo time), *CRNJR*, 56–61. See also Morinosuke Kajima, *The Diplomacy of Japan, 1894–1922*, vol. 1 (Tokyo, 1978), 154. Lamsdorf later told Kurino that Tsar Nicholas was taken completely by surprise by Japan's decision to terminate negotiations and sever diplomatic relations. See *Japan Times*, March 10, 1904.

17. WAR FOR KOREA

1. Cited in Julian S. Corbett, *Maritime Operations in the Russo-Japanese War, 1904–1905*, 2 vols. (Annapolis, MD, 2015), 2:383.

2. Corbett, *Maritime Operations*, 2:383.

3. Corbett, *Maritime Operations*, 1:66–67; Ian Nish, "Korea: Focus of Russo-Japanese Diplomacy, 1893–1903," *Asian Studies* (Manila) 4, no. 1 (April 1966): 70–83.

4. Alfred Mahan, "Retrospect upon the War between Japan and Russia," in *Naval Administration and Warfare: Some General Principles, with Other Essays* (Boston, 1908), 145.

5. V. K. Vitgeft, "War-Plan for Naval Forces of the Pacific Ocean in 1903," May 3, 1903, cited in Corbett, *Maritime Operations*, 2:399–403.

6. Nicholas Papastratigakis with Dominic Lieven, "The Russian Far Eastern Squadrons Operational Plans," in *The Russo-Japanese War in Global Perspective: World War Zero*, vol. 1, ed. John W. Steinberg et al. (Leiden, 2005), 224.

7. Pak Chon-Khe [Pak Chonghyo], *Russko-iaponskaya voina 1904–1905 gg i Koreia* [The Russo-Japanese War of 1904–1905 and Korea] (Moscow, 1997), 155.

8. Despite measures taken in January 1904 to increase railway capacity, progress was very slow. See E. H. Nilus, *Istoricheskii obzor Kitaiskoi vostochnoi zheleznoi dorogi, 1896–1923 gg* [A historical survey of the Chinese Eastern Railway, 1896–1923] (Harbin, 1923), 292–297.

9. *Täglishe Runschau*, February 16, 1905. Also *Japan Times*, March 15, 1904.

10. J. Kefeli, B. Bock, B. Dudorov, V. Berg, et al., *Port-Artur: Vospominaniya uchast-nikov* [Port Arthur: Memories of the participants] (New York, 1955), 52–53.

11. Pak, *Russko-iaponskaya voina*, 161–162; Corbett, *Maritime Operations*, 1:60.

12. The full letter from Makarov to Avellan, dated February 8, 1904, is reproduced in Corbett, *Maritime Operations*, 2:409–410.

13. Pak, *Russko-iaponskaya voina*, 155–156.

14. Nagayo Ogasawar, *Life of Admiral Togo* (Tokyo, 1934), 194; Corbett, *Maritime Operations*, 1:61; Pak, *Russko-iaponskaya voina*, 155–156.

15. Cited in Pak, *Russko-iaponskaya voina*, 157; Corbett, *Maritime Operations*, 1:62.

16. On February 6, the same day Kurino visited Lamsdorf to announce the break in diplomatic relations, Ambassador Baron Rosen was informed of the break by Komura. See John Albert White, *The Diplomacy of the Russo-Japanese War* (New Jersey, 1964), 129; Pak, *Russko-iaponskaya voina*, 160–161; Corbett, *Maritime Operations*, 1:86–87.

17. The *New York Herald* European edition ran a story on February 16 headlined "All Corean Wires Cut. All Code Messages Refused over Japanese Wires." See Margaret Maxwell, "The Changing Dimension of a Tragedy: The Battle of Chemulpo," *Historian* 39, no. 3 (May 1977): 491. Part of the reason for Russia's uncoordinated response may have been that all communications from Saint Petersburg went through the consulate staff at Chifu (Yantai). Kefeli et al., *Port-Artur*, 91.

18. Cited in Pak, *Russko-iaponskaya voina*, 162.

19. Cited in Maxwell, "Changing Dimension," 492.

20. NARA, RG 59, M-134, roll 20, Allen to Hay, January 12, 1904.

21. "The Fighting at Chemulpo," *North China Daily*, March 11, 1904.

22. "The Fighting at Chemulpo," *North China Daily*, March 11, 1904.

23. FO 305/3 [December 19, 1903–December 8, 1904], Jordon to Campbell, February 15, 1904, Sir Newell John Jordon Papers, NA.

24. NARA, RG 59, M-134, roll 20, Allen to Hay, February 12, 1904.

25. See Bella Park, "Rossiyskaya Diplomatiya i Koreya nakanunye i v gody Russko-Yaponskoi voiny" [Russian diplomacy and Korea on the eve of and during the Russo-Japanese War of 1904–1905], *Oriental Studies* 41, no. 1 (2019): 21–22. See also Dmitri B. Pavlov, "The Russian 'Shanghai Service' in Korea, 1904–05," *Eurasian Review* 4 (November 2011): 1–10.

26. *ERJW*, 4–5. See also H. W. Wilson, *Japan's Fight for Freedom*, vol. 1 (London, 1904), 302–303.

27. NARA, RG 59, M-134, roll 20, Allen to Hay, February 22, 1904; *ERJW*, pt. 2, 4. The decision by the Imperial Staff to land the troops at Inch'on was, shockingly, taken without consulting Admiral Tōgō. See Corbett, *Maritime Operations*, 1:126.

28. Nakai Kitarō, *Chōsen kaikō roku* [Memoir of Chosen] (Tokyo, 1915), 98–99. There were also problems housing the soldiers. Many Japanese settlers put up soldiers in their homes; Nakai himself took in eight (103). See also Peter Duus, *The Abacus and the Sword: The Japanese Penetration of Korea, 1895–1910* (Berkeley, 1995), 55–56.

29. Wilson, *Japan's Fight*, 1:302.

30. NARA, RG 59, M-134, roll 20, Allen to Hay, February 22, 1904.

31. Kobe Chronicles, *A Diary of the Russo-Japanese War*, 2 vols., vol. 1, pt. 2 (Kobe, 1904), 54.

32. Pak, *Russko-iaponskaya voina*, 180.

33. Horace Allen notes, February 15, 1905, Horace Newton Allen Papers, box 3, letterpress copy books no. 1–2, New York Public Library.

34. Hwang-hyŏn, *Yŏkju Maech'ŏn yarok* [Translation with commentary of the unofficial records of Maecheon], vol. 2 (Seoul, 2005), 156–159. This work was translated into

modern Korean by Lim Hyong-t'aek. On the whole, Hwang's writings about the war were very anti-Russian.

35. *ERJW*, pt. 3, 78.

36. *ERJW*, pt. 2, 5. See also Tani Hisao, *Kimitsu Nichi-Ro Senshi* [Confidential history of the Russo-Japanese War] (Tokyo, 1966), 141–143.

37. Kobe Chronicles, *Diary*, vol. 1, pt. 3, 72.

38. NARA, RG 59, M-134, roll 20, Report of Brigadier General Henry T. Allen, March 31, 1904.

39. Bruce W. Menning, *Bayonets before Bullets: The Imperial Russian Army, 1861–1914* (Bloomington, IN, 1992), 153–154.

40. Anton Denikin, *The Career of a Tsarist Officer: Memoirs, 1872–1916*, trans. Margaret Patoski (Minneapolis, 1975), 104–105; Francis McCullagh, *With the Cossacks: Being the Story of an Irishman Who Rode with the Cossacks throughout the Russo-Japanese War* (London, 1906), 121–122.

41. Denikin, *Career of a Tsarist Officer*, 104.

42. General Kuropatkin, *The Russian Army and the Japanese War*, vol. 2 (New York, 1909), 207–208.

43. Kuropatkin, *Russian Army*, 2:209.

44. Menning, *Bayonets before Bullets*, 172.

45. Kuropatkin, *Russian Army*, 2:209–211; Denis Warner and Peggy Warner, *The Tide at Sunrise: A History of the Russo-Japanese War, 1904–1905* (London, 1974), 253–255.

46. Pak, *Russko-iaponskaya voina*, 190–191. Just before Kuropatkin left for the front, he told a close friend: "During the first month, people will say I am inactive. The second, they will say I am incapable. The third, they will call me a traitor, for we are certain by then to have sustained serious defeats. Let them talk—I do not care. I refused to take the offensive till I have an overwhelming superiority in numbers. That will not be until July." *Japan Times*, July 19, 1904.

47. Warner and Warner, *The Tide at Sunrise*, 257.

48. George Alexander Lensen, *The Russo-Chinese War* (Tallahassee, FL, 1967), 10, 18.

49. Lensen, *Russo-Chinese War*, 206.

50. Pak, *Russko-iaponskaya voina*, 191.

51. Ian Hamilton, *A Staff Officer's Scrap Book during the Russo-Japanese War*, vol. 1 (London, 1906), 82; Pak, *Russko-iaponskaya voina*, 200.

52. Hamilton, *Staff Officer's Scrap Book*, 1:83–85. Hamilton, a British military attaché with the Japanese Army in Manchuria, was one of the first Western observers to publish an account of the war. His book is considered a classic.

53. NARA, RG 59, M-134, roll 20, Sharrock to Allen, 4/6 1904; Pak, *Russko-iaponskaya voina*, 197.

54. Hamilton, *Staff Officer's Scrap Book*, 1:84–85.

55. Hamilton, *Staff Officer's Scrap Book*, 1:86.

56. Tani Hisao, *Kimitsu Nichi-Ro Senshi*, 146.

57. Wilson, *Japan's Fight*, 1:419.

58. Hamilton, *Staff Officer's Scrap Book*, 1:87–88.

59. *ERJW*, 2:7–8.

60. Hamilton, *Staff Officer's Scrap Book*, 1:99; Warner and Warner, *The Tide at Sunrise*, 264; Hamilton, *Staff Officer's Scrap Book*, 1:259.

61. *Japan Weekly Mail*, May 14, 1904.

62. Hamilton, *Staff Officer's Scrap Book*, 1:106.

63. Hamilton, *Staff Officer's Scrap Book*, 1:106.

64. Hamilton, *Staff Officers Scrap Book*, 1:103.

65. *Japan Weekly Mail,* May 14, 1904.

66. On the Russian forces, see Pak, *Russko-iaponskaya voina,* 200.

67. Warner and Warner, *The Tide at Sunrise,* 82.

68. *ERJW,* 2:11.

69. Hamilton, *Staff Officer's Scrap Book,* 1:125–126. Frederick Palmer, a war correspondent for *Collier's Weekly,* described the scene as a "slaughter." Palmer, *With Kuroki in Manchuria* (New York, 1904), 93–94.

70. David Campbell, *Russian Soldier versus Japanese Soldier, Manchuria, 1904–05* (London, 2019), 40. The First Army Medical Corps listed the Yalu casualties (killed and wounded) as follows: Guards Division, 132; Second Division, 250; and Twelfth Division, 316; for a total of 708. This number swelled by roughly 300 by adding the casualties in the pursuit. *North China Herald,* May 20, 1904; Warner and Warner, *The Tide at Sunrise,* 268.

71. Alfred Stead, "The War in the Far East," *Fortnightly Review,* June 1904, 956.

72. B. D. Pak, *Rossiia i Koreia* [Russia and Korea] (Moscow, 2004), 365; Park, "Rossiyskaya Diplomatiya," 22.

73. Pavlov, "Russian 'Shanghai Service,'" 3.

74. Park, "Rossiyskaya Diplomatiya," 22; Pavlov, "Russian 'Shanghai Service,'" 2. See also Evgeny Sergeev, *Russian Military Intelligence in the War with Japan, 1904–04: Secret Operations on Land and at Sea* (London, 2007), 79.

75. Pavlov, "'Russian Shanghai Service,'" 4–5.

76. Pak, *Russko-iaponskaya voina,* 211–212.

77. Duus, *Abacus and the Sword,* 121; Andre Schmid, *Korea between Empires, 1895–1919* (New York, 2002), 47–48.

78. Chŏng Kyo, *Taehan kyenyŏsa* [Chronological history of Taehan], vol. 2 (Seoul, 1957), 174.

79. Vladimir Tikhonov noted that the hostile view of Russia widely promulgated by Japan was also shared by many pro-Japanese Korean reformers in the 1880s and 1890s. Vladimir Tikhonov, "Images of Russia and the Soviet Union in Modern Korea, 1880s–1930s: An Overview," *Seoul Journal of Korean Studies* 22, no. 2 (December 2009): 215–247; Yu Yŏngnyul, "Kaehwa chisigin Yun Ch'i-ho ŭi Rŏsia insik" [Yun Ch'i-ho's perception of Russia in the Enlightenment period], *Han'guk minjok undongsa yŏng'gu* 41 (2004): 94–121.

80. Vipan Chandra, "Sentiments and Ideology in the Nationalism of the Independence Club (1896–1898)," *Korean Studies* 10 (1986): 23.

81. Vladimir Tikhonov, *Modern Korea and Its Others: Perceptions of the Neighboring Countries and Korean Modernity* (New York, 2016), 27–28.

82. Chandra, "Sentiments and Ideology," 23; Yumi Moon, *Populist Collaborators: The Ilchinhoe and the Japanese Colonization of Korea, 1896–1910* (Ithaca, NY, 2013); Carl F. Young, *Eastern Learning and the Heavenly Way: The Tonghak and Ch'ŏndogyo Movements and the Twilight of Korean Independence* (Honolulu, 2012); Schmid, *Korea between Empires.*

83. Cited in Tikhonov, *Modern Korea,* 28.

84. Homer Hulbert, *The Passing of Korea* (New York, 1906), 215; Duus, *Abacus and the Sword,* 367–368.

85. Hwang Hyŏn, *Maech'ŏn yarok,* 184–185.

86. Gustav Mutel, *Mwit'el chungo ilgi* [Bishop Mutel's journals], vol. 3, *1901–1905* (Seoul, 1986), 365; Hwang Hyŏn, *Maech'ŏn yarok,* 195–196.

87. CIK, 23 kwan (541) [12826–12828], no. 686, Hayashi to Komura, September 23, 1904, http://db.history.go.kr/item/level.do?setId=146&itemId=jh&synonym=off&chinessChar=on&page=1&pre_page=1&brokerPagingInfo=&position=34&levelId=jh_023r_0020_5140.

88. Moon, *Populist Collaborators*, 86.

89. CIK, 22 kwan (76) [12651], no. 38, Yi Chung-ha [Provincial Governor of P'yŏngan-do] to the Ŭijŏngbu, September 17, 1904, http://db.history.go.kr/item/level.do?setId=978&itemId=jh&synonym=off&chinessChar=on&page=1&pre_page=1&brokerPagingInfo=&position=7&levelId=jh_022r_0030_0760.

90. Young, *Eastern Learning*, 34.

91. See Ōhigashi Kunio, *Ri Yōkyū no shōgai: Zenrin yūkō no sho ichinen o tsuranuku* [The life of Yi Yong-gu: Sticking to the original intention of maintaining good friendship with neighbors] (Tokyo, 1960), 31.

92. See Yumi Moon, "From Periphery to a Transnational Frontier: Popular Movements in the Northwestern Provinces, 1896–1904," in *The Northern Regions of Korea: History, Identity, and Culture*, ed. Sun Joo Kim (Seattle, 2010), 184.

93. Moon, *Populist Collaborators*, 86; Young, *Eastern Learning*, 54, 62; Vipan Chandra, "An Outline Study of the Ilchinoe (Advancement Society) of Korea," *Occasional Papers on Korea* 2 (March 1974): 43–72.

94. Yi Yong-gu, who went by several aliases (Yi Sang-ok, Yi P'il-u, and Yi Man-sik) had served as Chŏn Pong-jun's deputy during the Tonghak Uprising in October 1894. In Japan with Son Pyŏng-hŭi he was influenced by Sun Yat-sen's pro-Japanese reformist message. Tarui Tōkichi's book *Daito Gappōron* [On the theory of uniting the Great East] (1893) had a significant impact on Yi's involvement in the Russo-Japanese War. See Ōhigashi Kunio, *Ri Yokyu no shogai*, 31–40. See also Moon, *Populist Collaborators*, 150–152.

95. CIK, 22 kwan (2) [1291], Yokata Saburō to Hayashi Gonsuke, October 1, 1904, http://db.history.go.kr/item/level.do?setId=978&itemId=jh&synonym=off&chinessChar=on&page=1&pre_page=1&brokerPagingInfo=&position=19&levelId=jh_022r_0120_0020.

96. CIK, 22 kwan (2) [1291], Yokata Saburō to Hayashi Gonsuke, October 15, 1904, http://db.history.go.kr/item/level.do?setId=978&itemId=jh&synonym=off&chinessChar=on&page=1&pre_page=1&brokerPagingInfo=&position=19&levelId=jh_022r_0120_0020.

97. CIK, 22 kwan (2) [1291], Yokata Saburō to Hayashi Gonsuke, October 15, 1904, http://db.history.go.kr/item/level.do?setId=978&itemId=jh&synonym=off&chinessChar=on&page=1&pre_page=1&brokerPagingInfo=&position=19&levelId=jh_022r_0120_0020. The two groups formally merged on December 2, 1904; see Young, *Eastern Learning*, 79. Hwang Hyŏn was skeptical of the Ilchinhoe, stating that when the organization was established, Ilchinhoe members "deceived the people" by promising them "official positions in the central and local government for their contributions." Hwang Hyŏn, *Maech'on Yarok*, 4:198.

98. CIK, 21 kwan (34) [12655], no. 598, Chief of Staff of the Korean Army in Korea, Ochiai Tyosaburo, to Hayahsi, November 22, 1904, http://db.history.go.kr/item/level.do?setId=978&itemId=jh&synonym=off&chinessChar=on&page=1&pre_page=1&brokerPagingInfo=&position=5&levelId=jh_021r_0070_0340.

99. The numbers of Ilchinhoe members working on the railway for the month of October were: Hwanghae Province, 11,514; Pyŏngansamdo (southern P'yŏngan province), 64,799; P'yŏnganbukdo (northern P'yŏngan province), 72,900; for a total of 149,213 members. See Ōhigashi Kunio, *Ri Yokyu no shogai*, 45–46.

100. CIK, 22 kwan (4), no. 58 [12914], Vice Council of Chinnamp'o Someya Nariaka to Hayashi, November 12, 1904, http://db.history.go.kr/item/level.do?setId=978&itemId=jh&synonym=off&chinessChar=on&page=1&pre_page=1&brokerPagingInfo=&position=17&levelId=jh_022r_0110_0040.

101. CIK, 25 kwan (1), no. 1 [12630], Komura to Hayashi, January 10, 1905. Song Pyŏng-jun sent the letter to Yasuharu Matsuishi. Komura obtained a copy and sent it to

Hayashi; http://db.history.go.kr/item/level.do?setId=146&itemId=jh&synonym=off&chiness Char=on&page=1&pre_page=1&brokerPagingInfo=&position=73&levelId=jh_025r_0100 _0010.

102. Young, *Eastern Learning*, 81.

103. Roughly 115,000 members helped with the transportation of military goods in northern Korea, from Songchin on the northeast coast to Manchuria. Much of the cost of building the railway line was paid for by the Ilchinhoe members themselves, although some did receive an "employment fee" from Japan authorities. Ōhigashi Kunio, *Ri Yōkyū no shōgai*, 44.

104. On the Korean Garrison Army, see Tani Hisao, *Kimitsu Nichi-Ro Senshi*, 555–556. See also Park, "Rossiyskaya Diplomatiya," 24.

105. NARA, RG 59, M-134, roll 2. Allen report on the Korean Ilchinhoe Society, O1904. Yun Ch'i-ho remarked that the suppression of the Ilchinhoe had made Kojong extremely unpopular. "Today [December 19, 1904] the Ilchinhoe moved into their new quarters. The soldiers and police tried to dislodge them. Eleven Ilchinhoe were wounded [but] Japanese gendarmes and soldiers inter [vened] on behalf of the Ilchinhoe. The people now hate the [emperor] so much that they seem to welcome anything to humiliate and disappoint him. Nothing short of his total dethronement would satisfy the sense of justice or the feeling of disgust of the people." Song Pyŏng-gi, ed., *Yun Ch'i-ho ilgi* [Diary of Yun ch'i-ho], vol. 6, *1903–1906* (Yonsei Taehakkyo ch'ulp'ansa, 2011), 80. CIK, 22 kwan (47), no. 114 [12790], Hayashi to Komura, November 26, 1904, http://db.history.go.kr/item/level.do?setId=978&itemId=jh& synonym=off&chinessChar=on&page=1&pre_page=1&brokerPagingInfo=&position=23&level Id=jh_022r_0130_0470.

106. Moon, *Populist Collaborators*, 101–102.

107. *Yun Ch'i-ho Ilgi*, 6:79–80.

108. CIK, 23 kwan (357), no. 357 [12823–12825], Komura to Hayashi, December 30, 1904. Reports such as these reveal that, contrary to the opinion that the Ilchinhoe was a Japanese-designed organization, it was very much an organically created Korean organization; http://db .history.go.kr/item/level.do?setId=978&itemId=jh&synonym=off&chinessChar=on&page =1&pre_page=1&brokerPagingInfo=&position=27&levelId=jh_023r_0010_3570.

109. Hayashi to Komura, November 26, 1904. See also Hwang Hyŏn, *Maech'ŏn yarok*, 197–198. Beginning in November 1904, conservative local elites began launching concerted attacks on the Ilchinhoe; see Moon, *Populist Collaborators*, 199.

110. CIK, 23 kwan (592), no. 793 [12826–12828], Hayashi to Komura, December 31, 1904, http://db.history.go.kr/item/level.do?setId=158&itemId=jh&synonym=off&chiness Char=on&page=1&pre_page=1&brokerPagingInfo=&position=41&levelId=jh_023r_0020 _5920.

111. The Ilchinhoe's close links with the Japanese did not sit well with other elements of Korean society. Confucian scholars formed an organization called the Ch'angŭihoe to frustrate Japanese reform efforts and "exterminate the Ilchinhoe." See CIK, 26 kwan (4) [12917], no. 4, Miura Yagorō to Hayashi, March 29, 1905, http://db.history.go.kr/item/level.do?setId=146& itemId=jh&synonym=off&chinessChar=on&page=1&pre_page=1&brokerPagingInfo =&position=118&levelId=jh_026r_0050_0040; Ch'oe Ik-hyŏn, the Confucian scholar who played such a pivotal role in Kojong's reign, was a likely member. Moon, *Populist Collaborators*, 66; Han Woo-Keun, *The History of Korea* (Seoul, 1970), 432.

18. WAR IN MANCHURIA

1. Lieutenant-General N. A. Tretyakov, *My Experiences at Nan Shan and Port Arthur with the Fifth East Siberian Rifles*, trans. A. C. Alford (London, 1911), 21; H. W. Wilson, *Japan's Fight for Freedom*, 3 vols. (London, 1904), 2:491.

2. Tretyakov, *My Experiences*, 4–5, 20.

3. Denis Warner and Peggy Warner, *The Tide at Sunrise: A History of the Russo-Japanese War, 1904–1905* (London, 1974), 288–290.

4. Tretyakov, *My Experiences*, 22–23.

5. Ishimitsu Makiyo, *Bōkyō no Uta* [Songs of nostalgia] (Tokyo 2018), 18.

6. Reviel Netz, *Barbed Wire: An Ecology of Modernity* (Middletown, CT, 2009), 107; Felix Patrikeeff and Harold Shukman, *Railways and the Russo-Japanese War: Transporting War* (London, 2007), 68–69.

7. Warner and Warner, *The Tide at Sunrise*, 291.

8. Ishimitsu, *Bōkyō no Uta*, 18.

9. The Japanese infantry attacked en masse, following the German doctrine of "momentum." J. W. Westwood, *Russia against Japan, 1904–1905: A New Look at the Russo-Japanese War* (New York, 1986), 126–127.

10. Ishimitsu, *Bōkyō no Uta*, 19.

11. Ishimitsu, *Bōkyō no Uta*, 19.

12. Warner and Warner, *The Tide at Sunrise*, 294.

13. HistoryNet, "Russo-Japanese War: Japan's First Big Surprise," https://www.historynet.com/russo-japanese-war-japans-first-big-surprise.htm.

14. Tretyakov, *My Experiences*, 53.

15. Ishimitsu, *Bōkyō no Uta*, 21.

16. Tretyakov, *My Experiences*, 60.

17. Ishimitsu, *Bōkyō no Uta*, 22–25; E. K. Nojine, *The Truth about Port Arthur*, trans. Captain A. B. Lindsay, ed. Major E. D. Swinton (New York, 1908), 81–82.

18. Tretyakov, *My Experiences*, 66.

19. Rotem Kowner, *Historical Dictionary of the Russo-Japanese War* (London, 2017), 251. The "official" military statistics of the Sino-Japanese War indicate that more Japanese soldiers died of diseases, such as cholera and dysentery, than in battle. See Kyu-hyun Kim, "Sino-Japanese War (1894–1895): Japanese National Integration and Construction of the Korean Other," *International Journal of Korean History* 17, no. 1 (February 2012): 20.

20. Ishimitsu, *Bōkyō no uta*, 19; Warner and Warner, *The Tide at Sunrise*, 296–297.

21. Rotem Kowner lists Japanese casualties as 739 dead and 5,459 wounded. Other sources list Japanese losses at Nanshan as 4,204 killed and wounded. See Kowner, *Historical Dictionary*, 251; Wilson, *Japan's Fight*, 2:596.

22. Tadayoshi Sakurai, *Human Bullets* (London, 1999), 54–55.

23. General Kuropatkin, *The Russian Army and the Japanese War*, 2 vols. (New York, 1909), 2:257; *Japan Times*, May 18, 1904.

24. *Japan Times*, April 3, 1904.

25. Kuropatkin, *Russian Army*, 2:217–218.

26. Wilson, *Japan's Fight*, 2:204.

27. Yoshihisa Tak Matsusaka, "Human Bullets, General Nogi, and the Myth of Port Arthur," in *The Russo-Japanese War in Global Perspective: World War Zero*, vol. 1, ed. John Steinberg et al. (Leiden, 2005), 179–201; Doris G. Bargen, *Suicidal Honor: General Nogi and the Writings of Mori Ōgai and Natsume Sōseki* (Honolulu, 2006), 49–50.

28. Kuropatkin, *Russian Army*, 2:214–215.

29. Frederick McCormick, *The Tragedy of Russia in Pacific Asia*, vol. 1 (New York, 1905), 129.

30. Japanese losses were 1,163 killed and wounded. Wilson, *Japan's Fight*, 2:263. Rotem Kowner puts Russian losses at least 3,500 killed, wounded, or missing. Kowner, *Historical Dictionary*, 374.

31. Kuropatkin, *Russian Army*, 2:258.

32. Alekseev's proclamation appeared in the *China Times*, which then translated the original Chinese copy into English. See *Japan Times*, June 26, 1904.

33. *Japan Times*, June 26, 1904.

34. Keith Stevens, "Between Scylla and Charybdis: China and the Chinese during the Russo-Japanese War," *Journal of the Hong Kong Branch of the Royal Asiatic Society* 43 (2003): 132.

35. *Japan Times*, April 12, 1904. See also Roy V. Mager, "John Hay and American Traditions in China," *Social Science* 4, no. 3 (May–July 1929): 310.

36. Ian Nish, "Japanese Intelligence, 1894–1922," in *The Collected Writings of Ian Nish*, pt. 2 (Tokyo, 2001), 149–165; Inaba Chiharu and Rotem Kowner, "The Secret Factor: Japanese Network of Intelligence-Gathering on Russia during the War," in *Rethinking the Russo-Japanese War, 1904–5*, vol. 1, *Centennial Perspectives*, ed. Rotem Kowner (Leiden, 2007), 78–92.

37. Tani Hisao, *Kimitsu Nichi-Ro Senshi* [Confidential history of the Russo-Japanese War] (Tokyo, 1966), 669. See also Warner and Warner, *The Tide at Sunrise*, 355.

38. Nish, "Japanese Intelligence," 152. As a sixteen-year-old, Fukushima fought in the Boshin War (1868–1869) and later worked as a newspaper reporter and English language translator during the Satsuma Rebellion. Eventually, he was noticed by Yamagata Aritomo who appointed him as his intelligence chief in 1878, launching his career as a military officer. Fukushima became famous for his epic seventeen-month lone horse ride journey from Berlin to Japan via Siberia and Manchuria. Without ever having commanded a troop unit, his intelligence work carried him to the general staff and service in the Sino-Japanese War, the Boxer expedition, and the Russo-Japanese War.

39. French general Henri Frey singled out Japanese intelligence in the 1900 operation. See his *Français et Allies au Pe-Tchi-li: Campaign de Chine de 1900* (Paris, 1904), 84–88.

40. It is also referred to as the Newly Created Army. See Chi Hsi-sheng, *Warlord Politics in China, 1916–1928* (Stanford, CA, 1976), 13–14.

41. Tani, *Kimitsu Nichi-Ro Senshi*, 673.

42. Tani, *Kimitsu Nichi-Ro Senshi*, 280.

43. A. R. Colquhoun, "China in Transformation and the War," *North American Review* 179 (July 1904): 574–575. See also Patrick Fuliang Shan, *Yuan Shikai: A Reappraisal* (Vancouver, 2018); Stephen R. MacKinnon, *Power and Politics in Late Imperial China: Yuan Shi-kai in Beijing and Tianjin, 1901–1908* (Berkeley, 1980); Jerome Chen, *Yuan Shi-kai, 1859–1916* (London, 1961).

44. *Japan Times*, April 12, 1904.

45. *Japan Times*, March 9, 1904; *Japan Times*, January 24, 1905.

46. Tani, *Kimitsu Nichi-Ro Senshi*, 674.

47. Tani, *Kimitsu Nichi-Ro Senshi*, 673–674.

48. One soldier wrote: "We receive rice (70 percent rice, 30 percent wheat) from the kitchen. We make our own side dishes and receive rations every five days. What I received today was: one and a half chicken per person, meat, onions, canned beef, shaved Bonito Flakes, Kōya tofu, local tofu, fried salted sardines, and soft seaweed. For breakfast (rations) we receive Fukujinzuke (pickled vegetables), soya sauce, powdered miso, miso with sugar and sake, sugar, salt, and so on. What we receive varies from time to time. Four to five soldiers who share the same room cook whatever they want for themselves . . . We sometimes even have dessert." Ōe Shinobu, *Heishitachi no nichiro sensō: 500-tsū no gunji yūbin kara* [Soldiers of the Russo-Japanese War: Through 500 military letters] (Tokyo, 1988), 195.

49. Tani, *Kimitsu Nichi-Ro Senshi*, 676–677.

50. Tani, *Kimitsu Nichi-Ro Senshi*, 675.

51. Nish, "Japanese Intelligence," 151–152. See also Chiharu and Kowner, "The Secret Factor."

52. Ian Nish, "Japanese Intelligence," 156; Akashi Motojirō, *Rakka Ryūsui: Colonel Akashi's Report on His Secret Cooperation with Russian Revolutionary Parties during the Russo-Japanese War*, selected chaps. trans. Inaba Chiharu, ed. Olav K. Fält and Antti Kujala (Helsinki, 1988).

53. Tani, *Kimitsu Nichi-Ro Senshi*, 255. On Polish participation, see McCormick, *Tragedy of Russia*, 1:265–266.

54. On July 28, 1904, Minister of the Interior Vyacheslav von Plehve fell to an assassin's bomb in Saint Petersburg. See V. I. Gurko, *Features and Figures of the Past: Government and Opinion in the Reign of Nicholas II*, trans. Laura Matveev (New York, 1970), 253–254.

55. A. Votinov, *Iaponskoi Shpionazh v Russko-iaponskuiu voinu, 1904–1905 gg* [Japanese espionage in the Russo-Japanese War of 1904–1905] (Moscow, 1939), https://www.prlib.ru/en/node/392016, 11. It is not clear who exactly Votinov was or what position he held, but his report says his knowledge of Japanese intelligence was based on his experience in Mukden. Many of his observations are backed by Ishimitsu's and others' accounts of Japanese clandestine activities during the war. See also Evgeny Sergeev, *Russian Military Intelligence in the War with Japan, 1904–05: Secret Operations on Land and at Sea* (New York, 2007).

56. Votinov, *Iaponskoi Shpionazh*, 23.

57. Ishimitsu, *Kōya no Hana* [The flower of the wasteland] (Tokyo, 2017), 65–66.

58. Ishimitsu, *Kōya no Hana*, 176–196. Ishimitsu was in Harbin when the Russians swept over the city in August 1900 during the Russo-Chinese War.

59. Ishimitsu, *Kōya no Hana*, 264, 89. See also Ian Nish, "Spy in Manchuria," in *Collected Writings*, pt. 2, 136.

60. Ishimitsu, *Kōya no Hana*, 274–278. See also Nish, "Spy in Manchuria," 136; Sergeev, *Russian Military Intelligence*, 57.

61. Ishimitsu, *Kōya no Hana*, 328–329.

62. Votinov, *Iaponskoi Shpionazh*, 11–12.

63. Votinov, *Iaponskoi Shpionazh*, 39–40.

64. Kuropatkin, *Russian Army*, 1:226.

65. Votinov, *Iaponskoi Shpionazh*, 40. See also Frederick Palmer, *With Kuroki in Manchuria* (New York, 1904), 184–185.

66. Palmer, *With Kuroki*, 183–184.

67. Kowner, *Historical Dictionary*, 411.

68. McCormick, *Tragedy of Russia*, 1:183.

69. McCormick, *Tragedy of Russia*, 1:183.

70. Kuropatkin, *The Russian Army and the Japanese War*, 226–228.

71. Warner and Warner, *The Tide at Sunrise*, 374.

72. Matsusaka, "Human Bullets," 182.

73. The six-day assault on Port Arthur, on August 19–25, cost the Third Army fourteen thousand causalities, including twenty-three hundred dead. Matsusaka, "Human Bullets," 188, 194.

74. Warner and Warner, *The Tide at Sunrise*, 354; Kowner, *Historical Dictionary*, 206.

75. Sarah M. Nelson, *The Archeology of Korea* (Cambridge, 1993), 209.

76. Warner and Warner, *The Tide at Sunrise*, 321–323.

77. Ishimitsu, *Bōkyō no Uta*, 31–32.

78. Tani, *Kimitsu Nichi-Ro Senshi*, 427–430.

79. Warner and Warner, *The Tide at Sunrise*, 354–355.

80. Warner and Warner, *The Tide at Sunrise*, 362.

81. Wilson, *Japan's Fight*, 3:883–884; Capt. Carl Reichmann, "Report of Capt. Carl Reichmann 17th Observer with the Russian Forces," *Reports of Military Observers Attached*

to the Armies in Manchuria during the Russo-Japanese War, pt. 1 (Washington, DC, 1906), 208–209. Official dates for the battle of Liaoyang vary widely. My dates are based on Ian Hamilton, *A Staff Officer's Scrap Book during the Russo-Japanese War*, 2 vols. (London, 1906).[81] Warner and Warner, *The Tide at Sunrise*, 362–364.

82. Wilson, *Japan's Fight*, 3:910.

83. Ishimitsu, *Bōkyō no Uta*, 46–47.

84. Palmer, *With Kuroki*, 251.

85. Hamilton, *Staff Officer's Scrap Book*, 1:137.

86. Warner and Warner, *The Tide at Sunrise*, 372.

87. See William Maxwell, *From the Yalu to Port Arthur* (London, 1906), cited in "Literature of the Russo-Japanese War," *American Historical Review* 16, no. 3 (April 1911): 513.

88. Warner and Warner, *The Tide at Sunrise*, 373.

89. Anton Denikin, *The Career of a Tsarist Officer: Memoirs, 1872–1916*, trans. Margaret Patoski (Minneapolis, 1975), 122; Warner and Warner, *The Tide at Sunrise*, 401. On Alekseev's recall, see John C. O'Laughlin Papers, box 97, LOC.

90. Denikin, *Career of a Tsarist Officer*, 122.

91. Hamilton, *Staff Officer's Scrap Book*, 2:143.

92. Ōe Shinobu, *Heishitachi no Nichi-Ro Sensō*, 120–124. Ōe seems to suggest that another reason for the censorship had to do with spying and fears that soldiers might unwittingly give away vital information to the enemy.

93. Ishimitsu, *Bōkyō no Uta*, 55–57. War weariness was particularly acute for the lower classes of Japanese conscripts, who could not support their families at home. See Naoko Shimazu, "Patriotic and Despondent: Japanese Society at War, 1904–5," *Russian Review* 67, no. 1 (January 2008): 34–49.

94. David H. James, *The Siege of Port Arthur: Records of an Eye-Witness* (London, 1905), 49.

95. James, *Siege of Port Arthur*, 67.

96. Sakurai, *Human Bullets*, 230, 207.

97. Sakurai, *Human Bullets*, 155.

98. Warner and Warner, *The Tide at Sunrise*, 341–342.

99. Warner and Warner, *The Tide at Sunrise*, 346–352, 374.

100. J. Kefeli et al., *Port-Artur: Vospominaniya uchastnikov* [Port Arthur: Memories of the participants] (New York, 1955), 99.

101. Tani, *Kimitsu Nichi-Ro Senshi*, 203–204.

102. After the failure of the First Assault in August, Nogi ordered his soldiers to begin digging parallel trenches, each new line approaching nearer to the forts. Nojine, *Truth about Port Arthur*, 215.

103. Tani, Kimitsu *Nichi-Ro Senshi*, 204–205. Presumably Port Arthur still could have held out indefinitely as long as their ammunition lasted. *The Outlook*, December 10, 1904, 901–902.

104. See Tani, *Kimitsu Nichi-Ro Senshi*, 205–206. See also Matsusaka, "Human Bullets," 192. Other accounts credit Kodama with the plan of refocusing on 203 Meter Hill. See Warner and Warner, *The Tide at Sunrise*, 278.

105. Tani, *Kimitsu Nichi-Ro Senshi*, 211–13.

106. Tani, *Kimitsu Nichi-Ro Senshi*, 215–216.

107. Kowner, *Historical Dictionary*, 298.

108. Nagaoka was clearly extremely frustrated, but his rage turned to joy when he received the news that the Third Army had suddenly changed its strategy after the initial failed assault. Tani, *Kimitsu Nichi-Ro Senshi*, 228–230.

109. Tani, *Kimitsu Nichi-Ro Senshi*, 238. See also Matsusaka, "Human Bullets," 192–193.

110. James, *Siege of Port Arthur*, 184.

111. Alexsis M. Uzefovich, "The Fall of Port Arthur," *Military Engineer* 22, no. 122 (March–April 1930): 102.

112. Matsusaka, "Human Bullets," 193–194; James, *Siege of Port Arthur,* 204–205.

113. See Matsusaka, "Human Bullets," 194–195.

114. Kefeli et al., *Port-Artur,* 100.

115. Kowner, *Historical Dictionary,* 299.

116. As Matsusaka points out, few people could have imagined the lionization of Nogi after the war. See Bargen, *Suicidal Honor.* See also Richard Barry, "Nogi—Seer, Statesman, and Soldier," *Harper's Weekly,* September 28, 1912.

117. Ellis Ashmead-Bartlett, *Port Arthur: The Siege and Capitulation* (London, 1906), 448.

118. In his piece published in the *Times* on January 25, G. E. Morrison related that there was plenty of food and supplies for the Port Arthur garrison to have held out for many months longer. See G. E. Morrison, *The Correspondence of G.E. Morrison, 1895–1912,* ed. Lo Hui-Min (Cambridge, 1976), 289; also Morrison, "The Defense of General Stoessel," *North China Herald,* March 3, 1905. This evidence was corroborated by E. K. Nojine, a Russian correspondent who was in Port Arthur during the siege. See Nojine, *Truth about Port Arthur.*

119. Lt. Colonel Tsunoda, who accompanied Stoessel to Port Arthur after the general's interview with Nogi on the fifth, reported that he had asked both questions but received no definitive answers. *North China Herald,* February 2, 1905.

120. Ashmead-Bartlett, *Port Arthur,* 449.

121. In March 1904 Smirnov was appointed commanding officer of Port Arthur, but he was outranked by the previous commander, Anatoly Stoessel, who refused to relinquish his powers. See Kowner, *Historical Dictionary,* 356–357; Nojine, *Truth about Port Arthur,* 174–175.

122. Denikin, *Career of a Tsarist Officer,* 128–129.

123. Uzefovich, "Fall of Port Arthur," 103. See also Nojine, *Truth about Port Arthur,* 274–275. Poison gas was especially effective in driving the Russians from the tunnels. See Kefeli et al., *Port-Artur,* 129.

124. Tretyakov *My Experiences,* 288.

125. Tretyakov, *My Experiences,* 296, 298.

126. H. P. Willlmott, *The Last Sea Power,* vol. 1, *From Port Arthur to Chanak, 1894–1922* (Bloomington, IN, 2009), 90.

127. *North China Herald,* February 2, 1905.

128. When asked later what the besieged had found most formidable in the attack, Stoessel emphasized "the immensely destructive effects of the 28-centimeter guns. *North China Herald,* February 2, 1905.

129. A transcript of this meeting appears in Nojine, *Truth about Port Arthur,* excerpted transcripts of December 29 on 303–309. Smirnov was also against surrender, stating that the fortress could hold out for at least three more weeks (331).

130. Votinov, *Iaponskoi Shpionazh,* 59.

131. Nojine, *Truth about Port Arthur,* 309.

132. Viren was appointed commander of the Pacific Squadron on September 4, 1904. He issued orders for the remaining fleet to be scuttled rather than given up to the Japanese, See Kowner, *Historical Dictionary,* 409; Nojine *Truth about Port Arthur,* 327.

133. Nojine, *Truth about Port Arthur,* 332.

134. Maurice Paléologue, *Three Critical Years: 1904, 1905, 1906* (New York, 1957), 153.

135. Tretyakov, *My Experiences,* 299–300.

136. Ashmead-Bartlett, *Port Arthur,* 457.

137. Sergei Witte, *The Memoirs of Sergei Witte,* trans. Sidney Harcave (New York, 1990), 400.

138. Votinov, *Iaponskoi Shpionazh,* 59–60.

139. Votinov, *Iaponskoi Shpionazh*, 60; Warner and Warner, *The Tide at Sunrise*, 453.

140. Sidney Harcave, *First Blood: The Russian Revolution* (New York, 1964), 39.

141. Mikhail Zygar, *The Empire Must Collapse, 1900–1917* (New York, 2017), 166.

142. Zygar, *Empire Must Collapse*, 167. Grand Duke Vladimir (uncle of Nicholas II) claimed that German socialists were behind Bloody Sunday. Eddy to Hay, February 1, 1905, John Hay Papers, reel 8, LOC.

143. The official figure was 96 killed and 333 wounded, of whom 34 died later. These figures did not include the dead and wounded who were removed from the scene of the massacre. See Witte, *Memoirs*, 402–403.

144. Louis Fischer, *Life of Lenin* (London, 1964), 48–49.

145. Dominic Lieven, *Nicholas II: Emperor of All the Russians* (London, 1994), 145–146.

146. The first large cooperative demonstration by Russian and Korean workers was a strike at the Selemdzhisky mines in Amru's Oblast. On August 13, 1900, at the Zlatoust mine, about five hundred Russians and Korean workers went on strike. Boris Pak, *Koreitsy v Rossiiskoi imperii (Dal'nevostochnyi period)* [Koreans in the Russian Empire (The Far East period)] (Moscow, 1993), 160–161.

147. Pak, *Koreitsy v Rossiiskoi Imperii*, 159–160.

148. Pak, *Koreitsy v Rossiiskoi Imperii*, 159.

149. Pak Chon-Khe [Pak Chonghyo], *Russko-iaponskaya voina 1904–1905 gg i Koreia* [The Russo-Japanese War of 1904–1905 and Korea] (Moscow, 1997), 216–217. Instead of abandoning their position in northern Korea altogether, the First Nerchinsk Regiment was ordered to help form a Korean people's militia made up of regular army defectors, hunters, and ŭibyŏng [Righteous Army] guerrillas. Pak, *Russko-iaponskaya voina*, 214–215.

150. See Pak, *Russko-iaponskaya voina*, 215–216. In December, Ōki Yasunosuke, the vice counsel in Wŏnsan, complained to Hayashi that "most of the county's governors here in Hamgyŏng province are either pro-Russian or have earned their position with the help of the pro-Russian faction." CIK, 20 kwan (5), no. 22 [12877], Ōki Yasunosuke to Hayashi, December 17, 1904, http://db.history.go.kr/item/level.do?setId=19&itemId=jh&synonym=off&chinessChar=on&page=1&pre_page=1&brokerPagingInfo=&position=1&levelId=jh_020r_0120_0050.

151. Kojong continued to actively support the Righteous Army. "Using Kojong's imperial seal, Yi Pŏm-yun could do anything he wanted in Jiandao," wrote one exasperated Japanese official. "This included plundering and killing without worrying about Russian authorities as his deeds were all sanctioned by the emperor." CIK, 3 kwan (3) [22315], no. 5, Nomura to Tsuruhara Sadakichi, May 14, 1907, http://db.history.go.kr/item/level.do?setId=271&itemId=jh&synonym=off&chinessChar=on&page=1&pre_page=1&brokerPagingInfo=&position=9&levelId=jh_093r_0060_0030.

152. The Korean division was formed on July 7, 1905. Pak, *Russko-iaponskaya voina*, 217–220.

153. Karoly Fendler, "The Japanese Plan to Abduct Korean Emperor Kojong during the Russo-Japanese War of 1904–5: Ho Russian Diplomats Saved the Emperor," *Far Eastern Affairs* 38, no. 4 (2010): 136–139. See also Komatsu Midori, *Meiji Gaikō Hiwa* [The secret history of Meiji diplomacy] (Tokyo, 1966), 241.

19. MUKDEN

1. Lt. General Sir Ian Hamilton, on January 29, in General Staff War Office, in Hamilton, *The Russo-Japanese War: Reports from British Officers Attached to the Japanese and Russian Forces in the Field*, vol. 2 (London, 1908), 55.

2. Denis Warner and Peggy Warner, *The Tide at Sunrise: A History of the Russo-Japanese War, 1904–1905* (London, 2004), 461.

3. N. P. Linievich, *Russko-iaponskaya voina: iz dnevnikov A. N. Kuropatkina i N. P. Linievicha* [The Russo-Japanese War from the journals of N. P. Linievich and A. N. Kuropatkin] (Leningrad, 1925), 58–59, https://www.prlib.ru/en/node/363224.

4. Anton Denikin, *The Career of a Tsarist Officer: Memoirs, 1872–1916*, trans. Margaret Patoski (Minneapolis, 1975), 129. Linievich, *Russko-iaponskaya voina*, 58; Warner and Warner, *The Tide at Sunrise*, 461; Geoffrey Jukes, *The Russo-Japanese War, 1904–1905* (Oxford, 2002), 62.

5. Warner and Warner, *The Tide at Sunrise*, 459–462, 466.

6. The Russians refer to this as the Battle of Sandepu, after the village that was the object of the Russian offensive. The Japanese refer to it as the Battle of Heikoutai, for the site where they lost and then won the battle.

7. Warner and Warner, *The Tide at Sunrise*, 462–463.

8. Wilson gives 330,000 for Kuropatkin. H. W. Wilson, *Japan's Fight for Freedom*, vol. 2 (London, 1904), 1262–1263. Vladimir Zolotarev places Kuropatkin's force at 285,000 and Japan's at 200,000. See Vladimir Antonovich Zolotarev, *Tragediya na Dal'nem Vostoke*, [Tragedy in the Far East: The Russo-Japanese War of 1904–1905], 2 (Moscow, 2004), 562–563.

9. Tani Hisao, *Kimitsu Nichi-Ro Senshi* [Confidential history of the Russo-Japanese War] (Tokyo, 1966), 524–525.

10. The day before the offensive, Kuropatkin warned Grippenberg not to cross the Heikoutai line unless necessary. See Zolotarev, *Tragediya na Dal'nem Vostoke*, 563.

11. Linievich, *Russko-iaponskaya voina*, 60.

12. Wilson, *Japan's Fight*, 2:1228.

13. Warner and Warner, *The Tide at Sunrise*, 463.

14. Linievich, *Russko-iaponskaya voina*, 64.

15. Warner and Warner, *The Tide at Sunrise*, 464. Most of the region around Sandepu had been covered with a thin crust of ice, and thick fog confused the attacking troops. The commander of the Fourteenth Division of the Eighth Corps, S. I. Rusanov, received the good news that Sandepu was taken on the evening of the 26th. But it turned out that the Fourteenth Division had taken the village of Baotaizi, not Sandepu. See Zolotarev, *Tragediya na Dal'nem Vostoke*, 565.

16. Linievich, *Russko-iaponskaya voina*, 65.

17. Linievich, *Russko-iaponskaya voina*, 66–67. Stackelberg had initiated the offensive without permission from Grippenberg or Kuropatkin.

18. Wilson, *Japan's Fight*, 2:1232.

19. Tani, *Nichi-Ro Senshi*, 524–525.

20. Major Charles Lynch, ed., *Reports of Military Observers Attached to the Armies in Manchuria*, pt. 4 (Washington, DC, 1907), 391–392.

21. Lord Brooke, *An Eye-Witness in Manchuria* (London, 1905), 296. Tomita Zenjirō, with Kuroki's First Army in the east, wrote that "although the number of frostbite cases were fewer in comparison with the number of cases during the Sino-Japanese War, the cure rate for frostbite was still extremely low during the Russo-Japanese War." Ōe Shinobu, *Heishitachi no Nichiro Sensō: 500-tsū no gunji yūbin kara* [Soldiers of the Russo-Japanese War: Through 500 military letters] (Tokyo, 1988), 164–165.

22. Denikin, *Career of a Tsarist Officer*, 130.

23. Linievich, *Russko-iaponskaya voina*, 67.

24. Linievich, *Russko-iaponskaya voina*, 67.

25. Brooke, *Eye-Witness in Manchuria*, 297. On the increase in desertion, see Zolotarev, *Tragediya na Dal'nem Vostoke*, 566–567.

26. Linievich, *Russko-iaponskaya voina*, 69.

27. Rotem Kowner, *Historical Dictionary of the Russo-Japanese War* (London, 2017), 342.

28. Rotem Kowner qualifies this statement, writing that it was the longest land battle in military history until then (February 23–March 10, 1905). Kowner, *Historical Dictionary,* 245. An accurate count of the size of the two forces is elusive. Warner and Warner, *The Tide at Sunrise,* 466–467, gives for Russia 275,000 infantry and 16,000 cavalry, and for Japan 200,000 infantry and 7,350 cavalry. Geoffrey Jukes gives for Russia 275,000 infantry and 16,000 cavalry, and for Japan 200,000 infantry and 7,350 cavalry (*Russo-Japanese War,* 65). Bruce W. Menning gives only "total" figures of 276,000 for Russia and 270,000 for Japan (Menning, *Bayonets before Battle: The Imperial Russian Army, 1861–1914* [Bloomington, IN, 1992], 187). The consensus is about 275,000 infantry and 16,000 cavalry for Russia, and 200,000 infantry and 7,350 cavalry for Japan. The Russians had an advantage in artillery, with 1,219 pieces versus 992 for Japan.

29. Kuropatkin, *The Russian Army and the Japanese War,* 2 vols. (New York, 1909), 2:61. Linievich also noted in his journal on February 16 (OS, February 3) that Grippenberg "did not carry out orders from the commander in chief," and often "gave orders alongside or contrary to those given by Kuropatkin. He never reported anything to Kuropatkin, and in many cases, did not even ask his input or come to him for advice at all." Linievich, *Russko-iaponskaya voina,* 72.

30. Kuropatkin, *Russian Army,* 2:267.

31. Linievich, *Russko-iaponskaya voina,* 71–72.

32. Quoted in Warner and Warner, *The Tide at Sunrise,* 467.

33. Tani, *Kimitsu Nichi-Ro Senshi,* 562–563.

34. Kuropatkin, *Russian Army,* 2:269.

35. Wilson, *Japan's Fight,* 2:1264.

36. McCormick, *Tragedy of Russia,* 2:386.

37. Warner and Warner, *The Tide at Sunrise,* 467.

38. Linievich, *Russko-iaponskaya voina,* 76.

39. Linievich, *Russko-iaponskaya voina,* 74. See also Warner and Warner, *The Tide at Sunrise,* 468.

40. Linievich, *Russko-iaponskaya voina,* 76.

41. McCormick, *Tragedy of Russia,* 379.

42. Francis McCullagh, *With the Cossacks: Being the Story of an Irishman Who Rode with the Cossacks throughout the Russo-Japanese War* (London, 1906), 227.

43. Linievich diary entry for March 3 (OS February 18), 81.

44. McCullagh, *With the Cossacks,* 380–381.

45. Linievich, *Russko-iaponskaya voina,* 78; McCullagh, *With the Cossacks,* 293; Zolotarev, *Tragediya na Dal'nem Vostoke,* 570–571.

46. Linievich, *Russko-iaponskaya voina,*79.

47. Shiba Ryōtarō, *Clouds above the Hills: A Historical Novel of the Russo-Japanese War,* vol. 4, trans. Andrew Cobbing, ed. Phyllis Birnbaum (London, 2015), 65. The novel was originally published in eight volumes from 1868–1972. It was also made into a television series that aired on NHK (Nippon Hōsō Kyōkai) from 2009 to 2011.

48. Shiba, *Clouds Above the Hill,* 4:67.

49. Zolotarev, *Tragediya na Dal'nem Vostoke,* 570.

50. Ishimitsu Makiyo, *Bōkyō no Uta* [Songs of nostalgia] (Tokyo 2018), 73–74.

51. Ishimitsu, *Bōkyō no Uta,* 74–75.

52. Warner and Warner, *The Tide at Sunrise,* 474.

53. Linievich, *Russko-iaponskaya voina,* 86.

54. Linievich, *Russko-iaponskaya voina,* 81–82.

55. Linievich, *Russko-iaponskaya voina,* 86. See also Denikin, *Career of a Tsarist Officer,* 139; Warner and Warner, *The Tide at Sunrise,* 474; Wilson, *Japan's Fight,* 2:1296.

56. Warner and Warner, *The Tide at Sunrise*, 475.

57. McCullagh, *With the Cossacks*, 285.

58. McCullagh, *With the Cossacks*, 300–301.

59. Denikin noted that "by the 17th the Japanese offensive impulse was dissipating and the crisis had passed." Denikin, *Career of a Tsarist Officer*, 140.

60. Kobe Chronicles, *A Diary of the Russo-Japanese War*, 2 vols. (Kobe, 1904), 2:173.

61. Ishimitsu, *Bōkyō no Uta*, 86–87.

62. Kowner, *Historical Dictionary*, 247; Wilson, *Japan's Fight*, 2:1324–1325; Warner and Warner, *The Tide at Sunrise*, 480.

63. Warner and Warner, *The Tide at Sunrise*, 480.

64. Denikin, *Career of a Tsarist Officer*, 143.

65. Tani, *Nichi-Ro Senshi*, 632. Writing to John Hay on March 30 Roosevelt confided: "It looks as if the foreign powers did not want me to act as peacemaker. I certainly do not want to myself. I wish the Jap[anese] and Russians could settle it between themselves, and I should be delighted to have anyone except myself give them a jog to settle it." Elting E. Morison, ed., *The Letters of Theodore Roosevelt*, vol. 4 (Cambridge, 1951), 1150.

20. THE PORTSMOUTH TREATY AND KOREA

1. Shumpei Okamoto, *The Japanese Oligarchy and the Russo-Japanese War* (New York, 1904), 109.

2. Elting E. Morison, ed., *The Letters of Theodore Roosevelt* (Cambridge, 1951), 4:1115–1116.

3. Tyler Dennett, *Roosevelt and the Russo-Japanese War* (New York, 1925), 179.

4. Tyler Dennett, "American 'Good Offices' in Asia," *American Journal of International Law* 16, no. 1 (January 1922): 23.

5. Tani Hisao, *Kimitsu Nichi-Ro Senshi* [Confidential history of the Russo-Japanese War] (Tokyo, 1966), 564.

6. Tani, *Nichi-Ro Senshi*, 564–565.

7. Okamoto, *Japanese Oligarchy*, 111; Tani, *Nichi-Ro Senshi*, 564.

8. Cited in Okamoto, *Japanese Oligarchy*, 111.

9. Tani, *Nichi-Ro Senshi*, 564–565.

10. Okamoto, *Japanese Oligarchy*, 111; Raymond A. Esthus, *Double Eagle and Rising Sun: The Russians and the Japanese at Portsmouth in 1905* (Durham, NC, 1988), 31.

11. The occupation of Sakhalin began on July 7. The surrender of the island by Russian forces took place on July 31, and thus the entire island was in Japanese hands before the start of the Portsmouth Conference in early August. See Tani, *Nichi-Ro Senshi*, 566–567. See also Okamoto, *Japanese Oligarchy*, 223–224; H. W. Wilson, *Japan's Fight for Freedom*, vol. 1 (London, 1904), 1414–1416.

12. Esthus, *Double Eagle*, 31–32.

13. Okamoto, *Japanese Oligarchy*, 115–118.

14. Morinosuke Kajima, *The Diplomacy of Japan, 1894–1922*, vol. 2 (Tokyo, 1978), 231–232.

15. Morison, *Letters of Theodore Roosevelt*, 4:1158.

16. Morison, *Letters of Theodore Roosevelt*, 4:1156–1158.

17. Maurice Paléologue, *Three Critical Years: 1904,1905,1906* (New York, 1957), 112.

18. Paléologue, *Three Critical Years*, 125–126.

19. S. S. Oldenburg, *The Last Tsar: Nicholas II, His Reign and His Russia*, vol. 2 (Belgrade, 1939), 126–127.

20. Paléologue, *Three Critical Years*, 179–183.

21. Paléologue, *Three Critical Years*, 175–176.

22. Paléologue, *Three Critical Years*, 180; Raymond A. Esthus, "Nicholas II and the Russo-Japanese War," *Russian Review* 40, no. 4 (October 1981): 400.

23. Esthus, "Nicholas II," 400–401.

24. Kajima, *Diplomacy of Japan*, 2:217; Paléologue, *Three Critical Years*, 201.

25. Paléologue, *Three Critical Years*, 257; Esthus, "Nicholas II," 403–404.

26. Ishimitsu Makiyo, *Bōkyō no Uta* [Songs of nostalgia] (Tokyo 2018), 87–88.

27. Esthus, *Double Eagle*, 40.

28. M. A. de Wolfe Howe, *George von Lengerke Meyer: His Life and Public Services* (New York, 1920), 212–213.

29. Oldenburg, *Last Tsar*, 2:129.

30. Esthus, "Nicholas II," 405. Kuropatkin was also fiercely opposed to peace. See N. P. Linievich, *Russko-iaponskaya voina: iz dnevnikov A. N. Kuropatkina i N. P. Linievicha* [The Russo-Japanese War from the journals of N. P. Linievich and A. N. Kuropatkin] (Leningrad, 1925), 92.

31. Esthus, "Nicholas II," 405; Oldenburg, *Last Tsar*, 2:129.

32. Howe, *George von Lengerke Meyer*, 159, 161.

33. Sergei Witte, *The Memoirs of Count Witte*, trans. Sidney Harcave (Armonk, 1990), 421. Ambassador to Italy Nikolai Valarianovich Muravev was the nephew of the renown Count Nikolai Muravev-Amursky. He was not related to the former foreign minister Mikhail Nikolayevich Muravev who died in 1900.

34. Witte, *Memoirs*, 426.

35. Witte, *Memoirs*, 166, 425–426.

36. Cited in Okamoto, *Japanese Oligarchy*, 120–121.

37. Shumpei Okamoto, "A Phase of Meiji Japan's Attitude toward China: The Case of Komura Jutarō," *Modern Asian Studies* 13, no. 3 (1979): 435.

38. Okamoto, "A Phase," 436.

39. Esthus, *Double Eagle*, 59.

40. Cited in Esthus, *Double Eagle*, 59–60.

41. Shinobu reports a massacre of 180 Russian POWs on the island on August 31, well after General Lipunov surrendered to the Japanese. Araya Shintaku, a reserve officer of the Konoe Third Infantry Regiment of the Japanese First Army (Kuroki) assigned to POW guard duty in Korsakov, wrote that on August 15 his company received a special mission to eliminate remnants of the defeated Russian troops holed up on the western coast of the island. See Ōe Shinobu, *Heishitachi no Nichi-Ro Senso: 500-tsu o gunji yubin kara* [Soldiers of the Russo-Japanese War: Through 500 military letters] (Tokyo, 1988), 235–236.

42. Okamoto, *Japanese Oligarchy*, 118.

43. Esthus, "Nicholas II," 408.

44. Witte, *Memoirs*, 440.

45. Esthus, "Nicholas II," 307.

46. See Kajima, *Diplomacy of Japan*, 2:331–332; Vladimir Korostovets, *Mirniye Peregovori v Portsmutye v 1905 godu* [The Peace Talks in Portsmouth in 1905], vol. 3 (Saint Petersburg, 1918), 66.

47. Meyer diary, George von Lengerke Meyer Papers, box 2, LOC.

48. See Dennett, *Roosevelt*, 256. On Kaneko and Roosevelt, see Matsumura Masayashi, "Theodore Roosevelt and the Portsmouth Peace Conference: The Riddle and Ripple of His Forbearance," in *Rethinking the Russo-Japanese War, 1904–5*, vol. 1, *Centennial Perspectives*, ed. Rotem Kowner (Leiden, 2007), 50–60.

49. Roosevelt might not have wanted to inform the Japanese of the tsar's concession on southern Sakhalin because Nicholas was notoriously indecisive. See Tosh Minohara, "The 'Rat

Minister' Komura Juntarō and U.S.-Japan Relations," in *The Russo-Japanese War in Global Perspective: World War Zero*, vol. 2, ed. David Wolff et al. (Leiden, 2006), 2:563; Dennett, *Roosevelt*, 283.

50. Kajima, *Diplomacy of Japan*, 2:345–346.

51. Cyrus Adler, *Jacob H. Schiff: His Life and Letters*, vol. 1 (New York, 1928), 231–232. See also Richard Smethurst, "American Capital and Japan's Victory in the Russo-Japanese War," in *Rethinking the Russo-Japanese War, 1904–5*, vol. 2, *The Nichinan Papers*, ed. John W. M. Chapman and Chiharu Inaba (Leiden, 2007), 63–72; Matsukata Masayoshi, "Korekiyo Takahashi and Jacob Schiff after the Russo-Japanese War of 1904–5," *Studies in International Relations* (Tokyo) 23, no. 3 (2003): 15–42; Gary Dean Best, "Financing a War: Jacob H. Schiff and Japan, 1904–5," *American Jewish Historical Quarterly* 61, no. 4 (June 1972): 313–324.

52. Tosh, "'Rat Minister' Komura," 563.

53. Kajima, *Diplomacy of Japan*, 2:349–350.

54. Tani, *Kimitsu Nichi-Ro Senshi*, 663.

55. Cited in Esthus, *Double Eagle*, 157. The battle of Minatogawa is famous in Japanese mythology for the loyalty displayed to the emperor in the face of certain death.

56. Tosh, "'Rat Minister' Komura," 563–564.

57. Korostovets, *Mirniye Peregovori*, 73–74.

58. Witte, *Memoirs*, 440.

59. Komatsu Midori, *Meiji Gaikō Hiwa* [Secret stories of Meiji diplomacy] (Tokyo, 1966), 220. See also Dennett, *Roosevelt*, 260–261.

60. Korostovets, *Mirniye Peregovori*, 74.

61. Esthus, "Nicholas II," 410.

62. Korostovets, *Mirniye Peregovori*, 78–79.

63. Esthus, *Double Eagle*, 164.

64. Korostovets, *Mirniye Peregovori*, 79

65. Eki Hioki to Horace Allen, September 8, 1905, Horace Newton Allen Papers, box 3, letterpress copy books no. 1–2, MNN ZZ-23704-2, New York Public Library.

66. Korostovets, *Mirniye Peregovori*, 80.

67. There is no hard evidence to suggest that Roosevelt did this deliberately to undermine Japan; more probably he did not altogether take the tsar at his word. Had he passed on this information to the Japanese and it proved untrue, the entire peace process would have been ruined. See Tosh, "'Rat Minister' Komura," 565.

68. Boris Pak, *Rossiia i Koreia* [Russia and Korea] (Moscow, 2004), 374.

69. David P. Fields, *Foreign Friends: Syngman Rhee, American Exceptionalism, and the Division of Korea* (Lexington, 2019), 29–35. See also Michael Finch, *Min Yong-hwan: A Political Biography* (Honolulu, 2002), 166; Robert Oliver, *Syngman Rhee: The Man behind the Myth* (New York, 1954), 75; *Yun Ch'i-ho Ilgi* [Diary of Yun Chi-ho], vol. 6 (Seoul, 1903–1906), 51–52.

70. Fields, *Foreign Friends*, 3.

71. CIK, 26 kwan (171) [12829–12832], no. 268, Hayashi to Katsura, July 13, 1905, http://db.history.go.kr/item/level.do?setId=20&itemId=jh&synonym=off&chinessChar=on&page=1&pre_page=1&brokerPagingInfo=&position=7&levelId=jh_026r_0010_1700.

72. Morison, *Letters of Theodore Roosevelt*, 4:1112.

73. CIK, 26 kwan (9) [12960], A. W. Lucci report, June 19, 1905, http://db.history.go.kr/item/level.do?itemId=jh&levelId=jh_026_0090_0090&types=0.

74. Pak, *Rossiia i Koreia*, 374–375.

75. Pak, *Russko-iaponskaya voina*, 238–240.

76. Pak, *Russko-iaponskaya voina*, 239–240; Pak, *Rossiia i Koreia*, 376–377.

77. Kirk W. Larsen and Joseph Seeley, "Simple Conversation or Secret Treaty? The Taft-Katsura Memorandum in Korean Historical Memory," *Journal of Korean Studies* 19, no. 1 (Spring 2014): 61.

78. Esthus, *Double Eagle,* 93.

79. Douglas Howland, "Sovereignty and the Laws of War: International Consequences of Japan's 1905 Victory over Russia," *Law and History Review* 29, no. 1 (February 2011): 53–97.

80. *Meiji Tennō Ki,* vol. 11 (Tokyo, 1968–1977), 375–385.

81. CIK, 26 kwan (16) [12916], Kurozawa Kurasaku to Kumagai Yoritaro, September 23, 1905, http://db.history.go.kr/item/level.do?setId=75&itemId=jh&synonym=off&chinessChar=on&page=1&pre_page=1&brokerPagingInfo=&position=48&levelId=jh_026r_0040_0160.

82. CIK, 26 kwan (16) [12916], Kurozawa Kurasaku to Kumagai Yoritaro, September 23, 1905.

83. Eulsa refers to the year 1905. It is the forty-second year of the Sexagenarian cycle year of the Korean calendar.

84. CIK, 22 kwan (3) [12670], Itō's journal of his meeting with Emperor Kojong, November 2–December 1, 1905, http://db.history.go.kr/item/level.do?setId=24&itemId=jh&synonym=off&chinessChar=on&page=1&pre_page=1&brokerPagingInfo=&position=1&levelId=jh_025r_0070_0040. Hwang Hyŏn also described the meeting at the palace. See Hwang Hyŏn, *Maech'oˇn Yarok* [Collected works of Hwang Hyon] (Seoul, 2005), 4:250–252.

85. Hwang, *Maech'ŏn Yarok,* 257.

86. CIK, 24 kwan (108) [12627–12629], no. 258, Katsura to Hayashi, November 25, 1905, http://db.history.go.kr/item/level.do?setId=83&itemId=jh&synonym=off&chinessChar=on&page=1&pre_page=1&brokerPagingInfo=&position=27&levelId=jh_024r_0110_1080. Hayashi denied that any force was used or that Japanese soldiers entered the palace. CIK, 24 kwan (140) [12627–12629], no. 478, Hayashi to Katsura, November 28, 1905, http://db.history.go.kr/item/level.do?setId=83&itemId=jh&synonym=off&chinessChar=on&page=1&pre_page=1&brokerPagingInfo=&position=31&levelId=jh_024r_0110_1400. According to a Russian report, soon after Itō and Hasekawa arrived a palace sentry guard abruptly entered the emperor's chambers intending to assassinate Itō and was stopped by Korean officers. See *Rŏsiawa ilbonŭi chŏnjaeng kŭrigo hanbando* [The Russo-Japanese War and the Korean Peninsula] (Seoul, 2012), 199.

87. CIK, 24 kwan (66) [12627–12629], no. 246, Katsura to Hayashi, November 20, 1905, http://db.history.go.kr/item/level.do?setId=83&itemId=jh&synonym=off&chinessChar=on&page=1&pre_page=1&brokerPagingInfo=&position=23&levelId=jh_024r_0110_0660.

88. Chong-sik Lee, *The Politics of Korean Nationalism* (Berkeley, 1963), 76–77. While Hulbert was in Washington on Kojong's behalf, the Korean emperor was also soliciting help from the Russians. Pak, *Rossiia i Koreia,* 381–382.

89. Arthur Judson Brown, *Mastery of the Far East: The Story of Korea's Transformation and Japan's Rise to Supremacy in the Orient* (New York, 1919), 200.

90. Willard Dickerman Straight to Whitey, November 30, 1905, in Willard Dickerman Strait and Early U.S.-Korea Relations, Division of Rare and Manuscript Collection, Cornell University, https://rmc.library.cornell.edu/Straight/.

91. Hwang, *Maech'ŏn Yarok,* 4:262–265.

92. *Nŭngchi* was a traditional Chinese torture in which body parts are methodically removed with a knife over an extended period of time, ultimately resulting in death.

93. Chosŏn wangjo sillok [Annals of the Joseon Dynasty], Memorial of Ch'oe Ik-hyon, November 29, 1905 (lunar), http://sillok.history.go.kr/id/kza_14211029_004.

94. The effects of the Russo-Japanese War were galvanizing for young Chinese. Having been radicalized while studying in Japan, they looked to it as the model for China to follow. See Richard Howard, "Japan's Role in the Reform Program of Kang Youwei," in *Kang Youwei: A Biography and Symposium,* ed. Jung-Pang Lo (Tucson, AZ, 1967); Pamela Kyle Crossley, *The Wobbling Pivot: China since 1800* (Sussex, 2010), 144–145.

95. Dennett, "American 'Good Offices,'" 18.

96. Hwang, *Maech'ŏn Yarok,* 4:266–269; Finch, *Min Yong-hwan,* 175, and see 173–179 on Min's suicide and funeral.

97. Hwang, *Maech'ŏn Yarok,* 4:291, 262–274. Hwang provides many more examples of people who committed suicide in the aftermath of the signing of the Protectorate Treaty.

98. CIK, 24 kwan (181) [12627–12629], no. 124, Maruyama Shigetoshi to Hayashi, December 6, 1905, http://db.history.go.kr/item/level.do?setId=67&itemId=jh&synonym=off& chinessChar=on&page=1&pre_page=1&brokerPagingInfo=&position=7&levelId=jh_024r _0110_1810.

99. *Yun Ch'i-ho Ilgi,* 6:208–209.

100. Boris Pak, *Koreitsy v Rossiiskoi imperii (Dal'nevostochnyi period)* [Koreans in the Russian Empire (The Far East period)] (Moscow, 1993), 102–103. Many fewer Japanese settled in the north compared to the south. The north was much poorer than the rest of the country, prompting many Koreans to leave for Manchuria and the Russian Far East for economic reasons. See RICKH, 2:170–172.

101. On Ch'oe, see Pak, *Koreitsy v Rossiiskoi Imperii,* 164–166.

102. Pak, *Koreitsy v Rossiiskoi Imperii,* 168. On Yi Pŏm-un in Vladivostok, see CIK, 3 kwan (3) [12554], no. 5, Nomura [deputy director of commerce in Vladivostok] to Tsuruhara Sadakichi, May 14, 1907, http://db.history.go.kr/item/level.do?setId=271&itemId =jh&synonym=off&chinessChar=on&page=1&pre_page=1&brokerPagingInfo=&position =9&levelId=jh_093r_0060_0030.

103. *Yun Ch'i-ho Ilgi,* 6:174–175.

104. Kyung Moon Hwang notes that the new Japanese regime gave opportunities for advancement to members of the secondary status group, especially the *chungin* (commoner class). See Kyung Moon Hwang, *Beyond Birth: Social Status in the Emergence of Modern Korea* (Cambridge, MA, 2004), 347–349.

105. Song thus sought to differentiate the "substance of independence" from what he called "protected independence" (*poho tongip*) by prioritizing the reform of the government and the people's welfare over *formal* state sovereignty. See Yumi Moon, *Populist Collaborators: The Ilchinhoe and the Japanese Colonization of Korea, 1896–1910* (Ithaca, NY, 2013), 161; Carl F. Young, *Eastern Learning and the Heavenly Way: The Tonghak and Ch'ŏndogyo Movements and the Twilight of Korean Independence* (Honolulu, 2012), 104–105.

106. Song also reiterated Japan's language about securing "peace and security in Asia." CIK, 26 kwan (33) [12970–12972], Ilchinhoe bonbu [headquarters], November 12, 1905, http://db.history.go.kr/item/level.do?setId=280&itemId=jh&synonym=off&chinessChar =on&page=1&pre_page=1&brokerPagingInfo=&position=11&levelId=jh_026r_0100 _0330. See also Moon, *Populist Collaborators,* 141–142.

21. "ETERNAL PEACE AND SECURITY IN ASIA"

1. *Fortnightly Review,* June 1904, 964.

2. Masazo Ohkawa, "The Armaments Expansion Budgets and the Japanese Economy after the Russo-Japanese War," *Hitotsubashi Journal of Economics* 5, no. 2 (January 1965): 68–83.

3. Richard Chang, "The Failure of the Katsura-Harriman Agreement," *Journal of Asian Studies* 21, no. 1 (November 1961): 66–67.

4. Cyrus Adler, *Jacob Henry Schiff: A Biographical Sketch* (New York, 1921), 8–9. See also Larry Haeg, *Harriman vs. Hill: Wall Street's Great Railroad War* (Minneapolis, 2013), 41–64.

5. George Kennan, *E. H. Harriman: A Biography,* vol. 2 (New York, 1922), 1.

6. Lloyd C. Griscom, *Diplomatically Speaking* (New York, 1940), 263.

7. Kennan, *E. H. Harriman,* 2:5–7.

8. Chang, "Failure of the Katsura-Harriman Agreement," 67.

9. Naoko Shimazu, "Patriotic and Despondent: Japanese Society at War," *Russian Review* 67, no. 1 (January 2008): 47–48.

10. Griscom, *Diplomatically Speaking,* 264.

11. Chang, "Failure of the Katsura-Harriman Agreement," 68.

12. Kennan, *E. H. Harriman,* 2:14–15; Griscom, *Diplomatically Speaking,* 264.

13. Masayoshi Matsumura, *Baron Kaneko and the Russo-Japanese War (1904–05): A Study in the Public Diplomacy of Japan,* trans. Ian Ruxton (Morrisville, NC, 2009), 454–456; Chang, "Failure of the Katsura-Harriman Agreement," 71.

14. In 1904 Roosevelt instructed his Justice Department to bring suit against Harriman's Northern Securities Company, using the Sherman Anti-Trust Act. It was the first major trust busting of his administration. *Literary Digest,* October 12, 1912, 603–605. See also Haeg, *Harriman vs. Hill.*

15. The South Manchurian Railway was renamed by the Japanese after the war as the south branch of the Chinese Eastern Railway line, running from Changgchun to Port Arthur.

16. Chang, "Failure of the Katsura-Harriman Agreement," 71–72; Masayoshi, *Baron Kaneko,* 455–456.

17. Takihara Kogorō and Sergei Witte, "The Portsmouth Treaty: Official Documents," *American Journal of International Law* 1 (January 1907): 17–22. See also Frederick McCormick, "Japan, America and the Chinese Revolution," *Journal of Race Development* 3, no. 1 (July 1912): 43–54; Tyler Dennett, *Roosevelt and the Russo-Japanese War* (New York, 1925), 313; John V. A. MacMurray, ed., *Treaties and Agreements with and concerning China, 1894–1919,* vol. 1 (New York, 1921), 74–77.

18. Kennan, *E. H. Harriman,* 2:16–18.

19. Shumpei Okamoto, "A Phase of Meiji Japan's Attitude toward China: The Case of Komura Jutarō," *Modern Asian Studies* 13, no. 3 (1979): 455.

20. Jonathan D. Spence, *The Search for Modern China* (New York, 1990), 238–241; Daniel H. Bays, "Chinese Government Policies towards the Revolutionary Students in Japan after 1900s: Reassessment and Implications," *Journal of Asian History* 7, no. 2 (1973): 155.

21. Orville Schell and John Delury, *Wealth and Power: China's Long March to the Twenty-First Century* (New York, 2013), 151–152.

22. Mary Wright, ed., *China in Revolution: The First Phase, 1900–1913* (New Haven, CT, 1968), 3–4.

23. Bays, "Chinese Government Policies," 157–158.

24. Daniel Leese, "'Revolution': Conceptualizing Political and Social Change in the Late Qing Dynasty," *Oriens Extremus* 51 (2012): 25–61.

25. Spence, *Search for Modern China,* 240.

26. Sin-Kiong Wong, "Die for the Boycott and Nation: Martyrdom and the 1905 Anti-American Movement in China," *Modern Asian Studies* 35, no. 3 (2001): 565–588; Shih-Shan H. Ts'ai, "Reaction to Exclusion: The Boycott of 1905 and Chinese National Awakening," *Historian* 39, no. 1 (November 1976): 95–110.

27. Spence, *Search for Modern China,* 238; Akira Iriye, *Pacific Estrangement: Japanese and American Expansion, 1897–1911* (Cambridge, MA, 1972), 119.

28. The Chinese had even expressed a strong desire to participate in the Portsmouth negotiations but were assured by American minister to China W. W. Rockhill that Japan had no territorial ambitions in Manchuria. Hirakawa Sachiko, "Portsmouth Denied: The Chinese Attempt to Attend," in *The Russo-Japanese War in Global Perspective: World War Zero*, vol. 2, ed. David Wolff et al. (Leiden, 2006), 541.

29. "Memorandum by Mr. Hohler," November 22, 1904, in *British Documents on the Origins of the War, 1898–1914*, ed. G. P. Gooch and Harold Temperley (London, 1927), 4:64.

30. *NGB*, 38:1, 204.

31. *NGB*, 38:1, 204; the entire Sino-Japanese negotiations are at 38:202–406.

32. Asada Masafumi, "The China-Russia-Japan Military Balance in Manchuria, 1906–1918," *Modern Asian Studies* 44, no. 6 (November 2019): 1290.

33. John Albert White, *The Diplomacy of the Russo-Japanese War* (New Jersey, 1964), 335.

34. *NGB*, 38:1, 204.

35. *NGB*, 38:1, 204–23l; White, *Diplomacy*, 336; Asada, "China-Russia-Japan Military Balance," 1289–1290.

36. *NGB*, 38:1, 212.

37. Asada, "China-Russia-Japan Military Balance," 1290.

38. MacMurray, *Treaties and Agreements*, 1:554–555.

39. Komura also insisted that Japan be in charge of the railway line between Mukden and Hsinmuntun, to defend Manchuria. *NGB*, 38:1, 234–235.

40. *NGB*, 38:1, 237.

41. *NGB*, 38:1; White, *Diplomacy*, 337; MacMurray, *Treaties and Agreements*, 1:554.

42. Thomas F. Millard, *America and the Far Eastern Question* (New York, 1909), 177–178. On the cabinet meeting to resolve opposing views, see Masato Matsui, "The Russo-Japanese Agreement of 1907: Its Causes and the Progress of Negotiations," *Modern Asian Studies* 6, no. 1 (1972): 36.

43. Stewart Lone, *Army, Empire, Politics in Meiji Japan: The Three Careers of General Katsura Tarō* (New York, 2000), 123–124; Millard, *America and the Far Eastern Question*, 179–180; Yosaburo Takekoshi, *Prince Saionji* (Tokyo, 1933), 227–230.

44. M. A. DeWolfe Howe, *George von Lengerke Meyer: His Life and Public Services* (New York, 1920), 112; Dennett, *Roosevelt*, 310–311.

45. Dennett, *Roosevelt*, 311.

46. Matsui, "Russo-Japanese Agreement," 36.

47. Kennan, *E. H. Harriman*, 2:22.

48. *IHH*, 1:391–408, 392, 393–394.

49. *IHH*, 1:395–396.

50. *IHH*, 1:396.

51. *IHH*, 1:399–401.

52. *IHH*, 1:400–401, 407–408.

53. *IHH*, 1:408. Japan's policy toward Manchuria in 1905 signaled a *complete* reversal from what it had pursued before the war. Katsura made his position clear when he wrote to Itō on December 28, 1901: "If Japan desires to implement its policy of maintaining its prestige toward other countries, Japan cannot dominate any part of Manchuria or dominate it economically for Japan's own benefit." See *IHH*, 2:49–50 (append. 61).

54. Alvin D. Coox, *Nomohan: Japan against Russia* (Stanford, CA, 1985), 2; Lone, *Army, Empire*, 128. See also Ramon H. Myers, "Japanese Imperialism in Manchuria: The South Manchuria Railway Company, 1906," in *The Japanese Informal Empire in China, 1895–1937*, ed. Peter Duus et al. (Princeton, NJ, 1989), 101–132.

55. William C. Summers, *The Great Manchurian Purge of 1910–1911: The Geopolitics of an Epidemic Disease* (New Haven, CT, 2012), 45.

56. As president of Mantetsu, Gotō served in an advisory capacity to Governor-General Ōshima. See Yoshihisa Tak Matsusaka, *The Making of Japanese Manchuria, 1904–1932* (Cambridge, MA, 2001).

57. Just prior to the outbreak of the Sino-Japanese War, the Japanese navy had won organizational independence from the army and pressed for a position of seniority to determine the nation's strategic priorities. Navy Minister Yamamoto Gonnohyōe (Gombei) argued that a seaborne defense was much more likely to secure the nation's interests than one that was "static and land-oriented." Dismissing claims made by the army that Korea and Manchuria were vital links in Japan's security, Yamamoto even advocated abandoning them altogether. Like Alfred Thayer Mahan, Yamamoto referred to "command of the seas" as the essential component of imperial expansion, advocating the policy of "avoiding the continent and advancing on the seas" or a "southern advance" (*nanshin*) toward Southeast Asia as opposed to the army's alternative "northern advance" (*hokushin*) toward Manchuria. David C. Evans and Mark R. Peattie, *Kaigun: Strategy, Tactics and Technology in the Imperial Japanese Navy, 1887–1941* (Annapolis, MD, 1997), 133–151; S. C. M. Paine, *The Japanese Empire: Grand Strategy from the Meiji Restoration to the Pacific War* (Cambridge, 2017), 77–85.

58. On arguments for "peaceful expansionism," see Iriye Akira, "Heiwa-teki hatten shugi to Nihon" [The ideology of peace development in Japan], *Chūō Kōron*, October 1969, 74–94. See also Paine, *The Japanese Empire*.

59. Shin'ichi Kitaoka, "The Army as Bureaucracy: Japanese Militarism Revisited," *Journal of Military History* 57, no. 5 (October 1993): 74. See also Peter Duus, *The Abacus and the Sword: The Japanese Penetration of Korea, 1895–1910* (Berkeley, 1995), 203.

60. Millard, *America and the Far Eastern Question*, 261–262, 264.

61. Many members of the army general staff were strongly opposed to the resident-general of Korea having control over the Korean Garrison Army. See Ogawara Hiroyuki, "Nichirosensō to Nihon no Chōsen seisaku: Tōkan no guntaishiki-ken mondaini okeru bunbukan no tairitsu o chūshin ni" [Japan's Korea policy during the Russo-Japanese War: Focusing on the civil-military clash over the resident-general's right to command the military], *Chōsenshikenkyūkai ronbun-shū* 44 (October 2006): 49–51.

62. *IHH*, 1:314–316.

63. After the annexation of Korea in 1910, the Korean Garrison Army was first renamed the Chōsen Chūsatsugun, then the Japanese Korean Army (Chōsen-gun, literally "Korean military") in June 1918. Its main task was to protect Korea from possible Soviet incursions. See Matsuda Toshihiko, "Chōsen shokumin-chi ka no katei ni okeru keisatsu ikō (1904–1910)" [Police apparatus in the process of Korean colonization (1904–1910)], *Chōsenshi kenkyūkai ronbunshū*, 1993, 130–131.

64. This law stated that responsibility for the protection of the lines fell on each village and town, and that anyone who participated in the destruction or gave succor to the vandals was to be sentenced to death. See Matsuda, "Chōsen shokumin-chi," 131.

65. F. A. McKenzie, *The Tragedy of Korea* (London, 1908), 146, 152.

66. Homer Hulbert, *The Passing of Korea* (New York, 1906), 213–214. Koreans suffered the greatest indignity especially in matters of real estate. See also Thomas F. Millard, "When the Japanese Came," *New York Times*, May 25, 1908.

67. Hwang Hyŏn, *Maech'ŏn yarok* [Collected works of Hwang Hyon] (Seoul, 2005), 4:198.

68. CIK, 25 kwan (9) [12652], Head Office of the Ilchinhoe, January 6, 1906, http://db .history.go.kr/item/level.do?setId=9&itemId=jh&synonym=off&chinessChar=on&page =1&pre_page=1&brokerPagingInfo=&position=0&levelId=jh_025r_0030_0090.

69. Pak, *Rossiia i Koreia*, 383–386, and see 387–388 on the concession resolution.

70. Alexander Izvolsky, *The Memoirs of Alexander Izvolsky*, trans. C. L. Seeger (London, n.d.), 20–21.

71. Pak, *Rossiia i Koreia*, 392.

72. McKenzie, *Tragedy of Korea*, 157.

73. Pak, *Rossiia i Koreia*, 394.

74. McKenzie *Tragedy of Korea*, 157–158.

75. Komatsu Midori, *Meiji Gaikō Hiwa* [The secret history of Meiji diplomacy] (Tokyo, 1966), 242, 247. See also Pak, *Rossiia i Koreia*, 394–396.

76. Pak, *Rossiia i Koreia*, 396–397.

77. Itō was not taken completely by surprise by these events. See CIK, 3 kwan (15) [22315], no. 31, Itō to Hayashi, May 19, 1907, http://db.history.go.kr/item/level.do?setId=66&itemId=jh&synonym=off&chinessChar=on&page=1&pre_page=1&brokerPagingInfo=&position=15&levelId=jh_093r_0150_0150.

78. CIK, 3 kwan (2) [12556], no. 1661, Ikeda to Furuya Hisatsuna, July 12, 1907, http://db.history.go.kr/item/level.do?setId=66&itemId=jh&synonym=off&chinessChar=on&page=1&pre_page=1&brokerPagingInfo=&position=4&levelId=jh_093r_0050_0020.

79. George Trumbull Ladd, *In Korea with Marquis Ito* (New York, 1908), 417.

80. CIK, 3 kwan (2) [12556], no. 1661, Ikeda to Furuya Hisatsuna, July 12, 1907, http://db.history.go.kr/item/level.do?setId=66&itemId=jh&synonym=off&chinessChar=on&page=1&pre_page=1&brokerPagingInfo=&position=4&levelId=jh_093r_0050_0020.

81. Komatsu, *Meiji Gaikō Hiwa*, 249; CIK, 3 kwan (22) [12556], no. 37, Ikeda to Furuya, July 24, 1907, http://db.history.go.kr/item/level.do?setId=66&itemId=jh&synonym=off&chinessChar=on&page=1&pre_page=1&brokerPagingInfo=&position=10&levelId=jh_093r_0050_0220. According to Komatsu, the normally mild-mannered Itō blew up when told what Kojong had done. "It was the only time [I saw him] really angry," Komatsu recalled. Prime Minister Yi Wan-yong offered to tender his and his cabinet's resignations, but Itō stopped him, saying Kojong had acted independently of the cabinet and had "listened to some bad advice." To soothe matters, Yi offered to force Kojong's abdication "so as to appease Itō." See Komatsu, *Meiji Gaikō Hiwa*, 249.

82. Matsui, "Russo-Japanese Agreement," 47. On the United States and Manchuria, see Walter LaFeber, *The New Cambridge History of American Foreign Relations*, vol. 2 (Cambridge, 2013), 217–220; Matsusaka, *Making of Japanese Manchuria*, 122–125.

83. News of Kojong's abdication was received violently. See CIK, 3 kwan (18) [12556], Ikeda to Furuya, July 23, 1907, http://db.history.go.kr/item/level.do?setId=66&itemId=jh&synonym=off&chinessChar=on&page=1&pre_page=1&brokerPagingInfo=&position=9&levelId=jh_093r_0050_0180. Following Sunjong's ascension to the throne, Kojong was given the title "retired emperor" [太上皇帝]. See CIK, 3 kwan (10) [12556], no. 24, Ikeda to Furuya, July 21, 1907, http://db.history.go.kr/item/level.do?itemId=jh&levelId=jh_093r_0050_0100&types=r.

84. Chang Hui, *Ch'oehu ŭi mama yunbi* [Her last Majesty, Queen Min] (Seoul, 1966); Christine Kim, "Politics and Pageantry in Protectorate Korea (1905–1910): The Imperial Progress of Sunjong," *Journal of Asian Studies* 68, no. 3 (August 2009): 838; Robert Neff, "Sunjong's Unhappiness Shadows Turbulent Last Decades of Yi Dynasty," *Korea Times*, May 16, 2011.

85. The idea of disbanding the army had already been brought up in 1905. See Ogawara Hiroyuki, "Nichirosensō to Nihon no Chōsen seisaku," 58.

86. Boris Pak, *Koreitsy v Rossiiskoi imperii (Dal'nevostochnyi period)* [Koreans in the Russian Empire (The Far East period)] (Moscow, 1993), 172.

87. Matsusaka, *Making of Japanese Manchuria*, 97; Evans and Peattie, *Kaigun*, 135–141.

88. In 1919, following a reorganization, these became known as the Kantō Army. Its size remained at approximately 10,400 until 1931. See Asada, "China-Russia-Japan Military Balance," 1291.

89. Iriye, *Pacific Estrangement*, 91–125; Kitaoka Shin'ichi, "The Strategy of the Maritime Nation: From Yukichi Fukuzawa to Shigeru Yoshida," in *Conflicting Currents: Japan and the United States in the Pacific*, ed. Williamson Murray and Tomoyuki Ishizu (Santa Barbara, 2010), 39–44.

22. ANNEXATION

1. Boris Pak, *Rossiia i Koreia* [Russia and Korea] (Moscow, 2004), 400.

2. Akira Iriye, *Pacific Estrangement: Japanese and American Expansion, 1897–1911* (Cambridge, MA, 1972), 155.

3. John H. Latané, *America as a World Power, 1897–1907* (New York, 1907), 319.

4. *New York Times*, June 10, 1907.

5. *New York Times*, January 31, 1907.

6. David Brudnoy, "Race and the San Francisco School Board: Contemporary Evaluations," *California Historical Quarterly* 50, no. 3 (September 1971): 297. See also *Theodore Roosevelt: An Autobiography* (New York, 1916), 393–394.

7. *New York Times*, January 31, 1907.

8. Iriye, *Pacific Estrangement*, 135.

9. *North China Herald*, January 31, 1908.

10. Brudnoy, "Race and the San Francisco School Board," 298.

11. Lee Houchins and Chang-su Houchins, "The Korean American Experience in America," *Pacific Historical Review* 43, no. 4 (November 1974): 548.

12. Wayne Patterson, *The Ilse: First-Generation Korean Immigrants in Hawaii, 1903–1974* (Honolulu, 2000); Patterson, *The Korean Frontier in America: Immigrations to Hawaii, 1896–1910* (Honolulu, 1988).

13. In April 1908, however, the Japanese enforced press restrictions, and Korean newspapers published abroad were seized. See CIK, 4 kwan (103) [12688–12690], no. 36, Matsui Shigeru to Nabeshima Keijiro, December 10, 1908, http://db.history.go.kr/item/level.do?itemId=jh&levelId=jh_094r_0090_1030&types=r.

14. Syngman Rhee refused to act as interpreter at the trial, causing friction with An, possibly because he disapproved of the violent methods used in this case. David Fields, *Foreign Friends: Syngman Rhee, American Exceptionalism, and the Division of Korea* (Honolulu, 2019), 110; Houchins and Houchins, "Korean American Experience," 557.

15. CIK, 1 kwan (15) [12577], no. 127, Chinda to Tsuruhara, October 26, 1907, http://db.history.go.kr/item/level.do?itemId=jh&levelId=jh_091r_0040_0150&types=r.

16. CIK, kwan (19) [12557], no. 43, Terauchi to Sone, August 21, 1908, http://db.history.go.kr/item/level.do?setId=20&itemId=jh&synonym=off&chinessChar=on&page=1&pre_page=1&brokerPagingInfo=&position=15&levelId=jh_091r_0040_0190.

17. *New York Times*, July 13, 1908. On the Democratic Convention and Asian immigration, see The American Presidency Project, 1908 Democratic Party Platform, https://www.presidency.ucsb.edu/documents/1908-democratic-party-platform.

18. According to the organization's charter, any Korean man over the age of fifteen and "capable of good conduct" living in Korea or abroad could become a KNA member. See B. D. Pak, *Koreitsy v Rossiiskoi imperii (Dal'nevostochnyi period)* [Koreans in the Russian Empire (The Far East period)] (Moscow, 1993), 202–203.

19. Houchins and Houchins, "Korean Experience in America," 565–566.

20. The organization peaked in 1915, when there broke out a protracted factional controversy between Rhee and An Chang-ho and Pak Yong-nam, mainly over what means should be used to achieve Korean independence. Pak favored a militant approach, Rhee a slower course emphasizing education and diplomacy. Houchins and Houchins, "Korean Experience in America," 566–567; Fields, *Foreign Friends,* 110.

21. Ogawara Hiroyuki, "Nichirosensō to Nihon no Chōsen seisaku: Tōkan no guntai-shiki-ken mondai ni okeru bunbukan no tairitsu o chūshin ni" [Japan's Korea policy during the Russo-Japanese War: Focusing on the civil-military clash over the resident general's right to command the military], *Chōsenshikenkyūkai ronbun-shū* 44 (October 2006): 52–53.

22. Itō believed that Manchuria and Korea should be viewed as separate issues, because they presented different problems. Kodama, however, thought that the issues of Manchuria and Korea were inseparable, even arguing that the Japanese Garrison Army should be based not in Seoul but in P'yŏngyang, so as to expand its control northward and southward. Ogawara, "Nichirosensō to Nihon no Chōsen seisaku," 50–51.

23. CIK, 3 kwan (30) [12644], no. 14, Wakami Toraji to Furuya Hisatsuna, August 3, 1907, http://db.history.go.kr/item/level.do?setId=372&itemId=jh&synonym=off&chiness
Char=on&page=1&pre_page=1&brokerPagingInfo=&position=33&levelId=jh_093r_0090
_0300.

24. CIK, 3 kwan (2) [12633], no. 15, Itō to Chinda Sutemi, Vice Minister of Foreign Affairs, July 28, 1907, http://db.history.go.kr/item/level.do?setId=372&itemId=jh&synonym
=off&chinessChar=on&page=1&pre_page=1&brokerPagingInfo=&position=21&levelId
=jh_093r_0080_0020.

25. CIK, 3 kwan (2) [12633], no. 15, Itō to Chinda, July 28, 1907.

26. CIK, 3 kwan (30) [12644], no. 14, Wakami Toraji to Furuya Hisatsuna, August 3, 1907, http://db.history.go.kr/item/level.do?setId=372&itemId=jh&synonym=off&chiness
Char=on&page=1&pre_page=1&brokerPagingInfo=&position=33&levelId=jh_093r_0090
_0300. Also, CIK, 3 kwan (11) [12633], no. 11, Itō to Chinda, August 1, 1907, http://db
.history.go.kr/item/level.do?setId=372&itemId=jh&synonym=off&chinessChar=on&page
=1&pre_page=1&brokerPagingInfo=&position=31&levelId=jh_093r_0080_0110. See also Eugene Kim, "Japanese Rule in Korea (1905–1910): A Case Study," *Proceedings of the American Philosophical Society* 106, no. 1 (February1962): 58; F. A. McKenzie, *The Tragedy of Korea* (New York, 1908), 161–162.

27. CIK, 4 kwan (99) [12842–12844], Hasegawa to Itō, August 14, 1907, http://db
.history.go.kr/item/level.do?setId=372&itemId=jh&synonym=off&chinessChar=on&page
=1&pre_page=1&brokerPagingInfo=&position=57&levelId=jh_094r_0050_0990; Eugene Kim, "Japanese Rule in Korea," 58; George Trumbull Ladd, *In Korea with Marquis Ito* (New York, 1908), 439.

28. Kim, "Japanese Rule in Korea," 59.

29. According to a 1906 Russian report, southern Korea accounted for approximately 65 percent of the entire Korean population; there were few Japanese settlers in the north. See "1905 nyŏn malkwa 1906 nyŏn ch'o han'guksanghwang kaegwan" [An Overview of the Korean situation in late 1905 and early 1906] (Seoul, 2012); *RICKH,* 169–174.

30. Igor Saveliev, "Military Diaspora: Korean Immigrants and Guerrillas in Early Twentieth-Century Korea," *Forum of International Development Studies* 26 (March 2004): 149.

31. Pak, *Koreitsy v Rossiiskoi Imperii,* 166–167. On other organized groups, see Kim, "Japanese Rule in Korea," 59.

32. E. Smirnov, "Report 4.1, no. 241," May 14, 1908, *RICKH,* 264–265.

33. Pak *Koreitsy v Rossiiskoi Imperii,* 167.

34. E. Smirnov, "Report 4.6, no. 205," June 26, 1908, *RICKH,* 276–277.

35. Pak, *Koreitsy v Rossiiskoi Imperii*, 168. In 1907 there were 203 altercations between the Righteous Army and the Japanese garrison and *kenpeitai* forces in Korea. By 1908 the number increased to 1817, then tapered off to 779 in 1909. See Shin Ch'ang-u, *Singminji chosŏnŭi kyŏngch'algwa minjungsegye 1894–1919: 'Kŭndae'wa 'chŏnt'ong'ŭl tullŏssan chŏngch'imunhwa*] [Colonial Chosŏn police and the world of the Korean masses, 1894–1919: The political culture surrounding "modern" and "tradition"] (Seoul, 2019), 322–323; Pak, *Rossiia i Koreia*, 402.

36. Pak, *Koreitsy v Rossiiskoi Imperii*, 168.

37. E. Smirnov, "Report 4.7, no. 347," July 20, 1908, *RICKH*, 280–283.

38. CIK, 3 kwan (3) [12619], no. 5, Normura to Tsuruhara, May 14, 1907, http://db
.history.go.kr/item/level.do?setId=271&itemId=jh&synonym=off&chinessChar=on&page
=1&pre_page=1&brokerPagingInfo=&position=9&levelId=jh_093r_0060_0030. Smirnov
also reported that Yi Pŏm-yun had requested compensation from Russia as payment for efforts in the war. See Smirnov, "Report 4.10," June 16, 1910, *RICKH*, 297–298.

39. Pak, *Koreitsy v Rossiiskoi Imperii*, 167–168; E. Smirnov, "Report 4.6, no. 205," June 26, 1908, *RICKH, 274.*

40. Pak, *Koreitsy v Rossiiskoi Imperii*, 170. On Unterberger and Russian settlement of Priamursky Krai, see Pak, *Koreitsy v Rossiiskoi Imperii*, 107–108.

41. Pak, *Koreitsy v Rossiiskoi Imperii*, 170. See also E. Smirnov, "Report 4.9, no. 54," February 6, 1909, *RICKH*, 290–294.

42. Smirnov, "Report 4.8, no. 2057," August 24, 1908, *RICKH*, 286–289.

43. Pak, *Rossiia i Koreia*, 403.

44. Ōe Shinobu, *Heishitachi no nichiro sensō: 500-tsū no gunji yūbin kara* [Soldiers' Russo-Japanese War: Through 500 military letters] (Tokyo, 1988), 71–77.

45. McKenzie, *Tragedy of Korea*, 193.

46. McKenzie, *Tragedy of Korea*, 207.

47. Donald N. Clark, *Living Dangerously in Korea: The Western Experience, 1900–1905* (Norwalk, 2003), 35.

48. Clark, *Living Dangerously*, 35–36.

49. E. Smirnov, "Report 4.4. no. 297," June 19, 1908, *RICKH*, 266–268.

50. E. Smirnov, "Report. 4.9, no. 54," 6 February 1909, *RICKH*, 290–294. As would continue to be the case through the 1910s and 1920s, Korean partisan units often fought one another with the same gusto as they fought the Japanese, and often turned to banditry. See Michael Gelb, "An Early Soviet Ethnic Deportation: The Far-Eastern Koreans," *Russian Review* 54, no. 3 (July 1995): 393.

51. E. Smirnov, "Report 4.9, no. 54," February 6, 1909, *RICKH*, 290–294.

52. Ministry of National Defense, "1905 nyŏn malkwa 1906 nyŏn cho hankuk sanghwang kaekwan" [Survey of the Korean situation in late 1905 and early 1906], *RICKH*, 169–174; Kim, "Japanese Rule in Korea," 59; Peter Duus, *The Abacus and the Sword: The Japanese Penetration of Korea, 1895–1910* (Berkeley, 1995), 237–239.

53. CIK, 26 kwan (10) [12973], Uchida to Ito, April 15, 1907, http://db.history.go.kr
/item/level.do?setId=67&itemId=jh&synonym=off&chinessChar=on&page=1&pre_page
=1&brokerPagingInfo=&position=12&levelId=jh_026r_0110_0100.

54. Hwang Kyung Moon, *Beyond Birth: Social Status in the Emergence of Modern Korea* (Cambridge, MA, 2004). See also Yumi Moon, *Populist Collaborators: The Ilchinhoe and the Japanese Colonization of Korea, 1896–1910* (Ithaca, NY, 2013), 83–100; Jung Min, "The Shadow of Anonymity: The Depiction of Northerners in Eighteenth-Century 'Hearsay Accounts' [*kimun*]," in *The Northern Region of Korea: History, Identity, and Culture*, ed. Sun Joo Kim (Seattle, 2010), 93–115.

55. Moon, *Populist Collaborators*, 46–80.

56. William Newton Blair and Bruce F. Hunt, *The Korean Pentecost and the Sufferings Which Followed* (East Peoria, 2015), 63.

57. Arun Jones, "The Great Revival of 1907 as a Phenomenon in Korean Religions," *Journal of World Christianity* 2, no.1 (2009): 92.

58. Blair and Hunt, *Korean Pentecost*, 77–78.

59. Clark, *Living Dangerously*, 39.

60. Blair and Hunt, *Korean Pentecost*, 71–72; Jones, "Great Revival," 93–94.

61. Clark, *Living Dangerously*, 39.

62. Cited in Kenneth M. Wells, *New God, New Nation: Protestants and Self-Reconstruction Nationalism in Korea, 1896–1937* (Honolulu, 1990), 67.

63. Wells, *New God*, 67–68.

64. Pak, *Koreitsy v Rossiiskoi Imperii*, 205–206.

65. Komatsu Midori, *Meiji Gaikō Hiwa* [The secret history of Meiji diplomacy] (Tokyo, 1966), 253. Itō departed Korea on July 15.

66. Christine Kim, "Politics and Pageantry in Protectorate Korea (1905–10): The Imperial Progress of Sungjong," *Journal of Asian Studies* 68, no. 3 (August 2009): 842–843.

67. *Japan Times,* January 19, 1909.

68. Cited in Stewart Lone, "The Japanese Annexation of Korea, 1910: The Failure of East Asian Co-Prosperity," *Modern Asian Studies* 25, no. 1 (1991): 156.

69. *Japan Times,* January 16, 1909.

70. Lone, "Japanese Annexation of Korea," 157.

71. Lone, "Japanese Annexation of Korea," 157.

72. Kim, "Politics and Pageantry," 851.

73. *Japan Times,* January 29, 1909.

74. *Japan Times,* March 2, 1909.

75. *Japan Times,* March 2, 1909.

76. Komatsu, *Meiji Gaikō Hiwa,* 251.

77. Komatsu, *Meiji Gaikō Hiwa,* 255.

78. Herbert Bix, *Hirohito and the Making of Modern Japan* (New York, 2000), 35; Kim, "Politics and Pageantry," 843.

79. Gotō was selected by Kodama in February 1898 to head the Minseibu [Civil Administrative Bureau], a position he held until 1906. See Chang Han-Yu and Ramon H. Myers, "Japanese Colonial Development Policy in Taiwan, 1895–1896: A Case of Bureaucratic Entrepreneurship," *Journal of Asian Studies* 22, no. 4 (August 1963): 433–449.

80. Komatsu, *Meiji Gaikō Hiwa,* 262–263. See also *Japan Times,* January 6, 1909; Patrick Fuliang Shan, *Yuan Shikai: A Reappraisal* (Vancouver, 2018), 124–126.

81. Japan had claimed that the entire Kando/Jiandao area was Korean territory China had "illegally" occupied. See James Francis Abbott, "The Sino-Japanese Convention of 1909 and Its Significance," *Bulletin of Washington University,* February 1910, 85–110. See also *North China Herald,* October 9, 1909.

82. Komatsu, *Meiji Gaikō Hiwa,* 262–263; Count Vladimir Nikolaevich Kokovtsov, *Out of My Past: The Memoirs of Count Kokovtsov,* ed. H. H. Fisher, trans. Laura Matveev (Stanford, CA, 1935), 234.

83. *NGB,* 42:1, 197; Kokovtsov, *Out of My Past,* 233–234. Kokovtsov writes that An Chung-gŭn arrived on October 24.

84. Pak, *Koreitsy v Rossiiskoi Imperii,* 178–179.

85. Pak, *Koreitsy v Rossiiskoi Imperii,* 176–177. According to a Japanese report, the assassination plot was hatched sometime in July 1909. CIK, 7 kwan (331) [12761–12764],

Matsui Shigeru to Ishiukza Eizō, January 7, 1910, http://db.history.go.kr/item/level.do?setId
=87&itemId=jh&synonym=off&chinessChar=on&page=1&pre_page=1&brokerPagingInfo
=&position=70&levelId=jh_097r_0010_3310.

86. Kokovtsov, *Out of My Past*, 237.

87. CIK, 7 kwan (14) [12761–12764], no. 155, Komura Jutarō to Sone Arasuke, October 27, 1909, http://db.history.go.kr/item/level.do?setId=87&itemId=jh&synonym=off
&chinessChar=on&page=1&pre_page=1&brokerPagingInfo=&position=8&levelId=jh_097r
_0010_0140.

88. *NGB*, 42:1, 196–197; *New York Times*, October 27, 1909.

89. Yoshitake Oka, *Five Political Leaders of Modern Japan: Itō Hirobumi, Ōkuma Shigenobu, Hara Takashi, Inukai Tsuyoshi, and Saionji Kimmochi*, trans. Andrew Fraser and
Patricia Murray (Tokyo, 1979), 41.

90. Komatsu, *Meiji Gaikō Hiwa*, 271–272.

91. Komatsu, *Meiji Gaikō Hiwa*, 263–264; Pak, *Rossiia i Koreia*, 405.

92. E. W. Edwards, "Great Britain and the Manchurian Railways Question, 1909–
1909," *English Historical Review*, no. 321 (October 1966): 749. Louis Grave, *Willard Straight
in the Orient: With Illustration from His Sketch Books* (New York, 1922), 45.

93. Pak, *Koreitsy v Rossiiskoi Imperii*, 179–181. According to Japanese data, in July 1909
alone there were seventy-eight clashes between Japanese troops and *ŭibyŏng* detachments
with the main rebel headquarters in Vladivostok (173–174). Peter Duus notes that the insurgency also threatened the interests of the landholding elites in Seoul. Duus, *Abacus and the
Sword*, 225.

94. Ernst Batson Price, *The Russo-Japanese Treaties of 1907–1916* (Baltimore, 1933),
44–45; Pak, *Rossiia i Koreia*, 405.

95. On a plan to smuggle Kojong out of the country, see Pak, *Rossiia i Koreia*,
406–407.

96. E. Smirnov, "Report 4.10," June 16, 1910, *RICKH*, 296–300. Unterberger's fears
of Korean emigration were also motivated by his general fear of the Yellow Peril, and he called
for the speedy enactment of laws limiting the renting of land to Chinese and Koreans of foreign citizenship in Primorsky Krai. See Pak, *Koreitsy v Rossiiskoi Imperii*, 112. See also Saveliev, "Military Diaspora," 151.

97. So great was Russian consternation at the possibility of foreign financial inroads into
Manchuria that Russia considered going to war to annex it. George Alexander Lensen, "Japan
and Tsarist Russia: The Changing Relationships, 1875–1917," *Jahrbücher für Geschichte Os-
teuropas*, new ser. (October 1962): 344.

98. Price, *Russo-Japanese Treaties*, 56–57. Gotō Shinpei's response to the American proposal was dismissive. *North China Herald*, January 21, 1910.

99. Most scholars have overlooked Korea as a main factor behind Japan's desire for an
agreement with Russia in 1910, noting instead American maneuvers in Manchuria and Knox's
"dollar diplomacy." See Walter LaFeber, *The Clash: U.S.- Japanese Relations throughout History* (New York, 1998).

100. Komatsu, *Meiji Gaikō Hiwa*, 264–246.

101. Sŏ Yŏng- hŭi, "Kungminshinbot'erŭl t'onghae pon ilchinhoeŭi happangnon'gwa
happangjŏnggugŭi tonghyang" [The annexation theory of the Ilchinhoe and the movement
of the political situation as seen through the *Kungmin Sinbo*], *Yŏksakwa hyŏnsil* 69 (September 2008): 27–28. See also Vipan Chandra, "An Outline Study of the Ilchin-hoe (Advancement Society) of Korea," *Occasional Papers on Korea*, no. 2 (March 1974): 61.

102. Suh Yŏng-hŭi, "Kungminshinbot'erŭl," 37–38, 41–42. See also Ogawara Hiroyuki,
"Ichi-shin-kai no nikkangappō seigan undō to kankokuheigō : `Sei gappō' kōsō to ten'nōsei
kokka genri to no sōkoku" [The Ilchinhoe's petition movement for Japanese-Korean confed-

eration and Korean annexation: The "confederation" concept, the principle of the emperor system state, and how they clashed], *Chōsenshi kenkyūkai ronbunshū* 43 (October 2005): 189–193.

103. Komatsu, *Meiji Gaikō Hiwa,* 264–266.

104. Cited in Lone, "Japanese Annexation of Korea," 162.

105. Komatsu, *Meiji Gaikō Hiwa,* 266–267.

106. Komatsu, *Meiji Gaikō Hiwa,* 267–268.

107. Lone, "Japanese Annexation of Korea," 167; Komatsu, *Meiji Gaikō Hiwa,* 270.

108. Yi Yong-gu and Song Pyŏng-jun were flabbergasted, but the Japanese determined that the Ilchinhoe was no longer useful. Komatsu, *Meiji Gaikō Hiwa,* 251–252; Chandra, "Outline Study of the Ilchin-hoe," 66; Duus, *Abacus and the Sword,* 241.

109. Komatsu, *Meiji Gaikō Hiwa,* 276–277. Yi Wan-yong had even come up with a plot to assassinate Yi Yong-gu in December 1909, but the scheme was thwarted by the Japanese. See CIK, 8 kwan (24) [12796], December 7, 1909, http://db.history.go.kr/item/level.do?setId=105&itemId=jh&synonym=off&chinessChar=on&page=1&pre_page=1&brokerPagingInfo=&position=17&levelId=jh_098r_0020_0240.

110. Komatsu, *Meiji Gaikō Hiwa,* 277, 278.

111. Komatsu, *Meiji Gaikō Hiwa,* 293–295.

112. Jonathan D. Spence, *The Search for Modern China* (New York, 1990), 263.

EPILOGUE

1. Richard Overy, *Blood and Ruins: The Last Imperial War, 1931–1945* (New York, 2022), 2.

2. Hirakawa Sachiko, "Portsmouth Denied: The Chinese Attempt to Attend," in *The Russo-Japanese War in Global Perspective: World War Zero,* vol. 2, ed. David Wolff et al. (Leiden, 2006), 531–549.

3. S. C. M. Paine, *The Japanese Empire: Grand Strategy from the Meiji Restoration to the Pacific War* (Cambridge, 2017).

4. Thomas W. Burkman, *Japan and the League of Nations: Empire and World Order, 1914–1918* (Honolulu, 2007), 27.

5. After declaring himself emperor in 1915, Yuan was forced to resign and the government was placed in the hands of a cabinet headed by Duan Qirui, a former protégé of Yuan. See Jonathan D. Spence, *The Search for Modern China* (New York, 1990), 275–294.

6. Although Chiang turned his back on his Communist partners in 1927—massacring the very Communist labor leaders whom Sun Yat-sen had solicited to join the Guomindang a few years earlier—by 1936 he finally agreed to form a Guomindang-Communist United Front against the Japanese.

7. Alyssa M. Park, *Sovereignty Experiments: Korean Migrants and the Building of Borders in Northeast Asia, 1860–1945* (Ithaca, NY, 2019), 237–238; John J. Stephen, *The Russian Far East: A History* (Stanford, CA, 1996), 131–133.

8. The modern ideology of neo-Eurasianism associated with the works of Soviet historian Lev Gumilyov and Russian philosopher Alexandr Dugin, among others, traces its spiritual origins to the Eurasianist movement of the 1920s. Many contemporary adherents of the new ideology have become part of Vladimir Putin's inner circle. Dugin's rejection of Western hegemonic "universal values" and his championing of a vision of the world as one consisting of "civilizational blocs"—what Putin has called a "Eurasian Union"—is just one manifestation of neo-Eurasianism. According to Sergei Karaganov, widely recognized as Putin's foreign policy adviser, Russia "has a chance to attain a new status, not that of European periphery with possessions in Asia, but as an Atlantic-Pacific power committed to the future, as one of

the centers in rising Greater Eurasia." See Sergei Karaganov, "From East to West, or Greater Eurasia," *Russia in Global Affairs*, October 25, 2016, https://eng.globalaffairs.ru/pubcol/From -East-to-West-or-Greater-Eurasia-18440. See also Charles Clover, *Black Wind, White Snow: The Rise of Russia's New Nationalism* (New Haven, CT, 2016); Igor Torbakov, *After Empire: Nationalist Imagination and Symbolic Politics in Russia and Eurasia in the Twentieth and Twenty-First Century* (Stuttgart, 2018); Marlene Laruelle, *Russian Eurasianism: An Ideology of Empire* (Baltimore, 2008); and Mikhail Zygar, *All the Kremlin's Men: Inside the Court of Vladimir Putin* (New York, 2016).

9. Cited in David Schimmelpenninck Van Der Oye, "Russia's Asian Temptation," *International Journal* 55, no. 4 (Autumn 2000): 609.

10. Japan formally recognized the Soviet Union in 1925, extracting a Soviet pledge not to promote revolutionary activities in Korea and Manchuria. In order to placate Japan, the Soviet Union began a crackdown that culminated in 1926 with stopping all further immigration of Koreans (and Chinese) into the Russian Far East. See Michael Gelb, "An Early Soviet Ethnic Deportation: The Far-Eastern Koreans," *Russian Review* 54 (July 1995): 389–412; and Henry Huttenbach, "The Soviet Koreans: Products of Russo-Japanese Imperial Rivalry," *Central Asian Survey* 12, no. 1 (1993): 59–69.

11. Koreans in the Russian Far East in 1927 numbered 170,000, although unofficially there were at least 250,000. The largest Korean communities were in the Suchansk District, east of Vladivostok, and in the area of Pos'et, west of the city. According to official figures, Koreans made up an estimated 95 percent of the population in the Suchansk District. After 1937 the Soviet regime suddenly became fearful that some members of the Korean communities might spy for Japan, as had happened during the Russo-Japanese War, and ordered their deportation to Central Asia. The Soviets later drew from those Korean communities to help build the nascent North Korean state in 1945, even though Stalin chose Kim Il Sung, an anti-Japanese fighter based in Manchuria, to eventually lead it. See Boris Pak, *Koreitsy v Rossiiskoi imperii (Dal'nevostochnyi period)* [Koreans in the Russian Empire (The Far East period)] (Moscow, 1993); Jon Chang, *Burnt by the Sun: The Koreans of the Russian Far East* (Honolulu, 2016); Walter Kolarz, *The People of the Soviet Far East* (New York, 1969); Haruki Wada, "Koreans in the Soviet Far East, 1917–1937," in *Koreans in the Soviet Union,* ed. Dae-sook Suh (Honolulu, 1987), 24–59.

12. Suzuki Masayuki, "The Korean National Liberation Movement in China and International Response," in *Koreans in China,* ed. Dae-sook Suh and E. J. Shultz (Honolulu, 1990), 115–143; Erik Van Ree, *Socialism in One Zone: Stalin's Policy in Korea, 1945–1947* (Oxford, 1998); Andrei Lankov, *From Stalin to Kim Il Sung: The Formation of North Korea, 1945–1960* (New Brunswick, NJ, 2002).

13. Roughly 740,000 refugees from the north moved south between 1945 and 1949. Yumi Moon, "Crossing the 38th Parallel: Northern Refugees in Postwar South Korea, 1945–1950," unpublished paper.

14. After the Philippine-American War, imperialism lost much of its appeal for the American people and "peaceful" commercial expansion became a main priority. Akira Iriye, *Pacific Estrangement: Japanese and American Expansion, 1897–1911* (Cambridge, MA, 1972), 1–25.

15. Frederick R. Dickinson, *War and National Reinvention: Japan in the Great War, 1914–1919* (Cambridge, MA, 1999), 35.

16. Stanley K. Hornbeck, "Has the United States a Chinese Policy?," *Foreign Affairs,* July 1927, 622–623.

17. Walter LaFeber, *The American Age: United States Foreign Policy at Home and Abroad since 1750* (New York, 1989), 320.

18. Dickinson, *War and National Reinvention,* 236.

19. Akira Iriye, *After Imperialism: The Search for a New Order in the Far East, 1921–1931* (Chicago, 1990), 279.

20. Sheila Miyoshi Jager, "Competing Empires in Asia," in *The Cambridge History of America and the World*, vol. 3, ed. Brooke L. Bower and Andrew Preston (Cambridge, 2021), 247–267.

21. Walter Russell Mead, "The Return of Geopolitics: The Revenge of the Revisionist Powers," *Foreign Affairs*, May–June 2014, 69–74.

22. See, for example, Richard Haas, "Cold War II," *Project Syndicate*, February 23, 2018; and Evan Osnos, David Remnick, and Joshua Yaffa, "Trump, Putin, and the New Cold War," *New Yorker*, March 6, 2017.

23. Adam O'Neal, "Russia, China and the New Cold War," *Wall Street Journal*, March 18, 2022.

24. It is important to note that Russia did not recoup all of the territory it lost after the Brest-Litovsk Treaty in March 1918, even though that treaty was declared invalid under the terms of the Treaty of Versailles. Armenia, Azerbaijan, Georgia, and Ukraine would be reconquered by 1921, but Poland, Finland, and the Baltic States would keep their independence throughout the interwar period. The long-term consequences for Russia were profound. As Jörn Leonhard has argued, "revanchism became a central policy objective for all Soviet leaders after 1918." See Jörn Leonhard, *Pandora's Box: A History of the First World War* (Cambridge, MA, 2018), 730.

25. Cited in Torbakov, *After Empire,* 173.

26. Pushkin presents the Poles as wayward kinsmen who must be reunited with their Slavic family, headed by Russia. Of Europe, he writes in the third stanza: "And you hate us" [*I nenavidite vy nas*]—a stark accusation meant to ward off the possibility of European interference but that also underlines the persistent suspicion that the West is out to destroy Russia. Napoleon's invasion of Russia in 1812 gave credence to Pushkin's suspicions. See Edyta M. Bojanowska, "Pushkin's 'To the Slanderers of Russia': The Slavic Question, Imperial Anxieties, and Geopolitics," *Pushkin Review* 21 (2019): 11–19.

27. This point was brought home at the Nineteenth Party Congress of the Chinese Communist Party in October 2017, when Xi Jinping declared: "People on both sides of the [Taiwan] strait are one family, with shared blood . . . No one can ever cut the veins that connect us." For full text of the speech in English, see *China Daily*, November 4, 2017, https://www.chinadaily.com.cn/china/19thcpcnationalcongress/2017-11/04/content_34115212.htm.

28. The dispute arose after the end of World War II. Japan and the United States have claimed that the agreement reached at Yalta in February 1945 did not provide for the transfer of all of the Kuril Islands to the Soviet Union. The four islands south of the Kuril chain, referred to as the Northern Territories, are considered by Japan to be part of the Hokkaido Prefecture. See Bruce A. Elleman et al., "A Historical Reevaluation of America's Role in the Kuril Dispute," *Pacific Affairs* 71, no. 4 (Winter 1998–1999): 489–504.

29. Anna Zotéeva, "From the Russian Constitution to Putin's Constitution: Legal and Political Implications of the 2020 Constitutional Reform," *U Brief* (May 2020), https://www.ui.se/globalassets/ui.se-eng/publications/ui-publications/2020/ui-brief-no.-5-2020.pdf.

30. In a remarkable address to the nation on February 21, 2022, Putin attacked Russia's Soviet legacy for the first time. He specifically castigated Lenin for recognizing an independent status for Ukraine, Belarus, Armenia, and other republics in the creation of the Union of Soviet Socialist Republics, which paved the way for the Union Treaty of 1922 and the subsequent constitutional provision of 1924. Because the legal foundations of the Soviet state "were not promptly cleansed of the odious and utopian fantasies inspired by the revolution," the breakup of the Soviet Union, and the "collapse of historical Russia," was the inevitable result, which Putin later said was the "greatest geopolitical catastrophe of the twentieth

century." The entire text of the speech can be found at http://en.kremlin.ru/events/president/news/67828. See also *Moscow Times,* December 21, 2021. For a discussion of Lenin and the national problem, see Jeremy Smith, *The Bolsheviks and the National Question, 1917–23* (London, 1999), 175–189, 239–242.

31. Elizabeth Economy, "Xi Jinping's New World Order: Can China Remake the International System?," *Foreign Affairs,* January–February 2022, 63.

32. John Micklethwait and Adrian Wooldridge, "Putin and Xi Exposed the Great Illusion of Capitalism," *Bloomberg,* March 24, 2022, https://www.bloomberg.com/opinion/articles/2022-03-24/ukraine-war-has-russia-s-putin-xi-jinping-exposing-capitalism-s-great-illusion.

33. Launched in 2013, the initiative aimed to connect China to Asia, Europe, the Middle East, and Africa through three overland and three maritime corridors. See Andrew Chatzky and James McBride, "China's Massive Belt and Road Initiative," *Council on Foreign Affairs,* January 28, 2020, https://www.cfr.org/backgrounder/chinas-massive-belt-and-road-initiative. See also Economy, "Xi Jinping's New World Order," 57.

34. "China Is Reassessing Western Financial Power after Ukraine: Beijing Is likely to Speed Up Global Decoupling," *Foreign Policy Magazine,* April 15, 2022, https://foreignpolicy.com/2022/04/15/china-western-financial-power-ukraine/.

35. Christopher M. Dent, "Brexit, Trump and Trade: Back to a Late 19th Century Future?," *Competition & Change* 24, no. 3–4 (2020): 228–357.

36. "Interview with Ivan Krastev," *Der Spiegel,* March 12, 2022.

ACKNOWLEDGMENTS

Over the many years of researching and writing *The Other Great Game,* I have incurred many debts of gratitude to the countless people who made this book possible. My greatest debt goes to my husband, Jiyul Kim, who has been my closest partner in all my academic endeavors. He has been my severest critic but also my most enthusiastic cheerleader. If there is any one reader to whom all my writing is addressed, it is to him. I am also deeply grateful to my editor at Harvard University Press, Kathleen McDermott, who saw the potential of this project early on and supported my vision for it despite its ever-growing length. She not only read through every sentence of the multiple drafts but gently reshaped it into a more manageable size.

Help with translations was given by my friends, former students, and colleagues. Sadly, Choule Sonu did not live to see this book in print. Choule's translations of old Japanese texts was vital to the book's completion. He was born in P'yŏngyang in 1929 when Korea was still a colony of Japan, and this project was meaningful to him both personally and intellectually. Choule taught me so much about life, about resilience, and about friendship. His wisdom and encouragement are deeply missed. My former student Isak Saaf, who helped with the translations of Russian texts, was also invaluable—we have traveled a long journey together. I would also like to acknowledge the translation and research work of Heewon Seo, Shogo Ishikawa, Xun Zhang, Elsie Wang, Runhua Tang, Jingyi Yuan, Jie Zhang, Anna Fofanova, Dmitri Lee, and Ryo Adachi. This book would have been immeasurably weaker without their tremendous help and significant contributions.

A number of friends and colleagues have provided me with opportunities to present parts of the manuscript and have given valuable feedback and support over the years: Ezra Vogel, Rana Mitter, Christian Ostermann, Barak Kushner, Hans van de Ven, Mitch Lerner, Balázs Szalontai, and B. R. Myers. Sadly, Ezra passed away before the project was complete, but for me his spirit lives on in the pages of this book. For their hospitality and generosity, I am grateful to my friends Suh Hee-gyŏng and Kim Yŏng-su. They not only ensured that my research stay in Seoul was comfortable and productive, but their surprise guided tour of Kyŏngbok Palace, retracing the final hours of Queen Min's life, yielded unexpected revelations and remains one of my most cherished memories of that year.

I would also like to acknowledge my colleagues at Oberlin College, Hsiu-Chuang Deppman, Maia Solovieva, Liu Fang, Emer O'Dwyer, Ann Sherif, Leonard Smith, and David Kamitsuka, for their generous support. I owe a particular debt of gratitude to Diane Lee and Runxiao Zhu, excellent librarians, both at Oberlin College, who were able to track down numerous rare books and manuscripts over the years.

Funding for this project was provided by a Senior Fulbright Research Fellowship and a generous grant from the Smith Richardson Foundation. I was fortunate that Allan Song at the Smith Richardson Foundation took a chance on this project, though I fear that the end result is not exactly what he originally had in mind. Summer grants for domestic and overseas travel, as well as grants covering student research assistance, were covered by the Office of Foundation, Government and Corporate Grants at Oberlin College. I wish to thank Pamela Snyder, Elizabeth Edgar, and Wendy Beth Hyman, as well as other members of the Oberlin Research and Development Committee for their sustained and enthusiastic support of this project during all its various stages.

Finally, throughout the writing of this book, my children, Isaac, Hannah, Emma, and Aaron, have endured far more in the way of uneven temper and eccentric behavior than they had any right to expect. Emma spent a year with me in Seoul, even agreeing to enroll in a Korean middle school and learn Korean. Her good cheer and generally carefree demeanor made the research year joyful and memorable. Hannah provided excellent research and technical support, especially by helping me track down dozens of rare photographs at the National Archives in Kew, UK. Our research trips to Washington, DC, Boston, and London were some of the happiest highlights of my career, both as a scholar and as a mom.

INDEX

Anti-Russia Society (Tairo Dōshikai), 299, 540n56
Aoki Nobuzumi, 350, 351, 352, 354
Aoki Shūzō, 114, 115, 163, 263, 280, 446
Araya Shintaku, 558n41
Ariga (military correspondent), 156
Arrow War (Second Opium War; 1856–1860), 8–9, 11, 12, 21, 136, 265
Asahi Shimbun (newspaper), 162, 200, 460–461, 540n51
Ashmead-Bartlett, Ellis, 371
Austria, 81–82, 144, 244, 246, 530n42

Baitouzi, Battle of (1900), 322
Bakunin, Mikhail, 98–99
"balance of power" principle, 53, 59–60
Banzai Rihachirō, 350, 351
Barabash, Ia. F., 101
barbed wire, 343, 362, 363
Batarevich (Blagoveshchensk police chief), 253, 254, 257
Beiyang Fleet, 143–144, 145, 147, 175, 191, 194, 195
Beiyang Intendancy, 31, 129
Belinsky, Vissarion, 5
Bellonet, Henri de, 24–25, 27
Belt and Road Initiative, 482, 574n33
Beresford, Charles, 232–233
Berneux, Simeon François, 22–23, 24, 490n25, 491n29
Berthémy, Jules, 24
Bethell, Ernest Thomas, 416, 418
Bezobrazov, Alexander Mikhailovich, 274, 290–291, 292–295, 540n38
Bickmore, Albert S., 163
Big Sword Society, 239–240, 529n21
Bilderling, General, 385, 389, 391
Bingham, John A., 62
Binkley, Francis, 163
Biriukov, N. N., 377
Bismark, Otto von, 81–82
Black Ocean Society (Gen'yōsha), 116, 174, 508n93
Blagoveshchensk massacre, 252–258, 531n84, 532n89, 532n97, 532nn99–100, 533n119
Blair, William N., 456
Blaramberg, Ivan, 4
Bloody Sunday, 375–376, 554nn142–143
Boer War, Second (1899–1902), 121, 250, 265
Bogdanovich, E. V., 505n24

Bolshevik Revolution, 472–473, 474, 475
Bompard, Maurice, 401
Boxer Uprising (1900): introduction, 121; Anglo-Japanese Alliance and, 280–281, 536n12; beginnings and Chinese response, 241–242; in Beijing, 245; Big Sword Society and, 239–240, 529n21; Boxer Protocol negotiations, 263–264, 269–270, 351, 533n3, 535n39; Dagu Forts bombardment and declaration of war against foreign powers, 245–247, 530nn55–56, 530n58; international relief force, 243–245, 529n32, 530n42; Japanese contingent, 121, 244, 247–250, 249, 530n42, 531n71, 531n73; Korea and, 278–279, 280; looting by foreign powers, 270–271; Russian response to, 250–252
Brest-Litovsk Treaty (1918), 573n24
Briner, Boris Yuliyevich, 291, 538n4, 539n17
Britain. *See* Great Britain
Brooke, Lord, 383, 384
Brooks, S. M., 241, 242
Burtsev, Vladimir, 82
Butashevich-Petrashevsky, M. V., 99
Butzov, Eugene, 30

Cai Er-kang, 509n8
Calder, Captain, 149
Cassini, Arturo, 130, 214, 218, 219, 220, 234, 402
Catherine II (Catherine the Great; Russian tsarina), 2
Catholic Church. *See* Roman Catholic Church
Chaffee, Adna R., 249, 270–271
Chang Yanmao, 237
Ch'angŭihoe, 548n111
Ch'angŭikun, 518n52
Chanykhve (Military Organization), 465
Cheguk sinmun (newspaper), 318
Chemulp'o Bay, Battle of (1904), 308, 316
Cheng Biguang, 194
Chiang Kai-shek, 474, 571n6
China: "barbarians to control barbarians," 53, 130, 473; Beiyang Intendancy, 31, 129; boycotts against US exclusionary laws, 429–430; Christian tensions and persecution, 24, 240–241, 242; Cixi and Guangxu's deaths, 462; First Opium War, 3, 242; Hundred Days Reform, 237, 351–352; New China nationalism,

Itō Hirobumi (*continued*)
  Manchuria and Korea as separate issues,
  449, 567n22; Manchuria question and,
  430, 433, 434–436, 442; negotiations
  with Russia, 273, 282–283, 284–285, 302,
  306, 462–463, 537n26, 537nn29–32,
  537n34; Nishi-Rosen agreement and,
  226; Port Arthur massacre and, 162–163,
  164; proposed loan for Korea and, 523n87;
  protectorate treaty and, 168, 414–416,
  417–418; Russo-Japanese Convention
  (1907) and, 441–442; Russo-Japanese
  War peace negotiations and, 405, 408;
  Sino-Japanese War and peace negotiations,
  131, 189–190, 196–197, 198–199, 212–213;
  Sunjong's inspection tour and, 459–461;
  Tianjin Convention (1885) and, 79–80,
  93; Tonghak rebellion and, 127–128, 176,
  180; treaty revision and, 119, 123; Triple
  Intervention and, 200, 201; as tutor of
  Yi Ŭn, 462
Itō Sukeyuki (Itō Yūkō), 143–145, 147, 150,
  192–193, 194–196, 521n40
Ivan III the Great, 2, 487n3
Ivan IV (Ivan the Terrible; Russian tsar), 2,
  4–5
Ivanovich, Matvei, 331
Iwakura Mission, 35–36, 494n33
Iwakura Tomomi, 35–39, 48, 111, 494n47
Izvolsky, Alexander: Alekseev-Zengqi Agree-
  ment and, 266; foreign policy focus, 439;
  Korean policies, 280, 439, 445; Korean's
  Hague Conference delegation and, 440;
  Russo-Japanese Convention (1907) and,
  441; Russo-Japanese Treaty (1910) and,
  465–466; Russo-Japanese War peace
  negotiations and, 404; on Witte,
  104–105

James, David, 370
Japan: anti-Western "patriotic societies,"
  116–117, 508n93; continental expansion
  and expansionism debate, 437, 444,
  472–473, 477, 564n57; Iwakura Mission
  to Western powers, 35–36, 494n33;
  liberalization, 478; Meiji Restoration,
  28, 186; Open Door proposal and, 234;
  post-Other Great Game, 472–473,
  477–479; treaty revision (equal treaties)
  with Western powers, 75, 116, 119, 123,
  160, 514n98; WWII and, 471–472.
  See also Japanese-Chinese relations;
  Japanese-Russian relations; Japanese-US
  relations; Korea, under Japanese rule;
  Korean-Japanese relations; Russo-Japanese
  War; Sino-Japanese War
Japan Weekly Mail (newspaper), 159, 163,
  304, 522n72
Japanese Korean Army, 564n63. *See also*
  Korean Garrison Army
Japanese-Chinese relations: assistance against
  Boxers, 121, 244, 247–250, 249, 530n42,
  531n71, 531n73; Boxer Protocol and,
  269–270; Chinese-Russian Manchuria
  negotiations and, 268, 534n30, 534n33;
  consulted on Korean-Japanese relations,
  31, 32–34, 49–50, 51; Convention of
  Tianjin (1885), 54, 79–80, 88, 119, 127,
  129, 197, 508n93; Japanese appreciation
  for Chinese culture, 186–187; Japanese
  expansion into China, 351, 472; Jiandao
  agreement, 462, 569n81; Kapsin coup
  and, 79–80; Korean reform proposal and,
  128–129; Manchuria and, 434; Mongol
  attempts to invade Japan, 15; Russo-
  Japanese War and, 310, 350–352, 354;
  Shimonoseki Peace Treaty (1895), 196–199,
  213; Sino-Japanese Treaty (1871), 32, 33,
  49, 187, 493n21, 496n34; Sino-Japanese
  Treaty (1905), 430–432, 432, 473, 563n39;
  Tonghak rebellion and, 119–120, 126–128,
  509n20, 509n22; US mediation post-Other
  Great Game, 477–479. *See also* Sino-
  Japanese War
Japanese-Korean relations. *See* Korean-
  Japanese relations
Japanese-Russian relations: Alekseev-Zengqi
  Agreement and, 265, 266; Anglo-Japanese
  Alliance and, 273–274, 287–288; an-
  nexation of Korea and, 462–463, 464;
  attempted assassination of Nicholas II,
  110–116, 507n76, 508n94; equal rights
  agreements over Korea, 223, 526n38;
  Japanese backlash against Sino-Russia
  Secret Treaty, 222–223; Komura-Weber
  memorandum (1896), 526n38; Kuril
  Islands dispute, 481, 573n28; negotiations
  over Korea and Manchuria, 273, 280,
  282–283, 284–286, 302–303, 304–306,
  307, 536n21, 537nn26–27, 537nn29–34,

338–339, 547n101; Manchuria question and, 396, 427–428, 433; negotiations with Russia, 303, 305; Nishi-Rosen Agreement and, 226; Open Door rhetoric, 399; request for US to remove legation from Korea, 419; Russian relations and, 281; Russo-Japanese War and, 307, 350, 402, 543n103, 544n16; Russo-Japanese War peace negotiations, 401, 405–406, 407–408, 409, 411, 412, 413–414; Sino-Japanese Treaty negotiations, 430–432, 432, 563n39

Komura-Weber memorandum (1896), 526n38

Kondratenko, Roman, 372

Kongnip sinmun (newsletter), 447–448

Konoe Atsumaro, 299, 540n56

Kopitov, Rear Admiral, 212

Korea: Boxer crisis, 278–279, 280; Catholic converts and persecution, 12, 20–21, 22–24, 26–27, 172, 277–278, 490nn20–21, 490n25, 491n29, 491nn34–35, 535n1, 535nn3–4; conservative-progressive divide, 51–52, 66–67, 167–168, 172–173, 288–289; contemporary destabilization, 480–481; at Hague Conference, 440–441, 450, 565n77; Imo Uprising (*see* Imo Uprising); Independence Club, 292, 332, 335, 412, 457, 508n7; Japanese-Russian agreements about, 223, 225–226, 266, 279, 280, 526n38; Kabo-Ŭlmi reforms, 166–169, 516n3, 536n9; Kapsin coup (1884), 54, 77–79, 79–80, 90, 92, 172, 500n91, 500n95; Kwangmu Reforms, 279–280, 289, 536n9; Kyŏngbok Palace, 40–41, 44; linked with Manchuria in Japanese-Russian struggle for dominance, 273, 280, 282–283, 284–286, 302–303, 304–306, 307, 536n21, 537nn26–27, 537nn29–34, 537n36, 537n38, 542n76, 542n80, 542n89, 544nn16–17; modernization efforts, 63–64; neutrality, 280, 304, 307; North-South divide, 459, 476–477, 480, 572n13; post-Other Great Game, 475–477; Righteous Army (*see* Righteous Army); Russo-Japanese War peace negotiations and, 413–414; seclusion policy, 15, 17, 27, 65, 492n50; *sŏwŏns* (private Confucian academies), 41–43, 45, 495n10; Tonghak rebellion (*see* Tonghak movement

and rebellion); treaties with Western powers, 65, 498n40; "triumph" over French punitive mission, 24–25, 26, 27, 44, 491n42; two-king problem, 44–45, 69–73, 89–90. *See also* Imo Uprising; Kojong (Chosŏn king); Korea, under Japanese rule; Korean-Chinese relations; Korean-Japanese relations; Korean-Russian relations; Korean-US relations; Myŏngsŏng (Queen Min); Righteous Army; Taewŏn'gun; Tonghak movement and rebellion

Korea, under Japanese rule: commoners, 561n104; cultural nationalism, 457–459; decision to annex, 397, 459, 461–462; disbanding of Korean Army, 442–443, 449, 565n85; Hague Conference and, 440–441, 565n77; Ilchinhoe's annexation petition, 466–468; Itō and Kojong's protectorate meeting, 414–416; Itō's assassination, 463–465, 569n83, 569n85; Itō's resident-generalship, 437–438, 439–440, 459, 564n61; Japanese militarization and abuse of Koreans, 438–439, 564n64, 564n66; Japan-Korea Treaty (Protectorate Treaty; 1905), 395, 416–421, 421–422, 440–441, 560n86, 561n97; Japan-Korea Treaty (1907), 442, 448–449, 452; Japan-Korea Treaty (Annexation Treaty; 1910), 468–469, 472, 571n108; Kojong's abdication, 441; March First movement, 478; opposition to annexation, 442–443; population distribution, 567n29; press restrictions, 566n13; Protestants and, 455–457, 457; provisional agreements (1905), 168, 516nn11–12; Righteous Army insurgency, 449–455, 568n35, 568n50, 570n93; Russia and annexation, 462–463, 464; Sunjong's inspection tour, 459–461. *See also* Korean-Japanese relations

Korean Army (*hullyŏndae*), 207–208, 523n95

Korean Garrison Army (Kankoku Chusatsugun), 438, 448–449, 564n61, 564n63, 567n22

Korean National Association (KNA; Taehanin kungminhoe), 448, 458, 566n18, 567n20

Korean Provisional Government (KPG), 476

Korean-Chinese relations: advice on relations with Western powers, 46–47, 497n11; border disputes, 490n13; British occupation of Port Hamilton and, 87–88;

Korean-Chinese relations (*continued*)
changing Chinese policy, 72–73, 92;
Chinese consulted on Korean-Japanese
relations, 31, 32–34, 49–50, 51; commercial treaty (1882), 75; Imo Uprising
intervention, 69–73, 196, 499nn62–64,
499nn69–70; Kapsin coup and, 54, 78,
90; Kim Ok-kyun's assassination and,
124–125; Korean-US treaty (1882) and,
53–54, 62, 64, 65, 498n38; military
advisors issue, 88–89; Mongols and, 15;
Russian intrusion, 18; *A Strategy for Korea*
(Huang) and, 53, 59–61, 66, 91, 92,
497n21; Taewŏn'gun and, 71–72, 89–90,
133; Tonghak rebellion and, 126–128,
175, 509nn19–20, 509n22; traditional
relations, 11, 16–17, 489nn5–6; Yuan's
expansion of Chinese control, 77, 80,
90–92, 123–124, 132, 503n52, 510n45
Korean-Japanese relations: apology mission
for Imo Uprising, 73, 74–75; assassination
of Queen Min, 207–208, 208–210, 523n92,
524n106, 524n110, 524n116; assistance
to Korean progressives, 75, 76–77; Chinese
consulted on, 31, 32–34, 49–50, 51;
diplomatic missions to Japan, 57–58, 59,
61, 74; gunboat diplomacy, 39, 47–48;
Imjin Wars, 15–16, 140, 141, 169, 511n19;
Imo Uprising response, 69, 71, 72, 499n70,
499n74; Inoue's proposed loan to Korea,
203, 205–206, 523n87; Japanese reform
attempts, 128–129, 131–132, 165–168,
169–171, 202–206, 510n43, 522nn76–78,
523n80; Kanghwa Treaty (1876), 13,
51–52, 75, 131, 172; Kapsin coup and
subsequent Japanese policy, 54, 77–79,
93–94; Kim Ok-kyun's assassination and,
124–125, 125–126, 509nn11–12, 509n15;
Kojong's rapprochement with, 45, 46–47,
51–52, 495nn23–25; Korean neutrality
proposal, 304; Korean refusal to recognize
Meiji Restoration, 13, 28–29, 34, 493n28;
Osaka Incident, 94, 504n70; Russo-
Japanese War and, 318, 331–334; Seikanron
debate on punitive expedition, 13, 29–30,
35–36, 36–38, 494n40, 494n46; Shufeldt's
mission to Korea and, 62; Sino-Japanese
War and, 168–169, 175–176; Taewŏn'gun
and, 89, 132–133, 166–167, 168–169,
169–170, 510n46, 510n49; tensions with

Yuan and, 123–124; Tonghak rebellion
and, 126–128, 170–171, 174–175, 509n20,
509n22, 509n24; traditional relations,
29, 496n1; Triple Intervention and, 204;
Un'yŏ incident, 48, 50; Yalu ports issue,
298–299, 300–301, 301–302, 304, 306,
307, 543n100. *See also* Korea, under
Japanese rule
Korean-Russian relations: Kojong's appeals
for help, 91–92, 503n56, 503n59, 560n88;
Korean anti-Russian views, 332, 546n79;
Korean emigration to Russian Far East,
17–19, 21, 30, 421, 475–476, 561n100,
570n96, 572n11; on Korean neutrality, 304;
military instructors and, 88–89, 502n37;
Righteous Army and, 377, 451–452, 475;
Russian influence in Korea, 206–207,
210–211, 307; Russia's cautious approach
to, 92–93, 452, 502n36; trade demands,
21–22; Yalu timber concessions, 290–293,
294–296, 301–302, 332, 439, 539n17,
541n69
Korean-US relations: *General Sherman*
incident, 492n50; Kojong's appeals for
help, 305, 412–413, 419, 560n88; Korean
activism in US, 447–448; Roosevelt's view
of Korea, 399–400; US initial attempt to
open diplomatic relations, 33; US-Korean
Treaty and Korean backlash (1882), 53–54,
64, 65, 66–67
Korostovets, Vladimir, 405, 409, 410, 411
Korzhinsky, S. I., 98
Kowner, Rotem, 549n21, 549n30, 556n28
Koyama Toyatarō, 197
Krastev, Ivan, 482
Krestovsky, V., 101
Kropotkin, Pyotr, 97, 99, 500n2
Kumi Kunitake, 494n33
Kuril Islands, 30, 481, 494n38, 573n28
Kurino Shin'ichirō, 161, 163, 302–303, 306,
307, 542n89, 543n103
Kuroda Kiyotaka, 37, 48, 51, 496n32
Kuroki Tamemoto: advance to Liaoyang,
347; at Battle of Liaoyang, 362, 363; at
Battle of Mukden, 387, 390–391; at
Battle of Yalu River, 323, 325, 326, 328,
329, 330; Japanese troop landings in Korea
and, 317; at Port Arthur siege, 359
Kuropatkin, Aleksei Nikolaevich: arrival in
Liaoyang, 322; at Battle of Liaoyang,

Propper, S. M., 296
Protestantism, 455–457, 457. *See also* Christianity
Przhevalsky, Nikolay M., 18, 19, 22, 110, 490n10, 490n24
Pullman, George H., 163
Pukchŏp (Northern Assembly), 173, 178, 334
P'ungdo, battle of (1894), 134, 136, 139, 145, 175, 511n54
Pushkin, Alexander, 5, 480, 573n26
Putatin, E. V., 21–22
Putin, Vladimir, 475, 481, 571n8, 573n30
Puyi, 530n51
Puzhuan, 246, 530n51
pyŏlgigun (Special Skill Force), 67
P'yŏngyang: Chinese retreat to, 139–140; history of, 140; Sino-Japanese War battle, 140–142, 143, 169, 175, 511n15, 512n22, 512n26, 512n28

Qing, Prince (Yikuang), 246, 264, 266, 268, 430–431, 533n5
Qing Empire (1644–1912). *See* China
Qingdao, 221, 223–224, 240, 358
Qingnian hui (Youth Association), 429

racism: anti-Japanese agitation in California, 445–447; by Russians, 306; Yellow Peril, 446, 570n96
Radolin, Prince Hugo von (German ambassador to Russia), 223
"Revolutionary Alliance" (Tongmenghui), 429
Rezanov, Lieutenant, 17–18
Rhee, Syngman (Yi Sŭng-man), 412, 447, 448, 458, 476, 566n14, 567n20
Ridel, Félix-Claire Father, 24
Righteous Army (*ŭibyŏng*): banditry and in-fighting, 568n50; establishment, 377–378, 421; against Inchinhoe, 439; insurgency against Japanese, 397, 421, 443, 449–451, 452–455, 568n35, 570n93; relations with Russia and Soviets, 377, 451–452, 475
Rockhill, William W.: Boxer Protocol and, 263, 265, 266, 270, 535n39; on Li Hongzhang's death, 271; Open Door Notes and, 233, 234, 235, 528n31, 528n33, 533n1; Russo-Japanese War peace negotiations and, 563n28; US legation's withdrawal from Korea and, 419; on Yellow River, 236

Rodgers, John, 492n50
Roman Catholic Church: Korean converts and persecution, 12, 20–21, 22–24, 26–27, 172, 277–278, 490nn20–21, 490n25, 491n29, 491nn34–35, 535n1, 535nn3–4; tensions in China, 239–240. *See also* Christianity
Roosevelt, Samuel Montgomery, 426–427
Roosevelt, Theodore: California's anti-Japanese crisis and, 445, 446; expansionist philosophy of, 230; foreign policy towards Japan and Russia, 297–298, 395; Harriman and, 427, 562n14; Kojong's appeal to, 419; on Korea question, 399–400, 412; Russo-Japanese War peace negotiations (Portsmouth Treaty) and, 394, 401, 402, 404, 406, 407, 411, 413, 420, 425, 557n65, 558n49, 559n67
Root, Elihu, 419, 464
Rosen, Roman: on Bezobrazov, 290; break of Russo-Japanese diplomatic relations, 544n16; negotiations with Japan and, 299, 303; Nishi-Rosen Agreement, 225–226, 266, 279, 280, 540n51; on Russia's continued presence in Manchuria, 261–262; on Russo-Chinese bank, 213; Russo-Japanese War peace negotiations and, 405, 409, 410; Yalu timber concessions and, 298
Rouvier, Maurice, 404
Roze, Pierre-Gustave, 24, 26
Rozhestvensky, Z. P. Admiral, 368, 394
Rudnev, V. F., 314, 315, 316
Rusanov, S. I., 555n15
Russia: 1905 Revolution and Bloody Sunday, 355, 374–377, 397, 554nn142–143; Alexander III's reactionary regime, 84–86; Asian identity, 5; Bolshevik Revolution, 472–473, 474, 475 (*see also* Soviet Union); Boxer Protocol and, 263–264, 269–270, 533n3; Boxer Uprising and, 121, 244, 250, 530n42; on British occupation of Port Hamilton, 87–88; bureaucratic dysfunction, 295–296; Congress of Berlin and, 81–82; cooperative protests by Russian and Korean workers, 377, 554n146; Crimean War, 4, 6; Great Game in Central Asia, 2–3, 81, 83–84, 86–87, 99, 501n11, 501n13; invasion of Ukraine, 480, 481; Mahan on, 231–232; Mongol (Tatar)

—battles: Chemulp'o Bay, 308, 316; Chŏngju skirmish, 322; Liaoyang, 360–364, *361*, 365–366; Mukden, 309, 385–394, *386*, *388*, 556n28, 557n59; Nanshan, 341–346, *342*, *345*, 549n9, 549n21; Port Arthur siege and fall, 358–359, *365*, 366–371, *367*, *375*, 379, 551n73, 552nn102–104, 552n108, 553n118, 553n121, 553nn128–129, 553n132; Sandepu/Heikoutai, 380–385, *381*, 555n6, 555n8, 555n10, 555n21; Telissu, *348*, 349, 549n30; Tsushima, 402; Yalu River, 323–326, *324*, 328–330, *331*, 340, 546nn69–70
Russo-Turkish War (1877–1878), 58, 81, 100
Ryōjun. *See* Port Arthur

Sada Hakubo, 29–30
Saigō Takamori, 35–36, 37–38, 494n40, 494n46
Saigō Tsugumichi, 116, 201
Saionji Kinmochi, 205–206, 433, 434, 447, 472
Sakhalin: Japanese concerns about Russian occupation, 30, 37, 38; Japanese occupation during Russo-Japanese War, 406, 557n11, 558n41; Russian exploration and occupation, 3–4, 30; Russo-Japanese War peace negotiations and, 400–401, 403, 406–407, 408, 409, 411; Treaty of Saint Petersburg (Sakhalin-Kuril Treaty; 1875), 30, 48, 113, 481, 494n38
Sakharov, Viktor, 384, 403
Sakurai Tadayoshi, 346, 366, 368
Salisbury, Lord, 250
Samejima Shigeo, 369
San Francisco Chronicle (newspaper), 161, 163
San Francisco school board, 445–446
Sandepu/Heikoutai, Battle of (1905), 380–385, *381*, 555n6, 555n8, 555n10, 555n15, 555n17, 555n21
Sanjō Sanetomi, 34, 35–36, 37, 38
sarafan, 488n18
Satō Sasumi, 197
Satow, Ernest, 270, 281
Savelovka incident, 100–101, 505n26
Schelking, Eugene de, 531n78
Schiff, Jacob, 407–408, 424
Schweinitz, Hans Lothar von, 82–83
Schwindt, Captain, 370
Scott, Charles S., 287–288

Second Anglo-Afghan War (1878–1880), 81, 99
Second Boer War (1899–1902), 121, 250, 265
Second Hague Conference (1907), 440–441, 450, 565n77
Second Opium War (Arrow War; 1856–1860), 8–9, 11, 12, 21, 136, 265
Seikanron, 13, 29–30, 35–36, 36–38, 494n40, 494n46
Senba Tarō, 350, 351
Seredin-Sabatin, Afanasy, 206–207, 523n90
Sergei Alexandrovich (grand duke), 376
Seward, George Frederick, 31–32
Seymour, Edward, 243–244, 245
Shabanov (Blagoveshchensk police officer), 255, 256, 257–258, 532n100
Shandong, 239–242, 472, 473, 478
Shanghai Chamber of Commerce, 429
Shao Youlian, 189
Sharrock, A. M., 325
Shevich, Dmitry Yegorovich, 114, 115
Shiba Ryōtarō: *Clouds above the Hills*, 391–392, 556n47
Shibusawa Eiichi, 425
Shidehara Kojūrō, 405–406
Shimonoseki Peace Treaty (1895), 196–199, 213
Shipaev, V. I., 288–289
Shipov, D. N., 405
Shoushan, General, 258, 260
shubang (dependency), 33, 64, 493n21
Shufeldt, Robert W., 61–63, 64, 65, 498n37
Siberia, 2, 97, 99–100. *See also* Russian Far East
Siberia (newspaper), 97
Siberian Expedition (1918–1922), 474, 475
Sill, John M. B., 442, 523n80
Sin Hŏn, 65
Sin Ŭl-sŏk, 454–455
Sinminhoe (New Citizens Society), 458
Sino-French War (1884), 77, 79
Sino-Japanese Treaty (1871), 32, 33, 49, 187, 493n21, 496n34
Sino-Japanese Treaty (1905), 430–432, *432*, 473, 563n39
Sino-Japanese War (1894–1895): about, 120; British intervention proposal, 520n14; casualties, 345, 549n19; Chinese advantages, 136; Chinese peace gestures, 189;

comparison to Russo-Japanese War, 312, 346; contemporary impacts, 480; impetus and justification, 130–132, 134, 165, 300; Japanese landings at Dairen and Jinzhou, *148*, 148–149; Japanese perceptions of China, 187–189, *188*, 520n9; Japanese public support for, 135–136; Japanese strategy, 136, 138, 511n4; Japanese triumph, 186; Japanese troop movement, *137*; Japan's Korea problem and, 201–202; Korean impacts, 185; Korean support for China, 168–169; Li's attempts to prevent, 129, 130, 134, 510n53; Mahan on, 230; peace treaty negotiations, 196–199, 521nn46–47, 521n49; Pescadores Islands and, 521n42; Port Arthur massacre, 152–157, *153*, *155*, 158–161, 514n70, 514n74, 514n76, 514n78, 514n80; Port Arthur massacre, and US-Japan treaty, 160–161, 163–164, 515n99; Port Arthur massacre, Chinese accounts of, 164, 515n121; Port Arthur massacre, disinformation campaign to cover up, 160, 161–164, 515n105, 515n112, 515nn115–116, 515n120; requisition orders in Korea, 175–176; Tonghak suppression and, 170–171, 174–175, 176–177, 180–185, *181*, 518nn58–60, 519n64, 519n67; Triple Intervention, 120, 199–201, 204, 212–213, 230, 522n57; Yamagata's recall, 190, 513n51
—battles: Haicheng, 190; Port Arthur, 149–152, *151*, 157–158, 347, 513n68; P'ungdo, 134, 136, 139, 145, 175, 511n54; P'yŏngyang, 140–142, *143*, 169, 175, 511n15, 512n22, 512n26, 512n28; Sŏnghwan, 138–140, 175; Weihaiwei, 190–196, *195*, 520n20, 520n23, 521n32, 521n34, 521n40; Yellow Sea, 143–148, 512nn34–35, 513n45
Sino-Russian Secret Treaty (1896), 218–220, 220–222, 224, 525n32
Sino-Russian War (1900): Baitouzi battle, 322; beginnings of, 251–252; Blagoveshchensk massacre, 252–258, 531n84, 532n89, 532n97, 532nn99–100, 533n119; Haicheng battle, 322; negotiations over Manchuria, 267–269, 271–272, 287, 534n33, 535n45; Russian conquest of Manchuria, 258–262, *259*, 264, 532n113, 533n114

Sin-sŏp, 498n46
Skobelev, Mikhail, 83
Smirnov, E., 450–452, 454, 465, 466
Smirnov, Konstantin, 373, 553n121, 553n129
Smith, J. Gordon, 434
Sŏ Chae'il (Philip Jaisohn), 332
Sŏ Chae-pil, 508n7
Sŏ Jae-p'il, 500n95
Sŏ Kwang-bŏm, 74–75, 202–203, 500n95
Sŏ Yŏng-hŭi, 467
Society for the Celestial Salvation of the Oppressed (Ten'yūkyō), 174–175, 517n38, 518n39
Society of the Divine Word, 239–240
Soejima Taneomi, 30, 31–33, 36, 38, 49, 187, 493n25, 494n46
Someya Nariaki, 336
Somov, Aleksander S., 377, 452
Son Pyŏng-hŭi, 185, 334, 335, 336–337, 396
Sone Arasuke, 459, 462, 466–468, 536n21
Song Pyŏng-jun: annexation and, 467, 468, 469, 571n108; on Ilchinhoe's friendliness with Japanese, 336, 422, 547n101, 561nn105–106; outburst against Christians, 460–461; Sunjong's inspection tour, 459
Song Pyŏng-sŏn, 420–421
Song Si-yŏl (Uam), 41, 42, 495n4
Sŏnghwan, battle of (1894), 138–139, 175, 179
Sontag, Antoinette, 206–207, 524n106
sōshi (Japanese thugs), 207, 208, 523n94
South Manchurian Railway (SMR, Mantetsu), 425, 436, 473, 562n15, 564n56. *See also* Chinese Eastern Railway
Soviet Union, 459, 473, 474–476, 572nn10–11, 573n24. *See also* Russia
sŏwŏns (private Confucian academies), 41–43, 45, 495n10
Soyeda Juichi, 425, 427
Spanish-American War (1898), 121, 235, 477
Speyer, Alexey de, 292, 538n11
Spring-Rice, Cecil, 297, 410
Stackelberg, G. K.: at Battle of Sandepu/Heikoutai, 382–383, 384, 385, 555n17; at Battle of Telissu, 347, 349; Battle of the Yalu River and, 326; command at Port Arthur, 346; command of Southern Detachment in Liaodong Peninsula, 322
Stalin, Joseph, 475, 476, 572n11
Stead, Alfred, 330
Stein, Lorenz von, 113